SPEAKING FREELY:
A Guided Tour of American English from Plymouth Rock to Silicon Valley

Stuart Berg Flexner
and
Anne H. Soukhanov

New York   Oxford
Oxford University Press
1997

Oxford University Press

Oxford New York

Athens Auckland Bangkok Bogotá Bombay
Buenos Aires Calcutta Cape Town Dar es Salaam
Delhi Florence Hong Kong Istanbul Karachi
Kuala Lumpur Madras Madrid Melbourne
Mexico City Nairobi Paris Singapore
Taipei Tokyo Toronto

and associated companies in

Berlin Ibadan

Copyright © 1997 by Mountain Lion, Inc.
Published by Oxford University Press, Inc.
198 Madison Avenue, New York, NY 10016

Library of Congress Cataloging-in-Publication Data
Flexner, Stuart Berg, 1928–1990, and Anne H. Soukhanov, 1943–
    Speaking freely: A guided tour of American English from Plymouth Rock to
Silicon Valley.
    p. cm.
Based on Stuart Berg Flexner's I hear American talking and Listening to
America.
    ISBN 0-19-510692-X (alk. paper)
    1. English language—United States—Etymology.   2. English language—
United States—History.   3. English language—United States—Slang.
4. Americanisms.   I. Flexner, Stuart Berg. I hear America talking.   II. Flexner,
Stuart Berg. Listening to America.   III. Title.
PE2846.S59   1997
427'.973—dc21   97-15369
                                                                          CIP

1 3 5 7 9 8 6 4 2
Printed in the United States of America on acid-free paper

To

the memory of

Stuart Berg Flexner

March 22, 1928–December 3, 1990

who listened to America, heard America

talking, and brought the people's history

back to them—in their own words

I hear the sound I love, the sound of

    the human voice,

I hear all sounds running together, combined,

    fused for following,

Sounds of the city and sounds out of the city,

    sound of day and night . . .

I hear the chorus . . . .

—Walt Whitman

"Song of Myself"

CONTRIBUTORS

The following writers made important
contributions to this book: Leonard Ashley,
Colonel John Calabro, USA, Monica Collins,
Thomas Dalzell, Neil Jumonville, Robert Kyff,
Jeffrey McQuain, Casey Miller, Cullen Murphy,
Lee Pederson, James Shea, Kate Swift,
Sue Ellen Thompson, and David Weeks.

CONTENTS

INTRODUCTION

" . . . this is a book about the American language,
treating that language as an important part of
American history, of social history, and of the
biography of us all. The story of our words is also
the story of our century and our people."

—Stuart Berg Flexner
Listening to America

Though history teaches us much about our country and the many strands that
make its culture, the language of us, the people, is an uncompromising mirror of
that very history and culture, an unretouched record of the thoughts, feelings,
dreams, successes, failures, and intent of the people. For words are neither coined
nor used in a vacuum: we are what we say. In looking at the thousands of words
and phrases intimately linked with the growth and development of the United
States of America over four centuries, we cannot escape history, for it is our personal and national biography—written in our own words.

That biography is explored in this book, *Speaking Freely*, its thirty-nine sections
based upon Stuart Berg Flexner's bestselling *I Hear America Talking* (1976) and
Listening to America (1982), in which he recounted the tales of great events,
movements, decisions, and leaders as well as stories of everyday life in terms of
our ever-changing, colorful Mother Tongue. In so doing he drew a portrait of the
uncommon individualism of a not-so-common people. *Speaking Freely* is a fusion
of these two books, with the addition of entirely new sections reflecting changes in
our society, hence our language, since 1982.

And change we have! Consider just one instance—the new language of *cyberspace*. Aside from learning and talking about an entirely new "cybervocabulary,"
Americans talked about their new addresses as they plied the Information Superhighway. Thus, English took on a new meaning for a word over 400 years old, at
the same time conferring a new meaning on a punctuation mark once simply
called "a period," now a "dot," as in "dot com." A small example representing a
very large matter—the creation of yet a new frontier to American life, one following the wilderness of the 17th century and the frontiers of the 20th century
space program.

The sections of *Speaking Freely* are organized alphabetically by subject category
from "Advertising: Getting the Word Out" to "The Wild, Wild West." Illustrated
with over 350 photographs and other art, the sections clearly reveal a nation and
language in motion: as an example, "Food for Thought" takes you from the survival diets of the colonists (*Indian cake* and other parched-corn concoctions) to big
juicy *steaks* onward to *junk food*, thence to the choices of *vegans*, onward to multicultural menus of the 1990s—*mahimahi, sushi, tapas*, and all the rest, not omit-
ting the joys of *soul food*. Quotations in the margins show you, often in language
of the times, what people were saying, arguing about, or singing. As an example,
in "Fashions of the Times," a quotation from the *Brooklyn Daily Eagle* of 1883
remarks upon the "new" coinage *dude*, whose ultimate origin and date of first
appearance are still disputed.

The language, like the people, can surprise you every day. *Speaking Freely* contains many surprising insights into sociolinguistic history. For example, the modern word *hijack*, whence sprang *skyjack* and *carjack*, did not develop on highways or in rail yards; rather, it most probably evolved from under the soil—in the zinc mines of Southwest Missouri in the 1980s, as the section "Crime Watch" explains.

After most of the words and phrases under discussion are year or century dates or first recorded use, and whenever possible, brief notations explaining how they got into English. "First cited" in a specific century or year doesn't always indicate that the word might have been in prior oral, unrecorded use, however. Words whose origins are unknown are described as such, but sometimes interesting theories about their genesis are given, as in the cases of *jazz, cocktail, Yankee, scalawag,* and *hep.*

In preparation for writing, our team of writers used a collection of "citations" gathered ahead of time from a wide array of newspapers, magazines, and books to the extent possible according to the subject category. This is the standard practice of dictionary editors: It's the only way you can watch the language change and develop. We also relied on specialized books and journals dealing with specific topics; for example, snowboarding magazines, histories of costume, food histories, articles about the development of railroad cars, books containing recorded transmissions to and from astronauts, and encyclopedias of pop culture. We also relied heavily on such scholarly resources as the monumental *New Oxford English Dictionary*, the *Dictionary of American Regional English*, and the *Random House Historical Dictionary of American Slang.* Information in *Merriam-Webster's Collegiate Dictionary, 10th Edition*, the *American Heritage Dictionary of the English Language, Third Edition*, and *Webster's New World College Dictionary*, along with special articles in *Comments on Etymology*, edited by Gerald Cohen, University of Missouri-Rolla, was invaluable. And to Professor Cohen and all our other scholarly reviewers whose names are listed separately, we thank you for the hours of time you spent with our fledgling manuscript, giving us the benefit of your long experience and expertise.

Thanks to John Monteleone, President of Mountain Lion, Inc., which produced the book and to Randy Voorhees, Sales and Marketing Director. Also at Mountain Lion: Mark Gola, Production Editor; Joan Mohan, Office Manager and Text Input; Mark Goldman, Proofreader; Max Crandall, Designer; Doug Myers, Caption Writer. Also our appreciation to Margaret Trejo, Trejo Production, for page make-up; Ellen Pollak, photo research; Joanna Bruno, photo research at AP/Wide World. At our publisher, the Oxford University Press, Linda Halvorson Morse, Mary Kay Linge, Karen Murphy, and Paula Kakalecik deserve our appreciation.

In his role as senior consulting editor for *Speaking Freely*, Frank R. Abate, now Editor in Chief, U.S. Dictionaries Program, Oxford University Press, made the book all the better. Not only was his expertise essential, but his sense of humor and his understanding of the subtle quirks of English made him a grand colleague. To him we owe a very special thank-you.

To Doris Flexner, who, like our scholarly reviewers, read every line of every section, and who worked with us to preserve the style—and soul—of Stuart Berg Flexner's prose, our deepest appreciation.

Now turn the page and read your biography.

— Anne H. Soukhanov

ADVERTISING:
GETTING THE WORD OUT

*A*dvertisement, *literally that which causes one to turn toward and notice (from Old French* advertir, *"to notice," and ultimately from Latin* advertere, *"to turn toward"), meant any information or advice in Shakespeare's day. In British English* advertisement *is still pronounced* adVERTisment, *but the American pronunciation* adverTISEment *was well enough established to appear in Noah Webster's first dictionary published in 1806. By the year 1841 we had shortened the word to* ad, *and by 1860 our British cousins were clipping it to* advert, *which they pronounce with stress of the* ad-.

Early ads were painted picture signs beckoning mostly illiterate customers to taverns, inns, and shops on nameless streets without building numbers; handbills and posters; and short newspaper announcements of the arrival of shipments of coffee, tea, indentured servants, and slaves for sale, though by 1740 the *Boston News-Letter* carried ads of property for sale. In 1741, the first colonial magazines appeared, in Philadelphia, and so did the first magazine ad, a tiny notice for a runaway slave in Benjamin Franklin's *General Magazine and Historical Chronicle*.

In 1841 Volney B. Palmer started the first advertising agency in the U.S.—not on Madison Avenue in New York City, but in Philadelphia; it was then called an *advertising broker*. He sold what was even then called advertising *space* for newspapers, much in the same way that network account executives now sell *air time* for commercials, an occupation then already called *puffing*. When Palmer expanded his firm in 1850 to the American Newspaper Advertising Agency of New York, Boston, and Philadelphia, he introduced the term *advertising agency* just a year before *billboard* was recorded in its meaning of a roadside sign (it would be about 90 years later that *storyboard*, a panel or series of signlike pictures on which the action of a film or television commercial is roughed out, would appear).

An early print advertisement that violates at least four tenets of today's marketing: 1) depicting mortality, 2) requiring extensive attention from the audience, 3) attempting to sell the same product to multiple market segments at once, and 4) misspelling the manufacturer's name.

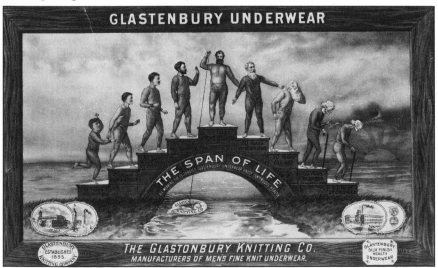

Five and 10's such as this one in WWII-era Baltimore are long gone, and Kresge's is now K-Mart, but neon endures.

In the 1880s new products and new methods of packaging and marketing led to changes in advertising. Thus the *sandwich board* (two sign boards strapped together at the top and hung over a person's shoulders with one in front and the other behind) is known as early as 1897; even earlier, in 1864, the *sandwich man* (the person wearing such signs) appeared—in print, at least. *Electric signs* were on the cutting edge in the 1890s, followed in the 1920s by the blazing glow of *neon* (from Greek *neos*, "new.")

Also in the late 1920s, people were talking about other types of *signage* (1976)—*road signs* and *skywriting*. The fondly remembered *Burma-Shave* series of road signs created by Allen Odell comically conveyed messages that literally turned motorists' heads.

During the mid 1920s *commercial* and *sponsor* took on new meanings with the wonder of home radio. The first *radio ad*, offering real estate for sale, was heard over Long Island's WEAF in 1922, and the *Eveready Flashlight Hour* first introduced "intermittent commercials" during its 1923 show. The term *television commercial* came forward in the late 1940s, with the 1949 *Texaco Star Theater* being the first major sponsored TV program. The concept of being *mersh*—that is, "to be commercial" (the word being a pronunciation respelling of *commerical*)—was clearly on its way, particularly in the new medium of television. Today, the once-familiar expression *And now a word from our sponsor* has a nostalgic air, while cable networks, and late-night TV are notorious for the *infomercial* (cited as early as 1981)—an extended, quasi-documentary commercial, three minutes to an hour in length, that imparts information to viewers while at the same time pitching a product. (Variants of the classic *infomercial* are the *documercial* and the *storymercial*.)

By the late 1940s people were calling anyone who worked in advertising a *huckster* (a word going back to the 13th century, coming to English from the Low German dialects of northern Germany, related to *hawker*, "peddler," and possibly borrowed from Middle Dutch *hokester*, "tradesman"), though as early as 1909 such a person had already been called an *adman*, and by 1926 a *pitchman*. As time went on, *copywriter* and *account executive* emerged, followed in the 1980s by *presenters*, those who pitch products in *infomercials*.

By 1952 we were using *Madison Avenue* figuratively to mean the U.S. advertising industry. Finally, by the mid 1990s, advertisers had moved into the *new media*; that is to say, they had begun to *build Web sites* and *home pages* on the World Wide Web, where elaborate *digitized cyberads* combined audio, animation, video, and, of course, product information for consumer *sampling*. This, then, became the new *online world* of advertising.

It pays to advertise, a fixture in American business parlance since 1914, represents the meaning of the word *slogan* itself, from Gaelic *sluaghghairm*, "war cry," a compound formed of *sluagh*, "army," and *ghairm*, "shout." *Slogans* came into prominent use in the 1840s in America, when patent medicine men, the first to "sell" rather than "announce" their wares, painted these expressions on their wagons. Slogans have been used to *pitch* (1530), *whoop up* (1885), *flog* (1919), or *tout* (1924) products, with the object being to hit the customer's *hot button* (an old street word once meaning "clitoris," now meaning "a key concern or issue known to influence decision-making").

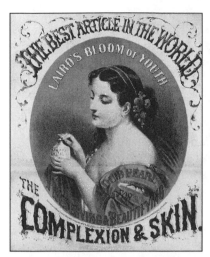

The promise of eternal youth is not an advertising technique unique to the latter half of the 20th century.

An Ivory Soap ad from 1913, its tag line—"99⁴⁴/₁₀₀% Pure"—already in its 35th year."

Getting the word out to customers today involves *pitches* much more sophisticated (and expensive) than those used in 1530, when "[They] did . . . take away . . . fyshe . . . , and *pyched* them in the parishe of Saynt Mary's, and their sette it to sale," where the form *pyched* (*pitched*) meant "to expose (wares) for sale."

Listen to the voices of American advertising from the 1840s to the end of the 20th century. They constitute a snapshot of our cultural history, from horse and buggy to cyberspace:

Harmless as Water from the Mountain Springs, 1840s, Hostetter's Stomach Bitters, recommended for the shakes, dyspepsia, colic, dysentery, nervousness, and gloom—and containing 44 percent alcohol!

Good for Man or Beast, early 1870s, Dr. Hitchcock's Kickapoo Indian Oil, an example of a *nostrum* coming from the Latin word meaning "our," and connoting the secrecy of the formulation.

It Floats—99⁴⁴/₁₀₀% Pure, 1879, Procter and Gamble's Ivory Soap, a batch of which had been accidentally stirred too long, permitting extra air to permeate the mixture, so that the soap actually floated in the tub. Harley T. Procter changed the soap's original name, The White Soap, to *Ivory*, inspired by the words of the 45th Psalm: "All thy garments smell of myrrh, and aloes, and cassia, and out of the ivory palaces whereby they have made thee glad." An element of that slogan survives in informal English to this day when we hear someone say, "I'm 99 and 44/100% sure I'm correct."

Let the Gold Dust Twins Do Your Work, 1880s, Gold Dust Washing Powder (in 1869 *washing powder* was the usual term for kitchen soaps and cleansers in powder form). This is an early example of ads using *you* or *yours* as a way of personalizing the product. AT&T used the same technique 100 years or so later in *Let Your Fingers Do the Walking*, promoting use of the Yellow Pages.

Good Morning, Have You Used Pear's Soap?, 1880s, one of the first appeals to personal hygiene, also using *you*.

Children Cry for It, 1880s, Fletcher's Castoria, a prime early example of a declaration conveying connotations of urgency, and if not that, guilt on the part of parents who do not care enough about their child's welfare to purchase this essential product.

More Than One Million Copies Sold!, 1882, advertising Dr. W. H. Parker's book *The Science of Life or Self-Preservation*, published by the Peabody Medical Institute. Variations on this slogan have been used for many books (and hamburgers) since then.

You Press the Button, We Do the Rest, 1889, George Eastman's slogan for *Kodak*, a meaningless trademark coined by him in 1888 because the letter *K* had "been a favorite with me—it seemed a strong, incisive sort of letter." It's been said that the pronunciation of the name also suggests the sound made by a camera shutter clicking. The Kodak became so popular that many people began to refer to all cameras as Kodaks, so, in order to prevent *Kodak* from becoming generic, Eastman adopted the slogan *If it isn't an Eastman, it isn't a Kodak*.

If You Keep Late Hours for Society's Sake, Bromo-Seltzer Will Cure That Headache, 1895, Bromo-Seltzer, an example of an early rhyming slogan, and one targeted to what we would call today *upscale markets*.

Dispense with a horse. 1898, Winton Motor Carriage Co., the first automobile ad to appear in a national magazine—the July 30th issue of

"Good to the last drop" Maxwell House competes with Schaefer beer, Spud cigarettes, and Chevrolet automobiles for the attention of drivers and pedestrians in New York's theater district.

Scientific American. Price of the car? $1,000. (The very first known automobile ad had been printed in 1896 in *Horseless Carriage*, promoting the Duryea Motor Wagon.)

A Room with a Bath for a Dollar and a Half, around 1900, created in rhyming form by hotel entrepreneur Ellsworth M. Statler.

There's a Reason, a message used from 1900 to 1924 for Charles Post's Grape-Nuts and Postum. The "reason" could be interpreted as the nutritious value of the products or their mildly laxative effect. In the 1950s Modess ran a series of similarly elliptical ads: *Modess because . . .* , as did Clairol in its *Does she . . . or doesn't she?* (around 1955), a double-entendre slogan for Miss Clairol hair dye (now called *hair coloring*), which invites speculation not only about hair color but also about sex life. All sound rather too-delicate in the 1990s, considering the now common ads for condoms, and the public service TV ad, *Don't get high; don't get stupid; don't get AIDS.*

Ask the man who owns one. 1902–56, Packard, one of the longest-running ads for any U.S. car.

Good to the Last Drop. 1907, Maxwell House Coffee, a blend created in the 1880s by Joel Owsley Cheek and served at the famous Maxwell House hotel in Nashville. The slogan is attributed to Theodore Roosevelt, who, while a guest in Nashville, was asked if he would like another cup of coffee. He is reputed to have responded "Delighted! It's good to the last drop."

When It Rains It Pours, 1911, Morton Salt, an example of an ad with the everlasting appeal of the 18th century proverb. It is still used generically to convey the idea that when one thing happens, it often sets in motion a torrent of associated events.

Pay as You Ride. 1916, Maxwell cars, introducing the purchase of a car on credit or on the *installment plan*; the wording plays on an old proverb attributed to Benjamin Franklin, *Pay as you go.*

Always Coca-Cola. Just not always so dainty.

Thirst knows no season, 1922, Coca-Cola, this slogan, created by adman Archie Lee, appeared initially with a drawing of skiers and was the first slogan pitching the beverage as a year-round treat. Coca-Cola's first advertising calendar (1881) pitched the beverage "For headache or tired feeling. Relieves Physical and Mental Exhaustion," and as late as 1935 Coca-Cola advertised itself as "A quick wholesome little lift when you need one," soon followed by the more innocent *The drink that makes a pause refreshing*, the forerunner of *The pause that refreshes*, used intermittently from 1929, followed later by others such as *It's the Real Thing* (from 1970), *Have a Coke and a Smile* (from 1979 to 1982), and *Coke Is It!* (1982).

Guard Against Intestinal Toxicity, 1929, Eno effervescent saline, an early warning among many others regarding the need for internal as well as external cleanliness, continuing the already-growing trend to better personal hygiene and *regularity*. In the 1930s came this rather alarming statement in a Fleischmann's Yeast ad: *Many Men are Failures because of INTESTINAL FATIGUE*, and a 1931 Scott Tissues ad showing a gowned and masked surgeon and nurse busily at work in an operating room was captioned *. . . and the trouble began with harsh toilet tissues*.

Call for Philip Morris. 1933, Philip Morris cigarettes, a memorable ad featuring (in print, and much later, television ads) a uniformed bellhop whose voice on the air intoned the slogan like a town crier, emphatically pronouncing *Morris* as MORR-REESS. Other famous cigarette ads in the days before the Surgeon General's warning of the health risks of smoking were *Lucky Strike Means Fine Tobacco* (1944), abbreviated to *L.S./M.F.T.*, and *Winston tastes good like a cigarette should* (from the 1960s), a rhyming sentence that sparked a huge usage controversy between linguistic purists and liberals over the

> "The philosophy behind much advertising is based on the old observation that every man is really two men—the man he is and the man he wants to be."
>
> — *William Feather*

Pedestrians in New York's Times Square in 1992 passed beneath "Joe Camel," the controversial piano playing cartoon camel featured in R.J. Reynolds advertisements for Camel cigarettes. Anti-tobacco groups want the cigarette manufacturer to discontinue use of the "Joe Camel" advertising, claiming it is a campaign directed toward children.

Quality is Job 1.

Ford Motor Company

FORD MERCURY LINCOLN FORD TRUCKS

The "Quality is Job 1" tag line helped erase the image of exploding Ford Pintos from the minds of consumers.

slogan's use of *like* as a conjunction. These were followed in the 1960s by *You've come a long way, baby*, for Virginia Slims, a slogan that took its cues from the emerging feminist movement. The 1990s witnessed a reappearance of the 1960s-era *Marlboro Man* with a new slogan, *Head Out, Ride Hard, Kick Back and Gear Up*, while the droll billboard image of *Joe Camel* (for Camel cigarettes) sparked controversy over the appeal of cigarette advertising to teens.

There's a Ford in Your Future, 1944, Ford Motor company, a slogan that foretold the planned post-World War II retooling of the company for civilian products. A later slogan was *Ford has a better idea*, similar to Avis's famous *We try harder*. In the 1990s Ford's long-running *Quality is Job #1* (from the 1980s) was often introduced by openers such as *Only your mother is more obsessed with your safety*, to tout the use of air bags and antilock brakes.

The first and only car designed for Your Majesty, the modern American Woman, 1950s, Chrysler Corporation, for the Dodge LaFemme, a pink car accented with pastel rose tapestry and coming with a matching parasol, purse, rain cape and boots, and a special storage compartment designed for the needs of women. No slipcover included.

We Do It All For You, early 1970s, McDonald's, followed by *You Deserve a Break Today*, 1980s.

Plop, plop, fizz, fizz, oh what a relief it is, 1977, Alka-Seltzer, an example of a slogan perfect for the airwaves, followed in the 1970s–1980s by *I can't believe I ate the whole thing*, voiced over by a person with acute gastrointestinal upset.

Humph! Din-din. I'll eat when I'm ready. . . . The cat who doesn't act finicky soon loses control of his owner, 1970s–1980s, 9-Lives Cat Food, voiceover for *Morris the cat*, a large yellow long-hair. The bored, jaded, sonorous male voice, the slogans and taglines, and the visuals showing Morris's pampered lifestyle generated all manner of spinoff products, even a biography of the cat. In the 1980s yet another animal—this time, a canine—became a famous "endorser": *Spuds MacKenzie*, the pit-bull *party animal* who marketed Budweiser.

Don't leave home without it, 1970s–90s, American Express, a slogan so famous that a reader or viewer/listener readily knows what *it* is without further context. This slogan, one of the "Great Warnings" in advertising during the era that gave us a new meaning of *plastic* (1980s)—"a credit card"—was an effective motivator. Similarly insistent wording is evident in Nancy Reagan's antidrug slogan *Just Say No* (1980s), Nike's *Just Do It* (1900s), AT&T's *Reach out and touch someone* (1980s) to promote long-distance calling, the rhyming coffee slogan *Fill it to the rim with Brim* (1980s–90s), and *Please don't squeeze the Charmin*, for toilet tissue.

Nothin' says lovin' like somethin' from the oven, 1970s–80s, Pillsbury, using a *g*-dropping rhyme to evoke the cozy atmosphere of home kitchens across the nation. Cast as a proverb, it finds a parallel in *Moms depend on Kool-Aid like kids depend on Moms*.

The Ultimate Driving Machine, BMW North America, bringing BMW—a *cult brand* of the 1970s—to an apex of sales in the 1980s, and targeted to upscale lifestyles—i.e., to the yuppie market. Use of *the* plus a word like *ultimate* that brooks no comparison (or competition), along with the very serious-sounding *driving machine*, reflected and typified the *serious* affluence of the 1980s.

A magazine advertisement for Absolut Vodka's 1988 Christmas campaign. The ad comprises an illustration covered in plastic pressing a clear liquid tight against the page, containing simulated snowflakes that float freely when shaken—not stirred.

What becomes a legend most?, 1970s–90s, for Blackglama furs, in ads depicting a celebrity swathed in a fur coat. The effectiveness of the slogan is attested by this headline in a January 1996 issue of the *New York Times* introducing a photo essay showing the dress styles adopted by New Yorkers during the Blizzard of '96: "What Becomes a Blizzard Most?"

Where's the Beef?, 1980s, Wendy's hamburgers, a question asked with querulous insistence by an elderly female character at a competitor's restaurant soon became not only a generic idiom, especially in the business world (to convey "Where's the essential element or meaning?") but famously used by Walter Mondale in the 1984 presidential race.

Our Most Important Package is Yours, 1994, FedEx, replacing *When it absolutely positively has to be there overnight* (1980s).

Our repairmen are the loneliest guys in town, 1990s, Maytag appliances, a slogan with such staying power that it spawned generic expressions such as "He's as lonely as the Maytag man."

Requires Great Skull, 1994, Nintendo, is an example of the style of advertising copy deemed attractive to a generation raised on electronic games and computer technology.

Start, 1995, Microsoft Corporation for its Windows 95 computer operating system.

Soup that eats like a meal, 1996, Campbell Soup Company for its Chunky soup, exhibiting a relatively rare intransitive use of *eat*, seen also in Shakespeare's *All's Well that Ends Well* (1601), "Like one of our French withr'd peares . . . it *eats* drily."

ABSOLUT NANTUCKET, 1996, V&S Vin & Sprit AB for its Swedish vodka Absolut, one in a series of ads juxtaposing the trademark *Absolut* with another word and illustrated by the image of the distinctively shaped bottle, itself tied in with the meaning of that second word—here, a photo of a boardwalk shaped like the bottle and leading through dunes to the shore. These ads merged culture with advertising to such a clever degree that people—especially teenagers—began collecting them like baseball cards. "Absolut Madness," remarked a *New York Times* headline of the phenomenon, which echoes the collection—in the 1880s and 1890s—of *stock trade cards* illustrating and advertising everything from agricultural supplies to Dr. Warner's Coraline Corset.

From The Computer "Bugs" at Orkin Pest Control . . . Welcome To ASK ORKIN http://www.orkin.com, 1996, a *Web Site* for the company that made "The Orkin Man" as famous as the Maytag man, with the site initially dominated by a graphic of a bug that crawls around on the computer screen as the *home page downloads*. This *welcome* is an example of the great shift in the late 1990s by advertisers to cyberspace, much like prior shifts to radio and television in earlier decades as those technologies became available to the mass market.

AMERICAN SPOKEN BY AMERICANS

*T*he American Language began to emerge to world view not when the first
English settlers arrived in the New World but when the Declaration of
Independence was written and then adopted on July 4, 1776. Its words and
ideas were the first indicators of the conversion of the English of America from
colonial expression into a national language, just as the document itself
represented conversion of the British colony into a new nation with an emerging
identity (20th century arguments about formally legislating English as our official
language notwithstanding). Through a rejection of British authority, the
Declaration transformed social relationships and redefined words, forming
American meaning through the Constitution (drafted in 1787; ratified in 1788)
and the Bill of Rights (ratified in 1791). With those three documents in place,
American culture developed a system of communication only superficially shared
by other speakers of the English language, whether in England, Canada, India,
Australia, or elsewhere. Our American language has continued to unite its
speakers through shared experience, from the Battle of Lexington (1775) to the
Million Man March (1995). As Mark Twain put it in "Concerning the American
Language" (1880), "A national language is a very large matter. It reflects
everything that happens to a people, the cultural forces that create ideas and
words, the content and form of regional and social expression."

*"The war produced one of the
most eloquent pieces of English
prose ever written (the Declaration
of Independence), a new sense of
American identity, in language as
well as politics."*

— *Robert Claiborne,*
Our Marvelous Native Tongue,
1983

Long before the War for American Independence, however, the
colonists had begun to modify their language according to their needs,
experience, origins, and habits. Early language developments reflecting
personal, ethnic, and social forces include:

(1) Coinages: *bobolink* (1774); *katydid* (1751); *whippoorwill* (1709)—all
   imitative of sounds made by these creatures

(2) Borrowings:
   from Native Americans: *hominy* (1634); *moose* (1603); *raccoon*
      (1608); *skunk* (1588)
   from Dutch: *boss* (1649); *scow* (1749); *sleigh* (1696)
   from French: *bateau* (1711); *levee* (1719); *portage* (1698)
   from African languages: *banjo* (1740); *buckra* ["white man"] (1736)
      chigger (1743). (See the subsection in this chapter titled "Black is
      Beautiful" for more)

(3) English dialect words generally retained in American:
   from Scottish: *drought*; Northern English: *sick* ["ill"]

(4) Obsolete English words generally sustained in America: *deck* (of
   cards);

(5) Changing meanings of preexisting English forms:

Form	"English" meaning	"American" meaning
bay	tree	bush
blackbird	merle	grackle, red-winged blackbird, etc.
beech [common genus *Fagus*]	sylvatica [different species]	grandifolia [different species]

Form	"English" meaning	"American" meaning
creek	an arm of the sea	a freshwater stream
hemlock	a poisonous bush	an evergreen
lark	a skylark	a prairie bobolink
laurel	a bay	an evergreen magnolia
oriole	a black and gold bird	a black and orange bird
partridge	a plump Old World game bird related to grouse and pheasants	a bobwhite, a grouse, or a quail related to the Old World partridge
rabbit	family Leporidae especially the domesticated Old World species or the cottontail	a hare—a mammal similar to the rabbits (family Leporidae); no native rabbits in North America
walnut	walnut	hickory nut (upstate New York)

Using these processes, Americans identified plants, animals, landscapes, living conditions, institutions, and attitudes seldom, if ever, encountered in England. Yet, Americans' continued widespread use of English dialect words was also natural: most Puritans came from England's southern or southeastern counties and spoke East Anglian dialects; most Quakers spoke Midland dialects; and, after 1720, many Scots immigrated to the New World and spread their dialects across the middle and southern colonies, from Pennsylvania to Georgia. The preservation of obsolete English forms, from both dialects and general usage, was also natural. Separated from the English cultural influence, American society and its speech had to advance independently. By the end of the 18th century, Americans had developed a distinctive pattern of expression that required only a formal set of cultural rules, a

The signing of the Declaration of Independence marks the beginning of the American language.

Thomas Jefferson foresaw the evolution of regional dialects.

constitution, to define its form and substance. (And so in 1756, a year after he published his *Dictionary of the English Language*, Samuel Johnson first recorded the term *American dialect*.)

In a letter (September 2, 1785) to Chevalier de Chastellux, Thomas Jefferson regionally distinguished the American population according to regional characteristics that he associated with climate:
In the North they are cool; sober; laborious; persevering; independent; jealous of their own liberties, and just to those of others; interested; chicaning; superstitious and hypocritical in their religion; In the South they are fiery; Voluptuary; indolent; unsteady; independent; zealous for their own liberties, but trampling on those of others; generous; candid; without attachment or pretention to any religion but that of the heart. Those characteristics grow weaker and weaker by gradation from North to South and South to North, insomuch that a traveller, without aid of the quadrant may always know his latitude by the character of the people among whom he finds himself. It is in Pennsylvania that the two characters seem to meet and blend and to form a people free from the extremes of both vice and virtue. Peculiar circumstances have given to New York the character which the climate would have given had she been placed in the South instead of the North side of Pennsylvania.
In the process, he anticipated four major dialect areas of the Eastern United States, Northern, Midland, Southern, and the powerful anomaly of Metropolitan New York City.

Although writing in French (1782), Jefferson's close friend Chastellux first used the term *American* to designate the language of the new republic. In 1802, the phrase *American language* appeared in the annals of the Seventh Congress. And in his *Compendious Dictionary* (1806), Noah Webster first recorded *American English*.

Did American English reflect good or bad usage? By 1735, the English had begun calling it "barbarous," sneering on Americanisms as *barbarisms*. When the anti-American Dr. Johnson used the term *American dialect* he meant it as an insult. Indeed, British contempt for American language and culture endured unabated through the Civil War. In "The Queen's English" (1863), a tract that went through eight editions, Henry Alford, Dean of Canterbury, harshly criticized American language, character, and abolitionism:

Look at the process of deterioration which our Queen's English has undergone at the hands of the Americans. Look at those phrases which so amuse us in their speech and books; at their reckless exaggeration and contempt for congruity; and then compare the character and history of the nation—its blunted sense of moral obligation and duty to man; its open disregard of conventional rights when aggrandisement is to be obtained; and I may now say, its reckless and fruitless maintenance of the most cruel and unprincipled war in the history of the world.
The English found much American usage merely colorful or quaint, terms such as *ground hog* and *lightning rod* and such borrowings as *opossum, tomahawk*, and *wampum* (from Algonquian languages); *waffle, coleslaw*, and *stoop* ["porch"] (from Dutch); *prairie, coulee*, and *voyageur* (from French); and *calaboose, hacienda*, and *rodeo* (from Spanish). But they condemned as unnecessary or illiterate hundreds of other American terms and usages, such as these:

allow, guess, reckon ("to think"), actually obsolete British English meanings.

bark up the wrong tree, an Americanism since 1832.

belittle, first used in print by Jefferson in 1787.

John Witherspoon (clergyman, president of what is now Princeton University, and signer of the Declaration of Independence) coined the term "Americanism."

"Our nationality which answers to the name of American is neither the center of a huge continent nor is it floating loosely around its East, West and Tropical coast lines and harbors. It is a language."

— Horace Gregory, preface, **William Carlos Williams' In the American Grain**, *1995*

"The people of the United States . . . speak, as a body, incomparably better English than the people of the mother country."

— J. Fenimore Cooper, 1828, in "Notions of the Americans"

Noah Webster's was the first American dictionary and it remains the standard nearly 200 years later.

---

bluff, in England, a headland along the sea; in America, a sharp rise of land by a river, stream, or lake, used in the South since 1687, and the first word criticized in England as an "Americanism."

bureau, chest of drawers, an obsolete meaning in British usage.

card, person who likes to joke, in American use since 1835.

clever, sharp-witted, an East Anglian dialect form, but used by all Americans.

fall, obsolete in English, replaced by *autumn*.

fork, branch of a road or river, only an eating utensil in England.

gotten, obsolete in England, where *got* serves as the past participle of *get*.

help, servants, an Americanism since 1630.

how? as an interrogative, "what did you say?" or "say what?"

loan, lend, as a verb, exclusively American.

seaboard, shore, an American coinage first recorded in 1788.

spell, a period of time, or of weather, a while, an Americanism since 1705.

wilt, droop, a verb first recorded in North Carolina in 1691, probably developed from *welk*.

And British observers also criticized our pronunciation and grammar. They rejected, even jeered at, much American usage: the vowel of "clue" in *show*, yielding the pronunciation "shew"; of "far" in *bear*, *there*, and *where*, yielding the pronunciations "bar," "thar," and "whar"; and of "can" in *angel*, *chamber*, and *danger*. (All these are limited today to American folk speech.) In the *American Democrat* (1838), James Fenimore Cooper recommended that Americans pronounce clerk as "clark," *cucumber* as "cowcumber," and *lieutenant* as "levtenant." Not surprisingly, he also advanced the pronunciations of *either* and *neither* as "eye-ther" and "nye-ther," pronunciations that endure today. Most of the other regionalisms identified by Cooper have disappeared. But sources of concern for both the English and the American Anglophiles endure, such as the stressed third syllable in *dilatory*, *missionary*, and *oratory*. In his visit of America in 1822, Charles Dickens observed a nasal drawl and "doubtful" grammar. In 1832, Mrs. Frances Trollope reported rarely hearing a correctly pronounced sentence during her American visit. Seven years later, visitor Captain Frederick Marryat found it remarkable how Americans had so "debased" the English language in such a short time. But a half-century earlier, Americans had declared their linguistic, as well as political, independence. And in 1778, the Continental Congress had recommended that, when the French minister visited, "all replies or answers" to him should be made "in the language of the United States" (not only as opposed to French but also as opposed to English). Objections such as those of Dickens, Trollope, and Marryat were, therefore, foreordained to futility. Noah Webster put it best: In his 1789 *Dissertations on the English Language*, Webster wrote that "the reasons for American English being different than English are simple: As an independent nation, our honor requires us to have a system of our own, in language as well as government."

SOME AMERICANISMS: PURE AND SIMPLE

OLD (1700s/1800s)	NEW (1900s)
bodacious	acid test
buncombe	air bag
cahoots	airhead
cattywampus	Baby Boomer
cowboy	Dagwood sandwich
electric chair	ego trip
enthuse (verb)	footsie
gerrymander	gobbledegook
Gilded Age	intelligence quotient/IQ
gulch	jaywalker
hornswoggle	jazz
horse sense	johnboat
lynch	jug band
maverick	juke box
monkey (verb)	junk food
rattlesnake	kewpie doll
root, hog, or die	kickboxing
scrub team	knucklehead
snollygoster	pink slip
stake and rider fence	trick or treat!
tintype	upside-down cake
Uncle Sam	white collar (attrib.)
whirligig	yuppie
yellow journalism	zipper

"English is destined to be in the next and succeeding centuries more generally the language of the world than Latin was in the last or French is in the present age."

— John Adams, 1780

One of our more rambunctious words is the Americanism *lallapaloosa* (1904, origin still uncertain), also spelled *lallapalooza* and *lollapalooza*, something large or remarkable. In "Reflections on slang *lallapaloosa*," *Comments on Etymology* (December 1994, Vol. 24, No. 3), Gerald Cohen remarks that "maybe—and this is just a guess—*lallapaloosa* was originally a *lulu appaloosa*, i.e., a humongous *appaloosa* (flathead catfish), perhaps even the one that got away."

DIALECTS

Although recorded in an English code of pronunciation, word forms, and grammar, American dialects have no counterparts anywhere in the world. The Northern, Midland, and Southern dialects reflect those same three patterns of regional culture identified by Jefferson more than 200 years ago. For example, Northern *headcheese* ("jellied hog sausage") is *pressmeat* in the Midlands, especially the South Midland, *souse* in the Upper South, and *hoghead cheese* in the Lower South. A *dragonfly* is a *darning needle* or *devil's darning needle* in the North, *snake feeder* in East and Southeast Midland regions of Pennsylvania, West Virginia, and Tennessee, *snake doctor* in the Southern Piedmont, as well as most of the Upper South, and *mosquito hawk* along the Atlantic and Gulf coasts, with the variant *skeeter hawk* most popular in the Piney Woods of the Lower South, from Florida to Texas. Some dialect expressions mark the spot you come from.

A basic North/South contrast emerged following the Civil War, Reconstruction, and Southern isolation. Some of the differences include these North/South terms, many now generalized because of travel, mobility, and the media: *hoe/chop* (weed, as of a crop); *corn on the cob/roasting ears*; *swill pail/slop bucket*; *frying pan/skillet*; *mud wasp/dirt dauber*; *firefly/lightning bug*; *skunk/polecat*; *teeter-totter/seesaw*; *pit* or *stone/seed* (of a cherry or peach); *bacon rind/bacon skin*; *woodpecker/peckerwood*; *peanut/goober*; *lima bean/butter bean*; *white potato/Irish potato*; *cherry tomato/tommyto*; *white bread/light bread*; *vermin/varmint*; *bluegill* or *sunfish/bream*; *carry* or *lug/tote*; *wishbone/pulley bone*; *trachea/goozle*; *Merry Christmas!/Christmas Gift!*; *creek/branch*; *tortoise/terrapin*; *crouch/hunker down*; *suspenders/galluses*; *ghost/haunt* (rhyming with *pant*); *pus/corruption*; *harmonica/French harp, mouth harp*; or *harp, burlap sack/tow sack, croaker sack*, or *crocus sack*; *barnyard/barn lot*; *andirons/fire dogs, dog irons*, or *dogs*. Although Americans in the North and South may not use some of these words as much today, most still are aware of them and usually respond with a smile.

AMERICA SPEAKS!

EXPRESSIONS THAT MARK THE SPOT YOU COME FROM

Regional American English still flourishes. The expressions listed here are "geographic markers"—by their very use they indicate where the speaker comes from, or, in modern terms, where the speaker has recently lived and picked up such expressions:

bear claw or *bear paw*, a pastry of chopped nuts and raisins, possibly originating in 1940s California, now commonly used on the Pacific Coast and into Nevada.

huli stomach, an upset stomach, use of which term identifies the speaker as a native or inhabitant of Hawaii, as does another expression among many, *manine-looking*, so wasted and thin-looking as to resemble the *manini* (a.k.a. *convict fish*), a common marine reef fish.

preacher, a partially submerged floating log in a river or other navigable body of water that constitutes a hazard to boats, a meaning of the word that is strictly Alaskan; in New England such an obstacle is a *deadhead*, while in Mississippi it is a *snag*, among other things.

cat's head, a large, light, fluffy hot biscuit, a term used in the South, as is *dead cat on the line*, something suspect or fishy, derived from the image of a dead catfish on a fishing line.

quahog, a large edible saltwater clam, the word from the Algonquian language of the Narragansett (a Native American people), a word whose *q*-spelling reflecting Algonquian *popquaΩhock* marks the user as a native or resident of the Narragansett Bay area of Rhode Island. The meat of the quahog is used in the preparation of a sort of deep-fried delicacy known locally as a *clam cake*, though it is actually a fritter. Those who spell the word *cohog* (reflecting its pronunciation) are folks from other parts of Northeast New England, most particularly Massachusetts, where *scrod* (probably from Dutch *scrood*, slice) is not a species of fish but the catch of the day.

neutral ground, a highway median strip, the use of which pegs the speaker as a native of Louisiana or southern Mississippi. Those who say *mall* for *median strip* come from upstate New York. If you say *boulevard, boulevard strip*, or *median*, you're from the Midwest. And if you say *medial strip*, in all likelihood you're from Pennsylvania. Under whatever name, many of these now often feature a concrete divider called a (*New*) *Jersey barrier* (or *divider*), a 1980s expression that has spread far and wide.

acequia, an irrigation ditch alongside a road, a term in the dialect vocabulary of South Texas.

shining, the hunting of game at night with a lantern or other lights, used in the upper reaches of the Midwest. *Jack-lighting* (as of deer) is the generalized word for it, though it was once used chiefly in the Northeast. And *spotlighting*, though once chiefly western, has progressed to the East Coast, an example not only of the longevity of dialect words but also their tendency to take root elsewhere in the nation.

storm house, an underground storm shelter, used by Mississippi Delta folk, as opposed to *storm pit*, used elsewhere in the lower reaches of the South, and *hidey-hole* (Oklahoma).

AMERICA SPEAKS! COMPASS POINTS OF THE AMERICAN LANGUAGE

Here are 11 sets of words for the same things that mark the origins of those who say them. In the Northeast if you have to replace the boards on your frame house, you order new *clapboards*; in the South and mid-Atlantic states, you order *siding*; in the Midwest, you ask for *weatherboards*; in the West, you need *batten*. These are but a very few of many differences in the way we still talk, from coast to coast.

Northeast	South	Midwestern	West
brook	branch	creek	creek
corn husks	corn shucks	corn husks	corn shucks/corn husks
cow lot	cow pen	cow lot	corral
devil's darning needle darning needle	snake feeder[1] mosquito hawk[2] skeeter hawk[3]	darning needle snake doctor[4]	dragonfly/snake doctor
faucet	spigot/spicket	tap	hydrant
johnnycake	corn pone	corn bread	corn bread
kindling	lightwood	kindling	sticks
pail	bucket	pail	bucket/pail
clapboards	siding	weatherboards	batten
Danish (now highly generalized)	sweet roll	long john/Bismark[5]	bear claw
tonic/soda	coke/cold drink	soda/pop	pop

[1]SE Highlands
[2]Coastal
[3]Piney Woods
[4]VA Piedmont, Upper South, Lower Mississippi Valley
[5]Metropolitan Chicago

Immigrants get their first glimpse of New York City.

". . . almost from the beginning,
the language of the nation has been
a various language of tongues
beyond number, mixing in the
melting pot."

— *Robert Hendrickson*, **American
Talk**, *1986*

*"Language is a heritage from the
past."*

— *George Harley McKnight*,
**English Words and Their
Background**, *1951*

*"The very idea that African-
American language is . . . separate
and apart is very threatening,
because it can encourage young
men and women not to learn
standard English."*

— *Maya Angelou on Ebonics, to*
The Wichita Eagle,
*quoted by the Associated Press,
December 22, 1996*

ETHNIC DIVERSITY: AMERICANS THEMSELVES

For a country that prides itself on its reputation as a *melting pot* (from the title of Israel Zangwill's 1908 play), the United States has not always been able to boast of harmonious relations among its various *ethnic groups* (a popular term since the 1960s; *ethnic* from Greek *ethnos*, people, nation). The tremendous influx of legal immigrants and *illegal aliens* over the past several decades added to the racial and ethnic tensions already brewing in areas of the country where the so-called natives—most of whom are descended from immigrants themselves—feared losing their jobs and their neighborhoods to newcomers who speak *English as a second language* (*ESL*). Even among *second generation Americans* there are regional biases: many New Englanders, also known as *Yankees*, poke fun at the way *hillbillies* from Appalachia talk; the *Anglos* in New Mexico look down on the speech of those of Mexican descent; and some *Angelenos* (from Los Angeles) think of New Yorkers as rude and unfriendly.

Although our language is rife with ethnic stereotypes, such as the *dumb Polack*, the *dumb Swede*, the *drunken Irishman*, and the *Jewish-American princess*, there is no denying that the presence of so many racial and ethnic groups has also enriched our *mother tongue*. Where would we be without expressions like "Hey man!" (Black English), "You should live so long" (Yiddish), and "Gesundheit!" (German, "health," ultimately from Old High German *gisunt*)? They may not realize it, but all Americans often use words and expressions that have been borrowed from their German-American, Hispanic-American, African-American, Italian-American, and other ethnic neighbors. Unfortunately, not all Americans appreciate what *diversity* (a 1990s term for America's ethnically varied population) has brought to their language.

BLACK IS BEAUTIFUL

The very first reference to African Americans or blacks (*black*, long-established; *African American*, much newer, with first instances from 1984) in America dates from 1619, when John Smith of Jamestown, Virginia wrote in his journal that a Dutch ship "sold us twenty Negars." The

Abolitionist Harriet Beecher Stowe's *Uncle Tom's Cabin* put Black English in print for the first time. The book has now been published in 20 languages.

term *black* was also widely used until the Civil War. But since *black* was considered a slave term, African Americans from the time the war ended until the late 1880s preferred to be called *colored*. From then until the 1930s they preferred to be called *negroes* (with a capital *N* after the late 1920s). During the Civil Rights Movement, especially in the 1960s, *black* again became the preferred word. Today, *African American* is an established term of first reference (having all but replaced the 1853 *Afro-American*, which enjoyed vogue during the 1960s–70s), employed exclusively by some, though the older terms are still appropriate in certain contexts—for example, the civil rights group known as the *NAACP* (*National Association for the Advancement of Colored People*).

The slaves who came to colonial America spoke many different African languages. Among the words we have taken from them—aside from *goober, yam,* and *gumbo*, discussed in the chapter on food—are *banana* (first recorded as a West African word from the Congo region in 1563), *Sambo* (a Hausan, north Nigerian word and name meaning "second son"; known to most colonists as a common African American male name by 1700 and used condescendingly by whites to refer to any black male by 1806), and *mumbo jumbo* (1738, perhaps from West African Mandingo).

Because most of them were never taught formal English, the early slaves developed their own dialect, or variety, of English and African words, pronunciations, syntax, grammar, tones, and speech rhythms (with some Spanish and French mixed in from the West Indies, Florida, and Louisiana). This dialect was first noted in 1702. It included African words such as *tote* (perhaps of Bantu origin, related to the Kongo *tota*, to pick up). The early black dialect also used pidginlike English words such as *sickey-sickey* and *workee* (for sick and work) and pronunciations and forms such as *berry* for "very," *de/dis/dat* for "the/this/that," and *gen'men* for "gentlemen." In terms of syntax and grammar, it simplified or dropped the use of some verbs, especially auxiliary verbs like *can, have, may, must,* and *will*. It often used *do* for *does* and *get* for *have/has* ("Do she gots a green dress?"), *be* for *is* ("It be rainin'," "He be right"), or dropped the *be* form altogether ("It rainin'," "He right"). This slave dialect had at least some influence on the white Southern dialect, espe-

Cutaway views of a fully-loaded slave ship.

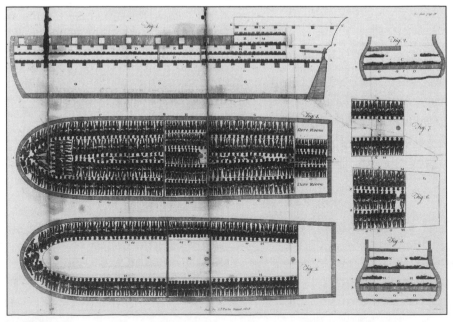

"Our scientific power has outrun our spiritual power. We have guided missiles and misguided men."—Rev. Martin Luther King, Jr. One of the greatest orators of the 20th century, he introduced the nation to the rhythms and phrasing of Southern Baptist preachers.

cially through the black *mammies* (a term of around 1800) who raised so many white southerners.

As succeeding generations of African Americans received more formal schooling, mingled more freely with whites, and moved to northern cities, this dialect of English and African elements changed, as all English has (and does). Today it is called *Black English* (a term made common among educators by Joey Lee Dillard's 1972 book which analyzes and explains it) or *African-American Vernacular English* (*AAVE*). In December 1996 the whole nation learned the word *Ebonics* (*ebon*y + phon*ics*), a synonym of *Black English*, used by the Oakland, California School Board, which voted to recognize it as a "second language" in its school system. The program, which was to train teachers to understand Ebonics and to help them teach students "proper" English, was a subject of national discussion in the late 90s.

During the Civil Rights Movement of the 1960s, *Black* (capitalized) replaced *Negro* as the preferred noun and adjective. The *Afro* (also called the *Natural*, a forward-combed, sometimes very full and rounded hairstyle for both men and women) was introduced in the late 1960s, when some young blacks began to wear it as a badge of *Black pride* and African identity. It was followed by *cornrow*s, rows of small, flat braids separated by half-inch parts. *Black is Beautiful* was the slogan during the 60s. Many colleges and universities instituted *Black Studies* programs, and many well-known African Americans (such as heavyweight boxing champ Cassius Clay, basketball player Lew Alcindor, and playwright Le Roi Jones) discarded their "slave names" and assumed *Black Muslim* names like *Muhammad Ali*, *Kareem Abdul-Jabbar*, and *Amiri Baraka* (the Black Muslims are a religious and political movement that advocates complete separation of the races in America). It was during this same period that *Oreo* became a derogatory word for a black who seemed to share white attitudes and culture rather than black ones (from the Nabisco company's chocolate cookie, which is black on the outside with white creamy filling on the inside). *Soul* (1962, meaning of, by, or for African Americans and their unique feelings and attitudes, from the 1950s term *soul music*) took on a new significance, giving rise to *soul food* ("down home" food; see FOOD FOR THOUGHT: AMERICA EATS, *soul brother* (a fellow black), and *soul food restaurants*.

THE REAL NATIVE AMERICAN RESIDENTS

The *North American Indians* (a term that originally referred to the inhabitants of the West Indies, then spread to include all the aboriginal peoples of the Americas) were here, of course, long before the African Americans and the whites were. In fact, many American place-names were originally Indian words. Indian words for plants, animals, and landscapes started to appear in our language soon after the colonists landed. Algonquian was the most widely spoken family of Indian languages in the eastern half of the U.S. Since the Indians hadn't yet invented writing, and since each local tribe might have its own pronunciation of any given word, the colonists had a hard time trying to spell and pronounce Indian words. Often they shortened the Indian word or phrase, or tried to pronounce the parts of the word like familiar English words (a process called *folk etymology*). Virginia's Captain John Smith introduced many

Wounded Knee. The aftermath of the U.S. Army's massacre of 200 members of the Sioux tribe (including unarmed women and children) on a reservation in South Dakota in 1890.

such words into English, begin-ning with his written description of Virginia in 1608. Today about 20 Algonquian words, mainly for plants and animals, are still in use, plus a sprinkling of words from other Indian language families, such as:

caribou (via Canadian French from Micmac *khalibu* or something that sounded like *maccaribpoo,* "he who paws the snow"), 1610.

chipmunk (Ojibwa or Chippewa *atchitamon,* "head first," from the way the animal descends a tree), 1832.

opossum (Powhatan *aposoum,* "white animal"), 1610. Shortened to possum by 1613.

Sequoia, named after the Cherokee Sikwayi (1770-1843) who invented an 85-syllable "alphabet" for recording the Cherokee language. *Sequoia* was first used as the genus name of a tree, which includes the giant California redwoods, by Hungarian botanist Stephen Endlicher in 1847.

tamarack, from an Algonquian word that sounded like *tamarack* or *hackmatack,* which is another word for this red larch, 1805, now mainly found in the names of summer camps and resorts.

Decades of westward expansion eventually left our American Indians—the preferred term now is *Native Americans*—confined to reservations. But in some areas the course of history is being reversed, with Native Americans expanding their real estate holdings with the profits they've made from gambling casinos. In fact, the economic success of some Native American tribes, combined with the efforts of poorer tribes to keep their culture alive, has increased Americans' sensitivity to words and expressions that capitalize on Indian stereotypes. Sports teams have been pressured to get rid of names like *the Braves* and *the Redskins,* and it is no longer common to address Indian men derisively as *Chief,* women as *squaws,* or babies as *papooses.* But there are other words that have been so wholeheartedly adopted by non-Native Americans that they aren't even aware that they're "talking Indian"—for example, *Podunk* (from *Podunk*, the name of a village in Massachusetts or a locality in Connecticut, 1666; of Algonquian origin, then used by whites to mean a small or insignificant town or rural region by 1841). (For more information on Native Americans and their contributions to our language and culture, see WILD WILD WEST.)

THE INUIT

The word *Eskimo* is now frowned on by many; *Inuit* is the preferred term because the source of *Eskimo*, the Micmac word *eskameege*, "eaters of raw fish," is considered insulting. (*Inuit* is the plural of *inuk*, "person.") The Inuit *mukluk* ("large seal") we use for shoes. *Mush!* is not Inuit: it comes from "mush on!" and ultimately from French *marchons!*

Aside from the familiar *igloo* (from *iglu*, "house"), the Inuit have also given us *kayak* (from *qajaq*).

THE JEWS

The nearly three million Ashkenazi Jews who came to America between 1880 and 1910 had a unique influence on the American language. They spoke *Yiddish* (from German *jüdisch*, Jewish), the 1,000-year-old language of these Central and East European Jews. It began when Jews from northern France first moved into the Rhineland and began to write German words with the letters of the Hebrew alphabet. Yiddish is still written in Hebrew, and its vocabulary is still based principally on German words, the rest being a mixture of Hebrew and words from various Slavic languages.

Yiddish flourished in the *ghettos* (defined in English in 1611 as a place where Jews dwell, from Italian) and the *shtetl* (literally "little city, village," a diminutive based on the German *Stadt*; it refers to a village of Jews, especially in Russia). Those who came to America brought with them words such as *chutzpah* (from Yiddish *khutspe*, from Hebrew "insolence; audacity"), *gelt* (from Yiddish, from Old High German *gelt*, recompense), *goy* (from Yiddish, from the Hebrew word for people, nation, non-Jews, applied to Gentiles), *kibitz* (via Yiddish *kibitsen* from German *kiebitzen*, from *Kiebitz*, the bird called a pewit), *klutz* (from Yiddish

Comedian Jackie Mason in 1990, autographing copies of his book, *How to Talk Jewish*. A magician revealing the tricks of his trade?

klots, from Middle High German *kloz*, lump), *kosher* (via Yiddish from Hebrew *kasher*, right, fit, proper), *mensch/mensh* (from Yiddish, human being, from Old High German), and *nosh* (from Yiddish *nash*, from Old High German). It was from these Jewish immigrants that Americans picked up the expression *Oy vay!* (which translates as "Woe is me," used as an exclamation of despair, fear, surprise, etc.), *schlemiel* (a bungler), *schlep*(p) (to drag, lug, carry, also to lag behind; one who is always dragging behind, a lazy, untidy person), and *schmaltz* (which originally referred to chicken fat, but is used in American English to mean excessive sentimentality).

Yiddish has also given us *schm-*, added to a repeated word to convey sarcasm or a "who cares?" attitude, as in *fancy-schmancy* or *dictionary-schmictionary*, and the noun-forming suffix *-nik*, as in *no-goodnik*.

THE GERMANS

What could be more quintessentially American than a good *delicatessen*? Every time we order up a corned beef on *pumpernickel*, we are recognizing the seven million German immigrants who have come to the U.S. since 1776. Common American words like *delicatessen* (from the German *Delikatesse*, delicacies to eat; as preserved and cooked meats, pickles, etc., 1893; as the store that sells such foods, 1903), *cookbook* (German *Kochbuch*, 1809), *coat hook* (German *Kanthaken*, 1848), and *cylinder* (German *Zylinder*, slang for a plug hat, 1860s), all have come to us by way of German immigrants. They started arriving in great numbers after the German Revolution of 1848, settling primarily in St. Louis, Cincinnati, Milwaukee, and Minneapolis. By 1860, the U.S. had 28 German-language daily newspapers in 15 cities. (And don't forget the *frankfurter* and *hamburger*—both discussed in FOOD FOR THOUGHT: AMERICA EATS, subsections Hot Dogs and Hamburgers.)

American English has scores of other German borrowings, many of them only partially naturalized, so we still associate them with Germans or things German, such as *hausfrau* (housewife), *knackwurst* (literally "sausage that cracks open when eaten"), *noodle* (German Nudel), *sauerbraten* ("sour roast," marinated roast), and *wienerschnitzel* ("Vienna cutlet"). Many common American exclamations also owe their origins to the Germans: *and how!* (1928, probably based on German *und wie*), and *ouch!* (German autsch, 1837).

FROM SPAGHETTI TO PASTA

One of the proudest ethnic groups in the U.S. is the *Italian-Americans*. Despite the fact that America was discovered by one Italian (Christopher Columbus) and named for another (Amerigo Vespucci) few Italians immigrated to this country until after 1865. Then over five million Italians came to the U.S., settling primarily in large northeastern cities.

Many of the Italian words in English entered the language during the Renaissance, when Italian culture was very much in vogue. Thus English has had *gondola* (from Italian *gondolar*, to rock) and *piazza* (Italian for public square, market square) since the 16th century; Italian musical terms such as *allegro*, *duet*, *opera*, *piano*, *staccato*, *trill*, and *violin*; and other words from Italian such as *balcony*, *cameo*, *granite*, *grotto*, *portico*, *stanza*, *umbrella*, and *volcano*. Words that have come directly into American English from Italian or our experience with Italians include:

pizza, an Italian word, perhaps from *pizzicare*, to pinch, prick, pluck, which also gives us the Italian musical term *pizzicato*, has grown in

Mulberry Street in New York's Little Italy, decorated for the annual San Gennaro Festival.

Migrant worker and United Farm Workers union leader, Cesar Chavez. His name became a household word in 1968 when he organized a national boycott of California grapes in his battle to improve the lot of farmworkers.

popularity among Americans since the 1940s; *pizzeria,* 1940s; *pizza parlor,* late 1940s.

spaghetti (Italian for "little string"), first common in America in the 1880s. The word entered both American and British English only in the 19th century.

tutti-frutti ice cream, 1876. It means "all fruits" in Italian.

We are particularly indebted to the Italians for some of our food-related terms, such as *café espresso* or *espresso* (literally "pressed out," by the steam), *cannelloni* (literally "big pipe"), *dulce* ("sweet"), *lasagna* (literally "cooking pot"), *ravioli* (literally "little turnips," from their shape), *spumone* ("spume, froth"), *vermicelli* (literally "little worms"), *minestrone* ("to serve, dish out"), *parmesan* ("from Parma"), *pasta* ("paste, dough"), and *al dente* (literally "to the bite" or "tooth," cooked enough to be firm, but not soft). Yuppies noted that when *spaghetti parlors* became restaurants specializing in *pasta,* prices soared.

HISPANIC-AMERICANS: THE NEW MAJORITY?

Perhaps the fastest-growing segment of the American population today consists of *Hispanics,* a term that covers Cubans living in Miami and New Orleans, Mexicans living in the Southwest, and Puerto Ricans living in New York City. It all started with the 16th century Spanish explorers and *conquistadors.* Coronado, Cortés, Ponce de Léon, Pizarro, and de Soto were the first Europeans to see many of the plants, animals, tribes, customs, and geological features of the Americas. They used Spanish names or borrowed the local Indian names for them, spreading their own Spanish words and their Spanish versions of Indian words to Europe and eventually into English. From the Spanish conquest of Mexico, including much of our own Southwest, we have such Mexican Spanish words as *bronco, corral, lasso, ranch, rodeo,* and *stampede,* now associated with American cowboys. Spain also ruled Puerto Rico, Cuba, and the Philippines, providing us with more Spanish words. Thus, from the early Spanish explorers to the exodus of Cubans from Castro's Cuba to the U.S. after 1959, Spanish has given us such words as *alligator* (Spanish *el lagarto,* the lizard, first recorded in America, 1682), *cockroach* (Spanish *cucaracha,* recorded in Virginia by Captain John Smith in 1624), *mosquito* (Spanish diminutive of *mosca,* fly, hence little fly, first recorded in America in 1656), *patio* (Spanish for courtyard, 1827), *savvy* (Spanish *saber,* to know, understand, 1850), and *vamoose* (Spanish *vamos,* "let's go," 1840s).

Most Americans were first introduced to the Hispanic-American subculture by the popular Broadway musical and a film *West Side Story* in the 1960s. Featuring music by the American composer Leonard Bernstein, *West Side Story* updated the Romeo and Juliet legend by moving it to New York City and the world of Puerto Rican gangs. Nowadays, most Americans are not only familiar with Hispanic food—thanks to the proliferation of *Tex-Mex restaurants* (see FOOD FOR THOUGHT: AMERICA EATS)—but also Hispanic-American celebrations like *Cinco de Mayo* and *Day of the Dead,* and Hispanic-American writers, athletes, entertainers, and politicians. In some parts of the U.S., particularly the area around Miami, southern California, and the Texas-Mexico border (where the

Tejano culture reigns), the Hispanic influence on all aspects of life is so widespread that it can no longer be defined as a "subculture." It's part of the area's culture.

ERIN GO BRAGH

Americans were calling an Irishman *Paddy* (an ancient nickname for Patrick) by 1748, *Irisher* by 1807, *Pat* (also from the common first name Patrick) by 1830, and an *Irish American* by 1836. Many Americans inherited an unfortunate condescension for the Irish from the English: by 1809 *to get one's Irish up* meant to get angry and by 1840 an *Irish pennant* meant the dangling end of a sloppily tied rope (first recorded in Richard Henry Dana's 1840 book *Two Years Before the Mast*). But it was the Irish Potato Famine of 1846—actually a widespread European famine caused by potato blight—that sent the wave of Irish immigrants to America that was to have such a wide and deep influence on our culture. By 1860 there were more than one-and-a-half million Irish immigrants in America, making it the largest foreign-born group in the country.

Unfortunately for them, these usually poor, uneducated immigrants found themselves competing for jobs with the better educated, more worldly German immigrants of the same period. Many Irish men ended up working as laborers, and many Irish women as servants or *Irish washer women*.

The first *St. Patrick's Day Parade* in America was held in 1779, and by 1818 *Paddy* had yet another meaning: the stuffed figure of St. Patrick carried in the *St. Paddy's Day Parade*. St. Patrick's Day (March 17), the traditional death date of Ireland's patron saint, also had many Americans saying *Erin Go Bragh* ("Ireland forever"), a Celtic toast that is still used on this day, and singing "When Irish Eyes Are Smiling" (1912). Incidentally, the *wearin' of the green* refers to the custom of wearing a *shamrock* (Irish *seamrog*, the diminutive of *seamar*, clover, hence "little clover") on this day because St. Patrick is said to have used its three-part leaf to illustrate the concept of the Holy Trinity. Other terms we associate with or have taken from the Irish include:

colleen, a young girl, 1828, from Irish Gaelic *cailin*, a diminutive of *caile*, girl. At St. Patrick's Day parades, *colleens* who are elected by officials, ride in the procession much like beauty and homecoming queens.

galore, 1628, in great abundance, from Irish Gaelic *go leor*, enough.

Paddy wagon, a police van, late 1920s, referring to the many Irish or "Paddy" policemen in such cities as Boston and New York.

shamrock, 1577, from Irish Gaelic seamr—g, diminutive of *seamar*, clover.

shillelagh, which has meant a club or cudgel in English since the 18th century, especially an oak or blackthorn one (originally made from the famous oaks of Shillelagh in County Wicklow, Ireland).

With immigration increasing rather than dying out, it seems likely that America will continue to be enriched by the contributions of all its ethnic groups. New Americans from Haiti, Asia, the Middle East, India, and elsewhere will inevitably add words of their own, making the language richer and, perhaps, eventually taking the "hyphenated" out of the popular expression *hyphenated Americans*—bringing us all closer together.

"Look at those (American) phrases which so amuse us in their speech and books; at their reckless exaggeration and contempt for congruity . . . "

— Henry Alford, A Pleas for the Queen's English, *1863*

BOOZE:
AMERICA'S LOVE AFFAIR WITH THE BOTTLE

*B*eer, hard liquor, and wine and the nature of their consumption in America form a colorful strand in the fabric of our social history, going back over the centuries. The histories of these beverages are apparent in the many expressions associated with them, and those very expressions speak to our nature as a society.

BEER, BEERGARDENS, AND SALOONS

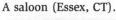

The *Mayflower* Pilgrims landed in Plymouth, because they were running out of "victuals . . . [and] beer." Otherwise they would have sailed on to Virginia as originally planned. Early colonists talked about making *corn beer, potato beer, pumpkin beer*, and even *persimmon beer*, but they mainly drank regular beer imported from England. (Only after it was found that native apples thrived in new England where grain did not, did *cider* replace beer as the colonists' major drink.) Early Americans drank their beer at home, but the men also drank it at inns, taverns, bars, alehouses, porterhouses, *beer cellars* (1732, from German *Bierkeller*), and *beerhouses*, which around the 1830s were sometimes simply called *houses* or *homes*.

Until the 1840s beer was darker, stronger, and fuller-bodied than the lager we have been used to since. Although some of it was *small beer* (1568)—weak, inferior, cheap beer, the term also coming to mean "unimportant matters; trivia"—most of it was ale, porter, "stout beer," or malt liquor.

A saloon (Essex, CT).

The Samuel Adams Brewhouse, a brew pub located in center city Philadelphia, opened for business in 1989. Owner David Mink, left, and brewer Jim Pericles hoist their product.

An early advertisement for Blatz lager.

In the mid to late 1980s *microbreweries,* or boutique breweries, began to produce *craft beers,* often locally distributed or available in a *brewpub,* at the brewery itself. A *microbrewery* is small by big domestic and international brewery standards, generally producing fewer than 10,000–15,000 barrels a year.

Here then are some of the types of beers that Americans have talked about over the years:

ale (before the 12th century). Until the 17th century ale was simply made of malted barley or other grains, yeast, and water. Then brewers began adding hops for flavor, making its formulation identical to beer.

beer (before the 12th century), always made with malted barley or other grains, hops, yeast, and water. In the 1840s the Germans introduced new yeast that allowed "bottom fermentation": the yeast sank to the bottom after doing its work. This combined with aging, gave us *lager beer.* Since then in America *beer* has technically meant the kind produced by bottom fermentation, *ale* that produced by top fermentation.

stout, 1677. Stout is from the 17th-century expression "a stout beer" or "a stout ale," meaning a strong one. It did not become a specific kind of beer until the 19th century. It's a strong, dark, malty ale with more hop flavoring than any other beer/ale.

porter, 18th century. Porter is short for *porter's ale* or *porter's beer,* so named because the porters who carried produce at London's Covent Garden market favored it. It's a strong, dark ale with a medium hop flavor and higher alcoholic content than other beer/ale. Porter was popular in early America and alehouses were sometimes called *porterhouses* (about 1814, Martin Harrison, the proprietor of a New York City porterhouse, popularized the *porterhouse steak*).

The "Bock Beer Maid" of Philip Best Brewing, 1886. Note the goat on her hat.

The German immigrants and their lager changed American beer, beer-drinking habits, and our beer vocabulary. We were now to have:

lager beer or *lager*, 1840s–50s, from German *Lager bier*, literally "storehouse beer," aged beer, a pale, light-bodied, medium hopped, comparatively weak beer that is more carbonated than older beers.

pilsner or *pilsener*, 1877, a name that comes from the famous *Pilsner Urquell* beer from Pilsen, Czechoslovakia, where the water gives it a clean, fresh, light-bodied flavor.

bock beer, or *bock*, 1856, from German *Bockbier*, originally *Einbecker Bier*, a special beer from the northern German city of Einbeck (*Einbeck* is pronounced "Einbock" in the dialect of Munich). The two-word expression *ein Bock* has an entirely different meaning in German: "a goat." Legend has it that during a drinking contest between two medieval German brewers, one of them passed out, only to claim later that he had been knocked down and out by a passing goat. The victor laughed, remarking that he had brewed the "Bock" that had floored his adversary. In terms of English, *ein Bock* or *Einbock* sounds like "ein buck." That's why we see some bock beer labels with pictures of bucks or goats on them, and that's why some folks started calling bock beer *buck beer* (1850s). Some bock beer has been called *double beer* (1867) because it can be twice as strong as lager. Some bock beer brands—German and American—end in the suffix *-ator*, e.g., *Optimator* (a German one) and *Illuminator* (a Philadelphia one).

dark beer, a brew (beer or stout) that is brown in hue because dark-roasted malt is used. When people ask for it, they often transpose the word *dark* so that it comes after the brand name, as in "I'll have a Beck's *dark*."

light (or *lite*) *beer*, once called *Vienna beer*, one in which lightly roasted malt is used. This variety of beer, with lower alcohol content and thus fewer calories, has become an established favorite among American beer drinkers.

malt liquor, a brew made with ingredients similar to other beers, but formulated to be higher in alcohol content than lager beer, up to 8%.

A 19th century brewery in Portsmouth, NH.

ice beer, a brew popularized in the 1990s, made with a process during which the beer is frozen and the ice removed, thus enhancing flavor. There are also *ice malt liquors* and *light ice beers.*.

Lager beer was the kind that made Milwaukee, St. Louis, and Cincinnati famous, the beer that men drank in the new *saloons* (1841, from French *salon*, hall) and made *saloon keepers* (1860) wealthy.

The saloons seemed full of children (and women) sent to get dad's (or hubby's) beer or apprentices sent to get it for a work gang. They brought in their buckets, cans, or pitchers called *growlers* (1885) (origin obscure and disputed). Fetching beer from a saloon in a growler was called *rushing* or *rolling the growler, working the growler, chasing the can* (or *the duck*), or *rolling the rock* from the late 1880s until Prohibition. It seemed that many men couldn't eat or work without their *bucket of suds* (1904), and many a man had a fat *beer belly* (early 1900s).

Until 1875 all beer had been *draft beer* (Old English *dragan*, to draw, as from a spigot on a cask). Draft beer was also called *shenkbeer* in the 1870s–80s, coming from the German word *Schenkbier* (from *schenken*, to pour). *Bottled beer* was first produced by Schlitz in 1875, giving us collateral expressions such as *a bottle of beer* and *beer bottle*. In Texas and other parts of the Southwest *beer bottle* came to be called a *longneck*, this word now starting to lose much of its regionality as its use today moves up the Atlantic Seaboard. An empty beer bottle has been called a *dead marine* or a *dead soldier* since about World War I. In 1935 Coors Ale gave us *canned beer* and by the end of World War II *a can of beer* and *beer can* were becoming household words.

How often do Americans talk about beer? No one knows. We do know that we are now the biggest beer-producing nation in the world. Unlike the *Mayflower* Pilgrims, we're not about to run out of it; but if someone does, that someone need only drop by the nearest *convenience store* (1965) and in the manner of *Joe Sixpack*, pick up a *sixpack* (1952).

> "During the years leading up to the Revolutionary War, rum became the distilled drink of Colonial America. . . . By the early 1700s, the colonists were consuming twelve million gallons of rum a year."
> — Joseph Earl Dabney, Mountain Spirits

> "When you absorb a deep swig of it [pure corn whiskey], you have all the sensations of having swallowed a lighted kerosene lamp."
> — Kentucky humorist Irvin S. Cobb, 1930s

When this photo was taken (1940), Schlitz had been producing bottled beer for 65 years. Beer in cans, on the other hand, was only five years old.

Brewing may have evolved into a $20 billion industry in the 90s, but its ingredients remain nothing more than barley (left), hops (right, being picked in 1941), yeast, and water.

BOOZE

To get the hard facts about the history of hard liquor in the United States it is necessary to dive into a barrel of words, some of which, like *liquor*, *booze*, *spirits*, and *alcohol*, were brought to America by the early settlers, if not the very first colonists:

liquor (about 1225). Originally the word meant any fluid; by about 1300 it had come to be used of any beverage or drink, but almost exclusively one created by fermentation, such as ale, or by distillation. Used in early America in the sense of a drink of an intoxicating beverage, *liquor* or *liquor-up* was considered slang.

booze (Middle Dutch *busen*, to drink or tipple), in English as a verb (*to booze*, drink) since the 14th century; the noun *booze*, liquor, dates back to the same century, and *booze* remains very common as a slang term in American English.

spirits, first recorded in 1610 in the sense of a liquid obtained by distillation, and as early as 1684 was used in the "hard liquor" sense.

alcohol, 1652, is from the Medieval Latin expression *alcohol vini*, fine powder, from Arabic *al-kuhul*, powdered antimony, a substance obtained by distillation, and used to tint the eyelids; it eventually came to be used of any distillate, and was finally specialized in popular speech to apply to intoxicating spirits.

rum, 1654, English word shortened from the obsolete *rumbullion*, which meant the same thing, but no one is sure where the long form came from: some theories are that the word referred to distillation, to the French chateau town of *Rambouillet*, or to *rum booze*, European argot for "excellent booze." Rum was made in the Caribbean almost as soon as the Spaniards landed and planted sugar cane. By 1639 our colonists were calling rum by the West Indies name *Kill-Devil*. The colonists also used *rum* to refer both to the specific drink and to liquor in general. New Englanders soon imported molasses and sugar from the West Indies to make their own rum, drank lots of it, and had a thriving business exporting the rest to the other colonies, Africa, and

The William Henry Harrison "hard cider" campaign of 1840.

elsewhere. New England ships traded rum for slaves on the African Gold Coast, then brought the slaves to the West Indies and traded them for molasses and sugar, which they brought back to New England to make more rum—making huge profits. This New England-made rum was called *Yankee rum* and *stink-a-bus*. It was the basic colonial liquor, and a dram or tot at breakfast was thought to be a preventive against the malaria that plagued the southern colonies.

The early settlers never heard of *rye* or *Bourbon*, much less *vodka*. They talked at first about their three most common alcoholic beverages—beer, cider, and rum—and also about wine and the less common brandy and gin. The history of American hard drinking thus really begins with rum and goes to whiskey and rye, then to Bourbon, Scotch (imported) and vodka, in that order. And that order of events brings together slave traders, a rebellion, taxes, moonshine, medicine, and the Russians:

whiskey and rye. The British imposed high taxes and import duties before the Revolutionary War, passing the restrictive Molasses Act in 1733 and the Sugar Act in 1764, then later imposed embargoes and closed harbors, thus crippling New England's rum industry. Fortunately, by that time the Scotch-Irish immigrants had arrived in force and were old hands with the *pot still* (*still* is a 16th century word; the formal *distillery* came later, in the 18th century, both from the verb *to distill*). By 1722 these Scotch-Irish had reached Pennsylvania, and especially the Shenandoah Valley, distilling their home-grown rye into whiskey. The Irish and Scots Gaelic words *beathadh* and *uisge beatha*, "water of life," were soon respelled as *whiskybae*, then shortened to *whiskey* (whiskey with the *-e-* is the American spelling, thus the way we spell our products *Bourbon whiskey* and *Irish whiskey*—whisky without the *-e-* is the British spelling, thus the way British products are spelled, *Scotch whisky, Canadian whisky*). From the mid 1730s through the Revolution, as the British made West Indies molasses and sugar more difficult to obtain, we turned from rum to this *whiskey* made of native rye. By 1785 *whiskey* had become a general term for all liquor, and if you wanted whiskey made form rye, you had to specify *rye whiskey*, which was not commonly shortened to *rye* until the 1890s. Some easterners, however, still have "rye" in mind whey they say "whiskey."

Rye whiskey soon met its own political fate. Money was short after the Revolutionary War, and the first Secretary of the Treasury, Alexander Hamilton, persuaded President Washington to levy an excise tax on domestic whiskey. those Pennsylvania Scotch-Irish resisted paying the tax, tarred and feathered some tax collectors, and in 1794, 13,000 militiamen were sent to quell the riots, which were called the *Whiskey Rebellion*. After that, some Pennsylvania rye-

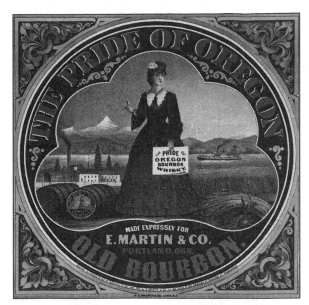

Though bourbon originated in Kentucky, here it's found its way all the way to Oregon by 1871.

Bootleggers frequently had to outrun federal agents in pursuit by automobile; for some bootleggers their second career was stock car race driver.

making farm families moved out of the tax collectors' reach, over the Appalachian Mountains into the new state and tall corn of Kentucky.

bourbon. When their rye crop was a little short these new Kentucky settlers started mixing some corn in their mash. This soon made *corn spirits* (a term first cited in 1764) a common drink all the way down the Ohio and Mississippi rivers to New Orleans. It had been called informally *corn whiskey* by 1780. The slang term *mountain dew* was known by 1878, but is no doubt much older. By the 1850s, Americans knew of it as *Bourbon County whiskey, bourbon whiskey,* or simply *bourbon,* named for Bourbon County, Kentucky, where Pennsylvania immigrants first made it famous in their log-cabin distilleries (the county name honors the French and Spanish royal family). Later, corn whiskey, often made illegally under cover of darkness, was also called *moonshine* (in the U.S., 1877), sometimes clipped to *shine* or *moon* as time went by. (*Moonshine,* traceable to 1785 in written contexts involving the activities of British coastal smugglers in Kent and Sussex, is said to have ultimately come from a preexisting [prior to the 1700s] word for a liquor smuggler on the British coast, *moonlighter.*) *Moonshine* was also known as *blockade whiskey,* as it was smuggled past naval blockades during the Revolutionary War, the War of 1812, and the Civil War. *Hooch,* first recorded in 1897, is a short form of *hoochinoo,* a distilled liquor made by the Hoochinoo (Hutsnuwu) people belonging to the Tlingit tribe, who inhabited the southeastern coast and islands of Alaska. (*Hooch,* which, over more than a century, has never lost its slang status, refers either to cheap, inferior liquor or illicitly distilled liquor.) Some African-American slang for *moonshine* that developed in the urban South include *alley bourbon, city gin, splo* (clipped from another clipped form *'splosion,* "explosion" in the drinker's gut), *cool water* (from its dilution with water in cheap bars), and *ruckus* (pronounced ROOK-us) *juice.*

gin. Americans have been drinking gin from colonial days. The word itself is an altered form of *geneva,* from Dutch *jenever,* juniper (ultimately from Latin *iuniperus*), the plant whose berries give gin its distinctive flavor. Gin was created originally as a medicine by a Dutch chemist and physician named Sylvius. William of Orange introduced it into England in the 17th century. Since it was easy to make, even in bathtubs (*bathtub gin,* 1920s-1930s), it became very popular during Prohibition and thereafter.

Scotch, made from malted barley, began to be exported from the Scottish Highlands after 1746. Except for travelers to England and a few wealthy people, Americans generally did not drink or talk about *Scotch* until the mid 1890s. Expensive to make and import, it gained further status during Prohibition, then became the sophisticated drink between World War II and the 1960s.

vodka, a Russian borrowing that first appeared in English in 1803, diminutive of Russian *voda,* water, was originally made from potatoes. It grew in popularity in America after World War II. In the late 1980s, pushed by American marketing, the Russian brand *Stolichnaya,* along with other imported brands, became even more stylish. A clipped form of *Stolichnaya, Stoly,* gained wide currency in American English.

A 1913 advertisement for Sandy MacDonald Scotch, emphasizing the drink's Scottish Highlands roots.

American colonists also drank *brandy* (1657), or, in full, *brandywine* (or *brandewine*, from Dutch *brandewijn*, distilled wine), a term noted for its use in hundreds of U.S. placenames.

Besides the more formal *liquor, spirits*, etc., we have called liquor—especially the strong, cheap, sometimes illegal stuff—many colorful things reflective of the American character, among them:

rotgut, 1633, for its supposed effect on the imbiber's gastrointestinal tract.

Jersey lightning (applejack), 1780; *lightning* (gin), 1891; *white lightning* (corn whiskey), 1915, also called *white mule* for its "kick," *white likker*, and *paleface*.

phlegm cutter, 1806, or *phlegm dispenser*.

blue ruin, 1811; *blue rum*, 1831, for cheap gin or whiskey; *blue pig*, 1840.

firewater, 1817, from the burning sensation it leaves.

red eye, 1819, because habitual drinkers tend to have bloodshot eyes; *red-eye special* (1922) was very cheap, strong whiskey sold in speakeasies during Prohibition.

eye-water, 1823, gin or whiskey.

lush, 1840, from the 1790 English use meaning any liquor.

coffin varnish, 1845.

forty-rod (or *fortyrod*), 1856, supposedly for its power to kill at 40 rods away.

tanglefoot, 1859, or *tangle-legs*, for its effect on one's gait.

busthead, 1857; also *bust skull*, 1860s, and *popskull*.

tarantula juice, 1861; *sheep dip*, 1865; *snake medicine*, 1865. These 1860s terms grew with the Civil War and are just a few of the Northern Army's many colorful words for the cheap or illegal whiskey the soldiers bought or made.

nose paint, 1881, referring to the red nose of some habitual drinkers.

mule, 1900s.

juice, 1920.

the sauce, 1920s.

panther sweat, 1929; *panther piss*, 1941 (*panther piss* is probably the older term, perhaps even very old, but its taboo nature prevented it from being recorded sooner), also called *tiger milk*.

Still more such terms are *joy water, whoopee water, crazy water, conversation water; sorrow drowner, bosom friend; courage, Dutch courage, liquid courage; tonic, medicine; cutthroat, stingo, stump puller, bottled dynamite, liquid fire, boilermaker's delight, who shot John; craw rot, poison, rat poison, scorpion juice, formaldehyde, widow maker, shellac*, and *embalming fluid*—the range and connotations being word-pictures of the effects of *the little brown jug, the cup that cheers, the nectar of the gods*, and *the flowing bowl*.

We have also called a drink of liquor *the hair of the dog (that bit you)*, going back to 1546 in England, first recorded in America in 1842. It's a drink of the same kind that gave one a *hangover* (1912) and that is used to cure the hangover. Others are *slug* (1762), *eye opener* (1817), *nightcap* (1818), *finger* (1856)—an amount equal to the width of a finger laid against the bottom of a glass—*pick-me-up* (1867), *snort* (1889), *snorter* (1891), *nip* (1891), *jolt* (1905), *shot* (1906), and *belt* (1921), with the verb *to belt* (to have a drink; to drink), first recorded in 1846 (both the verb and the noun go back to the 1830s expression *have a drink under one's belt*).

COCKTAILS, HIGHBALLS, GROG, ETC.

The American *cocktail* (1806) had spread around the world by the beginning of the 20th century, many countries having adopted our word and our drinks. The origin of *cocktail* is unknown, though unproved theories still circulate. And all attempts to trace the word to another *cocktail*, "a horse with a docked tail," have been futile. Some people think the word came from French *coquetier*, "egg cup," dating to the 1790s when a French-born New Orleans apothecary, Antoine Peychaud, dispensed tonics of Sazerac du Forge Cognac and his own *Peychaud bitters* in egg cups, the concoction then being called, after its container, a *coquetier*. Other theories are that *cocktail* is from the old British *cock tailings*, a mixture of the tailings from various liquor kegs, sold cheaply; from the British *cock ale* (1648), a mixture of chicken broth and ale; from *cock's ale*, an ale-and-liquor given to fighting cocks; or from a rum-and-fruit juice drink introduced to American officers by a New England innkeeper during the Revolutionary War, pronounced by French officers as *le coq's tail*, it having been decorated with the feathers of a neighboring Tory's rooster.

True cocktails originally had to be made of liquor, sugar, water, and bitters. In fact, in the early 19th century, cocktails were often called *bitter slings*, and the *Old-Fashioned* was so named because it is "an old-fashioned whiskey cocktail" made with bitters (it was invented, or reinvented, by a bartender in the Pendennis Club in Louisville, Kentucky). The word *cocktail* gives us such compounds as *gin cocktail* (1845), *rum cocktail* (1861), *whiskey cocktail* (early 1870s), and finally *champagne cocktail* (1870s). These drinks were mixed or shaken in makeshift shakers until the *cocktail shaker* (cited 1868) first appeared. (It is thought that one of the first shaken cocktails was created for the patrons of Increase Arnold's tavern in Providence, Rhode Island. It consisted of rum, sugar, milk, and cracked ice.) By 1905 we had formed the *cocktail habit*, using *cocktail glasses* (1907). In the 1920s and 1930s the celebration of sophistication, youthful stylishness, and romance that had by then been linked to cocktails began to be reflected in still more *cocktail* compounds—*cocktail hour* (1927), *cocktail party* (1928), *cocktail bar* (1929), *cocktail cabinet* (about 1933), *cocktail tray* (1934), *cocktail dress* (1935), *cocktail stick* (1937), and *cocktail lounge* (1939), followed in the early to mid 1960s by *cocktail pianist* and *cocktail table*. It is no coincidence that many of these *cocktail*-related compounds became popular during Prohibition (1920-1933). During that period hundreds of mixed drinks were invented in order to stretch supplies of the illegal liquor in speakeasies, but it was only in the late 1940s through the 1960s that the *cocktail* became established as a permanent social fixture here and abroad. Another indicator of the staying power of the modern mixed drink was the emergence in 1948 of the term *mixology*—the art and skill

A bartender plying his trade in 1941.

of making mixed drinks. After a relatively short period of declining popularity in the 1960s–70s, the cocktail made a comeback in the stressed-out 1990s, and many new ones were concocted, including a whole new class of cocktails called *shooters*, which are small enough to be drunk in one draft, and are often served in shot glasses.

Some of the mixed drinks Americans have talked about are:

the Bogus, *the Bumbo* (or *Bombo*), *the Meridian*, and *the Sampson*, all colonial concoctions, some recipes for which are unknown today, though we do know that *Bumbo*—the word possibly derived from baby talk—contained rum, sugar, nutmeg, and water. (George Washington, when running for the Virginia House of Burgesses in 1758, ensured that on Election Day the voters received 160 gallons of rum, a practice called "swilling the planters with *Bumbo*.") *Mimbo* was rum minus the nutmeg, and *mamm* (1600s) was rum, water, and sugar. Native Americans had a rum drink they called *coow-woow*, imitative of their war cry.

blackstrap, rum and molasses—a favorite colonial drink that, diluted with water, became something called *switchel*.

stonewall (or *stone fence*), rum mixed with cider.

punch, in colonial times a mixture of wine, liquor, milk, and hot water. *Punch*, first recorded in England in 1632, is said to have originally contained five ingredients: arrack, tea, sugar, lemon, and water.

julep, from Arabic *julab*, Persian *gulab*, rosewater, entered English around 1400 for a minted, nonalcoholic drink. Rum and brandy juleps were served in colonial days; *mint julep*, an American term of 1809 (almost 40 years before Kentucky's *Bourbon* became well-known), has become inextricably associated with the Kentucky Derby.

bounces and shrubs, made by pouring brandy or rum over fruit, sugar, and water, sometimes with citrus slices and spices, then allowing the mixture to sit or ferment for at least a week. *Shrubs* (probably from Arabic *shurb*, drink) had also been popular in England and sometimes differed from bounces only in that they were strained and sweetened with brown sugar before serving.

grog, named after British Admiral Edward "Old Grog" Vernon (1684–1757), who in 1740 ordered his sailors to take rum and water daily, instead of "neat spirits," to prevent scurvy (it didn't prevent scurvy). He was called Old Grog because he was famous for wearing a shabby old *grog*ram coat in foul weather. His drink became "Old Grog's drink," "Grog's drink," and then simply *grog*.

eggnog, made in England with ale (*nog* meant strong ale) or dry Spanish wine. The word was first recorded in America in 1775, by which time it was made with local rum or hard cider by most people, and with imported brandy by the rich.

syllabub, of unknown origin, though a popular theory has it that the word might derive from *Sillery*, in the champagne region of France, plus *bub*, an Elizabethan word for a "bubbling" drink. It became a wine eggnog in America, popular at Christmas, served chiefly to women and children instead of the stronger eggnog. It may be conjectured that the British made it originally with *champagne*, which is first recorded in English in 1664. By 1899 we were calling champagne *bubble water* or *bubbly water*, and by 1920 the other slang term *bubbly* had been established. Other words for it were *fizz* (1860), *gigglewater* (1926), and *giggle-juice* (1939), the latter persisting into the 1980s.

toddies (from Hindi *tari*, palm tree sap, which is distilled into a strong liquor), popular since the 18th century, though the word goes back to 1610 in English.

san garee (French *sang*, blood, from Latin *sanguis*, because the drink is dark red), what the colonists called their drink of red wine, fruit slices, citrus juice, sugar, and spices. We have known it as *sangría* (Spanish for "bleeding") since 1736; it was reintroduced into America from Spain by commercial bottlers in the 1960s.

flips, originally hot drinks for cold New England days. First a mug was filled with hot ale, liquor, or a combination of both, and sugar and spices were added. Then a red-hot poker would be thrust into it. The poker was called an "iron flip dog" (hence the name *flip*) or a *loggerhead* (all early Americans had these hung by their fireplaces). If a beaten egg had been added, the drink was called *a yard of flannel*, the egg and bubbling liquid having a fleecy appearance.

slings (*sling*—of unknown origin—had been English slang for any drink since 1768), popular since the early 1800s; *gin sling* was first recorded in 1800; *bitter sling* meant any cocktail in the early 19th century; *whiskey sling* appeared in 1880. Today they are usually made with gin or rum, to which brandy, sugar, and lemon juice are added; earlier Americans also added nutmeg.

Sazerac, a trademark. However, because Antoine Peychaud had used Sazerac du Forge brandy in his coquetiers, some people called any cocktail a *Sazerac* in the early 19th century.

cobblers (perhaps from *cobble*, "to put or patch together roughly"), recorded as early as 1809. They were drinks made out of wine, sugar, fruit, and juice mixed with cracked ice and popular in warm climes. By the 1830s *sherry cobblers* were in vogue; the term *whiskey cobbler* appeared in 1862.

cobbler's punch, last of the ale, liquor, sugar, and spice drinks still to be popular in the 1840s.

24-hour punch, originally an Asheville, North Carolina delicacy, consisted of corn whiskey, fruit juices, sugar, and fruit peelings marinated in big glass jugs for 24 hours.

sours, first popular in the 1850s. They were really simple *slings*, without the brandy. We still make them the same way, with liquor, sugar, and citrus juice. *Brandy sour* dates from 1861, *whiskey sour* from 1891.

fizzes, popular in the 1860s, are sours with soda water added. New Orleans' *Ramos gin fizz* became famous after 1888, when Henry Ramos bought the Imperial Cabinet saloon and introduced his complex, tasty gin fizz there.

the Manhattan, first recorded in 1890, and named for the New York City borough. It is basically whiskey and sweet vermouth with bitters. *The Bronx*, which substitutes gin for the whiskey, appeared in 1919.

gin rickey, 1895, is said to be named after a Washington D.C., imbiber by that last name. A drink of gin, soda, water, and lime (hence also sometimes called *lime rickey*), it's really a gin fizz without the sugar. If we put the sugar back in, or a syrup, and pour in a little more soda we have a *Collins* (a tall sour fizz). The original *Tom Collins* (1909) is said to be named after the bartender who invented it.

martini, first recorded in 1894, but people were drinking something called the *Martinez* in the 1860s; if the martini grew out of the Martinez it might be named after a famous hotel, restaurant, or bar by that name (there were several). Another theory has it that "Professor" Jerry Thomas invented it at San Francisco's Occidental Hotel while tending bar there in 1860–62, first making it for a thirsty traveler on the way to Martinez, California, or so the story goes in his book *The Bon-Vivant's Companion*. The more prosaic story is that the martini emerged in the 1890s under the auspices of Martini and Rossi vermouth, taking its name from the brand. The 1899 martini called for two parts gin to one of vermouth (strengthening the story that a ver-

"Awful calamity at the Park bird bath . . . when somebody discovered the birds were potted due to some members of the Mint Julep Association having emptied their julep glasses in the fountain."

— Baltimore Sun, August 14, 1943

mouth manufacturer was behind the whole thing). As a general rule of thumb, the martini has become one part more gin (or later vodka) for every 25 years of its history.

the Gibson, 1930, comes from a surname of that spelling, perhaps that of the illustrator Charles Dana *Gibson*. It is a very dry martini with a pearl onion instead of a lemon twist or an olive.

the Rob Roy, sometimes called a "Scotch Manhattan" since it is a Manhattan made with Scotch. It's named after Scotland's own Robin Hood, Robert MacGregor (1671–1734), popularly known as Rob Roy.

Bloody Mary, 1934, was a creation of Fernand Petior, the bartender at Paris's famous expatriate hangout Harry's Bar, where it was the favored drink of people such as F. Scott Fitzgerald and Ernest Hemingway. (When the drink first crossed the Atlantic to New York it was originally called a *Red Snapper*.) Its red color, from the tomato juice that is its chief ingredient, led to the name, from the nickname of the notorious Queen Mary I of England (1553–58).

Pina Colada, 1954, from Spanish, meaning "strained pineapple," is a concoction of rum, pineapple juice, and coconut cream that is reminiscent of some of the early colonial punches.

margarita, 1963, from the Spanish first name of that spelling, made famous in Jimmy Buffet's 1977 hit song "Margaritaville," is the cocktail that launched the still-current popularity of *tequila* (*tequila* is from *Tequila*, Mexico, and is made of the distilled agave pulque). It consists of chilled tequila, freshly squeezed lime juice, and triple sec, served in a chilled glass with coarse salt around its rim.

tequila sunrise (1965), a combination of tequila, orange juice, and grenadine.

DRUNK

Drunk has more synonyms than almost any other English word: at least 2,000 of them have been compiled. Benjamin Franklin, however, was the first American to publish a list of them, ending up with 228 terms in 1737, some of which are: *oiled, stewed, stiff, stiff as a ringbolt, soaked,*

A man who has quite literally been drunk "under the table."

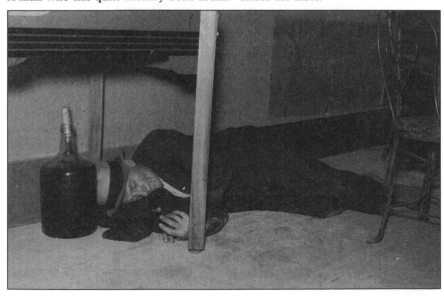

buzzed, bowzered, cockeyed, cocked, mellow, overset, jagged, have a brass eye, cherry-merry, flushed, frazzled, glaized, gold-headed, has his flag out, lappy, limber, loose in the hilt, lordly, moon-eyed, seen the devil, pigeon-eyed, topheavy, and nimptopsical.

Words for drunk run the gamut from tipsy to blotto, connoting the drinker's degree of inebriation—sort of a linguistic BAC (blood alcohol concentration). Here is a representative sampling of this drunk and disorderly lot in order of first written citation:

drunk, about 1340, from the older drunken (about 1050). Drunk came to be used (1779) as a noun to mean a drinking bout, or an intoxicated person (1852).

boozy, 1529; boozed, 1737.

intoxicated, 1576, from Latin intoxicare, from in- plus toxicum, poison, literally "poisoned with drink."

in one's cups, 1580.

inebriated, 1609, from Latin ebriu, drunk.

foxed, 1611 (spelled foxt then).

soused, 1613 (spelled soust then).

disguised, 1622.

high, 1627; elevated, 1748; high as a kite, 1939.

blind, 1630; blind drunk, 1775.

cut, 1650.

jolly, 1652.

wet, 1704.

rummish, 1760; rum-dum, 1891.

groggy, 1770; groggified, 1785; grogged, 1796 (literally "full of grog").

corned, 1785.

over the bay, 1787, with other nautically oriented expressions—(with) decks awash, half the bay over, and three sheets to the wind—eventually evolving.

slewed, 1801.

ginned, 1811.

lushy, 1811; lush, lushed, 1880s (lush, origin unknown, first recorded around 1790 and first meaning "liquor").

blue, 1818.

snuffy, 1823.

tight, 1830.

bent, 1833; bent out of shape, 1969.

half shaved, 1834.

screwed, 1838.

stinking, 1837; stinking drunk, 1926; stinko, 1927; stinko drunk, 1976.

full, 1840; full as a goose, 1883; full as an egg, 1887; full as a tick, 1892; full as a fiddle, 1905; full to the scuppers, 1915; full as a fiddler's fart, 1960.

pickled, 1842.

swizzled, 1843.

liquored up, 1845.

pixilated, 1848 (from *pixie*).

D and D (drunk and disorderly), 1855.

squiffed (or *squiffy*, origin unknown), 1855.

balmy, 1857.

damaged, 1859.

shot, 1864.

boiled, 1884 (spelled *biled* then); in current spelling, 1885; *as intoxicated* (or *drunk*) *as a boiled owl*, 1892.

cheered, 1886.

shikker, shicker, shickered (from Yiddish *shikker*, drunk, Hebrew *shekar*, strong drink), 1890s.

loaded, 1886; *with a load on*, 1890; *loaded for bear*, 1896; *get one's load*, 1902.

sozzled, 1886; *sozzled up*, 1904.

> "To take wine into our mouths is to savor a droplet of the river of human history."
> — Clifton Fadiman

Witches' Brews

Names and dangerous side-effects of moonshine sold during Prohibition:

happy sally; *jump steady*; *soda pop moon*, spiked with isopropyl alcohol that paralyzed its drinkers' tongues.

goat whiskey; *jackass brandy* (from peaches), this causing internal bleeding for $4.00 a quart!

sweet whiskey, made by boiling potassium nitrate.

yack yack bourbon, moonshine laced with burnt sugar, iodine, and other materials.

smoke, wood alcohol rectified by having been strained through old newspapers, causing its drinkers to go into a coma or become blind.

jake, an almost 90% alcohol fluid extract from Jamaica ginger, plus wood alcohol—a concoction that paralyzed the drinker's hands and feet. It was dispensed by some drugstores at 50¢ a two-ounce bottle, officially prescribed for "stomach distress." *Jake paralysis* affected at least 15,000 people.

sugar moon, distilled from sugar beets and causing an excruciating hangover, as was the case with *American whiskey*, made in Mexico from cacti and potatoes, smuggled into the U.S. where artificial color and flavoring were added.

cherry dynamite, Upstate New York, overripe black cherries soaked for twelve months in alcohol, a drink popular with summer visitors.

tanked up, 1893.

corked, 1895.

feeling good, 1888; *get good*, 1897.

woozy, 1897.

owly-eyed, 1900; *pie-eyed*, 1904.

have a bun on, 1901; *bunned*, 1901.

plastered, 1902.

pifflicated, 1905.

rosy, 1905.

frazzled, 1906.

spiflicated (or *spifflicated*), 1906.

jingled, 1908.

piped, 1912, first recorded, but probably much earlier.

polluted, 1912.

canned, 1914.

lit up, 1914; *lit up like a Christmas tree/church/the commonwealth/a lighthouse/a store window/the sky/Broadway/Times Square/Main Street*, all mid to late 1920s; *lit up like a cathedral/a Catholic Church/high mass/a kite/a skyscraper*, early 1940s.

blotto, 1917.

have a snoot full, 1918; *have a snootfull*, 1935.

gassed, 1919.

shellacked, 1922.

fried, 1923; *fried to the eyebrows*, 1925; *fried to the hat*, 1927; *fried to the gills*, 1942; *fried to the eyes*, 1947; *fried to the eyeballs*, 1964.

potted, 1924.

dead to the world, 1926 (from the meaning "fast asleep," going back to 1890).

crocked, 1927.

swacked, 1932.

batted, 1933.

looped, 1934.

feeling no pain, 1940s.

shitfaced, 1940s.

juiced (also *juiced up*), 1946.

sloshed, 1946.

boxed, 1947.

clobbered, 1951.

smashed, 1959.

bombed, 1959; *bombed out*, 1967.

> *"Good wine is a necessity of life."*
>
> — Thomas Jefferson

Typical nights at the dance hall such as this one in Butte, Montana helped the temperance movements gain momentum.

zonked, 1959 (probably imitative in origin).

wasted, 1984.

Others are these: *addled, afloat, bagged, beerified, blasted, buffy, bummed, buoyant, buried, busted, capernoited, comboozelated, corked, crashed, crocko, deleerit, flooey, giffed* (from *TGIF*, Thank God It's Friday), *gone, hammered, happy, hooted, illuminated, inebrious, jagged, jugged, loopy, lubricated, muddled, organized, orie-eyed, ossified, out, packaged, paralyzed, paralytic, petrified, pissed, primed, putrid, saturated, skunked, sloppy, snockered, snootered, sloshed, sozzled, stewed, swacko, tanglefooted, trashed, under the table, walleyed, wazzocked, whipped, wrecked,* and *zozzled*.

The results of a *spree* can be a *hangover*, also called the *katzenjammers* (1849), German for "cat distress" or "cats wailing"; *the shakes; the DTs* (1858, abbreviation of Latin *delirium tremens*, "trembling delirium"); *the jim-jams*, 1852; *the jitters;* the *heebie-jeebies* (coined by American cartoonist Billy De Beck in his strip "Barney Google," 1923); *the horrors; seeing pink elephants* (1940); and *the screaming meamies* (origin unknown, 1942).

We also have words for those who frequently get drunk. The first recorded *tipplers* were a John Jolivet and a John Smyth, listed as such when they came before authorities in England in 1396 for violating the liquor laws. (At that time *tippler* meant a tavern keeper; it later came to apply to the steady customers.) We have called a heavy drinker any number of things: *alcoholic, boozehound, boozer, dipsomaniac* (Greek *dipsa,* "thirst," plus *maniac*), *drammer, elbow bender, guzzler, inebriate, lush, lusher, rumhead, rummy, rumpot, rum sucker, shicker, soak, soaker, sot, souse, sponge, stiff, swiller, tank, toper, tosspot,* and *wino*. Antonyms? *Abstainer, teetotaler* (cited to 1834, origin disputed, possibly coined by a Richard Turner of Preston, England, around September 1833 in a speech promoting total abstinence from intoxicating liquors but also possibly of Irish or even U.S. origin), and *prohibitionist*.

Remaining abstemious, or at least responsible in one's drinking habits, has given rise to these few expressions: *sober as a judge/a deacon/a church/a shoemaker/a buck shad*, *cold* (or *stone*) *sober*, and for a former drinker, *on the wagon*. Joining these older expressions are the acronym *MADD* and the noun compound *designated driver*. *MADD*, which represents *Mothers Against Drunk Driving*, entered the American English lexicon in 1981, when the organization was founded. And *designated driver* (formed on the model of baseball's *designated hitter*), also a product of the 1980s, means a person chosen or volunteering not to drink on a night out in order to drive friends home safely. These terms are evidence of the rising concern, especially in the last two decades of the 20th century, over the effects of alcohol. The desire to have a drink socially yet still stay sober also led to the popularity of a large number of *nonalcoholic beers* in the 1990s.

PROHIBITION: JOE SENT ME

Thus began *the Prohibition Era* (*Prohibition* in this sense first recorded in the 1851 annual report of the American Temperance Union), the *dry era*, the *Noble Experiment* (President Herbert Hoover's 1928 term) which lasted from 1919 to 1933. It was brought about by the Temperance Movement (going back to the 1808 Temperance Society in Saratoga, New York, formed by a country doctor), which, from then on, advocated abstinence not only from hard liquor but also beer, wine, and hard cider—and ratified by the states. The 18th Amendment was immediately followed by legislation to enforce it. During the next 13 years we used such terms as:

bathtub gin, homemade or inferior bootleg gin, usually drunk with ginger ale or orange juice to kill the taste.

blind pig or *blind tiger*, any unlicensed saloon, words predating Prohibition.

An early form of public service advertisement, courtesy of the Women's Christian Temperance Union.

Temperance movements, such as the Woman's Holy War, began in the late 19th century.

bootlegger, a smuggler of illegal whiskey, because he hid the bottle in the leg of his tall boots. The word had become popular in the *dry* states of Oklahoma and Kansas in the late 1880s. *Bootleg whiskey*, 1904; to *bootleg*, 1906. It also gave rise to the famous *bootleg turn*, a 180-degree turn in an automobile as used by a bootlegger on the run from the law.

home brew. Though beer had always been made at home, this beverage and term became very popular during Prohibition. Hardware stores did a thriving business selling *bottle cappers* at $2.50 each and the sound of bottles of home brew exploding in the basement was heard throughout the land.

hospital alcohol, what bootleggers always told their customers they were getting—good, pure alcohol, not cheap denatured industrial alcohol.

near beer, 1909, as an imitation beer or beerlike soft drink containing less than $\frac{1}{10}$ of 1% alcohol. (In the 1900s *near* was first used to mean "nearly, almost.") During Prohibition near beer was made by reducing the alcohol content of real beer to the legal level of less than $f_{(l(1),l(2))}$ of 1% (sauerkraut contains more alcohol than this).

needle beer, needled beer, near beer or 3.2 beer into which grain alcohol had been illegally injected.

red ink, homemade wine. During Prohibition heads of households were legally allowed to make 200 gallons of wine yearly for home consumption. California and New York vineyards sold bricks of compressed grapes (e.g., *grape brick*) for winemaking and also an enormous quantity of grape juice in bottles, kegs, and in concentrate (e.g., *Vine-Glo*), which was not ostensibly for winemaking—but with which they thoughtfully provided detailed instructions on how *not* to make wine!

rum row, the line of liquor-laden schooners sitting offshore near most East Coast cities, supplying the *rumrunner* fleets of small motorboats, a precursor to the *go-fasts*, or *fastboats*, used by 1980s–90s drug smugglers. The ships carried Scotch and other whiskey from Canada and Bermuda, rye from Nova Scotia, and rum and alcohol from the West Indies and Cuba.

rumrunner, any person, ship, boat, car, truck, etc., engaged in smuggling whiskey. The overpowered motorboats unloading rum-row ships carried up to 70 cases at a time and could speed at 35 knots. The cars were often souped-up, oversprung, eight-cylinder touring cars, carrying up to 200 gallons.

speakeasy, 1889, in the dry state of Kansas; sometimes shortened to *speak* during Prohibition. The word may come from the English underworld *speak-softly shop* (1823), a smuggler's home or place of business. Many Prohibition speakeasies were "clubs," some charged a 50¢ entrance or membership fee; some issued much-sought after identification cards to their regulars, which could be flashed (a precursor to today's *carding* of youths attempting to enter bars) at the peephole or at the doorman; others were *key clubs*, giving door keys to regular patrons. If you weren't known, a simple "Joe sent me" would often do.

3.2 beer, a fairly weak beer containing 3.2% alcohol. Though it was sometimes confused with *near beer*, it was actually real beer by definition (3–6% alcohol). It was legalized April 7, 1933, shortly before Prohibition ended.

A rum runner at the end of the line in 1924. Rum running from Cuba to Key West was the centerpiece of Ernest Hemingway's *To Have and Have Not*.

By the late 1920s Prohibition was in shambles: liquor flowed, crime and corruption flourished, enforcement was lax or non-existent. Referendums showed the public was disgusted with the experiment. Repeal of the 18th Amendment, embodied in the *21st Amendment*, went into effect in December, 1933 during Franklin D. Roosevelt's first term.

WINE

Just as winemaking involves the use of many ingredients, so too is the linguistic history of American wine diverse. American winemaking was begun by early explorers and settlers from the Norse to the English to the Spanish to the French. It involved both coasts in two very separate stories, and its terminology is rich in foreign borrowings.

Viticulture (Latin *vitis*, vine, plus Middle English *culture*, cultivation, from Latin *cultura*)—the growing of grapes as a *vintner*, a winemaker (from Latin *vinum*, wine)—was practiced by the Egyptians and Assyrians (3500 B.C.) and later the ancient Greeks and Romans. Grapes came to be cultivated for wine across Europe. When Norseman Leif Ericson landed near Newfoundland over 1,000 years ago he discovered so many lush grapevines there that he dubbed it *Vineland the Good*. Trouble was, when the European explorers and settlers of America found the same thing, they also found that the grapes didn't taste good when made into wine. These grapes were too *foxy* (so called for their sour or musky flavor)— they yielded wine with a strong, even rank, aroma and taste.

Nevertheless in 1564 near what is now Jacksonville, Florida, the first American wine was successfully produced by French Huguenots using the native *muscadine* grapes, most probably the *scuppernong* variety— *muscadine* being an altered spelling of French *muscatel*, and *scuppernong* named after a North Carolina river of the same spelling. American *eno-*

A 19th century California vineyard in operation.

logical history, having started in Florida, had less successful roots on
Roanoke Island off the Virginia coast, home of the famed Lost Colony.

Though the settlers tried to introduce cuttings from European vines
in the New World, the transplants at first sickened and died. Nevertheless, the colonists persisted in their attempts to grow winemaking grapes
successfully.

Eastern winegrowing finally got off the ground when some of the
existing New World plants were accidentally hybridized with Europe's
Vitis vinifera (a species of grape brought over by the settlers as cuttings
and/or seeds). The results were the *Alexander*, the *Catawba*, the *Norton*,
the *Clinton*, and the *Lenoir*—all of them still foxy in taste and aroma. In
1843 Ephraim Bull of Concord, Massachusetts, planted a seed—thought
to be a cross between a wild grape and the *Catawba*—that eventually
yielded the now famous *Concord*, instantly popular not only in making
juice and wine but in jellies as well. It had taken 200 years to establish
even a rudimentary winegrowing industry in the East, an area stretching
as far as Cincinnati, where Nicholas Longworth introduced the first
American champagne.

California *enology* goes back to 1524, or 40 years before the Florida
Huguenots. When the Spanish conquistador Cortez was the governor of
Mexico, vines and cuttings were already being imported. Cortez had proclaimed that every Spaniard with a land grant had to plant 4,000 vines
for each Indian he employed. The Spanish Mission fathers were also a
driving force in developing vineyards, for they required wine for celebration of the Eucharist. Encountering an inhospitable climate, one grower,
a Jesuit priest named Juan de Ugarte, ventured to Baja California
[Mexico] in 1697 or 1701, where he started a vineyard at the Lareto Mission. By the time the Jesuits were expelled in 1767, this venture had
been successful enough to accrue a surplus, and the initial adventure of
the California wine had begun—in Mexico.

As the chain of Spanish missions moved north into California, more
and more vineyards were started, generating a grape variety called

Criolla, a Spanish word meaning "Mission." When the missions began to decline in the 1830s so too did their vineyards, reducing the production of what people called *ecclesiastical*, *church*, or *communion wine*.

Secular winemaking was driven by Joseph Chapman, California's first secular winemaker, followed by others who brought in new varieties. When the 1849 Gold Rush occurred, it triggered what was called the *grape-and-wine boom* on the West Coast, during which vintners first recognized the potential of places such as Napa Valley, Sonoma, and Santa Clara, plus the foothills of the Sierras, where vineyards moved to be conveniently close to the prospectors. After a huge number of *yards* were planted in the 1850s it was left to a Hungarian expatriate called Agostan Haraszthy (regarded as the Founding Father of the California Wine Industry) to bring in 100,000 cuttings in 300 varieties from Europe to get things moving. It worked: by 1862 California wines were being shipped to the East in such quantities that the Department of Agriculture issued its first bulletin recognizing a very real *winegrowing industry* in that state.

Sixty years of secular winemaking were, of course, destroyed in California and elsewhere in the United State with the institution of Prohibition. It was only in 1933 that the vineyards on both coasts—now in miserable condition—began a second, new life. And it was only in the mid 1960s, with changes, experimentation, and sophistication in the American diet, that table wines and later the popular *wine coolers* of the 1980s (chilled mixes of wine, fruit juices, and soda water) surged into the mass markets. *Boutique wineries*—those producing only small quantities of a single, excellent wine—became the latter-day trendsetters.

In 1971 Robert Mondavi gave America a new wine style called *Fume Blanc*; in so doing, he gave American English a new term for a wood-aged Sauvignon Blanc similar to the French Pouilly Fume. Americans have had to wrap their tongues around a number of foreign terms as European grapes and wines came to be produced domestically:

Chardonnay, dry white wine originating in Burgundy, now widely produced here.

Chablis, blended wine named after a village in north-central France where a very dry white Burgundy was and is made.

> # Descriptors of wine seen in tasting notes
>
> | | |
> |---|---|
> | *toasty oaky* | *to be sipped and brooded over* |
> | *vibrant with personality* | *rough and hard in its youth* |
> | *fleshy* | *flinty* |
> | *supple and smooth* | *robust* |
> | *lean, austere* | *noble* |
> | *producing fatness in the mouth* | |

Wine professionals sample wines at a 1985 tasting in New York.

Riesling, medium to full-bodied, sweetish or *off-dry* white wine similar to Rhine wine, the name altered in German from the obsolete *Rüssling*.

Zinfandel, called informally *Zin*, a dry California wine similar to claret, with the origin of both the vine and the word murky. Agostin Haraszthy probably tried to acquire the German vine, *Zierfandler*, but when the vine arrived it didn't at all resemble the vine he'd ordered. Nevertheless, the plant produced the full, fruity, unique wine that now bears the name *Zinfandel*. A totally American offshoot is the popular *white Zinfandel*, actually light pink in color, which mixes red and white wines in a sweetish, low-priced blend.

Chenin Blanc, fruity white wine with a touch of sweetness made from a grape bearing the same name.

Sauterne, originally *Sauternes*, a sweet to moderately off-dry wine named for the village in southwest France where a delicate sweet white wine of the same name is produced.

Chianti, dry, usually red table wine originally made only in Italy, which takes its name from the *Chianti* Mountains, a range of the Apennines.

blush wine, any one of various blends of white and red wines having a pink color and usually a light and fruity taste.

rosé wine, a pink wine made from red grapes whose skins have been removed during fermentation as soon as the desired level of color has been reached, *rosé* being French for "pink."

Gewürztraminer, a dry white wine with a floral aroma, from German *Gewürz*, spice, and *Traminer*, a grape variety, itself form Tramin, a winegrowing district in the southern Tyrol.

merlot, a dry red wine made from a grape introduced to the U.S. from southern Italy and France, now produced in California and Oregon. The word is French (*merle*) for a young blackbird, probably alluding to the dark color of the grapes.

pinot, a white or red wine (e.g., *pinot blanc*, *pinot noir*), the red having a cherry aroma with rich flavors, medium to light-bodied, made from any of various grapes grown in California and in France as well, a French word that is a variant of *pineau*, a diminutive of *pine*, from the shape of the clusters of grapes.

muscat, a sweet white grape used in making either wine or raisins; also, *muscatel* wine (a rich, sweet wine), a French word going back to Old Provençal *muscat*, from *musc*, musk, from Latin *muscus*.

American interest in wines and winemaking forced us to expand our stock of terms, and sent us off to the many handy pronunciation guides in wineries and liquor stores. America is now comfortable with pronunciations such as: SHAR-don-ay . . . SO-veen yawn-blonc . . . VEE-doll-blonc . . . REEZ-ling . . . PE-NWAH. We've come a long way from *smash, pluck, Virginia Dare* (a legitimate brand dating to Prohibition where it was advertised as an anemia tonic—22% alcohol), *muski, railroad whiskey,* and *sixteen-year-old aftershave*!

COMMUNICATIONS:
FROM SNAIL MAIL TO EMAIL

"DROP ME A LINE"

For the first two centuries after European colonization, communication in America depended on what the British generally call the *post*, but American English more commonly terms the *mail*. The British term is from French *poste*, "station" (from Latin *positum*, "positioned"); it originally referred to one of a series of stations which fast horsemen (*post-men*) traversed in delivering messages on the Crown's business. By the latter part of the 17th century it came to refer to the riders themselves, and eventually to the entire delivery system. English-speaking Americans used it for their earliest efforts: the first *postal system* operated from the home of Richard Fairbanks in Boston in 1639, a monthly *postal service* began between New York and Boston in 1672, the first *post office* was set up in Philadelphia in 1683, and in 1694 the Crown appointed Thomas Neale as *postmaster general* of all the colonies. The U.S. federal government's official *Post Office Department* began in 1782, becoming the independent agency known as the *U.S. Postal Service* in 1971.

Mail is of Germanic origin, from a word meaning "bag, satchel." How it came to have its modern sense is made clear by the early phrase *mail of letters*, "a parcel or package of dispatches," which also explains the common plural *mails*. In the 18th century *mail* was current as an official term in England, and so the American colonists used and kept it.

Carrier of news and knowledge

Instrument of trade and industry,

Promoter of mutual acquaintance,

Of peace and good-will

Among men and nations.

— Charles W. Eliot: Inscription on Post Office building, Washington, DC, 1905

Snail mail is still the way most of us receive our vital communications. In this case, the postman is none other than Postmaster General Marvin Runyon. Runyon took to the streets in a June 1995 salute to postal workers.

The original sense is still visible in the American term *mail carrier* (1790), and Noah Webster reported that *to mail* still meant "to inclose in a wrapper and direct to a post-office." *The mail* as a generic term did not appear until the 1840s, and by 1867 we had the etymologically redundant *mail bag*.

The mail has been delivered by every conceivable means of transportation: *mail coach* (late 1780s), *mail stage* (1792), *mail boat* (1796), *mail train* (1855), and *mail truck* (1924). By 1918 there was regular *airmail* service, modestly begun in 1911 (a flight from Garden City to Mineola, New York, less than five miles) but becoming well-established during World War I. The design for the modern *mail box* was patented in 1870, replacing earlier types sometimes called *letter boxes. Letter carrier* was known in America as early as 1825, but became more common in the late 20th century with more women in the job, hence the need for a gender-neutral alternative to the traditional *mailman* (1881).

In 1863, responding to increased demand as thousands of families wrote to those fighting in the Civil War, the Union's mail service introduced a scheme of dividing the mail into *first class, second class,* and *third class* materials. It also began providing *free delivery* in cities. This service was extended to *Rural Free Delivery (RFD)* in 1896, bringing newspapers, magazines, and mail-order catalogs to farm families, breaking their isolation and "urbanizing" the outlook of rural America. Other innovations included *special delivery* service (1885), *parcel post, insured mail,* and *COD service* (1913); numbered *postal zones* in cities (1943); and the 5-digit *ZIP code* (*Z*one *I*mprovement *P*lan, 1963). ZIP codes allowed the use of high-speed automated mail sorters, and since 1981 the Post Office further increased speed and efficiency by expanding ZIP codes from five to nine digits.

For a brief time in the mid 19th century, delivering the mail had its share in the romance of the American West. The *Pony Express*—affectionately called *the Pony Post* or simply *the Pony*—was established on April 3, 1860 as an attempt to win a mail contract by outperforming the Overland Stage. The object was to carry letters from St. Joseph, Missouri to Sacramento, California, nearly 2,000 miles, in ten days. There were 80 *Pony Express riders*, including "Buffalo Bill" Cody and "Pony Bob" Haslam, each of whom rode about 75 miles and changed mounts at each *station* along the route, roughly every 10 miles. For all its fame, the Pony Express lasted only 19 months, until October 24, 1861. Once the telegraph connected the east and west coasts, the service was rendered obsolete.

"SEND ME A WIRE"

In 1844 Samuel F. B. Morse used his *telegraph* to send a message from Washington to Baltimore at the speed of electricity through a wire. Generations later, schoolchildren still learned the text of his first famous message: *What hath God wrought.* By 1861, the *Western Union* telegraph company had extended its line from Omaha to California.

Communiqués sent by wire were called *telegraphic dispatches, telegraphic communications,* or *telegraph messages* until about 1850, when they began to be called *telegrams*; by World War I they were beginning to be called *wires.* A telegram sent by undersea cable has been called a *cablegram* since the appearance of such a service in the 1860s, and the shorter form *cable* came into use in the 1870s. After 1901, transatlantic messages could also be sent via Guglielmo Marconi's *wireless telegraph*

Samuel Morse, painter, sculptor, and inventor of the telegraph.

(1895) or *wireless* (1896) using radio waves; these messages were called *Marconigrams* by many, *radiotelegrams* by the more technical, and simply *radiograms* by 1910.

By 1920 telegrams were no longer being sent by Morse code but by the new *teletype,* which was faster and could print out messages in plain text, and then increasingly by the wireless version, *radioteletype.*

"GIMME A CALL"

Fast as it was, communicating by telegraph still not only required the services of a *telegrapher*; it also demanded that messages be written out (albeit as concisely as possible to save costs, hence the adjective *telegraphic*). But on March 10, 1876, Alexander Graham Bell exclaimed to his assistant, *"Mr. Watson, come here, I want you!"* Bell's assistant Watson, who was in another room out of earshot, heard Bell's words over a transmitter. The device was patented and dubbed the *telephone* (from Greek *tele*, "afar" + *phone*, "sound, voice"), the next great step in the history of communications.

In 1878, a *call* already meant a telephone call and by 1882 *to call* meant to reach via telephone. Although telephone service was very expensive during its first decades ($240 a year in Manhattan) there were already 60,000 phones in the U.S. by 1880. As service expanded, rate reductions led to even more widespread use: by 1910 there were almost 6 million phones in the U.S. and by the end of World War I over 10 million.

The telephone came to revolutionize our way of talking and living. Language for communicating at a distance now could be less formal than that of letters. The phone also made possible new types of communication, instant talk with anyone, anywhere, at any time. It broke the age-old isolation of the housewife at a time when almost all women were housewives. The telephone changed our use of language in another important way: it greatly decreased the amount we needed to write, while increasing the amount we talk. By the mid 1990s there were well over 200 million phone lines in service in the United States—and with the explosive increase in cellular phone use in the 90s, one phone line per American seemed a not-too-distant likelihood.

TELEPHONE TERMS
Since telephone technology was based on telegraphy, much of its early and basic terminology was actually from the telegraph:

telephone, in the 1830s, meant a sort of megaphone or speaking tube for conveying voices or music over a distance. Bell's invention, the "Electrical Speaking Telephone," was also called a *speaking telegraph* in the 1870s. The shortened form *phone* has been in use since the 1880s.

Bell Telephone Co. Formed in 1877 by Alexander Bell (1847–1922), his father-in-law, his assistant Thomas A. Watson, and three others, the name *Bell System* (once seen on pay phones everywhere in the U.S.) was first officially used in 1908. *Ma Bell*, an old familiar name for the Bell monopoly, became widely known in 1947 when it was used derogatorily during a strike against the company.

operator, late 1870s (it had meant a telegraph operator since the 1840s); *hello girl,* mid-1880s (widely used, originally humorously); *telephone girl,* 1893. The first women operators were Emma M. Nutt and her sister Stella A. Nutt, employed by the Boston Telephone Dispatch Co.

A telephone in 1909.

"Mr. Watson, come here, I want you!"

— *Alexander Graham Bell to Thomas A. Watson, March 10, 1876, the first intelligible words transmitted over a telephone.*

in 1878; both women had previously been telegraph operators. Women typically were hired as telephone operators because they were considered to have more pleasing voices and were more polite than men—and were also content to earn $10 a week.

switchboard, exchange, trunk line, central, late 1870s and early 1880s. When *exchanges* had few subscribers (the first, in New Haven, Connecticut, in 1878, originally had 21), they could all be connected by one operator. Soon larger *switchboards* (an 1860s telegraph term) were needed and often *switchmen* (usually boys) were used to plug in the connections at the far ends of a switchboard-filled room. By the 1880s *trunk lines* connected one exchange with another so that people could call out of their local area. By the late 1880s both a switchboard location and an operator were called *central*. When placing a call, a person would dial 0 for "operator" and then say, "Hello Central?," once a familiar expression for Americans, and still encountered in old song lyrics, etc. Manually plugging in a caller to the exchange, that exchange to another one, and from there to the person being called made "We've been cut off" a common complaint into the 1920s, after which time most switching became mechanized.

telephone number, Plaza-, Highland-, etc., early 1880s. *Telephone numbers* were first used in Lowell, Massachusetts, in 1879 during a measles epidemic, when a local doctor feared that the four operators might get sick and any substitutes would find it difficult to learn the names and connections of the subscribers. By the late 1880s *telephone number* was shortened to *number*: "Sorry, wrong number" became common by 1900. In the 1880s, too, some big-city exchanges began to use neighborhood or district names, such as *Nassau, Gramercy, Highland,* etc. In 1930, numbers were added to exchange names, so people began referring to exchanges such as *Plaza-1* or *Butterfield-8* (the title of a 1935 John O'Hara novel).

private line, party line. Although the first few lines of 1877 were all private, by the early 1880s almost all were shared, by as many as 20 subscribers. AT&T then offered *private lines* in 1886; the other, standard

Female telephone operators in Aberdeen, Maryland in 1941.

lines were called *party lines* by the early 1900s. *Party lines*, shared by several households in a neighborhood, each able to "listen in" on any call, had largely disappeared by the late 1950s.

night rates, an 1887 term, when the Bell System began to offer lower rates at night over some of its lines. Lower rates also applied as *Sunday rates* by 1936.

long distance. Inaugurated with a New York-Boston commercial line in 1884, long distance calling became truly long (1,000 miles) by 1892, when New York-Chicago service was initiated. Coast-to-coast service began in January 1915, requiring over 13,600 miles of wire, with a call taking 25 minutes to go through and costing a minimum of $20.70.

telephone directory and *phone book*, both well established by the 1900s. The first *listings* were in New Haven and New York City in 1878, and gave only names and addresses, numbers not yet being used.

telephone booth, late 1890s, when it was also called a *telephone box* or, in the early 1900s, a *telephone closet*. Though some enterprising men had gone into the business of charging others for use of their phones as early as 1878, the first practical public coin-operated telephone (called a *pay phone* by the 1930s) was installed in Hartford, Connecticut in 1889. Even in the 1990s some still say *It's your nickel,* meaning "you're paying for the call," which applied literally until 1951, when the 10-cent local call went into effect. Some cities began charging 25 cents for local calls in the early 1980s, and nearly all did by the mid-90s.

yellow pages, early 1900s. The Michigan State Telephone Co. of Detroit printed the first directory with classified advertising on yellow paper. *White Pages* for alphabetic personal and business listings and *blue pages* for federal, state, and local government listings emerged later.

give me a ring, I'll give you a buzz. By 1910 both *ring* and *buzz* meant a telephone call, and to *ring up* someone (now chiefly British) meant to call him or her on the telephone.

radiotelephone, 1909, pioneered by American inventor Lee De Forest, used to connect Montauk Point, Long Island, whose systems were quickly adopted for naval communications, and helped to save lives in the *Titanic* disaster of 1912.

dial, for most of telephone history, referred to the circular plate with finger holes, allowing numbers and letters to be selected to make a telephone connection. Such a *dial* was used in the 1879 patent for the device. *Dial telephone* and *dial tone* (the sound indicating a line is ready for a call) were first used in the 1890s, though it wasn't until 1919 that these terms came into widespread use, as the large number of calls swamping operators made new switching equipment and dialing necessary. The first *dial phones* went into general operation in Norfolk, Virginia, on November 8, 1919. The verb *dial*, meaning to call a certain number, never lost currency even as, by the 1990s, push-button phones had largely replaced those with finger-hole dials.

"At the tone the time will be . . ." New York City established the first time-service number in August, 1928.

the pipe, the horn, slang for telephone cited to the late 1950s.

"Throughout my childhood, it was clear that [phone] lines were not for conversation but for announcements. We were as likely to reach out and touch someone by telephone as we were to communicate by using a cattle prod. Casual planning was as rare as casual sex."

Ellen Goodman, "Casual Phoning and the College Student," Washington Post, February, 1989

Speakerphone, 1955. The phone incorporating a microphone and a loud-speaker allowed "hands free" calling, and it became a common method that business callers used to talk to several people in the same room.

area code, 1961, a three-digit prefix that identifies a telephone service area in the U.S. and Canada.

WATS line, 1961, an acronym for *Wide Area Telephone Service*, as provided to business or other customers placing many calls outside a local area so that each call is not handled or billed as a long-distance call.

Touch-Tone telephone, 1963. Eventually the dial was replaced by a panel of push buttons, each button generating a distinctive tone when pushed (*Touch-Tone* is a trademark). At first merely a more convenient way to dial the phone, Touch-Tone became a near-necessity by the 1990s as automated answering systems, providing directory information and extensive services such as *banking by phone*, virtually replaced human operators and telephone receptionists.

teleconferencing, 1974, the use of telephones and/or computers to hold a conference among people at remote locations; *videoconferencing*, 1977, the use of telephones and computers (employing audio and video signals) to hold such a conference.

hot line, early 1960s, a special direct line between the White House and the Kremlin so that the leaders of the two nuclear superpowers could communicate instantly to stave off nuclear crisis. By the late 1960s *hot line* was being applied to any specialized telephone information service, as one on which to ask urgently for help or advice.

911, the Bell System adopted this telephone number nationwide for police, fire, ambulance, and other emergency services in 1968.

telex, 1943 (*tele*type + *ex*change), a system of teletype machines connected through a central exchange similar to that of the phone system, used mainly by international business concerns.

cordless phone, a portable telephone using a short-range radio transmitter and receiver to communicate with a *base unit* that is *hard-wired* (physically connected) to the telephone line.

800 number, 1979, a special number with an "800" prefix allowing long-distance calls which the called party (typically a business firm) pays for. Special lines for long-distance *free calls* (as opposed to *toll calls*, 1929) were also called *WATS lines*, the acronym standing for *Wide-Area Telephone Service*. By 1995 the 800 service was so popular that most of the unique number combinations, some 7.7 million, were used up, so the new prefix 888 went into use in 1996, to be followed as needed by 877, 866, 855, 844, 833, and 822.

900 number, late 1980s, a special number with a "900" prefix allowing the called party to charge a fee to the caller. *900 numbers* were used for services from *phone sex* lines, psychics, and astrologers to weather forecasts, sports scores, and betting information. Several services cashed in on teenagers' propensity to talk on the phone by setting up *teen chat* lines, until parents' outcry over the resulting phone bills led to tighter controls on access to 900-number services.

telemarketing, 1980, mass marketing of goods or services by telephone. Computerized databases combined with automated dialing systems (for *automatic redial* and *speed-dialing*) and recorded sales pitches let *telemarketers* reach enormous, specifically-targeted audiences nationwide. Customer complaints about annoyance and invasion of privacy soon led several states to pass regulatory legislation.

I HEAR AMERICA DIALING

By the time of its hundredth birthday, the telephone was already ubiquitous in American life. By the mid 1990s, new technologies were using telephone connections to provide a mind-boggling variety of services.

"FAX ME"
One revolutionary new invention was the *facsimile machine*, a means of transmitting printed material directly over telephone wires or radio. The word itself (in the form *fac simile*, Latin, for "make alike") has been known in English since 1691, when it described a hand-written exact copy of a manuscript. A modern version using synchronized light beams was actually designed as early as 1843 by the Scottish physicist Alexander Bain, and a working system was constructed in Paris in 1861. But practical models had to await the development of photoelectric cells to convert light and dark areas on paper to electrical impulses. At first the technique was used mainly by the syndicated news *wire services* (1944), whose stories were often accompanied by photographs labeled with the trademark *Wirephoto*. But in the 1970s and 80s facsimile or *fax* technology grew cheaper and faster, fueled largely by developments in Japan, where it overcame the limitations of teletype for transmitting documents written in Japanese characters. Businesses worldwide found the new generation of *fax machines* irresistible and then indispensable. *Faxes* allowed text and illustrations, designs, and personal signatures to be transmitted almost instantly using phone lines, and within a decade it was rare to find even the smallest office without one. The market even expanded into private homes, and *fax me* became part of the language. What would once have been a redundancy, the terms *voice phone* and *voice line* came into use to distinguish the traditional use of the telephone from the faxes and growing array of specialized data devices that also used the phone lines.

"TALK TO MY MACHINE"
As the pace of business accelerated, the telephone's presence became more insistent. To avoid missing an important call, many people engaged an *answering service* (1961) to take messages when they were away from a phone. Though many doctors and other professionals employed a *service* to monitor their calls, most businesses and households relied on telephone *answering machines* (1961), some with electronic *voice mail* (1981) features, which could deliver outgoing messages to callers, record their answers, and allow the owner to call from a remote phone and play back the recorded messages. "Call my phone" and "talk to my machine" became meaningful phrases. By the mid 90s, it seemed unusual for a call not to be *picked up* at all, at least by a machine.

Another option for those who could not afford to miss a call was a *pager*. In the car, jogging, or on a golf course, a tiny, lightweight device clipped to a belt or carried in a pocket alerted the user to call their service for a message, or view a number to call displayed on a tiny screen. Doctors, emergency workers, technicians, and executives found the gadget—usually called a *beeper* (1970)—practical right away, but before long its popularity had spread to everyone.

" . . . the probable amplification of the facsimile system of Caselli, by which an exact copy of anything that can be drawn or written may be instantaneously made to appear at a distance of hundreds of miles from the original; and the countless other applications of electricity to the transmission of intelligence yet to be made—must sooner or later most seriously interfere with the transportation of letters by the slower means of the post."

— *from the U.S. Postmaster General's report to Congress, 1872*

"It shall be unlawful for any person within the United States to use any telephone facsimile machine, computer, or other device to send an unsolicited advertisement to a telephone facsimile machine."

— *U.S. Code, Title 47, Sec. 227[b][1][C]*

Research indicates that drivers with cellular phones are more likely, by one-third, to have an accident.

THE CELL PHONE CRAZE

In the fast-paced 90s even the beeper was not enough for many people. For many years a few of the more affluent had had *mobile phones* for their cars, boats, etc., but the service was very expensive and limited in range, based on radiotelephone technology. The floodgates of mobile phone service opened when *cellular telephone* systems became widely available. This scheme was based on a nationwide network of low-power, local-coverage microwave relay stations that would automatically switch an ongoing call from one "cell" to the next as either party moved or traveled, thereby giving *wireless*, like *to dial*, another sense. As the cost of the service fell and the phones shrank to palm-size in the early 90s, subscribership grew astronomically, from fewer than a million in 1985 to more than 60 million worldwide in the next ten years. Business deals were now done while driving or walking between appointments, and parents could call home when stuck in traffic.

One consequence of this explosion of new services, with *fax numbers, pager numbers,* and cell phones in demand, was that phone companies began to run out of numbers, especially in metropolitan areas. New *area codes* were added, and areas covered by one code reduced in size, but by 1995 the possible numeric combinations under the long-existing scheme were exhausted and had to be increased. The possibility of new four-digit area codes loomed large.

CELL PHONE LINGO

Americans using cell phones had to learn a new language of *wireless* technology:

airtime, the time one is on the phone; the user pays an *airtime charge*, incurred whether one *sends* or receives a call.

home area, the territory in which a user most often travels and uses the phone; *extended home* area, the territory adjacent to or surrounding one's *home area*.

roaming area, every locale outside one's *home* or *extended area*; rates are higher when one *roams*.

AMERICA GOES ONLINE

The end of the 20th century was an age of *electronic mail*, (See CYBER-SPACE: I HEAR AMERICA CLICKING). Learning to make their computers *interface* with the telephone service, users began to learn a number of new concepts and terms, two of the most important terms being these:

modem, around 1952, a blend of *mod*ulator/*dem*odulator, a device for converting digital data used by computers to the analog signal which telephone lines use, and back. A familiar term in the teletype industry since the early 1950s. By the 1990s, credit-card size *fax modems*, combining the function of both devices, were in widespread use.

fiber-optic cable, *fiber optics*, 1956; *fiber-optic* the adjective, 1961, began to replace copper telephone wire in many urban areas in the 1980s. Satellite and microwave technology also helped to make long-distance phone service remarkably clearer, cheaper, and more reliable.

CRIME WATCH

A mericans talk a lot about crime: they're worried about it, and with good reason. Americans remained particularly concerned about violent crime, which increased despite the efforts of gun control advocates. The annual murder rate, as a gauge of violence, remained at around 4 or 5 per 100,000 people throughout most of American history. But in the 1960s the rate suddenly began to climb, and by the 1980s it had more than doubled. And the result is that Americans are locking their doors, living in gated communities (1980s), purchasing security systems for their homes and cars, and establishing Crime Watch Neighborhoods or Neighborhood Watches.

> *"The American dream is, in part, responsible for a great deal of crime . . . because people feel that the country owes them not only a living but a good living."*
>
> *— psychoanalyst David Abrahansen, in the San Francisco Examiner & Chronicle, November 18, 1975*

In colonial days, it wasn't the government's role to control crime so much as it was to express the community's outrage and to punish the guilty. The usual means were torture and execution: Criminals were whipped, branded, scalded, mutilated, hanged, and stoned. But when the U.S. Constitution was written, its Eighth Amendment included a ban on "cruel and unusual punishments." The *penitentiary* was an American invention, designed to get convicts to work, pray, and read the Bible in hopes that "penitence" would bring them salvation.

The belief that prisons could *rehabilitate* criminals remained widespread right up to the 1980s. Then the public mood shifted, and Americans seemed willing once more to sacrifice crime control for punishment. The most striking example of this transition can be seen in the public's attitude toward the *death penalty*—punishing violent criminals by putting them to death in the *electric chair* (1889), in the *gas chamber* (1945), by the *firing squad* (1904), by *hanging*, or, more recently, by *lethal injection*. States began revising their laws regarding the death penalty in the 1970s, and by the 80s the majority of Americans were demanding the return of *capital punishment*.

Crime doesn't always pay. A Brooklyn crime boss is collared by the authorities in 1915.

Nearly 3,000 people were executed during the 30s and 40s, but this number dropped to single-digits during the 70s. One of these was convicted murderer Gary Gilmore, who actually sought as rapid an execution as possible by Utah authorities—even resorting to a 25-day hunger strike. His last words before facing the firing squad: "Let's do it."

"From Jesse James to Loeb and Leopold, from the perpetrators of the St. Valentine's Day massacre to the Lindbergh kidnapper and beyond, our celebrated delinquents have become a part of the national heritage."

— F.W. Dupree, New York Review of Books, February 3, 1966

There seems to be no end to the creativity of America's criminals. Just as prevention methods for one type of crime begin to pay off, another springs up in its place. *Hijacking* (1923, in the sense of stealing goods from a vehicle in transit, origin unknown) and *skyjacking* (1961, taking forcible control of a commercial aircraft and forcing it to take the *skyjacker* to a nonscheduled destination) resulted in the presence of *sky marshals* (1968) to protect passengers and airlines, but gave way to *carjacking* (late 1980s-1990s), in which armed criminals seize a car and drive off, sometimes with the passengers still inside. Though dictionaries give "origin unknown" as the etymology of *hijack*, Gerald Cohen has traced it most probably to the zinc mines of Southwest Missouri, in the 1890s or thereabouts (Gerald Cohen, *Studies in Slang, II* [1989], "The Missouri and Hobo Origin of *Hijack*"). The first *hijackers* (*high jackers*) were miners who pilfered *high jack* (a *high* grade of ore [zinc] called *jack*). Then the word began its passage into the general vernacular by way of the hobo jungles in the sense of a hobo who robs a fellow hobo while he is sleeping or someone who holds up a hobo, e.g., in a boxcar. *Larceny* (stealing another's personal property) is now supplemented by the theft of *intellectual property* (sometimes called *pirating*, after the 14th century outlaw sailors who roamed the high seas in search of *booty*), such as computer software and compact discs. And *robbing a bank* (a popular crime in the 1920s–30s) can now invole hacking your way into the bank's computer system and arranging an *electronic funds transfer*. In fact, *cybercrime* (a term that, along with *cyberthief*, became a permanent part of America's daily vocabulary when Kevin Mitnick, the most-wanted *computer hacker* in the world, was caught by a team of FBI agents with the help of a *computer security expert* in February 1995) became the new frontier for educated criminals, refining if not replacing *white-collar crime* (an older term defined as fraud, embezzlement, etc., committed by an individual in business, government, or a profession).

AMERICA'S MOST WANTED: THE LINEUP

Americans have a tendency to romanticize famous criminals—even cold-blooded murderers. *Billy the Kid* (William H. Bonney, 1859–81) has been talked about, sung about, even danced about (in the 1938 ballet *Billy the Kid,* with a score by American composer Aaron Copeland). Born in New York City and raised by his widowed mother in New Mexico and Colorado, he is said to have killed the first of his 21 victims at the age of 12. He went on to rob and murder Native Americans, hire himself out as a cattle-war mercenary, and become a quick-shooting *cattle rustler*. Billy was captured in 1880, but he managed to escape after killing two deputies. Sheriff Pat Garrett tracked him down and shot him dead in Fort Sumner, New Mexico, the following year.

Mr. and Mrs. Clyde Barrow were *bank robbers* in the 1930s who were later romanticized in the 1968 movie *Bonnie and Clyde.* Other famous bank robbers include *"Machine Gun" Kelly, "Baby Face" Nelson* (real name Lester Gillis), and *"Pretty Boy"* (Charles Arthur) *Floyd.* It was notorious criminals like these who made the *FBI* (Federal Bureau of Investigation, a name it assumed in 1935) famous. Originally established in 1908 under the Department of Justice as the *Bureau of Investigation,* its unarmed agents were known as *DJs* (from the initials for *Department of Justice*) or *Dee Jays,* as well as *Whiskers* (referring to Uncle Sam) and, by 1922, *G-men* (for *Government men,* a name popularized by "Machine Gun" Kelly when he was captured and said, "OK, G-men, you got me."). FBI agents didn't even carry guns until 1934, but they managed to kill

"Celebrated delinquent," Jesse James. His life of crime ended when he was shot in the back in 1882 by a member of his own gang who sought the $10,000 reward on James' head.

Bonnie Parker. The photograph is believed to have been taken by her partner in crime, Clyde Barrow, as part of their self-promotional efforts.

John Dillinger. Within a month of the posting of this reward, Dillinger would be dead. The notorious criminal once escaped from prison by using a fake gun carved out of wood.

"One small jump for D.B. Cooper; one giant leap that changed the face of airline travel, creating a paranoid world of metal detectors, luggage-screening machines, handheld body scanners, photo identification with ticket and baggage matching with passengers. Before Cooper, getting on a plane was as easy as getting on a bus. After his leap, it [was] like getting into Fort Knox."

— San Francisco Chronicle, *November 24, 1996*

As for identifying D.B. Cooper, this is still the best the authorities can do.

three well-known fugitives that year: Dillinger, "Pretty Boy" Floyd, and "Baby Face" Nelson.

Perhaps the most famous female criminal in American history was *Lizzie Borden*, who was put on trial for murdering her wealthy father and her stepmother in Fall River, Massachusetts. The double ax-murder was the most talked-about crime of the 1890s. Even though Borden was found to be not guilty, her alleged crime was immortalized in verse:

> *Lizzie Borden took an ax*
> *And gave her mother forty whacks;*
> *When she saw what she had done,*
> *She gave her father forty-one!*

In the 1930s, the name *Dillinger* struck terror throughout the Midwest. John Dillinger had been born in Indianapolis and led a fairly normal life until he was 22. Then he deserted the Navy, robbed a grocery, and was sent to a reformatory in 1924. He tried to escape and was sent to state prison, but within a month of being paroled in 1933, he and his gang were robbing banks and killing people in Illinois, Indiana, and Ohio. Attorney General Homer Cummings named him *Public Enemy Number One*—the only person ever to win this official designation. Others were merely at the top of the FBI's *Ten Most Wanted* list. Dillinger was eventually betrayed by a mysterious girlfriend, known to millions as *the woman in red*. He was shot and killed by FBI agents while leaving Chicago's Biograph Theater on July 22, 1934.

In the 1970s probably the most wanted man—later to become immortalized in verse, in song, in books, in a play, in a movie, and on T-shirts—was *D.B. Cooper*, the pseudonym of a still-unidentified man who, on November 24, 1971 skyjacked—and later parachuted out of—

J. Edgar Hoover ran the FBI for 48 years.

Serial killer David Berkowitz (Son of Sam) terrorized New York City during 1976 and 1977.

Northwest Airlines flight 305 going from Portland, Oregon to Seattle, Washington. Identifying himself as "Dan Cooper," this average-looking middle-aged *air pirate*—who wore a black suit, black tie, white shirt, and sunglasses and who threatened to blow the plane up with a briefcase bomb of dynamite—came to be called "D.B." when law officers later got his name wrong; the moniker stuck. After obtaining the demanded $200,000 ransom, Cooper took the cash and jumped out the aircraft's rear door two miles above the Oregon-Washington border into the rugged Cascade Mountains. He was never seen again, though in 1980 a young boy stumbled on $5,880 of the missing ransom on the banks of the Columbia River.

Regarded as a modern Robin Hood, D.B. Cooper was, and has continued to be, the talk of the nation, a cult hero of sorts. In 1996 the 25th anniversary of his sky piracy was celebrated in the small Washington town over which he bailed out (and in other locales as well), with the small town holding its annual festival called *D.B. Cooper Days*. *D.B. Cooper look-alike contests* were held, with men in black suits parachuting from aircraft.

The incident not only changed airline security forever, it also spurred creation of the eponymous *Cooper Switch*, a device on the air stairs of all U.S. commercial aircraft that prevents the stairs from being lowered while the aircraft are airborne.

More recently, Americans became fascinated with *serial killers* (murderers who kill repeatedly, without an apparent motive; coined by Robert Ressler, a former FBI agent). Not to be confused with *mass* or *spree killers*, who murder a number of people at one time (post offices were the sites of some of the worst *mass murders* in the 1980s–90s, leading to coinage of the idiom *going postal*), serial killers have been erroneously described as a uniquely American phenomenon. But the publicity that has accompanied the capture of such famous serial killers as Jeffrey Dahmer, John Wayne Gacy, and Ted Bundy, along with popularity of movies like *The Silence of the Lambs* (1992), certainly makes it seem as though the U.S. is the best place for serial killers to call home.

A well-known criminal of the 1990s was the *Unabomber* (so called because his earliest victims were associated with *u*niversities and *a*irlines), who, over a 17-year period beginning in 1978, sent 16 *mail bombs* (parcels containing sophisticated explosive devices) addressed to a variety of prominent people, including scientists, advertising executives, and lobbyists. The resulting explosions killed three and injured 23, some seriously. (See also the subsection Terrorists At Home in this chapter, which deals with *domestic terrorism*, a 1990s phenomenon of which the *Unabomber* was a contributor, albeit operating as a loner.)

THE MOB

While most crimes are committed by individuals acting independently, America has a long history of *organized crime*, a term first heard in the 1920s. *Al Capone*, popularly known as *the father of organized crime*, terrorized Chicago during Prohibition by organizing a gang of people willing to carry out criminal acts in exchange for money and the protection of other gang members. Referred to as "Scarface Al" from a razor slash he received while a youthful member of Brooklyn's notorious "Five Points Gang," Naples-born Alfonso Capone (1899–1947) helped Johnny Torrio corner the Chicago bootleg market by terrorizing and murdering the competition. By the 1930s, several large, well-organized groups controlled not only bootlegging but also gambling, prostitution, narcotics,

Mobster John Gotti was nicknamed "The Teflon Don" for his ability to earn acquittals. He is now serving a life sentence in a federal penitentiary.

and other illegal activities. These organized gangs were loosely called *Murder, Inc.* (although the name is often used in fiction to mean organized crime's *extermination squad*). One of the most talked-about gang leaders, *"Lucky" Luciano,* killed about 40 other gang leaders and reorganized Murder, Inc. into specific territories with subsidiary gangs. This has been called *the Mafia* since the 1950s. The original Mafia was a secret Sicilian society started in the 15th century to settle vendettas. Today's American Mafia is related to the Sicilian one only in its tradition of violence, blackmail, and murder, and in its emphasis on old-world family ties. In 1962, Mafia *informer* Joe Valachi introduced the term *Cosa Nostra* (Italian, "our concern") to the general public in his testimony before a congressional committee investigating organized crime.

Organized crime has popularized many terms, including *family* (referring to the relationship among those involved in the Mafia and its close-knit gangs), *contract* (an agreement for a hired gunman or *contract killer* to murder someone), and *hit* (the killing, to kill). A Mafia head is a *capo* (Latin, meaning "chief" or "head") or a *don* (a title of respect in Italian). The head don is the *capo di tutti capi* ("boss of bosses"), or, since the term was popularized by Mario Puzo's 1969 best-selling novel, *The Godfather.* A *consigliere* (Italian, from Latin *consiglio*, counsel; advice) is a (usually legal) adviser to a Mafia family or don. Other terms associated with organized crime are:

stool pigeon, 1830 (from the fowler's use of a pigeon tied to a "stool" or perch to decoy other birds); *stoolie*, 1931. Other words for informer and informing include *to peach*, 1848 (from *impeach*); *squealer*, 1891 (*to squeal*, to inform or confess since 1859); *fink*, cited to 1894 in the sense "a contemptible, unreliable person" and to the 1920s in the sense of a strikebreaker hired by a private detective agency. It is possible that *fink* comes from German *Fink*, a student who does not belong to the students' association, literally "finch," and thus "not one of the boys." *Fink* also may come from the German *Schmierfink*, a colloquial word meaning "a low, dirty person." Still others are *canary*, 1940s (because he *sings*, informs, confesses, 1930), and *snitch*, a police informant (1960s; a tattletale, around 1785, origin unknown).

shake-down, 1840s, extortion.

graft, 1859, originally meaning to earn a living dishonestly as a con man or robber; *grafter*, 1896; the variants *grift* and *grifter* came a little later.

hoodlum, 1871; *hood*, 1930. Originally *hoodlum* was "San Francisco hoodlum," an especially tough waterfront rowdy (from German-Bavarian dialect *hodalum*, rowdy). *Thug* is a 19th century British word, from the name of a religious organization of professional assassins in northern India (from Hindu *thagi*).

gangster, 1896, literally the member of a gang.

mobster, 1917; *the mob*, 1920s (*mob* entered English in the 19th century, from Latin *mobile volgus*, the fickle crowd).

take for a ride, 1920s. Until the late 1930s the term was usually the full "take for a one-way ride."

racketeering and *racketeer*, 1928. *Racket* meant a swindle or fraud by 1892, from the 1840s *grabracket*, a confidence game in which a *con man* grabbed money and ran while his accomplice distracted the victim by making a racket or commotion.

A flatfoot walks his beat in Philadelphia in 1972.

CALL THE POLICE!

Americans have been calling on the police (although they didn't actually use the word *police* until the 1780s) for help since colonial times. At first many settlements used a "watch and ward" system, in which private citizens patrolled at night, primarily to raise an alarm against fire and Indian attack. The first real policeman in the colonies was the *constable* (a 13th century English word via French from Latin *comes stabuli,* officer of the stable, chief groom), which was defined in 1630 as a man paid to organize a "constable's watch." *Constable* was a common word for any policeman well into the 1890s.

By 1646 the word *sheriff,* meaning a chief officer of a court charged with preserving the peace, was recorded in Massachusetts. *Sheriffs,* however, have existed since Anglo-Saxon times (Old English *scirgerefa,* the "reeve" or royal office of a "shire," hence a *shire reeve* or *sheriff*). By the late 1640s constables, sheriffs, and sheriffs' *deputies* were all being called *officer* (Latin *officium,* service, duty). The first real police force in the New World was an eight-man guard established by the Dutch in New Amsterdam in 1658; New York City then provided the first complete uniforms for its guard in 1693. By the 1780s Americans were beginning to use the word *police,* with *policeman* being in wide use by the 1830s. *Police forces* grew with the new industrial cities.

Since 1780 words associated with the police and their work have come thick and fast, including:

frisk, 1781 (the word once meant "lively, fresh").

nab (arrest), 1827; *pinch,* 1845; *collar,* 1879; *bust,* meaning a police raid, 1930s, coming to mean a police dispersal of a youth gang by 1949 (this was also called a *hassle*), and meaning to arrest by the early 1960s, originally by rebellious students.

Black Maria, 1840; *patrol wagon,* 1887; *Paddy wagon,* 1920s, refer to the vehicle used to transport people who have been arrested by the police.

chief of police, 1840s.

book, 1846, to enter charges against a suspect in a police register.

police station, stationhouse, late 1840s.

police commissioner, 1850s.

patrolman, 1860s.

traffic police, 1860, the year New York's famous "Broadway Squad" was formed to help people cross the street and to direct horse-drawn traffic; *traffic cop*, 1915.

third degree, 1890s, to interview someone regarding a crime.

desk sergeant, 1890s.

police captain, 1890s.

police blotter, 1900, a record of arrests and charges filed.

lineup (of suspects), 1907.

squad car, 1930s; *highway patrol* and *road block,* late 1930s.

Police and policemen have frequently been called by other, more colorful and less respectful, names. In 1835 they were simply *the law*. They weren't called *cops* until 1859, although *copper* dates back to 1846. Both of these terms may come from Old French *caper*, to seize. It has been

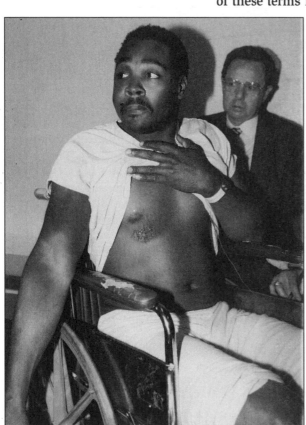

Rodney King displays the results of the beating he suffered during his arrest by the LAPD.

suggested that *cop* is an acronym for "constable on patrol," but it isn't. It is a short form of *copper*, one who *copped* (arrested) criminals. Although the term *pig* dates back to 1848, it was obsolete throughout the first half of the 20th century. In the 1960s it had a resurgence when radical students used it as a derogatory epithet for the police.

The term *bull* (1893) comes from the Spanish Gypsy *bul*, policeman. A *fly bull* (1907) was a detective or special duty policeman. A *cinder bull* (1910) was a railroad detective or guard. Railroad detectives were also called *yard bulls,* but by 1915 this term was being used for a prison guard. In 1913 policemen were called *flatfoots* (flatfooted from walking the *beat*), and in 1931 they were referred to as *fuzz,* (origin unknown), a term still in use.

We have also called policemen by the French term *gendarme* (French *gens d'arms,* men at arms) and have even used the informal British *bobby* (from Sir Robert Peel, 1788–1850, who instituted the Irish constabulary, called "peelers," and reorganized the London police force). *Detectives* became part of the American police force around 1840 (from the Latin *de-,* away, off + *tegere,* to cover, hence one who uncovers a crime or criminal). A *private detective* was called a *dick* (from condensing "detective") by 1900, a *gumshoe* around the same time (because a detective moves quietly, as if wearing gum-soled shoes), and a *private eye* or *P.I.* ("eye" being short for *I*nvestigator) by 1942. Raymond Chandler and other writers of *detective stories* (also known as *whodunits,* probably coined by Donald Gordon in the *American News of Books,* July 1930) popularized the private eye's image.

Today's *police officers* (an increasing number of whom are women) can be seen as villains as well as heroes. The *L.A.P.D.* (Los Angeles Police Department) is a good example. The L.A.P.D. suffered a tremendous loss of prestige in the wake of the *Rodney King incident* (in which

Los Angeles police officers were videotaped beating an African American who appeared to pose no immediate threat and was unable to defend himself). An independent commission headed by Warren Christopher concluded that the L.A.P.D. had racist, sexist elements, all too willing to use *excessive force*. When the four officers accused of beating Rodney King were found "not guilty," the controversial verdict launched the 1992 *Los Angeles riots,* which further denigrated the reputation of the city's *Blue Knights*.

The 1990s trend was toward *community policing* (getting to know the people who live in the community that the police officer patrols, and working with them to prevent crime). Police in many communities ride *mountain bikes* rather than cruising the streets in expensive *patrol cars* (also known as *squad cars, pandas,* or *black-and-whites,* if they're black and white). They're less likely to *strong-arm* a *suspect* (the once popular *carotid artery hold* resulted in the deaths of several suspects) and are more likely to show up at *Neighborhood Watch* meetings, where neighbors get together to discuss ways to protect their homes from burglars and make their streets safer. The *dragnet* approach to catching criminals (invented by L A. police chief James Davis in the 1920s; a *dragnet* is a net that is dragged along the bottom of a river or lake to catch fish), which consisted of stopping and questioning people to see if they had something to hide has been replaced by concern for their *constitutional rights* (see THE WORD OF THE LAW AND THE LAW OF THE LAND, subsection The Cases by Name). *Police brutality* hasn't disappeared altogether, but police officers who are the subject of *beefs* (complaints from the public) know that these complaints will end up in their *package* (personnel file) and count against them when they are up for promotion.

VIGILANTE JUSTICE

Americans have been taking the law into their own hands since the 19th century. *Vigilante* is a Spanish word for "vigilant" (from Latin *vigilans,* kept awake, wide awake) that was in common use by the 1830s when many communities, especially in the South, had "Committees of Vigilance" or "Vigilanty Associations." These not only maintained order by hanging murderers and horse thieves, but also helped maintain conformity by intimidating anyone suspected of immoral behavior or what was considered wrong thinking. Nowadays *vigilante* has more negative connotations. In the South before the Civil War, *vigilantes* came to mean organizations for intimidating African Americans and abolitionists. They were the forerunners of the *Ku Klux Klan* and other "night riders" (see ON THE FRINGES, subsection Racial Tensions). It was not until after the Civil War that lynching came to mean vengeful, often public executions, particularly by southern *lynch mobs,* who between 1882 and 1936 killed over 3,000 African Americans.

"A crowded police court docket is the surest of all signs that trade is brisk and money plenty."

— Mark Twain, 1872

DRUG SMUGGLERS

The *war on drugs* continued to escalate since the late 1970s when President Jimmy Carter endorsed the idea of *decriminalizing* (1969) marijuana as a way of taking the profit out of *drug trafficking* and reducing the amount of crime linked to *dealing* in drugs. In 1994 alone, United States Customs officials seized 204,000 pounds of *cocaine,* 559,000 pounds of *marijuana,* and 2,600 pounds of *heroin,* estimating that only 10 percent

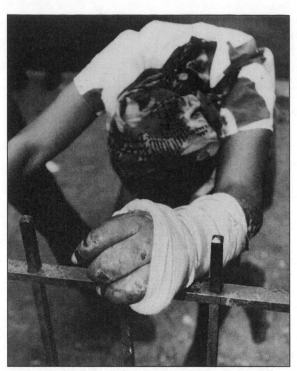

Washington, DC, 1989. The effect of narcotics and dirty needles.

of the *narcotics* coming into the country are ever seized! *Drug smugglers* (also known as *traffickers,* working for *drug lords*) can be wildly creative when it comes to thinking up new ways to sneak drug shipments past the watchful eyes of customs officials. Condoms filled with heroin and cocaine have been concealed in the stomachs of racehorses being transported across the Mexican border and smaller amounts in the body cavities of human couriers called *mules*, kilo bricks of cocaine have been hidden beneath the false bottoms of containers holding poisonous snakes, and surfboards have been hollowed out, packed with drugs, then painstakingly refinished. And highly-engineered *narco-tunnels* have traversed the Mexican-U.S. border. Finally agents along the Mexican border got wise to the *cone scam,* in which a smuggler takes a leisurely stroll across the border licking an ice cream cone in which cocaine or heroin has been concealed.

Back in the 1970s, America's drug of choice was *marijuana* (also known as *grass, weed, dope, hash* or *hashish, pot, reefer, bud, herb,* and dozens of other nicknames). It came from the *cannabis* plant, which was cultivated primarily in Mexico. But after American authorities began working with the Mexican government to spray Mexican marijuana fields with the herbicide *paraquat,* there was widespread concern about the safety of imported marijuana. With the Coast Guard and the U.S. Border Patrol stepping up their *drug interdiction* efforts, this crackdown encouraged smugglers to turn their attention from marijuana to *cocaine* (from the coca plant), which was both more lucrative and easier to conceal. Another unintended side effect of the effort to stop the flow of marijuana from Mexico was that it opened up the market for *home-grown* marijuana, primarily from California and Hawaii.

Ronald Reagan was the first American president to take a *zero tolerance* approach to the country's drug problem. Many Federal and state laws were rewritten to erase the distinction between marijuana (widely regarded as a *gateway drug* because it leads to the use of more serious drugs) and *hard drugs* like heroin (also known as *horse* or *smack*) and cocaine (*coke, snow, nose candy, blow)*. But the *drug culture* continued to flourish in the U.S.

Cocaine use reached epidemic proportions during the 1980s—particularly *crack cocaine,* a very potent form of the drug (also known as *rock, boulder, yahoo,* and *stone*) made by *free-basing* (1980, extracting, or "freeing," the alkaloid or base from a salt of the drug). Some people say the term *crack* comes from the sound the substance makes as it is being combusted. Others say it is the sound a *rock* makes as it hits the table after processing and cooling, or that it "cracks your head" when consumed. The publicity surrounding the problem of *crack babies* (children born to mothers who are *addicts*) drew attention to the innocent victims of *drug abuse*.

Yet another fad among drug *users* was methamphetamine or *meth* (also *speed, crank, crystal, tweak,* and *go-fast)*. It is made from ephedrine, a drug extracted from the ephedra shrub or made synthetically and used to help treat asthma. It helped soldiers in World War II fight fatigue and enhance their performance, and it was a favorite *recreational drug* among the *speed freaks* of the late 1960s. By the 1990s it was being smoked, injected, or *snorted* (introduced directly into the nose by being inhaled up a narrow tube). Though it is somewhat more expensive than cocaine, the *high* lasts four to five times longer. But frequent meth users have a tendency to become nervous and agitated, a condition described as *tweaking*, that makes them prone to violence. A number of brutal crimes were linked to methamphetamine use in the 1990s. A powerful form of methamphetamine known as *ice,* along with the emergence of *crank* (a meth derivative), provoked promises of new law enforcement strategies in the early 1990s.

Meanwhile, a series of new *designer drugs* (synthetically produced substances with a more "glamorous" reputation) gained popularity among upper and middle class young people, including *ecstasy* (along with its natural and entirely legal counterpart, *herbal ecstasy*) and *PCP* (phencyclidine, popularly known as *angel dust*, 1973). It seems that no matter how much money is spent on the *war on drugs,* Americans have found it more difficult than ever to *Just Say No.*

KIDNAPPED!

According to the National Center for Missing and Exploited Children (NCMEC), more than three-quarters of a million children under the age of 18 disappear in the U. S. every year. Most are only missing for a short time, but of the almost 6,000 active cases that end up in the Center's computerized files, most fall into one of four categories: *runaways, family abductions* (usually by the parent who does not win custody of the child after a divorce or custody hearing), *non-family abductions,* and a catch-all category known as "lost, injured, or otherwise missing." The vast majority of these *missing children* end up reunited with their parents. But many are found dead. The widespread publicity following the disappearance of Polly Klaas (see THE WORD OF THE LAW AND THE LAW OF THE LAND) focused the nation's attention on the security of children and the punishment meted out to their abductors.

TERRORISTS AT HOME

One of the most disturbing trends in crime at the end of the 20th century was *terrorism.* Once considered something that could only happen in foreign countries, *domestic terrorism* (crimes committed in the U.S. for primarily political reasons) became, in the 1990s, a real threat. The period between 1880 and 1920 saw an endless number of violent incidents, including the attempted murder of Carnegie Steel executive Henry Clay Frick (1892), a bomb explosion at the home of Woodrow Wilson's

Timothy McVeigh in custody in 1995, charged with the April 19 Oklahoma City bombing. April 19 was a vital date for anti-government extremists even before Oklahoma City. The seige at Waco ended on April 19, 1993.

attorney general, A. Mitchell Palmer (1919), and the bomb that set off the 1886 Haymarket Riot in Chicago. But the 1990s competed for designation as "the golden age of American terrorism." The bombings of New York's World Trade Center (1993) and of the Alfred P. Murrah Federal Building in Oklahoma City (April 19, 1995) set new standards for terrorism at home.

Just as *Oklahoma City* will forever be identified with domestic terrorism, the city of *Dallas,* Texas has never been able to shake off its association with the assassination of President John F. Kennedy in 1963. And *Waco,* another Texas town, has become synonymous with everything that can go wrong when government agents confront the members of an isolated and anti-government *fringe group* (see ON THE FRINGES).

JAILS AND JAILBIRDS

What does America do with all its *robbers, thieves, burglars* (all three terms were in the English language before colonial days), and *crooks* (1870s)? *Jails* were first established in the 12th century merely to hold people awaiting trial (by colonial times they were called *debtors' prisons*). Spelled either *jail* or *gaol* (in the 1640s the British, including our colonists, were using the *gaol* variant, but by 1776 the *jail* form was taking over in America), the term always had a less foreboding meaning than the 11th century word *prison* (via French from Latin *prehendere,* to seize). *Penitentiary* (literally "a place for penitents") is an American word dating from 1790, when the Quaker state of Pennsylvania built a special cell block to separate more serious offenders from lesser ones. We've had a lot of other words for jails and penitentiaries, including:

workhouse, a 1533 British term, first recorded in America in 1653.

the clink, an 18th century term (originally the name of a London jail) that became popular around 1918.

calaboose, 1792 (from Spanish *calabozo,* dungeon), but it didn't become common until cowboys popularized it in the 1860s.

reformatory, a common American word after the Elmira, New York, reformatory opened in 1807.

jailhouse, 1812.

the jug, 1815 (possibly from the *stone jug,* a reference to London's Newgate Prison).

the lockup, 1839.

hoosegow, an 1860s cowboy term from Spanish *juzgado,* sentenced, jailed.

pen, short for penitentiary, 1870.

the cooler, 1884, originally a special cell for "cooling off" drunks or violent prisoners.

the joint, a penitentiary, 1890s.

the big house, a penitentiary, especially Sing Sing, 1900.

the can, 1910.

the pokey, 1919 (from *pogy,* an 1891 word for a workhouse, poorhouse, or old people's home, from *poke,* to confine).

the tank, 1920s; *fish tank,* 1939, a large cell for holding suspects or new prisoners (*fish* had meant newcomer, novice since around 1900); *drunk tank,* 1943, a large cell for holding drunks overnight.

The slammer. Chicago, 1943.

The Rock, Alcatraz penitentiary, 1930s. Located on rocklike Alcatraz Island in San Francisco Bay, this was a military prison after 1858 and a federal prison from 1933 to 1963.

the slammer, the slam, mid 1930s. Long before that, *slammer* was the underworld slang for "door."

With a prison population today that threatens to overwhelm the available space, even Americans who've never been inside a *minimum security prison (maximum security prisons* are reserved for the most violent criminals) are more than familiar with some of the language that is used there. They know, for example that the *yard* (1777) is the place where prisoners get their fresh air and (sometimes) exercise, and that a *yardbird* (1920s) is a convict or *ex-con (con* meaning convict dates back to 1890). They know what it means to *do time* (1860), *to be sent up the river* (1930s, originally a reference to Sing Sing prison, which is up the Hudson River from New York City and is now known as *Ossining*), and to *take the rap (rap* had meant blame, rebuke, a "rap on the knuckles" since 1777) or *beat the rap* (get off scot-free). Other prison-related expressions include *frame-up* (1900) or *frame* (1914), *fall guy* (1906), and *two-time loser* (1930s, when a person who was convicted twice for major crimes faced mandatory life imprisonment for a third conviction, similar to the *three-strikes-and-you're-out* law).

We can thank the world of crime for hundreds of colorful expressions and catchphrases. Americans are constantly worried about getting *ripped off* (in thieves' slang, to *rip* has meant to rummage through or search for something to steal since at least 1816) or *mugged (to mug* is to hit in the face, *mug* having meant face since the 1840s, probably because drinking mugs were often made to resemble faces). Some of our expressions have slipped away from their criminal origins. To be put *on the spot,* for example, means pressed to perform under adverse circumstances. But it used to mean to put someone in a position so that he could easily be killed, that is, to make him a *marked man.*

The Rock. Originally named Isla de los Alcatraces (Isle of the Pelicans) by Spanish explorers, it is now part of the Golden Gate National Recreation Area.

CYBERSPACE:
I HEAR AMERICA CLICKING

*W*hen the first *personal computers (PCs) were introduced to the
American public in the early 1980s, no one knew that within a few
years millions of Americans would be getting* new addresses—*to which
we could send* email. *And just as society changed forever, so did the language—
the new, email sense of* address *and the new meaning and pronunciation of the
punctuation mark* • *("dot," as in "dot com," not "period") being prime examples.*

Soon we heard people talking about *bits* and *bytes* (*kilo-*, *mega-*, and
giga-), *RAM* and *ROM*, *CD-ROMs*, *hard drives* and *floppy disks*, *laser
printers*, and *mice*. People applying for jobs had to be *computer-literate*,
just as their children already were!

The *personal computer* (abbreviated *PC*) was so called because it put
real computing power into a device small and inexpensive enough for
individual users to afford, in contrast with the *mainframes* (around 1964)
and *minicomputers* (1968) that still ruled the high-end data processing
world; hence the alternate term *microcomputer* (1971). But the microcomputer did not stay "personal" for long. Business users soon found
that the power of their *desktop computers* (*desktop*, cited to 1958)
increased as they were connected together to pool their resources over
LANs (1982, *Local-Area Networks*) and then *WANs* (*Wide-Area Networks*). Hobbyists quickly discovered that they could do something similar, using the telephone line and a *modem* (around 1952, *mod*ulator-
*dem*odulator, a term borrowed from radioteletype) attached to each
computer.

IBM CEO Louis Gerstner was brought in to turn around the office products company in the early 90s. Despite inventing the "PC," Big Blue's weakened competitive position was due in large part to its failure to anticipate just how dramatic
the shift in demand from large, mainframe computers to desktop machines
would be. A company culture that had never fostered individuality in its workers
was blamed by many for IBM's failure to capitalize on the boom in "personal
computing."

> *"It was a seminal event of
> postwar science, one of those rare
> demonstrations that changes
> everything."*
>
> — *T.R. Reid,* The Chip, *1985,
> remarking on the development
> of the microchip, a thing and
> a word that people never
> stopped talking about*

Home electronic giant Sony entering the PC market in 1996 was a sign of The Apocalypse for some—proof that the transition of the PC from information tool to entertainment box was complete.

Born from *cybernetics* (1948), the science of automatic communication and control systems (from Greek *kybernan*, "to steer, control, govern"), the term *cyberspace* first appeared in 1982 in William Gibson's science-fiction novel *Neuromancer*. In Gibson's imagination, *cyberspace* was a place where one communicates with others, and interacts—often by means of a brain-computer *interface* device—with objects that are present not in reality, but *virtually*. (The noun *interface* in its computer sense is cited to the early 1960s; the verb, to the late 1960s.) A number of authors elaborated the idea in a science fiction genre known as *cyberpunk* (razor-edged, near-future visions of an urbanized world in which megacorporations have replaced governments, data has become the most valued commodity, and the boundary between humans and machines has been blurred). Efforts to create cyberspace environments in the "real" world involved the techniques of *virtual reality* (late 1980s-early 1990s) whose goggles-and-glove devices allowed users to see and manipulate objects in *virtual space*.

By the early 1990s, journalists were using *cyberspace* to mean the imagined space where electronic communication takes place across computer networks. Here, distance is wiped out, as users can exchange messages in seconds anywhere via *electronic mail* (1977)—*email* (1982, styled variously as *E mail* or *e-mail*)—and *access* limitless amounts of information by *logging on* to *remote databases* around the world.

In his 1992 vice-presidential campaign, Senator Al Gore popularized the term *Information Superhighway* to symbolize his vision of universal access to a huge interlinked matrix of computer systems through a highly developed communications infrastructure. (A less unwieldy equivalent, *Infobahn*, was soon borrowed from German; *Bahn* means "highway" or "road" in that language.) The basis for this new megasystem was to be the already existing *Internet*, a loosely organized global "network of networks" with its roots in the scientific, academic, and defense communities of the late 60s. Incidentally, the Internet's direct predecessor, was created as an attempt to facilitate communication between incompatible government computers being used in research; hence, distribution of information without a single center of authority.

Third-grader Anna Walter teaches a group of adults about the Internet.

That's why a lack of central control has become a characteristic of *Internet culture*. Americans have argued pro and con about this lack of control for years.

In 1994, interest in the Internet exploded with the maturing of the *World Wide Web (WWW)*, which allowed the Internet to carry *video clips*, sound, rich *graphics*, and specially coded documents in which a reader could, by activating a highlighted word in the text or area on the screen—a *hypertext link*, or *hyperlink*—jump directly to another document, which might *reside* in a computer halfway around the world. This scheme (based on a software language called *HTML*, *H*ypertext *M*arkup *L*anguage) was so powerful and easy to access that private and commercial users immediately tried to establish their presence "on the Web"; by the late 1990s the number of *web sites* had soared. Businesses, organizations, politicians, and private citizens alike all rushed to create distinctive *home pages* to advertise their wares, their services, or simply themselves. To many, the terms *Web, Internet,* and *cyberspace* became synonymous.

Before the Web, however, a number of sophisticated structures were already in place for communicating via computer. Over the years a growing number of computer users had developed their own style of interacting with each other, its language strongly influenced both by the world of technology in which so many of them worked, and by the nature of the new medium, which made it easy to exchange written messages at any distance without the delay of the postal service (*snail mail* also called *smail* or *s-mail*) or even the trouble of committing them to paper (hence the much-ballyhooed *paperless office*, predicted in the 1980s, though the ease and simplicity of *desktop publishing* [1984] actually made paper use soar).

THE COMPONENTS OF CYBERSPACE

Computer hobbyists learned early on that there were great advantages in linking computers together via modem. Some of them made their machines available as full-time *Bulletin Board Systems*, which others

Virginia Governor George Allen explores the state library's web site on a laptop computer.

could call any time to leave messages, *upload* (cited to 1983) or *download* (cited to 1980) files and *software* (1960), and *chat online* from keyboard to keyboard in *real time* (1953); the operators of these *BBSs* (also called *b-boards* or simply *boards*) were known as *sysops* (1983, for *sys*tem *op*erato*rs*). Many BBSs propagated discussion groups called *chat groups* (discussions taking place in virtual *chat rooms*) and *SIGs* (Special Interest Groups) or *forums* in which users with a common interest could share their ideas daily. Never before had it been so easy for a person to reach such a large audience so quickly. Commercial interests with more resources expanded on the BBS concept, creating *online services* (*online*, 1950) such as CompuServe, Prodigy, GEnie, Delphi, and America Online.

Members of the academic and research community began to pursue their interests over the steadily expanding Internet. The service was almost universally free to individual users, as costs were generally absorbed by institutional budgets and research grants. But here, too, commercial ventures sensed opportunity. Around 1990, a few services began to offer Internet access to the public for a monthly subscription fee. By mid-decade, competition in the *ISP* (Internet Service Provider) business was ferocious, as the major online services, the long-distance telephone companies, and numerous small *mom and pop ISPs* attempted to carve out niches in the rapidly expanding market.

From the beginning, the bedrock of Internet communication was *email*, a system that combined the speed and convenience of the telephone with the reliabilitiy of paper mail. As the medium grew, new tools for sharing and searching for information across the *Net* brought still more new words to Americans and new meanings for old terms. A sophisticated program called a *gopher* allowed you to jump from one *server* to another to find sites of interest. Files began to be stored in large collections, where you could retrieve them by *ftp* (*f*ile *t*ransfer *p*rotocol). To make it easier to search for files in these *archives*, the *Archie* program was developed. A related program for locating information on gopher sites was named *Veronica*, supposedly standing for *Very Easy Rodent-*

"The open society, the unrestricted access to knowledge, the unplanned and uninhibited association of men for its furtherance—These are what may make a vast, complex, ever growing, ever changing, ever more specialized and expert technological world, nevertheless a world of human community."

— Science and the Common Understanding, *1953*

Oriented *Netwide Index to Computer Archives*, but clearly inspired by the name of a teenage character in the popular nerd comic strip *Archie*. (Incidentally, *nerd*, cited to 1951, goes back to the name of a creature in the Dr. Seuss book *If I Ran the Zoo*, itself dated 1950.)

Probably the largest recognizable network before the World Wide Web was *Usenet*, which originated in the 1980s as a way of distributing news about the *UNIX* computer operating system (developed by AT&T) and other topics of interest to computer scientists. Much like the discussion forums on a BBS, each Usenet *newsgroup* was dedicated to a single topic, letting participants from institutions worldwide exchange views. The numbers of users and newsgroups grew steadily until by 1996 there were something like 20,000 separate groups dealing with everything from artificial intelligence to collecting Teddy bears.

From the start, Usenetters developed their own jargon, shared to some extent by the BBS community. Sending a message to a newsgroup was called *posting*, reflecting the system's bulletin board-like origins. A message to the group was an *article*, or alternatively a *posting* or *post*; posting the same article to multiple groups simultaneously was *cross-posting*. To *reply* to an article meant to send a message to the author by private email; responding to it publicly in the newsgroup was called *posting a followup*. A series of articles on the same subject was a *thread*. One who read the articles in the group but never announced his presence or posted articles of his own was a *lurker*—colorful, yes, but carrying little connotation of disapproval. When a newsgroup grew large enough that its experienced hands grew tired of new users repeatedly asking for the same basic information, someone would create and post a document providing answers to the most *Frequently Asked Questions*, after which *newbies* (newcomers to the newsgroup) were regularly enjoined to *read the FAQ*.

Other facets of the Internet less well known to the general public were pursued passionately by their devotees. *IRC* (*Internet Relay Chat*) let users carry on keyboard-to-keyboard conversations with others around the world; at any given time thousands of separate *channels* might be active with anything from scientific discussions to no-holds-barred bull sessions. Other users spent their time in *MUDs* (*Multi-User Dungeons*), where they could create identities and characters for themselves, compete in imaginary combat and adventure games, and cooperate in expanding the dimensions of the computer-generated world. For many, *mudding* became an obsession; true *mudheads* sometimes spent so much time at it that they lost jobs, alienated friends, and failed to obtain academic degrees in the quest to attain *wizard* status.

In the mid 1990s, the *World Wide Web* came to the fore as the preeminent method of *navigating* the Net. An elaboration of the gopher concept, the Web provided a unified method of locating most of the Net's resources by using a single *point-and-click* program, the *web browser*. This referred to the manipulation of a screen *cursor* by means of the buttons and movement of a computer *mouse*. As *browsers* rapidly grew in sophistication, users could *surf the Net* in search of ever more elaborately designed *Web sites* offering not only text, but all the features of *hypermedia* including integrated graphics, sound, and *full-motion video*. Businesses rushed into what they perceived as a new marketing frontier, creating *online shopping malls* to advertise and sell their goods and services to *cybershoppers*, who could *order online*. *Web design*, creating and maintaining *web pages* and their ever-shifting content, became a sought-after skill, entrusted to those with the newly created job title *Webmaster*.

PERSONALITIES OF CYBERSPACE

Much cyberspace jargon reflects the background and experience of its creators—an assortment of computer scientists, researchers, and students who built the structure as they went along. The most general designation for any denizen of cyberspace is *user,* a term originally used by programmers to refer to non-programmers, people who operate systems and programs without knowing how they work. (At MIT around 1975, a debate over whether such people should be described as *users* or *losers* was resolved with the compromise form *luser.*)

In the relationship between computers and society, few terms have been the center of as much debate as *hacker* (1950s). In computer circles, it means essentially an expert programmer, one who enjoys learning as much as possible about the details of programmable systems, solving problems and overcoming limitations with creativity and ingenuity. Naturally, in the course of events a certain number turned their efforts to the challenge of circumventing security safeguards on systems in the *real world,* such as telephone companies, banks, and university registrars' offices. Concern in the media first brought *hacker* in the familiar—negative—sense to the public consciousness, though within the hacker community the accepted term for these illegal activities was *cracking.* But beneath the distinction lay a fundamental difference in how hackers and the general public viewed privacy, security, and access to information. It was a common conviction among those who had developed the Internet

"You can salvage the hard work you've put into 16-bit DLLs by calling them from your 32-bit applications using a Windows 95 technique called flat thunking. Thunking allows your 32-bit VB app to call a 32-bit DLL which in turn calls your 16-bit DLL through the thunking layer—a kind of hyperspace leap where code reaches through a 32-bit thunking layer to grab 16-bit DL functions."

— *Steve Jackson, "Thunk Before You Port,"* **Visual Programmer's Journal,** *March 1996,* **an example of the jargon of the field; of the 65 expressions in these two sentences, about half (30) would not be understood by the uninitiated**

The web site of the American Film Institute, which aired its first classic movie online in January 1997. It's been a long, adventuresome trip for the Internet, which has evolved from a Defense Department communications system into a competitor of video stores and cable TV.

Revenge of the nerds. The richest man in America, Bill Gates, in 1992 with the product that helped get him there.

and the operating system on which it was based that information resources should be free and accessible to all. Many hackers extended this belief to include the view that system-cracking was ethically acceptable as long as the cracker didn't steal, vandalize, or breach confidentiality. Although it clashed profoundly with the concerns of security-minded and cost-conscious administrators in the real world, this view was a defining characteristic of life on the Net, until the influx of commercial interests began to overwhelm it in the mid 1990s.

A less complimentary term was *geek* (short for *computer geek*). It is difficult to improve on the *New Hacker's Dictionary*'s description: "One who fulfills all the dreariest negative stereotypes about hackers: an asocial, malodorous, pasty-faced monomaniac with all the personality of a cheese grater." (In an early U.S. sense [1928], *geek* referred to a carnival performer who bit the heads off live chickens and snakes.) Even on those occasions when geeks found themselves at social gatherings with non-computer types, they might find it difficult to avoid *geeking out*, or *byte-bonding* with fellow *propeller-heads* (a term alluding to the real or imagined popularity among hackers of beanie caps with mini-propellers on top). Depending on context and speaker, the term could be one of scorn or approbation, as could *weenie* (from *wiener*), one who has spent a great deal of time and effort at mastering a particular operating system or programming language. Likewise, the popular 1990s slang word *wannabe* meant one who aspires to the hacker lifestyle but lacks the experience or the sensibility to truly understand the mystique.

At the other end of the spectrum from hackers and experienced *Internauts* (or, less complimentarily, *net potatoes*, after the television-watching counterpart *couch potato*) were *newbies*, those who had yet to learn the ropes. Those whose errors were particularly serious, repeated, or *cretinous* might be tagged *lamers*.

As the number of users climbed and the complexity of the Net grew, the work of the *system administrator (sysadmin*, or simply *admin*), the person (or people) in charge of computer and network operations at each site, grew more difficult. Unlike the early users who accepted the new technology's experimental nature—and were often willing and able to solve problems themselves—paying subscribers to commercial services demanded reliable service and quick repairs when things went wrong. A large part of the *sysadmin's* work ended up as *firefighting*, intensive efforts to correct system malfunctions. Another important entity at many sites was the *postmaster*, to whom it was customary to direct complaints about users who abused the mail system.

CYBERSPACE CULTURE

From the beginning, the *online community* developed a body of accepted practices, especially in email and Usenet. On the Internet, adhering to the standards of *netiquette* mentioned in MANNERS & MANNERISMS was the sign of a well-behaved *netizen*. Most users also deplored practices like excessive *cross-posting* and over-large *signatures*, *sig blocks*, or *.sigs* (pronounced "dot sig").

The most common consequence of violating the standards of *netiquette* was to be subjected to *flames*, an acrimonious or hostile response from another user. If returned in kind, *flaming* could rapidly escalate into a public *flame war*, which if joined by enough third parties, could lead to the breakdown of an entire discussion forum. Antisocial folks were sometimes known to post *flame bait*, messages whose offensive content was deliberately intended to get the predictable response. A related, if less malicious, technique was *trolling*: posting an article that would deceive and embarass the *clueless* but which more experienced *netters* would recognize as a *troll*.

Perhaps the most widespread cause of net *flamage*, however, was *spamming*: flooding the Net with inappropriate, *off-topic* messages, often posted simultaneously to a huge number of unrelated newsgroups or electronic *mailing lists*. The name came from a popular comedy sketch by British comedy group Monty Python's Flying Circus—very popular among hackers—in which *Spam* (trademark for a canned luncheon meat) was repeated over and over. A relative rarity in the early days, the *spam* problem increased massively as the Net was opened to *non-techies* and subscribers to the major commercial online services. A common response to *spam campaigns* was *mailbombing*, the tactic of returning hundreds of copies of an offending message to its point of origin, in the hope that the resulting overload on the sender's system would lead to the cancellation of his or her account.

Acronyms and *emoticons* became two distinctive ways of conversing online. They suited the fast, impromptu style of writing electronic notes. A few are these:

AFAIK	As far as I know
AFK	Away from keyboard
BRB	Be right back
BTW	By the way
FWIW	For what it's worth
IANAL	I am not a lawyer (disclaimer used when giving legal advice)
IMHO	In my humble opinion
IMNSHO	In my not-so-humble opinion
IYKWIM	If you know what I mean
LOL	Laughing out loud
OTOH	On the other hand
PMFJI	Pardon me for jumping in
ROTFL(L)	Rolling on the floor laughing (loudly)
TTFN	Ta ta for now
YMMV	Your mileage may vary (a phrase from automobile ads); i.e., you may not get the same results I did

Impatience on the part of experienced experts, or *gurus*, with questions they considered asinine or unnecessary led to another extremely common acronym, the universally understood *RTFM: Read the Fucking Manual*. The only permissible rebuttal to this instruction is "I *did* RTFM; the answer wasn't in there."

Emoticons (from *emotion* + *icon*) are possibly the most original feature of online communication, neatly and creatively solving the problem of being unable to see facial expressions or hear tones of voice in typed correspondence. The basic form of the *emoticon* is a smiling face (hence the alternate generic term *smiley*), created from characters on the keyboard, and viewed by tilting one's head to the left: :-)
This sign was a convenient humor marker, added whenever a writer wanted to ensure that what he or she had written was intended to be ironic or all in good fun. Combining keyboard characters in various ways led to a great variety of smileys, from simple to elaborate:

;-)	Winking smiley
:-/	Skeptical smiley
:-(	Sad face

(-:	Left-handed smiley
:-o	Shocked smiley
:-x	My lips are sealed
:-)}	Man with beard
:-{)	Man with mustache
(:-)	Bald-headed man
{ :-)	Man wearing a toupee
:-)))	Double chin
8-)	Wearing glasses
B-)	Wearing horn-rimmed glasses
:-)X	Wearing a bow tie
:-?	Smoking a pipe
:-#	Braces on teeth
8:-)	User is a little girl
:-)-8	User is a big girl
C = :-)	User is a chef
+ -:-)	User is the pope
= |:-) =	Uncle Sam

CYBERSPACE AND SOCIETY

As the general public became aware of the cyberspace phenomenon in the mid 1990s, people began to worry about its effect on society at large. Access to this newest of our "new frontiers" was easy; anyone with a computer and modem could cruise the *fast lane* of the Information Superhighway, with little protection from nefarious activity, real or imagined. The fact that unsupervised youngsters could be exposed to sexually explicit or graphically violent materials prompted many groups to call for tighter restrictions on what could be placed on the Net, while advocates of free speech strongly resisted any such controls and condemned the efforts of self-appointed *net police.* As computer entertainment and television moved closer together at the end of the 20th century, similar worries over the potential content of *interactive TV* and *video on demand* led to the development of the *V-chip* (*V* for *violence*), a device to allow home users to set controls on what their home sets could display.

Another area of debate was *cybercrime,* the theft of information by computer. Because of the Internet's inherent structure, it was relatively easy for *cybercrooks* to intercept personal email and retrieve valuable data. Users accustomed to paper mail looked for tighter security, and businesses seeking to expand their markets sought ways of persuading potential customers that it was indeed safe to send their credit card numbers and other personal data over the World Wide Web. For many, the answer to problems of data security was to develop effective schemes for *encrypting* communications, so that only those who held the appropriate *keys* could decipher them. Many in the government, however, saw in encryption a threat of unrestrained and unmonitorable worldwide communications to the benefit of criminal and terrorist organizations, and so supported the development of the *Clipper Chip,* a device that would permit authorized agencies to intercept and monitor encrypted communications at need. A loosely organized group of encryption adherents called *cypherpunks* strongly opposed the plan.

More positive innovations also left their mark on the language. Speedier and more realistic interactions in cyberspace made it possible to do things that were once largely face-to-face: *cyberdoctors* could practice increasingly effective *telemedicine*; students could choose from a huge variety of *telecourses* and degree programs for *distance learning*. Far-reaching changes affected the American workplace, as workers and employers found advantages in *telecommuting*, creating a *virtual office* at home.

CYBERSPACE VOCABULARY

Partly because electronic communication is largely unrecorded and ephemeral, and partly because language innovation spreads through this large community in virtually no time, the vocabulary of cyberspace changes quickly. Terms with *click appeal* today may be gone tomorrow. Like any selection of representative terminology, then, the following list is a snapshot:

asbestos, material for protecting oneself from *flames*. Often in the form of *asbestos longjohns*, typically donned in advance by one who knowingly makes a inflammatory remark.

avatar, in *MUDs*, graphical chat environments, and *virtual reality* environments, a symbol, an icon, or a graphic that represents a user's character.

Bad Thing, an idea or action that cannot possibly make matters better. From the 1930 parody of English history *1066 And All That*. Conversely, a notion that is bound to be helpful is a *Good Thing*.

bamf. In *MUDs*, a representation of the sound made when one is magically teleported or transformed (from the *X-Men* comics).

bandwidth, 1937, a telecommunications term meaning roughly "the amount of information a transmission medium can handle per unit of time." In this sense the basic unit of measurement is *bits per second (bps)*. In cyberspace, it is chiefly a commodity which others are accused of "wasting" through *off-topic* remarks, unnecessary quoting, excessive *cross-posting*, over-large *signatures*, and general *lameness*.

baud, 1931, first printed reference—1929—in French, from the name of the French inventor and engineer Jean Maurice Emile *Baudot*, is the unit of transmission speed over a serial communications line. In general usage it is equivalent to "bits per second."

baud barf, the *garbage* (an unintelligible mass of characters) you see on the screen when the connection with another computer is disrupted.

bigot, a person zealously devoted to a particular type of computer, operating system, program, programming language, or the like. In contrast with the *weenie*, the bigot is reluctant to give up his attachment even when the system becomes obsolete.

bit, 1948, from *bi*nary + dig*it*, the basic unit of data in a digital computer system, representable by either a one or a zero.

bitraking, a type of investigative journalism practiced by reporters cruising the Net for breaking stories (after *muckraking*).

bogus, useless, wrong, stupid, silly, or lame. In hacker slang since the late 60s, it spawned a number of derivatives, for example the verbs *bogotify*, "make bogus," and *bogue out*, "act bogus." *Bogosity* is theoretically measurable on a *bogometer*; its basic quantum unit is the *bogon*.

boink, an event where Net users gather for social interaction in person or *face time*. From the general slang verb "to have intercourse with," itself going back to at least 1987, popularized by the television show *Moonlighting*.

bozon, the quantum unit of stupidity. From *bozo*, a clown, a loser. Adjective *bozotic*.

brain-damaged, *brain-dead*, so poorly designed or stupid as to be useless. Generally refers to lame or cretinous software, but may extend to humans as well.

brain dump, the act of telling someone everything one knows about a particular subject, typically before leaving for another job. From *core dump*, early mainframe term (perpetuated in the UNIX world) for a copy of the full contents of the computer's core memory, usually produced when a process is interrupted unexpectedly.

brain fart, the result of a *glitch* (1962, Yiddish, "slippery place"), or minor error, in brain activity. It is the result of a *braino*, another word for *thinko*, an unintentional error in thinking (by analogy with *typo*).

brochureware, nonexistent software that is advertised and promoted in order to stall prospective customers from purchasing an existing competitive product. Compare *freeware, shareware, vaporware*.

bug, an error or other flaw in a system or program. The word in the technical sense appeared as early as 1896 in *Hawkin's New Catechism of Electricity*, where it was defined as "any fault or trouble in the connections or working of electric apparatus," and was known in Edison's time as a word for an industrial defect.

It seems to have come from telegraphers' usage, but whether its ultimate origin goes back to the word for "insect" or the Welsh loanword meaning "scarecrow, hobgoblin" (as in *bugbear*) is uncertain.

clickstream (also *mouse trails*), the path a user takes from site to site while surfing or browsing the Web. Advertisers developed software to track this trail in order to gather demographic data on potential customers. Popular sites are said to have *click appeal* (as in *sex appeal*).

cobweb site, a web site that has not been updated recently.

cyber-, denoting practically anything having to do with computers and the *online* world. Although this prefix is disapproved of by Internet veterans and experienced users, it is highly productive. Representative examples: *cybernaut*, one who navigates cyberspace; *cybrarian*, one who makes a living searching online data resources, library catalogues, etc.; *cyberporn*, sexually explicit material available from online sources; *cyberdate*, a romantic interest one meets online, through chat forums and email; *cybercreep*, an obnoxious character encountered while looking for a cyberdate; *cybershopping*, viewing and purchasing goods through the World Wide Web; *cybercrime*, theft, fraud, or other crime committed over computer networks.

dead tree edition, the paper version of a newspaper or magazine that is also available in electronic, online form.

delurk, to post an article in a newsgroup where one has been *lurking*.

dot, the pronunciation of and now the name for a period in an Internet address. For example, "ftp.uu.net" is pronounced "F-T-P dot U-U dot net."

firewall, a computer, containing security and monitoring software but no critical or sensitive data, which serves as a connection point or *gateway* from the outside world to a networked computer system. A hacker can try to break into a firewalled system by defeating the security systems or by discovering a *back door*, an undocumented or unprotected alternate-entry method.

freeware, software that the author distributes at no cost. Compare *brochureware, shareware, vaporware.*

grilf, girlfriend. An example of a new word that started its life as a typo!

handle, a fictitious name used on an online service.

haque, an elegant example of *hacking.*

mode, the state one is in or what one is doing at a given time. Common examples are *sleep mode, work mode,* and *flame mode.*

munge, to garble information in transfer. "That newsreader *munges* the headers of Usenet articles." (Possibly from Scottish/North English dialect, "to chew up.")

robot or *bot*, an automated process that runs in the background. On *Internet Relay Chat*, robots perform such tasks as greeting new visitors to a channel with a personal message or ensuring that a user does not adopt a *nickname* that has already been claimed by another user. In *Multiuser Domains* robots are often written to appear to be real users. A more practical use of the robot concept is the *knowbot*, an automated software agent that actively searches the Net for specified kinds of information.

shareware, software that is distributed at no cost for evaluation puposes, thus saving the author the cost of advertising and packaging. Those who find the program suitable and use it are expected to register and pay for it. One technique for reminding users of this last condition involves a reminder screen which appears whenever entering or exiting the program, leading to the designation *nagware*. Compare *brochureware, freeware, vaporware.*

simulator sickness, the queasy feeling, akin to motion sickness or seasickness, experienced by some users of *virtual reality* headsets. Also called *barfogenesis.*

UNIX, widely used computer operating system, written in the C programming language so that it can run on a large number of computer system architectures.

URL, Uniform Resource Locator, a string of characters specifying the address of a document on the World Wide Web, for example "http://www.yahoo.com."

vaporware, software that is advertised as forthcoming but never appears. Compare *brochureware, freeware, shareware.*

virtual, denoting a simulated thing or event as opposed to its counterpart in the *real world*. Technically and originally, it refers to the addressing of physical devices, memory locations, and the like by "logical" names. This meaning is still discernible in *virtual reality*, a space where computer-generated *virtual objects* appear as (and are sometimes connected to) real ones. From this arose the general sense, essentially synonymous with *cyber-.*

virus, a program that propagates by copying itself into other programs on a user's computer, usually in order to do damage to data in the system. (A *virus* can also destroy the hard disk and program files.) Because viruses can be "caught" through the unprotected exchange of software, a large body of punning humor is devoted to the parallels between *Net SEX* (Software EXchange) and sexually transmitted diseases. One variation on the virus concept is the *Trojan horse* (an early use going back to a 1974 issue of *Datamation*), a program distributed in a glossy package and having the appearance of a commercial product but containing a virus—yet another term (here, going back to references to the infamous "wooden horse" of war in Homer's *Odyssey* [Book 8] and Virgil's *Aeneid* [Book 2]) that, in the development of an entirely new "sublanguage," has taken on its own specialized meaning.

In contrast to some of the more cyberspace-specific words in the previous list, Americans quickly picked up and began to use expressions like *GIGO* (garbage *i*n, garbage *o*ut, the acronym denoting the rule that the integrity of computer *output* depends on the integrity of the initial *input* by the operator), *rebooting* (turning a computer off and then on again to restart the computer's operating system), *z directories* (lists of the *files* on a disk), *scrolling* (to cause displayed text or graphics to move on the screen vertically or horizontally), and *user-friendly* (1977, easy to learn or use, a term that generated all manner of offspring like *user-unfriendly* and *reader-friendly*).

DIRTY WORDS:
PARDON MY FRENCH

*O*nce unprintable *(1860)* words are now everywhere in print, the subject of comment pro and con by Americans, and in heavy use by many of them as well. The average adult movie contains more dirty words *(late 1500s for this sense of* dirty*) than the collected comedy routines of the once notoriously risqué Lenny Bruce. Many Americans think the youth of the country need to have* their *mouths washed out with soap.*

WARNING: READER DISCRETION IS ADVISED

Throughout this X-rated section words are discussed that are generally considered *taboo, vulgar, obscene, low, vile, base, unspeakable, coarse, disgusting, not what you would say to your grandmother, not what you would use in polite company,* etc., including the *f-word* (and its derivatives). Words such as these have, in earlier years in America, caused books to be banned, or worse. As a result, the evidence for these words in print, hence the citational dating provided (if at all available), is a bit less certain than would normally be the case. Though dates are given for many terms, the actual first use of the words in question are highly likely to be much, much earlier.

In Britain—where Kenneth Tynan introduced *fuck* into serious discussion years ago—*The Economist* of June 22, 1996 editorialized on *swear words* (early 1400s at least, for this sense of *swear*):

Some swear words are now deployed so often they in effect become punctuation, a sort of comma substitute, and so lose their power to shock or relieve. . . . Swear words work best when used sparingly; more frequent deployment does not liberate, it devalues a wonderful means of expression. Pity the rebellious of today, groping for a way to shock. What can they possibly say?

A 1992 off-off Broadway play, Marion McClinton's *Police Boys*, employed *motherfucker* 274 *friggin'* times (*frigging*, 1820s), with *frig* having been used since the 15th century to mean "to thrash about" and since 1590 to mean "masturbate." It come from Old French *friquer*, to rub, from Latin *fricare*.

In unrefined conversation descriptions of the self or others are laced with *bastard, cocksucker, fucker,* and *asshole*—all nonspecific now because of such frequent use, as is the case with *schmuck* (cited to 1892, from Yiddish *shmok*, penis). The most overworked words, with innumerable meanings and innumerable combinations, are *fuck* and *shit*.

Fuck has been common in English—whether we like it or not—since the late 15th century; it was first recorded in an encrypted poem titled "Flen flyys," the encryption suggesting that the word was taboo even then. The form of the encryption was *gxddbov*; decryption yielded *fuccant*, a pseudo-Latin word meaning "they fuck," the "they" being the Carmelite friars of Cambridge, England, the subject of this spoofing poem: *Non sunt in coeli, quia gxddbov xxkxzt pg ifmk*, or "They [the monks] are

"Obscene" comedian Lenny Bruce returns to New York in 1963 after being refused entry by Britain.

not in heaven since *fuccant* [they fuck] *vvivys* [the wives] *of heli* [Ely, a nearby town]." Beyond that, scholars think that *fuck* is most probably the English form, or spelling, of a Germanic word, taking into account Middle Dutch *fokken*, to thrust, to copulate with; Norwegian dialect usage *fukka*, to copulate; Swedish dialect *focka*, to push, to copulate—with *fock* meaning penis; and German *ficken*, to copulate.

Screw came into English via Old French from the Latin *scrofa*, sow, which also gives us the woodworking *screw* and the word *scrofula* (the wood-working *screw* because its threads coil like a sow's tail and the word *scrofula* because the glandular swelling of this condition is rounded like a pig's back). But this Latin word *scrofa*, sow, was influenced by or melded with another Latin word, *scrobis*, ditch, whose Vulgar Latin meaning was "vulva"—and these two words "sow—vulva" gave us *screw*, to copulate.

There is, of course, no logical reason why *fuck, screw, make* (1922), or any other term should be "dirty," shocking, or taboo, no logical reason why they should be considered any different than such synonyms as *copulate* or *sexual intercourse*. It's a matter of conditioning and etiquette. *Fuck* appeared in poetry and scholarly dictionaries until the 18th century, but eventually it became strongly taboo. From then until after World War II no dictionary listed or discussed the word.

Because of the "blackout" between the 18th century and the 1940s, we don't know exactly when *fuck* and *screw* were first used in certain oaths, as expletives and intensives, or when they first took on some of their extended meanings, such as to cheat (*His business partner fucked/screwed him*), to bungle to confuse (*He fucked/screwed up that job*), or to loaf or malinger (*Stop fucking/screwing around*). We do know, however, that such uses first centered on *fuck*, with *screw* being substituted later. (*Fuck* may have come to mean cheat or take advantage of someone partly because of its similarity to the Old English *ficol*, false, treacherous.) In any event, the use of sex words to refer to cheating, confusion, failure, etc., undoubtedly has a connection with human experience and our society's often ambivalent attitudes about sex. (See THE AMERICAN WAY OF SEX.)

In the 1870s *obscenity* (Latin *obscenus*, filthy, repulsive) and *scatology* (Greek *skatos*, dung) began to increase. The 1870s saw the first widespread use of *fuck!* as an expletive of anger or annoyance, the angry rejection *go fuck yourself*, and the first recorded use of *like fuck!* and *fuck it all!*

The use of obscenity and scatology then increased greatly during World War I and became prolific during World War II. The use of the cursing modifier *fucking*, for *damned*, first reached epidemic proportions with British soldiers during World War I, by which time they were also using *fuck arse* (for a contemptible person, which American troops translated into *fuck ass*), *fuck me gently* (literally "don't take advantage of me too much, don't cheat me too blatantly"), *fuck 'em all*, and *make a fuck up of* ("bungle, ruin"). The loosening of language taboos between the wars is shown in the 1930 Canadian armed forces alliterative expression *fucked by the fickle finger of fate* and by a few daring books that represented *fuck* with the censored spelling *f**k* (this quaint form first used in Francis Grose's 1785 *Classical Dictionary of the Vulgar Tongue*). Use of these words by the armed forces spread to many other segments of the population during and after the war, helped by veterans bringing their vocabulary to college campuses and a wartime and postwar lessening of social restrictions. Other factors were increasing social mobility, new concepts of free speech, the sexual revolutions of the 1950s and 60s, and the Women's Liberation Movement in the late 60s. In 1959 Grove Press

"I remember my uncle, a farmer who had used four-letter words ten to the sentence ever since he learned to talk. One day he came too near the circular saw and cut half his fingers off. While we stared in horror, he stood watching the bright arterial blood pump from his ruined hand. Then he spoke, and he did not speak loud. 'Aw, the dickens,' he said."

— *Wallace Stegner, "Good-bye to All T——t!" in* About Language, *1989*

Members of the Army's famed 82nd Airborne Division are primed to enter Kuwait during the Gulf War. Many "colorful" words and expressions have originated from the military experience.

Francis Grose introduced fuck as an option in his *Classical Dictionary of the Vulgar Tongue*.

first printed the word *fuck* respectably in modern times, in an unexpurgated edition of D. H. Lawrence's 1928 *Lady Chatterley's Lover*; this caused a legal battle over obscenity that the publisher won in a 1960 court ruling.

In World War II there appeared the very popular acronym *snafu* (situation *n*ormal, *a*ll *f*ucked *u*p), meaning a mistake, bungling, or confusion, as well as other such acronyms, as: *fubar* (*f*ucked *u*p *b*eyond *a*ll *r*ecognition), *fubb* (*f*ucked *u*p *b*eyond *b*elief), *tarfu* (*t*hings *a*re *r*eally *f*ucked *u*p), *janfu* (*j*oint *a*rmy-*n*avy *f*uck *u*p), *fubis* (*f*uck *yo*u *b*uddy, *I'*m *s*hipping out), and, as "the last word," *fubio* (cited to 1946, the post-VJ Day acronym for *f*uck *yo*u *B*ub, *i*t's *o*ver). There were also abbreviations such as *F.O.* (*f*uck *o*ff), *F.T.A.* (*f*uck *t*he *a*rmy), and *G.F.U.* (*g*eneral *f*uck *u*p), along the lines of *S.O.S.* (*s*hit *o*n a *s*hingle). Later the Korean War helped to popularize *motherfucker*, now identified with Black English going back to the late 1930s, but in fact originally Southern Upland white speech. In any case, the word now spread. It soon became, and remains, American English's most intensely taboo sexual epithet. *Motherfucker* also produced popular euphemisms in the 1950s, that combined *mother-* with other two-syllable words substituted for *fucker*, such as *mothergrabber* and *motherlover*.

Vulgarities center chiefly on toilet terms such as *shit* (as in *shit out of luck, shit-head, bullshit*), *pee* (at least late 1800s, from the first letter of *piss*) and *piss* (as in *piss call*, the Navy reveille of the 1930s, *pissed*, drunk, and *pissed off*, angry—elaborated into *pissed off like a fly on a toilet seat*). Sexual kinkiness has introduced such terms as *shit-eater* (though *shit-eating grin* indicates sly defensiveness more than deviance) and *golden shower*, both of which occur in vulgar speech. Euphemisms such as *take a) whiz, drain a vein, take a slash*, and *see a man about a dog* (1867) are being replaced by the more direct *take a piss*, but *dump* is widely used for *shit*, and *dump on* someone (treat another badly, attack that one) is used by people who often never think of its scatological content, any more than they do with *brown nose* (a toady). *Poop* (cited in print only to 1965 but obviously much older, being from Middle English

Oh Shit!

Oh Shit! could be any scholar's cry of exasperation when trying to pin down the use and popularity of many taboo words (the noun *shit* cited to around 1585; the verb to around 1720). We know that the Old English *scitan*, to defecate, befoul, was spelled *shite* by the 14th century and *shit* by the 16th century. Until the late 19th century, however, written uses are so few that we don't know what expressions *shit* was used in. Then in the 1870s, terms such as *to fall in the shit* (to get into trouble) and the exclamation *shit and corruption!* were recorded. Also recorded in wide use between the 1870s and 1890s were both *shit* and *bullshit* meaning "nonsense, rubbish, lies" (*chickenshit* and *horseshit* were first recorded in the 1930s); *the shits*, diarrhea; *shit pot* and *shit face*, both referring to a contemptible person (*shithead* is known from 1915); *to shit on someone*, to treat someone badly; and *to beat the shit out of* someone. By 1910 *shit or bust*, to do or die, was common and so was (*either*) *shit or get off the pot*, a vulgar rephrasing of the old New England "fish or cut bait," meaning to do something or let someone else try, do something or give up. By 1918 *S.O.L.* was a common abbreviation for the older *shit out of luck*.

In World War I the old rural term *shithouse* became a popular soldiers' word for latrine, while *shit alley* was a particularly dangerous battlefield or position and *shit pan alley* was a military hospital (a pun on the 1914 *Tin Pan Alley*). World War II introduced *shit list*, a personal list of people one dislikes; and *shit on a shingle*, creamed chipped beef on toast.

poupen, to make a gulping noise, itself imitative), meaning to defecate, is another term that does not raise eyebrows. *Crap* (Middle English *crappe*, chaff, from Old French, from Medieval Latin, possibly of Germanic origin) and *crapper* are still widely used; and many scholars believe the rumor that the latter word comes from Victorian toilet manufacturer Thomas Crapper is no more true than the rumor that Union Army General Joseph Hooker gave us a word for whores. *Tail*, or *piece of tail*, is an equivalent of *poontang* (cited to 1929, possibly an altered form of French *putain*, prostitute), *piece of ass*, or *cunt* (14th century in the sense of the female sex organs, going back to Middle English *cunte*, literally a hollow space). And speaking of *hookers* (cited to 1845), consider the following

Pissing and Peeing

Written records show that Americans have been *pissing* and *peeing* since the late 1700s. It seems doubtful that earlier colonists *held their water* or merely used the word *urinate*. *Piss* has actually been part of the English language since the 13th century (via Old French from Vulgar Latin *pissiare*), its late recording in America being only because people didn't write such words. *Piss pot* was a 15th century word for chamber pot, and the expression "He hasn't got a pot to piss in" (is too poor to own a chamber pot) probably predates the sailing of the *Mayflower*. Because of delicacy and censorship, terms such as *pisser*, someone or something extraordinary; *pissed-off*, angry; *to be full of piss and vinegar*, full of energy; and *piss call*, the first call to get out of bed in the morning, especially in the Navy, didn't generally appear in writing until the late 1930s.

Pee, a children's euphemism formed by merely saying the first letter, *p*, is derived from *piss*. It was known in America at the time of the Revolutionary War. The children's terms *pee pee* and *wee wee* both appeared by the 19th century.

synonyms and related terms, some euphemistic, some slang, some standard, and at least one highly taboo:

baggage, suggesting a person viewed as low and contemptible, perhaps related to *(old) bag* (1890s).

B-girl, 1930s, one who hustles bar customers.

bagnio, 16th century, from Italian, "bath"; a brothel.

bawd, 14th century, via Middle English from Middle French *baude*, "dissolute"; related to a Germanic root seen in English *bold*, procuress, now usually called a *madam,* a manager of a brothel or a *call girl* (1940) ring.

bordello, 1590s, a brothel, suggesting Renaissance England's connection of whorehouses with Italians.

brothel, 15th century, from older *brothel-house* (Middle English *brothel*, "harlot; worthless person").

easy, offering little resistance to sex, as in the euphemism *woman of easy virtue*.

floozie/floosie, early 1900s, started from Victorian *flossy*, "shiny, showoff." The word then deteriorated in meaning.

gold digger, early 1900s, mercenary *slut* (14th century, from Middle English *slutte*, related to dialectal *slut*, "mud," and possibly a Norwegian

You Son of a Bitch!

Son of a bitch was first recorded in England in 1712, *bitch* (Old English *bicce*) having meant female dog since before the 10th century and an immoral woman since the 15th. By the 1780s *son of a bitch* was one of the most offensive and common American insults.

By the 1890s, however, American men could also use the term familiarly, as in calling an old friend "You old son of a bitch you." The euphemism *son of a gun* was common by the 1750s, while *son of a sea cook* appeared in 1825.

Son of a bitch was used so often by World War I American soldiers as an expletive or intensive that Frenchmen called them "les sommobiches." The abbreviation *S.O.B.* also appeared during World War I. When President Harry Truman first used *S.O.B.* publicly in 1948, it was highly controversial.

---

dialect term, *slutr*, "sleet; impure water"), looking for a (*sugar*) *daddy*, early 1900s, a lover who will support her.

harlot, originally a male rascal (12th century, ultimately from Medieval Latin *harlotus*, "vagabond"), as *fairy* was originally a female prostitute and *gay* a female *wanton*.

house, often short for *whorehouse* (14th century). There are also barrel-house (1880s, serving drinks, once drawn from barrels, as well as proffering sex, also notable for the jazz and blues music played there), *bed house, can house, cat house, chicken ranch, fast house, fuck palace, grind house, house of assignation/ill fame/ill repute, joy house, sporting house,* etc. Today TCB (taking care of business) may involve *escort services, call girls or boys, models, massage, role-playing, French lessons, telephone or phone sex, backroom sex* in bars and discos, even *inflatable dolls,* etc., not to mention *safe sex.*

hussy, 17th century in the "low woman" sense, once meant *housewife*, illustrating a word that, over time, has taken on a negative meaning.

hustler, early 1900s, once meant a male pimp or *pros* of either sex, now usually means a (male) dishonest dealer, swindler, or sharp salesman.

jade, 16th century, originally a worn-out horse, later a *clapped-out cunt*.

Jezebel, 16th century, a shameless, seductive woman, alluding to the biblical character (1 Kings).

mistress, title of respect but also "whore," more recently *top* in sadomasochism; a live-in one is a *shack job* (and foreign wars have provided foreign words to describe such women).

piece of dry goods, 1869, and *piece of calico*, 1880, merely "women"; now *piece of ass* can be male or female.

pimp (early 17th century use in Middleton's *Your Five Gallants*, 1607) has given rise to *pimpmobile* (cited to 1971) for any big, flashy car. *Pimp*, the verb, dates to 1636.

prostitute, 1613, from the Latin participle *prostituta*, "offered for sale."

street walker, late 16th century, elaborated into *pavement princess*.

tart, originally and still "a small pie," but that sense led, by the 1880s, to "whore" or any *cock teaser*.

trick, a prostitute's *john* or *client* or a gay person's casual sex partner (paid or not).

trollop, cited to 1621, possibly from *troll*, to wallow about; one who used to *troll* or *cruise* for *customers* or *pick-ups*; a whore is also a *trull* (1519, from German *Trulle*).

twat, 1656, origin unknown, the vulva; also used to denote a woman; highly offensive, though used by writers such as E.E. Cummings, Henry Miller, Norman Mailer, Philip Roth, and John Updike.

working girl, a *round heels* of either sex who lives *the life*.

Some terms are fluid: *swinger* can mean "in the swing" of fashion, a *spouse-swapper*, a *bi(sexual)* person. *Get off* can describe either sexual or non-sexual pleasure. *On the make* can describe predatory moves in business or in what used to be called *courting*. *Hot to trot* can be sexually or otherwise eager. *Partying* or *party* the noun can denote sexual or non-sexual activity. Any despised person of either sex can be a *bitch*, *cunt*, or *son of a bitch*. Often there is no sexual intent in usages such as *up yours*, *this sucks*, or *fuck you and the horse you rode in on*.

BLASPHEMIES AND THEIR SUBSTITUTES

Americans have developed a whole lexicon of exclamatory substitutes (or euphemisms) for blasphemies, from *gee* (elaborated into *golly gee*, *gee willickers*, *gee whiz*, etc.) to *gosh darn*, *garldurn*, and many more. On the other hand, we have the stronger *Jesus H. Christ*—cited in printed sources only to 1924, but in use much earlier according to references to it by Mark Twain, who had, before his death in 1910, reported that he had heard it as a boy (some 70 years before the 1924 citation); the *H.* is said to be somewhat casually and ignorantly derived from the *IHS* monogram seen in church art and on vestments, actually representing the first three letters of the Greek spelling of *Jesus*.

Here are some more euphemisms Americans are often heard using: *by George*, *by golly*, *darn*, *cripes*, *crikey*, *good grief*, *by cracky*, *by jimminy*, *jeepers creepers*, *I'll be blowed/dogged/jiggered/switched*, *consarned*, *dad-burned*, *doggone*, *a devil of a—*, *what in Hades*, *goodness gracious*, *deuced*, *Hell's bells*, *botheration*, *perdition*, *tarnation*, *how in blazes—*, *heck*, *Hail Columbia*, *holy smoke/cow/Moses*, *land's sake*, *lawsee me*, *what the Sam Hill?*, *by the great horn(ed) spoon*, *Great Horny Toads*, *by Godfrey/Jove/heavens/Jupiter/Judas/gum/gar*, *for Pete's sake/pity's sake/goodness sake*, *suffering cats/catfish*, etc. *Shucks!* this list could go on forever.

A FULL-FRONTAL LOOK AT ENGLISH

In 1933 the following words—aside from the term *sex* itself—were censored from movies: *alley cat*, *broad*, *damn*, *guts*, *lousy*, *madam*, *mistress*,

Comedian George Carlin's nine cable specials have given him ample opportunity to say on TV the seven words you can't say on TV.

nude, and *punk.* By contrast, at the end of the 20th century, movies were using *adult themes* with *adult language* (or *explicit language*). Society had seemingly become inured to the broad use of George Carlin's once notorious "Seven Words You Can't Say on TV" (*fuck, cunt, tits, shit, piss, motherfucker,* and *cocksucker*). *Dirty words, Anglo-Saxon monosyllables, four-letter words,* and *racial epithets*—many, fixtures in the language for centuries—showed, at century's end, no signs of pending oblivion.

NAMING THE ENEMY

In wartime, both soldiers and civilians tend to coin terms, often extremely derogatory ones, for their opponents. One function of the worst of the terms, of course, is to dehumanize or demonize the enemy, making him easier to hate and kill.

One good example of dehumanization is the term *savage,* used from colonial times through the middle of this century to label Native Americans. Some American colonists even considered the Indians to be creatures of Satan in his war against mankind, an idea that persisted in the use of *devils* in dozens of phrases describing Indians. The racist *redskins,* of course, pointed beyond a difference in skin pigmentation to a presumed lesser degree of humanity (also the color of the devil's skin in many depictions).

In the American Revolution, the more vicious tendencies of naming the enemy remained in check. Americans called the British troops *redcoats* (English use since 1520, American use since 1674), referring to their bright red uniform jackets.

During the Civil War, *rebel* (1861) denoted a Confederate civilian or soldier. *Reb* appeared by 1862, along with *Johnny Reb*—for which the southern equivalent was *Billy Yank. Copperhead,* which had named a snake since 1775 and by 1809 meant any hostile or vindictive person, denoted a Northerner who sympathized with the South (1862). *The Blue* or *the Federals* (both 1861) meant both the North and its army, with blue, of course referring to the color of that army's uniforms. Similarly *the gray,* 1861, denoted the Confederacy or its army, from the color of its official uniforms. *Butternuts*, 1861, was another name for Confederate soldiers because many wore homemade uniforms dyed with butternut extract.

The strong note of disparagement re-emerged with the Spanish-American War. *Goo-goo, gu-gu* was the word for a Filipino that American soldiers and Marines used after the occupation of the Philippines and during the subsequent guerrilla war. Perhaps a parody of Tagalog sounds or a reference to slanted eyes—*goo-goo eyes* having meant loving glances in the U.S. in the 1890s—the term may also have led to *gook* (exact origin unknown), common parlance for any Asian in World War II, the Korean Conflict, and Vietnam, and traceable in print to at least 1935.

Americans called Germans and German soldiers during World War I *Boche* (from a derogatory name used of Germans by the French meaning "head of a nail" or "blockhead,") *Hun, Kraut* (shortened from *Souerkraut*, a popular German dish) *Jerry,* and *Fritz*. During World War II, they mostly used *Nazis,* from the German shortening of *Nationalen Sozialisten*, the National Socialist German Workers' Party, founded in 1919 by Hitler and six others. (The German word seems to have first appeared in English in *The London Times* in 1930.) Americans also called the German enemy *Jerry* and sometimes *Kraut* in World War II, but seldom used *Hun* and *Boche*.

The Japs are what Americans called the Japanese during World War II, often in the phrase "the dirty Japs" (*Jap* had been a slighting term for a Japanese since 1886). They also called a Japanese a *slant-eye*, a disparaging term for an Asian since the 1930s.

In Korea and Vietnam, derogatory terms for the enemy or Asians in general proliferated. *Gook, Slant* and, *slant-eye* came along with the U.S. troops when they deployed from Japan to Korea. *Slope*, also alluding to slanted eyes, then updated *slant* and *slant-eye* in Vietnam.

Dink and *zip* were new Vietnam War terms. *Dink* may have come from the 1858 English dialect and 1887 U.S. use of *dinky/dinkey*, insignificant (though this origin is dubious). Since 1900, *zip* had meant zero, especially as a score in sports or mark in school, but Vietnam saw its first application to a person (it probably comes from the psychologists' acronym *zip* for *z*ero *i*ntelligence *p*otential).

Raghead, is a derogatory term for Iraqis and, at times, any Arab. It is derived from the appearance of traditional Bedouin headgear. The terms *raghead* or *towelhead* had been slang labels for Arabs long before the war, but in the Gulf they gained wide currency. The racist *sand-nigger* also named the enemy or an Arab ally during the war.

Radio star Arthur Godfrey with his ukelele in 1958. We've heard the words "hell" and "damn" on television since Godfrey blurted them out in the 60s.

DISASTER AREAS

*O*ur word disaster *(1591) came into English by way of French from the*
Italian word disastro. *The Italian word, a mix of* dis-, *meaning "to pieces,*
apart" and astro *meaning "star," was used to describe an evil stellar*
influence. It also describes events the Italians could not have known about. There
is not unanimous agreement as to the exact cause of the events that occurred
millions of years before humans evolved, but it is universally recognized that
something catastrophic ended the reign of countless species ranging from plankton
to dinosaurs, in a blink of the eye, as measured on the geologic time line *(1951).*

Theory holds that an asteroid or comet slammed into the earth about
65 million years ago, landing in the ocean near the Yucatan Peninsula in
Mexico and throwing up huge amounts of debris into the atmosphere.
The debris formed clouds that blocked sunlight and thereby killed off
plants and animals alike. An alternate theory backed by some paleontolo-
gists and paleobotanists claims that the meteor's impact raised the ocean
water temperature to the point where *hypercanes* (1995), forms of super
hurricanes, were spawned, reaching altitudes of 35 miles well up into the
stratosphere. Because of their extent these storms could have transported
water vapor, ice particles, and dust into the stratosphere, where they
would have blocked out sunlight and destroyed the life-protecting ozone
layer.

Scientists believe that *volcanoes* (1613, from Italian, from Latin
Volcanus, Vulcan, the Roman god of fire and metalworking) were responsible for injecting dust and debris into the upper atmosphere. Another
interesting hypothesis suggested in the 90s links the extinction to a huge
slow upwelling of gas from the oceans' depths.

VOLCANOES

Some of the material ejected from a volcano is fluid molten rock or *lava*
(1759); some is lighter and porous, *pumice* (15th century). Pumice from
Krakatoa's eruption in 1883 was thrown 50 miles and became a naviga-
tion hazard because this type of rock contains trapped gas and floats.
Tsunami (1897) waves 175 feet high traveling 400 miles an hour hit
Djakarta, Indonesia and destroyed the new harbor in Perth, Australia.
Mudflows (1900) crashed downslope at speeds of 50 mph or more.
Magma (15th century) from Mt. Vesuvius converged on Pompeii in
A.D.79 covering the hillside and city. Solidifying *lava* and *magma* form a
number of *igneous* (1664) products: *tufa* (1770) or *tuff* (1815)—both
from Italian; *volcanic glass* (1840); and various *pyroclastic* (1887) frag-
ments. Extinct volcanoes often end up with *craters* (1613) and *calderas*
(1691) over 1,000 feet deep.

Seamounts (1941) are submarine mountains rising from the sea floor;
they can be volcanic as well. Chains of volcanoes can be formed over the
centuries as the sea floor travels over a *hot spot* (1929), a *plume* of hot
rock rising from deep in the mantle. One such *hot spot* exists just west of
the East Pacific Rise, a boundary where two of Earth's crustal *plates*
(1960s) are separating with new sea floor forming between them (the

Residents of Moses Lake, Washington, dig out after large deposits of volcanic ash were dumped on the city from the 1980 eruption of the volcano Mount St. Helens.

term *plate tectonics* goes back to 1969; *continental drift*, to 1926). There are over 500 active volcanoes on earth along the boundaries of such *plates*. *Hot springs* (1669), *geysers* (1780, from Icelandic *Geysir*, hot spring, from *geysa*, to pour or rush forth, from Old Norse), and *fumaroles* (1811, from Italian *fumarola*, from Latin *fumariolum*, vent) are examples of similar activities when they occur on dry land.

EARTHQUAKES

Earthquakes (14th century), also known as *temblors* (1876, from Spanish, "trembling," from *temblar*, to tremble, from Medieval Latin *tremulare*) or *seisms*, are sudden movements of Earth's crust caused by the release of stress that accumulates along geologic faults under the earth, or by the activity of volcanoes. The relative frequency and distribution of earthquakes are denoted by the word *seismicity* (1902), going back to *seismic* (1858), an adjective from Greek *seismos*, "shock or earthquake," from the Greek verb *seiein*, "to shake." As those who "live on the fault line" well know, the language of *quakes* (first cited of earthquakes in 1881, but no doubt much older) is distinctive:

aftershock, 1894, a relatively minor shock that follows an earthquake's main shock; a warning shock is a *before-shock*.

epicenter, 1887, the point on the surface directly above the underground source of a quake; *hypocenter*, 1905, the source area itself.

Mercalli scale, 1921, named after 20th century Italian priest and geologist Giuseppe Mercalli, a scale of 1–12 that measures the force and intensity of a quake as it is felt in a specific location: 1 means it is felt only by a few, located at the epicenter; 12 means total destruction.

Richter scale, 1938, named after U.S. seismologist Charles F. Richter, whose 1930s work led to this open-ended logarithmic scale that measures the magnitude of an earthquake in terms of its energy. Typical readings: 1.5, *barely felt*; 3.5, *slight* damage; 4, *moderate* damage; 5,

Most of the damage from the April 18, 1906 earthquake in San Francisco was caused by the fires that burned for three days after the seismic activity.

considerable damage; 6, *severe* damage; 7, *heavy* damage; 8, *tremendous* damage. In April 1906 San Francisco sustained a quake measuring 8.3 on the Richter scale, and in 1964 Alaska had an 8.5 earthquake. The term also is used figuratively of anything with a powerful or devastating effect, as "The news was a shock equal to a seven on the Richter scale."

San Andreas Fault, a major area of fractures in Earth's crust extending along the California coastline from San Francisco to southern California. San Francisco experienced a noted quake in 1989.

seismogram, the record of an earthquake taken by a *seismograph* (1858).

seismology, 1858, the science of earthquakes and their detection.

LET IT SNOW, LET IT SNOW, LET IT SNOW

The historic blizzard of January 1996 covered 17 states from Kansas to Massachusetts, and set new single-storm records as well, and not just for *snowfall* (1821), but for losses of life and property. The "blizzard of '96" buried some areas with two-and-a-half feet of *snow* (before the 12th century, Middle English, from Old English *snaw*).

Though the press tends to characterize particularly severe and dramatic winter storms as "the Blizzard of the Century" or "the Blizzard of (year)," bad weather has long been a characteristic of this nation's meteorological history: though well acquainted with rain, sleet, hail, and snow in England, the colonists had not been forewarned of the severe New World climate. The Pilgrims realized they were in for trouble with it only when they lowered boats from the *Mayflower* and rowed through freezing rain and snow looking for a place to land. Later colonists going to New England were purposely misled by being shown accounts of the mild climate in Virginia or the Caribbean or by being told that New England was, after all, in the same latitude as sunny Spain. Thus early Americans talked with despair and horror about the weather and we've been talking about it, reading about it, and watching television coverage of it ever since.

"Year of snow
Fruit will grow"

— an old English rhyme

Children have been talking about building *snow forts* since 1853; New England farmers hoped for *sugar snow* (1861, a late spring snow slowing the flow of sap and extending the time for gathering maple sugar); and we now enjoy not only skis but *snowmobiles* (1934, first used to refer to experimental vehicles used by Admiral Byrd in exploring the Antarctic) and *snowboards* (1981). We named the *snow goose* by 1771 and the *snow* or *snowy egret* by 1895. People were said to be *snowed under* (overwhelmed) by 1880 and we overwhelmed people with exaggerations and lies called *snow jobs* by the 1940s.

But the most storied American "snow" word is *blizzard*. Though its history is somewhat murky, the word in its winter-storm sense was popularized over 100 years ago by the American press, and the story of its evolution brings together a small-town newspaper editor, a small-town character, Thomas Jefferson, a physician, and Davy Crockett. Tradition has it that the "violent snowstorm" sense of *blizzard* originated in the 1850s in the Northern Plains, where such storms are notorious. The term *blizzard* (spelled with one *z*) appeared in the local newspaper of Estherville, Iowa, the *Northern Vindicator*, on April 23, 1870, and again one week later (this time with the familiar two-*z* spelling). This word got into the *Vindicator* through its editor, O. C. Bates, who had gotten the term from one "Lightnin'" Ellis, a local character who hung out in the barber shop and the general store. *Blizzard* was thus established in the local press, and then began to appear in other Upper Midwest newspapers. In the winter of 1880–81 a series of severe snowstorms occurred across the country, and American papers freely used *blizzard* to describe them, thus propelling the word into the mainstream, thence across the Atlantic to England as well.

Before these meteorological usages, however, the ultimate origin of *blizzard* remains obscure. One theory has it that the word derives from German *Blitz*, "lightning." Yet another is that *blizzard* is onomatopoeic (its sound suggesting such words as *blow, blast,* and *bluster*). And evidence exists for a word spelled *blizz*, "a violent rainstorm," but no direct linkage between *blizz* (first cited in 1770) and *blizzard* has ever been established to the satisfaction of scholars.

A policeman to the rescue during a 1929 blizzard in the Midwest.

We do know, though, that in 1824 Thomas Jefferson invited Robley Dungilson, a German-educated medical doctor, to the University of Virginia to serve as a professor of medicine. Dungilson, who was a polymath, wrote a glossary of "Americanisms" published in 1829–30. In it the doctor defined *blizzard* thus: "a violent blow, perhaps from *blitz*," and ascribed the usage to Kentucky. The next early evidence for *blizzard* in American English resides in the 1834 autobiography of Tennessee-born frontiersman, Davy Crockett, who used it in the meaning of "a rifle shot." One year later Crockett used the same word again, this time figuratively, meaning "a stinging, crushing retort." Twenty-five years later during the Civil War *blizzard* had come to mean "a volley of musketry." That sense of a flurry of shots seems to have developed into the now-familiar weather term, first in the Upper Midwest perhaps, then spreading generally through English, thanks to editor Bates, his colorful source Ellis, the noted winter of 1880–81, and the power of the American press.

Blizzard-savvy Americans living in the *snow belt* (1874) know how to cope with snowy conditions. Some have suffered *snow blindness* (1748), have gotten caught in *snowstorms* (1771) and *snow showers* (1779), and have become *snowbound* (1814), run down by *snow slides* (1841), caught in *snowbanks* (1779) or in *snowdrifts* (14th century), *snowed in* (1859), or have simply stared dolefully at the *snowcaps* (1871) on the mountains. As is our nature, we have developed numerous and varied ways to avoid coming down with *cabin fever* (1918) while watching falling *snowflakes* (1734) and waiting for the spring *snowmelt* (around 1946). We walked with *snow shoes* by 1666; pushed it around with (manual) *snow plows* by 1792; built *snowmen* (1827), and stopped its drifting with *snow fences* (1872). We used it for a confection called *snow pudding* by 1876. In winter we donned *snow suits* (1937) and put *snow tires* on our cars to drive through it (1943). We've moved it out of the way with *snow blowers* (1950) and *snow throwers* (1954), and even started making it artificially (for ski slopes) with *snowmakers* in 1954. We know of *snowmobiling* on it as a sport, eating a form of it in *snow cones* by 1964.

By the early 1900s the slang sense of *snow* for cocaine and heroin was in use. Women who brought clients to dope peddlers became known as *snowbirds* (1938), the same term used for folks attempting to escape wintry weather by migrating South for the winters. (Jackson and Hellyers' *Vocabulary of Criminal Slang*, published in 1914, contained this explanation for the drug-related coinage, ". . . derived from the extremely flocculent nature of cocaine when pulverized." The *Policemen's Monthly* of December 17, 1915 contained the following colorful advice, "One day his pal found him depressed and told him to take a little sniff of *snow*, as heroin is known to [sic] the vernacular of the criminal.")

GREAT FLOODS

"There is an annual flood in the Nile and the Mississippi," said the 1855 edition of Noah Webster's *American Dictionary of the English Language* (revised by Chauncy A. Goodrich of Yale). Well, some floods are different from others: "Iowa Flood Leaves 250,000 without Drinking Water," was just one of many U.S. headlines in July 1993. The great Mississippi, a river that Mark Twain once called "this lawless stream" (1882), overflowed its banks in a fashion not seen for 70 years or more. (The word *flood* is first recorded in English in 825, meaning simply "a river or a stream"; it was spelled *flod*). In 1993 some 36,000 people living along the Mississippi fled their homes. Residents coped, however, *come hell or*

On May 31, 1889, the South Fork Dam in Johnstown, PA broke, unleashing a rolling wall of water 75 feet high and a half-mile wide. More than 2,200 people were killed.

high water (1930), despite tons of *gumbo* (1881, river mud) that covered everything. Whole towns *flooded out* in the disaster were actually moved *lock, stock, and barrel* (1842) to higher ground above the *floodplain* (1873) after the *floodwaters* (1791) had receded, well above the former *high-water mark* (1553).

Flood is one of a set of ten monosyllables denoting various kinds of inclement weather, each characteristic of northwestern Europe during the Middle English period (from around 1100 to 1500). All but one word in the set can be traced back to Old English (mid 5th century to the beginning of the 12th century). *Cloud, drought, hail, rain, sleet, snow, storm, wind,* and *flood* are all traceable to Germanic. The last, *fog,* probably comes from a Danish word of the same spelling that meant "a spray or shower."

We Americans also talk about other unique storms. Besides *cloudbursts* (1869) we talk about:

hurricanes (via Spanish *huracán* from the Carib *huracan, furacan,* meaning "big wind" and also being the name of the evil spirit of storms), first cited in 1555. The word was still so new in Shakespeare's day that he used it around 1601 in *Troilus and Cressida* to mean "waterspout." Hurricanes—warm-core tropical cyclones with minimum sustained surface winds of 74 mph or over—occur east of the International Date Line. When a hurricane loses wind speed ("strength"), typically after reaching landfall and/or cooler water, it is "reduced" to the status of a *tropical storm* (around 1945).

    The practice of giving hurricanes names has gone on for centuries, but was only systematized after World War II. By 1953 the U.S. weather services began assigning names from a list that was determined in advance for each *hurricane season* (June through November in the Atlantic, including the Caribbean and Gulf of Mexico; June through November 15 in the eastern Pacific); from 1953 to 1978 only women's given names were used. From 1978 men's given names were

The remains of a home in Homestead, Florida in 1992 in the wake of Hurricane Andrew.

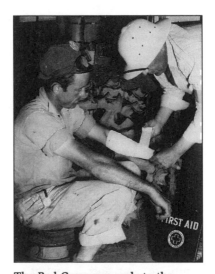

The Red Cross responds to the needs of the wounded in wartime, and the victims of natural disasters in peacetime. The American National Red Cross was founded by Clara Barton in 1881, and is currently supported by the efforts of 1.5 million volunteers.

introduced into use, alternating in each year's list with the women's names. Currently hurricane names are selected and agreed upon by the World Meteorological Organization, for both Atlantic and eastern Pacific storms, and have more of an international look. Names beginning with *Q, U, X, Y,* and *Z* are never used, apparently because so few names begin with these letters. An entire year's list of names may be repeated in later years, but if a particular storm is of historic proportion, a name will be retired from use. The National Hurricane Center in Miami assigns a name when a storm or *tropical depression* reaches sustained wind speeds of more than 39 miles per hour, making it officially a *tropical storm.*

Hurricanes are ranked by categories of strength according to the *Saffir-Simpson Scale*: *Category 1* (*central barometric pressure* of 28.94 in. or more; winds of 74–95 mph; 4–5 ft. *storm surge*; causes *minimal* damage); *Category 2* (pressure 28.50–28.93 in.; winds of 96–110 mph; 6–8 ft. storm surge; *moderate* damage); *Category 3* (pressure 27.91–28.49 in.; winds of 111–130 mph; 9–12 ft. storm surge; *extensive* damage); *Category 4* (pressure 27.17–27.90 in.; winds of 131–155 mph; 13–18 ft. storm surge; *extreme* damage); *Category 5* (pressure less than 27.17 in.; winds over 155 mph; 18 ft. + storm surge; *catastrophic* damage).

A *hurricane watch* announces to an affected area that those living there may be threatened. A *hurricane warning* indicates that the storm is expected in 24 hours or less. The *eye* of the hurricane is a fairly calm area in the center of the storm. The sky may be almost clear, with light winds.

tornado (an alteration of Spanish *tronada*, thunderstorm, from *tronar*, to thunder, from Latin *tonare*; *tronada* may have been influenced by Spanish *tornar*, to twist); in its original, now archaic, sense, "a tropical thunderstorm," cited to 1556; in its current sense, "a rotating column of air with a funnel-shaped cloud extending downward, its whirling vortex causing destruction as it touches the ground, is cited to 1804.

Similar to hurricane watches and warnings, a *tornado watch* informs the public, expecially those living in areas of the country dubbed *Tornado Alleys*, of the possibility of a tornado; a *tornado warning* means a storm is imminent or that a *funnel cloud* has been sighted.

Twister (1897) is colloquial for a tornado, and is also used for a *waterspout* (1738; basically, a tornado over water, with an accompanying cloud of spray) or for a *dust devil* (1888, a rather small dust- or sand-filled whirlwind).

cyclone, 1848, alteration of Greek *kykloma*, wheel or coil, from *kykloun*, to whirl or go around, from *kyklos*, circle), a storm with strong winds that rotate around a moving center of low atmospheric pressure; sometimes used in the U.S. to mean *tornado* and in the Indian Ocean to mean *hurricane*. *Cyclone cellar*, to which one flees during such a storm, is cited to 1887, *storm cellar* to the 1900s—both called *hidey-holes* in Southwest U.S. dialects.

When any of these storms cause widespread destruction, the governors of the affected states request that the areas be designated *disaster areas*, allowing local and state governments and citizens access to federal aid.

A tornado strikes Denver in 1988.

Weather Watch Boxes

On a television weather map a *watch box* is usually bright orange-red, indicating areas where severe, dangerous storms are occurring or are expected. Here is a language "watch box" with a few frequently occurring weather terms:

Beaufort scale, 1858, named after British admiral Sir Francis Beaufort (1774–1857), a system of code numbers, 0–12, classifying wind speeds into groups from 0–1 mph, or Beaufort 0, to those over 75 mph, or Beaufort 12.

Doppler radar, 1960, named after the Austrian physicist Christian Johann Doppler (1803–53), who articulated the principle called the *Doppler effect*; radar used especially in weather forecasting to locate, measure, and show the direction of storm winds and precipitation.

downburst, 1978, an extremely strong, violent, downward-moving air current, usually associated with thunderstorms and highly dangerous both to airborne aircraft and people on the ground; *microburst*, 1982, a sudden, extremely violent downdraft over a very small area, almost impossible to predict with standard weather instruments and extremely dangerous to aircraft during landing and takeoff; *wind shear*, 1941, a marked change in wind speed and direction between slightly different altitudes, dangerous to airborne aircraft, especially when landing.

dust storm, 1879, a whirling storm marked by wind speeds in excess of 30 mph, intense electrical activity, and flying dust reducing visibility to a half mile or less.

feeder band, a band of rain and wind squalls emanating from and feeding off a huge storm cell, such as a hurricane, and contributing to storm surges in coastal areas.

flash flood, 1940, a sudden flooding of rivers, streams, and surrounding ground areas resulting from heavy rains or rapid snowmelts.

freeze (at least 15th century in the weather sense), denoting a condition when surface air temperatures drop to 32° F. or below during the growing season; a *severe* or *hard freeze* indicates a *cold spell* or *cold snap* of at least two days or more.

frost (before the 12th century), the formation of ice crystals on surfaces; often used in weather-forecasting expressions such as *frost in low-lying areas*, *scattered frost*, and *heavy frost*.

gale, around 1547, origin unknown, a strong sustained wind of 39–54 mph, or 34–47 knots, as in the expression *gale-force winds*. New Englanders have called a gale from the northeast a *northeaster* (or *nor'easter*) since 1774. Americans have called a strong cold wind from the north a *norther* since 1776 (possibly suggested by a similar use of Spanish *norte*). People in the foothills of the Rockies have been talking about the *Chinook wind* since 1860, clipping it to *Chinook* (1876), named for the Native American tribe that lived west of the Rockies, whence came these dry winds accompanied by rapidly rising temperatures. The *Santa Ana* (1880, from the Santa Ana canyon in southern California, not from the Mexican general *Santa Anna* as some people incorrectly believe) is a strong wind—hot and dry— generally from the northeast or east in southern California. The

Chinook and *Santa Ana* winds are *foehns* (1861, a German borrowing)—warm, dry winds on the lee side of a range of mountains caused by compression as air moves down the slopes.

high winds, sustained winds of 39 mph or more, expected to continue for an hour or longer, often used in winter forecasting expressions like *high winds, and drifting and blowing snow.*

ice storm, 1876, a winter storm during which falling drizzle or rain freezes upon contact with the ground and objects on it.

isobar, around 1864, an imaginary line on a weather map that links points of equal atmospheric pressure.

orographic lifting, the lifting of an air current due to its passing up and over surface elevations such as mountains.

sandstorm, 1774, a storm, e.g., in a desert, with winds of 30 mph or more with blowing sand reducing visibility to a half mile or less.

severe thunderstorm, an electrical storm with associated surface winds or gusts of 53 mph or more, and/or such a storm that generates hail measuring three-quarters of an inch in diameter or larger.

smog (1905, a blend of *sm*oke and f*og*), polluted air that creates haze.

squall, 1699, probably of Scandinavian origin—related to Swedish *skval*, "rushing water"; a sudden increase in wind speed by at least 18 mph and increasing to 29 mph or more, lasting at least one minute or longer; used in expressions like *wind squall*, *snow squall*, and *rain squall*; *line squall*, 1887, a thunderstorm or a squall occurring along a cold front.

stadium effect, the counterclockwise motion of winds and clouds from the eye of a hurricane, as viewed in a satellite image.

storm surge, a sudden, significant rise above normal water level in low-lying coastal areas due to strong incoming winds and a drop in atmospheric pressure on the water's surface, as from a hurricane. The *storm surge* from a hurricane can extend hundreds of miles from the eye of the storm. A *storm tide* is the height of a storm surge or hurricane wave above the normal sea level. In Hugo, a Category 4 hurricane that hit South Carolina in 1989, the *storm surge* and *tide* extended hundreds of yards inland, carrying large trawlers with it to "dry land."

travelers' advisory, an alert to the public that weather will cause dangerous driving or flying conditions in a widespread area; *small-craft advisory*, a similar alert to mariners; *stockmen's advisory*, an alert to farmers and ranchers regarding extremely cold, hot, dry, or flooding conditions of possible danger to their animals. *Advisory* is upgraded to *warning* as conditions deteriorate.

windchill factor (or *index*), 1939, the cooling effect on skin of a combination of temperature plus wind. It is technically the loss of human body heat in kilogram calories per hour per square meter of exposed skin surface. Winter weather forecasts now regularly give the windchill to indicate that a 20° F. day may *feel* like −10° F. if there is strong wind.

wind field, the extended area of sustained winds surrounding and a part of *landfalling hurricanes.*

A fire in California's Pine Region in 1923. The state's dry climate makes it very susceptible to forest fires.

"You gave us beer,

now give us water."

— Dust bowl farmers' slogan to the government (Prohibition had been repealed in 1933)

The first widespread weather observations in America were made by a network of 600 telegraph stations under the direction of the Smithsonian Institution beginning in 1849. The first *weather forecasts* appeared in New York City newspapers in 1853. In 1859 the *weatherman* appeared, *weather forecaster* not recorded until 1909. A government *weather bureau* was widely discussed in 1857, but the *Weather Bureau* was not established by the Signal Corps until 1870, providing *weather maps* for the War Department by 1871. After being part of the Department of Agriculture from 1891 the Weather Bureau was moved to the Commerce Department in 1940, becoming the *National Weather Service* in 1970, a branch of the *National Oceanic and Atmospheric Administration* (*NOAA*, pronounced "NO-uh").

THE DUST BOWL

In the 1930s The Great Plains area of Kansas, Colorado, Oklahoma, New Mexico, and Texas had been farmed badly for decades beginning with trying to fill World War I demands for wheat. The *Great Drought* of 1933 destroyed crops and dried the land, and severe dust storms began in 1934, blowing huge dust clouds from this Great Plains area over Chicago and all the way to the Atlantic. Residents of the plains were talking about *dust pneumonia* by 1935, and by 1936 everyone was calling the stricken area *The Dust Bowl*.

"Okie use' to mean you was

from Oklahoma.

Now it means you're scum."

— John Steinbeck, The Grapes of Wrath, 1939

Thousands of farm families left their unproductive land or were forced off by mortgage foreclosures. They piled their belongings on jalopies or old farm trucks and headed west, swelling the roving ranks of the unemployed during The Great Depression. Since many were from Oklahoma, and were called *Okies*, the word began to conjure up an offensive image of uprooted unskilled farmers and their large, undernourished families traveling west like gypsies. Some eventually settled in shanty towns and city tenements, but many became itinerant, migrant farm workers. Other job seekers and local authorities cursed the arrival of the Okies, while some sympathized with their plight, or at least read and talked about John Steinbeck's description of it in his 1939 best-selling, Pulitzer Prize-winning novel *The Grapes of Wrath*.

"IT'S THE ECONOMY, STUPID"

*A*mericans worry about the federal deficit *and about* maxing out *(exceeding the credit limit on) their* plastic *(1980s, credit cards). People shop at* outlets *and* discount stores, *join clubs so that they can enjoy the benefits of* buying in bulk, *and wait for* sales *featuring* slashed prices. *Almost every American's heart beats a little faster upon hearing the words* On sale now! 50 percent off! Free gift! Today only!

John Kenneth Galbraith in 1975.

To pay for their purchases, many Americans borrow money at excessive *interest rates.* They pay *service charges* to get cash from *ATMs* (1981, *automated teller machines*). And poor, *unbanked* Americans pay extortionate service charges at *check-cashing* facilities. Millions of Americans are in debt—beyond the $60,000 or $70,000 that represents each family's share of the *national debt.* Some have already *tanked* or *gone down the tubes* (filed for bankruptcy), while others are merely *strapped for cash.* Those who live *hand-to-mouth* (1748) can only hope to *scrape by. Winning the lottery* is a long shot, but the sheer number of lottery tickets sold every day across the U.S. attests a widespread belief in *winning the jackpot* as the surest path to financial well-being.

There have always been some Americans who are *in the money* (1902), *in the chips* (1938), or have *money to burn.* It used to be that you had to be a *millionaire* before you were considered *filthy rich* (1940) in America. Now millionaires are *a dime a dozen,* and you have to be a *billionaire* (1861) to join the ranks of the truly *affluent* (a popular synonym for "wealthy" since John Kenneth Galbraith's *The Affluent Society,* 1958). Most Americans, however, can only imagine what it feels like to be *rolling in dough.* (See the subsection "Easy Street" in this chapter.) For them, it's *another day, another dollar.*

The automated teller machine (ATM) provides cash on demand and, reflecting the diversity of America's population, it does it in four languages. Money is, after all, the international language.

THE ALMIGHTY DOLLAR

The word *money* has been in English since 1330. It comes, via Old French, from the Latin *moneta,* meaning "coin" or "mint," after the temple of Juno Moneta on the Capitoline Hill, where Roman money was coined. *Dollar* comes from the German *t(h)aler,* an abbreviated form of *Joachimstaler* (meaning "of the Saint Joachim Valley"), a silver coin first minted in Joachimstal, Bohemia, in 1519. This original *t(h)aler* or *da(h)ler* became such a common European coin that it became the general name for any large silver coin. By 1851, the English spelling was *dollar.*

The early American colonists had the so-called *lion dollar* (or *lion*), a Dutch coin bearing the likeness of a lion and brought here by the original Dutch settlers around 1620. They also used the Spanish *peso,* which they called a *Spanish dollar* from at least 1684. Calling a peso a *dollar* is a habit that was retained: The Mexican peso was called a *Mexican dollar* in 1831, when it was the major *currency* (1699, from the Latin *currentia/currere,* to run, so called because it is the current, generally accepted medium of exchange) in the far West. It was Thomas Jefferson who suggested that the dollar be the basic unit of the new American *dollars and cents* currency in 1784.

The First Bank of the U.S. issued *paper money* around 1800. In 1862 the U.S. Treasury's *Bureau of Engraving and Printing* began printing *paper money,* but *bimetallism* (an 1876 English word referring to defining the dollar in terms of both gold and silver) lasted until 1873. Bimetallism and the *silver standard* (an 1896 term) were rejected in the elections of 1896 and 1900, in both of which the *silver Democrats* and their presidential candidate, William Jennings Bryan, were defeated. Thereafter the U.S. was effectively on the *gold standard* (an 1875 term), made official by the Gold Standard Act of 1900.

When the U.S. was taken off the gold standard in 1933, gold coins were removed from circulation, *gold certificates* (an 1863 term, the year Congress first authorized them) were called in, and our coins and paper money were declared *legal tender.* From 1878 until 1963 the government also issued *silver certificates,* paper money backed by silver dollars. Today, 100 percent of our paper money is in *Federal Reserve Notes.*
Old words for U.S. money include *eagle* ($10 gold coin) and *double eagle* ($20 gold coin). Slang terms include *deuce* ($2), *five spot* and *fin* ($5), *sawbuck* (1850, from the Roman numeral X for 10 on $10 bills), *ned* (same as an *eagle*), *half a C* ($50), *C Note* ($100 bill), and *grand* or *G* ($1000). *The day the eagle screams* or *shits* was payday in the military during World War II, the expression still in use in the 1980s. General slang words for money include:

beans, a *bean,* referring to any coin in 1810. It came to mean specifically a $5 gold piece in 1859, and by 1905 it meant $1.

bread, 1935 slang for money, then widely used by the Beat Generation in the 1950s, this use of *bread* suggested by *dough* (the idea that money is as basic and as necessary as bread); origin undetermined.

buck. Between 1700 and 1750 a quarter of a million to half a million *buckskins* were traded each year on the American frontier. By 1720 many hunters and traders were calling these animal hides *bucks* and reckoning their earnings and rates of barter in terms of bucks. Although *buck* wasn't recorded as meaning a dollar until 1856, a buck or buckskin had long been used as a unit of exchange and a measure of wealth in America.

cash, 1596 in England, when it also still meant money box (via the French *caisse*, the Italian *cassa*, cash box, from the Latin *capsa*, box).

change, smaller denominations exchanged for an equal amount of money, by 1622 in England (via the Anglo-French from Latin *cambium/cambere*, exchange); then by 1691 in England *change* meant any coin of a low denomination. Americans have used *small change* since 1819 to refer to coins of less than a dollar and since 1908 to mean insignificant.

clam, 1930s. No one knows the origin of this sense of the word. A tentative suggestion is that it comes from the 1890s beggar's use of *to clam*, meaning to beg for money or go about trying to grab some money.

dinero, late 19th century, the Spanish word for money.

dough, 1840, almost certainly from considering bread as the basic staff of life. *Do-re-mi*, as a pun on *dough* and the musical *do*, was first used in 1925.

gravy, money obtained without effort, especially political graft, appeared in 1900, while *on the gravy train* and *riding the gravy train* have been in use since the 1930s.

greenbacks, from the color on the backs of the first U.S. Treasury *demand notes*, issued in 1861. Union soldiers, among the first to receive such bills from the government, are said to have given the green-backed bills the name.

jack, 1859 as money, but at first used to mean only a small coin or a small amount of money. *Jack* had been English slang for a farthing since 1700.

legal tender, an English term of 1740 referring to bills or coins that must be accepted in payment of a debt when tendered.

long green, our green paper money, 1891. Since this earlier paper money was somewhat leaflike in color, it has given us slang words for money such as *kale* (1911), *lettuce* (1929), and *cabbage* (1942). However, the earliest of these vegetable terms, *kale*, could very well have come from the 1673 English slang *cole*, meaning money (coal, from the 15th century interjection, *precious coals!*), which, once misunderstood or pronounced as *kale*, could have led to our slang use of *lettuce* and *cabbage*.

loot, late 1940s. The money sense developed from the prime sense, spoils of war, around 1788, from Hindi *lut*, from Sanskrit, "he plunders."

mazuma, 1880, from Yiddish *mazume*, cash.

moola(h), 1930; occasionally shorted to *moo*, 1943, origin unknown.

scratch, 1929, money. The basic expression behind this term, *to scratch for a living*, goes back to 1847.

shekel, a piece of money. Though used in the Bible and by Shakespeare in *Measure for Measure* (1602), this word was first used as a general slang term for money, coins, or bills in 1871. It's from the Hebrew *sheqel*, weight, coin, from a Babylonian unit of weight and a silver coin weighing about two-thirds of an ounce.

shinplasters. Silver was scarce during the Civil War and silver coins so widely hoarded that shopkeepers found it almost impossible to make change. The Union first declared postage stamps legal tender and then, in 1862, issued stamplike paper currency in 3-, 5-, 10-, 25-, and

50-cent denominations. These flimsy, ugly little bills were contemptuously called *shinplasters* because they resembled the little pieces of paper soaked in vinegar, tobacco juice, or some other home remedy that people applied to their shins, feet, etc., to help soothe and heal small cuts.

spondulic(k)s, 1856, also spelled *spondulix* (1890), money, origin unknown.

wampum, first recorded in 1638 as the Algonquian word for Indian shell money (literally "string of white" shells); it has been considered general American slang for money since 1904.

wherewithal, 1809, in England, originally as the necessities or supplies to accomplish a desired end.

In contrast to these words for *money*, the mid 1990s brought Americans a host of new terms relating to the introduction of *electronic currency*, that is to say, the end of cash as we know it and the use of *smart cards* to effect transfer of *digital money* in commercial and personal transactions.

WORKING 9 TO 5

Most Americans have traditionally relied on their jobs for an income. But the exporting of jobs and *cost-cutting* led, in the early 1990s, to widespread *layoffs* (also known as corporate *downsizing*, the verb going back to 1975, and deriving from the auto industry's production of compact and subcompact cars) and to *downshifting* (being forced to accept a less-well-paid job). Another problem was the increasingly popular practice of farming out work to cheaper providers (*outsourcing*, 1982), which resulted in regular employees being *fired, laid off,* or simply *let go*. Although *middle management* was hardest hit by such cuts in the 1990s, few American workers at any level were immune to the prospect of being *dumped*.

Despite more than a century of strong earnings by his company, AT&T CEO Robert Allen helped make downsizing a household word in the mid-90s.

An unemployed construction worker, left, with tools in tow, stands in a Los Angeles unemployment office.

Hard-working Americans worried about their *financial security*. They were, and are, concerned about *buyouts* (where one company *buys out* another, often giving *pink slips* [1915] to many of its employees) and *golden parachutes* (1981, financial protection for company executives in the event of an unfriendly *takeover* by another firm). People want to protect their *IRAs* (1974, Individual Retirement Accounts), *401(K)s,* and other savings plans, and they wonder about whether *Social Security* will still be there when they reach *retirement age* (which used to be 65, but was pushed up to 70 for some occupations and eliminated altogether for others).

The solution for some was to start their own businesses. But not everyone can succeed as an *entrepreneur* (1852, from French) in a *start-up business* or *franchise* (14th century, ultimately from Old French *franc,* free), staying *in the black* and not *going into the red*. Not everyone can *get in on the ground floor* of a business that later *takes off,* or find life-long security in an established company and work there until it's time to accept a *gold watch* (the traditional retirement gift) or a *golden hand-shake* (1960, a *retirement package* so generous that it encourages the employee to retire). For many hard-pressed Americans, *penny-pinching* (1935) became a way of life to keep the *bottom line* (1972) looking good. They subscribed to *thriftzines* (magazines catering to people who are interested in living as economically as possible) such as the *Tightwad Gazette* and *Skinflint News*. They shopped in *thrift shops, consignment shops* (where secondhand clothing is sold on consignment), or *Sally Anne* (the *Salvation Army* thrift stores) and clipped *coupons* (enabling them to buy items at a discount or get *two for the price of one*).

By the end of the 1990s many Americans complained that they couldn't get work or that they didn't want the kind of work they could get. Many refused to *flip burgers* (a reference to minimum-wage work at a fast-food restaurant). They complained that because the *manufacturing economy* (based on factory jobs) was giving way to a *service economy* (where employees provide a service rather than producing goods), skilled factory jobs were disappearing, and that their training and experience were no longer valued. Another frequent complaint, particularly in California and the Southwest, was that illegal aliens were taking jobs away

It's nearing midnight on April 15, the last day for filing federal income tax returns. The IRS handles approximately 500,000 phone calls on the final day of the filing season.

"A man who has a million dollars is as well off as if he were rich."

— John Jacob Astor 4th, in the early 1890s. He went down with the Titanic in 1912, leaving a fortune of over $87 million.

from American citizens. Because they're often willing to work for less than the *minimum wage* and do not demand extensive *fringe benefits* (1948), *migrant workers* (who travel from one type of *seasonal work* to the next) and others lacking a *green card* (1969, a registration card, originally green, granting an alien permission to live and work in the U.S.) are cheaper to hire.

Even Americans with steady employment found themselves struggling to keep up with *inflation* (an increase in prices that causes a decline in purchasing power). In the 1990s most families had two wage-earners (*dual income* or *second paycheck* families) and still had a hard time *making ends meet*. With the exception of *DINKs* (early 1980s, *dual income, no kids*), working couples often found themselves *strapped for cash*.

EASY STREET

At the other end of America's economic spectrum have always been those who are *living on easy street* (1901). The first American to be worth the equivalent of a million dollars was probably plantation owner and banker Robert "King" Carter, whose father arrived in Virginia in 1635 and began acquiring rich farmlands. The son then expanded these holdings and owned over 300,000 acres, 1,000 slaves, and a mansion with 28 fireplaces and a library of 1,500 volumes. But "King" Carter was not called a *millionaire,* because the word didn't enter English (from French *millionaire*) until the 1820s.

Multimillionaire is an American word, first recorded in the 1850s and then widely used in talking and writing about only one man—John Jacob Astor (1763-1848), who had arrived in New York City from Germany at the age of 21 and, through his friendship and connections with Thomas Jefferson and other politicians and government officials who granted him exclusive trading rights, amassed more than $20 million from his 1808 American Fur Company and his 1810 Pacific Fur Company. Astor invested much of his money in real estate and had long been known as *the richest man in America.*

The word *billionaire* appeared in 1861. The world's first billionaire was John D. Rockefeller (1839–1937), who, while still a young man, owned 90 percent of all American oil refineries, all the oil pipelines, and all the oil cars carried by the Pennsylvania Railroad, forming the basis of Standard Oil. Our next two billionaires were probably Andrew Mellon (1855–1937), the banker and aluminum industrialist, and Henry Ford (1863–1947), mass-producer of the Model T car. Thus during the first half of the 19th century some people were amassing millions and during the second half of the century a few were amassing billions. There are now several hundred thousand millionaires in America, but considerably fewer billionaires, most of whom made their initial fortunes from oil. *Trillionaire* is a possible word of the future.

We have called a large sum of money a *windfall* (1464 in England, as trees and branches blown down, hence easy-to-obtain firewood; then used since 1542 to mean any unexpected acquisition or good fortune); a *mint* (1579 in England as a store of money, then used since 1655 to mean a *fortune*); a *pile* (1740, *to make one's pile* dates from 1850); *big money* (1876); and *megabucks* (1946, from Greek *megás,* large, powerful, especially as used in physics to mean a thousand times a given unit, as in *megawatt*). Once multimillionaires and billionaires appeared, fortunes

Real estate tycoon, gambling impresario, deal-maker, and consummate self-promoter Donald Trump.

could be large or small, with the somewhat contradictory term *small fortune* appearing in the 1890s. To *blow* (waste, spend) *a fortune* dates from 1874. *To strike it rich,* originally a gold- and silver-mining term, was first used in 1869.

Other terms we use when talking about wealthy individuals include:

Nabob, 1612, from Hindi *navab* or *nawwab,* the plural of *naib,* governor, viceroy.

Midas touch, 1883, the uncanny ability to make huge amounts of money; named after the fabled Phrygian monarch who had the power to turn everything he touched into gold.

mogul, 1613, from Persian *mughul. The Mogul* was first used in England to refer to the Grand Mogul, Emperor of Delhi and Hindustan, then came to mean any great or autocratic personage by 1678.

well-fixed, an American term first recorded in 1822. *Well-to-do* and *well off,* however, were both originally English terms (of 1825 and 1849 respectively).

rich as (or *richer than*) *Croesus.* Croesus, the 6th century B.C. Lydian king known for his wealth, and often considered to have been the first to issue gold and silver coins, has been an idiomatic expression for a wealthy person since the 1750s (originally in England). The names of other well-known rich people were later substituted, as in *rich as Rockefeller.*

tycoon (via Japanese *taikun,* shogun, military leader). The word was brought back to America from Japan in the 1850s. *Tycoon* was then used from 1861 as an affectionate name for President Lincoln (probably from its meaning "military leader") during the Civil War by some of his cabinet members, secretaries, and close political friends. Beginning in the 1870s it was applied to such powerful and wealthy men as John D. Rockefeller and the financiers Jay Gould and Cornelius Vanderbilt. Such *magnates* (a 1430 English word from Latin *magnus,* great) were also called *captains of industry* by the 1880s and sometimes *robber barons* by 1900.

high roller, 1881, one who spends recklessly or can afford to; literally, one who rolls the dice for high stakes; *to live high,* 1883, meaning to live luxuriously (the term *high living* wasn't recorded until 1934); *high stepper,* 1890s; *high flier,* 1904.

money bag(s), 1896, a wealthy person. The term wasn't usually plural until the 1920s, when the post-World War I boom and soaring stock prices seemed to give the rich more than just one bag of money.

living the life of Riley. This expression was first popular around 1910 but probably comes from Pat Rooney's 1883 comic song, "Is That Mr. Reilly?", which tells what Mr. Reilly would do if he suddenly became rich.

sitting pretty, since 1910, being in comfortable circumstances .

filthy rich, first recorded in 1940, although to be *filthy with* something has meant having plenty of *filthy lucre* since 1929.

No matter how *broke* (1820s, with *clean broke, dead broke,* and *flat broke* all appearing in the early 1840s) or *down and out* (1901) the rest of us might be, there is one overriding consolation: Americans are known for their *get-rich-quick schemes.*

A STROLL DOWN WALL STREET

Some of the wealthiest Americans have made their fortunes by *playing the market*—that is, investing in the *stock market*. The word *stock* had been used to refer to a business's capital in England during the 1620–1700 period to which so many of our basic financial terms can be traced. *Market* originally meant a gathering of people to transact business and the place where they met (via Old French from the Vulgar Latin *mercatus,* trade, marketplace, from *merc-/merx,* merchandise). By the mid 17th century it had acquired its special financial use. *The market* originally referred not to the entire securities market but, from the 1830s, to specific types of stocks, bonds, or commodities and their dealers. At that time, people spoke only of the grain market, the cotton market, or the market in railroad shares. A stock market expert was called a *market man* in 1895.

Wall Street has been used to refer to New York's financial district and America's financial establishment and overall securities market since 1836. Merchants, *brokers* (the term *Wall Street broker* was first used in 1836), and bankers had met on the streets and in the coffeehouses in the triangle formed by Wall, Broad, and New Streets in lower Manhattan for generations and, by the 1830s, many leading commercial houses and banks were located there. Wall Street itself goes back to the days of New York's original Dutch settlers. In 1653, these settlers built a wall along the northern boundary of their settlement, known as New Amsterdam, because they feared attacks from the Native Americans and the English. The wall rotted and fell down in a few years, and its outline became a short, narrow dirt road called *Wall Street*.

During the 50-year period from around 1830 to 1880, speculators and unscrupulous merchants and brokers developed ways to *beat the market*. The best way was to have advance information on value, prices, and price fluctuations by being or knowing an *insider* (1830, the term *inside*

The trading floor of the New York Stock Exchange on Wall Street in Lower Manhattan. The Exchange was founded in 1792. The price of membership increased from $17,000 in the war years after the Depression to $1,150,000 just prior to the 1987 market crash.

information dating from 1888 and *inside dope* from 1919). Other financiers and businessmen might try to *corner the market* (1849, to acquire a monopoly on a stock so as to be able to raise the price). Financier and railroad tycoon Jay Gould and speculator James Fisk were masters at this and made these stock market terms well known to many when, on September 24, 1869, they tried to corner the market on gold, thus triggering the country's first stock market *panic.* Another term added to the language by unscrupulous financiers and businessmen during this same period was to *water* stock (1863) by issuing more shares initially than the total was worth, or to dilute the value of existing shares by creating new ones. In the same period America's *bears* and *bulls*—those who expect the market to go down and those who expect it to go up—emerged. Contrary to popular belief, the terms have nothing to do with the fact that a bear attacks by sweeping its paws downward and a bull by tossing its head or horns upward. *Bear* in the stock market sense emerged in the early 18th century, probably coming from the phrase *sell the bearskin*, which originated in the proverbial expression "to sell the bear's skin before one has caught the bear." *Bull*, which emerged in the stock market sense somewhat later, was probably suggested by *bear*. They were speculating by buying *long* (in expectation that the stock price would go up) or *short* (a bear who sold stock before he owned it was called a *short*, 1849; by 1852 we would say he *sold short*) or by combining both strategies to *straddle* the market, especially in commodity *futures* bought on *margin* (these last three terms all from 1870). Dishonest brokers might open a *bucket shop* (1880 in the financial use, from the original 1875 sense of the word, referring to a place where one could buy liquor cheaply by the pitcher or bucket), claiming it was a legitimate broker's office or stock exchange affiliate and encouraging gullible investors to become small-time speculators and stock market gamblers by buying and selling small quantities of stock quickly with each market

"Junk-peddler" Michael Milken on his way into court in 1990. Milken would eventually pay $600 million in damages to settle felony fraud charges against him, and he has since dedicated himself to a life of philanthropy.

fluctuation. Big-time market *scalpers* (1886; *scalper* meant one who took scalps from an enemy's head by 1760 and one who sold or resold theater tickets at exorbitant prices by 1869) were also gambling on market fluctuations.

The stock market became much more reliable after the telegraph stock *ticker* (a device for recording stock market quotations on a paper tape—hence *ticker tape* [1902], *down tick*, and *up tick*) and the telephone became common, replacing the mails and messengers so that everyone had access to the same information at the same time. After World War II and a mild recession in the 1950s, the 60s and early 70s saw the public invest in the *glamor stocks*, especially those of new electronics and aerospace firms. The same period saw the growth of *mutual funds* (a 1798 term for an insurance company whose policy holders were also its shareholders), which pool the resources of individual investors to invest jointly in a variety of securities. Funds that were bought into quickly and with excitement were called *go-go funds* (from the early 60s *go-go dancers*, scantily clad young women stage performers in a discothèque); those who handled them were *go-go managers, go-go brokers*, or *go-go boys*. As inflation ran rampant, many investors first put their money into *CDs* (bank *C*ertificates of *D*eposit) and then into a new form of mutual fund, the *money market fund* (*money market*, 1950).

By the 1990s stock market information had become largely computerized, and individual *shareholders* could get up-to-the-minute price information on their home computers. But investors continued to rely on a multitude of market myths—for example, the *Nifty Fifty*, a term used during the *bull market* of the 1980s to describe a loosely defined group of stocks that always seemed to go up in value; or the *Dogs of the Dow*, the five highest-yielding but out-of-favor stocks of the 30 *Dow Jones Industrials* (named after Charles Henry Dow and Edward D. Jones, founders of the publishing firm of *Dow Jones and Co.*, pioneers in the compilation and dissemination of current and reliable stock market information). But the widely publicized downfalls of *junk bond king* Michael Milken (a *junk bond* [1976] being any bond that is rated below investment grade, making it risky to buy), various *inside traders* (1966, who buy and sell stocks based on information that has not yet been made public), and other Americans who have made fortunes by mastering the labyrinthine ins and outs of the securities business made it clear that no matter how sophisticated Wall Street's *white-collar criminals* become, sooner or later some of them may get caught.

BOOM TO BUST

The "Wall Street Lays an Egg"

— Variety *headline announcing stock market crash, October, 1929*

The American economy seems to operate in cycles. In the country's early days, most people were farmers or worked in small local businesses, often *bartering* (trading, exchanging) food, clothing, and services. Money was scarce and economic *depressions* or *hard times* merely meant less cash, not widespread suffering or unemployment. Although the words *panic* and *depression* had first been used in America during the Panic of 1819, it was only a financial panic, not a countrywide depression. There were also panics in 1837 and in 1857, when *inflation* and *bread riots* entered the language. Another panic happened in 1869 when Jay Gould and Jim Fisk tried to corner the gold market, resulting in the first *Black Friday*. (Other subsequent financial panics first became serious on Fridays, and so *Black + Friday*—indicative of a day of evil or disaster—came to mean any sharp drop, or *free-fall*, in the financial markets.) In

1873 *stock market crash* was used for the first time, followed in 1893 by yet another one and by the worst depression the country had ever seen (until 1929). There was another panic in 1901 when Edward Harriman tried to gain control of James Hill's Great Northern Railroad; and again in 1907, when the *rich man's panic* saw many banks and businesses fail. But the *Panic of 1929* was different: Now the country was larger and more industrialized, most people depended on *wages,* and many average people had invested or *speculated* in the stock market during what was becoming known as the *Golden Twenties.* The *boom* (an economic term in the 1870s) that was well under way in 1928 persuaded many experts that there might never be another *bust* (which had meant a *bankruptcy* in the 1840s and was first applied to an economic collapse in the Panic of 1893).

Then, on *Black Wednesday* (October 23, 1929), stocks began to fall. The wave of selling continued the next day and *the bottom dropped out* of the market on *Black Thursday,* the day of the *stock market crash.* The ensuing panic even caused some prominent businessmen and stockholders to commit suicide, and it led to the deepest economic depression in U.S. history. Thirteen million people (one-fourth of the labor force) were out of work, production was down 44 percent, foreign trade was at a standstill, and bank closings, bankruptcies, factory shutdowns, and farm and home mortgage *foreclosures* were at an all-time high. *The Great Depression* lasted until the outbreak of World War II in 1939, and it provided us with such terms as *Apple Annies* (who sold apples on street corners to feed their families), *rent parties* (with each guest bringing $2 to help pay the rent), *breadlines* (a word first used in 1900 when charities handed out loaves of bread and cups of coffee to the poor), and *soup kitchens* (which had originally been an 1855 army term).

It would be left to President Franklin Delano Roosevelt's New Deal (see AMERICA'S POLITICAL LANGUAGE) and the subsequent World War II war effort to drag the U.S. economy out of its depths of Depression. But some words we use today echo to the troubled times of the 1930s: the *FDIC* (Federal Deposit Insurance Corporation, 1933), which still insures deposits in member banks to prevent bank failures); the *TVA* (Tennessee Valley Authority, 1933, created to build 30 dams along the Tennessee River and its tributaries to supply hydroelectric power to the region); and *relief, case worker* (a social worker-investigator), *farm subsidy,* and *Social Security* (Old Age and Survivors' Insurance instituted by the Social Security Act of 1935).

The Federal Reserve is the "government's bank" and Alan Greenspan has been the chairman of its Board of Governors since 1987. With its influence on the country's monetary policy and economic health, Greenspan's may be the most powerful unelected office in America.

WELFARE REFORM

President Bill Clinton and his policy *wonks* (1954, origin unknown, possibly a backward spelling of *know*) ended six decades of guaranteed help to the nation's poor in August 1996, when he signed a sweeping welfare reform law. Hailed (and reviled by some) as the biggest shift in social policy since the Depression, the new law abolished *Aid to Families with Dependent Children,* the cornerstone of the government's welfare system, which provided monthly cash benefits to 12.8 million people, including more than 8 million children. It was replaced by a system of *block grants* to the states, giving them the authority to design their own welfare programs to solve the long-term problem of dependence on government *handouts* (1882). Requiring all welfare recipients to find work within two years of receiving their first *welfare check* and placing a five-year *lifetime limit* on cash benefits, the new law was designed to promote jobs and self-sufficiency. But many who were concerned about the new law's effect on children decried it as an election year ploy.

WHAT GOES UP . . .

Americans enjoyed a long period of relative *prosperity* following World War II, only to be confronted by *stagflation* (1965, a period during which the economy is stagnant while inflation continues) in the early 1970s, *galloping* or *double-digit inflation* in the 1970s and early 80s, and periodic *recession* (1929, in the sense of a temporary falling-off of business activity and public confidence in the strength of the economy). The *go-go 80s*, a very prosperous time for those Americans who had benefited from *Reaganomics* (also known as *supply side* or *trickle-down* economics), ended in the *Crash of '87,* the largest single-day drop in the *Dow Jones Industrial Averages* since *Black Thursday* in 1929.

The *go-go 80s* gave us lots of new vocabulary, some of it these words, whose very use characterizes the era:

antitakeover measures, moves by a company, such as staggered terms for its directors and high-affirmative-vote requirements among stockholders, intended to prevent hostile takeovers.

arbitrageur, 1870, shortened to *arb,* 1979, a person who engages in *arbitrage,* 1875, the simultaneous buying and selling of identical assets (e.g., stock) so as to make a profit on the price differential between the two. In the early '80s the *arbs* were the "fair-haired boys" on Wall Street, and people talked about the enormous profits they were amassing in this, the decade of the *corporate raider* or "takeover artist."

greenmail, 1983, a way to avoid a hostile takeover, by which the targeted company buys the raiding company's stock at a price higher than what other stockholders would pay.

poison pill, 1983, a tactic, such as increasing corporate debt, used to make a firm less vulnerable and attractive to a hostile takeover.

raider, either an individual or a company that seeks to gain controlling interest in a target company, fought off not only by greenmail but by *shark repellent* (any of several antitakeover measures, e.g., new stock issues or a major corporate acquisition running up the target company's debt), aided by *white squires* or *white knights.* (A *white squire* is an investor sympathetic with a target company's management and who held a large block of its stock; a *white knight* [1951] an individual or another company that bought a targeted firm out from under a raider attempting a hostile takeover).

takeover, cited to around 1917, the acquisition of controlling interest in a company, either *hostile* or *friendly.* These were the big words in finance during the 80s.

And two verbs characterized the 1970s and the 1990s, respectively: President Jimmy Carter's frequent use of *stimulate* (as in "a program that will *stimulate* the economy") and President Bill Clinton's use of *grow* (as in "*growing* the economy"). This transitive use of *grow* puzzled average Americans who were unfamiliar with its long use on Wall Street, a use that parallels *shop,* as in "The company is being *shopped*" (i.e., its owners are *shopping* it, seeking potential buyers).

"Whip Inflation Now" buttons, brainchild of the Ford Administration in 1974 when inflation hit 11%, its highest level since 1947. Tighter control of the money supply and the collapse of OPEC, the Arab oil cartel—not buttons— eventually helped whip inflation in 1982 and the years since.

ENGLISH ENGLISH

*P*ut briefly, the key differences between the two major "dialects" of English are in vocabulary, pronunciation, and spelling. The examples in this chapter—selected from hundreds—reflect the fact that the American and British cultures have developed largely independently in terms of domestic and leisure pursuits, in certain technologies, and in government. See AMERICAN SPOKEN BY AMERICANS for the explanation of the historical development of the American "dialect," and the social factors causing the two to diverge.

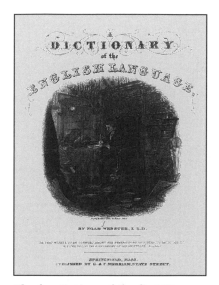

The frontispiece of the first "American" dictionary.

As a different people living in a different country and having different experiences, we Americans were bound to develop our own brand of English. What the English called *barbarisms* we proudly called *Americanisms.* John Witherspoon, a signer of the Declaration of Independence, coined this word in 1781, and defined it as any word or usage peculiar to English as used in America. He gave the first good list of American words, pronunciations, usages, and blunders. He noted our use of *mad* for "angry"; our cant use of *to take in* and *to bamboozle* for "to swindle"; our heavy use of such contractions as *ain't, can't, don't,* and *couldn't;* common mistakes as "lay" for "lie" and "knowed" for "knew"; and such pronunciations as "winder" for "window."

Throughout our history we have added an array of Native American and Spanish words, have borrowed words and intonations from immigrant groups, and have continued to coin new words and meanings, develop our own dialects and pronunciations, and manifest some characteristic grammatical and syntactical usages and misusages. Offsetting all these factors is, however, the modern influence of internationalism: Especially since World War II, best-selling books, movies, TV shows, popular songs, and tourism have spread American English to England and British English to the U.S. Politics, pop culture (notably rock music, whose styles and stars are known on both sides of the Atlantic), and telecommunications continue to bring the two "languages" closer together again. But marked differences do indeed remain.

> "American English is the greatest influence of English everywhere."
>
> — *Robert W. Burchfield, 1986, on completing* A Supplement to the Oxford English Dictionary

BRITISH THERE, AMERICAN HERE

VOCABULARY DIFFERENCES

The British say *fizzy drink,* we say *soda*; the British say *chucker-out,* we say (bar) *bouncer.* Should we "call the whole thing off"? Not at all, for it is fun to point out the differences between the two Englishes, at the same time noting that some of the word-markers separating the two no longer do: the British now also use *radio, run* (in a stocking), and *Santa Claus* as well as their own *wireless, ladder,* and *Father Christmas.* The lists that follow show some of the more interesting and typical remaining differences between British and American, with the British terms given first.

> *"England and America are two countries divided by a common language."*
>
> *— George Bernard Shaw*

Food, Drink, and the Kitchen

aubergine—eggplant
bangers—sausages
candy floss—cotton candy
chips—French fries
cooker—stove, range
corn—grain of any type
courgette—zucchini
crisp—potato chip
crockery—dishes
fizzy drink—soda
ice lolly—Popsicle
joint—cut (of meat)
lemon squash—lemonade
minced beef, mince—ground beef, hamburger
prawn—shrimp
swede—rutabaga
sweet, a—candy, a piece of
sweet, pudding, afters—dessert
tin—can
treacle—molasses
tunny—tuna
undercut—tenderloin or filet
vegetable marrow—squash

Domestic Terms

cellotape—Scotch tape
clothes-peg—clothespin
cot—crib (for a baby)
drains—plumbing (in a house)
drawing pin—thumbtack
dustbin—garbage can
dustman—garbage man
garden—yard
green fingers—green thumb
earth—(electrical) ground, grounding wire
estate agent—real estate agent
mains—power supply
moving house—moving (i.e., changing residence)
plaster—Band Aid
power point, points—outlet (electrical)
pram—baby carriage
pushchair—stroller
reel—spool (of thread)
removal van—moving van
skirting board—baseboard
standard lamp—floor lamp

Clothing, Fashion

bespoke—custom-made, made-to-order
bowler—derby (hat)
fringe—bangs (hairstyle)
grip—hairpin
jumper—sweater
knickers—underpants (women's)
nappy—diaper

off the peg—off the rack, ready-made
smalls—underclothes
trousers—pants, (in Britain, *pants* refers to underpants)
trouser suit—pantsuit
turn-up (of trousers)—cuff (of pants)
vest—undershirt
waistcoat—vest

Consumer Goods and Shopping
advert—ad(vertisement)
carrier bag—shopping bag
cash desk—checkout counter
chemist—druggist, drugstore
hire purchase—installment plan
ironmonger's—hardware store
jumble sale—rummage sale
trolley—shopping cart

Money and Banking
building society—savings & loan association
cashpoint card—ATM card
current account—checking account
deposit account—savings account
quid (pound)—buck (dollar)

Everyday and Miscellaneous Terms
anticlockwise—counterclockwise
bank holiday—national holiday
chap—guy
catapult—slingshot
catmint—catnip
chat show—talk show
chucker-out—bouncer (bar)
dialling tone—dial tone
ex-directory—unlisted (telephone number)
first floor—second floor
flick knife—switchblade
gangway—aisle (theater)
ground floor—first floor
hoarding—billboard
Joe Bloggs—Joe Blow
lift—elevator
loo—john (toilet)
lucky dip—grab bag
nought—zero
paraffin—kerosene
Plough, the—Big Dipper, the
porter, caretaker—janitor, custodian
ring (up)—call (on the phone)
rubber—eraser (for a pencil)
scribbling block—scratch pad
Sod's Law—Murphy's Law
spanner—wrench
Summer Time—Daylight Savings Time
surgery—doctor's/dentist's/vet's office
takeaway—take-out (food)
torch—flashlight

trunk call —long-distance call
vulgar fraction—common fraction
WC—toilet, bathroom
white wax—paraffin
zed—(the letter) Z

Sports, Games, and Entertainment
athletics—track and field
cannon—carom (billiards)
court card—face card (playing cards)
draughts—checkers
football—soccer
fruit machine—slot machine
fun fair—carnival
noughts-and-crosses—tick-tack-toe
patience—solitaire
peep-bo—peek-a-boo
press-up—push-up
rain off—rain out
ready, steady, go—ready, set, go
scenic railway—roller coaster
shovelboard—shuffleboard
trainers, plimsolls—sneakers

Cars and Road Transportation
accumulator—battery
bonnet—hood
boot—trunk
bottom gear, first speed—low (or first) gear
caravan—trailer, RV
dip switch—dimmer switch
diversion—detour
driving licence—driver's license
drop top—convertible top
dual carriageway—divided highway
dynamo—generator
estate car—station wagon
fascia—dashboard
flyover—overpass
give way—yield
lay-by—rest stop
level crossing—grade crossing
lollipop man, woman—crossing guard
lorry—truck
metalling—paving (of a road)
motorway—expressway, thruway, interstate
number plate—license plate
orbital—bypass, beltway
petrol—gasoline, gas
pink—ping (engine noise)
propeller shaft—drive shaft
ramp—speed bump
rank—taxi stand
reservation—median strip
ring road—beltway
roof lamp—dome light
roundabout—traffic circle

silencer—muffler
sleeping policeman—speed bump
slip road—on- or off-ramp
sparking plug—sparkplug
sump—oilpan
tailboard—tailgate
track—tread (of a tire)
turning (of a street)—corner
windscreen—windshield
wing—fender
wing mirror—side mirror

Rail Transportation
carriage, waggon—railroad car (passenger)
goods train/waggon—freight train/car
luggage van—baggage car
restaurant car—dining car
return ticket—round-trip ticket
single—one-way ticket
sleeper—cross tie
tie-beam—crossbeam
underground—subway (urban rail system: in Britain, a subway is an underground pedestrian walkway)

Education
faculty—school (that is, a group of departments at a university, not just teaching staff)
lecturer—assistant professor (roughly)
maths—math
public school—private school
read—major in
reader—associate professor (roughly)
school-leaver—dropout
staff—faculty (university)
state school—public school

Workplace
chargehand—foreman
holiday—vacation
made redundant—laid off
managing director—president, CEO
rise—raise (in pay)
situation—job

Law & Government
barrister; solicitor—lawyer; attorney (only a barrister has been "called to the bar" and may plead a case in court, while a solicitor handles other legal matters)
constable—police officer
Hansard—Congressional Record
identification parade—police lineup
Inland Revenue—Internal Revenue Service
rates—taxes
truncheon—nightstick
witness box—witness stand

ONE WORD: TWO MEANINGS

Aside from vocabulary or word choice, British and American semantically diverge, as shown by the following table listing single words having two totally different meanings.

BRITISH MEANING	WORD	AMERICAN MEANING
a great success	bomb	a total failure; a flop
a small desk	davenport	a sofa
the owner of a pub	landlord	the owner of any space for rent
to call for someone at their room or residence	knock up	to get a woman pregnant
woman's genitals (taboo)	fanny	buttocks (slang)

BRITISH OR AMERICAN (OR BOTH)?

Still other terms are now in use on both sides of the Atlantic, when in the past they might have been restricted chiefly or solely to one side or the other. But all of the "Briticisms" in the left column can and do occur in American speech and writing.

TYPICALLY BRITISH	TYPICALLY AMERICAN
anorak	parka
car park	parking lot, parking garage
cock	rooster
elastic (band)	rubber band
flat	apartment
holdall	tote bag
kipper	smoked herring
knave (cards)	jack
interval	recess, break, intermission
larder	pantry
lavatory	toilet
line	track (railroad)
lodger	roomer
overtake	pass (another vehicle)
post (a letter)	mail
pub, public house	bar, saloon, tavern
queue	line (of people)
railway	railroad
saltcellar	saltshaker
shop	store
whilst	while

DIFFERENCES IN PRONUNCIATION

The major differences in American and English pronunciation are in intonation or melody, vowel quality, and voice timbre. Typically we speak with less variety of tone than the English do. This may be due in part to the teaching of generations of American students to repeat and articulate every syllable in a word as given in Noah Webster's spelling book. Our voice timbre seems harsh or tinny to the English, theirs gurgling or throaty to us. English conclusion: Americans speak shrilly, monotonously, and like someone reciting. American conclusion: the English speak too low, theatrically, and swallow their syllables. Some specific differences include: (1) In many common words we use a flatter, shorter *a*. Thus most Americans pronounce the *a* in such words as *ask, brass, can't, dance, fast, grass, half, last,* and *path* short and flat, as in *gas*. English pronounce it more as the broad *a* in *father*. (2) We Americans are more scrupulous about clearly articulating certain unaccented syllables, especially *-ary, -ery,* and *-ory*. Thus the English say *melanc'ly, monast'ry, necess'ry, preparat'ry, secret'ry,* etc., while we fully articulate the final syllables. (3) We frequently move the accent or stress to the first syllable of a word, as in *DEfect* (the noun), *DEfense* (especially in sports), *EXcess, LAB'ratory, REcess,* and *REsearch* while the English say *deFECT, deFENCE* (note spelling), *exCESS, laBORat'ry, reCESS,* and *reSEARCH*.

On the other hand, there are certain words in which we accent a later syllable than do the English: we say *gaRAGE* and *adverTISEment*; they say *GARage* and *adVERTisement*.

DIFFERENCES IN SPELLING

Not until 135 years after the Pilgrims landed did English spelling have a guide in Dr. Johnson's *Dictionary of the English Language* (1755). This monumental work froze much of English spelling and, among other things, decreed that such words as *critick, logick, musick,* and *publick* end in a final *k* and such words as *colour, honour,* etc., end in *-our*.

England, including its colonies, began to follow Johnson's spelling; but, in 1758, three years after Johnson's dictionary was published, Noah

Webster was born, in Hartford, Connecticut, and 21 years after Johnson's dictionary the American Revolution began—two events that were to help separate English English and American English. After graduating from Yale, Webster became a teacher. He then compiled his three-part *Grammatical Institute of the English Language*, including an elementary spelling book (in 1783), a grammar (in 1784), and a reader (in 1785). Part I became fantastically successful as *The American Spelling Book*. Generations of Americans learned to spell and pronounce from it. It was known to millions as simply the "Blue-Backed Speller."

The success of his spelling book gave Webster the financial freedom to devote himself to his 1806 *Compendious Dictionary of the English Language*, the forerunner of his monumental 70,000-entry 1828 *American Dictionary of the English Language*, the predecessor of all modern American dictionaries.

Noah Webster grew to manhood during the period of increasing American patriotism preceding the Revolutionary War. He and other Americans of his generation wanted to create a new civilization, and were determined that the English language in America be a unique "national language" that would weld the 13 states into a unified nation. In 1789, in his *Dissertation on the English Language*, Webster challenged Samuel Johnson's English rules and practices. His friend Benjamin Franklin had convinced him that spelling reform was necessary, though Webster's reforms didn't go as far as Franklin's, which included six new characters, the dropping of all silent letters (*giv, wil, rong*), and a confusing array of respellings such as *obzerv, reezon* (reason), and *tong* (tongue). The Webster's dictionaries were the first to contain such American words or meanings as *Americanism, applicant, appreciate* (to increase, 1778), *barbecue, Congressional* (1775), *coop* (for chickens), *corn, crib* (for corn), *druggist, land office* (1781), and *lot* (piece of land). Webster also dropped the *k* that Johnson had added to such words as *critic, logic, music*, etc., and gave us many other American spellings still used today.

ENVIRONMENTAL STUDIES

Though America's awareness of the importance of environmental issues is not at all new, the mid 1970s saw a marked increase in environmentally related vocabulary, especially in general, as opposed to purely scientific or technical sources. This influx of new words was the result of what might be called a greening of America, i.e., the development of a heightened awareness of the finite nature of Earth's resources and a realization of the need to protect those resources—this greening associated with the title of the 1970 book The Greening of America *and itself the impetus for yet another more generalized sense, "the development of a less naïve attitude toward sociopolitical issues."*

Henry David Thoreau, America's first environmentalist.

As people talked pro and con about environmental issues they created new senses of the adjective *green* (dating to before the 12th century) and the noun *green* (13th century)—"concerned with and advocating protection of Earth's environment," and "an environmentalist or a member of an environmentalist political party," respectively. In 1971, *Greenpeace*, the international environmentalist pressure group, was founded in Canada and the U.S.

Fear of environmental harm, although alluded to in the 19th century (as in Charles Darwin's early work before moving on to evolutionary biology), did not become a major concern in the sense of "one's surroundings," then specifically "natural surroundings," until the second half of the 20th century. The term *environment* from the English verb *environ* ("to surround") goes back only to 1827, with Thomas Carlyle writing in 1874 that "the organism is continually adapted to its *environment*." Of course, whatever the terms used, even prehistoric humans graduated from adapting to the environment to outright manipulation and wholesale change.

Many environmental terms have been with us for some time:

climate, in the language since the 1300s, originally and still used to define both a geographic region with specific meteorological conditions as well as the average conditions that prevail in that region. Recently it has been used to describe the characteristics, as heat and humidity, in an indoor setting, such as in a *climate-controlled* building (and more generally, the prevailing character or atmosphere of a situation, for example, *a climate of fear*).

pollution, 1300s, the adverse effect on the environment of an unnatural, harmful substance. Pollution was later classified by subgroup of either area affected (*air pollution, water pollution*) or cause (*thermal pollution, noise pollution, light pollution*).

habitat, 1796, the place in which a plant or animal normally lives.

ecology, 1873, the science of organisms and their environment. Subsequently this came to be applied to people and their relationship with the environment and especially the preservation of the quality of its elements, such as air and water. In this newer meaning, *ecology* is synonymous with *environmentalism* as a philosophy of conservation and concern about the adverse effects human beings have on the environment. It was a vogue word of political activism from the 1960s and into the 70s.

Greenpeace's *Rainbow Warrior*. Its presence has called attention to incidents ranging from illegal whaling in the Atlantic to atomic testing in the Pacific.

"The most common trait of all primitive peoples is a reverence for the life-giving earth, and the Native Americans shared this elemental ethic: The land was alive to his loving touch, and he, its son, was brother to all creatures."

— *Stewart L. Udall, U.S. Secretary of the Interior,* The Quiet Crisis, *1963*

biosphere, 1899, the zone which contains all life. This received broad use and notoriety in 1993 as the name of an environmental project, *Biosphere II* (*Biosphere I* being the Earth, to project organizers), in which a group of people confined themselves in a 3.15-acre sealed habitat as an experiment.

rain forest, 1903, a dense, usually tropical forest in which rainfall exceeds 100 inches per year. Some of these forests have flourished for more than 40 million years. The existence in them of commercially valuable trees, such as mahogany and teak, has led to the *deforestation* (the term cited as early as 1884) of many rain forests, leading in turn to soil erosion, climatic changes, and threats to various plant and animal species.

biome, 1916, a major ecological community of living organisms, usually defined by the plant type with which it is associated, as a rain forest or grassland.

environmentalist, 1916, an advocate of environmentalism.

environmentalism, around 1922, advocacy for the environment and protection of it from pollution and other harmful effects.

biomass, 1934, the total mass of living matter in a unit area or volume in an ecosystem at a given time. It is usually expressed in terms of dry weight per unit area.

ecosystem, 1935, a particular community of plants and animals considered together with the surrounding physical environment with which it is in delicate balance.

ecosphere, 1953, an area inhabited by living organisms.

Human exploitation of the environment has led to occasional, and well-publicized, disasters (the 1970s evacuation at *Love Canal* near Buffalo, New York, owing to chemical contamination of the soil from a nearby plant; a similar episode at *Times Beach*, near St. Louis, Missouri, in the 1980s; and the less-than-occasional oil spill from supertankers, such as the notorious *Exxon Valdez* spill into Alaska's Prince William Sound in 1989), but although *ecology* as a distinct science emerged in the 1890s, it was a fringe study until the activist 1960s. The year 1970 saw the establishment of the *Environmental Protection Agency (EPA)*, an independent federal body to monitor the environment and how we were affecting it. EPA programs such as *Superfund* offered billions in federal dollars for environmental cleanups, while 1973's Endangered Species Act gave us the federal *Endangered Species List* to identify nearly extinct, rare, or threatened wildlife for protection from destruction by industrial or construction activity. Massive civil projects met delays awaiting *environmental impact statements* to be completed, filed, reviewed, and debated. In one case, the Tellico Dam on the Little Tennessee River was delayed through the 1970s over concern about destroying what was believed to be the only natural habitat of the *snail darter fish*. After completion of the dam in 1980, it was found that the species thrived in other Tennessee streams.

Environmental response became a great national concern through the 1980s following disasters that riveted our attention. The names for these still call up powerful images: *Bhopal*, in central India, where 2,000 people died and 200,000 were injured from a poisonous gas leak at a chemical plant in 1984; *Chernobyl*, a nuclear power plant near Kiev in Ukraine, where a *near-meltdown* and massive radioactive leak in 1986 led to many deaths and untold further consequences (far worse than the 1979 radioactive leak from the nuclear plant at *Three Mile Island*, near Harrisburg, Pennsylvania). Concern over nuclear accidents revived anxieties about the theorized *China Syndrome* (dramatized in a popular 1979 movie by that title), which suggests that a nuclear meltdown could eat through the Earth from this side to China. Such noted disasters, fictional and real, served as rallying cries, and indeed far tighter federal regulation followed, from the EPA, the industrial watchdog *OSHA* (pronounced "OH-shuh"; the acronym for *Occupational Safety and Health Administration*, which began operations in 1971), as well as the Fish & Wildlife Service, the National Park Service, and numerous other federal, state, and local bodies. The branch of law called *environmental law* also emerged.

As the first conservationist President, Theodore Roosevelt set aside 125 million acres in the West as national parks.

Public awareness of the damage being done to the environment by human activity might very justifiably be dated from the 1962 publication of Rachel Carson's *Silent Spring*, which detailed the destruction that common pesticides, such as *DDT* (subsequently banned in 1972), wreaked upon the environment. Since its ban, some bird species, including the bald eagle, peregrine falcon, osprey, and brown pelican, have made impressive recoveries. The book was a call-to-arms

Thoreau's *Walden* recounts the author's experiences from 1845–47 as he lived in a hut on Walden Pond near Concord, Massachusetts. Attempts in the mid-1980s by developers to build on the land near Walden Pond were halted by the protests of environmentalists, including rock star Don Henley.

for a whole generation of budding environmentalists, and its spirit was embodied in the pop tune of the 60s in which Joni Mitchell lamented: "They paved paradise and put up a parking lot." Another cause célèbre was *acid rain* (cited as early as 1858)—blamed for harming or killing fish in lakes and streams, stunting forest growth, and eating away at the facades of cathedrals, statues, and monuments, some centuries old.

The word *ecophysiology* is an American term of 1962 that focused our attention on an organism's physiology relative to its environment. The year 1969 introduced us to the possibility of *ecocatastrophe*, referring to a major destruction of the natural balance of things, such as that resulting from an oil spill. As a result of facing some of the realities of the problem, we began in 1970 to observe *Earth Day* to promote respect for our natural heritage; it continued as an annual event into the 1990s. Conservation associations such as Greenpeace and the Sierra Club encouraged us to become more *environmentally friendly*, or *ecofriendly*. The concept of *biodiversity* came in 1986, emphasizing the importance of preserving large numbers of different plants and animals. An army of activists, dubbed by some as *ecowarriors* and *tree-huggers*, practiced disruption of commercial activities deemed harmful to the environment; this

The contaminated dump in Love Canal, near Niagara Falls, New York.

disruption was criticized as *ecoterrorism*, *ecotage* (a blend of *eco + sabotage*), and *monkeywrenching* in the 1980s.

Recent decades have also witnessed our fighting personnel returning from war claiming to suffer the effects of *Agent Orange* (1970) and *Gulf War Syndrome* of the 1990s. The *oil crisis* of the 1970s forced us to explore *alternative energy* that derived from sources other than nuclear power or the burning of *fossil fuels* (1935) such as coal, oil, and natural gas. Examples included *geothermal energy, hydroelectricity, solar energy, tidal power, wave power,* and *wind power.* We spend our time avoiding *biohazards,* 1967, agents or condition that threaten life on earth and *hot spots,* where there were high concentrations of toxic chemicals or *hazardous materials,* now often abbreviated to *HAZMAT* (and no one wanted to see hazardous waste disposed nearby, hence the *NIMBY syndrome* of the early 1980s, the acronym for "*not in my backyard*"). Our automobiles became equipped with *catalytic converters (1964) to reduce toxic emissions. Releases of chlorofluorocarbons,* or *CFCs* (1949), chemical compounds of chlorine, fluorine, and carbon once used extensively as aerosol propellants and in refrigerants, were said to damage the *ozone layer* (1929). This layer of the upper atmosphere, between about 10 and 20 miles above Earth's surface, contains an abundance of ozone that blocks damaging ultraviolet radiation from reaching Earth. Concern persisted in the 1990s over the discovery of an *ozone hole* (1986) in the atmosphere over Antarctica, with chlorofluorocarbons implicated in the damage.

People also were talking about: *global warming,* 1980s, a gradual, long-term increase in the average temperature of Earth's atmosphere, attributed by many including some scientific studies, to the *greenhouse effect* (1937). The *greenhouse effect* is the warming of Earth as a result of

Workers bagging sea otters killed by the Exxon *Valdez* spill in Prince William Sound. The oil spill coated 1,100 miles of shoreline, the equivalent of Miami to Washington, D.C.

Nuclear family? Mother and child at play near the cooling towers of the
Three Mile Island nuclear plant located near Harrisburg, Pennsylvania.

the sun's radiational heat being trapped near the surface by carbon
dioxide, ozone, and certain other gases in Earth's atmosphere, similar to
the effect of the glass panels in a greenhouse. Carbon dioxide and other
gases including methane, nitrogen oxides, and ozone, are often referred
to collectively as *greenhouse gases*. The combination of widespread deforestation, burning of fossil fuels, and exhaust from motor vehicles has
increased carbon dioxide levels in the atmosphere to the extent that
many scientists believe the greenhouse effect may lead to melting of the
polar ice caps and a dramatic rise in the level of the seas, flooding coastal
lands.

Excessive irrigation, overcultivation, and forest clearance, possibly in
combination with naturally occurring processes, gave us *desertification*
(1974), the formation of new desert areas. The *food chain* (1926) was
now viewed in light of relationships within an ecosystem that could be
affected by physical or chemical factors such as drought or pollution.
Feeding high on the food chain even became generalized to refer to high
rank or power within an organization; being at the *bottom of the food*

chain was the reverse. *Overfishing* (1867), the depletion of once-rich fishing grounds, such as of cod and haddock in the North Atlantic, became a global concern as the human population continued to grow. Ironically, this concern was offset somewhat by a decrease in appetite for fish caused by the discovery of mercury and *PCBs* (1966) in many fish populations. *PCBs*, or *polychlorinated biphenyls*, are a group of toxic chemical compounds containing chlorine that are used industrially. PCBs are long-lasting environmental pollutants that accumulate in animal tissue, thereby working their way *up the food chain*. Such storage in tissue is known variously as *bioaccumulation, bioconcentration,* or *bio-magnification. Fallout* (1949), from atmospheric nuclear testing in the 1950s and 1960s, produced fear over the accumulation of *strontium 90* in cow's milk, and subsequently the human skeleton, as it replaced calcium.

At least one group was optimistic about the future; followers of the *Gaia theory* (1972), a proposal first offered by James Lovelock, saw Earth as a living organism, with built-in self-regulating controls. Named for the Greek goddess of Earth, the theory holds that Earth is a system of all

The spotted owl became a cause for environmental extremists when those seeking to protect its habitat clashed with the economic interests of timber companies and workers in the northwest.

Marine explorer Jacques Cousteau alongside his ship, *Calypso*, in 1986, before embarking on a five-year around-the-world expedition.

"If you want to clear the stream get the hog out of the spring."

— *American proverb*

living things that will re-establish equilibrium no matter how badly disturbed.

By the end of the 1980s environmental concern even turned to our homes, our places of business, and our public water supplies. The decade brought us the *sick-building syndrome*, *environmental* or *ecological illness*, *20th-century disease*, and *total-allergy syndrome*, all referring to chronic conditions attributed to *low-level exposure* to "safe" chemicals. Chemicals resulting from the *outgassing* of building materials, carpeting, paint, clothing, furniture, perfumes, and countless other sources were branded for their toxic effects, although baffling the medical community and defying diagnosis. The 1980s brought us *multiple chemical sensitivity*, or *chemical hypersensitivity syndrome*, an allergy to a broad spectrum of commonly occurring items in the air, water, food, housing, and drugs. Such sufferers are also known as *universal reactors* (1986). The medical discipline that treated such conditions was called *clinical ecology*, or *environmental medicine*.

Homes and schools exposed us for years to the dangers of *asbestos* in insulation; *benzene* from solvents; *biological contaminants* in the form of animal fur and dander, molds, and mites; and *carbon monoxide* from space heaters and furnaces. *Lead* in paint (banned in the 1970s) and *lead poisoning* from such paint were concerns many years after use, as children ingested paint chipped from long-neglected walls. *Radon gas*, the natural byproduct of the decay of radium, leaked into basements as an odorless gas, allegedly causing a higher incidence of lung cancer. Some worried about *electromagnetic (EM) fields* from electric power lines.

Even the weather was to blame. *El Niño*, 1925, an irregular flow of warm surface water along the western coast of South America, affects precipitation patterns in other parts of the world. Spanish for "the child," El Niño purportedly caused a warming trend every three to seven years as cold water did not upwell, affecting normal fish populations and triggering often severe weather disturbances. *Red tide* (1905) is the large-scale preponderance of red-colored sea plankton, producing a toxin poisonous to marine life and to humans consuming the contaminated shellfish.

Because of concern for the environment we began to talk about: the emergence of *agroforestry* (1977), land management for increased production of trees, food, and crops, an alternative to *slash-and-burn* (1942), agriculture; *aquaculture* (1867), or *fish farming*, the cultivation of fish, shellfish, or other marine life in small ponds or paddies; *biological controls* (1923), the use of natural means to control pests; the use of *biodegradable* (1961) materials; *bioregionalism* (1980s), a philosophy of living in harmony with the local environment; and *recycling* (1926), the careful disposal, often allowing re-use, of glass, metal, plastic, and paper.

In concluding this brief discussion of the *greening* of the American language it is worth mentioning a few more terms playing on the association of the color green with environmental friendliness: *green politics*

Strip mining—surface excavation rather than tunneling deep into the earth—is cheaper for mining companies and much safer for miners. It also thoroughly degrades the environment for years to come.

and *green parties* sprouted up in the 1980s to lobby for environmental goals; the *green revolution* (1968) pushed for large increases in food production through use of high-yielding crop varieties; and urban *greenways* (1968) gave us corridors of undeveloped land for recreational use near cities, along with *urban forests*, trees in city parks and other areas within city limits.

FASHIONS OF THE TIMES

A merica's fashion vocabulary illuminates no small part of our social history: our fashion trends and the words denoting them have consistently mirrored the needs and moods of the people over four centuries.

Calvin Klein has become more well known for his outrageous advertisements—including some condemned as child pornography and eventually pulled—than for the clothes he designs.

"Fashion, the semioticians keep telling us, is a language."

— Charles McGrath,
"It's Greek to Us,"
New York Times,
"Fashions of the Times,"
Spring 1996

THE 1600S–1700S

The Virginia Company advised each immigrant to the Jamestown colony to take with him "a *Monmouth cap* [1599, from an English county town of that name—a flat, round cap worn by sailors and soldiers], three shirts, one suit of canvas, one pair of garters, four pairs of shoes, three *falling-bands* [1598, fine lace-and-fabric collars], one waistcoat, one suit of *frieze* [a thick, warm, woolen cloth in use since the 14th century, going back to Dutch], one suit of *broadcloth* [15th century; a fine woolen cloth with a smooth surface], three pairs of silk stockings, [and] one dozen pairs of *points* [laces used in the 16th and 17th century to fasten clothing and secure men's hose]."

Men talked about and wore *doublets* (14th century; close-fitting, padded jackets with or without sleeves) under which they might wear *stays* (corsets stiffened with bones). They sported ruffs, *Holland shirts* (elaborate, loose shirts of Holland linen), and boots called *French falls* (floppy just above the ankle with large buckles at the instep). Men's *breeches*, typically of leather, were worn by all social classes. Working men wore canvas *jerkins* (1519, hip-length sleeveless jackets) and broad-brimmed hats of *thrums* (14th century; bits of warp thread left on a loom after the woven cloth had been removed) or of felt.

Women, who also wore ruffs and falling-bands at the necklines of their long gowns—as well as stays—supported their wide skirts with *farthingales* (1552, ultimately from Spanish—padded rolls of material worn around the waist to hold the skirts out on each side). By 1625 men were wearing earrings. And by 1689 both sexes carried *muffs* (1599). In the 1670s men had begun wearing flowing hairpieces called *periwigs* (cited to 1529).

By contrast, the Puritans, in accordance with a 1634 order by the Massachusetts General Court, were forbidden to buy "any apparell, either woolen, silke, or lynnen with any lace on it, silver, golde, silk, or thered." Two years later the Court forbade lace for any purpose, in effect moralizing fashion. The men wore *mandillions* of black cloth (1577, ultimately from Italian), or loose overcoats, now known as *Puritan cloaks*. Their falling-bands and wide-brimmed hats were generally unornamented, as were the women's clothes; both sexes wore shades of gray, lavender, brown, and, of course, black.

Here are some fashion terms in common use from the 1600s to the end of the 1700s, most now rare or obsolete, but one, *jean*, still very much with us today:

alamode, from French *à la mode*, "in the style," a soft, plain, glossy silk often mentioned in colonial newspapers, spelled variously as, e.g., *elamond, alamod*, or *arlimod*, used to make clothing throughout the century.

amazeen, a strong corded silk dating from the time of Elizabeth I through George III, often advertised in colonial newspapers.

biggin, 1530, possibly an alteration of French *beguine*, "nun," sometimes spelled *begin*, a close-fitting children's cap worn before 1700.

chicken-skins, gloves of chicken skin worn to bed to keep the skin white, a practice lasting as late as George II's reign.

crocus, a coarse cloth worn by working people and slaves, the word probably coming from the use of the material to package and ship saffron (*crocus*, the Greek word meaning "saffron," is ultimately of Semitic origin); cited in print as *crocus sack* to at least 1696, the term still in 20th century U.S. dialectal use in the South Atlantic states in reference to burlap bags.

drawers, used in colonial days of men's summer-weight breeches, not *underpants* (1925) or *undershorts* (1949).

duck, 1640, a strong linen fabric with no twill, still current.

gamoshes, leather leggings worn since the late 1500s (from earlier *gamash*, believed ultimately to derive from Ghahames near Tripoli, an early source of fine leather).

hum-hum, 1620, origin unknown, but thought by some to derive from Arabic *hammam*, a toweling cloth; a coarse cotton cloth imported (1750–70) from India, used for coat linings and advertised in colonial newspapers.

jean, 1577, a clipped form of *jean fustian* (*fustian*, 13th century, from Latin), from Middle English *Gene*, Genoa, Italy. The same fabric would, over 400 years hence, be the heart of "the U.S. uniform"—*blue jeans* (1901).

loo mask, 1690, from French *loup*, literally "wolf," a half-mask worn in winter by women.

moccasin, around 1612, from Virginia Algonquian *mockasin*, a soft leather heelless shoe with a laced-up U-shaped top, as still used today.

plumpers, 1690, thin, round, light balls inserted into the mouth to fill out hollow cheeks, worn even into the 1900s.

shoepack, cited to 1755, a truly "American" word like *moccasin*, also spelled *shoepac, shupac*, from Delaware [Native American] jargon *seppock, síppack*, "shoes," from Unami Delaware *cípahko*, "moccasins," influenced by English *shoe*; a moccasin-like shoe of tanned leather sometimes with a tongue and an added sole, worn during the American Revolution. In 20th century use, laced waterproof boots (also *shoepac*).

tabby, 1638, watered silk, from French *tabis*, ultimately from Arabic *'attabi*, itself from the name of a Baghdad suburb, *Al-'Attabiya*, where such fine silks were made.

THE 1700S–1800S

During the first half of the 18th century—the most prosperous time in the colonial era—European-influenced clothing became the centerpiece of a fashion-conscious society. The colonists talked about and wore rich fabrics, many with exotic names like *calico*, late 1500s, in various spellings; originally a silky cotton fabric imported from *Calicut*, India, whence its name; by the early to mid 1800s coming to mean in America a rather coarse printed cotton. They also imported *kincob* (1712, from

Bonnets.

Persian via Hindi), an Indian brocade, and *Nankeen* (1755, a respelling of *Nankin*, China, where this yellow cotton fabric was made). Men and women on the frontier, however, wore *homespun* (1607), a loose-weave woolen or linen fabric made from yarn spun at home; and *buckskins* (14th century), clothes made from deerskin.

During the first quarter of the 18th century men wore knee-length *Roquelaures* (1716), cloaks named after a French duke of that surname who served at Louis XIV's court. The colonists often respelled it *Roquelo*. (Later, it was worn in a longer version by both sexes.) Men's coats had big cuffs and big skirts. They were lined and stiffened with *buckram* (15th century, ultimately from *Bokhara* in Central Asia), a stiff cotton or linen. Kneebreeches, hose, and buckled shoes plus *tricorn* or *cocked* hats completed the ensemble. The long, flowing, curly hairpieces called *campaign wigs* (1693) went out of style in England and the colonies in favor of the *ramillie* (or *ramile*) wig (popular from the early 1700s, named for *Ramillies*, Belgium). This wig was powdered, braided (or queued) in back, and tied with a black ribbon. (Though powdered hair, in style for men from the 1690s, went out of fashion by the 1790s, the hair was still tied back in such a "pigtail.")

Women wore stays, hooped petticoats, and elbow-length sleeves on dresses with wide skirts, the backs of which were fitted with large overhanging box pleats called *Watteau saques* or *backs* (after the French painter [1684–1721] who represented people in this attire in his works). The word *bonnet* (from French) was used throughout the 18th century in reference to hoods and caps, but the bonnet as we know it came into vogue only in the latter half of the century: a 1798 citation notes that "straw bonnets were in full fashion."

THE 1800S–1900S

Americans continued to absorb the styles and vocabulary of European fashion, now via the monthly fashion magazines from London and Paris, which supplemented or replaced the *fashion dolls* shipped from abroad since the 1700s (tiny mannequins attired in miniature replicas of current designs).

Women's long, slender dresses with short, puffed sleeves, low necklines, and high waistlines (the *Empire* style associated with the first French Empire [1804–15] of Napoleon) began to emerge at the end of the 18th century and were worn for at least 10 years into the 19th century.

George IV's reign as Regent of England from 1811 to 1820 spawned an entire sublexicon as well as a special style. Examples included the *Regency wrapper*, a morning dress, long and flowing but tight-fitting in the torso with long, tight, epaulet-trimmed sleeves and a front laced up with a cord.

The first *leg-of-mutton sleeves*, held out with *sleeve cushions*, appeared in 1825. From 1825 to 1835 the sleeves increased in girth until they verged on the grotesque. The wearers were compelled to pass through doors crabwise. These and other fashions were illustrated in a magazine first titled the *Lady's Book*, initially published in 1830 by Louis Antoine Godey of Philadelphia. After 1837 it became known as *Godey's Lady's Book*. Among some of the styles talked about and illustrated was the *redingote*, popular in 1848, a walking dress that was buttoned down the front. (The word is a borrowing from French, and French *redingote* itself is a corruption of the English *riding coat*. This cross-Channel migrant dates in French to 1725.)

The 1850s were marked by two innovations with social import: *bloomers* and *denim* work clothes. The first, *bloomers* (see THE GENDER GAP), were a reaction against the hoopskirt. Named for Amelia Jenks Bloomer (1818–94), an activist in the *dress-reform movement*, these were trousers worn under a short skirt.

Levi Strauss (1829?–1902), a would-be gold prospector who had arrived in California in 1850, made a pair of work pants for a miner-

> *"A skirt reaching to about half-way between the knees and the ankles and not very full. Underneath the skirt trousers moderately full, and in fair weather coming down to the ankle and there gathered in with an elastic band."*
>
> — *Amelia Jenks Bloomer's definition of bloomers*

Hoop skirts (below) and the bloomers they inspired (left).

friend. The pants were so long-wearing that Strauss, realizing the commercial value of his creation, went to San Francisco and opened a factory. He ordered bolts of duck and *denim* (1695, from French *serge di Nîmes*, "serge of Nîmes," the city in France where a certain type of serge material was manufactured), the latter a firm, durable fabric of twilled cotton woven with a colored warp and white threads. The rest is history: the pants became known as *Levi's*.

The *hoop skirt*—a wide, circular, wire-stiffened undergarment, first cited in 1857—reached its apex in the decade of the 1860-70s. Decried not only by the *dress reformers* but also by those forced by fashion to wear it, this contraption gave rise to a new term, the *crinoline accident*. This was a situation in which the wearer of the hoop, topped with a *crinoline* —a full underskirt of open-weave cotton or horsehair, going back to Latin *crinis*, "hair," plus *linum*, "linen," cited to 1830 in the fabric sense—might be seriously injured or even killed if coming into contact with an open fire or candle spark.

The Gay Nineties witnessed the debut of the *Gibson girl* (see THE AMERICAN WAY OF SEX, subsection Dream Girls). This creation of illustrator Charles Dana Gibson (1867–1944) set the tone of women's fashion from head to toe from the early 1890s up to 1914. The Gibson girl had a soft, wide pompadour and wore a high-collared starched *shirtwaist* (1879)—also called a *Gibson girl blouse*—with narrowed leg-of-mutton sleeves, a dark ascot tie, and a floor-skimming flowing dark skirt.

The 19th century saw men's fashions transform into suits and long trousers, leaving all vestiges of colonial attire behind. By the 1830s narrow, full-length trousers—the precursor of the *business suit*—had evolved.

Reflecting the influence of "celebrities" on fashion was the *spencer* (1795). It was a close-fitting, short, waist-length men's jacket named for the English politician George John, 2nd Earl Spencer (1758–1834, and ancestor of 1980s-90s fashion plate Diana, Princess of Wales); emerging in the early 1800s, it was stylish into the first half of the 19th century. *Wellington boots* (1817)—with a loose top and the front arching to or above the knee—were named for Arthur Wellesley, 1st Duke of Wellington, the "Iron Duke" (1769–1852), who defeated Napoleon at

The eponymous Ambrose Everett Burnside.

Many men have forsaken the local barber for hair sytlists and salons.

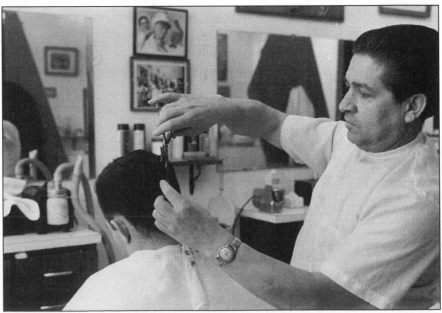

The Beard-box

In the 1600s and 1700s a pasteboard *beard-box* was worn by a man while sleeping in order to keep his *beard* (from a pre-12th century Old English word, related to Old High German *bart*, from Latin *barba*) in place. Among other terms Americans talked about with respect to male facial hair are these:

burnsides, 1875; *sideburns*, 1887, a mustache/side whiskers combination named after Union General Ambrose E. Burnside (1824–81).

Fu Manchu mustache, 1930s, a mustache extending straight down on both sides of the mouth to the chin, named for the Asian archvillain popularized in the Charlie Chan movies of 1929–39

handlebar mustache, 1933, a heavy mustache with upward-curving sections at each end (resembling the shape of bicycle handlebars).

Imperial, since 1841, a long mustache and chin tuft popularized by Napoleon III. The beard on the chin was the trimmed *spade* (since the 16th century); the related *goatee* (1844) first appeared on Uncle Sam in 1868.

military mustache, 1914–18, a pencil-thin mustache stylish with World War I officers and adopted by movie stars like Errol Flynn.

mustache, 1585, via French from Greek *moustaki*, a diminutive of *mystak-*, *mystax*, "upper lip, mustache," the hair on the upper lip. *Mustachio*, 1588 (sometimes still used in the plural), is from Spanish and Italian and derives also from the Greek word.

mutton-chops, *mutton-chop whiskers*, both 1865, side whiskers narrow at the temples but broad at the lower jaws, so called from their resemblance in shape to the cut of meat.

Van Dyke, 1894, a trim, pointed beard named after the 17th century Flemish painter whose portraits show many aristocrats wearing such beards.

Zapata mustache, a mustache that curves downward on each side, named after Mexican revolutionary Emiliano Zapata (1879?–1919), who captured Mexico City three times.

"A new word has been coined. It is d-u-d-e or d-o-o-d. . . . it has sprung into popularity within the last two weeks. . . ."

— Brooklyn Daily Eagle, February 15, 1883, remarking on dude—of uncertain origin— used to denote a rich, empty-headed young fop who wore tight trousers, "bell-crown English hats," pointed shoes, and high clerical-like white shirt collars, and who frequented the theaters. Dude also took on the sense "a city slicker or a tenderfoot," giving rise to dude ranch. And in Black English it came to mean first a pimp, later just a man or a guy.

Waterloo (1815). And *Bluchers* (1831)—which, like Wellingtons, still persist in fashion today—were named for Prussian general Gebhard Leberecht von Blucher (1742–1819), who also helped defeat Napoleon. These were and are boots or shoes having a one-piece tongue and vamp with the quarters lapped over the vamp and laced together.

The *Beau Brummell* look dominated 19th century male fashion from 1800 till around the 1830s. Named for George Bryan ("Beau") Brummell (1778–1840), a dandy and close friend of the then-Prince of Wales (later George IV), the style included *Hessian boots* (1809), high, tasseled boots reaching to just below the knees; foot-long *neck cloths*; and for the evening, *opera hats* and white waistcoats.

Knickers (cited to 1881, clipped from the 1848 *knickerbockers* [1859 in the clothing sense], itself from Diedrich *Knickerbocker*, the fictitious author of Washington Irving's 1809 *History of New York*) were loose-fitting, typically flannel, short trousers gathered at the knees, worn by boys and sportsmen. By the 1920s they had evolved into *plus fours*, so-called because they were four inches longer than regular knickers.

The *swallowtail* (1835)—also called the *tailcoat* (1847), the *cutaway* (1849), the *steel pen* (U.S., 1873), and the *clawhammer* (also U.S., 1879)—remained popular well into the 1860s: it was a coat whose skirts tapered from the front waistline to form "tails" at the back, worn day and evening.

The style we call the *business suit* (cited to 1870) first appeared in England, where, as the 1880s equivalent of the *leisure suit* (1975), it was initially sniffed at by the upper class because of its association with "trade." Not so, however, with the *bow tie* (1897) or the *smoking jacket* (1878), the latter a tailored, silk, brocade, or velvet jacket tied with a belt, worn at home.

The most influential arbiter of male style in this, the century of Spencer, Wellington, and Brummell, was Albert Edward, Prince of Wales, son of Queen Victoria, who became Edward VII. Known as the best-dressed man in Europe, this bon vivant lent his name to men's house slippers called *Prince Alberts* and to a long double-breasted frock coat called the *Prince Albert coat* (1884).

THE 1900S–2000

U.S. *ready-made* (1882) or *ready-to-wear* (1895) clothing came into its own in the early 20th century. New York City's *Seventh Avenue* became the nexus of U.S. clothing manufacturing and merchandising.

By 1920 narrow, knee-length skirts had replaced the post-World War I unconstructed, drop-waisted, calf-length frocks. These new, short, drop-waisted dresses were worn with the *cloche* (French, "bell")—a close-fitting, round-crowned hat with a very narrow brim. Gone were the tightly laced *corsets* worn in the Gay Nineties. In came *powdered knees*

Clothes make their way from designers' runways to consumers' closets via the streets of New York City's Garment District.

and *rolled stockings* just below the knee (rolled because neither *girdles* nor *garter belts* with points of attachment were then available). Gone, too, were the 10 yards of heavy flannel listed in an 1870s fashion book as essential in making a women's *bathing suit* (a term then coming into use, replacing *bathing dress* and *bathing costume*). Gone as well were the *bathing stockings*, required until 1907 at Atlantic City for all female bathers. When Jantzen introduced the skirtless one-piece bathing suit for women in 1913, it changed the trend of women's *active sportswear* forever. Men's *trunks* had been worn by professional swimmers and other athletes since the 1880s, but as late as 1935 men wearing trunks without tops were arrested at Atlantic City. And the *T-shirt*, first a man's collarless short-sleeved undershirt, made its debut in 1920, so called because, when spread out flat, its shape resembled a *T*.

With the entry of the U.S. into World War II the great majority of men were in uniform, a style emulated by women. Women's suits were severe and short-skirted. Hems were stitched at two inches, and skirts were limited to 72 inches around with no ruffles, no cuffs on coats, and only one patch pocket per blouse—a result of strict rationing. Since hose were virtually impossible to get during the war, many women used *leg makeup* and penciled "seams" on the backs of their bare legs.

The first *two-piece* women's *bathing suit* emerged in the early 1940s with the midriff bared a few inches. Skimpy playclothes called *rompers* were in fashion, as were *pedal pushers* (1944, mid-calf pants), and *wrap-arounds*, simple self-tied dresses created because of a lack of zippers. *Chinos* for both sexes emerged from military use, and the khaki cotton twill garment (its name from American Spanish *chino*, "toasted," for its color; the fabric is known from 1943) persisted in style through the 1990s.

During the war teenagers were for the first time recognizable as a cohesive group with its own sociology and style. The style was marked by *Sloppy Joes* (1942, loose-fitting cardigan sweaters), *bobby socks* (1943; also *bobby sox*; *bobby* may be from *bobbed*, that is, short, as they were often rolled down so that they barely covered the ankle), worn by *bobby soxers* (1944) often with *saddle shoes* (1939)—white or cream oxfords with a brown or black "saddle" across the middle and white laces.

The year 1946 marked the advent of the *bikini*—in Europe—created by Louis Reard, a Renault automotive design engineer. He coined the term by association with *Bikini*, the South Pacific atoll then in the news as the site of U.S. atomic bomb testing, because of the style's explosive effect on fashion. Though the bikini became an instant success in Europe, it managed to gain wide acceptance in the U.S. only in the 1960s, thereafter morphing into the *monokini* (first cited in 1964 in a European context as a bikini with top and bottom joined by a band; also, 1968, a topless bikini).

Though the *gray flannel suit* (worn in the 1920s and 30s) had, by the 1950s, come to symbolize staid male business attire, the period of the 1950s actually was the start of the *wash-and-wear* wardrobe. With *wash-and-wear* (1956), cotton, wool, and silk gave way to the use of synthetic fabrics such as nylon and polyester. In the 1950s people talked about:

Bermuda shorts, 1951, knee-length walking shorts for men and women.

button-down shirts, usually of *Oxford cloth* (1950s), dress shirts with long sleeves and collars fastened to the tops of the fronts by two small buttons; a term that eventually generated the form *buttoned-down*, meaning "traditionally businesslike and conservative."

"The 60s were open season on legs. Skirts moved higher, higher, and still higher, till many miniskirts barely covered the domain usually left to underwear. The concession to modesty, however, was the accompanying hosiery, either fishnet, glittery, opaque, ribbed, or knee-high."

— *The Changing American Woman: 200 Years of American Fashion*, Women's Wear Daily, 1976 special supplement

Jackie Kennedy and her European style in 1963. Ironically, the wife of the French Minister of Culture, to her left, is dressed more as a 1950s-era First Lady.

Capri pants or *capris*, around 1956, close-fitting, ankle length pants often with a side slit at the bottom, for women and girls.

crinoline, no longer of horsehair as in 1850s–60s, but used similarly as a half-slip worn often in multiple layers, especially by teenage girls, to give fullness to skirts and dresses.

Peter Pan collar, originally cited to 1908, in the 50s a round collar on a woman or girl's short-sleeved blouse, adorned with a *circle pin*.

Young men affected the *ducktail*—a hairstyle in which the hair was swept back on each side, held in place by liberal amounts of hair cream, and converging in an upswept point (hence the name) at the nape of the neck; also called the *D.A.* (for *duck's ass*). Many wore straight-legged *peg pants*, black boots with heel and toe taps, white socks, and black leather jackets for an urban tough-guy look. Those more conservative chose the *flattop*—a short haircut with the top brushed straight up and cropped in a flat plane. The white *sport coat* and the wool *crewneck* sweater were essential.

The 1960s were the most prolific in modern American fashion terminology. Certainly the fashion symbol of the early 60s was First Lady Jacqueline Kennedy. She single-handedly altered the look of the American woman from the dowdiness of the 50s to the European sophistication of the *Beautiful People* (1964). She popularized the *pillbox* (a high, round little hat set atop teased, bouffant, often windblown hair), the sleeveless *shift* (a simple, straight dress often adorned by a triple strand of pearls at the plain, round neckline), and a lace *mantilla* instead of a hat for church.

The early 60s also brought us *Christine Keeler boots*—tight-fitting, high-heeled, knee-length boots named for the "party girl" who brought down the career of British War Secretary John Profumo in a sex scandal. The wide popularity of these boots marked the beginning of a 30-year trend in tall boots for women. *Panty hose* (1963) came in about the same time, followed in 1964 by the first *pantsuits* for women.

In the early 60s hair styles were longer, often teased, lacquered, and piled high into the *beehive*, a look popularized by Farah, the young empress of Iran. Men, too, began letting their hair grow longer after the Beatles took popular music by storm in 1964, sporting their *mop-top* hairdos. As hair grew longer, skirts got shorter, all the way to the *miniskirt* (1965), with a hem several inches above the knee, and the *micromini* (1966). Short skirts and long hair were *mod* (around 1960, a clipped form of *modern*), the word and the style coming from Britain's youth culture.

Revolution and rebellion were typified by the *topless swimsuit* and the *braless* or *no-bra* look (bra, 1936, clipped from *brassiere*, 1911). But the fashions of the 60s are also associated with hippies. The hippie look became a style, even for the *radical chic* (1970)—socially prominent people who affected hippie hairstyles and attire and associated with those they perceived as radicals or "minorities." Young girls wore *granny dresses* (the word and the style actually dating to 1909)—long, high-waisted, loose frocks. Other terms on people's lips were *granny glasses* (1966, eyeglasses with small lenses and narrow metal frames); *flower children* (with "flowers in their hair"); *love beads* (1968, the symbol for love and peace during the Vietnam War); the *Afro* hairstyle, with curly hair teased to puff out, for African Americans; and the peace symbol.

In addition to *hip-huggers* (1960s)—pants with waistlines dropped below the waist to ride the hips, and usually with flared *bell-bottoms*—the late 60s saw the emergence of the *midi* (1967), or *midi-skirt*, which fell to mid-calf. African American men and women began to wear the *dashiki* (1968, a spelling modification of Yoruba [a Niger-Congo language of southwestern Nigeria] *dànsíkí*)—a long, collarless, flare-sleeved, usually brightly patterned robe. *Muumuus* (Hawaiian, "cut off")—loose, long dresses in bright fabric patterns—and for men, *Mao* jackets (after the Chinese Communist leader Mao Zedong [1893–1976]) were emblems of radical chic. *Tie-dyed* (1904) jeans and dresses (tied in knots, then dyed often with several colors to create light and dark patterns) were worn with *thongs*.

The 1970s ushered in *hot pants*—very tight, skimpy shorts worn by women with bright satin blouses and high heels. And along came the *string bikini*, which was soon abbreviated to the buttocks-baring *thong* (a second fashion sense of a word going back to Old English). Men cast off their love beads for gold chains and chest-baring shirts, symbols of the *macho* (cited to 1928 as an adjective, from Spanish "male," ultimately from Latin *masculus*) look. *The* fabrics of the 70s were double-knit *polyester* and the Japanese import *Ultrasuede* (trademark), both used to make pant suits, *jumpsuits, leisure suits*, skirts, and *shirtdresses*. *Palazzo pants* (which flared up to several yards at the hems), four-and-a-half-inch heels on *platform shoes*, and *fun furs* (jackets, vests, and coats of fox, raccoon etc.) plus the *maxi* (1967)—a skirt, dress, or double-breasted coat of floor length—were all stylish in the 1970s.

In the 70s the emphasis was on designers as much as designs: people talked about *designer clothes, designer sweaters, designer ties, designer dresses, designer perfumes, designer sheets*, and *designer towels*. The *designer* phenomenon roughly coincided with a trend, first among men, to "dress for success," a trend that would, in the 1980s, culminate in *power attire. Pinstripes*, monogrammed button-down Oxford cloth dress shirts, *three-piece suits*, and *regimental* (conservative, striped) *ties* took hold in the late 70s, then dominated the go-go 1980s. John Malloy's 1977 book *Dress for Success* encouraged career women to adopt a professional uniform similar to men's clothing. What emerged in the 80s for women was the severe, tailored suit, the white blouse, and the dark or colored scarf-tie analogous to the necktie. As both sexes moved into *power dressing* for *power lunches*, the noun *power*, like its predecessor *designer*, came to be used more and more as an attributive.

Paralleling power dressing was the *preppy* (or *preppie*) look for youth and adults at leisure. Blue *blazers* (the word cited to 1880) with gold buttons, khaki pants, crewnecks, kilts, flat shoes, longer skirts, and, for casual wear, *Top-Siders*—the trademarked soft leather or canvas boat shoe with rubber soles—were the look in a decade that was also moving toward *unisex* short haircuts. The fitness craze of this decade made *sweatpants* and *sweatshirts* (both cited to 1925), *sneakers* (1895), and *tennis shoes* (1886) a status-symbol look.

The *punk look* of the 1980s—black clothes, Doc Martens, black hose, clothing held together with safety pins, and *Mohawks* (men's hairdos with the head shaved on the side leaving only a narrow, central, often bizarrely dyed strip of high bristles)—gradually evolved into *grunge* in the 1990s. *Grunge* is a "back-formation" of the preexisting *grungy* (1965), its origin unknown, but possibly a blend of *grunt* in the baby-talk sense "to defecate," plus elements of *dingy* and *grimy*. The look involved wearing drab baggy clothes full of rips, holes, and signs of wear—the

Supermodel Claudia Schiffer wearing a product of superdesigner Gianni Versace.

"deconstructed" styling taking cues from hip-hop wear and from the "lumberjack" look of the Pacific Northwest. Youths were seen wearing *baggies*—below-the-knee oversized shorts—topped with oversized shirts, high-topped tennis shoes, and baseball caps worn backwards. *Birkenstocks*, thick-soled sandals with buckled cross straps, or *Doc Martens*, a brand of lace-up high leather boots with thick soles, dominated the footwear scene.

In the very late 80s office workers had begun to *dress down*, i.e., to dress casually without neckties or severe suits, on Fridays—a practice begun on the West Coast. By the mid 1990s *dress-down days* were being observed in work settings across the country.

The mid-90s saw a 60s revival. Short skirts came back along with other artifacts of the 60s like square-toed, square-heeled high boots, leather three-quarter-length *car coats* (1958, but then worn in a boxier shape), and *wraparound sunglasses*—this being dubbed *Modified Mod*. The 60s look in the 90s and other *retro* styles simply proved designer Anna Sui's point (1995): "Fashion is not . . . complicated—it's a pendulum. . . . It just goes from one extreme to another."

FIGHTING WORDS

War has its laws," wrote Cardinal Newman in 1864. So too does it have its own language, generalized to all combat, yet often specific to certain conflicts. In the case of American English many of the "fighting words" associated with specific conflicts have become permanent reminders of those struggles: The word **doughboy** recalls the Word War I trenches "Over There." **Blitz, D-day,** and **kamikaze** conjure images of World War II. **MASH, DMZ, 38th parallel,** and **chopper** gained widespread currency during the Korean War. **ARVN, in-coming, firebase, Ho Chi Minh trail, hot LZ** (a landing zone under enemy fire), **search-and-destroy, body count,** and **fragging** individually and collectively represent the military and social conflict that was the Vietnam War. Finally, **Scud, MREs** (meals ready to eat), and vehicles with a name pronounced "humvee" call to mind the **line drawn in the sand** (from George Bush, 1990—an extension of an 18th century phrase for setting a boundary) amidst the **fog of war** in Saudi Arabia and Kuwait in 1991, the conflict called **Desert Shield,** then **Desert Storm.**

"These are the times that try men's souls. The summer soldier and the sunshine patriot will, in this crisis, shrink from the service of their country; but he that stands it now, deserves the love and thanks of man and woman."

— *Tom Paine,* The American Crisis, No. 1, *December 23, 1776, with* summer soldier *and* sunshine patriot *referring not only to those who supported the Revolution only when the war was going well, but to those who took advantage of short enlistments to serve during the more comfortable months, returning home to bring in the fall harvest*

To look at the anvil that forged these fighting words is to look back to the year 1775. For it is in 1775 that the profound effect of bloodshed on American English is first to be seen.

NEW NATION FORGED IN WAR

The American Revolution began on April 19, 1775, when colonial *Minute Men* and *militia* lined up on the village green to fight the British at the *Battle of Lexington*, Massachusetts. Its end came with the surrender of Cornwallis to a combined American and French force at the *Battle of Yorktown*, October 19, 1781.

As usual in wartime, terms formerly restricted to military circles began intruding into the common speech of Americans. These included *barracks, bounty, draft, furlough, discharge, militia, outpost, rangers,* and *stockade.* Though some traced their origins to Latin, French, or Spanish, by the 1770s they had entered the English military lexicon, and the meanings they had acquired by the end of the conflict have remained rel-

"Stand your ground; don't fire unless fired upon, but if they mean to have a war, let it begin here." The words of Captain Parker to his 70 Minute Men before the Battle of Lexington, as 800 British troops advanced on the town.

Patriot Ethan Allen during his 3-year confinement by the British in Montreal. Allen and his Green Mountain Boys fought alongside Benedict Arnold as they captured Fort Ticonderoga in the early days of the American Revolution.

"There never was a good war, or a bad peace."

— *Benjamin Franklin, September 11, 1783*

Old Ironsides. Built in 1797, it can still be seen 200 years later at the Boston Navy Yard.

atively stable in American English. As parts of a vocabulary that continues to apply to all wars, they bring no particular war to mind. Some words and phrases, however, persist in bringing the Revolution to mind:

Minute Men, a phrase well known by 1774 to denote a special force of militia, ready at a moment's notice. Though first organized by Massachusetts and other colonies, the Continental Congress finally authorized them in 1775. Over time, the term came to be spelled *minutemen*. (See FRINGE GROUPS.)

Patriots, 1775, those Americans who supported the Revolution. Of the 21–22 million colonists, 67–80 percent were Patriots. The Loyalists called them *rebels* or "the rabble."

turncoats, 1557 English word for traitor, from the idea of a coat being worn right-side or wrong-side out according to circumstances. The name of the most famous turncoat of all, *Benedict Arnold*, eventually acquired the generic meaning of "traitor," at least in colloquial speech, where one might say of a betrayer, "He's a *Benedict Arnold*."

Yankees or *Yanks*, 1758; 1778, another term for the Patriots, of somewhat murky origin, possibly coming from the Dutch *Jan Kees*, "John Cheese," a disparaging European nickname for the cheese-making, cheese-eating Hollanders since the 1650s; possibly brought to the New World by the British, who used it with reference to Dutch pirates. It may also be from Dutch *Janke*, "little John," pronounced "yant-yeh," and a derogatory usage. In any case, British soldiers, who had been calling English settlers *Brother Jonathans*, implying a rustic simpleness, eventually began calling them *Yankees*. The colonists appropriated the insult, however, investing it with patriotic pride.

Though the Revolution was one of the most successful in history, it was incomplete and led inevitably to the War of 1812, which lasted from 1812 to 1815. The roots of this war lay in an Anglo-French conflict that began in 1793. Although the U.S. tried to remain neutral for the sake of its foreign trade and its shipping industry, neutrality proved difficult to maintain. For one thing, England had been angering America for years by subjecting U.S. citizens to *impressment* (1787). Claiming that British-born merchant sailors serving on American ships rightfully belonged to England, its navy would stop U.S. ships to remove them, *impressing* them into British service.

War Hawks had been coined by Jefferson in 1798 to refer to those Federalists who wanted war with France which, like England, had tried American neutrality severely. Now, as 1812 approached, *War Hawks* were what easterners called "war Republicans," congressmen from the South and West who, fueled by concerns about commerce and territorial expansion, directed their *war fever* (1812) against Britain. (*War Hawks* remained vital in the language through the Vietnam era, though by then usually shortened to *hawks*.)

Eventually war fever turned to flame. By the time it was extinguished, it had produced two of the most memorable sentences in American naval history: *Don't give up the ship*, a small variation on the actual words spoken by Commander James Lawrence during a battle off the New England coast (June 1, 1813); and *We have met the enemy and they are ours*, from Captain Oliver Hazard Perry's victory message after the Battle of Lake Erie (September 10, 1813). Finally, the war inspired a poem that would eventually become the lyrics of the national anthem, *The Star-Spangled Banner* (words from a poem by Francis Scott Key, who was inspired by witnessing the survival of Fort McHenry, near Baltimore, after a night bombardment on September 13–14, 1814).

"... my country, right or wrong."

— Kentucky Congressman John J.Crittendon, speech to Congress, May 1846, in reply to President Polk's request for a declaration of war

Equally dramatic, a new icon had captured the American imagination, *Old Ironsides*, 1815. The frigate *Constitution* was "Old" merely as a familiar nickname, having been launched in 1797; she was "Ironsides" because of her indestructible performance during the war, it being said that a seaman first called her that when he saw enemy shot rebound from her oak sides.

EXPANSIONIST CONFLICTS

In 1835, Americans in Texas, then a part of Mexico, joined what was originally a Mexican revolt against the dictatorial government of General Antonio Lopez de Santa Anna, took it over, and were soon fighting for independence. The most famous sentence from that conflict was, of course, *Remember the Alamo!* It memorialized the massacre, on March 6, 1836, of over 125 Americans after an 11-day siege of the Alamo (from Spanish *alamo*, cottonwood tree)—an old Spanish mission in San Antonio. After diplomatic negotiations with Mexico broke down, Congress declared war on May 13, 1846. The Mexican War brought the first widespread American military use of the word *chevrons*. The insignia, which appeared on the coat sleeves of U.S. noncommissioned officers at this time, traced their name to a 14th century English word for "rafters" and, ultimately, to the Vulgar Latin word for goat, *caprio*, from Latin *caper*, since rafters raised on end resembled butting goats.

"From the halls of Montezuma,

To the shores of Tripoli,

We will fight our country's battles

On the land as on the sea"

— *"The Marines' Hymn,"* 1850s, in which the halls of Montezuma *refers to the capture of Mexico City in the Mexican War*

THE GREAT FRATRICIDE

Southerners called it *the Revolution, the War of Independence,* and *the War of Secession* (all 1861 terms). After it was over, the Northern name *Civil War* (1861) dominated, though by the 1890s, people also called it the *War Between the States* and *the War Between the North and the South.*

With the firing on Fort Sumter on April 12, the war was on, and by the time it was over, many new terms had entered the language:

"Mine eyes have seen the glory of the coming of the Lord;

He is trampling out the vintage where the grapes of wrath are stored;

He hath loos'd the fateful lightning of His terrible swift sword;

His truth is marching on. . . ."

— *"The Battle Hymn of the Republic,"* Julia Ward Howe, November 1861, *after reviewing Union troops, first published in* The Atlantic Monthly, *1862*

The Alamo falls, March 6, 1836. Perhaps the most famous military defeat in American history.

Frontiersman Davy Crockett was one of those killed at the Alamo. He would not have been there had he been re-elected to Congress in 1835.

A.W.O.L. These became the initials for "absent without leave," popularized by Southern offenders having to wear placards so initialed. During World War I, people spoke the initials as "a-w-o-l," but later the initials were pronounced as a word, "Awol," the more common usage since World War II.

ante-bellum, 1867, before the war.

Confederate. The adjective in *The Confederate States of America* began appearing in other combinations in 1861, for instance *Confederate money*, *Confederate stamps*, and the *Confederate flag*, also called *the stars and bars* to distinguish it from the Union's *stars and stripes*.

draftee. Nationwide conscription came to America with the Confederate Conscription act of 1862 and the Union's Draft Law of 1863. Both allowed draftees to pay the government a fine in lieu of service or to hire *substitutes*. In the North, conscription led to *draft riots* in several cities, the worst in New York, July 13–16, 1863.

ironclads, 1867. Naval vessels which traced their ancestry to the North's *Monitor* and the South's *Virginia* (a captured and converted U.S. frigate formerly named the *Merrimac*) were called *ironclads*, armorplated with iron. The two fought a five-hour battle in Hampton Roads, Virginia, on March 9, 1862.

skedaddle (1861, origin unknown but possibly from Scots or Northern English dialect, perhaps related to Greek *skedannunai*, to split up). This word had entered American English in the 1820s but became popular when Union troops used it to describe Confederate forces fleeing from battle.

the Medal of Honor, the Congressional Medal of Honor. Congress established the medal for Union heroes in 1862.

unconditional surrender. Though now associated with the demands of the Allies in World War II, the phrase traces its origin to Union General Ulysses S. Grant who, at the Battle of Fort Donelson, Tennessee, on February 16, 1862, responded to General Simon Bolivar Buckner's request for terms, "No terms except *unconditional surrender.*"

war correspondent, 1861. The Civil War saw the emergence of the war correspondent, one of the most famous of whom was Winslow Homer, who accompanied the Union Army as a writer and artist.

CENTURY'S END

Rebels had fought against Spanish rule in Cuba between 1868 and 1878, and widespread fighting broke out again in 1895. Meanwhile, the *yellow journalism* (1898) appearing in William Randolph Hearst's *New York Journal* and Joseph Pulitzer's *New York World* whipped up American sympathy for the rebels through sensational, often exaggerated, stories of Spanish atrocities. Then, when the U.S. battleship *Maine* exploded and sank in Havana harbor on February 15, 1898, taking 258 American lives, *Remember the Maine* became the rallying cry that took the nation into the war on the side of the rebels. President William McKinley called it the *Spanish-American War* in 1899 when urging the Senate to ratify the peace treaty. Though brief, the war added its share of terms to the language, some of them foreign borrowings, for this was the first time our troops were exposed to, and had the opportunity to absorb, foreign languages:

Lee surrendering to Grant at Appomattox, marking the end of a war that left more than 600,000 dead. The final casualty, President Lincoln, would be assassinated five days later.

boondocks (via the Philippine Tagalog *bundok*, mountain), first used by U.S. Marines during the post-war campaign against the Filipino guerrillas (1899–1902). Having fought for independence against Spain, the guerrillas now began to fight the new oppressors, the Americans. Other foreign borrowings brought back by the troops were *padre, junta, machete,* and *incommunicado.*

boot, from the leggings sailors used to wear, first came to mean a navy or marine recruit during this war, and by World War I, *boot camp* named their training site.

the brass, referring to the insignia on officers' uniforms, came into widespread use during the Spanish-American war to mean high-ranking officers.

to bust, to reduce in rank, came into military usage in this war.

campaign hat, initially denoted the Rough Riders' khaki-colored felt hat. Other military units and law enforcement agencies soon adopted the dashing headgear.

khaki (from Urdu—an Indic language, the official literary language of Pakistan, also used by Muslims in India—and meaning "dusty"), the cloth of choice for the Rough Riders' uniforms, an idea borrowed from the British. When the cloth came in, so did a new word in American English.

the Rough Riders. *Rough rider* had meant a cowboy ever since Theodore Roosevelt had used it in its American English sense in an 1888 article in *Century Magazine.* Now the men who enlisted in his First U.S. Volunteer Cavalry Regiment said they were joining *Roosevelt's Rough Riders,* later shortened to *the Rough Riders.* In Cuba, the regiment earned lasting fame—and hero status for its commander—with its supporting attack on Kettle Hill during the Battle of San Juan Hill.

shavetail, term used by farmers and those in the army mule corps to describe a mule or ass (by 1846, because of the practice of shaving the tails of newly broken mules to distinguish them from the others). By the 1890s, it meant an inexperienced person, then narrowed to a newly commissioned lieutenant during the Spanish-American War.

WORLD WARS

Although World War I had been raging since June 28, 1914, the U.S. did not enter the fray until April 6, 1917. At that point, America joined *the Allies* in opposition to *the Central Powers*, so called because of their location in Central Europe. Initially, Americans followed the British lead in calling the conflict *the European War* (1914), but increasingly *the World War* came into use. Afterward, veterans termed it *the Great War*.

Because the airplane was a dramatic novelty in the war, it produced some of the most memorable additions to the language. These included *ace*, a pilot who had shot down at least five enemy planes; *parachute* (French, *para,* protecting against, preventing + *chute,* fall), along with *air drop* and *bail out*; *bomber* (British coinage, 1915); *fighter plane, fighter,* and *dogfight; formation* and *formation flying*.

Others popularized are these:

basket case, 1919, a quadruple amputee, originally British Army slang, later coming to mean mental, not physical, incapacity.

blimp and *zeppelin. Blimp* (1916) comes either from the designation of a British design for a dirigible, the type *B-limp* (*limp* meaning nonrigid, the gas bag supported solely by internal gas pressure), or from the sound made by striking the gas bag with one's thumb. Count Ferdinand von *Zeppelin* lent his name to the cigar-shaped rigid dirigible that he had perfected in 1900.

chow, which had been a slang word for food since 1856, became common in World War I, along with *chowhound,* one who was always first in the *chow line* at *chow time, chowing down*. Originating among sailors and Chinese railroad workers on the Pacific Coast, it probably traces its roots to Mandarin *ch'ao,* to stir, fry, cook, possibly via Chinese Pidgin English *chowchow,* food, from which it was clipped.

civvies, civilian clothes, going back to 1889.

dog tag, 1918, a disk worn on a chain around the serviceman's neck, for identification in case of injury or death, so called because it resembles a license tag on a dog's collar.

doughboy, a word that had seen some use in the Civil War, now became the common term for an American infantrymen. No one knows the origin for sure, though it may be an allusion to a type of fried sweet cornmeal cake called a *doughboy* as early as 1770. The globular brass buttons on some Civil War infantry uniforms resembled these cakes, and so the word was applied to the soldiers themselves.

dud, shell or bomb that fails to explode, probably from the 14th century. By 1919 it had broadened to mean anything that did not meet expectations.

flame throwers (a loan-translation of the German *Flammenwerfer*), first saw use in German hands at the Battle of Verdun on February 21, 1916. The term superseded the earlier British *flame projectors*.

gas, the poison gases the Germans began using in 1915, first against the Russians and later, the French and British, in defiance of the 1907

Mules and doughboys in France during World War I. Poison gas made masks standard equipment for both man and beast.

"Praise the Lord and pass the ammunition."

— *Chaplain Howell Forgy aboard the cruiser* New Orleans, *encouraging its crew to sustain a barrage while under attack at Pearl Harbor, December 7, 1941. It became a set wartime phrase and the title of a pop song by Frank Loesser*

Hague Conference's proscriptions. *Gas mask* (1915), too, came into the language, along with the names of the gases, *phosgene* (going back to 1812), *tear gas* (1917), and *mustard gas* (1917), which became household words.

gobs and swabbies, what Americans called sailors in World War I. By 1909 people in the Navy were using *gob*, origin unknown, but possibly from *gobby*, which had meant a coastguardsman since 1890. *Swabby* comes from *swab/swabber*, used since the 18th century to mean a merchant seaman, among whose duties was to swab the deck (*swab* meant "mop" by the 16th century, probably from the Middle Dutch *swabb*).

goldbrick, a brick or bar of gold in the U.S. by 1853, then a valueless brick appearing to be made of gold by the 1880s. By 1914, it meant a second lieutenant, very likely because of the brick-shaped gold bars denoting the rank. More specifically, it meant a lieutenant appointed from civilian life, without training or experience. By the end of the war it came to mean anyone who didn't do his share, and *to goldbrick* meant to shirk.

sabotage, from French *saboter*, a verb meaning "clatter with sabots (wooden shoes)," or "botch." Having entered English (first recorded in 1910), the word saw wide use during the war to refer to destruction by enemy agents.

shell shock, 1915, originally a British coinage, found wide use by Americans even though the official military term was *battle fatigue*.

slacker, one who tries to avoid military service. Americans acquired the word from the British, though as the war went on, they tended to prefer an old Americanism (1833) *shirker*, going back to *shirk* (origin unknown). In the late 1980s and early 90s *slacker* made a return appearance to refer to a lazy, unambitious young adult.

tank, British Colonel Sir Earnest Swinton's code name for this new weapon during its development. The parts of a tank, *turret*, *hatch*, *hull*, etc., have nautical names because the British Admiralty originally sponsored it.

trench warfare (first recorded in print in 1917), marked the grueling three years that followed the First Battle of the Marne in 1914. *No-man's land* (going back to the 14th century) lay in the crossfire zone between opposing front lines. *Trench warfare* also produced *trench coat* (1916), *trench knife* (1915), *trench mortar* (1915), *trench fever* (1915, transmitted by lice), *trench foot* (1915, a form of frostbite), and *trench mouth* (1918, a form of gingivitis).

submarines, *U-boats, torpedoes,* and *periscopes. Submarine* has meant "under the sea" in English since 1684 and an undersea boat since the 1890s. The short form, *sub*, emerged in 1914, first recorded in print in 1916. The Germans were the first to use submarines on a large scale, and during World War I people called a German submarine a *U-boat* (1913, from the German *Unterseeboot*, undersea boat.) *Torpedo* was the Latin name for a raylike fish that delivers a numbing electrical charge (from Latin *torpere*, to be stiff, or numb, which also gives us *torpor*). The fish was a *torpedo* in English by 1520; then, in America in 1786, a *torpedo* came to mean a percussion shell and by 1807, a mine or attachment device for blowing up ships. The self-propelled torpedo first appeared in World War I, and soon became what most people meant when they said *torpedo*. *Periscope* (Greek *peri*, all around + *scope*, an instrument for observing) was in English by 1822 to name a

147

device for looking over or around obstacles, but it came to be associated especially with submarines during this war.

After the Armistice that took effect on November 11, 1918, the *Treaty of Versailles*, signed on June 28, 1919, ended the war. At the peace conference, President Wilson had proposed his *Fourteen Points* as the foundation of "just and generous peace," including the formation of a *League of Nations*.

Neither the League nor the peace lasted for very long, however. Called "the war to end all wars" after 1918, the so-called Great War was followed by an even bloodier one, World War II, only 21 years later. Critics of the Versailles Treaty had in fact said that the war just ended would be but *World War I* and that a second would follow. The U.S. armed forces did not officially use the name until 1942, by which time the fighting had reached around the world.

The period between September 1, 1939—when Germany attacked Poland and France and England responded by declaring war—and America's actual entry into the fighting, witnessed reverse after reverse for *the Allies*. France's supposedly invincible *Maginot Line* (1936, named after French war minister André *Maginot*) proved useless as the Germans flanked it by invading the Low Countries; then after the "miracle of *Dunkirk*," the fall of France in May 1940, and the commencement of *the Battle of Britain*, it became obvious that if Germany were to be halted, the U.S. would have to surrender its neutrality and play at last the role of *The Arsenal of Democracy* (coined by Jean Monnet, the French ambassador to the U.S. but popularized by Franklin D. Roosevelt in a December 29, 1940 speech). The Japanese attack on Pearl Harbor, of course, brought America actively into the war, and gave to American English the expression *day of infamy*, President Roosevelt's reference to the December 7, 1941 attack, a reference that brought *infamy*, relatively rare in terms of wide American usage, to the fore. As one of the *Allies* fighting against the *Axis* in Africa, Europe, and the Pacific, the U.S. eventually helped bring about the *unconditional surrender* of Germany on *V-E Day*, May 8, 1945, and that of Japan on *V-J Day*, August 15.

Additions to the language that came out of World War II include:

amphibious landing, an invasion by sea. Large *landing ships* brought troops and vehicles close to shore. Then smaller *landing craft* took them to the beach where they secured an initial site, a *beachhead*, before additional troops and supplies came ashore.

the Battle of Britain, the air attacks on English cities that began with a raid on London in September 1940, and continued almost every night for two years. People also called it the *London Blitz* or simply the *Blitz* (1939, from German *Blitzkreig*, also 1939 with *Blitz* meaning "lightning" and *Krieg* meaning "war," itself an overpowering high-speed armored attack). The attacks brought on the use of such terms as *air raid*, *air raid shelter*, *air raid warden*, *blackout*, and *bomb shelter* (more common than *air raid shelter* in 1940).

the bazooka (perhaps from the Dutch *bazuim*, "trumpet;" perhaps from the slang *bazoo*, meaning "big or loud mouth" since 1860), originally a homemade trombone made in 1905 by Bob Burns, a comedian, from two pieces of stovepipe and a whiskey funnel. By the 1930s, the bazooka had become a popular stock feature in Burns's act, and in 1943, U.S. Army Major Zeb Hastings named the infantry's new anti-tank rocket launcher after it.

the black market, as originally used in World War II, meant the market in stolen military supplies, but soon came to mean the illegal market in rationed or scarce items such as cigarettes or silk stockings.

A general purpose vehicle on training maneuvers in North Carolina, a month before the Japanese attack on Pearl Harbor brought America into World War II.

concentration camp, which has been in the language over a hundred years, nowadays refers mainly to the prison camps where Germans tortured, starved, and killed millions of people during World War II. Though hints of their existence had emerged as early as the 1930s, Americans discovered the full horror only in 1945 when Allied forces began liberating these *death camps* (attested to 1944) and discovering the *gas chambers* (1945) and other features of the German attempt at *genocide* (1945, from Greek *genos*, race + *-cide*, killing, killer).

Dear John (letter), early 1940s, a letter to a soldier from his sweetheart, fiancée, or wife, announcing that she was breaking with him, usually because she had found another.

ersatz, a borrowing of the German word for "substitute," used widely by 1940 to denote the artificial foods and synthetic items that were replacing war-scarce natural ones on both sides of the conflict.

flak, antiaircraft fire, 1938 (from the German acronym for *Flieger Abwehr Kanone*, "aircraft defense gun"). *Flak jacket*, a padded vest worn by air crews as body protection against flak.

GI Joe. In the 1920s, *G.I.* meant a heavy army garbage can, from the abbreviation for the material it was made of, galvanized iron. By 1935, however, *G.I.* stood for *General Issue* (some say *Government Issue*), the initials stamped or stenciled on everything issued to soldiers. Meanwhile, from the 1920s through the 40s, *Joe* began to rival *John* as the name for any typical male. Lieutenant Dave Berger combined *G.I.* and *Joe* in his June 17, 1942 comic strip for *Yank*, the Army weekly. Soon *GI Joe* became the name for any American soldier, often shortened to just *GI*.

gizmo, *gismo*, 1943, a thing whose name is unknown; the word seems to have originally been used in the Navy, but its origin is unknown.

gung ho, 1942, a motto used by some U.S. Marines in Asia, from Mandarin Chinese *gonghé*, to work together, short for the Chinese name for the Chinese Industrial Cooperative Society, with *gong* meaning "work" and *hé*, meaning "together," coming to be an adjective in American English meaning "enthusiastic."

Jeep, an army word which the rest of America first heard on February 22, 1941, the day this tough, agile vehicle was publicly exhibited. The origin is in dispute, but strong influences on the name include both the Ford Motor Company's initials for this military vehicle, *GP*, for "general purpose," and E. C. Segar's *Eugene the Jeep*, an animal that first appeared in his *Popeye* comic strip on March 16, 1936, making the peeping noise "jeep, jeep," and able do almost anything.

a kamikaze, *kamikaze pilot* (Japanese from *kami*, "divine, godlike" + *kaze*, "wind"), one of the Japanese *suicide pilots* ready to die for their emperor-god and the glory of Japan. They crashed obsolete planes, each carrying a 55-pound bomb, into American ships and other targets. Americans learned the word *kamikaze* in October 1944, when the pilots first attacked U.S. Navy ships in the Battle of Leyte Gulf.

liberate and *liberation*. At a press conference in May 1944, a month before D-Day, President Roosevelt said that after the invasion of Europe began, Americans would be using the word "liberation—not invasion." Thus, the *liberation* labeled the Allied advance against the Germans in Western Europe, and Allied troops *liberated* cities rather than capturing or occupying them. U.S. forces also used *liberate* in connection with the spoils of war; they "liberated" bottles of French wine or "liberated" watches from captured German soldiers.

The painting of a combat artist, from the memory of a kamikaze attack made on the *USS Hornet*.

Liberty ship. This was the standardized World War II cargo ship of 11,000 tons deadweight capacity built by Henry J. Kaiser's West Coast shipyards, using assembly-line methods.

Mae West, a canvas and rubber inflatable life vest worn by air crews. Royal Air Force aviators first bestowed the name on it because, when inflated, it gave one a chest size reminiscent of American entertainer Mae West.

POW, the common abbreviation for *prisoner of war* during World War II, giving us the term *POW camp.*

radar. One of the most important inventions of the war, it was developed by Scotland's Robert Alexander Watson Watt, an Air Ministry adviser on telecommunications. It was first used by the British—but they called the device, which uses high-frequency radio waves, a *radiolocator*. The U.S. Navy called it *radar* (an acronym for *ra*dio *d*etecting *a*nd *r*anging) when it publicly revealed the device in the spring of 1943.

Remember Pearl Harbor!—recalling *Remember the Alamo!* and *Remember the Maine!*—became the initial war slogan and battle cry of the U.S. after 360 Japanese planes attacked U.S. naval and air bases in Hawaii at 7:55 Sunday morning December 7, 1941.

roger!, used by pilots to mean "your message received and understood" in response to radio communications; later it came into general use to mean "all right, OK." *Roger* was the code word for the letter *R*, which in this case represented the word *received.*

sack, almost completely replaced the word "bed" among our servicemen in World War II (*bed sack* had meant a sack to carry bedding in since 1661, and colonial beds were often just long sacks of cornhusks, hay, leaves, etc.). By 1943 *to hit the sack, to sack out,* and *to sack in* all meant to "go to bed," or "go to sleep."

sad sack, originally a 1930s term for a blundering, unpopular student, became a common World War II label for the citizen as a misfit in military life—confused, put upon, and unkempt. George Baker began his *Sad Sack* comic strip for armed forces publications during the war.

shack up, 1940, to set up housekeeping and live with a local woman near one's military base; a woman with whom a man shacked up was called a *shack job.*

snorkel (German *Schnorchel*, "air intake, spiral"), introduced during World War II, when it meant a retractable tube for ventilating a submarine as it cruised slightly below the surface. By the late 1940s it came to mean a breathing tube used while swimming face down in the water on or close to the surface.

storm troopers, members of the Nazi party's *Sturmabteilung* or SA (*Sturm*, "storm, attack" + *Abteilung* "division, department"), organized in 1921 as the party's strong-arm squad. Storm troopers wore brown shirts as part of their uniform and were thus also called the *Brownshirts.*

SS troops, members of Hitler's *Schutzstaffel* ("protective echelon"), formed around 1923 as an elite corps of storm troopers who served as bodyguards for Nazi leaders. Under Heinrich Himmler, the SS men were Hitler's "Secret Police." They assassinated and tortured prisoners into making confessions, and arrested and shipped non-Aryans to concentration and death camps, which the SS built and ran. They wore black shirts as part of their uniform, so became known as the *Blackshirts.*

task force, a naval attack force on a special mission or patrol. The public first heard the term in news reports of the task force carrying out the amphibious landings in North Africa in November 1942.

tin can. Destroyers were called *tin cans* because they were the smallest fleet vessels and had the thinnest armor. A *rust bucket* meant any old ship, but in World War II it especially meant a destroyer.

the underground, the loose network of small groups throughout Nazi-occupied Europe that continued to resist the Germans. The French underground was the largest and was called *the resistance*, its members often termed *resistance fighters*. Guerrilla groups that continued to fight against the Axis after their countries were defeated, especially in Greece and Yugoslavia, were called *partisans*. Those who accepted and worked with the Nazi conquerors were called *collaborators.*

walkie-talkie, a radiotelephone combining a receiver and transmitter in one unit light enough to be carried by one man (thus it both "walked" and "talked"). It was developed by the Signal Corps in 1933, and the Army had used the name before the war.

The war that began with a *blitzkrieg* ended with the *atomic bomb*. The U.S. detonated the first of these in the desert at Alamagordo, New Mexico, at 5:29:45 A.M. on July 16, 1945. It was the beginning of the *Atomic Age*. Three weeks later, on August 6, 1945, as many as 66,000 people died in Hiroshima when the B-29 Superfortress *Enola Gay* dropped the first atomic bomb used in war. Three days later, a second bomb killed some 36,000 in Nagasaki. Japan surrendered on August 14, and World War II was over.

People immediately shortened *atomic bomb* to *atom bomb*, which then became *A-bomb* or simply *the bomb* before the year's end. *Fireball*

"I was the first American commander to put his signature to a paper ending a war when we did not win it."

— General Mark W. Clark, October 21, 1953, upon his retirement as Supreme Commander, UN Forces, Korea

took on a new meaning and *mushroom cloud* came into use. *Nuclear weapons* (soon shortened to *nukes*) filled the postwar news, and things became even more ominous in 1950 with something under development called an *H-bomb*, a *hydrogen bomb*.

The U.S. and USSR had emerged from the war as the planet's two *superpowers*, leading the *Free World* and the *Communist Bloc* in *the Cold War* (1946), a struggle that featured such things as the doctrine of *massive retaliation* (1954, the threat to meet foreign military aggression with a nuclear response), and the research and diplomacy aimed to give one's side an advantage in the *nuclear arms race*.

RESISTING COMMUNISM

On June 25, 1950, with full approval of the Soviet and Chinese leaders, North Korean troops crossed the *38th parallel* and invaded South Korea. The U.S. immediately sponsored a resolution in an emergency session of the UN Security Council which declared North Korea an aggressor and, on June 27, the Council called upon the UN's 52 member nations to repel the invasion.

At his first news conference after American entry into the fighting, President Truman was quoted as saying that the U.S. was not at war but engaged in a *police action* under UN authority. Since America never declared war—though Truman himself later used the phrase *limited war* in referring to the fighting—Congress termed it the *Korean Conflict* in passing various military appropriations. Within a year, however, most Americans called it the *Korean War*.

Any list of Korean War terms shows one obvious thing: there are not many of them. The war made little impact at home. Americans were not emotionally involved. The new words used by our armed forces include several from the Japanese—such as *honcho*—because at the beginning of the war, the U.S. rushed troops into Korea from Japan, where they had been serving as Post-World War II occupation forces:

brainwashing, a new word of 1950, first used to refer to a combination of physical torture, threats, intimidation, promises, and around-the-clock indoctrination used by Communists to break down the loyalties of anti-Communist resistance fighters (it seems to be a loan-translation of the Chinese Communist term for it, *hsi nao*, *hsi* meaning "wash" and *nao* "brain"). At the end of the war, Americans learned that some U.S. prisoners of war had been successfully *brainwashed*.

Boeing's B-52 bomber has been in service in five different decades, from the 50s to the 90s. Along the way, it's given its name to a ladies' hairstyle, a liquor drink and a rock band.

"1, 2, 3, what are we fighting for? Don't ask me, I don't give a damn. My next stop is Vee-et-NAM."— from a popular protest song of the late 60s.

chopper and *whirly bird*, common terms for a helicopter during the Korean War, the first war in which the aircraft saw extensive service in transporting troops and supplies. *Helicopter* (from Greek *helix*, "spiral" + *pteron*, "wing") had been in the language since 1887 (the Wright brothers built and experimented with helicopters), and the synonym *gyroplane* (1907) had been popular in the 1930s.

DMZ, the abbreviation of *de*militarized *z*one, referred to the area on both sides of the *38th parallel* separating North and South Korean troops. Many also used it to mean the 38th parallel itself. Similarly, in Vietnam, the *DMZ* meant the demilitarized zone centered on the 17th parallel or that dividing line itself. Another abbreviation inextricably associated with the Korean War and used subsequently in Vietnam was *MASH*—*m*obile *a*rmy *s*urgical *h*ospital, to which the wounded were *choppered* for treatment.

germ warfare, a science-fiction term until early 1952 when it appeared in newspaper headlines. After serious epidemics swept North Korea early that year, the population blamed the Communists for lack of proper medical care, food, and shelter. The Communists tried to shift the blame by charging the United Nations with "germ warfare," torturing and brainwashing 78 captured American pilots until 38 of them confessed—falsely—to dropping loads of cholera-infested insects on North Korea.

honcho (1947, from Japanese *han*, "squad" + *cho*, "leader," literally "squad leader," a corporal or sergeant), saw wide U.S. armed forces use in Korea to mean "leader, boss, man in charge," and soon entered general American slang.

Mama-san, literally "boss mother," was used by U.S. troops to mean a brothel madam. *Papa-san*, "boss man, the man in charge," was also used, the suffix -*san* being added to many English and pidgin words in imitation of Japanese use.

Just 13 years after the cease-fire that ended the Korean War on July 27, 1953, the U.S. was again sending ground forces to Asia, this time to Vietnam. Between the late 1950s and 1965, Americans termed it *the war in Viet Nam*, but once U.S. troops began fighting there in 1965, most called it the *Vietnam War*. As with Korea, America never officially declared war, so some politicians employed such euphemisms as the *Vietnam conflict*. However, with more U.S. troops involved than in Korea and more tons of bombs dropped than during all of World War II, it was certainly a war.

The important names and terms of the Vietnam War include:

advisers, *military advisers*. As the Communist pressure on South Vietnam increased through the late 1950s, President Eisenhower finally agreed to help train its troops. In 1961, after the *Viet Cong* had entered the fighting, South Vietnam asked for still more help, and the new president, John F. Kennedy, sent *Special Forces* as *military advisers*, often simply called *advisers*, to direct the defense of villages and military outposts. By mid 1965, when our troops first entered combat, 23,000 *advisers* were in South Vietnam.

airmobile, 1965, referred to U.S. infantry units equipped with their own helicopters to fly them into battle.

counterinsurgency, a new word in 1961, the year the U.S. established a *Counter-Insurgency Committee* to devise ways to meet the Communists' techniques of unconventional warfare. In the early 60s it appeared with a hyphen, *counter-insurgency*, and some used the acronym *COIN* (from *counter-in*surgency). Originally the concept included psychological warfare and political reforms, but soon it merely meant fighting guerrillas with guerrillas of one's own.

defoliate, to spray chemicals or use incendiary bombs on trees or crops in order to deprive enemy forces of concealment or food. This term acquired notoriety during the 1964 presidential campaign when the Republican Barry Goldwater suggested that small atomic bombs might be used to destroy areas of the Vietnamese jungle to deprive Communist guerrillas and supply columns of places to hide. And *Agent Orange* (1970, so called from the orange identification stripe on its storage barrels)—the dioxin-containing *defoliant* widely used in this war, became a word-symbol for the *defoliation* mission.

firebase, late 1960s, probably 1968, an artillery emplacement with its own troop protection, ammunition, and supply dumps, which often sustained *in-coming* (i.e., in-coming enemy fire). With no front lines at which to mass fire power, U.S. forces often established the bases near strategic cities and supply lines.

fire fight, used in U.S. military communiqués to replace the 14th century English word *skirmish*.

fragging (first recorded in print only in 1970), originally named incidents in which soldiers killed an officer by rolling a *fragmentation grenade* (hence *to frag, fragging*) into his tent, but by the late 1960s, it denoted the killing of one's officer by any means. Soldiers usually *fragged* officers whom they considered overzealous in seeking out and pursuing the Viet Cong, especially after mid 1969, when the U.S. began withdrawing, and no soldier cared to take unnecessary risks when he would soon go home.

grunt, late 1960s. Originally, U.S. Marines used the term to refer to an infantryman; then the foot soldiers themselves used it, referring to the usual complaints grunted by soldiers in response to the hard work of hiking and fighting in the jungle.

gunship, an old Navy term, meant by the mid 1960s a helicopter armed with cannons and rockets and serving as flying artillery to support ground troops.

hooch (from Japanese *uchi*, "house"), used by U.S. troops in the Korean War primarily to mean the hut, house, or room of a prostitute or a house where a serviceman set up housekeeping with his native girlfriend. In Vietnam, it first meant a typical Vietnamese jungle hut, and later, any living quarters, especially a barracks or *Quonset hut* (the last being a trademark named after Quonset Naval Base in Rhode Island where it had been developed from a British design many years before). (See BOOZE, section Booze and Bars)

KIA and *MIA*, long been military abbreviations for *killed in action* and *missing in action* but now came into wide use in news reports and conversation. The abbreviations also became nouns, with a serviceman labeled a *KIA* or *MIA* if killed or missing in action. With reference to slaying the enemy, *body counts* and *kill ratios* became familiar through news accounts. Joining these was *body bag*, euphemized during the 1991 Persian Gulf War to *human remains pouch*.

napalm (from the chemical name *na*phthalene *palm*itate). Flamethrowers and incendiary bombs had employed this jellylike mixture containing gasoline since World War II, but it now gained wide notoriety when

"It was the defining event . . . and remains a thousand degrees hot."

— *John Wheeler,* Touched With Fire, *1985, on the Vietnam War*

antiwar groups denounced its use on enemy troops and Communist-controlled hamlets.

SAM, the abbreviation for *surface-to-air missile* since the 1950s, but during the Vietnam War, it became the pronounceable acronym, "sam," for such a missile. Russian-built SAMs defended major targets in North Vietnam.

the Viet Cong, *V.C.*, and *Charlie*, as opposed to the *ARVIN*, pronounced "ARvin," an acronym for *A*rmy of the *R*epublic of *V*iet *N*am (South Vietnam). In 1960, North Vietnam announced the formation of the National Liberation Front of South Vietnam Communists. Often called the *NLF* in the early 1960s, this organization, its members, and especially its uniformed soldiers and nonuniformed guerrillas, soon acquired the label *Viet Cong* (a short form of the Vietnamese for "Vietnamese Communist"), or simply *the Cong*. Americans abbreviated *Viet Cong* to *V.C.* Then, since the military code word for the letter *V* is *Victor* and for *C* is *Charlie*, they also called the Viet Cong *Victor Charlie* or just *Charlie*. The *Viet Cong* and the *North Vietnamese Regulars* plied the *Ho Chi Minh trail* (late 1950s onward)—their network of jungle supply routes from North Vietnam through Cambodia and Laos into South Vietnam.

The end was stark: on April 30, 1973, U.S. helicopters ferried the last 395 American diplomats and advisers from Saigon to U.S. warships waiting offshore. Within hours, South Vietnam announced its *unconditional surrender* to the Communists.

AFTER VIETNAM: NEW MISSIONS

"Almost fifty years ago, we began a long struggle against aggressive totalitarianism. Now we face another defining hour for America and for the world."

— President George Bush, January 1991, referring to the impending Persian Gulf War in his State of the Union address

In 1983, for example, American forces conducted "Operation Urgent Fury," an invasion of Grenada. A coup in 1979 had installed a Marxist government headed by Maurice Bishop that allied the nation with Cuba. The subsequent overthrow and execution of Bishop led to the invasion by the U.S.—with token forces from other Caribbean nations—to restore democratic rule. The U.S. government justified the invasion in part as a *rescue operation* meant to ensure the safety of Americans studying at a university on the island.

In late 1992, for another example, the U.S. sent troops to fulfill a *humanitarian mission* in Somalia. Their specific charge was *famine relief* in a country where the population had been decimated by starvation. Another sort of *intervention* undertaken by the armed forces was *peacekeeping*. One of the earliest such efforts had begun in the early 1980s after the withdrawal of Israeli forces from Egyptian territory in the Sinai Desert. There, Americans made up part of a United Nations command whose job was to ensure that the parties formerly in conflict kept their distance and maintained the peace. Another American *peacekeeping intervention* began during the winter of 1995–96 when U.S. forces, along with troops from other Western nations, went to Bosnia to enforce a cease-fire among the belligerents—Muslim and Christian, Serb, and Croat—who had been slaughtering one another with such ferocity that charges of *genocide*, euphemistically called *ethnic cleansing* by the perpetrators, had long since begun appearing on the pages of newspapers.

The most dramatic American military operation during this period, however, was the *Persian Gulf War*, which began as a political crisis after Iraq's invasion of Kuwait in August 1990 and ended with a dramatic "100-hour" land offensive in February 1991, that routed the Iraqis—while leaving their leader, Saddam Hussein, in power.

American Troops in Saudi Arabia in February 1991. While television brought the Vietnam War "up close and personal" into America's living rooms and fueled anti-war sentiments, advances in military technology allowed the Gulf War to be fought and viewed from a distance. It proved to be an unparalleled military success and one of the year's highest-rated television programs.

Though other American military operations of the period left no strong impress on the language, this war produced several terms with potential staying power:

Gulf War syndrome, the complex of symptoms suffered by some veterans of the war, who alleged exposure to Iraqi *chemical weapons*.

hummer, from *HMMWV*, pronounced "HUMM-vee," the acronym for the U.S. forces *High-mobility Multipurpose Wheeled Vehicle*. The *hummer*, ubiquitous in the Gulf War, had replaced the jeep during the 1980s.

Mother of All Battles. In a speech on January 11, 1991, Saddam Hussein insisted that his aim in resisting the U.S.-led forces arrayed against him was to conduct a holy war. He called on all Islamic leaders to prepare the "masses" for "the great *mother of all battles*"(as it was translated from the Arabic) against the allied *Coalition*. After wide media coverage of the speech, *the mother of all* (e.g., *storms, blizzards, flus*) came into heavy use.

Scud, a ballistic missile used by the Iraqis against targets in both Saudi Arabia and Israel. Developed by the Russians in the 1950s, it was a direct descendant of the German V-2 used against allied cities in 1944–45. The Iraqis fired a total of 81 Scuds. The U.S. countered with the *Patriot Missile*, soon shortened to the *Patriot*.

smart bomb, an aircraft-delivered munition guided to its target by a laser beam. During the Gulf War, television featured gun-camera footage of these bombs homing in on their targets with what seemed to be pinpoint precision. Actually, guided bombs were no recent addition to the American arsenal. Crude ones had been developed during World War II, and during the Vietnam War the U.S. employed roughly 21,000 such weapons against the North Vietnamese.

FIT AS A FIDDLE

*O*besity has always been an American problem, with one out of three Americans qualifying as **obese** (defined as 20 percent or more above a person's desirable weight) in 1990. Even with the recent growth of fitness facilities and fitness awareness since the 1970s, and the amount of publicity that health and fitness receive, the fact remains that only a very small percentage of the American population actually engages in serious exercise on the recommended "two or three times a week" basis.

Jogging, which swept the nation in the mid 1970s, was the *exercise fad* credited with launching the modern fitness movement. By the mid 1980s the favorite form of exercise was *aerobics* (1967)—group exercise classes, frequently to music, aimed at keeping the heart beating at 60 to 90 percent of its maximum for at least 20 minutes, three times a week. Participation in exercise decreased 10 percent between 1985 and 1990, due largely to conflicting reports in the media about the benefits, fear of injury, lack of time, and the economic downturn. In the 1990s, the focus of fitness programs shifted to *strength training* and less joint-jarring, more accessible forms of exercise like walking.

THE FITNESS GURUS

A graduate of the College of New Jersey (now Princeton University) by the age of 15, Dr. Benjamin Rush was a signer of the Declaration of Independence and surgeon general of the Continental army. In addition to physical fitness, Rush also advocated the medical practices of bloodletting and purging.

Dr. Benjamin Rush, one of the signers of the Declaration of Independence and probably the best-known colonial physician in America, was—along with Wiliam Byrd—an early advocate of the benefits of physical exercise. Later came Sylvester Graham (of the *Graham cracker* fame), who attained national prominence in the 1830s as a nutritional reformer who advocated exercise, vegetarianism, and non-strenuous sex between long-term partners as the best route to a long and healthy life. Graham recommended that Americans go to the nearest *gymnasium* (from the Greek *gymnazein,* meaning "to train naked") and "swing upon and climb the poles and ropes and ladders and vault upon the wooden horse." He also ran a series of boarding houses where people came to regain their health.

If Graham's pre-Civil War push for fitness can be considered the first American *fitness craze,* then the second arrived after the war was over. German immigrants, many of whom were doctors, arrived in this country with an enthusiasm for *calisthenics* (from the Greek meaning "beautiful strength") and *water cures* (a loan-translation of German *Wasserkur,* first cited in English in 1842; German spas were famed for their mineral baths where one would "take the waters"). There was an explosion of interest in football, baseball, and other team sports. It was also during this period that Americans—particularly the well-to-do workers of the Northeast— bought the first *rowing machines* (1872, a stationary exercise device that simulates the motion of rowing a boat), ate "Granula" cereals, and started frequenting indoor gyms.

The third fitness craze began in the period of prosperity of the Roaring Twenties, when ethnic and racial tensions were rising, crime in cities was increasing, family farms were disappearing, labor unions were gathering strength, and women had won the right to vote. The surge in the number of Americans who exercised reflected not only their interest

If running is more a way of life than a sport, then Dr. George Sheehan was the Emerson to Jim Fixx's Thoreau.

in health but the growing need for regeneration; exercise was seen as both good for the spirit and an antidote to the evils of urban life.

Charles Atlas (born Angelo Siciliano in 1893) embodied the early 20th century ideal of fitness. The stereotypical *90-pound weakling* who had had sand kicked in his face by the Coney Island lifeguard who stole his girlfriend, Siciliano started building up his muscles by lifting weights. By 1922 he was dubbed "America's Most Perfectly Developed Man" at a *physical culture* exhibition held at the original Madison Square Garden in New York City. After seeing a statue of Atlas, the Titan in Greek mythology compelled to support the heavens on his shoulders, Siciliano changed his name to Charles Atlas and, with the help of a young advertising man named Charles P. Roman, started marketing a highly popular mail-order *body building* course. The home-study program combined *isotonic* exercises (from the Greek *isos*, "equal," and *tonos*, "tension" or "tone"; the term refers to lifting certain fixed amounts of weight, keeping the tension on the muscles equal during the exercise) and nutrition tips.

During the 1930s, most Americans were too worried about their jobs and basic necessities to frequent tennis courts, ball fields, and swimming pools. But after World War II, interest in fitness and health picked up again under the leadership of three American presidents who showed a personal commitment to physical activity. Harry S. Truman was known for taking his daily "constitutional," or brisk walk. Dwight Eisenhower, whose love of golf was legendary, founded the *President's Council on Youth Fitness* in 1956 to raise the fitness level of American school children to that of European youngsters. The Council became even more important under the Kennedy administration. John F. Kennedy was not only the second youngest American president (albeit one who suffered from chronic back pain) but the one who put physical fitness on the map, advocating *fitness testing* for all school-age children and vigorous *phys ed* (abbreviated form found in the early 1950s; the full form, *physical education*, known from 1858) programs in the nation's elementary and high schools. In fact, Kennedy came to be associated with the word *vigor* (14th century), which he pronounced "VIG ah" in the typical Boston r-dropping manner.

The first modern *fitness guru* was Dr. Kenneth Cooper, whose 1968 book *Aerobics* sold more than 12 million copies over the next decade. A physician and exercise physiologist, Cooper believed that a high level of *aerobic fitness* (meaning exercise so vigorous that it requires the maximum consumption of oxygen by the body) was essential for a long, healthy life. To achieve it, he recommended walking three miles in less than 45 minutes, five days a week, or running two miles in less than 20 minutes, four times a week. Cooper's standards became the basis for aerobic exercise programs across the country, and his Institute for Aerobics Research performed studies showing that a *sedentary lifestyle* was comparable to the hazards of high cholesterol, high blood pressure, or cigarette smoking.

George Sheehan, a New Jersey cardiologist, began running to stay in shape while recovering from a broken hand. His lectures, columns, and books (which include *This Running Life* and *Running and Being*) promoted *jogging* in the mid 1970s but warned that exercise regimes must be "respected, not worshipped." One of his most devoted readers was James F. Fixx, a magazine editor who had injured himself playing tennis at the age of 35 and had starting running to strengthen his legs. Before long, Fixx had quit

At various times, Jane Fonda has been a college drop-out, sex-kitten movie star, anti-war activist, Academy Award winning actress, billionaire's wife, and exercise guru. Her fitness career has been far more successful than her foreign policy initiative, and she's still "going for the burn" in her 50s.

smoking two packs of cigarettes a day, lost 60 pounds, and published *The Complete Book of Running* (1977), a user-friendly fitness manual that became a number-one best seller. Fixx's unexpected death at age 52 from a heart attack while he was out running struck a telling blow to the fitness movement and to the millions of Americans who had helped him make jogging its symbol. But autopsy results showed that Fixx was suffering from advanced atherosclerosis, a progressive circulatory disease. He was fit when he died, but not healthy.

The experts who launched the fitness movement of the 1970s were replaced by television and movie stars promoting their own exercise regimes on *fitness videos*. Actress and political activist Jane Fonda started the celebrity trend with the publication of *Jane Fonda's Workout Book* in 1981, admonishing her readers to *Go for the burn*, the burning sensation experienced when a muscle has been used very strenuously. Fonda went on to make a number of exercise videos and to open a chain of *fitness centers*. Exercising at home in front of the television was particularly appealing to people who didn't have the time or money to join a *health club*, and the availability of VCRs, which began to appear in American homes in the early 1980s, gave the exercise video movement a boost. With titles like *Buns of Steel*, these home exercise videotapes encouraged Americans to turn their living rooms into fitness centers.

Richard Simmons, who had a serious weight problem himself before dieting and exercising his way to thinness, was one of the first non-celebrity figures to earn a nationwide reputation by advocating weight loss through exercise. Known for his sympathetic, upbeat approach to helping overweight women, Simmons made a fortune in the 1980s from his books and television appearances, and continued to promote his approach (and his videos) into the 1990s.

There are also exercise videos for *people with disabilities* ranging from spinal cord injuries to cardiopulmonary disease, multiple sclerosis, Parkinson's disease, and the aftereffects of stroke. Most of these videos are put out by hospitals and health care companies.

FITNESS FADS

Running and jogging peaked as fads and lost some popularity, but Americans still seek ways to exercise that bring maximum health benefits with minimal risk or effort. Various new forms of exercise and specialized exercise equipment have from time to time captured the health-conscious American's attention. Here's a brief glossary of America's favorite fitness fads represented by the words Americans used as they talked about them:

aerobics. One of the most popular ways for women to get fit in the early 1980s was by taking *aerobic dance* classes. Usually led by attractive young female instructors wearing skin-tight *Spandex*, these classes were particularly popular among women in their 20s and 30s. Dance routines incorporating vigorous arm and leg movements kept the heart beating in its *target zone* (calculated by subtracting your age from 220, then multiplying by 65 to 85 percent) for at least 20–30 minutes. *Step aerobics*, introduced in the late 1980s, involved following an instructor through routines that incorporated stepping on and off a small platform of adjustable height, thus adding the benefits of stair-climbing to regular aerobic exercise. *Double step* and *power step* aerobics soon followed, offering an even more intense aerobic *workout.*

The early aerobics classes were *high-impact*, meaning that they included moves like *jumping jacks* where both feet were off the ground simultaneously. Because of the stress that high-impact movements placed on the knees, hips, and ankles, *low-impact* aerobics (where one foot is always on the floor at any given time) largely replaced these more jarring movements. But in the mid 1990s, just when yoga and other less stressful forms of exercise were beginning to catch on, high-intensity aerobic classes made a comeback. Most gyms and health clubs now offer both high- and low-impact classes.

Aerobic classes usually begin with a *warm-up*, a period of stretching and moderate exercise that gradually raises the pulse rate to its target zone. The class ends with a *cool-down*, another period of less intense exercise that gives the heart time to return to normal. Such classes may incorporate *floor exercises* as well. *Crunches* (an abdominal exercise that has largely replaced traditional *sit-ups*), *push-ups*, *leg lifts*, and other exercises performed while lying down on an *exercise mat* help tone specific muscle groups and are usually performed at the end of the class, after the *cardiovascular workout* has benefited the heart.

Aerobics are popular with men as well as women, and this type of exercise is widely regarded as a means of promoting *cardiovascular fitness* and endurance. While the term usually refers to group exercise classes, any form of exercise that is rhythmic, sustained, and uses the *large muscle groups*—such as brisk walking, jogging, cross-country skiing, swimming, cycling, or jumping rope—qualifies as "aerobic exercise" if it increases the heart rate to its optimum *training level* (or target zone) and keeps it there for the magic minimum of 20 minutes, three times a week.

Some aerobics classes integrate dance steps with more traditional exercise moves. *Jazzercise* and *aerobic dance* were among the earliest trends in this direction. More recently, *funk* (a form of movement that incorporates ballet, jazz, hip hop, and modern dance with an African flavor) offers a low-impact aerobic workout for people who don't have any technical dance training.

slide-board training. This is the ultimate in low-impact aerobic exercise. The exerciser wears fabric booties over regular aerobic shoes that enable him or her to slide easily back and forth on a specially-coated exercise mat. *Sliding* provides a rigorous workout for the lower body, simulating the movements used in *speed skating* or *skate-skiing* (on lighter, shorter cross-country skis). It is known for working those muscles that other forms of exercise often neglect.

fitness walking. This is walking at a pace that provides *aerobic exercise.* It offers all the health benefits of running, but with a much lower risk of injury. The recommended pace is at least four miles per hour for at least 30 minutes.

marathons (a running race of just over 26 miles, 395 yards, approximately the distance that the ancient Greek Pheidippides covered when he ran from Marathon to Athens to bring news of the victory over the Persians in 490 B.C.), *biathlons* (which usually consist of running and biking) and *triathlons* (usually running, biking, and swimming) are

Neither cold nor snow deters this jogger from her appointed rounds.

endurance contests that used to attract only *hard-core athletes* but are now popular with amateur athletes all over America. One of the most famous is the *Iron Man Triathlon*, held in Hawaii. These *endurance events* spawned *ultramarathons* with up to 100-mile races, as athletes tested human limitations.

walking poles. These are aluminum poles with special ski pole grips and rubberized tips which are spring-loaded so that the pole retracts slightly when planted on the road or walking surface and reduces jarring in the hands, arms, and torso. Walking with poles is not unlike using a cane or walking stick. It increases the aerobic benefits of walking and is particularly good for people with foot or knee problems because it reduces stress in the joints.

walkshaping. This combines walking with *body sculpting* (using light *dumbbells* and *ankle weights* to firm and tone all the muscles of the body). It is another variation on regular walking. Its routines are made up of walking movements with exaggerated arm and leg swings to maximize the benefit of the wrist or ankle weights.

biking. Between 1870 and 1900, cycling had become America's first real fitness fad. Even middle-class women took up the sport. In much the same way that jogging and *health clubs* would reinforce the growing equality of women in the 1970s and 80s, cycling offered turn-of-the-century women physical mobility and the opportunity to pursue fitness as men had been doing for some time.

Cycling went through a number of changes since the early 1900s. In the 1970s, everyone was buying *ten-speed bikes* (bikes with thin tires, lightweight frames, and ten gears of speed to enable cyclists to get up steep hills). In the 1980s Americans turned to *mountain bikes*, which had wide, treaded tires (*fat tires*) and gears that enabled cyclists

"Daisy, Daisy, give me your answer do/I'm half crazy, all for the love of you/It won't be a stylish marriage/I can't afford a carriage/But you'll look sweet upon the seat/Of a bicycle built for two"—from a popular song of 1892.

In many parts of America, mountain bikes are now the choice for off-road workouts and races.

to ride *off-road*. Then came the *hybrid bike*, with rugged frame and treaded tires, but lightweight like *street bikes* or *racers*, and sporting up to 21 gears. *Stationary biking*, which had been around *health clubs* for many years, became even more popular in the 1980s. Stationary cyclists aboard their machines (some even computer-controlled with preset courses available at the touch of a button) could avoid boredom by watching television, reading, or listening to music while they exercised.

spinning. A variation on indoor stationary biking, *spinning* became, in the 1990s, the biggest new exercise fad since the introduction of step aerobics in the late 1980s. The modified bicycles used for spinning were built with the pedals below the seat—unlike *stationary bikes*, built with the pedals slightly in front of the exerciser, or *recumbent bikes*, on which the exerciser leaned back and extended his or her legs to pedal. They also had a fixed gear so that the exerciser could maintain a set speed while going into a stand-up position and not lose balance. The specialized equipment used in spinning was developed in 1987 by California long-distance cyclist Johnny Goldberg. He patented his spinning routine in 1990.

Spinning is a group activity, with an instructor, and it includes moves like *running* (cycling while standing on the pedals), *jumping* (alternately standing up quickly, then sitting down), *going up hills* (using increasingly harder resistance), and *rhythm presses* (pressing the upper part of the body toward the handlebars). It provides a high-intensity cardiovascular workout.

in-line skating. Though most American adults had abandoned their roller skates in fourth grade, many began, in the late 1980s, to buy expensive new *in-line skates*, trademarked as *Rollerblades* (the earliest successful brand), which combine the rigidity of a downhill ski boot with the lightness and comfort of an ice skate. But instead of having two sets of wheels front and back, in-line skates have all the wheels in a single row down the center, enabling the exerciser to skate on pavement with a smooth, rhythmic motion much like skating on ice. Starting as a fitness and recreation item, in-line skates also came to be used by urban commuters and delivery people, who could beat the traffic and still move at efficient speed.

Exerlopers.® These are a cross between a pogo stick and an in-line roller skate. Developed by Gregory Lekhtman, a Russian neurophysiologist looking for a less stressful alternative to jogging, the molded plastic boots have two elliptically-shaped springs with a tension band sandwiched in between them. As the exerciser walks or runs in the boots, the springs cave together, then bounce apart, lifting the foot slightly off the ground with each step. The higher the leap (or lope), the more spring there is to each step. The springing motion slows the loper down, but also gives a better workout in a shorter amount of time.

yoga. This form of exercise, known in India and East Asia for thousands of years, first became popular in the U.S. within the *hippie culture* of the 1960s, and in the 1990s found its way into the mainstream of American fitness. Although the pace is slow and the emphasis is on concentration and breathing, yoga sessions can also be quite rigorous, causing the exerciser to break into a sweat while standing almost perfectly still. The typical yoga class consists of *asanas* (postures), stretching, and breathing exercises. Each posture is designed to stimulate the circulation in a particular part of the body and to improve the health of certain muscles and internal organs. The posture known as the *shoulder stand*, for example, entails lying face up and lifting the legs and hips into the air, supporting the bulk of the body's weight on the shoulders. This is believed to improve circulation in the thyroid gland, which is located in the neck.

There are a number of different approaches to yoga, each based on the methods of a particular *yogi* in India. *Hatha yoga* is most common in the United States, but even here there are three different types: *Astanga*, which repeats a set sequence of postures; *Iyengar*, which focuses on precision of form in the postures; and *Kripalu*, which teaches awareness of one's inner self while holding the postures. By the 1990s many aerobics teachers had integrated yoga into the *cool-down phase* of their classes.

As part of its journey from Hindu philosophy to yuppie calisthenics, yoga made its first American inroads with the hippie culture.

urban yoga, a combination of yoga stretches, balancing routines, and slow, strenuous calisthenics. It evolved in the 1990s as yuppies, stressed out from their high-pressure jobs, decided to relax, stretch, and focus on breathing rather than further exhausting themselves in aerobics or spinning classes.

t'ai chi. Known by the full name of *t'ai chi ch'uan*, this ancient system of postures and exercises was developed in China as a form of self-defense and as an aid to meditation. It involves slow, relaxed, sweeping movements and requires great patience. But it can result in improved physical fitness, mental alertness, and spiritual awakening. The term is cited in English to 1954.

aquacize, another form of low-impact exercise that avoids placing stress on the joints and is very popular with senior citizens. Aquacize classes are usually held in public or community swimming pools and involve jogging and performing various exercises with most of the body submerged in water. Such workouts have also proven beneficial to athletes recovering from injury.

kickboxing. Popular among both men and women, kickboxing is a *martial art* (like karate) that has been modified to provide a vigorous aerobic workout. In fact, kickboxing can burn more calories that cycling, running, or rowing. The basic moves include *bobbing and weaving* (darting continuously from side to side and back and forth); throwing punches like the *speed jab*, the *right cross*, or the *left hook*; and kicking high in the air in a way that works the muscles without placing stress on the joints.

exercise machines. Exercise machines can be found today in gyms, community centers, and health clubs as well as in private homes. *Ski machines* simulate the motions of *cross-country skiing*, working the upper as well as the lower body. *Stair climbers* enable the exerciser to duplicate the leg and foot movements required to walk up stairs while standing in one place and holding on to a handrail for balance. *Climbing machines* require moving the arms and legs simultaneously.

treadmills, a popular alternative to walking or jogging outdoors. The mid 90s witnessed an explosion of popularity for various *body shapers*, machines that promise, in only "a few minutes a day," to give the user *washboard abs* (well-defined abdominal muscles), *tight buns* (a shapely posterior), *great pecs* (developed pectoral muscles), or just help attain good muscle tone.

strength training, the process of building muscle power by lifting *free weights* (such as *dumbbells*) or working against resistance by using equipment like *Nautilus*, *Soloflex*, or *Universal* machines. While *aerobics* was the catch-word of the 1970s and 80s, *strength training* became the exercise trend of the 1990s. It results in improved performance in other sports, greater endurance and stamina, lower *body-fat content*, and gain of *lean muscle*.

In addition to dumbbells and *barbells*, strength training may use *ankle weights* or *wrist weights*, and elasticized *exercise bands* (which resemble giant rubber bands and come in different thicknesses). The rule is to start with fairly light weights and a limited number of *reps* (repetitions), gradually increasing as the muscles grow stronger.

resistance machine, found in most commercial gyms and health clubs, each machine is designed to build strength in a particular muscle or muscle group. The language of body strengthening is full of "clippings," or short forms: There is usually a machine that works the *abs* (abdominal muscles), one that builds strength in the *pecs* (pectoral muscles of the chest), and one that concentrates on the *hams* (hamstrings at the back of the thighs) and *glutes* (gluteus muscles of the buttocks). There are machines for the *quads* (quadricep muscles on the front the thighs) and *lats* (latissimus dorsi muscles than run below the shoulder blades to the waist) as well. The user performs an exercise or movement that forces the muscle to use its *full range of motion* against the resistance provided by the machine. The amount of resistance can be adjusted by adding or subtracting weights, bands, or other devices in various increments. Each movement is performed until the point of *momentary muscular failure* is reached (the point at which the build-up of lactic acid prevents further muscle contraction)—usually one *set* of 8 to 12 reps. As the muscle gets stronger, more resistance is added.

Many fitness advocates of the 1990s encouraged both professional and amateur athletes to *cross-train*—that is, to vary workouts with one favorite sport or activity by alternating with other forms of exercise. People who don't do anything but jog, for example, tend to *over-train* certain muscle groups while neglecting others. Cycling, swimming, and weight training, for example, are considered a great way for runners to cross-train. Special shoes, *cross trainers*, are sold to serious aficionados. *Circuit training* is another way to introduce more variety into a daily exercise routine. Circuit training classes usually alternate brief periods of aerobic exercise with weight lifting.

In-line skater Raphael Sandoz hams it up for the camera. Originally a sport of the young, in-line skating is attracting more and more mature Americans as a fun way to stay fit.

GYMS AND HEALTH CLUBS

In the early 1900s, Bernarr Macfadden (1868–1955) became the first American to see exercise as something that could be marketed. His *Physical Culture* magazine, which had more than 100,000 subscribers, was filled with articles not unlike those found in our modern health and fitness publications. With titles like "Owning Our Bodies" and "What's Wrong with Doctors?" they associated fitness with enhanced attractiveness and sexuality. Macfadden was a true crusader in the fitness movement, and he can be credited with many of our existing ideas regarding fitness.

Macfadden opened a chain of *Healthatoriums* in major American cities, which he promoted by putting on *physical culture shows.* Young women in tight leotards (tame precursors of the *thongs* originating in the 1970s and increasingly popular in the 1990s) demonstrated how the body could be improved through exercise, self-control, and positive thinking. Of course, gymnasiums were not new; but the idea of marketing them as a place where men and women could show off their bodies was. Macfadden was particularly interested in displaying women's bodies. In 1900 his second magazine, *Beauty and Health: Women's Physical Development*, organized an extensive series of contests to discover the most perfectly developed woman in America. Macfadden's determination to bring an end to prudery by linking sexuality to exercise is the forerunner of today's sexually-oriented *health clubs*, exercise clothing or *fitness wear* (including not only *thongs*, but *bike pants*, *unitards*, *compression shorts*, *tank tops*, *muscle shirts*, and other body-revealing garb), and exercise videos.

Health clubs have been through a number of changes since the days of Macfadden's Healthatoriums. In the 1960s and 70s, only fanatics or *health nuts* belonged to health clubs, but since the mid 1980s memberships doubled. The intimate *aerobic studio*, with mirrors on the walls and an instructor on a platform leading the class through its routines, gave way to the *supergym* where dozens of people crowd into large rooms filled with treadmills and stair climbers.

In an effort to boost memberships and offer subscribers a more pampered approach, some health clubs are now expanding their offerings to include a variety of *New Age* treatments. A sampling:

massage. Although massage (from the French verb *masser*, which may have been adopted from the Portuguese *amassar*, "to knead") is nothing new—most large health clubs have a *masseur* (male) or *masseuse* (female) on call—but a number of specialized approaches based on massage became popular at health clubs across America. *Shiatsu*—cited in English to 1967—is a Japanese approach to therapeutic massage using pressure points on the body to prevent and alleviate physical problems. (*Shiatsu* is a short form of *shiatsu-ryoho*, where *shi* means "finger," *-atsu* means "pressure," *ryoho* means "treatment.") *Cranio-sacral therapy* is the manipulation of the head, scalp, and nerve endings at the top of the spine. And *Rolfing* (1965–70, named for the American physiotherapist and inventor of the technique, Ida P. *Rolf* [1897–1979]) is the sometimes painful manipulation of muscle sheaths to realign tissue and bones.

reflexology, popular among the Amish, is an ancient Egyptian therapy based on the belief that the body's control panels are in the feet. It was rediscovered in America around 1870. Having one's feet rubbed by an experienced *reflexologist* has been known to alleviate all sorts of physical ailments. Some claim that it is as effective as *acupuncture*. Rubbing the middle of the right foot, for example, is supposed to relieve certain symptoms involving the liver. Walking barefoot is considered natural reflexology.

aromatherapy, a term coined by a French scientist named Gattefossé at the end of the 19th century to describe "the therapeutic use of odoriferous substances obtained from flowers, plants, and aromatic shrubs, through inhalation and application to the skin." This, too, was invented by the Egyptians, who built laboratories to study odors and develop highly specialized perfumes. Lavender, for example, is supposed to promote relaxation; rosemary, when massaged into a woman's breasts, is believed to break up fibrous tissue.

As commercial health clubs competed with each other for membership dollars, the struggle to come up with new gimmicks escalated. Those able to afford the membership fee at some clubs, for example, enjoyed swimming in an Olympic-sized pool wired with an *underwater sound system* or visiting a *sports simulation center*, well-equipped with computerized machines that allowing the exerciser to simulate the

"Stop the madness." Susan Powter (right) used this tag-line to tap into consumer disenchantment with diet and fitness programs in order to sell her own diet and fitness program.

motions of skiing down a mogul-studded mountainside while watching film footage of the terrain at a popular Colorado ski resort. In the mid 1990s even more complex exercise equipment exploiting new technologies like *virtual reality* and *biofeedback* were planned.

THE PERSONAL APPROACH

Affluent Americans began hiring *personal trainers*. A *personal trainer* is a fitness specialist who designs a personalized training program, based on the individual's fitness goals, and then comes to the home to oversee exercise sessions and make changes in the routine if necessary. A professional trainer is usually *H.F.I.C.-certified* (health fitness instructor certification from the American College of Sports Medicine or an equivalent organization) and trained in *CPR* (cardio-pulmonary resuscitation) and *nutritional science* as well.

The use of personal trainers became so widespread among Hollywood celebrities that many of the trainers themselves became stars, based on the success they had in whipping celebrity bodies into shape.

THE TREND TOWARD MODERATION— OR NO EXERCISE AT ALL

Many Middle Americans contented themselves with light or infrequent exercise (if any)—without personal trainers. They seemed willing to go on, at best, as *weekend athletes*, living with their *middle-aged spreads*, *spare tires*, *love handles*, and *front porches* (over ample waistlines), enduring scorn for *cottage-cheese thighs* (showing pockets of *cellulite*) and *double* or *triple chins*, content to do only *twelve-ounce curls* (lifting a beer can) as an *armchair quarterback* or a mere *couch potato*.

FOOD FOR THOUGHT:
AMERICA EATS

*T*he language of American food (before the 12th century, from Old English foda) is a study in dietary and linguistic contrasts. The words range from names of foods eaten for survival to those eaten for good health or merely for their good taste, from home-grown to international, from soul food to comfort food to junk food.

In the U.S. from the 1980s to the end of the century, terms like *lite, low-fat, no salt, meatless, fat-free, caffeine-free, sugar-free, low-* or *no-cholesterol,* and *low-cal,* sustained widespread currency. But people continued buying *snack foods* like the *Moon Pie* (the 1920s vintage chocolate-and-marshmallow cake "as big as a moon"), washing it down with an RC, *RC* standing for Royal Crown Cola.

And as new vocabulary entered American English, especially from the mid 1970s to the end of the century, some established vocabulary began to disappear. Going, going, almost gone by century's end were shouted lunch-counter instructions like "Hold the hail!" (of a soft drink, "no ice"). This is the very argot that gave us the familiar *BLT, mayo, combo,* and *coffee blonde* or *brunette* (with or without cream or milk, respectively). Replacing such expressions are voices from boxes at drive-thru fast-food outlets—"Original or crispy?"—and at upscale restaurants, *waitstaff* (early 1980s) who recite menu selections like these: "Tonight we are serving baked Manila clams with breadcrumbs and porcini, riscaldata (reheated) slices of bread sautéed in olive oil, grilled leeks in puff pastry. . . ."

But one category—purely American—has remained a favorite, transcending economic status and food fads. It is *soul food* (cited to 1964, but much older). Created by slaves in the Deep South, soul food is an expression of a culture.

People—black and white—talked about and enjoyed *collards* (1755, an altered form of *colewort,* and being a kind of kale), *likka* (pot liquor left from boiling collards and served especially to young children to keep them healthy), *trotters* (pigs' feet) served in vinegar and hot sauce, *hog jowls, hog maw* (the throat or gullet of a pig), *corn oysters* (fried fritters made of corn kernels), *cracklin's* (fried hog-fat crisps), *poke sallet* (an altered form of *poke salad,* the greens of pokeweed eaten as a salad), *black-eyed peas* (1728, cowpeas, originally grown for forage and green manure), *yams* (1657), and *okra* (1679)—both of African origin—*prawlines* (an altered form of *pralines*), *red-eye gravy, gumbo, jambalaya,* and *chitlins*

WAKE-UP CALLS: BREAKFAST FOOD

Breakfast food can, of course, be anything from "just a cup of coffee," as preferred by Lincoln, to *bagels* (1932, from Yiddish, ultimately from Old High German), to *Danish* (1928 in the pastry sense), to the large old-fashioned American breakfast of steak, eggs, and fried potatoes. Many colonials and early Americans ate *porridge* (oatmeal or other meal boiled in milk or water), but most made it out of cornmeal and called the dish *mush* (1671).

Shopping for cereal at the grocery store in 1970. In addition to the familiar "Cheerios" and "Wheaties," her options include "Sugar Jets" and "Sugared Frost O's: Sugar-Charged Oat Cereal."

Although *Cream of Wheat* had been packaged as a hot-cereal or porridge mix as early as 1893, *breakfast food* took on a new, specific meaning when a packaged cereal, *Ralston's Health Club Breakfast Food*, was advertised in 1899. Within the next 10 years *breakfast food*, *breakfast cereal*, and *cereal* had all come to mean packaged cold cereal.

DOUGHNUTS

Doughnuts (around 1809) are so called because they were originally small, solid balls or "nuts" of fried sweetened dough. The Pilgrims learned to make the solid ones during their stay in Holland, 1607–20, and brought them to New England; the Dutch, who called them *olykoek* (oily cake), soon brought them directly to New Amsterdam. (The form *olicook* is still used as a dialect word in the Hudson River Valley.) The New Amsterdam Dutch also introduced *crullers* (cited to 1818, from obsolete Dutch *krulle-koken*, a rolled-up cake) to America. These pieces of sweet egg batter fried in fat were "often shaped into *love knots*. (*Cruller*, still a U.S. dialect word, is now used chiefly in New England and Pennsylvania.) Our round, hole-in-the-middle doughnuts were first introduced by a 15-year-old Camden, Maine baker's apprentice in 1847.

PANCAKES, HOECAKES, JOHNNY CAKES, FLAPJACKS— AND WAFFLES

Early American *pancakes* (14th century) were made of ground parched corn or cornmeal. The earliest was the *Indian cake* (1607), made of parched cornmeal, water, and salt, also called a *no cake* (1634, from Narragansett *nokehick*, "it is soft," the soft batter being thrown and shaped from one hand to the other). *No cake* had become *hoe cake* by 1745, perhaps a mispronunciation of *no cake* or perhaps because it was sometimes cooked on a hoe blade (*hoecake* is still in use in parts of the South). If cooked in the ashes of a fire, it is also called an *ashcake* or *ashpone* (1810).

By 1739 people were eating the somewhat sweeter *johnny cake* (also spelled *jonnycake*). Its name may come from *jonakin*, a Native American dish of flat, thin cornmeal cakes fried in grease. *Shawnee cake* and *journey cake* were also common names for it, with *journey*, too, probably from *jonakin*.

By the 1740s Dutch-style *buckwheat cakes* had come to the colonies. We were calling both our cornmeal cakes and our wheat cakes *slapjacks* by 1796 (one slapped them into shape or into a skillet). Pancakes, also called *flapjacks* since around 1600, were called *flap cakes* and *battercakes* by the 1830s and *griddle cakes* by 1840.

Waffles (Dutch *Wafel*, wafer) were known to the *Mayflower* pilgrims from their stay in Holland and were later popularized in New Amsterdam by the Dutch themselves. *Belgian waffles* are still a popular menu item into the 1990s. (The verb *waffle*, "to act evasively," is probably a repeated form of the obsolete word *waff*, which meant "to yelp," and so is unrelated to the food term.)

AMERICAN CHEESE—AND BRIE

During the Revolutionary War, Americans missed the good imported English cheese they were used to, especially *cheddar* (around 1661, named after the English village where it was first made). Thus *American cheese* was a proud post-Revolutionary name of 1804, showing that we could be independent of British products. (The term *American cheese* later came to mean, by 1916, "processed" cheese.) By the 1860s our American cheddar was called *store cheese* or *factory cheese*; then in the 1920s and 30s we also began to call it *rattrap cheese* or *rat cheese*. Meanwhile, *bonny clabber* (1616), drained and pressed milk curd, was being made in America, forms of it called *pot cheese* by 1812, *smearcase* or *smiercase* by 1829 (from German *Schmierkäse*, smearing cheese or spreading cheese), and *cottage cheese* by 1848.

When, in the late 1970s and early 80s Americans began to take keen interest in what they felt were "exotic" foods, one cheese became inextricably associated with upscale eating: *brie*. This cheese is named for *Brie*, a district in northern France, and the word is cited in English to 1876.

SPREADING IT ON THICK: BUTTER, MARGARINE, AND PEANUT BUTTER

Butter dates to before the 12th century, via Middle and Old English from Latin *butyrum*, from Greek *bouturon*, cow + *turos*, cheese.

Oleomargarine (Latin *oleum*, oil + Greek *margaron*, pearl, from the pearl-like luster of a glyceride erroneously thought to be an ingredient) was in American English by 1873. It was called simply *oleo* by 1884. By World War II's end the word *margarine* (cited to 1873) had taken over.

Florence Fabricant, writing in a May 1986 edition of the *New York Times*, called *peanut butter* (cited to 1903) "the pâté of childhood." Whether smooth or crunchy, this staple of American spreads, and the groundnut of which it is made, have been enjoyed for decades by millions of American children and adults.

IS IT A BISCUIT OR A CRACKER?

Biscuit (Latin *bis*, twice + *coctus*, cooked) still means a crisp, flat cracker or cookie in Britain. By 1818, however, *biscuit* had come to mean a softer, raised breadstuff in America; as Noah Webster noted, American biscuits were "fermented" (leavened).

Retired ship captain Josiah Dent introduced the first "water biscuits" to be called *crackers* (1801, so called because these crisp "biscuits" of unleavened, unsweetened, rolled dough made a crackling noise when chewed), created in his Milton, Massachusetts bakery. *Crackers* (Dutch *krakelin*), as we know them, were called *soda crackers* in the U.S. by 1830. The small, round *oyster cracker* was a latecomer, dating from 1873. America's love affair with the *snack* (1757, from Middle English *snak*, bite, ultimately from Dutch) had begun.

BREAD: THE STAFF OF LIFE

Colonists ate and talked about Indian-style bread, made only from cornmeal, water, and salt, and called *pone* (1634, from Virginia Algonquian *poan*, *appoans*, cornbread, from an Algonquian word "to roast or bake"), *Indian bread* (1654), *pone bread* (1770s), and later *corn pone* (1859). When made with milk and eggs this became the fancier *corn bread* (1750). New Englanders ate a bread of rye flour, cornmeal, molasses, and yeast called *rye 'n' Injun* (*Injun* meaning "Indian meal," or cornmeal). Hunters, trappers, and others on the move ate *hardtack* (*tack* is an 18th century word for food).

In the 1830s and 40s everyone was talking of the new, light *salt rising bread*, also called *salt bread*; *salt rising bread* is still sold in the South. In the 1860s people were talking about the soft, white, bleached-flour *store-bought bread* or *bakery bread*. By the 1880s—over 100 years before the appearance of the first *bread machine* (1987)—it was cheaper to buy such bread than make other kinds; thus *white bread* became the American staple (and about 100 years later the adjective *white-bread* came to denote the blandness associated by some critics with the American middle class). *Sourdough bread* became associated with Alaskan gold rush prospectors soon after 1896 and a *sourdough* came to mean such a prospector.

Early Americans also ate some of their bread as *toast* (the English had eaten toast since the 14th century), made on *bread toasters*, long-handled forks to hold the bread over the fire. *French toast* was first a popular American dish and term in the 1870s. Almost the last word in toast was the electric *toaster* (1909). The first automatic *toaster* was developed in 1919. It would be left to the 1990s generation to invest *toast* with a new slang sense, "done for; finished; washed up," as in "That candidate is *toast*."

THE SANDWICH

The *sandwich* was named for John Montagu, the fourth Earl of Sandwich (1718–92). It was so called by 1762 because the earl had allegedly spent 24 hours nonstop at the gaming tables, during which time he ordered some meat and slices of bread, holding the meat between the bread slices and eating it while continuing to gamble.

Food Fact
Anadama bread, a New England term, denotes a loaf of white cornmeal, and molasses. Though its origin is unknown, it is said to come from "Anna, damn her!", uttered by a fisherman angry at his wife for always serving cornmeal and molasses. He allegedly added flour and yeast, baking the mixture while cursing her.

The first uniquely American sandwich was the *western sandwich* (now a sandwich with a *western omelet* as a filling). It was created when pioneers crossing the hot western plains found the eggs they carried with them quickly getting "high," so they mixed them with onions and served them on bread to cover up the strong flavor. The next widely discussed American sandwich was the *reception sandwich* accompanying the afternoon tea parties of the 1870s. These dainty sandwiches developed into our *finger sandwiches*, which accompanied 1920s cocktail parties (*finger food*, 1928). Our American *club sandwich* (1903), sliced chicken or turkey breast, tomatoes, lettuce, bacon, and mayonnaise with two or three pieces of bread, was also first widely popular in the 1920s, then associated with country clubs. It has been suggested that the first *club sandwich* was made in 1894 at the Saratoga Club in Saratoga Springs, New York or that it was created on a U.S. passenger-train club car.

In the 1930s people began making tall sandwiches of multiple layers called *Dagwood sandwiches*, named after Dagwood Bumstead, the comic-strip character in *Blondie* who made them on his midnight forages in the family refrigerator.

In the later 19th century, New Orleans tourists had begun to talk about the local *po' boy* or *poor boy*—fried oysters, French sausages, chicken salad, fried eggs, bacon, chopped green peppers and onions, and anything else available, that made a complete meal on a small loaf of French bread split horizontally. *Po' boys* are said to be named because they were given to young men begging for food.

Closely related to the *po' boy* is the *hero sandwich* or merely the *hero* by the 1920s, especially in New York City; *hero* by the 1990s had become generalized in use. It's also called a *grinder*, especially in Boston and other areas of New England; a *spuckie* (origin unknown) in the Italian section of Boston; a *hoagie* (possibly from *hog*), especially in Philadelphia and southern New Jersey; a *zep* (possibly a clipping of *zeppelin*, from its shape) in New Jersey; a *bomber* in Upstate New York; an *Italian* or *Italian sandwich* in Maine and parts of the southern Midwest; a *sub* or *submarine*, for its shape, now generalized; a torpedo, also because of its shape, in parts of New Jersey; a *wedge* or *wedgie*, especially in downstate New York and in Connecticut and Rhode Island; and a *Cuban sandwich* in Miami and Tampa, Florida.

In the 1980s into the 1990s one new sandwich was the *pocket sandwich*, often reduced to *pocket*. It was made of *pita* (1951, Modern Greek)—a flat, thin, oval bread easily separated into two layers forming a "pocket" into which a filling could be placed.

HOT DOGS

The American *hot dog* (1894, at Yale) has long been the most popular food at outdoor events. Originally the larger, beef *frankfurter* (1894, after Frankfurt, Germany) and the smaller, pork-and-beef *wienerwurst* (1889, "Vienna wurst") or *Vienna sausage* (around 1902) were two different sausages, especially in German neighborhoods—but they soon combined to become the American hot dog. *Frank* is cited to 1904, not becoming widespread in use until the late 1920s, with *hot dog stand* in wide use by 1920.

Ten cents in 1939 could get you a dog and a soda.

HAMBURGERS

Food Fact
In 1830 the first known recipe for *ketchup* American style appeared in the *New England Farmer*. By 1837 it sold in bottles of varying sizes priced from 33¢ to 50¢.

Hamburger (1884, "chopped or ground beef") takes its name from Hamburg, Germany, a city famous for chopped-meat dishes. *Hamburg steak*, always cooked and served as a steak, appeared in the U.S. around 1884 and was soon called *hamburger steak*. The English physician J. S. Salisbury, himself a food faddist, helped popularize it and *Salisbury steak* (1897). By 1912 enough people were finally putting their hamburger steaks on a bun so that *hamburger* came to mean the sandwich. *Cheeseburgers* appeared around 1938, with just *burger* in 1939.

THE CATCH OF THE DAY

"Birds Eye [has] brought out fish sticks (fresh fish coated with a special batter, breaded, fried, packed and then frozen)."

— Time, *October 12, 1953*

Aside from *catfish* (1612), *bass* (before the 12th century), and *shrimp* (14th century, from Old Norse, "to shrivel up"), one term captures the essence of 20th century American fish eating: *fish sticks*. *Fish sticks* entered American English (and the kitchen) in the 1950s, the term cited to 1953.

And then there's *scrod*, cited to 1841, a New England term for a young cod or haddock—the catch of the day—split and boned for cooking. This word is from Dutch, "slice." New Englanders joke that newcomers to the region often think that *scrod* is a kind of fish, like *tuna*.

A CHICKEN IN EVERY POT

"It takes a tough man to make a tender chicken," or so it's been said of poultry mogul, Frank Perdue.

Food Fact
Buffalo wings—fried chicken wings with hot sauce and blue cheese dressing—are named for Buffalo, New York.

On the frontier, domestic chicken was fancy eating; its presence on the table indicated that hardworking farmers and housewives had arrived. In 1838 *chicken fixings* meant any superior meal; this, in contrast to *common doins'*.

Southerners have been talking about *fried chicken* since 1710. *Southern*, *Maryland*, and *Kentucky fried chicken*, however, didn't become household words until the 1930s. Our American dish and term *chicken salad* have been around since 1841, and *chicken (pot) pie* since 1845, while southerners have enjoyed *chicken gumbo* since at least 1867, and *chicken à la king* was introduced in the 1880s.

STEAK AND PORK

Steak (from Old Norse *steik*, stick) has meant a strip of meat or fish cooked on a stick over a fire since the 15th century. From the earliest colonial times until the 1860s a steak was called a *beefsteak* (1711). By the 1760s some colonial eating establishments were billing themselves as *beef steak houses*. Since the mid 1860s *steak* has meant beefsteak. By the end of the 1860s the *beef steak house* was simply called a *steak house* (cited to 1762).

Various types of steaks are:

porterhouse steak, around 1758, from a now archaic sense of *porterhouse*, an alehouse or a chophouse, the first native American steak and steak name to become widely known, popularized as the "porterhouse beefsteak" around 1814.

tenderloin steak, around 1828, the choice and most expensive cut.

T-bone steak, around 1916, the most popular steak until after World War II.

A hog farm in Missouri.

sirloin steak (sirloin, 1554, a cut of beef from a section of the hindquarter in front of the round). *Sirloin* is a modern spelling of *sur-loin* (Old French *surlonge, sur*, over + *longe*, loin, hip, hence "over the loin," a hip cut).

Popular taste now demanded a *thick sirloin*, broiled over charcoal if possible. Thus in the late 1940s and 50s restaurants often advertised their *charcoal-broiled steaks*, later clipped to *charbroiled* (1968).

Pork products were a colonial staple from the first days of the Virginia Colony:

Virginia hams, also called *Tidewater hams*, were being exported to England under these names as early as the 1630s, though the names then meant any hams from Virginia or the Tidewater region. Not until 1824 did *Virginia ham* mean the meat of a peanut- or corn-fed hog, dry-cured, smoked, and aged.

Smithfield ham, from Smithfield, Virginia, an early colonial settlement, was talked about long before 1908, when the term came to mean only ham from the region's peanut-fed hogs, cured in hickory, oak, apple, and peanut-shell smoke, then aged for about a year.

sugar-cured ham was in the language by the 1820s, for a ham cured in brown sugar and smoked over green hickory. *Country ham* is the common, saltier variety of smoked ham, black on the outside from hickory smoke. *Ham* is a 17th-century word from Old English *hamm*, hollow of the bent knee, later the thigh and buttock.

People didn't talk about *ham and eggs* as one dish until the 1830s. *Jambalaya* (cited to 1872, from Louisiana French) was popular in New Orleans as a Creole dish of rice, seafood, often ham, and fowl. The term *red-eye gravy* was not common until the 1930s, first cited in print in 1947. (After pan-frying a slice of country ham, the cook removes the ham, then adds water and, in the South, a bit of coffee to the pan. The bits of leftover ham fat show up as little "eyes" in the gravy as it is stirred, giving the gravy its name.) *Chitlins*, or *chitterlings*, are pieces of batter-dipped small intestine fried in deep fat. Though the word seems very "soulfully" southern to us today, it goes back to the 13th century, from Middle English *chiterling*, itself probably a diminutive of Old English *cieter*, intestines. We have been talking about *side bacon* since 1850 and *side meat* since 1873 (referring to the bacon or pork from the side of a hog), with *fatback* (the top of a side of pork, free of meat and bone) not cited until 1903.

Barbecue comes from American Spanish *barbacoa*, which Spanish explorers and adventurers of the 1660s had gotten from the Taino tribe of Haiti, where it meant a framework of sticks on which to roast or smoke meat. By 1709 in America *barbecue* meant a whole animal carcass—pork, east of the Mississippi; beef, west of the Mississippi—roasted over an open fire, by 1733 a social gathering to roast and eat it, and by 1800 a political rally at which barbecue was served. *Cookout* is cited only to 1947.

Philadelphia scrapple has been a legendary mainstay of the upper-class Philadelphia breakfast for generations. It contains pork shoulder and neck meat—ordinary *scrapple* (1855) uses scraps from hog butchering—boiled with cornmeal, onions, herbs, and spices, chilled into a loaf, then fried in slices.

EAT YOUR VEGETABLES

KING CORN
Corn saved the Virginia and Massachusetts colonists from starvation. This plant, called *maize* after the West Indian Taino word for it, *mahiz*, came to be called *corn* in 1617 by the colonists. (*Corn*, which goes back in English to before the 12th century in the sense "a small grain," comes from Old English.) The colonists talked about *roasting ears* by 1650 (not called *corn on the cob* until around 1753), and by 1810 *sweet corn* had been designated as table fare, as opposed to *field corn* (1856).

Southerners talked about *corn dodgers* (1834, origin unknown), *hush-puppies* (cited to 1918, origin also unknown), and *corn muffins* (1844), not to mention *corn pudding*.

> *"Where the corn is full of kernels*
> *And the colonels full of corn*
>
> — William James Campton,*
> Kentucky

BEANS!
The early colonists found the Native Americans growing corn and beans together, with the cornstalks serving as beanpoles. The Native Americans

Corn being harvested in the heartland.

cooked the corn and beans together in bear grease to make what we call *succotash* (1751, from Narragansett *msíkquatash*, boiled kernels of corn).

Bostonians have been called *bean eaters* since 1800. The dish of beans cooked with saltpork and molasses wasn't widely called *Boston baked beans* until the 1850s.

Green beans were called *string beans* by 1759 (from the stringlike fiber along the side of the pod) and *snap beans* or *snaps* by 1770 (from the sound the uncooked pod makes when broken). *Green bean* is cited to 1847, and *wax bean*, the yellow variety, to 1897.

Butter beans, originally a tropical vegetable, got their name around 1819, but in 1756 had already been called *lima beans* after Lima, Peru. *Navy beans* (1856) got their name because of their extensive use in the Navy, and *pinto beans* (1916) got theirs from American Spanish *pinto*, spotted, painted, because the bean has a spotted pattern.

Soybeans, also spelled *soya beans* (cited to 1802, *soy* or *soya* from Japanese *shoyu*), were introduced to the U.S. in 1802, but were not widely grown and used here or there for over 100 years (*soybean oil* emerging around 1916).

Bean sprouts (1920–21), the sprouts of the *mung bean* (1910, Hindi, from Sanskrit) got their first commercial boost in 1920 when La Choy Food Products started selling them in glass jars and cans. Today *bean sprouts* are used regularly in a nation that has adopted Asian food as a national delight.

POTATOES AND RICE

Potato (1565, from Spanish *patata*, itself from the West Indian Taino word *batata*, sweet potato) meant only a sweet potato to the early colonists, who knew no other kind: thus the longer term *sweet potato* wasn't necessary or in use until the 1750s. Though native to the New World, what we call a *potato* was first brought to Boston by Irish Presbyterians in 1718 and planted the next year in Londonderry, New Hampshire. But for the next 100 years these *Irish potatoes* were used mainly for fodder, being considered by many unsophisticated people as a powerful aphrodisiac. Until the 1820s this potato was always called an *Irish potato* or a *white potato*. *Taters* (1759), a clipping, is a dialect form still in use in the upper reaches of the South. And *spuds* has been around since the 1840s but didn't become popular until the 1890s (it comes from a mid 17th century English word *spud*, a narrow-bladed or pronged spade used in digging up roots).

The Pennsylvania Dutch also ate white potatoes, including *mashed potatoes*, which were first known as a Pennsylvania Dutch dish early in the 18th century and until the 1850s were often called *Dutch potatoes* or *German potatoes*. And Thomas Jefferson learned about *French fried potatoes* while ambassador to France and served them at Monticello. They didn't become a sought-after delicacy until the 1870s and weren't common until the 1900s. Their name became *French fries* in 1918 and, increasingly, just *fries* since the late 1960s.

Potato chips (1840s) were originally much thicker than we know them today. The first modern-style thin potato chips were often called *Saratoga chips* or *Saratoga potatoes* in the 1870s and 80s because they were invented by, and were a specialty of, George Crum, a Native American chef at Moon's Lake Lodge at New York's fashionable 19th century spa, Saratoga Springs. According to the story, he created these paper-thin chips in a rage in 1853 to satisfy a customer who kept returning orders of French fried potatoes, complaining they weren't thin enough.

In 1565 rice from Spain was introduced as a food in St. Augustine, Florida—the first European colony in North America. True *rice* (13th century, from Middle English *rys*, ultimately of Iranian origin) was supposedly first planted in America in 1671 by Dr. Henry Woodward in the Carolina colony but it was then talked about only as a local curiosity, as no one knew how to clean it. *Piedmont rice*, important because it can be grown without irrigation, was introduced from its native northern Italy to America by Thomas Jefferson who, according to the story, had procured the seeds while traveling in Italy and brought them home in his pockets (a crime punishable by death). *Wild rice* (1748) is not a true rice but the seed of an aquatic grass that the Native Americans grew and ate. Americans also called it *water oats* and *water rice* (both 1817 terms), *Indian rice* (1843), and *Meneninee*, from the Chippewa name *manomin*, good berry. It was originally harvested by the Manomini River near Green Bay, Wisconsin by the Manomines, another Algonquin tribe.

VEGETARIANS AND VEGANS

Vegetarianism (around 1851) as practiced by *vegetarians* (1839) or *vegans* (1944, one who avoids eating or using animal products) who go to *vegetarian* restaurants (adjective cited to 1849), increased markedly from the 1970s into the 90s. In the early 70s *salad bars* (cited to 1973) appeared in many restaurants. Here one found herbivores and omnivores *grazing* (this sense, eating a little of this and a little of that, going back to the early 1980s) on *lettuce* (14th century), *radishes* (15th century), and *onions* (14th century)—all going back to Latin via Middle English. Also on the bar would be *tomatoes* (1604, an altered form of an earlier word spelled *tomate*, itself from Spanish, from the Aztec Nahuatl *tomatl*)—more often than not *cocktail tomatoes* or in the 90s the smaller *toy tomatoes*. All in all, whether the meal included *spinach* (15th century, from Middle English, ultimately from Arabic) or *chard* (1664, from French, ultimately from a Latin word meaning "thistle"), it made for a great *nosh* (cited in English to the 1950s, from Yiddish).

HASH, STEW, AND CHILI

The noun *hash* (around 1663) was a brand new English word when some of the colonists brought it to America (from the verb [1590], itself from Old French *hachier*, to chop, also the root of *hatchet*). It meant chopped food in general, especially a mixture of leftover chopped meat heated with vegetables. *Corned beef hash* is an American dish and term dating from 1902.

We have called a cheap restaurant a *hash house* since 1869, and a person who worked in one a hash slinger also since the late 1860s. *Hash browns*, boiled, diced potatoes mixed with chopped onions and shortening, fried until brown, are cited to 1951.

Stew (from Old French *estuver*, to steam) meant a stove, a heated room, a hot bath, and a brothel in the 14th century. It didn't get around to meaning a dish of stewed meat and vegetables until 1756.

Until the late 1820s *chili* (1604, Spanish *chile*, from the Aztec Nahuatl *chilli*) meant only the pepper itself. Then it came to mean various Mexican dishes and sauces using the pepper, especially a dish of the peppers stuffed with meat. Around 1828, Mexicans living in what is now Texas invented *carne con chili*, meat chunks with chili, which by 1858 had evolved into a stew of meat, chili peppers, beans, and tomatoes, with

Food Fact

Chowder (1751), like many other stews and soups, goes back to the fishermen's and hunters' custom of throwing an assorted catch into a big pot for cooking. The word comes from the French *chaudière*, kettle, cauldron, and moved down the Atlantic Seaboard from Newfoundland and Nova Scotia via the French Canadians.

the American Spanish name *chili con carne* ("chili with meat"), *chili* for short. A bowl of this chili was probably the spiciest, hottest dish Americans ever ate. The now-familiar tame bowl of chili didn't emerge until 1902. *Chili powder* is cited to 1938; *chili dog*, a hot dog topped with *chili*, is cited to 1969, though undoubtedly is much older.

SWEETS

PIES AND CAKES

Dessert (1600, from Medieval French *desservir*, to clear the table, as after the main course) had just become a popular English word when the Pilgrims sailed for America. *Pie*, however, goes back to a Middle English word, used since the 14th century. Beyond that point, its true origin is uncertain. *Pie* meant a meat pie to the English and the first colonists, with *tart* being their word for the pastry filled with fruit, berries, or jam—but colonists were soon calling both dishes *pies*. The English *gooseberry fool* was also popular in colonial America, *fool* being a 16th century word for clotted cream but by the 18th century meaning a dish of crushed or puréed fruit served with clotted or whipped cream, sometimes topped with macaroons.

Pumpkin pie was one of the first native New England dishes. The dish, however, wasn't called *pumpkin pie* until 1654; before that, and for some time after, it was usually called *pumpkin pudding* because it was baked without a top crust. *Apple pie* has been an American favorite since the 1760s. (But when we say something or someone is *as American as apple pie* we may not know that one of the earliest references to *apple pie* is dated 1590, where the Englishman using the term spelled it *applepye*.) By the 1840s and 50s we were talking about deep-dish *cobblers; duff* (a 19th century pronunciation of *dough* to rhyme with *rough*), which was fruit pudding, sometimes with a bottom crust; and *slump*, raised dough with a sweetened fruit filling. *Grunt* was a dish of berries steamed with biscuit dough dropped on top of them.

Key lime pie (*key lime* being a West Indian lime grown in Florida) appeared in the 1850s, inspired by the introduction of condensed milk. *Pie à la mode* (French *à la mode*, "in the fashion," in the latest fashion) has been around since the 1880s.

When people talked about *cake* before the 1870s they meant something different from what we usually do today. Modern light cakes couldn't be easily baked in fireplaces, in primitive hard-to-control ovens, or without good artificial leaveners. (When one side of a cake was burned and "fell," the other side virtually uncooked, it was called a *sad cake*.) To the colonists *cake* meant such dishes as *strawberry bread* and various shortcakes, with *strawberry shortcake* being a popular term by the 1830s. *Gingerbread* was a popular American cake throughout the 19th century, differing in its soft moist texture from the older European variety that is thin and hard like a cookie. It was rivaled by *pound cake* (1747), so named because early recipes called for a pound each of flour, sugar, butter, and eggs.

By the late 1870s and early 80s people were talking about *layer cake*; later on, about *angel food cake* (1920) and *devil's food cake* (1905). The last word in cakes is *cake mix*, an American term common since World War II.

Some birthday cakes are not baked so much as constructed.

In 1986, Betty Crocker, the first lady of the kitchen, let her hair down, lost some of her primness and got younger in a makeover that turned the homespun housewife into a dress-for-success yuppie. She was created at General Mills in 1921 and first pictured in 1936.

COOKIES AND BROWNIES

The word *cookie* (1703, from Dutch *koekje*, a diminutive of *koek*, cake) was brought to Niew Amsterdam (New York) by the Dutch colonists. But the most "American" of all cookies has to be the beloved *chocolate chip cookie*. The original, first called the *Toll House cookie*, was a culinary accident created by Ruth Wakefield in 1930. Wakefield, a Whitman, Massachusetts housewife and keeper of the Toll House Inn, added, on impulse, some bits of chocolate to her "Butter Do Drop" batter, thereby creating an American legend.

The origin of *brownie*, another American culinary accident, is obscure, but food historians have traced it to the first recorded recipe, dated 1897. It seems that a careless cook who had failed to add baking powder to cake batter concocted the heavy, chewy dough that today is baked in square pans all over America.

ICE CREAM, SORBET, SHERBET, AND YOGURT

People have been eating ice cream for 3,000 years, originally as flavored snow or ice. Early colonists poured maple syrup over snow. Both Washington and Jefferson owned a "cream machine for making ice" and Dolly Madison's White House dinner parties were talked about for the "large shining dome of pink ice cream" as the centerpiece. Colonists had been talking about going to *ice cream houses* since the 1700s, which weren't generally called *ice cream parlors* or *ice cream stands* until the late 1870s.

Since immediately after the Revolutionary War, ice cream lovers had been praising *Philadelphia ice cream*, originally made without eggs. Early ice cream was prepared and hand beaten until frozen in a pot placed in a pan of ice and salt. In 1846 Nancy Johnson, a Philadelphia dairy maid, invented the hand-cranked *ice cream freezer*. *Neapolitan ice cream*, different flavored layers frozen together, was first being talked about in the 1870s.

People began to ask each other if they had tried one of the new *ice cream sodas* soon after they were introduced at the semicentennial celebrations of Philadelphia's Franklin Institute in 1874. In the 1880s *ice cream cake* and *floats* appeared. Sometime in the 1890s the *ice cream sundae* came into being (*sundae* is cited to 1897). *Sundae* is probably a respelling of *Sunday*, but of uncertain origin. One theory holds that the dish was originally sold only on that day; another story goes that it was originally an ice cream soda without the soda water, which some areas would not allow to be sold on Sundays; and yet another says the chocolate syrup made it an expensive, "only on Sunday" dish. *Frappés* (French *frapper*, to ice) appeared in 1903, first meaning a partially frozen fruit juice drink, then a liqueur served over shaved ice, finally—in New England dialect—a thick milk shake pronounced "frap."

After the 1904 St. Louis World's Fair people started asking for *ice cream cones*, invented at the fair when an ice cream vendor ran out of dishes and a nearby vendor of the crisp pastry, salabria, twisted it into a cone to hold the ice cream. And in 1904 Strickler's Drug Store in Latrobe, Pennsylvania served the first *banana split*.

The trend toward so-called homemade ice cream began in 1959 with the introduction of *Häagen-Dazs* (a trademark created by a Bronx entrepreneur to look Danish even though it wasn't). Along with others, like Ben & Jerry's (created in 1978 in a converted Burlington, Vermont garage by hippie entrepreneurs Ben Cohen and Jerry Greenfield), it came to be known as *superpremium* ice cream.

An ice cream parlor in Southington, Connecticut in 1942.

With advances in chocolate technology, it's become hard for a skilled dipper to find a place to ply her trade.

Also reflecting the discerning, "superpremium" tastes of the upscale consumer of the 1980s and 90s was the popularity of *sorbet*. *Sorbet* (1585, from French, from Italian *sorbetto*, ultimately from Ottoman Turkish *sherbet*) is a fruit-flavored frozen dessert originally eaten between courses of a meal to freshen the palate.

Sherbet or *sherbert* (1603 in the sense of a cold drink of diluted, sweetened fruit juice) got into English also from Ottoman Turkish *sherbet*, thence from Persian *sharbat*, ultimately from Arabic *sarbah*, to drink. In its frozen dessert sense, *sherbet* is first cited to 1891.

Yogurt or *yoghurt* (1625, from Turkish *yogurt*)—so popular in the health-conscious 1980s and 90s—was slow to catch on in the U.S., not gaining wide acceptance until *soft frozen yogurt* was introduced at Bloomingdale's in 1974, though the first yogurt of this variety dates to 1971.

CANDY

Candy is short for the redundant 15th century *sugre* ("sugar") *candy* (ultimately from Arabic *qandi*, candied). Early colonists talked about their *sugar plums* and *maple syrup candy* or *maple candy*, about the New Amsterdam *marchpane* (later called by the German name *marzipan*), and in the 1720s about the new British *caramels* (via French, Spanish, and Portuguese to Latin *calamellus*, small reed). American children were asking for *lollipops* (1784, perhaps from British dialect *lolly*, tongue + *pop*, the noise) soon after they became popular in England. *Pralines*, 1723, originally almonds coated with white sugar, were created for and named after French diplomat César du Plesses-Praslin (1598–1675); but Americans began to make them in the 1800s and the Creoles of French New Orleans substituted native pecans and brown sugar.

By the 1820s any larger piece of hard candy was called a *sucker* (the term *all-day sucker* having been used around 1906). In the 1840s *candy pulls* became popular, being called *taffy pulls* by the 1870s. *Taffy* (British *toffee*) was simple to make, from molasses or brown sugar and butter. *Salt water taffy* became associated with the Atlantic City Boardwalk by the 1880s.

At the same time, adults were talking about the new *milk chocolate*, invented in Switzerland in 1875. The new candy that college girls were talking about in the 1890s was *fudge*. *Fudge* had meant to devise as a fake since 1674, origin unknown. (White *divinity fudge* wasn't heard of until around 1910, and *chocoholic* was not cited until 1968.) By 1905 children spoke of *jelly beans*. *Candy bars* became an American institution during World War I when they were mass-produced for the doughboys. New types, names, and brands of candy continued to emerge, including *cotton candy* in 1926. The tricolor, kernel-shaped *candy corn* (top, yellow; middle, orange; bottom, white)—the most long-lived Halloween treat—was introduced in the late 1920s. All this goes to prove one point: Americans have a big *sweet tooth* (14th century).

" . . . correct measurements are absolutely necessary to insure the best results."

— Fannie Farmer

COOKBOOKS

FANNIE FARMER AND THE LEVEL TEASPOON

Though *The Compleat Housewife* (1742, Williamsburg, Virginia) was the first cookbook published in America, it was left to other women to write

Fannie Farmer, the mother of level measurement.

such useful—and famous—cookbooks that they themselves became household names. Amelia Simmons published her 47-page *American Cookery* in Hartford, Connecticut, in 1796. It was the first American *cookerie book*, our term *cook book* being an Americanism of German origin dating from about 1809. Early collections were also often called *culinary reviews* or simply *recipe*, or *receipt*, *books*. In subsequent editions until the 1830s, Amelia Simmons' book was talked about and used by thousands of American women; it was the first to include recipes for such American dishes as pumpkin (she spelled it "pomkin") pie, and was the first to use such Americanisms as *molasses*.

In the 1840s Catharine Esther Beecher, a pioneer in women's education, gained fame with *Miss Beecher's Domestic Receipt Book* (1846). It contained not only recipes but hints on buying and storing food, using the ovens and utensils of the day, feeding a child, etc.

Fannie Farmer, officially titled *Fannie Farmer's Boston Cooking School Cookbook*, has been a watchword in American kitchens since the first 3,000 copies were printed at the author's expense and published in 1896. Fannie Merritt Farmer (1857–1915) gained neighborhood fame cooking in her family's Boston boardinghouse before becoming the Boston Cooking School's most famous student, then its director. After her cookbook appeared, she established her own Miss Farmer's School of Cooking in 1902, gave public cooking demonstrations widely reported in the press, wrote a cooking column for 10 years in *The Woman's Home Companion*, and lectured to women's clubs. (The *Fannie Farmer* tradition was carried on later by such "celebrity TV chefs" as Julia Child.) Before her death Fannie Farmer had changed American kitchen terminology from "a pinch" and "a dash" and "a heaping spoonful" to her own precise, standardized, scientific terms. To Fannie Farmer, we can attribute the popularity of such precise everyday kitchen terms as *level teaspoon* and *½ teaspoon*.

THE LANGUAGE OF THE AUTOMATED KITCHEN

Though the first real *pressure cooker* was invented in 1681 by French physicist Denys Papin, who called it "The New Digester, or Engine for Softening Bones," the first modern pressure cooker was not introduced to consumers until the 1934 World's Fair. The device, which cooked foods in one-third the ordinary time, freed up women to do other things; it remained popular until after World War II, but an increased number of explosions yielding "meals on ceilings" hastened its eventual disappearance.

The language of cooking was to change forever along with the process of meal preparation with the appearance of two devices—the *microwave oven* and the *food processor*—both in the early 1970s. The *microwave*, available to and affordable by consumers in 1974, was developed in 1945 by Raytheon technician Percy L. Spencer, who noticed that the *microwaves* (1931) he was studying had melted a chocolate bar in his pocket. In 1953 Raytheon made the first such oven for commercial use. The verb *to microwave*, often replaced by the slang synonyms *to nuke* or *to zap*, appeared in 1973, with *microwavable* or *microwaveable* and *microwave-proof* and *-safe* also emerging.

The *food processor* (1973), which supplemented the much earlier *mixer*, arrived in American kitchens with the advent of the *Cuisinart*, introduced at a Chicago exposition. It was an improved version of chef Pierre Verdun's 1970 "food preparation machine." The *food processor* thus further advanced the cycle of kitchen automation started by the Waring *blender* (1936). Serious cooks learned how to use their *processors' feed tubes, blades* and *discs*, and *food pushers* in order to grind/chop/shred/purée/slice/grate and knead, *pulsing* the machine on and off.

The food processor contributed directly to the popularity of home-prepared *nouvelle cuisine* (1974), a "new cuisine" that includes light, low-calorie sauces and stocks and little flour or fat, emphasizing the use of fresh, in-season produce. The machine also encouraged the emergence of *food stylists*—professional and amateur designers of attractive meal *presentation*.

CANNING, FREEZING, AND TUPPERWARE

CAN IT!
The word *can* (before the 12th century, Old English *canne*, cup) meant a container for liquids long before tin cans were invented. Americans have been using *tin can* for a large open tin container since 1770, but it wasn't until 1812 that the sealed *tin can* as we know it was invented. By the 1850s *to can* was a verb. But it was the Civil War that made canned food common: since it didn't spoil, such food was supplied to troops fighting in the hot southern summers. *Canned soup* started to become a popular term in 1869.

I'M FREEZING!
Francis Bacon had experimented with freezing chickens by stuffing them with snow in 1626 (he died that year from exposure suffered during the experiments), and in the 1840s some meat, fish, and poultry were frozen with natural ice for storage and shipping. However, it wasn't until after 1917 that practical *quick freezing* was achieved by Clarence "Bob" Birdseye, an explorer and scientist who had observed how Eskimos froze food in Labrador. Most people first heard of *frozen food* (1920s) through his *Birdseye* products. In the 1930s the top compartment of the new refrigerators was called a *freezer* (which had meant "ice cream freezer" since the 1840s), *freezing compartment*, or often *ice cube compartment*, the forerunner of the separate *home freezer* of the 1940s.

A family canning apples in 1942.

World War II was the proving ground that made *frozen food* common. Frozen foods were shipped to American servicemen all over the world.

Beginning in 1951, *precooked foods* were also frozen and sold, leading to complete frozen-meals-on-a-tray that could be heated, served, and eaten with little attention, the first being Swanson's 1953 *heat-and-serve* frozen turkey dinner in an aluminum tray. For a few years all America seemed to be heating and eating such meals on *TV trays* while watching television. The C.A. Swanson company obtained the trademark for such a meal—the *TV Dinner*, introduced in December 1953; *food technologist* Betty Cronin was the creator. In the late 1960s, new *dehydrated frozen food*, needing no refrigeration and called *freeze-dried*, was much talked about. (And in the 1990s the sophisticates were talking about *sun-dried fruits* and vegetables.)

YOU'RE INVITED TO A TUPPERWARE PARTY

When chemical engineer Earl S. Tupper (1907-83) purified and adapted a World War II oil refinery byproduct into polyethylene containers with an airtight seal that would ensure freshness, and named the product *Tupperware*, he created (1946) an American icon. After 1951, the famed *Tupperware parties* at which housewives would gather at a neighbor's house to view the products and receive a small "free gift" had become integral to women's evening social life in U.S. suburbs. In 1979 Tupperware became *dishwasher-safe*.

EATING OUT, TAKE-OUT, AND FAST FOOD

RESTAURANTS

Colonial men might eat in *taverns* and *inns* when they were single, away from home, or wanted to meet and talk with other men. But after the Revolutionary War our young nation loved its French ally and the French Revolution; hence, French customs, words, and food. Thus, from the time of Independence, many fine American eating establishments have had a French flavor. As early as 1794, Bostonians were talking about Jean ("Julien") Bapiste Gilbert Payplat's fine eating establishment, Julien's Resorator. It helped make *restorator* (French, "restorer, resting place") an early American word both for restaurant and restaurant keeper. The French word *restaurant* ("restoring") was first used to mean an eating establishment in Paris in 1763, then recorded in America in 1827, several years before it was used in England.

Early restaurants were often expensive and often still associated with inns or hotels (the first American inn or tavern to be called a *hotel* was New York City's Corre's Hotel of 1790). They introduced many terms to America. As an example, in 1855 Harvey Parker's new Parker House in Boston introduced the term *à la carte*, serving any dish all day long and not just meals at fixed hours. But the Parker House is best remembered for its soft, warm, folded *Parkerhouse rolls* (widely known by the 1870s).

During the 1830s Americans had begun to ask to see the *menu* (1837, French) introduced during that decade. Since 1840 people had also been talking about New Orleans' Antoine's, which made *gumbo Creole* famous (*gumbo*, 1845, Louisiana French *gombo*, of Bantu origin, related to another African word meaning "okra"). The word *restaurant* was a part of everyone's vocabulary between the late 1820s and 1855 and, during that

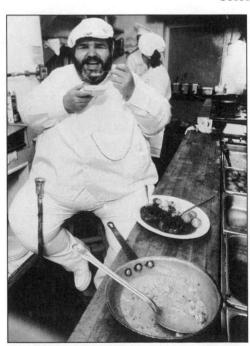

Chef Paul Prudhomme of K-Paul's Louisiana Kitchen in New Orleans. Prudhomme, famous for this early-80s discovery of blackened redfish, has become widely known as food programming has proliferated on television.

same period, we added still other French terms to our vocabulary: *filet*, *bisque*, *table d'hôte*, *maître d'* and *à la* this or that.

LUNCHROOMS AND LUNCH COUNTERS

Forty years after the Revolution some American businessmen and city workers were already forgoing large midday dinners in favor of quick, convenient, cheap lunches at *lunchrooms* (1830) or *lunches* (1812). After the Civil War these hash houses were also called *lunch stands* (late 1860s), *lunch counters* (by 1873), *lunch joints* (by the 1880s) and finally *luncheonettes* (by 1924) and *snack bars* (by 1930).

Even in fine restaurants a *short order* meant an *à la carte* serving of one dish by the 1890s, and by 1920 there were *short-order restaurants* and *short-order cooks*. By 1910 some cheap eating establishments didn't bother to call themselves anything, putting up a sign advertising EATS.

COFFEE SHOPS AND CAFETERIAS

Both *coffee shop* (1836) and *cafeteria* (1839, American Spanish for "coffeehouse") had meant a coffeehouse in America. By 1885, New York City had a complete self-service restaurant, for men only, but the modern *cafeteria* originated in Chicago to feed hungry tourists quickly and cheaply during the 1893 World's Columbian Exposition. The spelling was often *caffeteria*.

The first *Automat* (Greek *automatos*, self-acting) opened in Philadelphia in 1902. These vending-machine/cafeteria combinations eventually became associated in many people's minds not with Philadelphia but with New York City.

COFFEEHOUSES

In the 1990s modern *coffeehouses* (1612), places that sell coffee and other refreshments while often offering other entertainment (e.g., stand-up comics, guitarists, and the like) gained increasing popularity. High-school and college students in particular would go there to enjoy a cup of *espresso* (1945, Italian *caffè espresso*, "pressed-out coffee") or *cappuccino* (1948, also Italian, "Capuchin," from the similarity of its color to a Capuchin friar's habit), the latter an espresso mixed with frothy hot cream or milk.

DINERS AND DRIVE-INS

Chuck wagons—the precursors to diners—not only accompanied cowboys on the cattle drives of the 1860s and 70s but often followed them into the cow towns. These cowboy *chuck wagons* and the local *lunch stands* of the 1860s combined to give us the *lunch wagon* in the 1880s. Some stayed open until late at night and by the late 1880s were called *night owls* (*night owl* had meant a person who stays up late since 1846). When New York City, Boston, and Philadelphia sold many of their horse-drawn streetcars in 1897 and replaced them with electric ones, local lunch-wagon owners bought many of the old streetcars and converted them into *lunch cars*, sometimes called *diners* during the early 1900s. The in-town *diners* did not become truly popular, however, until they were joined by *roadside diners* during the early 1930s.

Curb hopping, serving food to customers seated in their cars at the curb, seems to have originated in Miami during the Florida land boom of 1925, and by 1930 it had led to the terms *car hopping, car hops, curb service*, and *drive-in restaurant*. All this opened the door to *take-out* (cited to 1965) food and *fast food* (cited to 1951).

Food Fact
In 1973 the first Mr. Coffee, an automatic drip coffeemaker, was introduced, replacing in most households the percolator, which had dominated the market since around 1890.

A business lunch, circa 1870. Cowboys at a chuck wagon.

FAST-FOOD LINGO

The language used by Americans who eat out at or take out food from *fast-food* outlets is replete with brand names like "It's *a Wendy's*" or "We're going to *the Colonel's* [Colonel Sanders of Kentucky Fried Chicken] tonight." But from the standpoint of language, McDonald's was the source of a host of new slang terms spun off in the 1990s from the company's own use of *Mc* in naming some of its fare, e.g., *Chicken McNuggets*. Examples are the *McPaper*, a term used by college students for a hastily contrived, poorly thought-out term paper; and *McJustice*, unfair summary treatment in the courts. McDonald's also gave us the first *drive-thru* window, tested in 1956 in Columbus, Ohio. The rest is history.

One of the first McDonald franchises, its 1953 design surviving into the 90s.

AMERICA'S MELTING POT

The *foodies* (1982) of the later 20th century, in their excellent adventure into *gourmet* (1820, French) cooking, triggered an increased use of foreign borrowings, taking the language far beyond the *fondue* craze of the 1960s (*fondue*, 1878, from French *fondre*, to melt). Though some "real men didn't eat *quiche*" (1941, French), upscale diners did, along with *gravlax* (1977, from Swedish *grave*, to bury + *lax*, salmon, from the original process of burying it in the ground)—an appetizer of salmon cured with salt, pepper, dill, and aquavit. They dug into *hummus* (1950, from Arabic, "chickpea"), a puréed chickpea paste. They flocked to *sushi bars* (*sushi*, 1893, Japanese) to taste bits of raw fish or shellfish mixed with cold rice and seasoned with vinegar. Still others experienced *calamari* (around 1961, Italian, the plural of *calamaro*, squid, from Latin *calamus*, the inky substance secreted by the squid), and enjoyed the Spanish hors d'oeuvres *tapas* (1953, from Spanish, "cover, lid"). All manner of *pasta* (1874, Italian, from Latin) was consumed, and people separated "A-list" pasta (made from fresh dough) from the more plebeian, "processed" stuff. At the bottom of the "snob scale" but at the top of the average person's *comfort food* (1980s) level were *macaroni* (1599, Italian from a dialect word for *dumpling*) and *lasagna* (1846, Italian, from a Vulgar Latin word, "cooking pot or its contents," ultimately from Latin *lasanum*, chamber pot).

And so Americans wrapped their tongues around a host of foreign borrowings (and dishes), many quite old to the rest of the world:

arugula, 1967, an Italian dialect word from Latin *eruca*, colewort; a Mediterranean salad green.

bok choy, 1938, Chinese, "white vegetable"; also called *Chinese cabbage* (1842).

couscous, 1759, French, from Arabic kuskus; steamed semolina served with meat or vegetables.

daikon, 1876, Japanese, from *dai*, big + *kon*, root; a large hard white radish.

empanada, around 1922, American Spanish, from Spanish *empanar*, to bread, from Latin; a turnover with a savory filling, e.g., of chopped meat or of vegetables.

enoki, around 1977, Japanese; a small white edible mushroom.

kiwi, 1966, this sense, the fruit of the Chinese gooseberry, introduced into New Zealand at the start of the 20th century and renamed for the New Zealand bird (the kiwi) after the fruit's introduction to the U.S.

kohlrabi, 1807, German, from Italian *cavolo rapa*, cabbage turnip; an extra large cabbage with a huge, edible turnip-like stem.

mahimahi, 1943, Hawaiian; meat of the food fish dolphin.

mirliton, around 1909, French; long used in Creole cooking, a pear-shaped fruit from a West Indian plant of the gourd family, eaten as a vegetable.

morel, 1672, from French *morille*; an edible fungus with a cap and a pitted surface.

Ethnic cuisine in America is not a modern phenomenon.

phyllo, around 1950, from Greek *phyllon*, very thin pastry sheets.

pesto, 1937, Italian, "pounded"; a sauce of fresh chopped basil, pine nuts, garlic, oil, and grated cheese.

radicchio, 1968, Italian, "chicory," from Latin; a red chicory eaten as a salad green.

shiitake, 1877, from Japanese *shii*, Japanese chinquapin + *take*, mushroom; a black mushroom with an edible cap.

At the same time Americans continued to *scarf* (around 1960, an altered from of *scoff*, to eat greedily, itself from the now obsolete *scaff*) Tex-Mex food: *nachos* (1969, American Spanish, from a Spanish word meaning "flat-nosed"), *refried beans* (1957), *salsa* (1962, Spanish, "sauce," from Latin), *tacos* (1934, American Spanish), *tostadas* (1939, American Spanish, from Spanish *tostar*, to toast), and *tortillas* (around 1699, American Spanish, from Spanish, a diminutive of *torta*, cake).

And when all else failed, we called out for a *pizza*. (See AMERICAN SPOKEN BY AMERICANS subsection Ethnic Diversity .)

ON THE FRINGES

*D*o you remember the **Branch Davidians** *(1993) and the* **Montana Freemen**
(1996)? How about the **Viper Militia?** *Although we like to say that the*
majority rules in America, in some ways every American is a minority of
one. We as a nation are a great collection of **fringe people** (fringe *meaning*
"peripheral, odd, not usual" since the 17th century). But what is considered
"fringe" is constantly being redefined, necessitating a distinction between the
lunatic fringe *(cited to 1913, radical extremists) and those who simply* **march to**
the beat of a different drummer *(a paraphrase of a line from Henry David*
Thoreau's 1854 work, Walden*).*

> *"There is apt to be a lunatic*
> *fringe among the votaries of any*
> *forward movement."*
>
> — *Theodore Roosevelt, 1913*

A tarot card reader waiting to ply
her trade. Tarot readers are among
the wide range of occult practitioners that includes gypsy palmers,
astrologers, and psychometrists.

The 1990s brought complaints about the decline of the *nuclear family*,
the erosion of *family values* (a phrase popularized by Vice President Dan
Quayle in the early 1990s), and the dissolution of *Mainstream* (or
Middle) *America*. Myriad *special interest groups* (*special interest* cited to
1910) of *concerned citizens* lobbied, protested, and fought for what they
believed to be basic American rights and standards. Such groups have
been around since before the founding of the Republic, and at times
some of them have exhibited the *extremism* (1865) of Anthony Comstock
(1844–1915, from whom we have the term *Comstockery* [1905], the
zealous suppression of works of art and literature alleged to be offensive
or dangerous to public morals), or Senator Joseph McCarthy in the 1950s
(hence *McCarthyism*, the use of indiscriminate and unproven accusa-
tions, innuendo, and investigative methods to ruin the reputations of
political opponents).

FROM JOE SIXPACK TO INDIVIDUALIST

Who represents *John Q. Public* (1945), *John Q. Voter* (1948), and *John Q.*
Citizen (1947)—not to mention the 1990s *Joe Sixpack*—against whom we
should measure digression from the norm? In a society that has traditionally cherished independence, it seems that no one wants to be average
any more. But as small town life yielded to suburban sprawl, and as
Main Street USA gave way to the shopping mall, the American ideal of
individualism was forced to find new expression. Many yearn for
freedom or *libertarianism* of the sort advertised on license plates in New
Hampshire, which invite us to *Live Free or Die*. A more belligerent American motto, *Don't Tread on Me* (seen on Revolutionary Era flags), came
back into fashion as well. Trying to cope with economic pressures, an
emerging global economy, and the pace of technological change, many
Americans at the end of the 20th century yearned to be more self-sufficient, to return to the kind of rural or small-town life their grandparents
had. *Dropping out* came into vogue in the 1960s and 70s, when young
people started setting up *communes*. Thirty years later, it was not
unusual to hear about a stockbroker who turned his or her back on a
six- or seven-figure income to teach in a rural school, a practice called
topping out. Modern pioneers were apt to run off to the wilds of the
Rockies or to Alaska, grow their own food, and become *back-to-the-lan-*
ders.

You didn't have to flee to the boondocks or belong to some *off-the-*
grid (1990s) or *last-frontier* community to join the many Americans who

had abandoned the mainstream. You could be an *urban cowboy,* or you could just wear your cap backwards to signal dissent. Or you could try *body piercing* (popularized by the *punk movement* of the 1980s)—earlobes pierced multiple times, nose rings and nipple rings, pierced eyebrows, lips, tongues, and even bellybuttons were a youthful declaration of independence from the beauty standards of an earlier generation. Even *tattoos* (1777, from Tahitian), once the fashion only among sailors and Hell's Angels types, became so popular among young people that the sight of a person tattooed from head to toe was no longer uncommon. You could live an *alternate lifestyle* just about anywhere, though tolerance or acceptance was greater in (certain) cities than in *small-town America,* where tradition did, and still does, tend to rule.

The 1990s saw some new kids on the block—the *street punks*—many also called *trustafarians* for their *trust funds* and *Rastafarian* hairstyles (the latter, cited to 1992). These young people, typically upper-middle-class whites, male and female, dropped out of society and lived intentionally on the streets, panhandling and eating out of garbage cans.

RACIAL TENSIONS

Some fringe groups have been motivated by racial prejudice. The secretive *white supremacists* known as the *Ku Klux Klan* (1865, said to be based on Greek *kuklos,* "circle, assembly" + *clan* spelled with a *k*—a vogue at the time, with Walt Whitman spelling *Canada* as *Kanada,* etc.) have stirred up trouble since the end of the Civil War. They tried to reassert *white supremacy* (1867) during Reconstruction by intimidating, flogging, tarring and feathering, *lynching,* murdering, and burning African Americans (and sometimes carpetbaggers and whites). *Night riders* (1875) were members of any Klan-like group who rode at night to do these terroristic acts. A larger group, the *Knights of the White Camelia,* merged with the Klan in 1867 to form *The Invisible Empire of the South.* There have actually been three groups named *Ku Klux Klan,* the most recent founded in 1915 by Colonel William J. Simmons, who

A Klan rally. Some have suggested that the name Ku Klux Klan was derived from the sounds made when a bullet is loaded into the chamber of a rifle.

A standoff in Ruby Ridge, Idaho ensued when federal officials came for Randy Weaver's guns. His wife and son would eventually be killed in the siege. Here Weaver (left) confers with his attorney, Gerry Spence, before offering his testimony to a Senate subcommittee on the 1992 standoff.

proclaimed it a "high class mystic, social, and patriotic" society devoted to the protection of womanhood and the supremacy of White Protestants, but who personally considered it a money-making venture (he later sold out his share in the Klan to a Texas dentist for $90,000). It was this Klan that became famous for *cross burning* as a warning. A *Klavern* (*Klan + cavern*, around 1924) is a local unit of the Klan; a *Ku Kluxer* (1880) is a member or supporter. The *Neo-Nazis,* the *Aryan Nation,* and bands of racist *skinheads* (the term in this sense and the "style" coming from 1960s England) also did their part to keep racism alive and well in America, which Mark Twain once called "The United States of Lyncherdom."

Separatism survived in the *survivalists* (gaining notoriety in the early to mid 1980s)—mostly whites who wanted to live free from government interference and the tyranny of technology. (The armed resisters were called *militias*.) Some were religious extremists who regarded the bar codes used for pricing and product identification as the *mark of the beast* (from the biblical book of Revelation) and came to refer to the period before the turn of the century as the biblical *end of time* or *end times*. They pointed to signs of the arrival of the *Antichrist* in the *New World Order,* the latter an expression used by President George Bush in 1990, and in *one-world government* (Wendell Willkie's high ideal, which can be traced back to Alfred, Lord Tennyson's "Parliament of Man" and "the federation of the world"). They denounced the activities of the United Nations and the Trilateral Commission (an international relations group of notable private citizens who promote greater cooperation among industrialized nations in the "trilateral" area: North America, Western Europe, and Japan). They saw both kinds of activities as evidence that *Armageddon* would be coming soon. Apocalypse Now—or at least at the millennium—seemed to be their focus.

A LEXICON OF CONSPIRACIES AND GUNS

Although labeled in American slang as *weirdos, freaks, sickos,* or *kooks,* the *fringe elements* have had a way of enriching our American vocabulary. *Conspiracy theory* buffs saw *black helicopters* (big government's *eye in the sky,* particularly feared by *right-wing militias*) hovering. Theories about the Kennedy assassination (was it Castro? the Mafia? J. Edgar Hoover? take your pick) were supplanted in the minds of some by fears about *international bankers* (an anti-Semitic code word among some conspiracy theorists) taking over the world. Suspicions were directed toward other international groups (such as the International Red Cross and the World Health Organization). And they resisted the Freemasons, the Vatican, agrarian reformers, and the traditional political parties.

Those lobbying for gun control and the banning of assault weapons faced strong opposition from the gun lobby. While very few relish being called a *gun nut,* many Americans insist on taking advantage of their constitutionally-guaranteed "right to bear arms." Along with increased government intrusion into private life, soaring crime, *domestic terrorism,* and widespread paranoia about personal safety came a whole new language revolving around weapons and violence. The 1990s gave new meaning to terms such as *blood games, citizen army,* and *head shots,* the last of which used to refer only to glossy black-and-white publicity photos. *Head shots* came to mean aiming for the target's head, as most law officers were routinely wearing *body armor* such as bullet-proof vests.

A NEW AMERICAN REVOLUTION?

The Minutemen of the American Revolution boasted that they could be ready "in a minute" to defend their country's liberty. Their 1990s compatriots were just as responsive regarding their own personal freedoms when usurped by Big Government. George Eaton's *Patriot Report* and other publications asserted that it was in the best American tradition to prevent *gummint* (a jocular spelling of *government,* reflecting a widespread pronunciation of the word, and often a negative attitude toward federal power) from interfering too much in the lives of private citizens.

> "A few angry men formed a Virginia militia because they were afraid of the federal government. Soon enough, the federal government was afraid of them, too. . . . They were in many ways average guys, but they were armed and angry, and they aimed their anger at the federal government."
>
> — Washington Post Magazine, *October 13, 1996*

> "We are at war with the System, and it is no longer a war of words."
>
> — The Turner Diaries, *a book called a "blueprint for an end-of-century race war," widely read by white separatists*

Nation of Islam leader, Louis Farrakhan (left), on *The Arsenio Hall Show* in 1994.

Unabomber suspect Theodore Kaczynski in Helena, Montana, the day after his arrest for possession of bomb components.

Privacy, threatened by *phone taps,* sophisticated electronic *snooping devices,* and other gadgets, as well as by federal dossiers and databases, found its champion in *private armies.* Words recurring in tracts written by, and discussions about, such militia groups were *modern Minutemen, call to arms, the operation, dangerous missions, treason, Zionist Occupied Government, the revolution, gorilla* [sic] *warfare, Aryan Nations, the Order, Christian Identity, white survival, resistance-type groups, federal whores, security, seditionist,* and *RepublicansandDemocrats* (the federal government and all career politicians—the terms purposely run together).

Most Americans want their government to be strong enough to prevent terrorism—like the explosion that rocked the World Trade Center in 1993, killing six and injuring 1,000, or the one that leveled the Alfred P. Murrah Federal Building in Oklahoma City in 1995, killing 169—and smart enough to catch the *Unabomber* (whose mail bombs killed three and wounded 23 from 1978 through 1995). But at the same time they want law-abiding citizens to be left alone. The tension between these two strongly held beliefs was reflected in the rhetoric used by politicians of the times and by the words Americans used in often heated discussions of the issues.

CULTS

In the final decades of the 20th century people talked about the activities of religious or quasi-religious *cults.* The word goes back to 1617 in its original sense, "formal religious worship or veneration," and it come from Latin *cultus,* worship (itself from the verb *colere,* to cultivate). By 1679 *cult* had taken on another meaning, "a particular form of religious worship with reference to its external rites," as in *the cult of Aphrodite.* From there, it was a short step, by 1711, to yet another meaning, "devotion or homage to one particular person or thing, openly professed by a group of followers." By the late 1970s, however, an even more narrowed—and quite negative—sense had begun to emerge, "a religious

What was left of the Branch Davidian compound in 1993, two weeks after the government ended the siege by burning it down. Eighty-seven men, women, and children, including cult leader David Koresh, were killed in the fire.

sect generally regarded as false or extremist, with its adherents living in an unconventional way (as in an armed, self-sufficient commune) under the direction of a charismatic, authoritarian leader." Parents worried about their teenage children in particular being attracted to, and taken in by, cults, resulting in their having to extract the kids and *deprogram* (1973) them; that is to say, to try to counteract the effects of religious or *cultic* indoctrination, often using coercive techniques.

Two of the most high-profile *cults* of the latter part of the 20th century were the *Peoples Temple* and the *Branch Davidians*. People talked about Jim Jones, the Peoples Temple leader who, with 912 of his followers, died in a mass murder-suicide in Jonestown, Guyana, on November 18, 1978. This tragedy propelled *Jonestown* (like the much later *Waco*) into the language as a word symbolizing such an event ("We don't want another *Jonestown*"). And people watched in horror television coverage of the fiery ATF/FBI attack on the *Branch Davidian compound* in Waco, Texas, in April 1993. Led by David Koresh, 80 *Branch Davidians* died in the assault, which occurred after long-term negotiations between Koresh and federal agents broke down, the Justice Department being concerned about alleged sexual assaults on small children and the possibility of "a *Jonestown*-type mass murder-suicide."

FUELING THE FIRES

*H*umankind has been burning wood to keep warm for over 200,000 years. Wood still provided 90 percent of America's fuel a hundred years ago. Although the Old English word wood (then spelled wudu/wuda) meant "tree" when first cited in the year 725, it very soon was applied to "firewood" (cited 888). Since wood was basically fuel for so long, the word firewood itself, implying other uses for wood, seems not to have been necessary until many years later, being first recorded in English in the 14th century (kindling is a 1513 English word, originally meaning only the material for lighting a fire).

"The happiness of the domestic fireside is the first boon of Heaven. . . ."

— Thomas Jefferson, letter to John Armstrong, 1813

Thus for untold centuries, heating depended on wood for fuel. The words *heating, log* (from Middle English *logge*, tree limb, fallen tree) and *fuel* (via Old French *feuaile* from Latin *focalis*, hearth) went together. All three words were first recorded in English in the same 1398 manuscript.

THE FAMILY HEARTH

Until the 11th century most European dwellings had dirt floors with a fire burning on a hearth in the center, this *hearth* (cited to before the 12th century and going back to Old English *heorth*) being nothing more than a flat stone or stone platform or a pit, the smoke from the fire escaping through an opening in the roof. Then, beginning in the 11th century, the first multistoried castles were built, their fortresslike walls and upper stories preventing smoke from escaping from a room with a simple hearth. This was no problem in the smaller rooms, which were heated only when occupied and then only by individual metal heating baskets, braziers, or fire pans in which charcoal or wood was burned. But something

The more things change, the more they stay the same. In addition to wind and solar power, firewood in the 1970s became a popular alternative to expensive oil and dirty coal.

A fireplace that is being used for both heating and cooking.

better than a large smoking hearth in the center of the floor had to be devised for the castle's great halls. They were heated by something new, large hearths actually built into the thick outside walls which, in turn, were specially constructed with tunnel-like openings through which the smoke could escape. Such hearths and wall tunnels finally led to the *chimney*. Spelled as *chimenai* (via Latin *caminus*, fireplace, from Greek *káminos*, heating chamber, furnace), the word was first recorded in English in the 14th century and then meant both the hearth or *fire hearth* and the special opening through wall or roof to let the smoke out. Later *chimney* meant only the smoke-funneling structure, especially that part of it above the roof (the chimney was also called a *flue*—origin unknown—in English by 1582). The word *fireplace* was in use by the late 1600s.

Until well into the 18th century almost all American colonists heated their dwellings as the English at home did, by burning firewood in some type of fireplace with a hearth and chimney. There was usually a *grate* (14th century, from Latin *grata*, grating) and *andirons* to hold the logs (*andiron* is also a 14th century English word, from Middle English *aundiren*, an alteration—influenced by Middle English *iren*, "iron"—of Old French *andier*, itself of Celtic origin). They have also been called in the U.S. South and Midlands *fire dogs* since 1792 and in some other U.S. dialects *dogs* or *dog irons*, so called because of their dog-like shape when viewed from the side. We also tended the fire with *fire tongs* (dating back to the year 1100) and a *poker* (1534), though as early as 1637 we also called the poker a *firestick* and the tongs *firesticks*. By the 15th century the English were using and talking about the *fire screen* in front of the fireplace; we began calling it a *fire fender* and a *fire guard* (the latter by 1833). A family would close off their fireplace in the summer with a *fireboard* (1855).

We had a variety of names for the timber, or long stone, supporting the masonry above the fireplace or the shelf it made or supported, using the English terms *mantle tree* (15th century, *mantle*, a variant of *mantle*, cloak, hood), *mantle* itself (1519), *mantlepiece* (1686), *mantleboard*

(1825), and *mantleshelf* (1828). In America *mantle tree* was considered to be a New England term, *mantlepiece* was seldom heard west of the Mississippi, and *mantleboard* was considered a rustic southern term. We also added our own American terms to these English ones, coining *mantleplace* (1870) and *chimney shelf* (1881).

In America we also had the often fringed or lacy *chimney cloth* (1744) valance around the mantel or chimney piece, both for decoration and to keep some of the fireplace smoke out of the room; and spoke of our native *chimney swallow* (1789, which is actually a swift that nests in chimneys and which John J. Audubon more accurately was to call a *chimney swift* in 1849).

The fireplace wasn't very effective for warming a person or a room, much less a family or a house. By definition and tradition this fireplace was built into the wall of a house, warming at best one side or area of one room only. The bigger the fire the more heat it gave. Thus many early colonial fireplaces were as large as 6 feet high and 10 feet wide, sometimes taking up an entire wall, and burned huge quantities of wood—most of the heat going right up the chimney. Many colonial homes had only one fireplace, in the kitchen for both heating and cooking. Thus, in winter, the kitchen served as a one-room house for most activities. People with one-room cabins were as warm or warmer than those with larger houses.

Even some of the earliest colonial houses did, of course, have more than one *fireroom* (1708, a room containing a fireplace), the second one usually being a sitting room with a fireplace back-to-back with the kitchen fireplace, the two fireplaces sharing a common chimney. Any extra fireplaces, however, meant that extra wood was needed and extra *wood cutting* (1683) had to be done or extra money available to pay someone else to cut and haul it. If one didn't want to keep the wood piled outdoors, additional fireplaces and their extra wood also meant that a larger *wood house* (1274), *woodshed* (1844), or *wood room* (1855) had to be built.

It was best to have a separate *wood lot* (1643), later sometimes called a *wood patch* (1856), to ensure there would be enough inexpensive fuel as the trees near houses and settlements were cut down. The large supply needed for churches, schools, or an elderly or sick householder was often provided by a community gathering to chop wood, such a gathering called a *wood bee* (1857), *wood spell* (1864), *wood chopping* (1872), or *wood frolic* (1889). The dates of these terms show how long wood remained an important fuel. However, early New England meeting houses didn't need any wood, because they had no fireplaces at all. The Puritanical congregations endured the cold with wraps, foot warmers, boxes of hot coals, and heated soapstones, perhaps basking in fire-and-brimstone sermons about the torments of hell.

STOVES

Even when the first colonists landed at Jamestown and Plymouth a heater existed that worked better and used less wood than the fireplace. It was called a *stove* (from Middle English "hot-air sweating room," through either Middle Dutch or Middle Low German, probably from a Latin word *extufa*, referring to steam or smoke, ultimately from Greek *typhein*, to give off smoke). The English word *stove* had been in use since the 1450s, first for a sweating room, then meaning a portable apparatus for burning fuel (by 1591), an oven (1640), and finally (by 1702) an enclosed fireplace, which is what a modern stove is.

"Heap logs and let the blaze laugh out."

— *Robert Browning,* Paracelsus, *1835*

"What matter how the night behaved?

What matter how the North wind raved?

Blow high, blow low, not all its snow

Could quench our hearth-fire's ruddy glow."

— *John Greenleaf Whittier,* Snowbound, *1866*

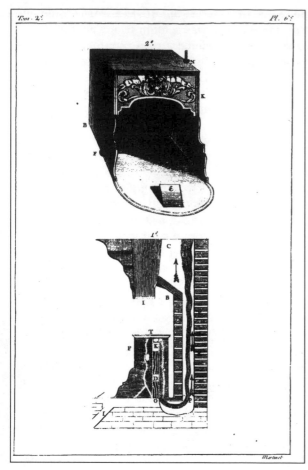

A drawing of the stove Benjamin Franklin invented.

The original colonists didn't use stoves because a stove couldn't be built by oneself as a fireplace could and because, in the 17th century, stoves were little known and less loved by traditional Englishmen. Yet our early colonists did know that stoves existed, and some of the Pilgrims, who had spent 12 years in Holland, had probably been well acquainted with Dutch stoves. A few of the early colonists actually did experiment with and build stoves. The first *cast-iron stove* (actually just a box-like brazier with no grate) to be given that name in America was made in Lynn, Massachusetts, in 1642; a larger boxlike cast-iron stove, probably based on an enclosed stove the Pilgrims had seen in Holland, was manufactured in Saugus, Massachusetts, in 1647; and a patent on such a stove was issued to John Clarke by the General Court of the Massachusetts Bay Colony in 1652.

Other American colonists were trying to improve the fireplace itself, first by building fireplaces narrower and lower; then, around 1700, by putting a large cast-iron plate, called a *firebank*, behind the fireplace fire to reflect more heat into the room (also called, by 1847, a *fireback*); and finally by adding not only firebanks but also hearths and sides of iron. This last development led to detached iron fireplaces, not built into the wall but set into the old fireplace opening and using its chimney. Between 1700 and 1740, some of these iron fireplaces were built on legs and placed in the middle of the room. During this 40-year period we had the:

fire frame, a four-sided iron box on legs, but with no front or back, and set into the fireplace. Its popularity increased even after Benjamin Franklin invented his five-sided *Pennsylvania fireplace* in 1744.

German fire-place, a five-sided box on legs, having a back but no front. At first it had no smoke pipe and was set in the fireplace, using its chimney; later some versions of it had a smoke pipe so that it could sit in the middle of a room. The Pennsylvania Dutch introduced this *German fire-place*, also then called a *German stove*, to America in the early 1700s, and it was manufactured in quantity in Pennsylvania from 1741 to 1768. It was called a *German fire-place* or *German stove*, because the Pennsylvania Dutch (who were German immigrants) decorated their stoves with illustrations of Biblical subjects with titles in German.

Holland fire-place, a six-sided iron box, usually about three feet high and on six-inch legs or a foot-high stand. The sixth side, or front, was an iron fuel door and the top had a hole for a smoke pipe. Though this completely enclosed stove was to be eclipsed by the open-front German stoves and *Franklin stoves* until almost the mid 19th century, it was constantly improved and constantly useful, also being called the *close stove* (1725, closed stove), *box stove* (1820), and *six-plate stove* (also 1820). When made of brick, with an iron door, it was called a *brick stove* (1809).

Were such cast-iron devices fireplaces or stoves? By 1740 some Americans were calling them both *fire-place* and *stove* but seemed to prefer *fire-place* if they were set directly on a stone or brick hearth or floor and *stove* if they were set on legs, especially if on legs and moved out from

"We keep fires to sit by seven months of the year . . . wood, our common fuel, which once might be had at everyman's door, must now be fetched near 100 miles in some towns, and makes a very considerable article of expense."

— Benjamin Franklin, "Account of the New Invented Pennsylvania Fire-Place," 1744

the old fireplace opening. Thus a "new invented iron fire-place" was advertised for sale in the *Pennsylvania Gazette* in 1741, the first recorded use of the term *iron fire-place*. The most famous and certainly one of the best designed and made iron fireplaces was the one Benjamin Franklin introduced in 1744. It was a large cast-iron box with an open front which had a tonguelike grate extending out from it to hold andirons and the small logs used. Being without legs, it was meant to be set in a fireplace or on a stone or brick hearth, with a flue pipe running up through the chimney opening, the rest of the regular fireplace and chimney to be closed off.

Franklin himself always called his invention, which originally had no legs and was meant to be placed inside the traditional wall fireplace, the *Pennsylvania fire-place*, but others were to call it or later versions of it the *Franklin stove* (1787), *the Franklin* (1818), and even the *Franklin heater* (1839) and the *Franklin furnace* (1846).

FUELS

Some of the inventors who tried to improve the fireplace and perfect stoves had, of course, experimented with burning *coal* (first recorded in English before the 12th century, through Middle English from Old English *col*, related to Old High German and Old Norse *kol*, "burning ember"). The Native Americans had used coal in pottery-making, and colonists had found it along the James River in Virginia in 1649 and mined it there from about 1750, as it was in demand by blacksmiths and iron makers. Early experimental coal-burning stoves often used *soft coal* (1789) or *bituminous* (from Latin *bitumen*, mineral pitch, asphalt; *bituminous* had been used to mean such pitch or asphalt, even petroleum, in England since 1620 but wasn't to be widely used to refer to soft coal until around 1830). Such soft coal was messy, did not burn cleanly, and needed constant attention. What was needed was a stove that could withstand the higher heat of burning *hard coal* (1846), or *anthracite* (1812, from Greek *anthrakítes*, coal-like, from Greek *anthrax*, coal; *anthracite* had been used in English since 1604 to mean a rubylike stone but wasn't to be used to refer to hard coal until 1820). Hard coal was cleaner to

A coal train.

A wood stove.

handle and burnt slower, longer, and more completely, leaving fewer ashes.

In 1821 the Lehigh Valley Coal Mine Company sent a small sample of coal to the Reverend Dr. Eliphalet Nott (1773–1866), asking him to design a stove to burn it efficiently and cleanly. Nott developed his first base-burning coal stove, which contained a special coal grate, a firebox made of *firebrick* (1793), an ashpit, and even a mica window. He called his first coal-burning stove the *Saracenic grate* (probably for the connotation of the Saracens and hot Arab climates) and by 1839 had 14 patents on coal stoves. By the late 1820s and early 30s the few coal stoves to be seen were often called *Nott's patent stoves* or simply *Nott stoves*.

Coal stoves became truly popular, however, only after Jordan L. Mott, Sr., of New York City improved and simplified Nott's base-burning design, obtaining a patent on a pyramid-shaped stove with a slanting coal grate in 1833, the coal sliding down from the upper part to be burned at the bottom. Mott's stove and grate were designed to burn *nut coal*, which was then very cheap. He made his stoves, which the public called *Mott stoves* by 1838, at his J. L. Mott Iron Works at Mott Haven, New York (now part of the Bronx in New York City). His stoves and those of his competitors were so successful that soon *stove* didn't mean "wood stove" anymore: we had to distinguish between wood-burning and coal-burning by using the full terms *coal stove* (1834) and *wood stove* (1847).

Wood was, of course, still used in many stoves, especially cookstoves, long after the Civil War, as shown by such late-occurring terms as *stove wood* (1867), *stove length* (1881, as wood cut to the size of a stove's fuelbox), and *stove stick* (1888, a stick of stove wood). However, terms such as *stove board* (1875, a protective metal plate or mat on the floor under a stove, especially found under parlor or sitting-room stoves), *stove lid* (1876, the usually round metal plate for covering the opening on top of a cookstove), and *stove lid lifter* (1886, for picking up the hot stove lid) might apply to either a wood or coal stove.

Many people who could afford stoves resisted them, regarding them as dangerous "redhot monsters" (Charles Dickens' term for the stoves that overheated him on a visit to America in 1842) that made the room too hot, dry, and stuffy, causing headaches.

The round or cylindrical stove had the best shape for heating a large room evenly. The cannon stove had been the first round stove in America, and Isaac Orr had a squat rounded stove in Philadelphia and Washington during the first three decades of the 19th century. Mott's early rounded stoves were called *pot-bellied baseburners* and *pot-bellied stoves* by the late 1840s (*pot-bellied* had first been used in England in 1657, to refer only to people, with the adjective being applied to bottles and other rounded objects by the 1820s); however, such a rounded stove was more apt to be called a *globe stove* during the late 19th century and was sometimes called a *barrel stove* (1904) during the early 20th century. The most famous pot-bellied stove was actually a globe stove made for schools, stores, and railroad stations, with the "Station Agent" being for years the most common stove found in railroad stations. It was usually around such a large pot-bellied stove that the *stove league* (1914) or *hot stove league* (1915) gathered, these terms referring to those rustic or neighborhood idlers who sat around the stove in a general store, basking in its warmth while discussing baseball, politics, and local news and gossip.

Famous stove models and homey stove names persisted for years; the "Station Agent" was in use in some of New York City's Sixth Avenue elevated railroad stations until 1939 and the U.S. Army used a "Warm Morning" baseburner in some of its camps during World War II. There were also specialized stoves, as the small, portable coke-burning *salamander stove* (1852) used for heating small rooms, drying plaster, etc., and so named because the salamander is supposed to be able to withstand extreme heat; and the *Yukon stove* (1898), a small sheet-iron box stove and oven with a telescoping smoke pipe, as carried by prospectors to the Yukon during the Klondike gold rush, which began in 1897.

A few fireplaces, stoves, and *heaters* (1688) had been designed to heat more than one room, such as the back-to-back fireplaces heating two rooms; the five-plate stove fed from one room and projecting into another, heating both; the *Russian stove,* developed in Russia and first mentioned as being used in the U.S. in 1811, which had multiple flue pipes radiating heat to as many as four rooms; the American *drum stove* (1833), which heated a ground-floor room in the normal way but which also had a flue pipe running through a sheet-iron drum in a second-floor room or sleeping loft to warm it (such a drum stove was also called a *dumb stove* by 1851, both because people confused "drum" and "dumb" and because the upstairs heating drum was "dumb" in that it had no fire of its own); and the *Latrobe Heater (*invented by John Latrobe in the 1850s) and *Sanford's Challenge Heater* (first manufactured by the National Stove Works in New York City in 1858), which were stoves with stovepipes for heating several rooms.

CENTRAL HEATING

Modern *hot-water heating* was developed in France in the early 18th century, where it was first used in a greenhouse and then in a chicken hatchery. Word of its success spread, so that by 1792 it was used to heat the Bank of England in London. Meantime, James Watt (1736-1819), the Scottish inventor of the modern steam engine in 1765, experimented with heating by steam in 1784 and a Halifax, Nova Scotia, inventor patented a *steam-heating* unit in 1791, such units being used to provide *steam heat* in some British factories by 1822. Both hot-water and steam-heating systems were introduced into the U.S. in a few theaters and in public rooms of some of the more plush hotels in New York City and Boston in the 1820s, 30s, and 40s, with Boston's Eastern Exchange Hotel of 1846 being the first to have every room heated by steam. However, it wasn't until the 1870s, 80s, and 90s, with newly perfected valves, return-line piping systems, and other components, that the terms *hot-water heating* and *steam-heated* (1884) became well known.

Both systems used a *boiler* (meaning a vessel for boiling water since 1725 and a vessel for boiling water to steam for a steam engine since 1752, both meanings first recorded in England) to produce the hot water or steam which is fed via a *hot-water pipe* (1842) or a *steam pipe* (1857) to a room *radiator* (1836 in the generalized sense "something that radiates," e.g., heat) or a *steam radiator* (1879). Since a valve is needed on each radiator to allow air to escape when the heated water expands in a hot-water system or when the steam enters in a steam-heating system, there could be a loud *knock* (1869 as the sound of mechanical parts striking together, the word first recorded in the year 1000 in English to mean the sound of a blow or rap). The two systems evolved almost simultaneously.

At the same time as boiler-fed hot-water and steam-heating systems were developing, so was the hot-air furnace. For just as the fireplace had been enclosed in iron and moved to the center of the room to become a stove, the stove was to be fitted with hot-air pipes and moved to the basement to become a *furnace* (first recorded in England in the 13th century meaning an enclosed structure for producing heat, from Latin *fornax*, oven, kiln, related to Latin *formus*, warm). The term *hot-air furnace* was first recorded in America in 1841, *warm-air furnace* in 1846, and *furnace fire* in 1859 (though it had been used in English since 1645 to refer to a fire in a smelting furnace). Hot air welled up through brass *registers* (1845 with this meaning) in the floor.

FURNACES

By the 1890s most new homes and apartment buildings for the upper and middle classes were being built with boilers and steam or hot-water radiators or with *coal furnaces* and hot-air registers. Thus *central heating* came to America, though the term itself was not recorded until 1906. Not only did central heating change the way we kept warm, but by heating the entire house it changed home design and construction, interior design, dress styles, and living habits. Drafts were no longer as much an issue as before, though such new terms as *heat loss* and *heat insulation* were being discussed by the 1880s, and *heat flow* entered the language by 1902, showing that new concerns had to be taken into account. One could wash, bathe, and shave in a warm room and hence did so more frequently—and in a separate bathroom, complete with its own sink and tub, instead of near the fire (*hot running water* from a *hot-water pipe*, 1897, was, of course, often a companion to central heating and many families began to enjoy both). The family had gained a larger, fully usable house, but the social value of the hearth—the fireplace or stove around which the entire family gathered and shared its life, the focal point that kept the family and its various generations, activities, and interests together—had disappeared. The American family would never be the same again.

The *coal-fed furnace* (1880s) started to become a common home feature. Everyone knew that coal came from a *coal mine* (1613). Home delivery of coal might be through a *coal hole* (1854) in the sidewalk. We also were often calling a coal scuttle a *coal bucket* by 1887. Coal was delivered to most homes by wheelbarrow, cart, horse-drawn wagon, or

"*Coal is a portable climate.*"

— *Ralph Waldo Emerson,*
The Conduct of Life, *1860*

truck, then carried to the coal cellar or shoveled or dumped down the chute into the basement *coal bin* (1864), each such home delivery leaving a trail of broken coal on streets, yards, and driveways and a fine film of *coal dust* (1597) over the furniture. Father or an older son rose early every winter morning to walk down cold basement steps to shake down the ashes from the furnace grate to the ashpit and remove the *furnace clinkers* (1853) or *clinkers* that wouldn't fall through the grate (*clinker* had been used in English since 1641 to mean a paving brick, from the Dutch *klinker*, a type of kiln-hardened brick, then by 1769 was used to mean a piece of slag formed from impurities in coal). Then he stirred the fire with a long poker and carried buckets or shovelfuls of coal from the coal bin to the furnace, stoking the fire to a roaring pitch to warm the house before the rest of the family rose to dress. In the evening the day's ashes and clinkers were removed and a roaring fire could be going again before the children undressed for bed and then the fire would be *banked* for the night (since at least 1860 to *bank* a fire has meant to add fuel and restrict the intake of air to keep it burning slowly for a long time, to *bank* having meant to pile up in English since 1590, from the 13th century English noun *bank*, a raised ridge).

By the late 1930s, however, some lucky families had homes with furnaces fed by an automatic *stoker* (originally used in English in 1660 to mean one who stokes a furnace, then first recorded in 1884 as a mechanical device for doing this). This stoker was usually a large screw, or *worm*, that carried small lumps of coal, usually specially shaped *briquettes* (1883, a direct borrowing from the French, a diminutive of *brique*, brick), from a specially filled hopper in the basement coal bin directly into the furnace. It and the flue draft were automatically activated when the temperature fell below a predetermined level by a *thermostat* (cited to 1831, from Greek *therme/thermo-*, heat, hot, + Greek *states/-stat*, constant, set, something that stops or steadies). The first thermostat used in home-heating systems had appeared on Elisha Foote's airtight stove of 1849; it was a bi-metallic rod that expanded with heat to close the draft automatically.

FORCED AIR HEATING
Though various methods to create a *forced draft* (1865) or *forced air* (1880) had been attempted in stoves and early furnaces, not until 1930 did *forced warm air heating*, as it was then widely called, begin to come into use. It used a motor-driven fan to force the warm air through smaller, usually rectangular *ducts* (the word used in England since 1713 to refer to a channel for liquids, then used in America to refer to furnace pipes since 1884).

The smaller, neater furnace ducts meant that the basement was no longer cluttered with big, cumbersome pipes, but could be a neat usable area, even paneled to serve as a *rumpus room* (1939), *family room* (which term had been used to mean an informal living room or second parlor since 1853), or *recreation room* (1854).

The same motor-driven fan that pushed hot air through the ducts could also be used to push heavier cool air through them, making *central air conditioning* much cheaper and more common (*air conditioning* cited in the building-cooling sense to 1930).

OIL AND GAS HEAT
Oil and gas furnaces appeared at almost the same time in American homes in the 1920s and 30s. Though the *oil stove* (1865, in the first U.S. patent for it) had appeared after the Civil War and the *kerosene heater*

and *kerosene stove* had first been talked about and used in the 1870s, *fuel oil* (1893) was first used on a large scale in *oil burners* or *oil furnaces* to provide *oil heating* on the West Coast in the early 1920s and became fairly widespread in the 1930s. Most families then still used coal furnaces, but spoke longingly of installing *oil heat* if the Great Depression ever ended and they could afford it.

Oil (via Middle English and Old French from Latin *oleum/olea*, oil, originally olive oil, olive tree, from Greek *elaía*, olive) has been in the English language since the 13th century, while *petroleum* (from the Latin, *petr/petra*, rock + *oleum*, oil) was first cited in the 15th century. Originally, however, *oil* meant only mineral and vegetable oils, then also fish and whale oil, before coming to mean petroleum and some of its products.

Oil was soon rivaled by gas as a heating fuel. The term *gas heater* had appeared in 1866, *gas-heated* in 1877, and *gas furnace*, in England, in 1879, with the early gas heating fixture often being in the shape of a *gas log* (1885), a gas burner manufactured in the shape of a log and installed in the fireplace to create a *gas fire* (1910) that looked like a wood fire. (The first *gas well* in the U.S. had been drilled to a depth of 27 feet near a "burning spring" in Fredonia, New York in 1821, though the term *natural gas* was not recorded until 1825.) People also liked the idea that one paid for the metered gas (*gas meter* was an 1815 English term) after it was used instead of having to pay for it beforehand. Many people were using *bottled gas* (also *LP gas* or *LPG*, for *liquefied petroleum gas*, 1920s) as well.

The main competition for gas became electric heating, the term *electric heater* having appeared in 1877 and *electric furnace* in 1885. However, many electric heating systems use no furnace but electrical resistance coils or panels to provide *baseboard heating* or radiant *panel heating* (both 1954 terms, *baseboard* in this sense being cited in 1853), which had been developed in England around 1915. During the 1960s use of electric heating began to increase rapidly, being even easier to use and simpler than gas furnaces, though the cost of electric heating as compared with that of gas and *fossil fuels* (an 1835 English term, referring to coal and oil) was usually high.

An oil derrick.

Solar panels.

In the early 1970s, with the U.S. importing more and more oil, much of it from the politically volatile Middle East, people began to talk about a future *oil shortage*, and oil prices soared as the *Organization of Petroleum Exporting Countries (OPEC*, officially organized November 14, 1960) raised oil prices dramatically. The cost of heating gas and electricity soon followed the spiral of inflation upward. The oil shortage was indeed an *energy shortage*: our own sources, including *off-shore oil wells*, developed since the early 1950s, seemed no longer sufficient; the *atomic power plants*, which since the late 1940s had promised such ready and cheap electricity, were horribly expensive to build, required years to license, were increasingly considered too dangerous to control, and produced radioactive wastes, which could not be suitably disposed of. Americans who heated their homes with electricity or oil told horror stories of spending several hundred dollars a month on heating bills—and wondering if or when Middle Eastern politics would disrupt the world's oil supply, or if the depletion of fossil fuels would leave them without a reasonably affordable source of heat.

Thus, from the late 1970s through the 80s many Americans returned to wood-burning stoves. Others talked of the future possibility of using newer, cleaner types of coal, such as *pulverized coal*, which could be delivered through pipelines, or of processing oil from *oil shales* (1873). Still others spoke of using *windmills* (first recorded in English in the 14th century) to generate household electricity or using geothermal heat from the ground to generate electricity for homes or cities. Newly popular too, was *solar heating*, though an experimental *solar boiler* had been talked about as early as 1884. The new interest in solar heating had us talking about collecting *solar energy* in metal coils or in *solar panels* (1961) on the roof or the outside walls of a house to heat circulating water.

Many Americans also turned down their central heating devices to conserve fuel and lower heating bills, such *energy conservation* considered not only the sensible and economical thing to do but also a patriotic way to "reduce our dependency on foreign oil." Turning the heat down began to change our dress styles again, and more Americans returned to wearing warmer clothing indoors, including *layering*, or wearing multiple thin layers of shirts, sweaters, vests, etc., adjustable for comfort. To supplement the lowered central heating system various modernized types of oil, kerosene, and electric heaters called *space heaters* (1925) were used only to heat the area or space in a room actually occupied, leaving the rest of the room and house cool—just as fireplaces and stoves had once done. People began to install much more insulation (sometimes so much that their houses became "sick" from lack of air circulation) to attain a greater degree of *energy efficiency*.

NEW HEATING TRENDS

In contrast to the *oil crises* of the 70s, the *oil glut* of the 1980s sapped much of America's motivation to develop *alternative energy sources*. Still, interest in new energy systems did continue to grow: *geothermal heating* (*geothermal*, 1875) became a fast-growing category of heating and air-conditioning equipment (in the industry called *HVAC*, for heating, ventilation, and air conditioning) in America. *Geothermal* refers to using the heat energy of the Earth's interior. Below the first two or three feet, the soil remains at a relatively constant temperature the year round. Geothermal systems work by extracting heat from deep within the ground, using a *heat pump* (1894) linked to a *heat exchanger*. These systems transfer heat to and from the ground through water-filled polyethylene loops installed in vertical bores or horizontal trenches. Geothermal heat pumps, or *GHPs*, use some electricity yet typically deliver three to four times more energy than they consume. More traditional *heat pumps*, which extract heat from the air, became popular in the 1970s. The use of *solar energy* for heating also made steady progress over the last two decades of the 20th century. Solar, in addition to geothermal and wind, is known as a *renewable resource* because it is available from natural, ongoing processes and not exhaustible. Current solar energy designs are categorized as *passive* or *active systems*. *Passive systems* collect, store, and radiate solar energy absorbed in specially engineered building components. *Active systems* have solar panels or *solar collectors* (1955) and storage/distribution subsystems using water or air to transport heat. Sunlight can be converted directly into electricity by a *solar cell* (1955), a *photovoltaic* (1890) device that converts light into electrical energy, sometimes stored in *solar batteries* (1954). *Solar ponds* (1961) are pools of salt water heated by the sun and used to supply heat directly or to generate electricity. *Solar cooking* is the use of concentrated solar radiation on a heating plate to cook food.

Wind turbine (1909) technology may prove the most economically viable alternative energy source. The potential of wind power is enormous—just one percent of Earth's wind power could meet the entire world's energy needs. By the 1970s, people living by choice "off the power grid" had begun using wind turbines to produce power for their homes. The machines entering the market in the 1990s generated 300–750 *kilowatts* (1884) per turbine, using lighter and more aerodynamic blades made of synthetic materials, improved hubs and drive trains, and more advanced electronics. *Wind farms*, complexes with many wind turbines driving electrical generators, have been with us since 1980. *Wind farmers* work *power farms* (1995), harvesting renewable electricity. So successful have been some home operations that they can sell excess electricity back to the power company. Among the most creative schemes is the installation of wind turbines along highways to take advantage of the wind created by passing cars and trucks.

Instead of burning wood and generating heavy pollutants, *pellet stoves* (1993) burn low-emission manufactured wood pellets. *Pelletization*, the formation and compaction of various materials into pellets, began in 1942, first with ores and later with coal and plastics. Wood pellets are made from wood waste products that are ground, dried, and compressed.

"The early exhaustion of our fossil fuels will require the use of such other sources of power as water, wind and sun."

— Scientific American,
May 14, 1921

IT'S YOUR FUNERAL

*T*he slang expression It's your funeral, *meaning "prepare to take the consequences," and the oft-heard* It was a lovely funeral, *referring to the arrangements for a deceased person, are Americanisms pure and simple. The second of the two could have become a cliché only after the 1860s when* embalming, *the fancy* casket *(no longer a* coffin*) for the common man, and the typically black funeral* wreath *all came into vogue. "Dr." Thomas Holmes, "the father of American embalming," who is said to have made a fortune embalming 4,028 slain soldiers at $100 apiece during the Civil War, brought the American funeral trade out of what one wag called the* Ice, *or* Glacial Age, *when bodies were preserved prior to burial in or on ice. (Holmes's embalming fluid—called* Innominata—*was "guaranteed to contain no poison"; over 130 years later it was discovered to have contained heavy amounts of arsenic.) And it was in 1863 that Nathaniel Hawthorne denounced the distinctly American—and new, euphemistic usage— of* casket, *calling it "a vile modern phrase [sic] which compels a person to shrink from the idea of being buried at all." The 1860s also gave English* funeral train, *it being first used in 1865 to refer to the train bearing Abraham Lincoln's body on a circuitous 12-day, 1,700-mile route from Washington, D.C., to Springfield, Illinois, on what could only be deemed a national viewing. (Funeral train came back into wide use 80 years later when Franklin D. Roosevelt's body was borne by train from Warm Springs, Georgia, to Washington, D.C.).*

"BURIAL ARTS" IN AMERICA

Embalming (about 1340, from Old French *embasmer*, from *en-*, "to put in or into," and *basme*, "balm") changed the style of the American funeral, and with it, the role of the *undertaker* (1698, also called in the 18th century a *dismal trader*, the word *dismal* coming from Medieval Latin *dies malii*, "unlucky days," and used formerly in the plural as a noun, *dismals*, to mean *widows' weeds* or mourning garments). The undertakers originated in one of three funeral support trades: running a livery stable (horses, wagons, carts), working as a carpenter (building coffins as well

Abraham Lincoln's funeral train in 1865.

Jackie Kennedy, in mourning, at her husband's state funeral, escorted by brothers-in-law Bobby (left) and Teddy (right).

as cabinets), and serving as a church sexton (ringing bells, digging graves). In early colonial days there were no full-time undertakers: the funeral was strictly a family-run affair. The body was cleaned, prepared, and *laid out* at home; it was buried usually in a church cemetery or on a plot designated as a family cemetery if on a farm or estate; a social gathering was held at the house for friends and relatives; and a sermon was preached—if at all—on the Sunday after the burial. Oftentimes clergy, especially in Puritan-dominated New England, were not even present at the burial. (It was only by the mid 19th century that it became common for clergy to perform pre-burial and burial rites.) Flowers were not used (they were frowned upon by the clerics), but *mourning jewelry* was passed out to relatives, friends, and helpers in the form of hair from the decedent woven into rings, pins, watch guards, or locket contents. Gold *mourning rings*, symbolizing the "marriage" between body and soul, were also given out, as were gloves, which were supposed to keep the spirit of the deceased from entering the body of a mourner, should that mourner touch the casket. And *mourning women*—essentially *professional mourners*—could be hired to sit near the coffin of an unpopular decedent and weep. A *passing bell* tolled to call the locals for prayers and to drive off any evil spirits that might have gathered for the funeral.

The African American funeral was also a family affair. A *cooling board* (typically an ironing board) was used, for example, in the Low Country of South Carolina, on which to lay out the body in the home. The grave was frequently dug along an East-West axis, recalling the West African taboo against burying someone North-South, or *crossing the world*. (The body needed to face East to allow it to arise on Judgment Day.) The clergyman did not *officiate*; rather, he *preached the funeral*. Graveyard dust in some communities of the South was *goofer dust, goofer* being of African origin, related to the Mende word *ngafa*, "ghost." *Ring shouts* were performed by those gathered for the funeral. Also called *the plantation walk-around*, these were counterclockwise circle dances with the participants' feet shuffling one in front of the other, never lifted from the ground. Members of *praise* (or prays) *houses*—used for midweek services, socials, and political meetings—would often oversee funerals and maintain the burial plots before the Civil War. After the war, *burial soci-*

"The Dead Shall Be Raised." Words of comfort for the mourners.

eties, *burial lodges*, and later urban *burying* leagues and *burial associations*, with *marshals* in charge of arrangements, would guarantee their dues-paying members proper funerals. Today, some such organizations are called *death-care corporations* and *funeral societies*.

By the mid 1880s the *undertaker* (from *undertake*, as in "to take upon oneself a [usually unpleasant] duty," a verb created on the model of Middle English *undernim*, which had the same meaning), had transformed into a *funeral director* (1886) who worked in or ran a *mortuary* (1865, from Latin *mortuatris*, "of the dead," from *mortuus*, "dead") and who, by 1895, had further transformed into a *mortician* (from Latin *mors*, "death"). By 1926 *mortuary* had been renamed *funeral home*, this transformation representing the demise of the *home funeral* in a newly urbanized culture wherein small apartments afforded scant room for laying out the dead, conducting services, and holding wakes.

Over time, the terminology associated with death softened by euphemism. Families and undertakers in American began to talk about:

the loved one, *the departed, the dearly departed,* and *the decedent* instead of *the dead person, the deceased,* and *the deceased person;*

the remains and *the cremains* instead of *the body, the corpse,* and *the ashes;*

the baby or *the infant* instead of *the stillborn child;*

the preparation room instead of the (funeral-home) *morgue* (1821, from French);

preparing the decedent instead of *handling the body;*

clothing instead of *shroud* (1570 in the sense of "winding-sheet for a corpse");

selection room instead of *backroom, showroom, salesroom, casket display room,* or *casket room* (in order to palliate the aura of funerary commercialism);

memorial counselor instead of *cemetery-plot salesman;*

slumber room, *reposing room, parlor* instead of *laying-out room in a funeral home*, with *reposing room* echoing another use of repose in

Carrying the casket into the church (right) and to the gravesite (left).

mortuary jargon—that is, the ***repose block*** used by undertakers to support the neck of the decedent during embalming;

service, memorialization, celebration of life, memorial instead of *funeral*, noting also that *funeral* by definition means the presence of the decedent while *memorial service* by definition indicates absence of the decedent (*funeral* going back to about 1523, from Middle French *funerailles*, ultimately from Latin);

coach, professional car instead of *hearse* (a 14th century word from Middle French *herce*, "a harrow; a frame for holding candles," ultimately from Latin);

service car instead of *body car* (used in transporting a decedent to the funeral home from the site of death, or from the funeral home to, e.g., a medical institution);

open/close a grave instead of *dig/fill a grave*, with *grave* attested before the 12th century and going back to Old English *grafan*, meaning "to dig," so that *open* doesn't soften the wording at all if one knows the history;

inter instead of *bury* (with *bury* dating to before the 12th century and coming from Old English *byrgan*, related to Old High German *bergan*, "to shelter," also related to Russian *berech*, "to spare"; *inter* from the 14th century, from Middle English *enteren*, assumed ultimately from Vulgar Latin *interrare*, "to put into the ground"—another instance of the failure of euphemism, for the seemingly softer *inter* has the harsher historical meaning, whereas the seemingly harsher *bury* has the softer historical meaning);

vital statistics form instead of *death certificate*;

cremation chamber or ***vault*** instead of *retort* (1605, from Middle French, ultimately from Latin);

strew the cremains instead of *scatter the ashes*.

And instead of to *die*, people began to say *expire, succumb, pass away, pass on, depart, depart this life, repose, go to sleep with the Lord* (or *the angels*), *quit this world, go to Heaven, be gathered to one's fathers, rest*

"Funeralese has had its ups and downs. The word "morticians," first used in Embalmers Monthly *for February, 1895, was barred by the* Chicago Tribune *in 1932, 'not for lack of sympathy with the ambition of undertakers to be well regarded, but because of it. If they haven't the sense to save themselves from their own lexicographers, we shall not be guilty of abetting them in their folly.'"*

— *Jessica Mitford,*
The American Way of Death

A service at the gravesite.

with one's ancestors, *meet one's Maker, go to the happy hunting ground, meet one's (untimely) end, make one's exit, end one's days, fall asleep, close one's eyes, take one's last sleep, put out to sea* (from the verse of Tennyson), *go the way of all earth* (Biblical), *go home (at last), join the choir invisible, pass over Jordan,* and *awake to life immortal.*

In a separate development, slang expressions—many jocular—synonymous with *die* sprang up: *be ten toes up, bite the dust, cash in, cash in one's chips, check out, conk (out), cop out, croak, curl up one's toes, feed the worms, go home feet first, go to the last roundup, kick in, kick the bucket, kick off, peg out, kick up one's heels, ring down the curtain, pop off, snuff out, swelt,* and *turn up* or *push up one's toes to the daisies.*

Similarly, *cemeteries* (15th century, from Middle French *cimetiere*, ultimately from Greek *koimeterion*, "a sleeping room; a burial place") replaced *graveyard, burying* (or *burial*) *ground*, and as the 20th century memorial parks (around 1928) evolved with their in-ground markers, the soothing English of what Shelley once called "the lone couch of . . . everlasting sleep" came full circle with these expressions designating America's cities, or gardens, of stone and/or the "neighborhoods" within them:

Perpetual Rest	Memory Gardens
Perpetual Care	Kindly Light
Perpetual Repose	Brotherly Love
Perpetual Sleep	Sweet Repose
Everlasting Love	Sheltering Hills
Abiding Love	Lilac Corridor
Enduring Faith	Sunshine Garden
Loving Kindness	Sunset View
Eternal Peace	Heaven of Peace
Eternal Memory	Gates of Heaven
Beautiful Memory	Blessed Promise

With growing numbers of people engaging in *pre-need funeral arrangements* and many choosing the previously stigmatized *cremation* (from *cremate,* 1874), the *cremains* (1947) from the *crematory* (1876) or the *crematorium* (1880) began to be placed into *cinerary urns* (*cinerary,*

Advertising the benefits of Rosedale Memorial Park: "The Cemetery Beautiful."

1750, from Latin *cinerarium*; *urn*, 14th century, from Latin *urna*) for *disposition* (another euphemism) in *niches* (1611, from Middle French *nicher*, "to rest," ultimately from Latin) located in *mausoleums* (or *mausolea*)—15th century, from Greek *mausoleion*, after Mausolus, the c.353 B.C. Greek ruler of Caria, whose widow constructed the first mausoleum for him. Other sites were *cinerariums* (or *cineraria*)—1880, from Latin, meaning "a place to receive the ashes of the cremated dead"—and *columbariums* (or *columbaria*)—1846, structures of vaults lined with niches for the urns. Most modern "gardens" now offer a variety of interment possibilities.

GARDENS AND CITIES OF STONE

Just as advancements in embalming techniques changed funerary practice in America and hence the language used by Americans, so too did the ideals of American living affect, tangentially at least, the landscapes of cemeteries, culminating in the memorial parks or gardens with a 20th century suburban look—far different from the colonial church graveyards, which, prior to the end of the 18th century, had been regarded by the colonists as unattractive, foul-smelling, and unhealthy. By the mid 19th century, public health reformers—regarding such cemeteries as breeding grounds for disease—advocated the *urban cemetery* and the *rural cemetery*. The first, located typically at a town or city's outskirts, was managed by a sexton, had a formal garden design, and contained for the first time three-dimensional *tombstones* (1565), monuments, and sculpture of stone or marble. (The first planned urban cemetery, the Grove Street Cemetery in New Haven, Connecticut, was established in 1796.) The colonists' markers had been wood, stone, or slate, often adorned with rather stark representations of grinning skulls and crossbones, the Grim Reaper, death's-heads, and coffins.

The second—the *rural cemetery*—emerged in 1831 and flourished through the 1870s. It was an *ornamental cemetery*, a botanical garden, a national-historical-architectural-artistic museum, and an arboretum all in one—located in the suburbs of cities, and featuring three-dimensional markers, monuments, and sculpture in granite and marble, along with mausoleums, some quite splendid. Owned privately, it was managed by a superintendent, and often was a place to which entire families would go by horse tram for a Sunday outing, as was the case with the *urban cemetery*.

By 1855 and into the 1920s the *lawn-park cemetery*, a commercial operation targeted to middle-class tastes, emerged. Sited in a rolling country field, it discouraged the clutter of big monuments and limited the number of individual markers. It encouraged close-to-the-ground markers, especially ones of bronze, a heretofore unused marker material.

The *memorial park* (1971) and its entrepreneurial salespeople, its flush-with-the ground markers and centralized sculptures (called *features*), was a natural extension of the *lawn-park cemetery*. It imitated in death the lives of suburbanite subdivisional living. Themes were often chosen for *burial courts* or *patios*, e.g., the *Court of Freedom* in Forest-Lawn in Southern California (America's first *memorial park*).

All these manicured burying grounds are far different from the infamous *potters' fields* (1777, from the mention in Matthew 27:7 of the purchase of a *potter's field* for use as a graveyard for foreigners). A famous *potter's field* on Hart Island (reachable from New York City only by ferry with special permission beforehand) is a stark strand a half mile east of the Bronx, where fully 750,000 souls repose on 45 acres, buried in 75-foot-long trenches, 6 feet deep, dug by convicts. These trenches are mass graves to be closed only after each one has been filled with coffins to which the decedents' names have been added (Markers, if any, are just about as primitive as the colonists'.)

Though also containing many souls, the nation's *national cemeteries* stand in strong contrast to places like Hart Island. Designed to honor the nation's military dead, the *national cemeteries* came into being during the Civil War. The most storied one was established in 1863 after the Battle of Gettysburg. By 1989 there were 110 of these, most featuring identical white markers, with officers and enlisted people buried in separate sites. Arlington National Cemetery, the best-known, was established in 1864 on 612 acres with over 20,000 trees and over 170,000 headstones.

THE MODERN LEXICON OF DEATH CARE

Some of the expressions Americans use today with respect to funeral arrangements reflect the arid tone of the technocrat as well as the aura of the New Age. Today, Americans talk about:

pre-need planning, early decisions on one's own funeral arrangements (type of disposition, costs, services) made with a funeral director, often prepaid with a contract.

grieving or *bereavement fare*, discounts by airlines from 20 to 60 percent off normal rates for transport of immediate family members to and from a funeral, requiring documentation from a funeral home.

at-need arrangements, funeral arrangements made at once as a result of a death.

direct disposition, burial or cremation immediately after death with no storage, embalming, or visitation.

P.O., please omit (flowers).

"Death, the stern sculptor, with a touch

No earthly power can stay,

Changes to marble in a hour

The beautiful, pale clay"

— *Louisa May Alcott*

"Imperishable Limoges porcelain portraits preserve the features of the deceased. They set firmly in to the stone and remain permanent forever."

— *Sears-Roebuck catalog, 1900–10*

Mourners placing flags and flowers at Arlington National Cemetery, resting place of President Taft, President Kennedy, Robert F. Kennedy, General Pershing, Admiral Peary, William Jennings Bryan, and Joe Louis. The cemetery was built on what had been the estate of Confederate General Robert E. Lee, and for 30 years after the Civil War it served as a settlement for freed slaves.

restorative artists also called *dermasurgeons* (sometimes corrupted to *demisurgeons*), facial and other reconstructive artists/technicians who attend to makeup, hairstyles, reconstructive modeling of face and hands, etc., as part of the preparation of the body prior to *viewing*.

perpetual care, a one-time charge by a cemetery for a burial plot.

back care, accrued charges for the unpaid maintenance of a cemetery plot;

vault, an outer receptacle to protect the casket and its contents as much as possible from the elements, usually made of pre-asphalt-lined concrete, aluminum, a copper-asphalt-concrete amalgam, or fiberglass.

memory picture, the last glimpse of a made-up, dressed, and embalmed decedent in an open casket.

funerary portraiture, photographs of deceased people baked onto enamel or porcelain, then affixed to tombstones, first used in France in 1855, common in the U.S. by the 1890s, still in use today.

vanity tombstones, technically called *personalized headstones*, tombstones designed by shape, color, and content of inscription to reflect the lifestyles, favorite activities, valued possessions, or tastes in drink, etc., enjoyed in life by those now buried under them. Typical designs have been a granite motorcycle, a luxury car, even an overflowing beer stein.

grief counselors, professionals who assist mourning families in dealing with complex feelings upon the death of a loved one, working as part of, e.g., a funeral home's *after-care* program.

grief therapy, the catharsis that is supposed to occur when family members view the deceased during visitation prior to interment.

closure, a coming to acceptance of death in terms of working through feelings of shock, fear, anxiety, frustration, denial, and perhaps guilt as well as grief. In the 1990s *closure* was used with such frequency by Americans that it became a single-word cliché, along with the phrase *get on with (one's) life*.

celebrity exhumation, the exhumation, typically after many years, of famous or notorious corpses, usually with the expressed intent of performing modern forensic tests, such as on samples of DNA, to determine the real cause of death in disputed cases or, in the case of people like the Western outlaw Jesse James, to determine if the interred corpse is in fact that of the person it is thought to be.

"If you don't go to other men's funerals they won't go to yours."

— *Clarence Day*

GENDER GAPS

*S*ince colonial times Americans have used the word sex to refer to either of the two main biological categories of people. "Your sex are naturally tyrannical," Abigail Adams wrote to her husband, John, when he and his compatriots were conferring about the federal government they would soon create. "In the new code of laws . . . remember the ladies," she told him, adding, "[we] will not hold ourselves bound by any laws in which we have no voice or representation." Although the Founding Fathers ignored her plea, the Constitution they created was finally amended 144 years later to state that the right of citizens to vote shall not be denied "on account of sex."

Hillary Rodham Clinton has challenged the stereotype of the politician's wife in many ways—from being the primary breadwinner for the family for most of her life, to reclaiming her maiden name, to becoming the first First Lady actively involved in policy.

Americans have used *sex* in expressions about women such as *the fair sex, the weaker sex, the gentle(r) sex,* and simply *the sex*—which defines half the population from the perspective of the other half. *Gender,* although sometimes used humorously as a synonym for *sex,* was long a technical term employed mainly by linguists.

In the *sexual revolution* of the 1950s and 1960s, people began to speak freely and publicly about acts of sex. With the increased emphasis on its erotic meanings, the word *sex* became less useful for differentiating between men and women in nonsexual (nonerotic) contexts. So by the 1970s, when people talked about the culturally constructed differences between females and males, they spoke of *gender characteristics, gender roles,* and *gender bias.* This apparently simple replacement signaled the direction of further linguistic change in America over the next quarter century: it might be called the Great Gender Shift.

Of the many words we use for an adult male person—some complimentary, others disparaging—the most common and nonjudgmental is *man.* It comes from the Old English word *man* which meant a human being, regardless of gender. Collectively, *man* (also spelled *mann*) meant humankind or humanity as well. Around 1000, *man* came to be used of a male person as well. (Before that, the words *wer* and *wif,* or the compound words *wœpman* and *wifman,* had denoted a male person and a female person, respectively.) After a few centuries, *man* replaced *wer* as the word of choice for a male person.

Words used for an adult female person include many that reflect a concept of her as childbearer, cook, or a mere extension of man:

woman, from Old English *wifman,* combining *wif,* then meaning woman, and *man,* then meaning person, hence "woman person." In Middle English times *wifman* became *wimman,* the reason for the new word's coinage unknown. It replaced *wif,* which lives on today as *wife.*

female, ultimately from Latin *femella,* diminutive of *femina,* woman. It was borrowed by Middle English (from Anglo-French) as *femelle* but as early as the 14th century it became *female* by association with *male.*

lady, from Old English *hlæfdige,* loaf kneader, bread maker. It has meant the mistress of a household since the 13th century, when it was also first used as a title of rank. In the 19th century it came to mean any well-mannered or admired woman, and in the 20th acquired an ironic sense of condescension in such expressions as *cleaning lady* and *lady politician.*

girl, from Middle English *gurle,* a young person of either sex (around 1300). Since around 1375 it has meant a female child, but has also been used informally of a woman of any age, sometimes demeaningly and offensively, as when an adult employee is called a *girl.* Contrary to perceived notions, however, *girl*—especially when used by women and amongst women of and to one another—is not offensive. Rather, in the 90s *girl* gained wide acceptance (influenced by its use as vernacular among African-American women), especially among younger women. This was a word-with-attitude, used in these typical contexts: "Get a life, *girl!*" and "Hey, *girl,* what's up?" Specialized uses of *girl* are found in the fashion industry, where female models have been and continue to be called *girls: big girls* are successful models, supermodels are *huge girls;* to discover a teenager with star potential is to *find a girl;* to make her a star model is to *make a girl. Gal,* an alteration of *girl* since the 1770s, became common in 20th century America as the female equivalent of *guy.*

mistress, Miss, Mrs., Ms., all deriving from Old French *maistresse. Mistress* was the female equivalent of *master* in the 15th century before it came to mean a female paramour. *Master* became *mister* and was first abbreviated as the title *Mr.* in the 16th century, while *mistress* was shortened to the noun *miss* and to the titles *Miss* and *Mrs.* in the 17th century. *Mr.* identified a man but not his marital status. But by the 19th century *Miss* and *Mrs.* were the titles used for an unmarried and married woman, respectively, as if her identity depended on whether or not she was a wife. To break this lopsided distinction, some women in the late 1960s began to use *Ms.,* still another abbreviation of *mistress* (occasionally recorded in colonial America), as a title unrelated to marriage.

poetess, sculptress, etc. The *-ess* suffix (from Old French *-esse*) was in use by the 12th century to denote females, but it wasn't until the 16th or 17th century that such words as *poetess, sculptress, actress, adventuress,* and *murderess* came into common use. In the 19th century some women's rights advocates favored the *-ess* ending, as in *doctress, lecturess,* and *conductress,* perhaps because it called attention to women's expanding roles. Today, *-ess* forms (except *actress*) are scrupulously avoided.

usherette, drum majorette, etc. The *-ette* suffix (from Old French) is used in English as a diminutive, as in *cigarette* and *statuette.* It also came to designate a woman, often implying that women were acting as small, cute men, as in such 20th century Americanisms as *farmerette,* 1902, and *bachelorette,* 1938.

"When the Constitution of the United States was completed on the 17th of September in 1787, I was not included in . . . 'We the people.' But through the process of amendment, interpretation, and court decision I have finally been included in 'We, the people . . .'"

— *Barbara Jordan,*
The Decade of Women, *1974*

English common law, with the full sanction of religion and society, kept colonial women subservient to men. The wife of a free man—although theoretically protected by law from the sort of abuse that could be inflicted on a slave—had the same legal status as her minor children. Her money and all her property were owned by her husband, who had the legal right to punish her in the same way he did any of their children. Yet early American free women shared in the economic life of their communities. Most husbands worked at or near home, and wives were in fact, if never legally, partners in what was really a family occupation, whether working on the farm or in a trade.

With the Industrial Revolution, more and more men began to be employed in offices, factories, and shops. Many women were left at home to do the *woman's work* of raising children, cooking, and cleaning and were largely cut off from community affairs. The one area of public life in which a woman might participate was charitable work. Many joined in the great humanitarian movement of the era, the abolition of slavery.

Pre-Civil War *female reformers* and abolitionists included the Grimké sisters, Sarah (1792–1873) and Angelina (1805–79). Daughters of a South Carolina slave-holding family, they were Quaker converts who lectured against slavery and became pioneers for women's rights. The charismatic mystic Sojourner Truth (c.1797-1883), a freed slave, traveled throughout the North preaching God's love, abolition, and women's rights. From the 1820s until the Civil War, the movement led to such new terms as:

female academy and *female seminary*, private boarding schools for women. Popularizing these terms was the pioneering educator Emma Willard (1787–1870), who in 1814 opened her first female seminary (used in a nonreligious sense for *school* with a curriculum similar to that of male institutions of higher learning). Dozens of new seminaries followed, many of which became four-year colleges, including Wheaton, Mount Holyoke, and Mills. *Coeducation* didn't enter the language until the 1850s. *Coed* was well established by the 1890s.

women's rights, also, often, *woman's rights,* in increasing use after the first women's rights convention, held at Seneca Falls, New York, July 19–20, 1848. The event, which marked the beginning of the women's rights movement in America, was organized by abolitionists Lucretia Mott (1793–1880) and Elizabeth Cady Stanton (1815–1902). The convention adopted 12 resolutions spelling out the rights women must be granted, including the right to the elective *franchise* (14th century, from Old French), as they called the right to vote, and the option of working at any job or profession.

business woman, 1844; *sales lady*, 1856; *salesgirl*, 1887.

bloomers, 1851, named for Amelia Jenks Bloomer (1818–94), who published patterns for them in *The Lily*, her magazine devoted to temperance and women's rights. In protest against the painful cinch-waisted stays and layers of petticoats then in fashion, Bloomer and other women activists (called *bloomers*) adopted a reform dress usually worn with a loose coat and broad-brimmed *bloomer hat* (1859). (See FASHIONS OF THE TIMES, subsection The 1800s–1900s.)

After the Civil War the women's rights movement gained momentum. Women who had worked for abolition and supported the Union's war effort now had time for their own cause. Also, expanding industry and cities offered more jobs for women, many of whom became clerks, teachers, nurses, and doctors, while others took newly created jobs like that of *typist* (1885), *telephone girl* (1893) or *telephone operator* (1894), and *stenog*, short for *stenographer* (1909). Between the Civil War and 1900, we had the following new terms and names:

woman suffrage, *female suffrage*, not common until the 1860s. *Suffrage* (Latin *suffragium*, the right to vote) entered English around 1500. It was first recorded in the U.S. in 1787 in the Constitution, which never denied women suffrage but left to each territory and state the right to set its own voter qualifications. When the 14th Amendment granted citizenship to former slaves, many women who had worked for abolition were incensed that for the first time a gender distinction was introduced into the Constitution: the amendment used the word *male* with reference to the right to vote. Women's rights advocates then tried to have the word *sex* added to the proposed 15th Amendment, which prohibited denial of suffrage on account of race, but the effort failed.

"Robbed of the fundamental privilege of citizenship, I am degraded from the status of a citizen to that of a subject; and not only myself individually, but all of my sex, are, by your honor's verdict, doomed to political subjection under this, so-called, form of government."

— Susan B. Anthony addressing the judge who found her guilty of voting in 1873 "without the legal right to vote." He sentenced her to pay a fine of $100 plus legal costs, which she refused to pay.

Susan B. Anthony was a leader in the early fight for women's suffrage. Born in 1820, she organized the National Woman Suffrage Association in 1869 and was a lecturer and active campaigner up until her death in 1906.

suffragist, a familiar term by the 1880s for either a man or a woman who advocated woman suffrage. *Suffragette* was coined by a London newspaper reporter in 1906 to disparage militant British suffragists, who then adopted the term, making it respectable in England. In America *suffragette* appeared in articles ridiculing women's rights but was seldom used by suffragists themselves.

National Woman Suffrage Association (NWSA), founded in 1869 by Elizabeth Cady Stanton and Susan B. Anthony (1820–1906). Stanton and Anthony shared a larger vision of equal rights for women and men in law, marriage, organized religion, and other areas about which they wrote in *The Revolution*, a weekly newspaper they started in 1868. The *American Woman Suffrage Association* (AWSA) was founded six months later by Lucy Stone (1818–93) and others. By 1890, when the two organizations merged to form the *National American Woman Suffrage Association* (NAWSA), the women's rights movement had become, in effect, a one-issue crusade. Stanton was elected the first NAWSA president, succeeded in 1892 by Anthony.

the new woman and *the emancipated woman*, popular terms in the 1890s. Such a woman might wear *trouserettes* (full-cut men's-style pants), engage in strenuous sports, smoke, and attend *emancipation teas*. Women's rights advocates used *emancipation* increasingly after President Lincoln's 1863 Emancipation Proclamation ended slavery.

Women won the right to vote, for the first time in the U.S., from the territorial legislature of Wyoming in 1869. But by 1900 women were still denied suffrage in all but five states. That year new leadership revitalized the NAWSA when Carrie Chapman Catt (1859–1947) became president. In 1913 a young activist, Alice Paul (1885–1977), formed a radical group

Women suffragists marching on Fifth Avenue, New York, in 1915.

bent on using militant tactics, including hunger strikes and mass demonstrations. By the end of World War I, in which thousands of women proved their value to the national cause, the tide had turned. The 19th Amendment, dubbed "the Anthony Amendment" for its late champion, Susan B. Anthony, was passed by Congress in 1919 and ratified on August 26, 1920.

During the early decades of the 20th century, people spoke of:

birth control, a term coined in 1914 by Margaret Sanger (1879–1966). As a maternity nurse working in New York's Lower East Side, Sanger saw the plight of impoverished women who were unable to control pregnancies and who often died in childbirth or from botched abortions. In 1916 she opened a network of birth control clinics and in 1921 formed the American Birth Control League, later the Planned Parenthood Federation of America. After being arrested several times, she won a federal court ruling in 1936 that allowed doctors to prescribe *contraceptives* (1891). Sanger popularized the term *diaphragm* by promoting the 19th century invention, also called a *Dutch cap*, previously called a *womb veil*. Incidentally, a sheathlike device worn since the 16th century by men to prevent venereal disease was reinvented in the 18th century as a contraceptive called a *condom* (origin unknown).

Lucy Stone League, founded in 1921 to help women with the legal and bureaucratic problems of keeping their own surnames after marriage. Stone was the first well-known American to do so when she married fellow abolitionist and women's rights advocate Henry Brown Blackwell in 1855. She kept her *maiden name* (late 1600s) as a symbol of her identity, but chose to be known as "Mrs. Stone" to show that she was married. Women who followed her example were called *Lucy Stoners*.

"I call myself a feminist in that I believe there are cultural, social and economic boundaries set for women which are immoral and unnecessary and which should be resisted publicly and privately."

— **Elizabeth Hardwick, around 1985, in a** New York Tmes Magazine *interview*

Women construction workers at a site near Oakland, California. By 1993, women made up eight percent of America's construction workforce, which is considered well above normal for occupations traditionally dominated by men, and a symbol of the growing numbers of women pursuing careers in the building trades.

feminism, from French *feminisme,* first used in the 1880s by women's rights advocates in France. *Feminism* was adopted in the U.S. in the early 1900s by women's rights activists whose aims went beyond winning the vote. They were committed to equality of the sexes on every level. Feminism did not die with the suffrage victory, but it was largely dormant for some 50 years.

In the first half of the 20th century women joined the paid work force in ever growing numbers. During World War II, women were recruited to fill better-paying jobs vacated by men entering military service, especially in defense plants. "Rosie the Riveter" became a national icon. The government even funded *day care* (1940s) for the children of women working in war industries.

With the war's end, women were laid off or demoted in droves as men returned to civilian jobs. Child-care centers and training programs closed down. Coeducational colleges, flooded with ex-servicemen studying at government expense, had little room for women, particularly in graduate and professional programs. In the postwar decade a powerful revival of the image of domesticity glorified the role of housewife. Although women continued to enter the job market, typically in low-paying "women's jobs," the mass media reflected a negative view of wives who worked outside their homes, especially if they had young children. But the 1960s brought new methods for women to control their fertility:

oral contraceptives, as *birth-control pills* were called when being tested in the 1950s. They went on the market in 1960, and soon everyone was speaking of the method, and of what came to be known as *the Pill.*

intrauterine device, 1964, a plastic or metal loop or shield placed in the uterus to prevent conception. It was quickly abbreviated as *IUD.*

The resurgence of feminism in the 1960s is associated with several organizations, individuals, and groups that had varying priorities. Professional and business women, some in government, were instrumental in establishing the President's Commission on the Status of Women in 1961 and carrying out its study of "barriers to the full realization of women's rights." The commission's 1963 report, *American Women,* thoroughly documented women's second-class status. Out of these efforts was born, in 1966, the first new feminist organization in almost 50 years, the *National Organization for Women,* or *NOW* (the acronym pronounced "now"). Its key leader, Betty Friedan, had given impetus to the resurgence of feminism with her 1963 best seller, *The Feminine Mystique,* which punctured the post-World War II myth of the happy, fulfilled suburban housewife and at the same time attacked the social attitudes that kept women inferior.

Many younger women who received their political education in the civil rights and anti-Vietnam War movements experienced being treated as subservient to men. Talking among themselves of the need for *women's liberation* (a 1964 term), they used the militant rhetoric of the civil rights and peace movements (and the word *movement* itself) to pioneer the *women's liberation movement,* which surfaced in the late 1960s and became a subject of keen discussion, debate, and sometimes heated action. Germaine Greer's *The Female Eunuch* (1970) made women's *sexual freedom* an element in the vanguard of the movement, and the attendant controversy. By the mid 1970s, there had evolved a multifaceted wave of feminism, which came to be called simply *the women's movement,* and gave us such terms as:

Gloria Steinem in 1969. On why she never married: "I can't mate in captivity."

sexist, 1965, a person having prejudices based on gender; (adj.) showing gender-based discrimination, especially against women; *sexism* 1968.

bra burner, 1968, used as a derogatory term for a feminist, though it was purely a media invention. At the 1968 Miss America pageant, demonstrators protested the demeaning image of women as sex objects by tossing into a "freedom trash can" such stereotypically feminine items as spike-heel shoes, false eyelashes, and brassieres. Though the items were never burned, reporters covering the demonstration—the first event of the women's liberation movement to receive nationwide media attention—mentioned burning in their stories (alluding to the *draft-card burning* protests of the same era), and the label stuck.

women's lib, 1969, a trivializing abbreviation of *women's liberation*, and *libber*, 1971, a disparaging term for a feminist. The shortened forms were widely used by opponents of the movement.

sexual politics, 1970, social conduct through which members of one sex exploit or oppress the other, from the title of Kate Millet's book published that year.

male chauvinist, 1970, a sexist man, one who thinks, assumes, or acts as if males are superior to females. *Chauvinist*, 1870, originally meant a fanatical patriot (via French *chauvinisme*, for Nicolas Chauvin, a soldier blindly devoted to Napoleon). The more derisive *male chauvinist pig* (*MCP*), 1972, borrowed *pig* from radical student activists of the 1960s, who used it contemptuously of the police.

By the late 1990s the women's movement was a pervading force in American life. The movement also worked to eradicate the stigma traditionally attached to being a *single mother* or childless woman, favored *choice* in childbearing, and advocated child-care centers for working parents. The resulting social ferment profoundly influenced the American family, work force, politics, and education, as well as our language:

Title VII of the federal Civil Rights Act of 1964 prohibited discrimination in employment on the basis of race, color, religion, national origin, or sex (opponents had added the word *sex* with the aim of killing the bill, but the move backfired). The *Equal Employment Opportunity Commission* (*EEOC*) was created to enforce Title VII.

affirmative action, 1965, an active effort to redress past discrimination by improving employment or educational opportunities for minority groups and women. Originating in federal government directives, the phrase became common in help-wanted ads identifying the advertiser as "an equal opportunity/affirmative action employer." Political and legal challenges came from people whose opportunities the policy curtailed, such as *AWMs* (1992), the abbreviation of "*angry white males*."

ERA, for the proposed *Equal Rights Amendment* to the Constitution, first introduced in Congress in 1923. Congress passed the ERA in 1972, but it was not ratified by three-fourths of the states before its 1982 deadline.

mommy track, 1989, a career path that allows a mother flexible or reduced work hours but tends to slow or block advancement.

sexual harassment, 1975, unwanted and offensive verbal or physical behavior toward an employee because of sex.

reproductive freedom, mid 1970s, first used by Gloria Steinem to mean the individual's right to decide to have or not to have a child.

gender gap, early 1980s, a measurable difference between the sexes in outlook, income, etc. The term entered the political vernacular after polls showed a clear divergence in voting patterns between women and men, and was also used when referring to the marked discrepancy between men's and women's average take-home pay. The rallying cry of those challenging the gender gap in income was "Equal pay for equal work."

glass ceiling, 1986–87, an "invisible" obstacle in an organization that bars women (or minority) employees from promotion to higher-level posts.

The Great Gender Shift taking place during the last decades of the 20th century both reflects and reinforces changes the women's movement has brought about in the American social scene. Traditional *gender roles* are much in question. In eradicating superficial gender distinctions, many individuals and institutions have dropped such gender-tagged terms as *chairman* and *chairwoman* on the grounds that they emphasize the person's sex rather than the position itself. Expressions like *woman doctor* and *male nurse*, which imply that those so designated are deviations from an accepted standard, have been largely discarded. And most of the *-ess*, *-ette*, and *-trix* words for women—*sculptress*, *usherette*, *testatrix*, etc.—have gone the way of the horsecar *conductress*. In restaurants, *waitress* is giving way to *server*, *waitperson* (1976), *waitron* (late 1970s), or simply *waiter*, a *unisex* (1968) term suitable for both sexes. And by the late 1990s the pronoun *s/he* was regularly used on forms and legal documents.

Some once-gendered terms have become unisex among the young, who in the 1990s began to speak of a cool guy as a *babe*. (Since at least the early 1900s the noun *babe* was in slang use for an attractive female.) Even the informal *guy* is now often unisex, especially in the plural, as when girls or women address one another as "you guys."

Equal rights advocates propose that gender-tagged job titles be scrapped by simply replacing *man* and *woman* with *person*, as in *salesperson*, used since 1901. Although the 1970s binge of neologisms like *personhole* (for a utility-access *manhole*), *oneupspersonship*, *woperson* (for *woman*), etc., were talked about more by adversaries of the women's movement than by its proponents, some ardent feminists still avoid the ubiquitous affix *-man* entirely, even in *woman*, where the etymological sense of *man* as *human being* is actually at work. Others have adopted *womyn*, *womon*, and the plural *wimmin* as alternative forms, and several of these have entered major dictionaries. Other supporters would describe themselves as *womanist*: first used with reference to a black feminist by the writer Alice Walker in the 1980s, it has since come to mean having a belief in or respect for women and their abilities beyond the boundaries of race and class.

TALKIN' 'BOUT MY GENERATION

W e may not know it, but we Americans talk about two kinds of generations: intellectual and demographic. Intellectual generations are not really generations at all, but are movements (the Beat Generation, for example), sometimes spanning only a decade—so that the same people might be called part of one generation one decade and another generation the next. Demographic generations (like baby boomers) are closer to what we usually mean when we say generations: a group of people born in a 20- to 30-year period, most of whom, we presume, share some experiences and values characteristic of their age.

INTELLECTUAL GENERATIONS

Generation gaps were not invented in America, but it was here that intellectual generations surfaced immediately. The Puritans had no sooner arrived in New England in the early 17th century than they began to fret, with good reason, that they might not pass the intensity of their religious vision to the second generation. Worried about the gradual corruption of their *mission*, the Puritans complained about the *declension* (decline) of society.

Similarly, tensions between intellectual generations arose during the founding of the United States. In the 1760s and 1770s, the "Revolutionary generation," with leaders such as Thomas Jefferson and Thomas Paine, were interested in diffusing the power held centrally by the English Crown to decentralized independent states, the former colonies. In the 1780s and 1790s a younger "Constitutional generation," with leaders such as Alexander Hamilton and James Madison, worked to create, in the U.S. Constitution, a federal government with enough centralized power to bring strength and efficiency to the weak collection of former colonies.

But America's intellectual generations made their strongest impact about the beginning of the 20th century, after the Industrial Revolution had sparked a national network of communication and transportation. Beginning then, young people, in a culture with national instead of merely regional or local horizons, began to identify with their own generation instead of their own region.

The first intellectual generation to think of itself, self-consciously and artistically, as a distinct entity emerged during and after World War I, and it was the first group of Americans to have been raised in a post-regional culture following the Industrial Revolution. This group of intellectuals, branded the *Lost Generation*, featured writers such as Ernest Hemingway, John Dos Passos, and F. Scott Fitzgerald. They adopted the bohemian lifestyle.

Gertrude Stein said she had heard the term *lost generation* in a conversation with a French garage owner. After hearing it from her, Ernest Hemingway used it in the epigraph to his 1926 novel *The Sun Also Rises*, which became a bible to the rootless, disillusioned young adults who came to maturity during World War I. The shocking death and destruction of the war, which made pre-war values seem futile, created an intellectual climate of alienation and cynicism about traditional American ways and Victorian-era values. This *lost generation* became a landmark concept and a model for subsequent American cultural phenomena, such as *the Beat Generation* and the *hippies* of the 1960s *counterculture*.

> "He acknowledged that the 'generation gap' is difficult both for the younger and the older generations."
>
> — an early usage, from the Boston Globe, May 10, 1967

> "'You are all a lost generation'—Gertrude Stein in conversation."
>
> — Ernest Hemingway, epigraph, The Sun Also Rises, 1926

AMERICA GETS "HEP"

As early as 1903, some Americans were using *hep* to mean "informed; in the know." *Get hep* appeared by 1906; *hep to the jive*, hep to jive musicians' talk, was popular by 1925. In the early 1920s jazz and jive musicians began calling each other *cats*, possibly an allusion to the style of a tomcat, but with music as their howling. *Hep* and *cats* were combined to form *hepcats*, the word everyone was using in 1935 to describe frenetic dancers to jive music. A few insiders, however, such as entertainer Cab Calloway, called these dancers not *hepcats* but *hepsters*.

By 1931 *hep* was occasionally being pronounced *hip*. This led to calling hep girls *hip chicks* and calling *hepsters* (jive dancers and fans) *hipsters* by the late 1930s. Thus turn-of-the-century *hep* became *hip*, now the usual form. No one knows exactly where *hep* comes from: some say it referred to an all-knowing Chicago bartender of the 1890s, Joe Hep; some say that *hip* was the original word (from the opium smoker's *on the hip*, "smoking opium," which was done lying on one's side or hip), and there is even the theory that *hepcat* is from the West African "Wolof word *hipicat* ("one who has his eyes wide open"), presumably then with origins in the African ancestry of early jazz musicians. If actually may derive from the Southern English form of *help*, pronounced *hep*. When you need assistance, Southerners advise you to "git hep." A jazzman whose technique was not up to snuff might have received similar advice—"get hep" from another jazz musician.

By 1945 *hip* had almost completely replaced *hep* in American slang, cat had come to mean any aware person (by the 1950s it was to mean any person at all), and *hipster* (cited to around 1941) was beginning to mean a devotee of the new "progressive jazz" from the West Coast. This intellectual, nonemotional jazz was also called *cool jazz*, as opposed to the *hot jazz* of the 1920s. It was *cool* or *beat*, both meaning unemotional, aloof. (*Beat* had meant exhausted, physically and emotionally drained, since 1834; as a verb *cool* has meant "to calm down" since Old English, and, as an adjective, the sense "unemotional" is similarly long-established.)

During the decade of 1945–55 *hipster* drifted away from its jazz meaning and was applied to anyone considered hip or cool. The cool jazz fan's vocabulary also moved into general student use, so that some of the youthful catchphrases most frequently heard were *cool, real cool, crazy, far out, gone, real gone, nervous, out of sight*, and *wild*—all vaguely meaning "great, wonderful, satisfying, exciting, or unique."

THE BEAT GENERATION

By 1957, when Beat novelist Jack Kerouac published *On the Road*, and even more clearly by November 1959 when Kerouac, accompanied by Steve Allen's piano, read his poetry on NBC's *The Steve Allen Plymouth Show*, we began to talk about a new American type, *the Beat*, originally with a capital *B*. The Beat seemed an extension of the *super cool* college-age youth, not only repelled by post-World War II, atomic-age American materialism but one who rejected bourgeois career-oriented life and traditional American values and rationalism to seek his own identity. The stereotypical *Beat* led a spontaneous, roving life (on his motorcycle, by hitchhiking, or from an old car) with the aid of drugs, jazz, poetry, and casual sex. *Beat* writers expressed themselves well and loudly, as in Allen Ginsberg's long 1955 poem *Howl* and Kerouac's other novel *The Dharma Bums* (1958). *Beat* became a widely used word in 1957; we spoke of *beat life*, and those who were part of *the Beat Generation*. They called themselves *beat* because they identified with the down and out, the marginalized in society, the people who were homeless or junkies or

Scat-cat and hepster Cab Calloway struts his stuff in 1934.

"In the swing period, 'hep' was widely used by musicians to mean 'in the know,' 'possessed of good taste,' or to indicate simple understanding. . . . The boppers quickly changed the word to 'hip.' Use of 'hep' was then regarded as a sign that the speaker was not the right sort."

— N.D. Hinton, Publications of the American Dialect Society, 1958

"As Cannonball Adderly has said, 'Hipness is not a state of mind. It is a fact of life.'"

— Black Scholar, 1971

"The Bop musician's use of 'cool' instead of 'hot' [is] a word of the highest praise."

— Harper's, April 1992

A "be-in" in Philadelphia in April 1967. At the time, the mainstream press still referred to these people as "beatniks," with "flower children" establishing itself as a phrase a few months later during the "summer of love."

wanderers: the *beaten* people, or the *beat* people. But Kerouac spoke of *Beat* as a shortened form of the word *beatific*, meaning "radiantly enlightened." Then on April 2, 1958 the *Beats* were first called *beatniks*, unflatteringly, in Herb Caen's popular "Bagdad-by-the-Bay" column in the *San Francisco Chronicle. Beatnik* was one of the early and most popular -*nik* words, based on Yiddish.

THE HIPPIES AND THE 60S

By 1957 the true *Beats* had followers, a growing number of *hipsters* who were the first to be called *hippies, anti-establishment* youth often from affluent homes who were, or idealized being, *dropouts* from school and society. The older beats looked down on *hippies* as not being true free spirits but merely college kids on their own but still living a consciously patterned life. The hippie was widely viewed as a *rebel without a cause*, an allusion to Robert Lindner's 1954 book *The Fifty-Minute Hour* and the name of the popular 1955 James Dean movie.

One side of *the Movement* of the 1960s pushed for rebellion in cultural areas such as style, dress, literature, gender relationships, living arrangements, and the sexual revolution. This side, referred to as the *counterculture* (1968), owed much to the Beats of the 1950s. Their most notable area of cultural expression was the *music scene* (this sense cited to a 1949 *Ebony* article about jazz), *alternative* living in communes, and the pursuit of *mind expansion* and broader consciousness through Eastern religion or *mind-expanding* (1963) psychedelic drugs. Increased personal liberation was their goal, and such movements as *black liberation, women's liberation, gay liberation,* and *liberation theology* were partly the result of this *countercultural* side of *the movement.*

In the hippie counterculture of the 1960s, *groovy* (a 1930s jazz term meaning "playing or able to play jazz or similar music brilliantly;

swinging, sophisticated") meant something like "wonderful and exhilarating." A person who was worried or insistent on being conventional was *uptight*. Conversations or situations were *heavy* (another 1930s jazz term) if they were deeply significant or burdensome. A good point, a good connection in conversation, or a statement "with which you were in complete agreement, was *right on*, a borrowing from Black English.

Through the 1960s everyone was talking about the hippies and their attitudes and *lifestyles*, including their temporary *crash pads* and their permanent *pads* ("apartments, rooms," originally an opium addict's term for a couch or bed, then in jazz musician's use by 1915). Parents talked about ways to keep their teenagers from the hippie *drug culture*, from *dropping out* (of society) or running away to hippie meccas like the Haight-Ashbury section of San Francisco (also *the Haight* or *Hashbury*, a blend of the names of the district's two key crossing streets reinforced by the popular slang *hash* for the drug *hashish*), or to New York's East Village. If you liked hippies you called them *flower children* (1967) and approved of their *flower power* and *love is* slogans; some who hated them called them *beatniks*, but the word *hippies* was the most popular. By the end of the 1960s many hippies had settled in *hippie communes*, or had completely disappeared into the world of drugs, while some returned to a more traditional life. (Evoking the enduring legacy of the children of the 60s was the 90s *lifestyle liberal*, a political liberal who advocates the legalization of recreational drugs.)

THE PROTEST MOVEMENT

The other side of *the Movement* was more outwardly political and comprised the various *New Left* (1960) protest groups with agendas that promoted antiwar activity, free speech, greater racial and economic equality, and an end to university military research. Those associated with the *New Left* and other political persuasions opposed the Vietnam War, castigated police as *pigs*, and advocated *people power*, open government, and *participatory democracy* (older liberals wanted *representative democracy* instead of *direct* or *participatory democracy*).

The *peace movement* referred to the various groups and individuals who protested against the Vietnam War, using *peace marches, peace demonstrations*, and *teach-ins* (1965). One of the largest student protest groups was the *SDS* (Students for a Democratic Society), an early *New Left* group organized in 1962 on college campuses by leaders of the *Berkeley Free Speech Movement*.

A *draft-card burner* was any draft-aged male who burned his draft registration card publicly at an antiwar demonstration. Similarly, a *draft evader* was one who ignored the call of the draft, sometimes by fleeing to Canada or Sweden. Antiwar sympathizers preferred this new term to the older *draft dodgers*, with its connotations of cowardice.

In the mid-to-late-1960s a *teach-in*, a term based on the *sit-ins* of the Civil Rights movement (itself going back to 1937 in the sense of a labor strike or demonstration), was an all-night session in a college or university classroom at which students, professors, and guest speakers argued against the war.

During the August 1968 Democratic National Convention, thousands of antiwar demonstrators clashed with Chicago police, who in turn clubbed some demonstrators and bystanders. The most publicized of the demonstrators was a small group led by Abbie Hoffman and Jerry Rubin, humorously called the *Yippies* (for the acronym of the Youth International Party, influenced by *hippie*).

The silent majority referred to that majority of Americans who didn't protest or demonstrate against the war and later came to mean average,

"It is time for America's silent majority to stand up for its rights. . . . America's silent majority is bewildered by irrational protest— and looking at the sullen, scruffy minority of student protesters . . . [who seem to] prefer the totalitarian ideas of Mao or Ho Chi Minh. . . ."

— Vice President Spiro Agnew, speech, May 9, 1969

John Travolta starred as a disco-dancing lady's man in the 1977 film "Saturday Night Fever," a movie exploring the restless and explosive generation of the seventies.

Two proud yuppies "networking" at a 1985 Yuppie Cotillion.

middle-class Americans. The term, which was not new—in the 19th century it meant "the deceased"—became popular when President Nixon used it in a television address on November 3, 1969, just 19 days after the antiwar *moratorium* in Washington, D.C. The purpose of the President's address was to counter or subdue the mounting dissent against the war. He said, "If a vocal minority . . . prevails over reason and the will of the majority, this nation has no future as a free society. . . . And so tonight—to you, the great *silent majority* of my fellow Americans—I ask for your support."

THE ME GENERATION

During the 1970s, the decade that novelist and social critic Tom Wolfe branded as the period of the *Me Generation*, the *social consciousness* of the 1960s was replaced by *self-realization*. Instead of healing society, individuals sought to heal their own inner wounds and nurture their own *inner child* with *self-help* techniques and therapies: Primal Scream Therapy, EST, Lifespring, and others.

The alienation felt in 1970s youth culture gave rise to a pride in rebellion. The opposition culture of the young made rebellion admirable, and so the pose of the rebellious outlaw began to be adopted. As such, first among African Americans and then among the hip young, *bad* (usually pronounced with elongation of the vowel) meant good.

OF YUPPIES AND DINKS

Through the 1980s concern for self was still much in evidence. Bumperstickers proclaimed: "He who dies with the most toys wins." Michael Milken promoted high-risk junk bonds on Wall Street. Young elites who for years had been known as *preppies* (for attending private college *prep schools*) were now joined by individuals known widely in the 1980s as *yuppies* : *y*oung *up*wardly-mobile *p*rofessionals. The acronym game blossomed quickly, dubbing various self-indulgent "types." *Dinks* were couples with *d*ouble-*in*come, *no k*ids, and so a lot of disposable income. *Oinks* were those with *o*ne *in*come, *no k*ids. (See IT'S THE ECONOMY, STUPID.)

All these 20th century social and intellectual generations were populated, and their causes articulated, mainly by rebellious youth. To discover the newest "new" generation, we have always to look to those aged 15 to 25. Malcolm Cowley—a member and chronicler of the *lost generation*—once remarked that the dissatisfaction of youth finds a continually renewed fund of causes and principles that define them. In 1920 Cowley said that rebellious youth were *Dadaists*, in 1927 *Surrealists*, in 1932 *proletarian writers*, in the late 1940s *Existentialists*, and in the 1950s *Beats*. To his list we can add the 1960s *counterculture* and *New Left*, and the *Me Generation* of the 1970s, the *yuppies* of the *Greed Generation* of the 1980s, and in the 1990s *Generation X*, the disaffected children of yuppies and Baby Boomers.

DEMOGRAPHIC GENERATIONS

There have been three major demographic generations identified in the past century: the *Children of the Depression*, the *Baby Boom Generation*, and *Generation X*. For ease of reference, though it doesn't fit the facts precisely, we talk of the first as being born between 1920 and 1945, the

Californiaspeak

The psychobabble of Marin County, California (an affluent residential area north of San Francisco associated with a free hedonistic lifestyle), picked up many strands from the voices of the counterculture, as well as Black English, jazz, rock music, and sports. This lingo, in use well into the 70s, was typified by these recurring expressions:

trip, an experience taking LSD, also an obsession, a lifestyle; as a verb, often *trip out*, to get high, especially on LSD. A *bad trip* was a psychotic reaction to LSD.

ego trip, power trip, and other attributive + *trip* combinations, a (specified) obsession or focus of interest.

alternative partners, sex partners in a promiscuous lifestyle.

laid-back, relaxed; easygoing.

getting (or *staying*) *in touch with* (*oneself*), engaging in realistic self-examination.

space, as in "personal space," adequate physical or mental leeway.

where (*one*) *is at*, one's position, intention, or views, as in "We still don't know *where he's at* on the war issue," also expressed as *where* (*one*) *is coming from*.

getting inside (*one's own* or *another's*) *head*, understanding, as in "I'm still trying to *get inside Don's head* on the marriage thing."

run something by (*someone*), to present (e.g., an idea) to (someone else) for reaction or approval.

off the wall, weird.

wig out, to go nuts or have a fit of anger or hysterics.

freak out, to have a bad drug trip, or to have a fit of hysterics.

Baby Boomers between 1946 and 1965, and *Generation X* between 1965 and 1985.

CHILDREN OF THE DEPRESSION

The *Children of the Depression*, or *Midcentury Generation*, who came to maturity at midcentury, were born between World War I and the end of World War II. They are also known as the *Interwar Generation* or *WWII Generation*, or occasionally the *Depression Generation* or *New Deal Generation*, and intermittently the *Affluent Generation*. For most, the 1930s Depression of their youth was a defining experience. Many fought in World War II or Korea, faced Hitler's fascism and the Cold War, bought houses in the expanding 1950s suburbs, and experienced the rapid growth in income and production following World War II.

BABY BOOMERS

With the postwar prosperity of the mid-to-late-40s, the rate of birth spiked up to historically high levels, hence the *Baby Boom*. As children in the 1950s and 1960s, most *boomers* enjoyed relative affluence compared with Depression-era children. But many a *child of the 60s* grew disillusioned about the *American Dream* (1931) as the era of the War on Poverty (1964), the civil rights movement, and the Vietnam War exposed the discrimination and hypocrisy of Cold War America.

As millions of *boomers* moved toward middle age, many preferred to hide their true age and retain a semblance of youth, referring to themselves as *thirtysomethings*. Yet through the 1980s and beyond *boomers* started families and moved into positions of power.

Though their spending habits involved the purchase of expensive "toys," some of the 1960s idealism remained with boomers in middle age. They became environmentalists. Other boomer issues were fought out in the late-century *culture wars*, staged mainly in the universities and by intellectuals in the media. In these battles the forces of tradition (which promoted what was disparaged as a *dead white male* culture), often supported by an older generation, fought the primarily boomer *postmodernists*. The postmodernists were often allied with those promoting *multiculturalism*, emphasizing ethnic and cultural diversity, and empowerment of all races, classes, and once-scorned subgroups.

GENERATION X

In the late 1980s a new demographic generation, *Generation X*, began to be noticed. The name was derived from the book *Generation X* (1964), by Charles Hamblett and Jane Deverson, who interviewed alienated British mods and rockers and let them speak for themselves. British rock star Billy Idol saw the book and named his band after it. In the late 1980s Canadian public opinion pollster Allan Gregg gave a speech on this new demographic group and tagged it with the name of Billy Idol's former band. Then Douglas Coupland, a young Canadian cartoonist and author, borrowed Gregg's *Generation X* speech title and created for *Vista*, a business magazine, a comic strip based on his generation. The strip featured young workers who were smarter than their boomer bosses but caught in dead-end jobs. When the 29-year-old Coupland published his novel *Generation X* in 1991 the image and name gained increasing recognition.

Alternate names for *Generation Xers* proliferated. Some called them *13ers* from the idea advanced by boomers Neil Howe and William Strauss that Xers were the *13th generation* since the states ratified the U.S. Constitution. Less appreciated as names, because they were derivative and

"Mr. (Gary) Hart seems to have drawn much of his support from young upwardly mobile people and young urban professionals—yumps and yuppies, as they are called."

— The Economist, March 17, 1984, also illustrating yump, *a word that never sustained continued use*

An outdoor rave, 1996.

were invidious comparisons to the boomers, were *twentysomethings* (a takeoff on *thirtysomethings*) and *baby busters* or *busters* (because they were part of the demographically smaller generation following the baby boom). Still another collective description—the *Angry Generation*—was suggested by some George Mason University fans of rock singer Kurt Cobain, whose 1994 suicide was seen as symbolic of the despair and frustration felt by the young people.

Xers complained that they faced a list of unique obstacles in life. They had been raised in an age of divorce as *latchkey kids* (*latchkey child* going back to 1944) who had to let themselves into empty houses after school while a *single parent* (often a *working mother*) toiled outside the home. Sex was not free in the era of *AIDS*. Journalist Hunter S. Thompson despaired for the fate of a generation for whom "sex is death, and rain is poison."

Further, *Xers* objected to being the first generation in 20th century America to face a worse economic future than their parents. Previous generations had created a huge national debt to repay, but *Xers* had only the prospect of *McJobs* (dead end, low-level jobs, such as those at McDonald's) or working as *microserfs* (another Douglas Coupland coinage in reference to overworked young employees of Microsoft Corporation). *Xers* argued that they couldn't break into the market for good jobs held by boomers.

The typical image of *Xers* was unflattering. In the national imagination, Xers skateboarded through life, affected a booted, flannel-shirted, ripped-jeans style of dress called *grunge* (adopted from the Pacific Northwest), wore their baseball caps backwards as a sign of defiance, spent their leisure watching *music videos* or *Beavis & Butthead* on *MTV*, worked as a *temp*, or worse, at a job where they asked, "You want fries with that?" or "You want paper or plastic?"

The language of Generation X was portrayed as bankrupt. Asked a question, *clueless* Xers answered *whatever* and registered their disagreement with something by exclaiming *"as if!"* From boomer to *Gen X* culture the slang usage of *like* proliferated. In the 1960s, boomer *hippies* used *like* as a sort of prefatory punctuation in a comparison or statement:

"It's, *like*, really cool to see you here" or "I'm, *like*, freezing." Xers continued to use *like* liberally, but also characteristically as a marker of reported speech, as in: "My mom is *like*, do you want to go to the store with me? And I'm *like, as if*!"

GENETIC ENGINEERING . . .
AND LINGUISTIC REENGINEERING

*T*he language of *genetics (1905) points us into the past and into the future all at once. From advances in genetics comes an entirely new, developing vocabulary. Though specialized, many terms originating in this field cross into the general language because the advances denoted by the words have global interest and impact:* clone, DNA fingerprinting, obesity gene, *and* genetic engineering, *to mention only a few. Certainly this would have been no surprise to Wilhelm Johannsen, who first used* gene *in English in 1911, writing in* American Naturalist: *"I have proposed the terms 'gene' and 'genotype' to be used in the science of genetics. The 'gene' is nothing but a very applicable little word, easily combined with others, and hence it may be useful as an expression for the 'unit-factors,' 'elements' or 'allelomorphs' in the gametes, demonstrated by our modern Mendelian researches."*

"This genie can't be pushed back into the bottle."

— *David N. Leff,* Biotechnology Newswatch, *March 15, 1987, on the impossibility of halting genetics research*

With the announcement in 1953 by Nobel Prize winners (1962) James Watson and Francis Crick of their proposed model of the DNA molecule, the *double helix*, they marked not only the culmination of years of research by many scientists but the figurative launch of *genetic engineering* that followed in 1966. (In so doing, they ensured linguistic perpetuity of their surnames in the scientific compound *Watson-Crick model*—cited to 1958—the term denoting their discovery.) Watson and Crick's model for *DNA* (1941), the molecular basis of heredity, gave us a plausible picture of a molecule that could both replicate and deliver to the next generation a complete and accurate copy of itself. The scientific basis of the model, with its four distinct base pairs—*adenosine* (1909), *thymine* (1894), *cytosine* (1894), and *guanine* (1850)—is rooted in, and serves to justify, centuries-old theories of cell biology. What was to

Francis Crick (shaking hands on the left) and James Watson (standing center) at the Nobel Prize ceremonies in 1962.

follow, however, with *genetic code* (1961), *gene counseling* (1968), *gene therapy* (1974), and *gene splicing* (1978), was like something out of *Frankenstein*.

Scientists have long employed their knowledge of plant and animal husbandry to produce "new and improved" species to better serve humankind. *Biotechnology* (1941), by the USDA's definition, is the "use of living organisms, cells, subcellular *organelles* [1920], and/or parts of those structures, as well as their molecules, to effect biological, chemical or physical changes." This definition includes not only *genetic engineering* but most of the traditional breeding techniques in use for many centuries. The *crossbreeding* (1640), *cross-fertilization* (1876), *cross-pollination* (1882), *interbreeding* (1859), and *backcrossing* (1904) of animals and plants to enhance desirable characteristics have produced many important successes. But traditional *hybridization* (1845) takes time, sometimes a decade or more to produce successful results. Scientists have long searched for faster, more efficient techniques to improve the process. The 1970s produced just such efficiencies as new discoveries enabled researchers to transfer genes from one organism to another, and *genetic engineering* was added to the definition of biotechnology. Recent applications of biotechnology center on the modification of nuclear DNA in bacterial cells to produce drugs, e.g., antibiotics, the virus-inhibitor *interferon* (1957, *interfere* plus the suffix *-on*, denoting a component), and hormones, e.g., insulin and human growth hormone. Genetic engineering has permitted commercially desirable characteristics to be conferred on organisms, producing crops resistant to specific diseases and pests and bacteria that can concentrate metals from low-grade ores. Biotechnology has also been applied to processes such as the breakdown and recycling of waste in order to minimize environmental damage.

The first *bioengineered* animal, developed by Philip Leder at Harvard University and patented by DuPont in 1988, was dubbed the *Harvard oncomouse* and was programmed with a gene predisposing it to cancer. The subsequent controversy over what people began calling the *patenting of life* united religious groups, environmentalists, and animal rights activists in grand protest. In a February 1993 *Los Angeles Times* article, "Building a Better Mouse for Testing," Michael Schrage wrote: "Much as sculptors carve stone and cinematographers light film, molecular biologists now struggle to manipulate their animals genetically into research masterpieces."

Cloning pioneers Jerry Hall (left) and Robert Stillman in 1993.

"Dolly," the world's first clone of an adult mammal. Dolly was developed by a team of scientists at the Roslin Institute in Edinburgh, Scotland.

"I therefore suggest clone (plural clones) as the correct form of the word."

— C. L. Pollard, Science, July 21, 1905 setting the form of the word clone, which was early on also spelled clon

"It was the galloping and bearded centaur—part man, part horse—that was mythology's equivalent of mixing genes between species. But the Greeks only imagined what scientists now are attempting: the transfer of human genes into a range of barnyard creatures. . . . The animals are called 'transgenic' because they carry transferred genes. And their commercial use in medicine is known as 'pharming'."

— Orlando Sentinel Tribune, April 11, 1993

On October 13, 1993, researchers Jerry L. Hall and Robert J. Stillman announced pioneering work that could lead to the *cloning* of a human embryo. There was a great deal of controversy over this, having to do mainly with the definition of *cloning*. Stillman says "the method they used goes by a variety of names, including *twig cloning, embryo twinning,* or simply *cloning*." In theory, the method could create identical twins or triplets. Some observers conjured up visions of Aldous Huxley's *Brave New World*, while others condemned the work as perverse. Even the researchers' own university (George Washington University Medical Center) denied knowledge of their work inasmuch as it involved potential human life and presented a more-than-casual ethical dilemma, but Hall and Stillman dismissed these concerns, claiming the experiment relied on abnormal human embryos that could not develop properly and had been slated for disposal anyway because they were not suitable for in vitro fertilization. Incidentally, the word *clone* (1903)—which people talked about especially in 1997 when the first-claimed successful *cloning* of a vertebrate, a sheep, occurred—is derived from Greek *klon*, meaning "twig," and suggests the practice of slicing off a piece of a plant to let it develop its own roots. Widespread discussions of *clones* and *cloning* in the scientific context led to extension of the meanings of the words "exact copy" and "to imitate," respectively.

Another rapidly growing field of genetic research and development is called *pharming* (1992), the word being a pun on *pharmaceutical* and *farming*. With *pharming*, researchers inject human genetic material encoded to produce chemicals normally generated only in the human body into pigs, cows, and other domesticated animals. The goal is to produce blood, proteins, and transplantable organs from the fully grown animals, which then can be used in medicines, in treating emphysema and bone-marrow disease, and in cross-species organ transplants. With the promise of unlimited supplies of such medically critical products as drugs, organs, and blood, the race is on to reshape the future. Many of us already use genetically engineered products. Most are medicines, such as insulin to treat diabetes or interferon to treat cancer. Others are foods. For example, by the end of the 1990s some two-thirds of the cheese manufactured in the U.S. was made with a genetically engineered enzyme called *chymosin*, an exact copy of *rennin*, the animal enzyme traditionally used to coagulate milk.

In genetic engineering's application to health in the 1980s and 90s, researchers were frustrated by the failure of gene therapy to cure disease, but tried new approaches to overcome the biggest current obstacle: getting healthy or reengineered genes in the right places in the body. Geneticists experimented with artificial human chromosomes, synthetic *minigenes*, DNA *biocapsules* made of a permeable membrane that lets useful gene products flow out but keeps large immune-system molecules from getting in, and *cassettes* that can slip past the body's natural defenses and stick around long enough to repair or replace faulty genes.

As we watched with awe the results of genetic reengineering and speculated about what the 21st century would bring, there was also irony in that the same technology might take us back to a time predating humankind. The premise of the best-selling novel and hit movie *Jurassic Park*—that DNA from dinosaur blood could be preserved in a mosquito trapped in amber, and cloned to re-create a living dinosaur—might not be all that far-fetched. Not only have scientists extracted bits of DNA from the bone marrow of a 65-million-year-old Tyrannosaurus rex fossil, but they also have recovered intact DNA from an insect trapped in amber in the Mesozoic era, 130 million years ago. As scientists look backward as well as forward in their research, one thing is clear: terms associated

DNA is injected into a mouse embryo in a research institute in Great Falls, Montana.

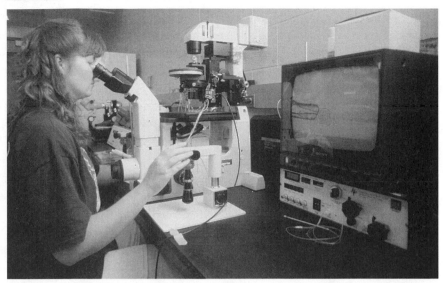

with genetics will continue to proliferate, and our vocabulary will expand in proportion to these new technical discoveries.

Here are some of the more interesting, fanciful, and essential words used in *genetic engineering*, all first occurring in the 20th century.

nucleotide, 1908, the basic structural unit of nucleic acids, DNA and RNA.

allele, 1928, any of the alternate forms of a gene that can occur at a given point on a chromosome. There is usually a pair of alleles for any one gene, one from each parent. (*Allele* is a short form of *allelomorph*, 1902, its predecessor, with the same meaning.)

genome, 1930, the total genetic content of an organism (from German *genom*, 1920).

bovine somatotropin, 1941, a growth hormone used to stimulate milk production in cows. Also called *recombinant bovine somatotropin* or *rBST* and trademarked *Posilac*, this hormone is feared by some for its unknown side effects on people. (*Somato-* comes ultimately from Greek *soma*, "body," and *-trophin* means "hormone.")

DNA, 1944, or *deoxyribonucleic acid*, the molecular basis of heredity consisting of repeating units of nucleotides arranged in a double-helix formation.

genetic drift, 1945, the random fluctuation in gene frequencies that occurs from one generation to the next.

RNA, 1948, or *ribonucleic acid*, any of various nucleic acids that are involved in the manufacture of proteins.

plasmid, 1951, a small circular loop of DNA that transfers genetic information, some of which confer characteristics such as resistance to antibiotics. It replicates independently within a cell. In the 1980s it also came to be known as *naked DNA*.

adenovirus, 1956, one of more than 40 DNA-containing viruses that act as vectors carrying genetic material to the lungs, for which they have a natural affinity. Some adenoviruses infect the respiratory tract and cause colds (*adeno-* from the Greek *aden*, meaning "gland").

genetic code, 1961, the genetic information contained in the nucleotide sequences in DNA. It is the biochemical basis of heredity and appears to be uniform for all forms of life.

messenger RNA, 1961, or *mRNA*, any of the single-strand molecules of RNA responsible for transporting coded instructions for the manufacture of proteins from DNA.

operon, 1961, a group of closely linked genes on a chromosome that produces a single messenger RNA molecule in transcription. Operons are more common in bacteria than in higher organisms (from French *operon*, based on the French verb *operer*, "to bring [something] about," plus *-on*).

codon, 1963, any of a number of specific nucleotide sequences that determine protein makeup and synthesis. (*Codon* comes from *code*, "sequence, system," plus *-on*).

liposome, (from Greek *lipos*, "fat," plus Greek *soma*, "body"), 1968, a tiny, usually multilayered droplet of fat that can deliver medicine or genetic material in the body.

oncogene, 1969, a gene that causes a normal cell to develop into a cancerous cell or to multiply in an uncontrolled manner. More than 60 *oncogenes* had been discovered by the mid 1990s, given fanciful names such as *erb*, *fes*, *myc*, *ras*, and *sis*. *Myc* is a respelling of M^c in McGene (an allusion to the ubiquitous fast-food chain, an intrusion of pop culture into the language of high science).

housekeeping gene, 1970s, a gene responsible for all life-sustaining actions of a cell. Among other things, it is responsible for waste removal.

recombinant DNA, 1975, genetically engineered DNA produced in cells of a host orgnism by incorporating desired genes from another species into the DNA of the host.

retrovirus, 1975, any of a group of viruses with genetic material consisting of RNA rather than DNA, including many carcinogenic viruses as well as the HIV virus.

biosafety greenhouse, 1977, a specially designed greenhouse, sealed to assure that no pollen from a transgenic variety of crop contaminates other varieties in nearby fields.

exon, 1978, a segment of a gene that carries coded instructions (a blend of *ex*pressed sequencer, plus *-on*).

intron, 1978, gene segment that is located between axons and that does not function in coding for the synthesis of proteins (loosely based on *in*tervening sequence, plus *-on*).

biofood, 1980s, food, such as tomatoes, genetically engineered to withstand harsh conditions. Critics charge that genetic changes making the tomatoes disease-resistant also makes tomato cells immune to the antibiotic kanamycin, a characteristic some people fear could be passed on to human beings.

bubble boy disease, 1980s, formally severe combined immunodeficiency disease (*SCID*), named *bubble boy disease* because its most famous victim was encased in a plastic bubble during his short life to protect him from infection. One form of SCID, called *ADA deficiency*, is caused by a defect that blocks production of a key enzyme, the absence of which immobilizes important immune-system blood cells. Several years ago physicians began to treat affected patients with a form of bovine enzyme, which proved to be partially successful. In the world's first approved gene-therapy trial, white blood cells extracted from two young Ohio girls with the disease were equipped with normal genes and reinjected into the girls. The blood cells began producing enough natural enzyme to boost the immune system measurably.

gene probe, 1980s, a fragment of DNA that is labeled with a radioactive isotope so that it can be easily detected, used to identify or isolate a gene.

genetic screening, 1980s, the determination, prior to birth, or at any age, of the genetic diseases to which a person is susceptible.

imprinted gene, 1980s, any of a class of genes that some believe, if inherited from one parent, are much more active than if inherited from the other. Imprinted genes inherited from the father seem usually to act to encourage growth, while those inherited from the mother act to slow it, often by directly opposing the effects of the paternal genes.

junk DNA, 1980s, vast sequences of nucleotides situated between genes that do not seem to code for any proteins, alluding to *junk mail*, 1954; *junk food*, 1971; and *junk bonds*, 1980s.

mighty mouse, 1980s, experimental product of genes for human growth hormone transplanted into the fertilized egg of a mouse. The egg was inserted into the reproductive tract of a female mouse and resulted in the birth of a mouse twice the normal size. This work on *transgenic* mice was done in 1982 by Dr. Ralph Brinster at the Pennsylvania School of Veterinary Medicine (again, the pervasive influence of pop culture from the cartoon *Mighty Mouse*).

minos, 1980s, a new transposable element, a sequence of DNA that can transport a new gene into hosts' sperm and egg cells. As with other transposable elements, *minos* has two important characteristics: it can replicate inside its host's chromosomes, and it produces an enzyme, *transposase* (1970s) that enables it to jump into different chromosomes in its host.

pseudogene, 1980s, a segment of DNA that resembles a gene but is inactive. *Pseudogenes* may be leftover dead, failed, or old genes.

transgenic, 1982, or *trans-species*, referring to a cell with genetic material introduced, usually in the form of DNA, from another species. The process of such cells at work is called *transgenics*. One biotech company reported that its *transgenic* calf, Herman, had sired 18 offspring, eight of whom carried the same gene as Herman's for human *lacto-ferrin* (a milk protein with antibacterial and iron-transport properties, a possible additive for infant formula). A second firm reported that three second-generation goats from a *transgenic* doe produced a *clot-busting* protein in their milk in high concentrations.

DNA fingerprinting, 1984, or *genetic fingerprinting*, a method of precise personal identification by determining the unique sequence of base pairs in the DNA of a person. Analysis is done in two ways: *RFLP*, or *restriction fragment length polymorphism*, uses pieces of DNA that are illuminated with radioactivity and captured on x-ray film as dark bands. If two DNA samples share a pattern of bands, they are considered a match. *PCR* or *polymerase chain reaction*, which can be performed on much smaller blood and tissue samples, is less conclusive. PCR has been described by forensic scientists as *molecular xeroxing* because individual genes are replicated millions of times in the laboratory and then compared for certain common chemical sequences. Although most often used in criminal cases such as the O.J. Simpson

DNA "detective" Henry Lee in 1992. He had participated in several thousand homicide investigations prior to his role as a defense witness in the O.J. Simpson trial in 1995.

murder trial, which brought *RFLP, PCR* and many more such terms to general public attention, *DNA fingerprinting* made international head-lines in 1993 when it was used to positively identify the remains of Russia's Czar Nicholas II, seemingly ending the mystery of the fate and remains of the Romanov family, murdered following the Russian Revolution of 1917–18. Queen Victoria, described as the grandmother of Europe's royal families, passed her DNA along to her grand-daughter, Alexandra, the wife of Nicholas II. Alexandra's sister, Princess Victoria of Hesse, passed it on to her children, one of whom was the mother of Prince Philip of England. DNA from samples of Prince Philip's blood were compared with samples of DNA taken from the bone, enhanced through *PCR*, suspected of being the czar's. The remains were declared to be Nicholas II's, with nearly 99% proba-bility.

Human Genome Project, 1990, an international joint effort to identify, map, and sequence all of the approximately 100,000 genes in the human body.

anti-freezing protein (AFP2), 1990s, a gene normally found in cold-water fish, such as flounder and Atlantic salmon, which, in an experimental procedure, is being copied synthetically and introduced into the cells of strawberries, citrus fruit, and tomatoes in an attempt to make the plants resistant to frost damage and to improve the quality of the fruit after it is frozen and thawed.

damper gene, 1990s, a gene that controls the cell-growth cycle (a bor-rowing from the language of mechanics).

designer molecule, 1990s, genetically engineered test-tube molecules that can intervene in the progression of diseases, such as cancer (the use of *designer* borrowed from the pop-culture sense seen in *designer jeans*).

endocrine cascade, 1990s, the sequential effect that a drop in production of one hormone, especially as a result of aging, has on the production of other hormones in the body.

obesity gene, 1990s, or *fat gene*, a gene that is thought to convey a tendency toward obesity.

retrotransposon, 1990s, bits of a cell's own DNA which, like retroviruses, can copy and slot themselves into other sites in the cell's genome.

stealth virus, 1990s, a virus that isn't picked up by the body's defenses and so can deliver its genetic "payload" (from the military use of *stealth*, as in *stealth fighter*).

stuttering gene, 1990s, a sequence of nucleotides that spells out the same genetic message again and again. The normal version of this gene contains anywhere from 11 to perhaps 34 copies of this three-letter "stutter." In Huntington Disease, the defective gene has from 37 to about 100. Both onset and severity seem to be linked to the number of repeats. In people with 80 to 100 repeats, for example, the disease comes swiftly—often in childhood.

suicide gene, 1990s, a gene which, when triggered, kills the cell it sits in. *Vectors* take these genes into the cells where the trigger is pulled and the cells die along with some of their neighbors. A related approach might be used to "booby-trap" the immune system against AIDS, using *suicide genes* that will kill any cell infected by the AIDS virus before the invader can reproduce.

gay gene, 1992, a gene, which, if inherited from one's mother, hypothetically conveys a tendency toward homosexuality. The scientific merit of such a discovery was mired in controversy by the subsequent talk of *gene therapy* and *eugenics*. Critics worried that parents might exploit such discoveries in attempts to screen children who might be homosexual.

protein library, 1993, an electronic "warehouse" of protein sequences.

bioscanner, 1994, an ultrasensitive molecular imaging instrument that provides quantitative images of molecular samples.

genosensor, 1994, a *bioelectronic* (1980s) microchip sensor capable of high-speed analysis of DNA sequences, consisting of a microcircuit-like array of synthetic *DNA probes*.

Xenomouse and *HuMab-Mouse*, 1994, trademarks of GenPharm International for genetically engineered laboratory rodents having both mouse and human genetic material. When these mice are injected with certain substances they will produce human antibodies, which, it is hoped, can be isolated and used to fight human diseases, such as cancer (the prefix *xeno-* from Greek *xenos*, "stranger").

jumping gene, 1995, or *transposon*, 1974, a transposable element of DNA that can insert itself into a gene. Their apparent ubiquity and ability to move around have earned *transposons* other nicknames, such as *pogo*, and *gypsy*, and *mariner*. The *mariner* transposon, which was thought to invade only insect genes, was recently found to occur in people as well and was linked to an inherited nerve disease, in this case one caused by having a partial duplication of a particular chromosome. The "break and enter" character of these genes also inspired the name *selfish DNA*, 1995. *Transposons*, with their ability to cut and enter genes, may be used someday to convey desirable genetic material to cells.

mean gene, 1995, a gene that conveys a hypothetical tendency toward violence or aggression.

GEOGRAPHY:
IT'S ON THE MAP

THE STATES

We proudly emphasized the unity of our country when we stopped saying "these United States *are*" and began saying "the United States *is.*" The states—thirteen to start, fifteen in 1792, twenty-six in 1837, thirty-eight by the centennial of 1876, forty-eight from 1912 to 1959, fifty now—derive their names from six basic sources: twenty-eight from Native American languages (one Inuit, one Hawaiian); eleven from English; six from Spanish; three from French; one (Rhode Island) from Dutch; and (Washington) from "The Father of His Country."

Here are the sources for the of names of *states*-—a term first used in British colonies here (1634)—and their nicknames and/or *booster names* (seen on license plates, etc.):

Alabama (1819, 22nd state), *alba ayamule* ("I open the thicket" to obtain food, Choctaw). Once *Alabama Territory. The Cotton State. The Heart of Dixie.*

Alaska (1959, 49th state), *alakshak, Ayayeks* ("great land, mainland," Inuit). We use the Russian version of the name. Previously *Russian America. The Last Frontier. The Land of the Midnight Sun.*

Arizona (1912, 48th state), *arizonac* ("small spring place," Pagago). *The Grand Canyon State.*

Arkansas (1836, 25th state), from Sioux for "south wind people (place)." Formerly *Arkansaw* and still pronounced so. *The Wonder State. The Land of Opportunity.*

California (1850, 31st state), an imaginary island in a Spanish romance. Previously *Alta California* (Upper California, contrasted with *Baja California*, Lower California in Spanish). *The Golden State.*

Colorado (1876, 38th state), "red" (earth) in Spanish. Previously *Colorado Territory. The Centennial State. The Silver State.*

Connecticut (1788, 5th state), *quinnitukqut* ("at the long tidal river," Mohican). *The Nutmeg State* (for the cheating by Connecticut peddlers of selling carved wood for nutmeg). *The Constitution State.*

Delaware (1787, 1st state), for colonial governor Lord de la Warr (1644). Previously *New Sweden, South River. The First State. The Diamond State.*

Florida (1845, 27th state), "flowery" in Spanish (referring to Easter, 1513, when Spanish explorer Ponce de Leon named it). Previously *Florida Territory. The Sunshine State.*

Georgia (1788, 4th state), for George III (1732). *The Empire State of the South. The Peach State. The Goober State.*

Hawaii (1959, 50th state), native name *Hawaiki* or *Owyekee* ("homeland"). Previously *The Sandwich Islands* (after an English earl). *The Aloha State.*

"There is overwhelmingly decisive evidence that Chicago means wild garlic, leek, or onion."

— *Virgil J. Vogel, "Indian Place Names in Illinois," Pamphlet Series No. 4, Illinois State Historical Society. The author goes on to present evidence that a great quantity of wild garlic grew in the woods, and that the native residents, the Miami, may have given Chicago its name.*

Montana came by its name naturally.

Idaho (1890, 43rd state), from Shoshone for "light on mountains." *The Gem State. The Gem of the Mountains. The Panhandle State.*

Illinois (1818, 21st state), via French from *illiniwek* ("men, warriors," Algonquian). *The Prairie State.*

Indiana (1816, 19th state), *indian + a* (country). Previously *Indian Territory. The Hoosier State.* Origin of *Hoosier* unknown, possibly from English dialect *hoozier*, "big or large thing."

Iowa (1846, 29th state), *ayuba* ("sleepy one," Dakota), denigrating a Native American tribe. *The Hawkeye State* .

Kansas (1861, 34th state), via French (1673) for Sioux, "south wind people (place)." Previously *Kansas Territory. Bloody Kansas* (Civil War). *The Sunflower State. The Jayhawk State.*

Kentucky (1792, 15th state), *kentake* ("meadow," Iroquois). Previously *Kentucky County* (Virginia). *The Dark and Bloody Ground* (Indian No Man's Land). *The Bluegrass State.*

Louisiana (1812, 18th state), for French King Louis XIV, *Louisane* (1681, French). *The Pelican State. The Creole State. The Sugar State.*

Maine (1820, 23rd state), for a province of France. Previously *Province of Maine. The Pine Tree State.*

Maryland (1788, 7th state), originally *Marieland* for Henrietta Maria, queen of Charles I of England (and sister of Louis XIII of France). *The Free State. The Old Line State.*

Massachusetts (1788, 6th state), from Algonquian for "at the big hill." Officially *The Commonwealth of Massachusetts.* Previously *Massachusetts Bay Colony. The Old Colony State. The Bay State.*

Michigan (1837, 26th state), *mica gama* ("big water," Chippewa, referring to Lake Michigan). Previously *Michigan Territory. The Wolverine State.*

Refugees of the Oklahoma dust bowl arrive in San Fernando, California in 1935.

Minnesota (1858, 32nd state), from Dakota Sioux for "sky-tinted water" (either cloudy or sky-blue). Previously *Minnesota Territory. The North Star State. The Gopher State. The Land of 10,000 Lakes.*

Mississippi (1817, 20th state), *mici sibi* ("big river," Chippewa, referring to the Mississippi River). *The Magnolia State.*

Missouri (1821, 24th state), from French for Algonquian, "canoe." The Peoria Indians called Missourians "the Canoeists" (*We-missouri-ta*); the root *missouri* was picked up by the white traders and missionaries who spoke with these Native Americans. Previously *Missouri Territory. The Show Me State.*

Montana (1889, 41st state), Spanish for "mountainous." Previously *Montana Territory. The Treasure State.*

Nebraska (1867, 37th state), *ni-bthaska* ("river in the flatness," Omaha language, referring to the Platte River). Previously *Territory of Nebraska. The Beef State. The Cornhusker State.*

Nevada (1864, 36th state), Spanish for "snowy" or "snowed upon." Previously part of *Washoe [Mountains] Territory. The Sagebrush State. The Silver State.*

New Hampshire (1788, 9th state). Named for *Hampshire*, England (1622) by grantee Capt. John Mason; this grant also included present-day Maine and parts of Vermont. *The Granite State.*

New Jersey (1787, 3rd state), for Jersey, the island off the British coast. One of the grantees of this formerly Dutch land was previously a governor of Jersey. *The Garden State.*

New Mexico (1912, 47th state), *Nuevo Mexico* of Spanish explorers, 1562. Previously *New Mexico Territory. The Sunshine State. The Land of Enchantment.*

New York (1788, 11th state), the Dutch *Nieuw Nederland* renamed for Duke of York (1664), brother of Charles II. *The Empire State.*

North Carolina (1789, 12th state), *the Province of Carolina* (for Charles II) of 1619 was divided into *North Carolina* and *South Carolina* in 1710. *The Old North State. The Tar Heel State.*

North Dakota (1889, 39th state), from Sioux for "friends, allies." Previously part of *Dakota Territory. The Flickertail State* (for the bird). *The Sioux State.*

Ohio (1803, 17th state), Iroquois *oheo,* "beautiful," for the Ohio River. *The Buckeye State* (for the horse chestnut).

Oklahoma (1907, 46th state), Choctaw for "red people." Previously *Indian Territory. The Sooner State.* (Some settlers jumped the April 22, 1889, date to claim Indian land sooner.)

Oregon (1859, 33rd state). Algonquian *Waregan,* "beautiful water," for the Colorado River, or possibly *Wisconsin* ("grassy place" or "beaver place")—Algonquian having been misspelled on a French map and thus creating the name of another state. *The Beaver State.*

Pennsylvania (1787, 2nd state), *Penn* (for founder William *Penn*) + *sylvania* (Latin *silva,* "woods"). Officially a *Commonwealth. The Keystone State.*

Rhode Island (1790, 13th state), from Dutch for "red (clay) island." Officially *The State of Rhode Island and Providence Plantations.* Previously *Isle of Rhodes. Little Rhody. The Ocean State.*

South Carolina (1788, 8th state). The *Province of Carolina* (for Charles II) of 1619 was divided into *South Carolina* and *North Carolina* in 1710. *The Free State. The Palmetto State.*

South Dakota (1889, 40th state). *Dakota* is a Native American name for the Sioux. Previously part of the *Dakota Territory. The Sunshine State. The Coyote State.*

Tennessee (1796, 16th state), for a Cherokee settlement the Spanish called *Tenaqui* (1567; meaning unknown). Previously *Franklin* (1784-88). *The Volunteer State* (30,000 men volunteered for the Mexican War).

Texas (1845, 28th state), local Native American word *texia* ("friend, ally" against the Apaches), in Spanish *Tejas* (1541). Previously *The Republic of Texas* (1836-45). *The Lone Star State* (said to be from a star on a coat button Sam Houston used as the Republic's seal).

Utah (1896, 45th state), land of the Ute Native Americans, or possibly Navaho for "higher (land)." Previously *Utah Territory.* The Mormons wanted to call it *Deseret,* a name from *The Book of Mormon. The Beehive State* (related to *Deseret* and communal industry).

Vermont (1791, 14th state), French *vert* ("green") + *mont* ("mountain"), but French would prefer the reverse order. Previously *New Connecticut. The Green Mountain State.*

Virginia (1788, 10th state), for England's Queen Elizabeth I, "The Virgin Queen" (1607). Officially a *Commonwealth. The Mother of Presidents. The Old Dominion.*

Washington (1889, 42nd state). *Washington Territory* (1853) named for George Washington. *The Evergreen State.*

West Virginia (1863, 35th state). For the western counties that seceded from Virginia in the Civil War out of loyalty to the Union. It is often affectionately referred to by its residents as *West By God!* [or *Gosh!*] *Virginia,* or simply as *West by Gosh,* as in "We just drove in from West by Gosh." *The Mountain State.*

Wisconsin (1848, 30th state), see Oregon. *The Badger State.*

Wyoming (1890, 44th state), Algonquian, *mache-weaming*, "at the big flats." *The Equality State.*

THE REGIONS

The *-villes* (from French, from Old French ville, village) in American English are many. These are a brief sampling: *chillsville* (1955), *dullsville* (1960), *endsville* (1959), *funsville* (1959), *gloomsville* (late 1950s) *gonesville* (1959), *hangoverville* (1955), *hitville* (1956), *ho-humsville* (1956), *lonelyville* (1959), *movieville* (1955), *quitsville* (1953), *sadsville* (1956), *splitsville* (1954), *weirdsville* (1955), *yawn-* or *yuksville* (1952). And Tommy Dorsey coined *squaresville* in 1942.

Americans also talk about large, regional areas such as *the East* (from 1654), *East Coast, West Coast, the Western Shore,* and the more recent *Left Coast, Dixie* or *the South* and *the Deep South, the Middle West* (from 1898, when *the Far West* was news) and *Middle America* (from 1923, suggesting traditional American values), *the Middle Border, the Plains States, the Northeast* (1789), *the Northwest* (1690, once called *the Northwest Territory*), *the Southwest* (originally as two words, 1853), *New England,* and so on. And in Alaska they refer to the *Lower Forty-Eight.* Less formally and sometimes even more difficult to describe exactly are the likes of *the Frontier* and *Out West* (historical), *the Bible Belt* (the part of the Midwest, Southwest, and South where fundamentalist Christianity is strong), *the Sun Belt* (states of the South and West with generally sunny climates), *the Rust Belt* (areas with decaying heavy industry), and *the Flyover* (a waggish reference to the entire area from the *Eastern Seaboard* to California, which executives fly over on their commutes between coasts), not to mention much smaller units such as the *Four Corners* (the place where the borders of Arizona, Utah, Colorado, and New Mexico meet—the only such spot in the U.S.), *the Beltway* (around Washington, often used to allude to the federal bureaucracy), *the Boston-Washington Corridor* or *Northeast Corridor* (often abbreviated simply to *BosNYWash*), *Silicon Valley* (suggesting the California computer industry around San Jose), various *Chinatowns,* many a *Little Italy,* and other ethnic enclaves. We name parts of cities such as *the Loop* in Chicago (because of the circular route of its elevated railroads), *the Village* (Greenwich Village) in New York City (along with *SoHo, Tribeca, Loisada* [formerly the Lower East Side] and the *Alphabet City* of Brooklyn's Avenues A, B, C, etc.), and *Foggy Bottom* (the area of the District of Columbia where the U.S. State Department is located; also refers to the Department itself). Of course there are the somewhat vague terms: *Atlantic States* (1789) and the

Evangelism in the Bible Belt before TV (Georgia 1940).

San Francisco's Chinatown, home for decades to one of the largest Chinese populations outside of Asia.

Atlantic Seaboard (1788), the *Pacific States* (1820) and *Pacific Coast* (1872) and *Pacific Northwest* (1889), the *Gulf States* (1870) and *Gulf Coast* (1889), *the West Coast* (1850), and *the Great Lakes* area. Some states have regional designations: *the Northern Neck* and the *Tidewater* (Virginia), *the Arrowhead* and *the North Woods* (Minnesota), *the Great Dismal Swamp* (North Carolina), *the Gold Coast* (affluent coastal communities in several states), etc. Some terms change their meaning: *Down East* now means specifically Maine, but in 1819 it was used in reference to all of *New England.*

Slang has also given us disparaging terms for neighborhoods and small towns, such as *the Boondocks, Nowheresville, East Jesus,* and the comic strips' *Dogpatch U.S.A.* (See POP CULTURE) and *Gasoline Alley.* The reputations of *U.S.A.* places are suggested when we use terms such as *New York minute, go Hollywood, Chicago overcoat,* and *Minnesota mule.* We speak of a *Florida room* (sun room) and see signs that say "Don't *Californicate* Oregon." We speak casually of our cities and towns as *the Big D* (Dallas), *P-Town* (Provincetown, Massachusetts), *LA* (Los Angeles), and NOLA (New Orleans, Louisiana), as well as of *the Big Easy* (New Orleans), *Hotlanta* (Atlanta), and *Motown* (Detroit). Among some of the geographically related terms Americans have put on the map are these:

Aleutian Islands, named by the Russians from the Aleut *aliuit* ("beyond the shores"), which seems like a good place for islands. We all know the Aleut word *parka,* which came originally (via a Russian dialect) from Nenets, a Samoyedic language of northern Russia for a reindeer skin. Warm clothes were made of such skins. Later, fur-lined or -trimmed hoods were attached for greater warmth.

America, for Italy's Amerigo Vespucci (Latin *Americus Vespuccius*) who gave his name to the Americas thanks to the German cartographer Martin Waldseemüller, 1507, who literally put America on the map. Florentine explorer Vespucci's accounts of four trips to the New World (1497–1503) were published in Waldseemüller's *Cosmographiae Introductio,* with maps that showed the name as *America* for the first time. In the 19th century *America* was occasionally used as a female first name in the U.S. Canadians (who call us *the States*) and Mexicans (who want us to be *Norteamericanos,* which of course confuses us with Canadians) both object to us calling ourselves *Americans.*

George Dallas, vice-president under James Polk, is just one of many relatively obscure Americans whose names adorn major U.S. cities.

Appalachian Mountains, for *appalachee* (Choctaw, "people on the other side") which gave its name to this 1,600-mile chain of low mountains, stretching from Maine to Alabama. "West" in our country once meant west of these mountains; for some, the "real" America is only to be found there. In *Appalachia, hillbillies* (first cited in 1900) and *mountaineers* (from 1834) lived in poverty.

badlands, from a Native American term we translated for these desolate (and sometimes sacred) lands that were bad to cross, in western South Dakota and Nebraska.

bayous, after Le Sieur de la Salle claimed Louisiana for the French in 1682, the first French word from the area of any importance in English was *bayou* (1766), from *bayuk* (by which the Choctaw could mean "creek" or "stream"). We use it for those and for a marshy inlet, or even a dry riverbed. Shortened to *bok* and French *bogue,* it also gave us English *bog(ue)* and place names like *Bogue Chitto, Bogue Sound,* and *Bogalusa.*

Bayou St. John in New Orleans, 1910.

Italian explorer Amerigo Vespucci. If German cartographer Martin Waldseemuller had put Vespucia on his map instead, would the name have stuck?

cajuns, an altered form of *Acadian* that caught on by 1858. The Cajuns refused to pledge allegiance to the British crown in eastern Canada, called *Acadia,* and went to Louisiana in 1755. They speak *Bougalie* ("Bog Talk") *French.* Their *Mardi Gras* ("Fat Tuesday," the carnival before Ash Wednesday and Lent) is world famous. Costumed merry-makers parade in New Orleans, and festivities are also held in other Louisiana *parishes* (counties) and in Alabama's Mobile.

Highly spiced, highly hyped *Cajun* cuisine has caught on in some trendy places where blackened fish is served. *Cajun* cuisine also gave us *jambalaya* and *mudbugs* (crawfish), among many delicacies.

New Orleans, with its *Vieux Carré* that English speakers call the *French Quarter,* its *beignets* (fried dough), boozers (*fried* denizens on Bourbon Street), and its long history of French, Spanish, and American rule, has given the language a number of words. Spanish *la napa* (from Quechua *yapa*) gave us, via Louisiana French, "the little something extra" called *lagniappe,* and French *picaillon* (a tiny coin of the Piedmontese) denoted the Spanish half *real* (about 6 cents), which, around 1800, became the *picayune* (also the name of a famous local newspaper). New Orleans was called *the Creole City* by 1880—now *the Crescent City* for the Mississippi's bend there—and by about that time all residents of Louisiana were called *creoles,* whether black or white. The original creoles (Spanish *criollo,* "native") were white French and Spanish settlers. Then their slaves were also called *creoles* because they shared their owners' sophistication and language. By 1800 any black with any trace of French or Spanish blood was a *creole* (while those with some white blood other than French or Spanish could also be called *quadroon, octoroon,* etc.). By 1829 *creole* meant any African American as opposed to a native African. *Creole* was then taken to Alaska, meaning "mixture." In the late 1860s it had come to mean a person of mixed Russian-Inuit blood.

Broadway, the New York City street synonymous with "theater." Other such geographical metaphors are *Wall Street,* "the U.S. financial interests"; *Madison Avenue,* "the U.S. advertising industry"; *Seventh Avenue* "the U.S. garment industry"; *Hollywood,* "the U.S. motion-picture industry"; and *the Hill,* "the U.S. Congress."

Cajuns in the French Quarter in New Orleans.

Combat Zone, when Boston threw an ostracizing cordon around what used to be called its *red-light district*, it gained this informal name. It has since been greatly improved, or *gentrified*. Other *porno* areas have other names: New York City's once infamous 42nd Street (more respectable in the 1990s) is *the Deuce*.

Erie Canal, whose opening in 1835 connected Lake Erie to the Hudson River (Buffalo to Albany) via a 363-mile, 40-foot wide, 4-foot deep road of commerce, brought the farm and forest produce of the eastern Great Lakes area to the thriving East and took settlers to the Northwest Territory. New York became a more important city than Boston or Philadelphia because of this *Big Ditch* or *Clinton's Ditch* (New York's governor, DeWitt *Clinton*, had talked the state into financing it). By 1840, there were over 3,000 miles of canals in America, including: the

Broadway in the 1990s.

Neck of Land Falls.

Chesapeake and Ohio (also *Potomac Canal*), following the Potomac from Washington, D.C., to Cumberland, Maryland, but once planned to go all the way to Ohio; the *Morris Canal,* 60 miles from Jersey City to the Delaware River; the *Delaware and Raritan,* New York to Philadelphia; and the *Wabash and Erie,* completed 1856, running 450 miles from Evansville, Indiana, to Toledo, Ohio, the longest of the U.S. canals. The Panic of 1837, overbuilding, and the birth of railroads spelled doom for the canals. George Washington had pushed for them as a way to ship goods cheaply, transport *deck passengers,* or provide comfortable transit on *packet boats.* The *tow boats* were pulled by *boat horses* or *boat mules* at a mile and a half an hour along *towpaths* (1788). The *packets* moved at four miles an hour. The cry of *Low bridge!* was first heard on the canals.

falls. Americans seem to prefer *falls* to (*water)fall,* as in *Niagara* (Iroquois, "neck of land") *Falls,* but we do have *Fall River,* Massachusetts. *Falls City* was a nic name (1859) for Louisville, Kentucky, at the *falls* of the Ohio River.

French, spoken by intrepid French explorers and *coureurs de bois* ("runners in the woods") gave us many American geographical terms: *ravine* ("mountain torrent" but to us a gorge or cleft in the mountains, 1781 in George Washington's diary), *Grand Teton* ("'big breast"), and so on. Place names such as *Lake of the Woods* (not *Woods Lake*) betray translation from French. *Lake Superior* was the "upper" one of the five Great Lakes.

Generic markers, a whole set of generic terms for places and regions have evolved in American English as a direct result of spoken and written usage. Thus, a person who lives on *the wrong side of the tracks* (that split 19th century towns into rich and poor districts) does not have a *good address.* Other examples are these: *the burn* (a burned-out area), *wetlands, kudzu* (unrestrained sprawl, like the plant of this name), *downtown* and *the hub, tent city* (related to *Hooverville* of the Depression but also for modern political protests), *depressed area* and *gentrification area, changing neighborhood, hurricane path, disaster area, speed trap,* and many more. (See HOMELESS ALONE, section The Urban Homeless)

ghost towns, completely or nearly deserted towns, many of them the detritus of western mining, produced by *boom and bust* development. (Some have been revived as tourist attractions in recent years.). A really famous one, *Virginia City* (named for a local character called "Ol' Virginny" from his place of origin), declined from a thriving silver town into a relic of the Old West. The term *ghost town* is also used to denote resort towns after "the season" and its influx of summer visitors end.

gold rush. Though the most famous strikes were farther west, early settlers looked for gold and our first real *Gold Rush* was in Dahlonego County, Georgia, in 1828. Others followed in Illinois, Mississippi, Iowa, around the Great Lakes, westward all the way to the most famous, in California, when at Sutter's Mill on the American River gold was discovered at Sutter's *Nueva Helvetia* settlement. *Gold fever* (1847) hit, the *gold rush* was on, and *forty-niners* reached the village

San Francisco in 1846, three years before the Gold Rush changed the face of the city forever.

of San Francisco by steamer on February 28, 1849. The next year San Francisco was a city of 50,000, a *boom town* with a raucous *Barbary Coast* of saloons, brothels, gambling dens, etc. The claims where some people had a *lucky strike* and *struck it rich* bore colorful names such as *Chucklehead Diggings, Angel's Roost, Jackass Gulch, Puke Ravine,* and *Greenhorn Canyon*, with a *greenhorn* being a *tenderfoot* or *raw-heel* newcomer.

Later rushes went to Colorado (the *fifty-niners*), Nevada (the *Comstock Lode*), and Arizona. *Tombstone* was named by prospector Ed Schieffelin because he was told by soldiers that if he invaded Indian territory he would need a tombstone. Montana and eventually Alaska (the *Klondike* and the *Yukon*) saw spectacular finds by prospectors. Tombstone's own tombstones were on *Boot Hill*. Dodge City, Kansas, also had its own *Boot Hill*.

John Soule wrote in the *Terre Haute Express* in 1851, "*Go West, young man! Go West*," and in 1865 Horace Greeley (who spent his life in the East but saw opportunities for others *out West*) echoed the same in his *New York Tribune*: "*Go West, young man*, and grow up with the country." The Gold Rushes certainly got many to grab a *grubstake* (1863) and, like Mark Twain's Huck Finn, to strike out for the territories.

Great and *grand* are clues to a name's origin. Great (English,"big") signals English naming: the *Great American Desert*, the *Great Divide*, the *Great Lakes*. *Grand* (French, "big"), reflecting names given usually by French speakers, is found in the *Grand Banks*, the *Grand Canyon*, and *Grand Rapids*.

Greenbelt, to prevent *urban sprawl* and preserve or at least evoke park-like amenities, planners created Greenbelt, Maryland, Green Hills, Ohio, and Greendale, Wisconsin. A *greenbelt* preserves part of the Front Range of the Rockies near Boulder, Colorado. Another idea was the *Garden City* (as on Long Island, New York) and *planned communities* such as Reston, Virginia. In the 1980s and 1990s *edge cities* (developed areas at the fringes of metropolitan areas) such as Tysons Corner, Virginia, evolved.

Reston, Virginia, one of America's first planned communities, in its earliest stages.

housing developments. Often names such as *Deer Run* are used when no deer have been seen in the vicinity for many years. "Early American" is just one category of such commercial names. Often all the streets will bear related names taken from almost any source, including *The Arabian Nights*, carrying out the chosen theme of the developers. Lately the trendy and upscale developments, or those wishing to appear so, have names in the pattern "(The) ___ at ___," where the first name is an idyllic or pastoral term and the double name after the *at* suggests a rural setting, such as "*The Brook* at *Settler's Green*."

neighborhood names once prevalent in local areas have tended to die out, though *South Boston* is still called *Southie*. Among ones still in general use are *Nob Hill* (a fashionable neighborhood in San Francisco), contrasted with *the Back of the Yards* (*yards* referring to the stockyards), a none-too-fashionable address in Chicago. And words like *the Projects* mean low-income, government-subsidized, government-built, poorly maintained, usually dangerous *public housing projects* in *inner cities*.

plaza, a Spanish word which achieved increased use in the 20th century, now can also refer to tollbooth areas on *parkways, thruways, freeways,* and *turnpikes* (the last named from the old habit of having a swinging pike as a barrier to stop people so they would pay the tolls).

retirement communities. These often have names suggesting leisure activities such as golfing, relaxation, the security of being a *gated community. Sun City* in Arizona may be the most famous. Another is *Leisure World* near Washington, D.C.

Spanish spoken by Spanish explorers gave us such geographical terms as *arroyo* (in Spain wet, in America dry), *canyon* (from the Spanish *cañón* for "tube"), *mesa* (tableland), *savanna* (via Spanish from Taino *zabana*, "grassy plain" or "lowland"), *sierra* (Spanish *serra*, for a jagged range of mountains), etc. The Spanish language also gave us many saints' names used for cities and towns: *San Diego, San Francisco, Santa Clara, San Gabriel, San Luis Obispo, San Juan Capistrano,* and many more. We mangled Spanish grammar in many place names: consider *El Mesa*. And fake Spanish names include *Altadena*.

streets. William Penn started the American custom of naming streets after trees (*Walnut, Elm, Oak*, etc.). New York City has a famous *grid system* with many numbered *crosstown* streets and *uptown-downtown* avenues, these also famous for *gridlock* (1980). Some places have put streets in alphabetical order, named them for U.S. presidents and states in order, and used other similar arrangements. The commonest street name in the U.S. is *Second Street*, many of the *First Streets* having been renamed *Front, Main, High*, or after a hero such as John F. Kennedy or Martin Luther King, Jr.

toponymic terms. From Britain we borrowed *barren* (1651) and *pine barrens* (1731), *bottom* (1624) and *bottom land* (1728), *chimney* (1832), *divide* (1806), *everglade* (1823, glades that go on forever!), *flats* (high, level land as in "The Outcasts of Poker Flats" by Bret Harte, who brought a lot of western words to general notice), *gap* (1635) and *water gap* (1756, as in Big Stone Gap or Delaware Water Gap), *gulch* (1842), *gully* (1637), *hollow* (1649) and *holler, hummock* (1589, for a tract of knoll or high ground, originally a small English holding anywhere), *lick* where deer, buffalo, etc., licked salt (as in Big Lick, now called Roanoke, Virginia; and French Lick, Indiana), *natural bridge* (1775, the *Natural Bridge* near Lexington, Virginia), *neck of land* (1553), *oxbow* (U-shaped river bend as in the famous Ox-Bow of the Connecticut River, near Northampton in western Massachusetts), *panhandle* (first used in Virginia, most famous in Texas), *pass* (as in the *Donner Pass* with its tragic story of 1846), *painted desert, petrified forest, pond* (in Britain always man-made, not so here, as in *Walden Pond*), *plain, ridge* (not common until 1780s), *scrubland* (1779), *sinkhole* (1709), *spring* or *springs* (source of one of the most common U.S. place names, *Springfield*, and many names such as *the Springs, Palm Springs, Hot Springs*, etc.), *tidewater* (1722, especially in Virginia), *wash* (eroded area 1835, dry watercourse 1861), and *watershed* (1874).

United States. We are not the only *United States* around. Think of The United States of Mexico and The United States of Brazil, for instance, or the proposed United States of Europe. But from the time that Tom Paine allegedly created the term *The United States of America* and the Declaration of Independence used it, it has been common, and official, since the year 1788. (Before that we were officially *The United States of North America*, as Canada was *British North America*.) The abbreviation *US* was written by George Washington in 1791, *U. S. A.* followed in 1795, and *U.S. of A.* is a 20th century term with somewhat rustic, rural connotations. Once they wanted to call us *Usonians*. Or *Columbians*. Aside from the formal-sounding *U.S. citizens*, the usual group term is *Americans*, used even by Canadians. And in the military the 48 contiguous states are called *CONUS*, an acronym for *Continental United States*.

wilderness, a vague area on the eastern border of Kentucky (1792) and a forested area south of the Rapidan River, Virginia, in 1799 where the Civil War *Battle of the Wilderness* was fought. By 1890, *wilderness* had a precise definition: fewer than two residents per square mile; by 1934 a *wilderness area* had become a national forest (at least 100,000 acres) set aside for recreation.

TO YOUR HEALTH!

*I*f *language reflects life, then the changing language of medicine is a clear mirror of the nation's health and the ways by which health care is delivered. Gone is the* country doctor *who, like the old-time ministers and judges, rode a "circuit" on horseback or by buggy in bad weather and good, treating the sick at home—making* house calls. *And in those days when no doctor was available, people had to "make do," which might mean treating a spell of arthritis by drinking a mixture of honey, vinegar, and moonshine, or stopping bleeding by putting a spider's web over the wound. Such remedies are related in* The Foxfire Book *(1972), which goes on to quote a rural lady to this effect, regarding the use of home remedies (now called* self-care *by 1990s families who consult handbooks advising them how to perform minor treatments to avoid expensive emergency room visits): "It was a chancy business. . . . If it hit, it hit; and if it missed, it missed."*

"It is the disease that robs the mind of the victim and breaks the hearts of the family."

— *Jerome H. Stone, President, National Alzheimer's Disease and Related Disorders Association, to the* New York Times, *November 23, 1983*

Also largely gone, except in the most inaccessible rural reaches of our nation and in the medical underground, are the old-time *midwives* (14th century, from Old English), also called *granny women* or *neighbor ladies*—replaced by highly trained and licensed *nurse-midwives* (1952), *nurse practitioners* (1969), and *physicians' assistants* (1970) working under the supervision of *board-certified* OB/GYN physicians or internists, using not only standard *delivery rooms* but the newer *birthing rooms* (furnished to look like bedrooms) where *natural childbirth* can take place in a hospital setting, often via the *Lamaze method* (1965, from the French physician Fernand *Lamaze* [1890–1947], childbirth involving prior physical and psychological preparation to help the mother deal with pain).

The *hospital* (14th century, from Middle English, ultimately from Latin *hospes*, host) originally denoting a charity institution for the aged, the infirm, and the needy, is now likely to be run by a *health care corporation* "reengineered" along *service delivery lines* by top management to cut costs in delivering a *product* (clinical care) along *clinical pathways* (stipulated sets of procedures done by specific people at specified times) to *customers* (you, the patients). With the advent of *managed care* in the

This doctor is among a diminishing number of American physicians who pursue careers as family physicians, or general practitioners.

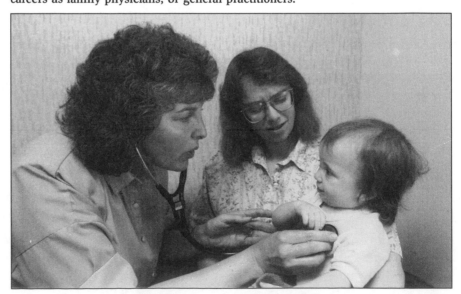

Dr. Jonas Salk in 1955, three years after his research into a flu vaccine resulted in the discovery of a vaccine to treat poliomyelitis. As a result of immunization, polio cases in the United States have dropped from 58,000 in 1952 to virtually none today.

"Every citizen will be able, in his productive years when he is earning, to insure himself against the ravages of illness in his old age."

—President Lyndon B. Johnson, July 1965, signing the Medicare Act

late 1980s and early 1990s the system and the language as well were *reengineered*.

Other reflections of life are to be seen in the broad array of immunological and virological terms that have made their way from the annals of medicine into general English because of the *AIDS (Acquired Imume Deficiency Syndrome) epidemic*; many of these terms, some listed in a boxed feature in this chapter, date only to the late 1970s and the mid 1980s.

But whether the terms we hear, learn, use, and argue about are *Kaposi's sarcoma, assisted suicide, Salk vaccine, surrogate mothers, test-tube babies, organ transplants, assisted care facility, Alzheimer's* or *Legionnaires' diseases, Ebola virus, botulism, lumpectomy* or *mastectomy,* or in the later 1990s *late-term* or *partial-birth abortions* (called *intact dilation and evacuation* by those performing them during the second half of a woman's pregnancy), the very mention of them brings up recollections of health or ethical issues of major continuing concern to the American people.

HEALTH CARE AND MANAGED CARE

Health care delivery systems constitute one of America's largest and fastest-growing industries. It is difficult to think of another area in which technological advances have occurred at such a rapid rate—with prices rising accordingly. Many Americans spend more on health care during the last few years of their lives than their parents spent in a lifetime. Physicians' fees and hospital costs skyrocketed, as did the cost of the *health insurance* that is supposed to cover such exceptional expenses. Relatively minor surgical procedures performed on an *outpatient* basis (i.e., in a doctor's office or a hospital clinic where patients do not spend the night) can still cost thousands of dollars, and the *drug regimen* used to treat *catastrophic* illnesses like AIDS can easily exceed five figures a year. Is it any wonder that *national health insurance* became a hot political issue in the 1990s, or that Americans are haunted by the prospect that *Medicare* and *Medicaid* (federally subsidized health insurance programs for the elderly and the indigent, respectively) will bankrupt the nation?

Most Americans have health insurance as a benefit of employment. Though care was traditionally provided on a *fee-for-service* basis, the trend among 1990s employers was to offer their employees *managed health care,* a broad term covering *HMOs* (Health Maintenance Organizations, which contract with physicians and other *health care providers* to provide medical services on a prepaid basis; the term *Health Maintenance Organization* was coined around 1970 by Paul Ellwood, M.D., regarded as the father of *managed care*) and *PPOs* (Preferred Provider Organizations, which agree to charge lower-than-average rates in return for a more predictable volume of business). The uninsured often rely on *emergency rooms* at *not-for-profit* or *private* hospitals and worry about paying their bills later.

The phenomenon known as *the graying of America*—in other words, the disproportionate increase in the number of older Americans as a result of improvements in medical technology (many people now live with once-fatal conditions like heart disease, cancer, and stroke) and the huge, aging baby boom generation—has contributed to the *health care crisis.* A popular slogan, often heard on the street or seen on T-shirts, says "I'm not getting older, I'm getting better." But no one has quite figured out how *wellness* can be maintained in an ever-deteriorating body whose genes are programmed for ultimate destruction. *Gerontology,* the study of aging, has led to many improvements in health care for the elderly, but even sophisticated operations like a *coronary bypass* (a surgical procedure in which sections of vein from elsewhere in the patient's body are used to shunt around blocked coronary arteries) or a *hip replacement* (in which the *ball-and-socket* hip joint is replaced with a metal-and-plastic one) can do little more than postpone the inevitable.

BETTER LIVING THROUGH CHEMISTRY

Early in the 20th century, people suffering from various physical and mental ills found solace in a variety of *opiates* and *narcotics* that were widely available and perfectly legal. Now *hard drugs* like cocaine and heroin are, of course, recognized as deadly, and *recreational drugs* like marijuana are illegal (though some states have tried to legalize it for therapeutic purposes). The term *controlled substance* was propelled into the nation's vocabulary in 1971 when The Comprehensive Drug Abuse Prevention and Control Act ("the controlled substance act") was put into effect. It was intended to control distribution and sales of all depressants, stimulants, and any other abusable drugs.

America's love affair with *vitamin supplements* can be traced back to post-World War II years, when an increasingly fast-paced ("No time for breakfast") American lifestyle made *One-A-Day* vitamins and *Geritol* supplements seem necessary. Dr. Linus Pauling made *Vitamin C* every American's favorite vitamin, believed to cure the common cold and prevent cancer. *Vitamin E* is widely ingested and applied to combat the effects of aging, and *beta-carotene* (one of the much-vaunted *anti-oxidants*) is

Dr. Linus Pauling (shown here in 1993) was only the second person to win two Nobel Prizes—one for chemistry for his work on sickle cell anemia, the other for peace for his work on the hazards of nuclear fallout. His work with Vitamin C was not as favorably received by his peers.

Managed Care: Some Words

The managed care *system has spawned all manner of jargon, but these few general terms of the 1990s illustrate how language mirrors harsh reality, and the ways people maneuver to confront that reality:*

drive-by delivery, 1995, a slang term no doubt developed by association with the pre-existing *drive-by shooting*, denoting a very short (e.g. 24-hour) hospitalization of a postpartum mother and newborn—a practice stemming from insurance carriers' and health care providers' zealous attempts to cut costs and save money; legislation to curb it was introduced in 1996.

insurance technician, cited to 1992, a registered nurse who is an employee, as of a health insurance company, and who monitors and reviews under physician supervision, hospitalized patients' care, using established company treatment guidelines and length-of-stay stipulations. This oversight, a form of *peer review* when the insurance-company physician intervenes, is regarded by many *primary care physicians* as intrusive and counterproductive; it was the subject of much general discussion and argument in the late 1980s-early 90s.

MSA, 1990s, abbreviation for *m*edical *s*avings *a*ccount; legal in many states in the 1990s, it allows self-employed individuals to make tax-deductible contributions to a fund reserved strictly—on pain of a 15 percent penalty—for the payment of medical expenses down the road.

self-care, 1996 in this specific sense; the treatment of minor medical complaints at home rather than in a medical setting, using handbooks, *dial-a-nurse* services, and computer networking. The practice, intended to save money, is a new take on the old method of using home guides to family medical care such as I.D. Johnson, M.D.'s *Guide to Homeopathic Practice: Designed for the Use of Families and Private Individuals* (1913), which gave advice on everything from "Rush of Blood to the Head" and "Buzzing in the Ears" to "Gum-Boil" and "Bites of Mad Dogs, etc."

viatical settlement, cited to 1988, increased usage in late 1990s; an insurance settlement by which an investor or a firm buys life insurance policies from terminally ill patients, giving those patients the needed cash for, e.g., paid *home health care*, with the purchaser/investor then profiting from the assigned policy when the insured dies; *viatical*, from *viaticum*, first recorded in English in 1562, "Last Communion," itself from Latin, "traveling money; Roman soldiers' booty." In English *viaticals* came to mean "articles for a trip" and in botany, "plants growing along frequented places, such as roadsides." This plural form, labeled "rare" as far back as the 1934 *Webster's New International Dictionary* (unabridged), is an example of the infrequent instance when a very old, heretofore disused word regains currency—resuscitated, as it were, by the force of circumstances (such asAIDS) while at the same time taking on a new, previously nonexistent meaning.

believed to inhibit the effects of environmental pollution. *Calcium supplements* are taken by millions of American women to combat the loss of calcium from bones that can lead to *osteoporosis* and *fractures*, especially after menopause. The minerals *selenium, zinc, potassium,* and *iron* all have their advocates. But American doctors remain largely skeptical about the benefits of supplements, recommending a *balanced diet* and regular exercise in place of costly vitamins.

The *New York Times* reported in March 1995 that about 3.4 percent of the 2.2 billion prescriptions for drugs written by doctors each year in the U.S. were for *NSAIDs* (pronounced "En-seds," for *n*onsteroidal *a*nti-*i*nflammatory *d*rugs), taken for pain relief and used to treat *arthritis* (inflammation of the joints). These include *Indocin* (acetic acid) and *Feldene* (an oxicam) as well as *over-the-counter pain-relievers* like *aspirin* (once Bayer's trademark for *salicylic acid* but now generic) and *Motrin* (proplonic acid).

From time to time a new drug is introduced that Americans are convinced is a *panacea* (from the Greek *panakeia,* healing all). This was true of *Valium,* the popular tranquilizer introduced in 1963, and of *Prozac* in the 1980s and 90s (*Go take a Prozac!* all but replaced, in the early 1990s, the earlier slang expressions *Chill out!* and *Get a life!*). Parents whose children have trouble focusing in school are sometimes counseled to have them put on *Ritalin,* widely prescribed in the 1990s to treat *ADD* (attention *d*eficit *d*isorder) and *ADHD* (attention *d*eficit *h*yperactivity *d*isorder), conditions unknown or undiagnosed a decade earlier.

DISABILITIES UNLIMITED

What once were regarded as behavioral problems came to be seen as *disabilities.* Alcoholism (1860) came to be recognized by the medical community as a disease, perhaps an inherited one, entitling those suffering from it to obtain treatment in *rehab* (rehabilitation) or *detox* (detoxification) *centers* without losing their jobs or being stigmatized. The passage of the Americans with Disabilities Act in 1990 changed attitudes toward a wide variety of physical and mental problems formerly blamed on the sufferer; those affected by the conditions spelled out in this law are part of *protected groups.* Even *drug addicts* are regarded as having a *chemically induced disability.*

In this sense, America's most widespread self-induced disability is *nicotine addiction,* otherwise known as *smoking.* Though tobacco has been a cash crop and tobacco producers a potent political force since colonial times, the *Surgeon General's warning* (1964, progressively more detailed and dire over the years) on cigarette packs and other tobacco products, a total ban on broadcast advertising of tobacco products (since 1971), as well as increasingly more troubling evidence of the dangers of smoking brought about a general decline in tobacco use since 1970 (which reversed itself, especially among teens, in the mid to late 1990s). Many who puffed *a pack a day* ("He's a *pack-a-day* man" was once a common expression) when they were in their 20s and 30s demanded, by the 1990s, a *smoke-free environment.* Smoking has been banned on all domestic airline flights since 1990, and in many public facilities; most restaurants long ago set aside *nonsmoking sections* for patrons whose appetites are ruined by *secondhand smoke* ("Smoking or non?"—a common abbreviated form of "Do you prefer a smoking or nonsmoking section?"—is now a standard restaurant question). Smoking became so politically incorrect that there was no cure too exotic or expensive—from hypnotism to *nicotine patches* (called *the patch* in the same manner that

The Language of Alcoholics Anonymous

Alcoholics Anonymous *doesn't define itself as a* support group *(1969) per se. Rather, it defines itself as "a* fellowship *of men and women who share their experience . . . with each other that they may solve their common problem and help others to* recover *from alcoholism." AA was founded in 1935 by Bill W., a New York stockbroker, and Dr. Bob S., an Ohio surgeon, who had both been "hopeless drunks." The name* Alcoholics Anonymous *had not been coined then; people came to know it in 1939 when Bill's book,* Alcoholics Anonymous, *was published by the fellowship. Members call this volume the* Big Book. *In this book words like* recovery— *so popular in the literature of late 20th century* self-help *move-ments—occur, as do:*

The Twelve Steps, among them *admission* of a powerlessness over alcohol; creation of a personal *moral inventory*; *admission* to one-self and to others the exact nature of one's misdeeds; *listing* the names of all those one has harmed; *making amends* to all those one has harmed; and so on.

spiritual experience, awakening, a profound, usually not imme-diate, alteration in the *recovering alcoholic's* reaction to life, aided by belief in and submission to a *Power greater than oneself*. This is called *God-consciousness* by the more religious members of AA.

24 hours of sobriety, referring to the *one-step-at-a-time* approach to the goal of staying sober from one day to the next.

My name is _____, and I'm an alcoholic, admission of the situation, using only the first name, followed by one's *story*.

". . . stress is rapidly spreading throughout the world. Or at least the word for it is. . . . The history . . . of the spread of the English word 'stress' has yet to be documented although it is . . . a borrowed term . . . in . . . lexicons for Russian, Polish and Bulgarian and in . . . Japanese. . . . In Spanish it is pronounced 'ess-TRESS,' in Russian 'STRESS-a.' In Japanese 'su tor es u.'"

— New York Times, January 26, 1997, the quotation illustrating the process of "foreign borrowing" of an English word into another language.

birth control pills came to be called *the pill*)—for those who wanted to *kick the habit,* and for whom the *Great American Smokeout* (an annual event to get smokers to quit, even if just for a day—the third Thursday in November) didn't work. But despite the medical evidence that smoking causes lung cancer, emphysema, and a host of other maladies, *stogies* (cheap cigars), *cheroots* (cigars with square-cut ends), *smokeless tobacco* (chewing tobacco), and *cigs* (cigarettes) remained popular, particularly among young people.

MEDICAL TALK

The world of health care has its own language, much of it highly tech-nical and baffling to the general patient. But there is a lighter side, too, in doctors' and nurses' slang, such as *left-sided appendicitis, heir-condi-tioned,* and *responding to treatment* (all terms for pregnancy). Hypochon-driacs or malingerers are *gomers* (for *G*et *O*ut of *M*y *E*mergency *R*oom), and some individuals are said to suffer from *high ceramic content* (in other words, they're *crackpots*). On the darker side, a *gork* (of disputed origin, possibly an acronym for *G*od *o*nly *r*eally *k*nows, referring to the mysterious cause of a catastrophic medical event) is a patient who has lost all brain function; the verb *gork off* and an adjective *gorky* are also in

"The ancients used the word [cancer] in reference to malignant tumors. The allusion, doubtless, was to the manner in which invasive neoplasms firmly grasped the tissues in which they grew. . . . Galen (A.D. 131–201) observed, probably of a breast cancer, 'Just as a crab's feet extend from every part of the body, so in this disease the veins are distended, forming a similar figure.'"

— *William S. Haubrich, M.D.,*
Medical Meanings:
A Glossary of Origins, 1984

common use. To *flatline* is to lose all cardiac functions, exhibiting this on a "flat" *EKG* (electrocardiogram) trace; a *flatliner* is the patient so affected. And a *horrenderoma* is slang for a large malignant mass impossible or extremely difficult to treat.

Doctors also use a multitude of acronyms. Consider *ECT* (electroconvulsive therapy, *IBW* (ideal body weight), *NYD* (not yet diagnosed), and *DOA* (dead on arrival). The most common medical abbreviation may be the *Rx* on prescriptions, used since medieval times for Latin *recipe,* meaning "take," the first word in Latin *recipes* or formulas for prescriptions. Most Americans feel comfortable bandying about such medical acronyms as *PMS* (pre-menstrual syndrome, 1982), *MRI* (magnetic resonance imaging, early 1980s, a diagnostic scan using a magnetic field), and *CFS* (Chronic Fatigue Syndrome, mid 1980s, believed to be caused by the Epstein-Barr virus). If they haven't had a *CAT* or *CT scan* (computer-

Cancer Ward

Cancer, *a direct borrowing from the Latin word meaning "crab; cancer," is a malignant tumor (or a disease caused by one) that expands locally by* invasion *and systemically by* metastasis *(1663, ultimately from Greek* methistanai, *to change;* metastasize, *1907, to spread).*

Cancer *and many words associated with it were much used during the 20th century and even earlier, as the word itself indicates: people were and are dying of it, while researchers attempt to devise preventions, treatments, and cures. Some of the more important, and widely used, cancer terms—a good many coming from Greek and based on the Greek suffix* -oma, *formation, mass, and coming to mean "tumor" in Medical English—are these:*

biopsy, 1895, *bi-* from Greek *bios*, mode of life + *opsy*, from Greek *opsis*, appearance or sight; the removal—for study, analysis, and diagnosis—of cells, fluids, or tissue samples from a living body.

carcinogen, 1853, based on Greek *karkinos*, an ulcerous sore, literally "crab"; a substance or other agent that induces or causes cancer.

carcinoma, around 1751, a malignant tumor originating in epithelial tissue; people wear sun blocks and avoid sunburn to avoid *squamous-cell carcinoma* (*squamous cell* the noun compound, around 1947), a form of skin cancer.

chemotherapy, typically clipped to *chemo*, full form dating to 1910; the combined use of drugs and serum to treat cancer.

hospice, from French, ultimately from Latin *hospes*, host, and going back to 1818 in its original sense, "a lodging place for students and other young people"; a program (not a building) that offers terminally ill patients medical, emotional, and spiritual care at home or at an in-patient facility.

leukemia, around 1855, from Greek *leukos*, white + *emia*, from *haima*, blood; an acute or chronic disease marked by an abnormal increase in the white blood cell count.

lymphoma, 1873, a tumor of the lymph-node tissue, or tumorous growth thereto; *Hodgkin's disease*, 1865, named after the British physician Thomas *Hodgkin*, 1798-1866, is a type of lymphoma.

mammography, 1937, the radiologic examination of the breasts to detect cancerous or precancerous lesions.

melanoma, 1830, a usually (but not always) malignant tumor with a dark pigmentation.

oncology, around 1857, from *onco-*, Greek, "mass" + *-logy*, from Greek *logos*, study; the branch of medicine that studies, diagnoses, and treats tumors.

polyp, 1742, from Medieval French *polype*, octopus, or nasal tumor, via Latin from Greek *polypous*, itself from *poly-*, from *polys*, many + *pous*, foot; a tumor with a pedicle, not commonly occurring in the uterus, rectum, or nose.

> *radiotherapy*, 1903, called *radiation* or *radiation treatments* by most folks, the use of x-rays and other radiologic techniques to treat disease, particularly cancer.
>
> *sarcoma*, 1804, from Greek *sarkoma*, fleshy growth, from *sarkoun*, to grow flesh; a malignant tumor in connective tissue, bone, cartilage, or striated muscle.
>
> *tumor*, 1597, from Latin *tumere*, to swell; an abnormal—benign or malignant—tissue mass that arises and grows without restraint and without obvious cause from pre-existing cells, and that has no physiologic function.

"Today I consider myself the luckiest man on the face of the earth."
—New York Yankee first baseman, Lou Gerhrig, on the 4th of July, 1939, 23 months before his death.

ized *axial tomography*, early 1970s, used to produce a series of x-rays providing a three-dimensional picture of the body), they probably know someone who has, and almost everyone has had an *FUO* (*fever of unknown origin*) or an *EKG* (or *electrocardiogram*, 1904, which produces a graph of the heart's activity; it is also called an *ECG*, though *EKG* is more prevalent, the latter being from the German spelling for the procedure, *electrokardiogramm*, since the earliest machines were from Germany). An *MI* (*myocardial infarction*, a failure of part of the heart muscle, causing a *heart attack*) can land you in the *ER* (*emergency room*), the *ICU* (*intensive care unit*), or the *CCU* (*cardiac care unit*).

It is a medical tradition to name diseases, syndromes, and conditions after the individual(s) who first described their symptoms, such as *Alzheimer's* and *Tay-Sachs diseases, Parkinson's* and *Down* or *Down's syndrome*. On the other hand, *Lou Gehrig's disease*, or amyotrophic lateral sclerosis, was named after the U. S. baseball star who died from it.

Radiologists at the University Hospitals of Cleveland monitor a patient undergoing magnetic resonance imaging, or MRI.

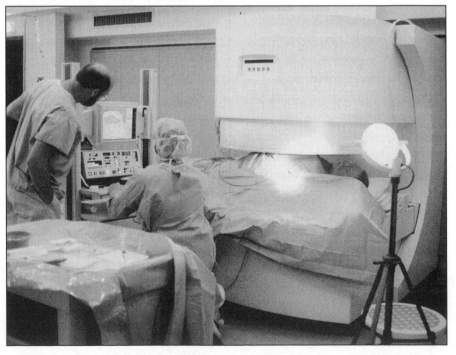

An acupuncturist inserts needles into the ear of his patient. The technique is often used to relieve pain or to help cure addictions, such as to heroin or nicotine.

CONSIDER THE ALTERNATIVES

Ever since *quacks* (early 1600s, shortened from a Dutch borrowing *quacksalver,* one who "quacks," or boasts, about the virtues of his salves or ointments) and *snake-oil salesmen* (1920s) went from town to town in early America hawking their nostrums, Americans' interest has been piqued by *alternative medicine,* known today as *alternate therapies*, these therapies gaining more and more accptance in the 1990s:

acupuncture, 1684, a technique for relieving pain or inducing regional anesthesia in which thin needles are inserted into the body at specific points.

Basketball legend Magic Johnson in November 1991, announcing that he was HIV-positive and retiring from the NBA. He would go on to be the MVP of the 1992 NBA All-Star game, win an Olympic Gold Medal, be an NBA head coach, and come out of retirement in 1996 to lead the Los Angeles Lakers into the playoffs.

biofeedback, 1970, the use of monitoring devices to furnish information regarding a bodily function, such as heart rate or blood pressure, in an attempt to gain some voluntary control over that function.

chiropractic, 1898, manipulation of the spine and other parts of the body. This is the most established and widely used of the alternate therapies. (The word is formed of *chir-*, Latin, from Greek *cheir-*, related to Hittite [an extinct language] *kessar*, hand + Greek *praktikos*, practical).

herbal medicine, use of traditional *folk remedies* based on common herbs, roots, and preparations made with them. Many are known by medical science to have therapeutic effect.

homeopathy, 1826, the administration, usually in very small doses, of drugs that would produce in a healthy person symptoms very similar to those of the disease being treated.

hydrotherapy, 1876, external use of water in localizing infections, relieving pain, and improving circulation, for example.

hypnotherapy, 1897, using hypnosis, especially for the treatment of *chronic pain*, *addition*, or *phobias*.

lomilomi (Hawaiian for "rub rub"), a style of massage originating in Hawaii.

naturopathy, 1901, based on a theory that disease can be cured by assisting natural healing processes without surgery or synthetic medicines. Naturopaths use special diets, fasts, massage, vitamins from natural sources, herbs, etc.

transcendental meditation or *TM*, 1966, popularized by India's Maharishi Mahesh Yogi, advocates deep concentration and meditation including repetition of a *mantra* to ease stress and anxiety.

Dr. Death with his suicide machine in 1991.

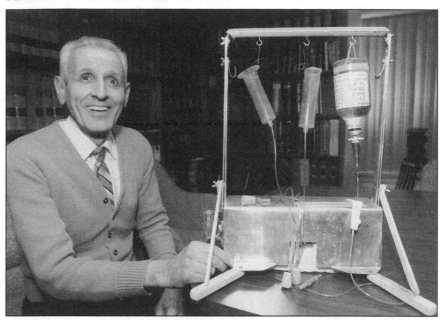

THE RIGHT TO DIE

Ever since Karen Ann Quinlan went into a ten-year coma in 1975, Americans have been arguing over who has the right to *pull the plug* on a patient who is on a *respirator* or other *life-support system,* and whom medical experts agree has suffered *irreversible brain damage* (also referred to as *brain death,* 1964) and, being *brain-dead,* is unlikely to recover. The controversy over an individual's *right to die with dignity* was re-ignited in the 1990s, when Dr. Jack Kevorkian (soon referred to in the press as *Dr. Death*) began traveling around Michigan using his *suicide machine,* which, when the patient chose to activate it, administered lethal doses of medication, allowing the terminally ill patient to choose when he or she wanted to stop living.

Although practiced openly in countries such as the Netherlands, *physician-assisted suicide,* or simply *assisted suicide,* remains the most highly controversial if not illegal (depending on local law) act in the U.S. Every doctor is required to swear fealty to the *Hippocratic Oath,* which includes the vow not to administer any "poison" or do anything else that constitutes harm to a patient. But physicians have in many cases quietly permitted their terminally ill patients to die by withholding treatment, sometimes at the instruction of the patient or family, expressed in a *living will* (early 1970s, a legal document specifying that no *extraordinary,* or *heroic, measures* are to be used to save a dying patient; such a patient in a hospital is called a *no-code,* meaning that at the point of expiration, no emergency "codes" will be called to summon resuscitation teams). The line dividing *euthanasia* (1869, Greek, "easy death") from murder is narrow, a matter of ethics and the law that remains unclear.

THAT HOLIDAY SPIRIT:
RED-LETTER DAYS

*T*he American calendar is crammed with special days for celebration or commemoration. The most important we call holidays, which give us a good excuse to take a day off from work. Though the word holiday itself, the first part of which is related to holy, originally referred to religious feast days in Anglo-Saxon times, the word early on began to secularize, so that by the Middle Ages it applied to any sort of day free from work, often given over to merriment. The term red-letter days, appearing as early as 1704, originally referred to holidays, alluding to the medieval practice of writing important saints' days in red on religious calendars.

A young couple dancing in the Cinco de Mayo parade in San Francisco's Mission District on May 5, 1996. Cinco de Mayo commemorates a Mexican military victory over the French in 1862.

THE "STANDARD SIX" HOLIDAYS

Most Americans have a day off on the "Standard Six" holidays: New Year's Day, Memorial Day, the Fourth of July, Labor Day, Thanksgiving, and Christmas. Other *legal holidays* (used as early as 1867, of a celebration of the anniversary of Lincoln's birthday) or *public holidays,* which are days off of work for many, vary by state or local area.

The *federal holidays,* when all U.S. federal government offices, post offices, and most banks are closed, include:

Veterans Day, November 11, was originally *Armistice Day* (so proclaimed by President Wilson in 1919), and commemorated the armistice that ended fighting in World War I on November 11, 1918, which began at "the eleventh hour of the eleventh day of the eleventh month." Declared a federal holiday in 1938, November 11 was officially designated *Veterans Day* by Congress in 1954 to honor all veterans of the armed services. From 1971 through 1977 the fourth Monday in October was observed as *Veterans Day,* but thereafter observance was restored to November 11.

A Veterans Day parade in Connecticut in 1940, back when it was still called Armistice Day.

Washington's Birthday, observed on the third Monday of February, is now more often than not celebrated as a "combined" holiday called *Presidents'* (or *President's*) *Day* or *Washington-Lincoln Day.* It commemorates the birthday of President George Washington (February 22, at least on the Gregorian calendar, though George himself was actually born on February 11, 1732, when the English and their colonies were still using the old Julian calendar) and, as a combined holiday, the birthday of Abraham Lincoln (February 12).

Martin Luther King, Jr. Day, observed on the third Monday in January (that nearest his birthday, January 15), honors the great civil rights leader and 1964 Nobel Peace Prize winner. King, whose August 28, 1963 "I Have a Dream" speech is universally praised for its eloquence, was assassinated on April 4, 1968. The federal holiday was declared by Congress in 1983.

Election Day, the first Tuesday after the first Monday in November, with *federal elections* every even-numbered year and *presidential elections,* also called *national elections,* every fourth year.

The federal holidays were the first to be regularly celebrated as *Monday holidays,* those always observed on a Monday, as established in 1968 by the passage of Public Law 90-363, the "Monday Holiday Law."

THE HOLIDAY SEASON

No time of year in America has grander or more extensive celebration, spirit, ritual, and consumerism associated with it than the time from Thanksgiving to New Year's. This period is often simply known as *the Holidays.*

THANKSGIVING, TURKEY, AND DRESSING
Thanksgiving (1533) was a familiar word to the early colonists in its sense of giving thanks to God. Local ministers and colonial governors proclaimed many a "day of thanksgiving" for the recovery of a sick person, the end of an epidemic, the safe arrival of a ship, a truce, or a good harvest.

Thanksgiving in 1858, before President Lincoln reestablished it as a national holiday.

"Our harvest being gotten in, . . . for three days we entertained [many Native Americans] *and feasted, and they* [the Native Americans] *went out and killed five deer, which they brought to the* [Plymouth] *plantation and bestowed on our governor, and upon the captain and others."*

— *Edward Winslow, Plymouth, Mass., letter of December 21, 1621, to George Morton in England, detailing in a sole original account the facts of America's first* Thanksgiving

The first real *Thanksgiving* was celebrated in Plymouth, Massachusetts between September 21 and November 9, 1621, and the celebration lasted over a three-day period. This was 10 months after the Pilgrims had landed there. The first winter and its "General Sickness" (probably scurvy) had killed nearly half the original 102 Pilgrims. Then summer had given the survivors new hope and the harvest of flint corn (a variety with small hard grains) brought them relief and rejoicing, especially since their European crops had failed. This was the native corn that Squanto had taught them to plant, with fish as fertilizer. Four Pilgrim men were sent out to hunt wildfowl and brought back enough to last a week. The Pilgrims' good friend, Chief Massasoit of the Wampanoags, was invited and came with 90 of his men: thus there were many more Native Americans than Pilgrims at the first Thanksgiving.

Everyone feasted on venison, wild ducks, geese and perhaps even swan with *pudding in the belly* (stuffing), cod, sea bass, watercress, flint corn, beans, squash, wild onions, American and Beach plums, raspberries, wild cherries, strawberries, and American crab apples, to name but a few items attested by historians. The Pilgrams drank beer, as did their children. They ate with knives and a few spoons, but no forks. Most of the cooking and eating was done outdoors, with the game roasted on spits.

The Pilgrims' intermittent Thanksgiving grew into a New England tradition. In 1676 the first formal proclamation of Thanksgiving was made in Charlestown, Massachusetts, followed in the years 1777-1783 by Continental and U.S. Congress proclamations, seven in all. (The first day of Thanksgiving was proclaimed by the Continental Congress for December 18, 1777.) It was left to President George Washington to issue the first National Thanksgiving Proclamation establishing Thursday, November 26, 1789 as the holiday. The custom waned under Thomas Jefferson. In 1827, however, Mrs. Sarah Josepha Hale, first as the editor of Boston's *Ladies Magazine* and later of its widely read successor, *Godey's Lady's Book* of Philadelphia, started a crusade to make Thanksgiving Day a nationwide observance. Her campaign eventually led President Lincoln to proclaiming August 6 as a national Thanksgiving Day in 1863. He made another *Thanksgiving Day Proclamation* in 1864:

> [I] invite my fellow citizens . . . to set apart and observe the last Thursday of November next as a day of thanksgiving and praise to our beneficent Father who dwelleth in the heavens.
>
> Abraham Lincoln, October 3, 1863

Thus Lincoln established Thanksgiving as a national holiday and made it the fourth Thursday that November. Each year from 1864 to 1939 the President of the United States proclaimed Thanksgiving as the fourth Thursday of November. Then in 1939 President Franklin Roosevelt changed the date to the third Thursday in November, to help the economy by giving stores an extra week of Christmas business between Thanksgiving and Christmas. Although Lincoln's first nationwide Thanksgiving of 1863 had been on August 6, by 1939 the fourth Thursday of November seemed sacred to many Americans. There were so many cries of outrage during the next three "early" Thanksgivings that Congress passed a Joint Resolution in December 1941 permanently changing it back to the fourth Thursday in November.

Now, how about Thanksgiving *turkey*? Our North American bird was erroneously named the *turkey* by European explorers as early as 1587 in confusion with the European turkey cock, a completely different bird (a mere guinea fowl, which got its name because it was introduced into Europe from Guinea through Turkey). Other stories, that our word *turkey* comes from some Native American word for it, or from the doctor on Columbus' ship shouting *Tukki!* (Hebrew for "big bird") when he first saw one, are spurious. Our term *Thanksgiving turkey* didn't appear until 1829, and it wasn't called a *Thanksgiving bird* until 1870. Thanksgiving itself wasn't referred to as *Turkey Day* until 1916.

We called the southern brown vulture a *turkey buzzard* by 1672 and a *turkey vulture* by 1823. We were shooting turkeys for prizes at *turkey shoots* in the 1840s and calling fowling pieces *turkey busters* by the 1860s. New England colonists called salted cod *Cape Cod turkey*, and in the 1920s and 30s *Irish turkey* was a humorous term for corned beef and cabbage, as well as a hobo and army term for stew or hash with unidentifiable ingredients.

CHRISTMAS

Christmas (before the 12th century, from Middle English *Cristemas*, from Old English *Cristes Mflsse*, Christ's Festival) is very much a time of music, including traditional *Christmas carols*, especially on December 25, the day it is celebrated. In the 1300s the word *carol* referred to a ring-dance, a circle of dancers with joined hands, often accompanied by choral singing and great merriment. By the early 1500s the English already were referring to *Christmasse carolles*, and now *carol* is almost never used of any other holiday. Even Handel's *Messiah*, intended as Easter music, is now associated with Christmas by many. It is very often the music of the season that puts one *in the Christmas spirit*.

Here are some of the more notable symbols of Christmas and the terms denoting them:

Christmas trees. The practice of bringing a tree into the home at Christmas was brought to this country from Germany by immigrants. From 1838, with "the introduction into the new country of the spec-

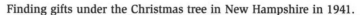

Finding gifts under the Christmas tree in New Hampshire in 1941.

Santa Claus (1773–).

tacle of the German *Christmas-tree*," to 1855, when the "selection and adornment of the *Christmas tree*" is spoken of, and, 1856, when "anxious children gathered round the *Christmas tree*," it is easy to see that the new custom took hold strongly and rapidly. It is likely that the practice became widespread sooner here than in England, where the German-influenced court of Queen Victoria popularized the custom.

Christmas stockings. The word *stockings* now seems quaintly old-fashioned to Americans. The famed Clement Clark Moore poem (almost always called "'Twas the night before Christmas" even though it is actually titled "A Visit from St. Nicholas") written in 1822 and first published in 1823 has the well-known reference to "stockings hung by the chimney with care." This would lead us to believe that the practice was already well-established. Today the stockings are still hung, and Christmas shopping includes getting some small, usually inexpensive *stocking stuffers* (1948) to put in them.

Christmas cards. The custom of sending holiday good wishes on illustrated greeting cards originated in England in the 1840s, soon after the introduction of the penny post in 1840. Sending a postcard, or one enclosed in a letter, became an inexpensive way to send *Season's Greetings.* In the 1870s a German immigrant, Louis Prang, began to have great success selling his richly lithographed cards, produced with designs Prang commissioned at his printing plant in Roxbury, Massachusetts, near Boston. Until that time, most Christmas cards sold in America were imported. Prang turned the Christmas card business into a thriving enterprise, and began in 1880 to award large cash prizes ($2,000 and more) in annual competitions for the most appealing design. From Prang's success with Christmas cards the entire greeting card industry developed.

Santa Claus. The jolly fellow in the red suit crying "Ho, Ho, Ho" brings Christmas gifts to children on his sleigh pulled by reindeer. He is one of the most enduring and well-loved of all our holiday symbols. The legend originates with St. Nicholas (hence the alternate name for Santa, *St. Nick*), a 4th century bishop of Myra, a coastal city in the ancient country of Lycia (southwestern Turkey of today). Many miracles were attributed to him, but the defining legend involves St. Nicholas secretly throwing a purse of gold on each of three nights into the house of a poor man whose three daughters had no dowry. The man discovered Nicholas on the third night, but the saint made him promise not to reveal his munificence. The legend, his association with generously and unselfishly helping children, and his popularity grew throughout the Christian world. Though his feast day is actually December 6, in German folklore he was transformed into a sort of patron of Christmas. In America the legend grew still further, and his name was modified under the influence of Dutch Protestant settlers in New Amsterdam (New York), who called him *Sinterklaas* (from Dutch for *saint* plus a clipped form of his Dutch name, *Niklaas*). *Santa Claus* first appeared in print in the *New York Gazetteer* of 1773.

NEW YEAR'S
Only one week after the end of the *Christmas rush* comes *New Year's Eve* and *Day,* often simply *New Year's. New Year's Eve* traditions include the singing of *Auld Lang Syne* (Scottish dialect for "old long ago"), popping corks and drinking champagne, and kissing other revelers at New Year's Eve parties. In sober attempts to counter the alcoholic revelry long part of New Year's festivities, several American cities, following Boston's lead

A 1906 New Year's Eve toast. The revelers have been duly warned by the signs that the "the throwing of confetti is strictly prohibited."

in 1976, have sponsored *First Night* celebrations, typically with artistic events, fireworks displays, and other family entertainment.

New Year's Day is notorious for *New Year's resolutions* (notoriously soon forgotten by their *resolvers*), *morning-after* hangovers for those who overindulged the night before, and a spate of parades and college-football bowl games on TV from early morning till late night.

SUMMER HOLIDAYS

Three holidays mark the *summer season* for Americans and are popularly seen as truer denoters of summer than the "official" ones, the summer solstice and autumnal equinox. In many parts of the country—except, as in the Northeast, where *February vacation* (*winter break*) and *April vacation* (*spring break*), create mid-winter holidays and make the end of school mid-June—Memorial Day is just about the time that *school's out for summer*. The Fourth of July holiday is taken as summer's halfway point. After the *Fourth*, many people go on *summer vacations* or *family vacations* (for the well-to-do, *summer* is a verb, too: "We *summer* on the Cape"); the American *vacation season* lasts through August. Right around *Labor Day* it is *back-to-school time*.

MEMORIAL DAY

Memorial Day was originally set aside to remember the Civil War dead of the North by decorating their graves with flowers; hence the two names *Memorial Day* and the older, now fading term *Decoration Day*. Although Boalsburg, Pennsylvania claims to have had a Memorial Day in 1864, Waterloo, New York is usually credited with having the first true Memorial Day observance on May 5, 1866, which included flying the village flags at half-staff, a veterans' parade, and a march to the village cemeteries where speeches were made. The first nationwide *Decoration Day* was planned and held in 1868 by the *Grand Army of the Republic*,

"In Flanders fields the poppies blow

Between the crosses, row on row

— "In Flanders Fields," a very popular World War I poem written for the London Punch, December 8, 1915, by John McCrae, a Canadian who commanded a dressing station at the Second Battle of Ypres and who was later killed in the war. The American Cemetery in Flanders, at Waereghem, Belgium, contains 368 American graves.

formed by Union Army veterans in 1866 to get Congress to provide veterans' pensions and aid to soldiers' widows and orphans. It was

> *for the purpose of strewing with flowers or otherwise decorating the graves of the Comrades who died in defense of their country during the late rebellion and whose bodies lie in almost every city, village or hamlet churchyard in the land.*
>
> —Order sent to local posts of the Grand Army of the Republic by its commander-in-chief General John A. Logan for observing May 30, 1868, as Decoration Day.

Memorial Day color guard in Maine in 1943.

The date, May 30, had no real significance, though it is roughly the anniversary of the surrender of the last Confederate Army (General Kirby Smith's, on May 26, 1865). A *Confederate Memorial Day* was soon observed in some southern states, varying from April 26 (the date of the surrender of General Joseph E. Johnston at Durham Station, North Carolina, 1865) to June 3 (Jefferson Davis' birthday).

After World War I the *American Legion* (chartered in 1919) took over planning the observance, which became a memorial day for American servicemen from all wars. Soon, however, it was also known as *Poppy Day*, for the flowers that had become the symbol of the tragedy of World War I because they bloomed profusely in French battlefield graveyards. Poppies had originally been sold on street corners during World War I for the benefit of French and Belgian war orphans; then in 1922 the Veterans of Foreign Wars conducted the first nationwide "poppy sale" for disabled and destitute American war veterans. In 1971 Memorial Day was changed to the last Monday in May, making it one of several official *three-day weekends*.

FOURTH OF JULY—INDEPENDENCE DAY

> *Yesterday [July 2]. . . . A resolution was passed . . . that these United Colonies are, and of right ought to be, free and independent States. . . . The second day of July, 1776 . . . ought to be commemorated . . . by solemn acts of devotion to God Almighty. It ought to be solemnized with pomp and parade, with shows, games, sports, guns, bells, bonfires, and illuminations—from this time forward for everyone.*
>
> —John Adams, letter to his wife Abigail, July 3, 1776

Adams was right about celebrating, but not about the date. The Continental Congress did approve a resolution for independence on July 2, but adopted the formal Declaration of Independence on July 4, while the famous signing of "the Declaration of Independence" took place in Philadelphia on August 2, after the document had been transcribed on parchment. Thus the birthday of American Independence could just as fairly be celebrated each year on July 2, July 4, or August 2. Philadelphia chose July 4th and that date became the focus of our most patriotic expressions.

The first Fourth of July celebration was on the first anniversary of the Declaration of Independence in 1777. Boston celebrated mainly with sermons; many places celebrated not at all. But Philadelphia, the Revolutionary capital, had a major celebration, including sermons, the ringing

Fireworks over the East River, with Manhattan providing the backdrop.

of bells, candles lit in every window, bonfires, 13-gun salutes, speeches, an official dinner, a captured Hessian band playing—and fireworks. Here, on this very first Fourth of July celebration, the term *the Glorious Fourth* was first used. Though Philadelphia was occupied by British troops in 1778, the celebrations spread to other areas. By the late 1790s the day was also called *Independence Day,* by the 1820s it was often simply called *the Fourth.*

By the 1840s *Fourth of July picnic* was a popular term, and sports and games, such as potato races, catching a greased pig, and watermelon eating contests, were popular. *Fireworks* have always been associated with the Fourth, partly because they represented the musket fire and rockets of the Revolution, partly just for the fun of it. In fact the word *fireworks* was first recorded in America in 1777 in connection with the first Fourth of July celebration (before that they had been called *rockets*; after 1820 those that were made to be heard rather than seen were called *firecrackers*).

LABOR DAY

As the American Federation of Labor (AFL) was being organized and began to grow, the Department of Labor and *Labor Day* were also becoming established. On June 27, 1884, Congress established a *Bureau of Labor* in the Department of Interior, then in 1888 gave this bureau independent status as the *Department of Labor* (in 1903 it became part of the *Department of Commerce and Labor,* then in 1913 became the separate Department of Labor again, this time with its head serving as a member of the President's cabinet as the *Secretary of Labor).* Meantime, machinist Matthew McGuire of Paterson, New Jersey and carpenter Peter J. McGuire of New York City, who had helped form the United Brotherhood of Carpenters and Joiners (both unrelated), played major roles in organizing the Central Labor Union's first *Labor Day Parade* in New York City in September 1882. Oregon became the first state to make *Labor Day* a legal holiday in 1887; President Grover Cleveland made it a national holiday, with the first national Labor Day celebration held the first Monday in September 1894.

A postman delivering Valentine's Day mail in 1859. Contrary to the belief of many men, the holiday was not invented by the greeting card and chocolate industries.

MINOR HOLIDAYS

Other holidays through the year are observed with their own, often intentionally silly or childish rituals, including Groundhog Day, Valentine's Day, April Fool's Day, and Halloween.

GROUNDHOG DAY
February 2 is annually noted in newspapers across the land with a story about *Punxsutawney Phil,* the *groundhog* (that's pure American for *woodchuck* or *marmot*) who emerges from his burrow on this day near Gobbler's Knob, just outside the borough of Punxsutawney (population 6,782) in west-central Pennsylvania. The story is that if the sun is shining and "the groundhog sees his shadow, there'll be six more weeks of winter." The legend explains that Phil is frightened by his shadow, and so goes back in his hole if he sees it; this is said to portend more winter weather to come. The folk origins of this go back to Europe, with similar rituals in England and Germany regarding bears, badgers, and other winter-hibernating animals emerging on this day, also called *Candlemas* (before the 12th century). Only cynics observe that, since winter officially ends with the vernal equinox around March 21, there are always six more weeks of winter anyway.

ST. VALENTINE'S DAY
Contrary to widespread and persistent popular myth, various ancient Roman festivals are not the source of *Valentine's Day.* Rather, Geoffrey Chaucer was most probably the very first to make the association between the saint's day and choosing one's sweetheart. There is no proven historical linkage prior to Chaucer's time but afterwards such linkages abound. The best piece of evidence from Chaucer dates to around 1300 in his *Parlement of Foules*: "on Seynt Valentynes day,/Whan every foul cometh there to chese [choose] his make [mate]."

Be My Valentine does not, of course, mean "Be My St. Valentine" but "Be My Love, Be My Gallant." by 1450, *Valentine* meant the person whose name was picked from a box or who was chosen to be one's sweetheart or special friend for that day; it meant a folded paper with the special person's name on it by 1533; a gift to the special person by 1610; and finally a verse, letter, or message to that person by 1824.

The first Valentine message is said to have been sent in 1415 from the Duke of Orleans from his cell in the Tower of London to his wife. Be that as it may, by the 16th century young gallants were sending their sweethearts poems on Valentine's Day; they often copied verses from special books, such as the very popular 1669 British *A Valentine Writer* (young men in America also used it widely). In the early 1800s young British and American men might still draw names from boxes to choose Valentine partners; if the young men were truly smitten, they might wear the slips of paper with their lady's names pinned to their sleeves for several days (by the early 1600s this had already given English the phrase *to wear* [one's] *heart on* [one's] *sleeve).*

By the 1800s, too, commercial woodcuts and lithographs of cupids, turtledoves, bleeding hearts, etc., began to replace or accompany the poems, with the first store selling such *valentines* opening in London in 1809. However, it was not until the introduction of penny postage and envelopes in England that delicately ornate or lace paper *valentines*, as we know them, came into wide use. These were soon imported from England into the U.S., and we were beginning to talk about and send *valentine cards* by the late 1840s and manufacturing them in America by 1850.

Valentine's Day, February 14, one of the most commercially exploited of American holidays, set the example for *Sweetest Day*, the third Saturday in October, for giving (especially store-bought) candy, flowers, cards, and other gifts to *the love of one's life*. A spate of other invented holidays followed. Some of these holidays, observed to varying degrees around the country, include *Grandparents' Day* (first Sunday after Labor Day), *Mother-in-Law Day* (fourth Sunday in October), and *Professional Secretaries' Day* (Wednesday of last full week in April). But *Mother's Day* (cited to 1908), the second Sunday in May; and *Father's Day* (cited to 1927), the third Sunday in June, are nationally promoted.

APRIL FOOL'S DAY

April Fool! has been shouted by small children since the 1600s, starting in England just before *April Fool's Day* was brought to America by the early settlers. The origin is uncertain, but the custom may well have to do with the changing of the New Year from April 1 (in older calendar reckoning) to January 1. In places where this change had recently been adopted, the original April Fool's trick was to pay a mock New Year's Day visit on April 1 to someone who might have forgotten the new date. Thus, *April Fool!* meant "I fooled you; it's not New Year's Day at all!"

HALLOWEEN

Halloween (also spelled *Hallowe'en*, reflecting its origin in *All-Hallow Even*, the evening of *All-Hallow Day*, former term for *All Saints' Day*; *hallow* [related to *holy*] deriving from the Old English word for *saint*), on October 31, has religious origins, as it is associated with the ancient Celtic harvest festival of *Samhain*, and is the eve of the Christian *All Saints' Day*. Hoary tradition has it that ghosts and goblins haunt the land on this night.

A jack o'-lantern under construction in 1917.

The day is now observed with humor and good fun, despite the spooky *jack-o'-lanterns* and *Halloween costumes* of skeletons, ghosts, monsters, and witches that are associated with it. Halloween has long been a favorite time for children, though in recent years many adults, too, have taken to wearing costumes in fun on *Beggar's Night,* going along with the kids, knocking on doors in residential areas in early evening, shouting *"Trick or Treat!"* and collecting *Halloween treats,* especially candy. In a number of regions (Detroit being one of the more notorious of the cities), the night before Halloween, October 30, is known variously as *Devil's Night, Mischief Night, Cabbage Night, Cabbage Stump Night, Corn Night, Goosie Night, Mystery Night, Picket Night,* and *Ticktack Night.* It has been known for serious and sometimes deadly vandalism, such as cars overturned and fires set, that goes far beyond the original mission of those participating: to hurl pumpkins or cabbages onto people's porches. This has led to police-enforced *dusk-to-dawn curfews* on both nights.

RELIGIOUS HOLIDAYS AND OTHER CELEBRATIONS

One favorite among these is certainly *St. Patrick's Day,* March 17, when everyone is said to be Irish for the day, and all might partake of *the luck o' the Irish.* The day is observed with the *wearin' o' the green* (green sweaters, ties, hats, or ornaments, with *green beer* served at some bars to celebrants, some of whom even sport green hair); *St. Paddy's Day parades* in more than 100 cities, including those best known for their Irish immigrants, Boston (which had the first celebration in 1737) and New York (the largest parade, often with more than a million spectators); shouts of *Erin Go Bragh* ("Ireland forever" in Gaelic) and *Cead Mile Failte* (the traditional Gaelic greeting, "a hundred thousand welcomes"), and feasting on *corned beef and cabbage.*

The "wearing of the green" in 1874, 137 years after the first St. Patrick's Day parade.

Rolling Easter eggs, 1993.

Columbus Day, observed the second Monday in October (traditionally October 12, the day Columbus first made landfall in the *New World*), was once widely celebrated, especially with *Columbus Day parades* honoring Christopher Columbus, who "discovered" America. Recent reconsideration of Columbus' achievement, and charges that he really only blundered upon the *New World* thinking it to be India, have led to embarrassment if not vociferous protests over celebration of this day. Some locales have gone so far as to rename the day *Indigenous People's Day.*

There are four major Jewish holidays:

Hanukkah, also spelled *Chanukah,* called the *Feast of Lights* and the *Feast of Dedication.* First cited in English in 1891, *Hanukkah* comes from the Hebrew word meaning "dedication." This eight-day holiday comes in December. It commemorates the victory, in 165 B.C., of the Maccabees over Antiochus Epiphanes (around 215–164 B.C.) and the rededication of the Temple of Jerusalem after it had been sacked and defiled by this Syrian. Observers light a *menorah* (cited to 1888 in English, from Hebrew)—a candelabrum—every night for one week, recalling the legend that when the temple was rededicated its lamps miraculously burned without any oil for one week.

Passover, also called *Pesach.* First recorded in English in 1530, *Passover* is a translation of the Hebrew *pesah,* to pass over, the reference being to the exemption of the Israelites from the slaughter of first-born males in Egypt (described in Exodus 12:23-27). *Passover* is an eight-day Jewish holiday commemorating the Exodus of the Israelites from slavery in Egypt. At the Passover *Seder* (cited in English to 1865, from Hebrew, "order, arrangement")—the feast held on the first two nights of this holiday—symbolic foods prepared in a *kosher* (1851, Yiddish, from Hebrew *kasher,* fit and proper) kitchen are eaten. (During the holiday only unleavened bread—*matzo* [1846, Yiddish, from Hebrew]—is eaten.) The story of the Exodus is read throughout the holiday.

Rosh Hashannah, Jewish New Year. Pronounced "rosh-huh-SHAH-nuh," this term is cited in English to 1846. It comes in September or October.

Jews gather to cast bread upon the water, an ancient custom representing the casting off of sins. Rosh Hashanah marks the first day of the Jewish New Year. It is observed for one day by Reform and Israeli Jews and for two days by Orthodox and Conservative Jews, starting the first day of the lunar month of Tishri.

Yom Kippur, pronounced "YOHM ki-POOR" or "YOM KIP-uhr," also called in English the *Day of Atonement*. Not a "joyous" holiday in the least, *Yom Kippur*, which in Hebrew means "day of atonement," is a day of fasting and atonement for sins. It comes in the autumn eight-days after Rosh Hashannah; the days between them are days of penitence as well. *Yom Kippur* is cited in English to 1854.

Kwanzaa (Swahili for "first fruits [of the harvest]") is a fairly new celebration of African-American culture, with each of seven days (December 26 through January 1) given over to honoring seven principles: *umoja* (Swahili for "unity"), *kujichagulia* (self-determination), *ujima* (collective work and responsibility), *ujamaa* (cooperative economics), *nia* (purpose), *kuumba* (creativity), and *imani* (faith). *Kwanzaa* was created in 1968 by Maulana Karenga of California State University in Long Beach, who drew on African traditions of first-fruit celebrations.

In multicultural America people can look at a calendar and find (and celebrate) a host of special days—from *Chinese New Year* (when the new year is dubbed *The Year of the Snake*, *The Year of the Tiger*, and so on) to Islamic *Ramadan* (cited in English to around 1595). Like the languages of food and fashion in particular, the language of our holidays reflects the spirit and cultures of the nation's varied and diverse peoples.

Muslim men kneel in prayer during Ramadan, a month of fasting to celebrate the revelation of the Koran.

Chinese Americans celebrate the Chinese New Year for 1989, the year of the snake.

HOMELESS ALONE

*T*he dark underside of the American Dream has been the American Nightmare of homelessness. Homelessness has been a problem in America ever since the first English colonists settled here, and many of the terms used by the homeless, or used to describe them and their plight, have become part of the American lexicon.

One oddity of homelessness and language involves the word *homeless* itself. Though the adjective *homeless* is first recorded in English in 1615, the use of *homeless* as a noun, as in *the homeless*, did not occur until the mid 20th century and did not become widespread until the early 1980s when *homelessness* —the word and the condition—gained increasing public attention in the United States.

THE COLONIAL PERIOD

Colonial communities, emulating the precepts of the Elizabethan Poor Laws in England, tended to distinguish between two groups of homeless: recognized members of the community who were usually provided with shelter and assistance, and outsiders who were treated much less generously.

One of the most common methods of sheltering local poor was the *putting out system*, through which towns paid freeholders to provide room and board for the homeless, usually for a period of one year. Money paid out to assist the homeless was called *outdoor relief, out relief,* or *home relief.* In 1644, for instance, the town of Portsmouth, New

> " . . . an Object in Human Shape, half starv'd with Colde, with Cloathes out at the Elbows, Knees through the breeches."
>
> — *a 1737 letter to Peter Zenger's* New York Journal, *describing a typical street urchin*

A 38-year-old New Yorker leaving his home in the morning, two blocks from Madison Square Garden and the 1992 Democratic National Convention.

Hampshire took measures to pay £9 annually to a local citizen for providing room and board for "ould John Mott."

Colonial towns were less hospitable to the non-local *wandering poor* who moved from community to community, often as agricultural laborers in a manner similar to 20th century migrant farm workers. Enforcing vagrancy laws modeled on those of England, town officials would order transients to leave town. This process was known as *warning out*. A more charitable procedure was *binding out*, through which transients were ordered to work as *indentured servants* (1723) for families in need of laborers, a system not unlike *workfare* (1968).

Eventually, however, the major seaboard cities experienced such a rapid influx of immigrants, sailors, and refugees from Indian wars that these systems proved inadequate. Most cities were forced to build special structures to shelter the homeless. Boston completed an *almshouse* in 1662, which at first housed both the *honest poor* and criminals. Philadelphia Quakers constructed a *Bettering House*, a communal workhouse presuming that homeless people needed moral improvement. In the 1730s New York City built a two-story brick structure called *Poor House, Work House*, and *House of Correction*.

THE URBAN HOMELESS

The rapid industrialization and urbanization of the northeastern U.S. during the 19th century led to increased homelessness. Because more people were now dependent on factory jobs for their livelihoods, the number of homeless people increased significantly in times of economic recession and depression. Similarly, because more Americans now lived in cities, homelessness fluctuated with the availability of urban housing. The Depression of 1819 and the Panic of 1837 led to dramatic increases in the number of urban homeless. In the late 1840s New York City alone had at least 10,000 homeless children.

Many cities were forced to build more and more almshouses and *poor farms*. Sometimes these institutions mixed different categories of homeless people together; orphaned children, for instance, were often housed with drunks, vagrants, prostitutes, the infirm, and the mentally ill. Often the city contracted with a private entrepreneur to operate such an institution at a profit. Also used to provide shelter for the homeless was an *auction system* by which destitute men, women, and children were auctioned off to the bidder willing to accept the least amount of money to shelter and feed them.

Societies and associations were formed to provide private shelter for orphans, widows, and other *paupers* (1516, from Latin, "poor"). During the 1840s, New York City had nearly 40 almsgiving societies and *bread-lines* (1900), which dispensed food to the needy. In the 1880s and 1890s, several advocates for the poor established *settlement houses* (1907) in crowded urban neighborhoods, not as places for the homeless to live, but as resource centers to provide nurseries, instruction, advice, recreation, and companionship—precursors of the 20th century centers, some called *women's resource centers*, that assist single mothers in need and/or battered women. (The term *settlement house* came from the fact that the relatively well-to-do social workers who lived there "settled" in indigent neighborhoods among the people they were there to help.)

The rapid expansion of industrialization, immigration, and urban growth following the Civil War led to increased urban congestion and homelessness. Concerned about controlling this *dangerous class*, many big cities turned increasingly to their police departments to round up and

"Under the auction system, men, women, and children were placed on the block, much as Negro slaves, and auctioned off to the person willing to accept the lowest amount for his case."

— *Sidney Lens,*
Poverty: America's Enduring Paradox, *1969*

A flophouse.

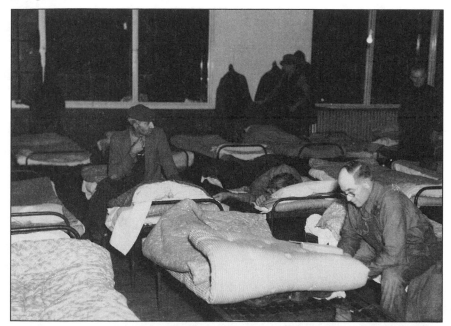

shelter vagrants and tramps. Under this system of *police lodging*, homeless people—mostly men—slept in bunks, in jail cells, and on the floors of police stations. Many reformers condemned police lodging as inhumane; by 1900 the use of local jails for lodging the homeless had been discontinued in most major cities.

Cheap boarding houses then became the main form of shelter for the destitute. These were called *flophouses* (1916), *flops* (1910, originally "a bed," then extended to mean "a free place to sleep"), or *flea bags* (1920s; originally a *flea bag* [1839] meant a bed or mattress). The depression years of the 1890s caused a massive increase in the number of homeless;

A "panhandler" in 1974.

by 1894 there were 105 flophouses in New York City with spaces for 16,000 people. Costs for one night's lodging ranged from 3 to 35¢. Those who couldn't find shelter in flophouses moved to *shanty villages* (1858) or *shantytowns* (1876).

The term *skid road* or *skid row* for the area of a large city inhabited by homeless derelicts did not come into common usage until the 1930s and 1940s. *Skid road* first appeared in the Pacific Northwest in 1890, where it referred to a corduroy road used to haul or skid logs to water. Early in the 20th century, an abandoned skid road in Seattle became a run-down strip with cheap bars and flophouses frequented by vagrants, and soon similar areas in other cities were being referred to as *skid roads* or *skid rows*.

Reformers persuaded cities to build more municipal lodging houses where trained staff could assist the homeless. At about this same time, many churches and religious groups established *rescue missions* (1902). *Orphanages* (1865 in the institutional sense) proliferated.

Many of the homeless were *moochers* (1857 in the "beggar" sense, probably from a French dialect word *muchier*, to lurk or hide) who knew the best places to *mooch* (cited to 1857, "beg, sponge"; in the 17th century a *moocher* meant an offender a truant). Many were also *panhandlers* (1897) who preferred to *panhandle* (1903) on what they called the *main stem* (1890, "main street" the best street to beg) or *main drag* (1900). *Panhandle*, the act of begging, goes back at least to 1849; its origin is unknown but it may simply be an allusion to a pan held out on a handle for begging.

In 1890 Danish-born journalist Jacob Riis published *How the Other Half Lives*, a book exposing the horrible conditions of the homeless on New York's Lower East Side. Riis documented the overcrowding in squalid *tenement houses* (1858), the practice of dispersing orphaned infants (known as *pay babies*) to women paid money to raise them, and the horrors of *baby farms* (1868), run by unscrupulous mercenaries who took money from orphan asylums to care for several babies and then allowed them to suffer malnutrition, disease, or neglect. Riis' book also described in detail the lives of homeless boys known as *street arabs* (1859), tough, wily orphans and runaways who survived by their wits and fists in alleys, outbuildings, and cellars.

In response to the plight of such homeless children, the *child-saving movement* evolved during the late 1800s. By 1900 it had achieved a number of substantial reforms, including the establishment of juvenile courts, reformatories, and state schools. A cornerstone of the child-saving movement was the *Children's Aid Society*, which not only provided lodging houses for orphans, but also made arrangements to ship many of them by rail to families in western states to begin new lives. This relocation system was known as *placing out*, and the trains that carried the children to new homes were called *orphan trains*. Between 1853 and 1929 at least 200,000 children and several thousand adults were "placed out" to the West.

HOBOES, TRAMPS, AND BUMS

The American hobo was created by the railroad and the Civil War. The war uprooted many men and enamored some of camp life; when it was over some "homeward bound" soldiers took to aimless wandering and soon were *pounding the rails*—walking the railroad right-of-way— because there were no laws against it. From here it was but a jump to

A hobo hops a freight in 1905.

riding in boxcars, where at first the men were accepted as worthy war veterans. But as the years went by, pilferage and damage to railroad property caused the railroads to order train crews to get rid of them and to hire guards called *bulls* (1893), also called *cinder bulls* and *yard bulls*, to keep them out. This drove the wanderers from the boxcars to more dangerous ways to *bum a ride* (1896), by *hopping a freight* (1880s) and:

riding the rods, riding the rails, 1880s, riding the connecting or draw rods below the body of the cars.

riding blind baggage, 1887, riding in the door frame or niche of the locked or doorless front end of the *blind baggage car* (1883), the baggage or mail car right behind the engine tender.

trucking it, 1890s, riding or clinging to the trucking hardware between the wheels. This may have contributed to the jitterbug's use of *trucking* (also meaning to leave or move on in the 1930s) and to the popular phrase of the 1960s *keep on truckin'*, keep moving, keep trying, keep "doing one's (own) thing" with good cheer.

By now the train-riding veterans had been joined *on the road* (1890s) by other chronic wanderers, by itinerant misfits and criminals, and by migratory harvest workers and lumberjacks. By 1905 there were 60,000 men on the road. They were variously known as *down-and-outs* (1889) or *down-and-outers* (1909), *driftwoods*, and *mushers*, a "corruption" of the French command *marchons*, "walk." Other names included:

bindle stiff, cited to 1892; *bindle man*, 1900; *bindle bum* (used by John Steinbeck in his 1937 *Of Mice and Men*); and also *bundle stiff, blanket stiff, jungle stiff*, and *railroad stiff*. They were called *bindle stiffs* because they carried a *bindle* (1880, perhaps from "bundle" or from German *Bündel*, "bundle," or from Scots *bindle*, a hemp or straw cord for binding something), a blanket roll or bedroll containing one's possessions. *Stiff* had meant "contemptible person" or just "fellow" since 1882, "penniless man" since 1899, and "hobo" by 1897 when in combination with *bindle*.

bum (probably a clipping of *bummer*), a lazy, dissolute loafer, first recorded in Oregon, 1855, suggesting an original application to wanderers from the 1849-50 California gold rush or to migratory workers and lumberjacks. It soon came to mean a vagabond or tramp; the verb *bum*, 1863, "to wander around, loaf," is also recorded with the meaning "to ask for or obtain (something) by begging"; by 1896 it meant to ride a train without a ticket. The original wanderers had also been called by the full term *bummer* (probably an alteration of German *Bummler*, a laze or loafer) since 1855. It had come to mean a foraging soldier by 1861, with this Civil War use then applied to the wandering Civil War veterans.

hobo, first recorded in Washington State in 1889, origin unknown, by which time *bo* was already in use as a short form for it. Like *bum*, *hobo* may have come from the Pacific Northwest as a term for migratory harvest workers and lumberjacks. In fact, as late as 1913 the former labor union called the Industrial Workers of the World defined *hobo* as a migratory worker and such men formed a large part of its membership During the Depression, a *hobo* differentiated himself from being called a *bum* by working for his keep.

knight of the road, 1665, may sound romantic but it is straight from the British underworld: it meant a robber or highwayman, as did *knight of the post* or *knight of the blade*, with a "cutpurse" having been called a *knight of the knife*, 1614. These combinations owe their origin to 16th century thieves' cant, in which *knight* meant "a vagabond who lives by his wits."

tramp, British use since 1664, meaning one who tramps from place to place, as a wandering vagabond, beggar, or thief.

vagabond and *vagrant* are both 15th century English words for a homeless wanderer or itinerant beggar (from Latin *vagabundus*, from *vagari*, to wander; *vagrant* from Middle English *vagraunt*, probably an alteration of Medieval French *waucrant*, wandering, ultimately of Germanic origin). *Vag*, a clipped form of *vagrancy* or *vagrant*, and the verb *vag*, to be arrested for vagrancy, as in "I got vagged," can be traced to 1891.

yegg or *yegg man*, 1903, a safecracker or a burglar, origin unknown; U.S. slang that also meant a tramp or hobo.

Hoboes liked to *rustle up a meal* (1871) and *get a rustle on*, to move or work energetically (1892), both referring to the rustling sound of movement. One way was to ask for a *handout* (1882) of leftover scraps at back doors. They also called a handout a *pokeout*, food handed out in a bag, or a *lump*, or a *bald lump* if the food were given to them unwrapped. Much of this food was literally *crummy* (1567, "crumbly," and by 1903 in the spelling *crumby* the word meant "inferior").

They carried some of the food back to their *hobo jungle* (1908), a deserted area near a railroad yard. Hoboes who scrounged from other hoboes but didn't contribute to the communal pot were *jungle buzzards*. These *jungles* (1910) were the hoboes' base, where they ate, swapped stories, and made fun of the *gay cats* (1907), those inexperienced or dilettante hoboes who would soon return home.

In the jungle the older hoboes, known as *comets*, broke in the *road kids* (1890)—runaway teenagers who had gone *over the hill* (1870) and *hit the road* (1894). Another word for a *road kid* was *prushun* (1893, origin obscure), with *profesh* referring to an experienced bo who "protected" the *prushun*. The *profesh* taught the youth how to beg, scrounge, and steal—and often practiced pederasty.

Other hobo terms include *rattler* (a train); *drag* (a slow freight); *hot shot* and *manifest* (a fast freight); *tea pot* and *hog* (locomotive); *batter, buzz, pling,* and *throw the feet* (beg); *nickel flop* (all-night movie house); *dip* (a pickpocket); *graveyard* (hash); *headlights* (eggs); *glims* (spectacles); *jolt* (penitentiary sentence); *kip* and *pound the ear* (to sleep); *sand* (sugar); *slides* (shoes); *angel food* (a mission sermon); *mission stiff* (man who "gets saved" to receive free flops and food); *clover kicker* and *plough jockey* (farmer); *pearl diver* and *deep-sea chef* (dishwasher); *splinter belly* (carpenter); *sky pilot* (mission house minister); *woodhead* (lumberjack); and *town clowns* (town policemen).

THE GREAT DEPRESSION

The Great Depression of the 1930s brought a dramatic increase in homelessness. In 1934 the number of homeless people in the U.S. was estimated to be 1.5 million, including entire families and abandoned children. As during the colonial era, the transient homeless were moved out of town by local officials unable to provide for their support.

A Depression-era soup kitchen.

Many resorted to living in shantytowns called *Hoovervilles* (1933) in mockery of President Herbert Hoover, who served as a scapegoat for the Depression. Old newspapers vagrants slept under were called *Hoover blankets*, rabbits shot for food were *Hoover hogs*, shoes with holes in the soles were *Hoover shoes*, worn-out autos pulled by mules were *Hoover cars*, and an empty pocket pulled inside out was a *Hoover flag*. The thousands of dispossessed women who by then had joined men on the road were called *road sisters*.

THE NEW HOMELESS

The relative prosperity of the 1950s, 1960s, and early 1970s reduced economic hardship in the U.S. and brought a decline in the number of homeless. But homelessness captured public attention again in the late 1970s and even more so in the 1980s as the worst economic recession since the 1930s took hold. The weak economy, combined, some say, with cutbacks in federally-funded public-assistance programs, produced a dramatic increase in homelessness. At the same time, a trend toward the *deinstitutionalization* (1969) of residents in mental-health facilities released many people who were now expected to fend for themselves. A rise in hard-drug use aggravated the problem.

Increased public awareness of homelessness in the U.S., widely reported in the news, led to the proliferation of several new terms:

bag lady, bag man, bag people. The term *bag lady* (1979), shortened from *shopping bag lady* (1976), refers to a homeless woman who roams city streets carrying all her belongings in shopping bags. *Bag man*, which since the 1760s meant a traveling salesman or a person who collects or distributes illegally obtained money, took on a new meaning as the male equivalent of *bag lady* during the 1980s, when *bag people* also appeared.

A "bag lady" and her wordly possessions in 1978.

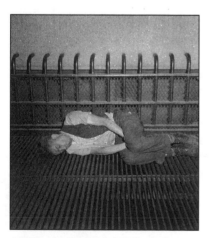

A "Bowery bum" in 1942. Today he'd be considered one of the "grate people."

grate people, 1980s, homeless people who slept on sidewalk steam grates because these openings provided warmth.

Greyhound therapy, a modern-day equivalent of the colonial practice of *warning out,* whereby local officials give unwanted transients a one-way bus ticket out of town.

skel or **skell,** a New York City police term for a vagrant or a panhandler who lives in the subway (also called *mole people*). *Skel* might derive ultimately from the now obsolete English verb *skelder* (1601, "to beg; to live by begging, especially by passing oneself off as a wounded or disabled soldier"). Quite a few New York City *skels* pretend to be ill or disabled in order to elicit sympathy and get money.

squats, a place where homeless people live, short for *squatters' shacks* or *squatters' habitation.*

street triage, 1992 (from the medical usage for screening large numbers of sick or injured patients), the process used by some homeless shelters to separate the homeless into categories based on the type of assistance they need. Also called *creaming,* as in taking the cream off the top.

The homeless of the 1980s and 1990s also devised their own terms for ways of surviving. Some went *Dumpster diving, scrounging* (1909, to beg or rummage about for something; to steal, probably an alteration of English dialect *scringe,* to pry, and gaining currency via World War I servicemen's use) through large trash receptacles (from *Dumpster,* a trademark). Others went *canning,* collecting and returning cans and bottles for their redemption value, and *ground scoring,* picking up scraps of food from garbage cans or off the ground.

The socioeconomic dislocation of the 1980s also created several new categories of homeless and marginally homeless people. *Couch people*

> "Emergency room workers call it 'granny dumping,' a phenomenon that they say is becoming familiar across the country as families crumble under the strain of caring for relatives who are living longer than ever."
>
> — Chicago Tribune, November 19, 1991

A homeless man in Colorado is rescued from a dumpster. He had been sleeping inside when trash was unloaded on him.

> "Orphanage is not a dirty word. It is a composite of love and care and hope. It was a support system outside the cottages where we stayed, where a gatekeeper kept out the bogeyman."
>
> — Elmer Gertz, Chicago attorney who grew up in an orphanage, in the Chicago Tribune, December 8, 1994

(1987) were homeless families who drifted from place to place, living temporarily with friends or families, often sleeping on their hosts' couches or floors. Single homeless people *couch surfed*, often exchanging money or sex for a night's lodging. *Granny dumping* (1991) referred to the practice of leaving an aged parent on the doorstep of a nursing home, church, or hospital emergency room. Some other terms applied to the less fortunate of society during the 1980s–90s:

boarder baby (mid 1980s), an infant, often the child of an AIDS victim or a drug addict, who remains at a hospital for several weeks or months after birth, awaiting placement in a home. A 1993 report of the Department of Health and Human Services estimated that there were 22,000 boarder babies in the U.S.

zero-parent children (early 1990s), children whose parents were deceased, jailed, or absent. Children who roamed the streets after running away from home or being abandoned by their parents were called *throwaways* or *throwaway children* (1980s).

squeegee kid (1989), an inner-city youngster who attempts to wash the windshield of a car stopped in traffic without being invited to do so, expecting a tip in return. In many cities, squeegee kids were soon replaced by *squeegee men* (or *squeegee guys* or *squeegee beggars*). While only a small portion of squeegee kids were homeless, a large percentage of squeegee men were likely to be.

The increasing numbers of homeless children precipitated a national debate over the term *orphanages* in late 1994. When Speaker of the House Newt Gingrich suggested putting children in *orphanages* to get them off welfare, he was assailed by President Clinton and others for whom the word *orphanages* conjured up Dickensian images of soulless warehouses for unwanted children. But others defended orphanages as an alternative to allowing drug-addicted or abusive parents to raise children. As the debate over the word *orphanages* showed, part of the challenge of dealing with homelessness in America remains a matter of finding the right words to use.

THE WORD OF THE LAW AND THE LAW OF THE LAND

Justice, ideally, is blind.

"It is my belief that there are 'absolutes' in our Bill of Rights, and that they were put there on purpose by men who knew what words meant and meant their prohibitions to be 'absolutes.'"

— U.S. Supreme Court Associate Justice Hugo Black, April 14, 1962 interview, American Jewish Congress

"The people made the Constitution, and the people can unmake it. It is the creature of their own will, and lives only by their will."

— U.S. Supreme Court Chief Justice John Marshall, Cohens v. Virginia, 6 Wheaton (19 US) 264, 389 (1821)

The law embodies the story of a nation's development through many centuries.

Oliver Wendell Holmes, Jr., *The Common Law*, 1881

WE THE PEOPLE

The United States Constitution—by Article VI, section 2, "The Supreme Law of the land"—written in 1787, is the bedrock of American justice. The Bill of Rights—the first 10 amendments to the Constitution, with roots going back to the Magna Carta (1215), ratified on December 15, 1791—contains the legal language that protects people's rights and specifies the principles on which our nation was founded. Therefore it is not surprising that over time people have talked about and used certain key expressions that derive directly or indirectly from the Constitution, and the Bill of Rights as cases involving court interpretations of the framers' intent arise:

freedom of speech, press, and religion, also called First Amendment rights, embodied in the First Amendment's words, which we repeat, so as not to forget the source: "Congress shall make no law respecting an establishment of religion, or prohibiting the free exercise thereof; or abridging the freedom of speech, or of the press; or the right of the people peaceably to assemble, and to petition the government for a redress of grievances"—the *five freedoms* that we still talk about.

right to bear arms, as it is usually referred to in short form, is found in the Second Amendment: "A well regulated Militia, being necessary to the security of a free State, the right of the people to keep and bear Arms, shall not be infringed." Interpreted variously as a statement of a basic right ensuring that individuals can defend themselves, this amendment became hugely controversial in the latter years of the 20th century. As worded, the amendment provides for militias, which in the context of America's early days asked individuals to bring their own weapons when called on to serve. But as society became increasingly horrified with clear evidence of gun violence, the free, unregulated availability of guns was limited by *gun-control legislation*.

unreasonable search and seizure, probable cause, and search warrants. These rights are all covered in the Fourth Amendment: "The right of the people to be secure in their persons, houses, papers, and effects, against unreasonable searches and seizures, shall not be violated, and no warrants shall issue but upon probable cause, supported by oath or affirmation, and particularly describing the place to be searched, and the persons or things to be seized."

self-incrimination, capital crime, indictment, grand jury, double jeopardy, and due process of law. These are enumerated in the Fifth Amendment, colloquially dubbed *the Fifth*, as in "The witness *took the Fifth*": "No person shall be held to answer for a capital, or otherwise

The courtroom and a jury of one's peers.

infamous crime, unless on a presentment or indictment of a grand jury, . . . nor shall any person be subject for the same offense to be twice put in jeopardy of life or limb; nor shall be compelled . . . to be a witness against himself, nor be deprived of life, liberty, or property, without due process of law." When witnesses refused to testify before the House Committee on Un-American Activities in the McCarthy era (see POLITICS: No Term Limits), and when Los Angeles Police detective Mark Fuhrman was ensnared on cross-examination by defense attorney F. Lee Bailey during the O.J. Simpson murder trial (1994–95) and refused to testify further, they were invoking their Fifth Amendment right of avoiding self-incrimination.

a speedy trial by an impartial jury (of one's peers), used commonly as a set phrase, is derived from the wording of the Sixth Amendment: "In all criminal prosecutions, the accused shall enjoy the right to a speedy and public trial, by an impartial jury of the State and district wherein the crime shall have been committed, . . . and to be informed of the nature and cause of the accusation; to be confronted with the witnesses against him; to have compulsory process for obtaining witnesses in his favor, and to have the assistance of counsel for his defense." This wording set the stage for the eventual establishment of *public defenders* (1918), or *court-appointed lawyers*, who defend those unable to pay for private counsel.

bail, fines, and cruel and unusual punishment. These issues are treated by the Eighth Amendment: "Excessive bail shall not be required, nor excessive fines imposed, nor cruel and unusual punishments inflicted." *Cruel and unusual punishment* came to include —in the minds of many—*capital punishment*, or the *death penalty*, and legal challenges kept many prisoners on *death row* for years on end.

John Marshall, the fourth Chief Justice of the Supreme Court, helped bring credibility and power to the court. The Liberty Bell cracked when tolling for his death.

slavery and *involuntary servitude* were finally addressed by the Thirteenth Amendment, adopted in 1865: "Neither slavery nor involuntary servitude . . . shall exist within the United States."

equal protection under the law, the usual modern wording, is articulated in the Fourteenth Amendment (1868). It bestowed rights and citizenship on formerly disenfranchised African Americans: "All persons born or naturalized in the United States, and subject to the jurisdiction thereof, are citizens of the United States and of the State wherein they reside. No state shall . . . deny to any person within its jurisdiction the equal protection of the laws."

suffrage (see THE GENDER GAP), was broadened in the Fifteenth and Nineteenth Amendments, adopted in 1870 and 1920, respectively. These amendments extended *voting rights* to African Americans and to women. So says the Fifteenth, with the wording of the Nineteenth parallel: "The right of citizens of the United States to vote shall not be denied or abridged by the United States or by any State on account of race, color, or previous condition of servitude."

ALL RISE: HERE COME THE JUDGES

Many of the words and concepts used in arguing American legal issues have often derived from the rulings of noted U.S. Supreme Court justices.

Though not the first Chief Justice, John Marshall (1755–1835) made the high court the *Marshall Court*. As a *judicial activist*, using today's parlance, Marshall identified and clarified the Constitution's ambiguities, filled in its omissions, and added reach to its powers in the tradition of what came to be known as *broad* or *loose construction*—a free interpretation taking into account the needs of the country, the spirit of the times, and the values of the justices—as opposed to *narrow* or *strict construction*—a literal interpretation of the framers' wording.

John Marshall Harlan (1833–1911), an associate justice, is linked with the statement so often quoted in 20th century *civil rights* cases: "Our Constitution is *color-blind*, and neither knows nor tolerates classes among citizens. . . . In respect of civil rights, all citizens are equal before the law" (dissent, *Plessy v. Ferguson* [1896]).

Oliver Wendell Holmes, Jr. (1841–1935), also an associate justice, gave us the expression *clear-and-present danger test*, in reference to the government's power to restrict free speech, in *Schenck v. United States* (1919):

> The most stringent protection of free speech would not protect a man in falsely shouting fire in a theater and causing a panic. . . . The question in every case is whether the words are used in such circumstances and are of such a nature as to create a *clear and present danger* that they will bring about the substantive evils that Congress has a right to prevent.

Those words formed the basis of what we like to call *free-speech law*. It was Holmes, too, who was responsible for the now oft-used expression the *marketplace of ideas*.

Associate Justice Louis D. Brandeis (1856–1941) is most often talked about in terms of protecting citizens' *right to privacy*. In *Olmstead v. United States* (1928), Brandeis dissented in a decision upholding the use of wiretaps, arguing for the first time that a constitutional *right of privacy* can be inferred:

NAACP attorney Thurgood Marshall enters the Supreme Court building in 1958 to file papers in the Little Rock school integration case. Nine years later, he would be a member.

Sandra Day O'Connor, the first woman to serve on the Supreme Court, on the steps of the Capitol in 1981 after her unanimous confirmation.

University of Oklahoma law professor Anita Hill in October 1991, as she prepares to testify before the Senate during Clarence Thomas's confirmation hearings.

"The police must obey the law while enforcing the law."

— *U.S. Supreme Court Chief Justice Earl Warren, unanimous opinion, June 22, 1959, holding that confessions obtained under duress must be excluded from criminal proceedings*

"I am for the First Amendment from the first word to the last. I believe it means what it says."

— *U.S. Supreme Court Associate Justice Hugo Black, April 14, 1962 interview, American Jewish Congress*

They [the framers] conferred, as against the government, the right to be let alone—the most comprehensive of rights and the right most valued. . . . The greatest dangers to liberty lurk in insidious encroachment by men of zeal, well-meaning but without understanding.

Associate Justice Benjamin Cardozo (1870–1938) is associated with his articulation of the principle *freedom of expression*, in the *Palko v. Connecticut* (1937) decision: "*Freedom of expression* is the matrix, the indispensable condition, of nearly every other form of freedom."

Hugo Black (1886–1971) is regarded as second only to John Marshall for his influential interpretations of the Constitution, affecting *First Amendment rights, civil liberties, civil rights*, and the development of *First Amendment religious guarantees*. Black, like Jefferson, believed in the *wall of separation* between church and state, leading to his famous ruling that banned *school prayer* from public schools (a controversial topic through the 1990s). In Black's words: "The First Amendment has erected a *wall between church and state*. That wall must be kept high and impregnable." (*Emerson v. Board of Education* [1947]).

Chief Justice Earl Warren (1891–1974) led the most judicially active court of the 20th century. The *Warren Court*, as people called it, rewrote a great deal of our constitutional law, taking a liberal bent, ruling that public school segregation was unconstitutional (*Brown v. Board of Education* [1954]).

William O. Douglas (1898–1980) was best known for saying that "the Constitution is not neutral. It was designed to take the government off the backs of the people." Douglas strongly upheld the First Amendment rights of anti-Vietnam War protesters and civil rights activists of the 60s and 70s. A great distruster of governmental and corporate bureaucracies, Douglas said that, if left unchecked, these would create "a nation of clerks."

Thurgood Marshall (1908–91) became a household name as the NAACP attorney who destroyed the South's notorious *Jim Crow laws* and who successfully argued *Brown v. Board of Education* of Topeka before the Supreme Court. He championed minority rights under the principle of equal protection. He is also associated with the *not guilty by reason of insanity plea*—still hotly debated across the nation.

Sandra Day O'Connor (1930–) made her mark in 1992 in *Planned Parenthood v. Casey*, when the Court decided that it was legal for the states to make abortion harder to obtain or more costly, but not to outlaw the practice—affirming the *Roe v. Wade* abortion decision despite vociferous public protests to the contrary.

Clarence Thomas (1948–), appointed to the Court in 1991 by President George Bush, remained famous for the stormy televised confirmation hearings that attended his controversial nomination. An entire nation watched as allegations of sexual harassment were made against Thomas by a former employee, attorney and law professor Anita Hill. Thomas eventually won Senate confirmation by 52 to 48, avoiding what had come to be called *being Borked* (1987), i.e., to be defeated in a partisan confirmation process. The term derived from the surname of federal judge Robert H. Bork, whose nomination to the Court by President Ronald Reagan was defeated after a ferocious confirmation hearing.

IN RE: THE WORDS OF THE BIG CASES

Most Americans talk about issues represented in major cases, but lawyers talk about cases by name. Some key national issues embedded in Supreme Court cases are these:

constitutionality of an act of Congress. This phrase was coined in *Marbury* v. *Madison* (1803) an announcement by the Marshall Court that an act of Congress is void if it is inconsistent with the Constitution. The high court established the principle that it is the judiciary's "province and duty" to say what, in fact, the law of the land is. Since then, the U.S. Supreme Court has been the final arbiter on questions of the constitutionality of federal statutes.

defendant's right to counsel. *Gideon v. Wainwright* (1963) was a Warren Court decision that firmly established the rights of felony defendants to attorneys. Clarence Earl Gideon, an indigent, was charged in Florida with breaking into a pool hall. When Gideon asked for a court-appointed lawyer, the judge denied him one because under Florida law such attorneys were supplied only in capital cases. Gideon ran his own defense and lost the case. Gideon wrote a letter to the U.S. Supreme Court from jail in the manner of a *jailhouse lawyer* (1969), claiming he had been denied a fair trial. Associate Justice Hugo Black wrote the majority opinion, adopting and affirming the principle that all defendants are equal before the law. In 1972 the Burger Court extended the ruling, guaranteeing an attorney for every person facing a prison term.

freedom of the press. This right was strengthened in *New York Times Company v. United States* (1971) a landmark decision in which the Supreme Court held that the federal government could not stop publication of the Pentagon Papers despite the contention that such publication would jeopardize conduct of the Vietnam War, and that the materials had been illegally removed from Defense Department custody. This decision also established the doctrine that *prior restraints* on speech or publication (here, on national security grounds) are impossible to justify. Also at that time, states enacted various *shield laws*

(1971) granting the press immunity from subpoenas demanding the names of confidential sources.

Libel was the subject of the notable case *New York Times* v. *Sullivan* (1964), in which the Court ruled that *public officers* (1925) cannot recover damages from a story relating to their official duties unless they can prove actual *malice* (14th century, Middle English, via Old French, from Latin *malitia*, based on *malus*, bad). To establish malice, the *plaintiff* (14th century, from Middle English, from Anglo-Norman *pleintif*, from Old French *plaintif*, aggrieved) has the *burden of proof* to show that those responsible for the story really did know it was false, or published it in *reckless disregard* of whether it was true or false. This decision reversed a prior *libel* (14th century, Middle English, "litigant's written declaration," via Old French, from Latin *libellus*, a diminutive of *liber*, book) verdict against the *Times* in an Alabama court.

Chilling effect, now a stock phrase, actually has its roots in a Supreme Court decision. *Chilling effect* denotes a situation or action that inhibits exercise of a constitutional right such as free speech, or that threatens to intimidate or limit the press in pursuing the facts of a story. Justice William Brennan, writing in *Dombrowski* v. *Pfister* (1965), used the term in its now most common sense. The case involved a challenge by a Louisiana civil rights group that the state's Subversive Activities & Communist Control Law had caused the group be harassed by local lawmen. The Court found that harassment, hence intimidation, had been integral in "the existence of a penal statute susceptible of sweeping and improper application. . . . The *chilling effect* upon the exercise of First Amendment rights may derive from the fact of the prosecution, unaffected by the prospects of its success or failure."

right to privacy. this phrase appeared in *Griswold* v. *Connecticut* (1964) in which the Supreme Court expanded the right to privacy. An 1897 Connecticut law forbade any use of contraception or supplying anyone with information pertaining to the use of contraception. When two Planned Parenthood officers were convicted under this law of giving married couples information on birth control, the high court decided that the state law was unconstitutional.

separate but equal. In *Plessy* v. *Ferguson* (1896) the Supreme Court upheld the constitutionality of segregation under the infamous *separate but equal* doctrine. An 1890 Louisiana law provided for "equal but separate accommodations for the white and colored races" on its railroads. In 1892 African American passenger Homer Plessy refused to sit in what was then called a *Jim Crow car*. Judge John H. Ferguson of a New Orleans criminal court upheld the state law, which was then challenged in the U.S. Supreme Court on grounds that it conflicted with both the Thirteenth and the Fourteenth Amendments. By a margin of 7-1 the Supreme Court upheld the Louisiana law, with John Marshall Harlan the single dissenter. The decision was reversed in 1954.

unreasonable search and seizure. In *Mapp* v. *Ohio* (1961) the Supreme Court extended Bill of Rights protections against *unreasonable search and seizure* to apply in cases of state law prosecution. Dollree Mapp had been prosecuted for possession of illegal materials seized by Ohio law enforcement officers from her residence without a *warrant* (1450, "a writ or order by a magistrate authorizing a law officer to make an arrest, search, or seizure"; Middle English *warant*, deriving from an Old French root *guarant*, seen also in English *guarantee*). One result was a marked increase in requests for *search warrants* (1818).

Five Supreme Court cases are so historically significant that they are commonly referred to by name, in the legal style, using the abbreviation *v.* for *versus* (15th century, from Medieval Latin, "against, toward," from Latin *vertere*, to turn), pronounced by many simply as "vee," but by most lawyers as "versus."

Bakke v. *University of California*, 1978, also shortened to *Bakke* or the *Bakke decision*. This case involved *affirmative action* (1965) and *reverse discrimination* (1969). Allan Bakke, a white man, was denied admission to the University of California's medical school, which had allegedly admitted African American candidates with weaker academic credentials. The Court found the university's admissions policy unconstitutional because it established and relied upon a *quota*—that is, a rigid numeric standard favoring admission of African Americans on the grounds that it compensated them for 200 years of discrimination: "The guarantee of equal protection cannot mean one thing when applied to one individual and something else when applied to a person of another color. If both are not accorded the same protection, then it is not equal."

Brown v. *Board of Education*, 1954, also called *Brown* or the *Brown decision*, a unanimous Warren Court decision that reversed *Plessy* v. *Ferguson* (1896) and forever ended federal acceptance of racial segregation under the *separate but equal* doctrine articulated in *Plessy*. The Court said, "We conclude that in the field of public education the doctrine of 'separate but equal' has no place. Separate educational facilities are inherently unequal." In 1955 the Court issued *implementation guidelines*—as hotly discussed as *separate but equal* and *Brown* itself— that ordered federal district courts to supervise public school desegregation "with all deliberate speed," an expression that also was the topic of spirited debate, with some people calling it an oxymoron. After protracted argumentation over the meaning of *all deliberate speed*, Justice Hugo Black remarked as late as 1964 (when certain Virginia counties chose toi close their schools rather than integrate them), that "there has been entirely too much deliberation and not enough speed. The time for 'deliberate speed' has run out." In many school districts across the country, federal judges imposed desegregation plans, often involving *court-ordered busing*.

Dred Scott, who was found to be "property" by the Supreme Court in 1857.

Dred Scott v. *Sanford* [misspelled *Sandford* in court records], 1857, also called the *Dred Scott Decision* or *case*, spurred national divisiveness, Lincoln's election, and the outbreak of the Civil War. Dred Scott, a black slave, had been taken in 1834 with his owner to live in the free state of Illinois, and then in Wisconsin Territory, where slavery was forbidden under the Missouri Compromise. After his owner died, Scott sued his new owner, one John Sanford, claiming that he was a free citizen, having lived on "free soil." The case went to the U.S. Supreme Court, where Chief Justice Roger B. Taney wrote the infamous 7-2 majority ruling that descendants of Africans imported as slaves into this country were property and could not be regarded as citizens. It also ruled that the 1820 Missouri Compromise, which prohibited slavery in certain territories, was unconstitutional, in that it deprived people of their property rights (in this case, slaves). The Court and the country were polarized over the issue of slavery.

Miranda v. *Arizona*, 1966, also known as the *Miranda ruling* or simply *Miranda*, a 5-4 decision that Fifth Amendment protection against self-incrimination applies to a person in police custody. The Court ruled that to safeguard this right, all suspects, before police questioning, must be informed of what are now called their *Miranda rights*: the right to remain silent, that anything they say may be used against them in court, that they have the right to the presence of an attorney, and that if they cannot afford one, an attorney will be provided before questioning if they so desire. Any statement obtained without a suspect first having been *read his rights* is inadmissible in a court of law, as is the fact that a suspect/defendant chooses to remain silent. The surname of the plaintiff in the case, Ernesto A. Miranda, eventually spawned a verb *Mirandize*, used by law enforcement people to mean "to read a suspect his or her rights."

Roe v. *Wade*, 1973, also known simply as the *abortion ruling*, is among the most controversial cases in the Supreme Court's history. In a 7-2 ruling the Court found that a woman, as part of her constitutional right to privacy, could choose to end a pregnancy before the fetus reached a state of development allowing survival outside the uterus, but that the government had an interest in protecting the fetus after that, when it became able to live, or *viable*, on its own. This ruling, which extended the right to privacy already articulated in *Griswold* v. *Connecticut* (1965), struck down the antiabortion laws of the individual states.

From the early 70s through the 90s public debate raged over the abortion issue, which became a *litmus test* in political races and judicial confirmations and also brought into wide currency terms like *pro-life* (1961), *antiabortion* (1971), *pro-abortion* (1972), *right-to-life* (1975), and *pro-choice* (1975), as well as *reproductive rights*.

In 1989 *Webster* v. *Reproductive Health Services* presented a challenge to *Roe*, and generated a record number of *amicus curiae* (1612, New Latin, "friend of the court") briefs, arguments filed by parties that are not actual participants in a litigation but are allowed to advise the court. Though the Supreme Court did sustain *Roe*, it suggested that the states reconsider individual solutions to problems generated by the law.

The issues treated in *Roe* remain the most socially divisive since the days of the *Dred Scott Decision* and are punctuated now, as then, by violence.

> *"I will not give to a woman an instrument to procure abortion."*
>
> — *The Hippocratic Oath, taken by medical students on receiving their degrees, and supposed to have been drawn by Hippocrates, c. 400 B.C.*

BY ACT OF CONGRESS

Americans have talked so much about some congressional acts that shorthand references to them are familiar:

the Brady Law, incorporated in the 1993 Omnibus Crime Law, is named for former White House press secretary James Brady, who was grievously wounded during a 1981 assassination attempt on President Reagan. The first federal *gun-control* legislation since 1968, the Brady Law requires a waiting period and a background check before a gun dealer can sell a firearm to a customer. *Gun-control laws* can be traced to pre-Civil War *Slave Codes*, which prohibited slaves from owning or possessing firearms. After the 1911 assassination attempt on New York City's mayor, the *Sullivan Law* passed by the New York state assembly required a *police permit* (now a *gun permit*) for owning and carrying a pistol. Over the next 30 years most states passed some form of the *National Revolver Act*, requiring a permit to carry concealed weapons. Sawed-off shotguns and machine guns were prohibited in the 1930s by

Former Republican James Brady gives a "thumbs-up" at the 1996 Democratic National Convention in Chicago. He survived being shot in the head to become a powerful symbol of gun control legislation.

the *National Firearms Acts. The Gun Control Act of 1968* stopped the sale of certain guns by mail or to out-of-state residents, and restricted ammunition sales.

the *Civil Rights Act of 1964* outlawed segregation in public facilities and racial discrimination in employment and education, with a 6-3 ruling by the Supreme Court in 1987 adding that gender would not form the basis for employment determinations.

the *Freedom of Information Act*, 1966, gave the right to request records from the Executive Branch of the federal government to any U.S. citizen or foreign national legally residing in this country. The term *full disclosure*, used by lawyers and citizens seeking their own personal files under an *FOI request*, is used in this Act, borrowed from the Securities Act of 1933.

Megan's Law, 1996, is an amendment of the Violent Crime Control and Law Enforcement Act of 1994, known by the first name of crime victim Megan Kanka, a seven-year-old killed by a twice-convicted child molester who lived in her New Jersey neighborhood. Megan's Law requires *community notification* when a convicted sex offender moves into a neighborhood.

the *Pure Food and Drug Act*, 1906, was vehemently opposed by the so-called Beef Trusts and the patent-medicine manufacturers, it prohibited foreign and interstate commerce in adulterated or fraudulently labeled foods. The Act evolved from "the embalmed beef" scandal that arose during the 1898 Spanish-American War, when U.S. soldiers were fed substandard meals. But it was Upton Sinclair's novel *The Jungle* that led to passage of the Act—probably the first time a novel has been a legislative catalyst. Sinclair exposed the appalling conditions of workers in the Chicago meatpacking industry and stockyards, including such details as the grinding up of poisoned rats in products for human consumption. Within six months of the book's publication, and the ensuing national outrage, the Act passed.

the Taft-Hartley Act, 1947, officially the *Labor-Management Relations Act*. This law was passed by a Republican Congress over the veto of President Harry Truman. Sponsored by Fred Hartley, Jr. of New Jersey in the House and by Robert A. Taft of Ohio on the Senate side, it made the *closed shop* (labor union membership as a condition of being hired or employed) illegal and prohibited secondary boycotts. Its most talked-about section was 14(b), which allowed the states to pass *right-to-work laws*, enabling them to regulate the number of union shops in their jurisdictions. The most important provision in the Act was the President's power to order a *cooling-off period* to help resolve strikes that threaten the national security or economic health of the country, such as those by rail workers or airline employees.

motor-voter law, a federal law that took effect in 1995, allowed citizens to register to vote when applying for driver's licenses. It expanded the potential number of eligible voters.

HIGH-PROFILE STATE LAWS

Four kinds of state laws are often talked about in generic terms, as issues involving them come to public notice:

*anti-stalking law*s, 1989, widely enacted after the murder of television actress Rebecca Schaeffer, who had been followed and harassed by a *stalker*. The first *anti-stalking law* was passed by California in 1991.

blue laws, 1781, originally regulated behavior in colonial New England, but the term was later generalized to mean state and/or local regulations banning certain activities on Sundays. The origin of the term is uncertain, but it may have derived from the color of the paper on which the colony of New Haven, Connecticut printed its laws. Blue laws prohibiting Sunday retail sales have largely been repealed in recent decades. Some states still prohibit the Sunday sale of beer, wine, and hard liquor, even Sunday boxing, polo, hunting, and clam digging; some enforce Sunday closure of barbershops.

sunshine laws, 1972, measures forcing the conduct of public business into an open forum, prohibiting *executive sessions* of governing bodies. The Florida *Sunshine Act*, proposed in 1961, finally passed after no less than a six-year debate. Other states followed with what are also called *open-meeting laws*.

three-strikes-and-you're-out laws, 1994–96, passed as part of the Omnibus Crime Law federally and adopted previously in varying forms in various states; these mandate lengthy prison sentences of convicted criminals guilty of a third felony. Its 1994 passage in California was achieved through a referendum vote driven by public outrage over the October 1, 1993 kidnapping and murder of 12-year-old Polly Klaas, who was killed by a paroled ex-convict with a prior conviction for kidnapping and assaulting a woman. The state of Washington was the first to adopt a *three-strikes law* (1993), and since then the legal terms *second-* and *third-strike convictions* have evolved—all deriving from baseball.

"Publicity is justly commended . . . as a remedy for social and industrial disease. Sunlight is said to be the best disinfectant and electric light the most efficient policeman."

— Supreme Court Associate Justice Louis D. Brandeis

DIVORCE LAW AMERICAN STYLE

In the 17th century America's divorce laws varied markedly from colony to colony. Divorces could be granted for adultery, long absences, and cruelty, but they were relatively few. In the South, however, divorces were virtually nonexistent, legal separations coming chiefly under the jurisdiction of ecclesiastical courts. Slaves couldn't legally marry, and indentured servants couldn't marry without the master's consent.

Early in the 19th century some state legislatures began to expand the grounds for divorce to include intemperance as well as cruelty. The 1850s saw an increased frequency in divorce, for it was easily obtained in the western states and territories. In the same decade *divorce lawyers* began advertising their services in getting *legal out-of-state divorces*. As rates of divorce climbed in the late 19th century, the exodus to Nevada for a *quickie divorce*, or a *Nevada divorce*, later called a *Reno divorce*, began. People who went there to get divorced were called *six-month settlers*. The divorce rate reached an all-time peak in 1946, when issues of *child support* and *alimony* (1656, from Latin *alimonia*, sustenance) were much discussed. After a leveling off in the 1950s, the rate soared again in the mid 1960s with the advent of the *no-fault divorce*, *no-fault* having been first recorded in 1967 with respect to auto insurance plans, then being used to denote a divorce in which neither party is held responsible for the break-up.

Associated with matrimonial law is *common-law marriage* (1900), a concept that came to be linked with live-in couples who when splitting up, might go to court over issues of *palimony* (1977, first spelled *pal-imony* in a *Los Angeles* magazine headline in its October issue and coined by the magazine's editor Lew Harris, not by famed divorce lawyer Marvin Mitchelson).

"Draw up the papers, lawyer,
and make 'em good and stout,
For things are running crossways,
and Betsey and I are out."

— Will Carleton,
Betsey and I Are Out, 1873

"TRIALS OF THE CENTURY"

O.J. Simpson . . . Rodney King . . . Charles Manson . . . these notorious cases and others reflect the celebration of sensationalism in a culture informed by mass media and cameras in the courtroom. But for several centuries Americans have had various *trials of the century*.

THE SALEM WITCH TRIALS
These occurred in the late 17th century, and in them this passage from Exodus 22:18 was oft repeated as the basis for executing defendants charged with witchcraft: "You shall not permit a sorcerer to live."

The Salem Witch Trials are among the most talked-about events of our colonial history, though witch trials themselves were never common in America. The term *witch trial* had been in use in England since the 13th century, and witchcraft was punishable by death according to English law from long before the Pilgrims landed until 1736.

In the late 17th century, English excitement over witches spread to the colonies. It was heightened as the famous Puritan clergyman, statesman, and president of Harvard College, Increase Mather (1639–1723) and his son Cotton Mather (1663–1728) both published books "proving" the existence of witches. Then in February 1692 two girls had fits in Salem Village (now Danvers), Massachusetts, and accused townspeople of bewitching them. Mass hysteria prevailed. Soon, 150 men and women had been accused of being possessed by the devil. A special commission led by jurist Samuel Sewall investigated and conducted the *Salem Witch Trials*: 19 "witches and wizards" were hanged (none was burned), and one was pressed to death between weighted planks for refusing to plead guilty or not guilty, while 10 others were convicted but not executed.

Increase Mather himself was the first to criticize the trials and helped halt them; his son Cotton never protested, though he did call for fairer rules of evidence; and Judge Sewall later repented the part he had played as presiding judge.

After this one witch-hunting orgy, witch trials practically disappeared from the colonies. In 1692 Massachusetts colonial governor William Phips set strict evidentiary guidelines for handling these cases, the result being a vast majority of acquittals.

SACCO AND VANZETTI

This trial had all America talking in the 1920s. Nicola Sacco and Bartolomeo Vanzetti were self-proclaimed anarchists who had immigrated to America from Italy in 1908, one a shoe worker, the other a fish peddler. In 1920 they were arrested for murder and robbery, charged with having killed a shoe-factory paymaster and his guard in South Braintree, Massachusetts, while taking the $16,000 payroll.

Sacco and Vanzetti were convicted in Judge Webster Thayer's court after a six-week jury trial in the summer of 1921. Socialists and radicals claimed the trial was not fair, and many others felt the two men had been convicted for their radical beliefs rather than on the basis of prejudicial evidence against them. Supporters claimed the two men had been falsely identified, and in 1925 a convicted murderer, Celestino Madeiros, confessed that he had taken part in the crime with the Joe Morelli gang. A worldwide stream of protests and mass meetings urged clemency. In June 1926 Governor A. T. Fuller appointed Harvard President A. Lawrence Lowell, MIT President Samuel W. Stratton, and a former judge, Robert Grant, to review the case. They found the trial fair, both men guilty, and advised the governor not to exercise clemency. Demonstrations again took place and radicals set off bombs in New York City and Philadelphia. Sacco and Vanzetti were executed on August 23, 1927, still protesting their innocence.

Nicola Sacco and Bartolomeo Vanzetti in 1927, four months before their execution.

LEOPOLD AND LOEB

The *Leopold and Loeb* trial was the sensational topic of 1924. Everyone talked about the two youths from wealthy, respected Chicago families—18-year-old Nathan Leopold and 17-year-old Richard Loeb—who had killed a friend and neighbor, 14-year-old Bobbie Franks. Leopold did it to prove he could commit a "perfect crime" involving kidnapping, ransom, and murder. The pair picked up young Franks after school. Leopold drove the car with the victim sitting next to him in front. Loeb sat in back and killed Bobbie by hitting him on the head with a chisel. Many newspapers described the pair sensationally as wealthy young "thrill seekers." Their lawyer, Clarence Darrow, introduced serious psychiatric evidence for the first time and saved his clients from the death sentence. (They were sentenced to life imprisonment.)

"[It is] *unlawful for any teacher in any of the . . . public schools of the state, to teach any theory that denies the story of the Divine creation of man as taught in the Bible, and to teach instead that man has descended from a lower order of animals.*"

— *State of Tennessee anti-evolution law, March 13, 1925*

THE MONKEY TRIAL

The Monkey Trial, also known as the *Scopes Monkey Trial*, 1925, was one of the most sensational, most talked-about trials in American history. It pitted Darwin's theory of evolution against fundamentalism, a battle that still rages between humanists and creationists regarding the teaching of evolution in the public schools.

Clarence Darrow at the Scopes Monkey Trial in 1925, later dramatized in the play and movie, *Inherit the Wind.*

It all began in 1921 when Baptist Rev. Dr. J. W. Porter, head of the Anti-Evolution League of America, had a bill introduced in the Kentucky state legislature banning "the teaching of Darwinism, atheism, agnosticism, and evolution " in state-supported schools. The press called it "the monkey bill," and it became a national issue. William Jennings Bryan urged its passage "to drive Darwinism from our schools," evangelist Billy Sunday praised it, and so did the violent, ranting Rev. J. Frank Norris. Kentucky's House of Representatives defeated the bill by one vote, but similar *monkey bills* became law in Oklahoma, Texas, and Tennessee.

The American Civil Liberties Union publicly offered to help anyone challenging one of the *monkey laws.* George Rapplyea, a drugstore owner in Dayton, Tennessee, a county seat of 3,000 souls, thought such a challenge would put Dayton on the map. He recruited John T. Scopes, a teacher of general science and athletic coach of Rhea County High School, to initiate the test case by claiming that he had taught Darwinism. The prosecution had the eager services of William Jennings Bryan. The ACLU countered with big-city agnostic Clarence Darrow, fresh from the *Leopold and Loeb* trial. The trial—the first jury trial brought before the public via radio—was a raucous carnival lasting from July 10 to 21, 1925. Dayton teemed with special correspondents, including H. L. Mencken of the *Baltimore Sun,* newsreel teams, hot-dog vendors, and a souvenir seller hawking toy monkeys. The American Association for the Advancement of Science sent expert witnesses to defend evolution—and when two showmen exhibited trained chimpanzees in town, the defense lawyers invited one of the chimps to lunch. Dayton was on the map, and the whole world was talking about it.

The trial ended after Bryan had taken the stand himself as an expert witness on the infallibility of the Bible. But the judge announced that he would not consider any testimony on the validity of evolution: the case, he ruled, was merely to decide whether Scopes had violated the state law or not. By all testimony he had, and the jurors found him "guilty as charged." The judge imposed a $100 fine, later set aside by the state supreme court on a technicality. Bryan died five days after the trial—and Arkansas and Mississippi passed "monkey law" bills the following year.

THE LINDBERGH KIDNAPPING

The most talked-about criminal case and trial of the 1930s, this one was the precursor, in terms of sensationalism and national fascination, of the O. J. Simpson trial some 60 years later.

In March 1932 German-born Bruno Hauptmann allegedly kidnapped two-year-old Charles Augustus Lindbergh, Jr., from his parents' house in Hopewell, New Jersey, later murdering the child. The toddler was the son of two of the nation's best-loved celebrities—aviation hero Charles Lindbergh and his wife Anne Morrow Lindbergh—and there was sensational press coverage of the crime, Hauptmann's arrest over two years later, and the 1935 trial in the small town of Flemington, New Jersey. Over 300 reporters attended the trial, among them big names such as Walter Winchell and Edna Ferber. In the manner of today's television *legal analysts*, criminal lawyer Samuel Leibowitz gave daily radio commentaries. And as would be the case with many later "celebrity trials," celebrities of the day such as Ginger Rogers and Jack Benny attended. Crowds mobbed the courthouse screaming "Kill Hauptmann!" And street hawkers sold, for a dime apiece, tiny wooden ladders like the one the kidnapper had allegedly used to get into the baby's second-floor nursery; women wore these as pins or bangles.

After a six-week trial the jury deliberated for 11 hours, 14 minutes before returning a guilty verdict. Hauptmann was executed in the electric chair on April 3, 1936, still proclaiming his innocence (echoed by his wife Anna up to her October 1994 death). As a direct result of this case, kidnapping was made a federal offense under what was popularly known as the *Lindbergh Act*.

THE ROSENBERGS

The *Rosenberg* espionage *case* of 1953 was one of the most controversial in the history of U.S. criminal law—the conduct of the trial of husband and wife Julius and Ethel Rosenberg after their July 17, 1950 arrest for atomic spying is still challenged by some legal scholars and retried by law students in *moot courts* (1788; *moot*, before the 12th century, from Middle English, "meeting," from Old English *mot*, *gemot*).

After a jury found them guilty in federal court, Judge Irving Kaufman sentenced them to death. The U.S. Supreme Court declined to hear their appeal, though in June 1953 Associate Justice William O. Douglas granted them a stay of execution. In an extraordinary session the Supreme Court voted 6-3 to allow the execution. The Rosenbergs were executed in the Sing Sing electric chair on June 19, 1953. The trial created a public uproar. To this day many people talk about the *Rosenberg executions* as a gross miscarriage of justice, while others defend the process that led to those deaths.

THE CHICAGO SEVEN

"Your honor, are we going to stop this medieval torture?"

— *William M. Kunstler to Judge Julius Hoffman, Chicago Seven trial, just as the judge had ordered Bobby Seale shackled and gagged*

The *Chicago Seven*, were political radicals accused of inciting the riots that marred the August 1968 Democratic National Convention in Chicago. Protest against the Vietnam War and social injustice were the catalysts as 10,000 demonstrators fought violently with Mayor Richard Daley's police, all televised before a stunned nation. Originally there were eight defendants: David Dellinger (a pacifist), Rennie Davis and Tom Hayden (leaders of the SDS, the Students for a Democratic Society; Hayden would later be elected a congressman), Abbie Hoffman and Jerry Rubin (leaders of the Yippies, the Youth International Party), John Froines and Lee Weiner (organizers from Chicago), and Bobby Seale (cofounder of the Black Panthers).

Chicago Seven member, manic-depressive, and self-proclaimed "orphan of America" Abbie Hoffman turning a somersault as he arrives for his trial for inciting a riot at the 1968 Democratic National Convention. Claiming that he wanted to be tried not for rioting, but for "having long hair," Hoffman's antics would continue inside the courtroom. He would be driven underground a year later after an arrest for drug dealing.

The trial, starting in September 1968, lasted five months, and brought to public attention the *Weathermen* (a pro-violence off-shoot of the SDS)—a group that declared *Days of Rage* outside the courthouse.

Defense attorney William M. Kunstler (1919–95) became a household name in representing this roster of radicals. This flamboyant advocate brought into the courtroom singers, artists, and socio-political activists to testify about the flaws in U.S. society requiring remedy. Bobby Seale, in the meantime, conducted his own defense, and the eight became the *Chicago Seven*. After a stormy trial the Chicago Seven were found guilty in February 1970, but an appeals court overturned that conviction in the fall of 1972, citing judicial hostility to the defendants and procedural errors. The fame of the *Chicago Seven* led to subsequent use of a place-name-with-a-number to designate a group of defendants, especially in trials involving civil rights protest.

THE O.J. SIMPSON CRIMINAL TRIAL

In a trial lasting from September 26, 1994 to October 3, 1995, former professional football star and TV and movie personality Orenthal James (O.J.) Simpson was *in the dock* (1580s, originally a cage or pen for animals, applied to the enclosure used to confine "the prisoner" in a British court; the term, though not the practice, came to America). He had allegedly stabbed to death his ex-wife Nicole Brown Simpson and an acquaintance, restaurant waiter Ronald Goldman, on the night of June 12, 1994 on the steps of her residence in the Brentwood section of Los Angeles. The entire nation was obsessed with the case. Many seemed to talk of nothing else, asking one another, "What happened with O.J. today?" They followed the televised coverage as they worked, attempted to understand complex DNA testimony by expert witnesses, even got updates from airline pilots on flights.

Some legal analysts remarked that the trial was "a lesson in civics for the nation," and others cited the exorbitant cost of the trial in calling for sweeping court reform. The focus here is on the terminology of the law

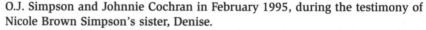

O.J. Simpson and Johnnie Cochran in February 1995, during the testimony of Nicole Brown Simpson's sister, Denise.

used in the trial, much of it involving *Law French*—vocabulary of Anglo-Norman origin dating from the years following the Norman Conquest of Britain in 1066. Many other legal terms are a mix of Latin and French, still others directly from Latin.

The Simpson "Trial of the Century" made the following terms part of everyday language:

coroner, around 1630, Middle English "crown officer," from Anglo-Norman *corouner*, ultimately from Latin *corona*, crown. The *corouner* was a royal judicial officer, officially called in Latin *custos placitorum coronae*, meaning "guardian of the Crown's pleas," a 12th century record-keeping functionary. The coroner also investigated suspicious deaths among the Norman ruling class; the latter function persists today among modern coroners, *medical examiners*, *forensic pathologists*, and *criminalists*. In the Simpson case the treatment of the *chain of evidence* by police and medical examiners alike came under harsh criticism by the defense.

judge, 14th century, from Middle English *jugen*, from Anglo-Norman *juger*, based on Latin *iudicare*, a verb whose root is Latin, *iudex*, judge. Judge Lance A. Ito was roundly criticized for unnecessarily lengthening the proceedings by not controlling his courtroom.

juror, 14th century, from Middle English *jurour*, via Anglo-Norman from Latin *iurator*, swearer, from *iurare*, to swear (whose root is *ius*, *iur-*, law). The Simpson trial had a *downtown jury* (referring to its ethnic, racial, and gender make-up). Over time 10 of the original jurors were either excused or dismissed, creating worries that a *mistrial* would result as the *jury pool* was exhausted.

jury, 15th century, from Middle English, *jurie* (same origin as *juror*). After only four hours of deliberation, the predominantly African-American Simpson jury returned a verdict of not guilty on all counts of murder in the first degree. The verdict created a storm of controversy, spurring spirited discussion of *race-based jury nullification*, that is, a jury's disregarding evidence presented in an effort to redress racial injustice. But the verdict did vindicate the *jury selection* done by the defense's jury consultant, who had advised them on which jury candidates to challenge.

trial, first cited in 1577 in the sense of a judicial tribunal, from Middle English *triall*, a testing, from Anglo-Norman *trier*, based on an Old French verb meaning "to sift or cull." The Simpson murder trial began on September 26, 1994, more than three months after his *arrest* (Middle English *aresten*, via Anglo-Norman from a Vulgar Latin verb meaning "to stop"), followed by his *indictment* (based on Middle English *enditen*, via Old French from Latin *indicere*, to proclaim) and *arraignment* (Middle English *arainen* via Anglo-Norman and Old French, ultimately from Latin *ratio*, reason). The arraignment is the formal procedure where the reason for the *indictment* or sworn accusation of crime made by a *grand jury* is presented in court, and the accused offers a *plea* (Middle English *ple* via Old French from Latin *placitum*, an opinion or decree, in this case the defendant's formal answer to the charge).

verdict, from Middle English *verdit*, from Anglo-Norman (*ver*, true, from Latin *verus*; + *dit*, speech, from Latin *dictum*, a form of *dicere*, to say). When the Simpson verdict was read "the country stopped," as a *New York Times* reporter noted. New York's Consolidated Edison discovered that at that moment, 745,000 more televisions than normal were on, based on a 93-million-watt surge in electrical consumption over normal usage.

voir dire, 1676, *voir* from Anglo-Norman, from Latin *verus*, true, and *dire* from Latin *dicare*, to say. *Voir dire*, integral to the outset of both the criminal case and the later 1996–97 *wrongful-death* civil suit brought by the Goldman family against Simpson, is a preliminary examination to determine the competency of a juror or a witness. Most Americans had no idea how to pronounce this term, having never encountered it before. Legal analysts varied in their own pronunciations, some saying *dire* as in "dear," others saying it as in "ire."

When lead defense attorney Johnnie Cochran, speaking to the jury of a bloody glove the defendant had been unable to don during a prosecution demonstration, said, "If it doesn't fit, you must *acquit*," he used a 13th century word of French and Latin origin. Though the courtroom language in the Simpson case was free of Latin expressions like *ex malita sua praecogitate* ("with malice aforethought") certain other English terms of Latin origin occurred often:

accuse, 14th century, via Middle English from Latin *accusare*, to call to account: *ad-* + *causa*, lawsuit.

prosecute, 15th century, "to pursue to the end," from Middle English *prosecuten*, from Latin *prosequi prosecui-*, *pro-* meaning "forward" and *sequi* "to follow."

subpoena, 15th century, from Medieval Latin *sub poena*, under penalty.

summation, 1836, "a summing up," from Late Latin *summatus*, from *summare*, to sum up, from Latin *summa*, sum.

In their closing arguments and numerous *sidebar* conferences with the judge, plain English was the rule when the *lawyers* (14th century, Middle English *lauier*, from *law*, itself based on an Old English word meaning "that which is laid down") talked. Three other legal terms of totally English origin used in the trial are these:

guilt, before the 12th century, from Old English *gylt*, crime.

oath, before the 12th century, from Old English *ath*.

witness, before the 12th century, "attestation of fact," going back to Old English *wit*, knowledge.

More contemporary English expressions that, when mentioned, conjure images of the Simpson trial are *rush to judgment*, used chiefly by the defense to characterize the prosecution's actions and statements regarding the defendant; and *race card*, as in *play the race card*, a focusing by the defense on the racial aspects of the case, especially as a means to influence the jury.

The team of defense *attorneys* (14th century, from Middle English *attourney*, from Old French *attorner*, to appoint) were called the *Dream Team* after the 1992 U.S. Olympic basketball team that had included Michael Jordan, Magic Johnson, and Larry Bird.

CLOSING ARGUMENTS

Whether the phrasing be Latin as in *habeas corpus* (15th century, Latin, "you shall have the body," the guarantee that an accused must be presented physically before the court with a statement demonstrating suffi-

---

"In Chicago, WGN-TV said its live coverage from the Santa Monica, California courthouse Tuesday night drew the highest audience share in the country's third-largest city, when most other stations were carrying [President] Clinton's speech to a joint session of Congress. Simpson . . . was found liable in a [wrongful death] lawsuit filed in the slayings of his ex-wife . . . and her friend."

— Washington Post,
February 6, 1997, on "O. J. II,"
or "Simpson II," as the civil trial
was colloquially dubbed,
the verdict handed down on
February 4, 1997

"'I'm totally O. J.-ed out,' said Walt Grimes, 44, adding a new verb to the nation's vocabulary."

— Washington Post,
February 12, 1997, on the O. J.
Simpson civil trial verdict

---

cient cause for arrest, thereby preventing indefinite imprisonment without charges) or whether it be strictly English, as in *Son of Sam Laws* (state laws preventing convicted felons from gaining monetary benefits from the sale, e.g., of book or film rights, named after a New York murderer who called himself "the Son of Sam"), the language of American law, like that of its English cousin, is both technical and traditional, reflecting the conjunction of cultures and languages that make up our legal system. In Oliver Wendell Holmes, Jr.'s words to the Suffolk (Massachusetts) Bar Association in 1855: "The Law, wherein, as a magic mirror, we see reflected not only our own lives, but the lives of all men that have been!"

MANNERS AND MANNERISMS

*T*he complaint that manners in America are continuing to degenerate has
been a recurring one. If anything, people used to behave much worse.
When Frances Trollope (mother of Anthony, the 19th century English
novelist), published **Domestic Manners of the Americans** in 1832, she commented
on the fact that people not only shoveled food into their mouths with knives, but
often blew their noses on their silk cravats and pulled a pocket knife out to clean
their teeth after a meal. She was particularly outraged by Americans' behavior in
the theater. The audience—largely male—routinely took off their jackets and
rolled up their sleeves, sprawled in their seats, chewed tobacco, and spat
everywhere. If they didn't like the performance, they chanted, jeered, shouted,
and hurled dead animals on the stage. They even entertained prostitutes in the
balcony.

*"Some people are very fond of
affecting a rude coarseness of
manners, and despise politeness . . .
as though it were inconsistent with
freedom and sincerity. . . . True
politeness, without compromising
any thing that duty or fidelity
requires to be brought forward,
observes proper times and seasons
for saying and doing things; every
thing is beautiful in its season,
nothing is beautiful out of it."*

— The Young Husband's Book,
1836

Americans have always prided themselves on a certain forthrightness
and egalitarianism in their social behavior. But they have never been
able to do away with standards of *etiquette* (1750, from the Old French
estiquette meaning "ticket" or "label") altogether. When the first colonists
arrived in the 17th century, it was clear that the old European social
rules were unsuited to conditions in the New World. Thanks to the vast
tracts of available land and the growth of new crops like tobacco,
landowners who had arrived with no social standing at all suddenly
found themselves quite prosperous. And wealth, rather than formal education or ancestry, was the key to social prominence in colonial America.

Of course these newly prominent landowners, bankers, and businessmen were not always well versed in the ways of polite society. So
they turned to books on manners and etiquette, hundreds of which
appeared during the mid 1800s. For example, *The Art of Good Behavior*
(1845) advised those who were unfamiliar with the rules governing

A six-year-old "little lady" carefully pours punch during the tea party at the final
class at the "Little Lady and Perfect Gentleman" manners class on August 14,
1996, in Bourbonnais, Illinois.

behavior in genteel society "to be cautious, pay attention, and do as he sees others do, who ought to know what is proper."

By the 1880s, the codes of behavior such books promoted had become quite elaborate. Guests at a Victorian dinner party were expected to show up in formal dress, gather in the drawing room before dinner, and, when summoned by a servant, form a procession into the dining room. The food was passed by servers in uniform, the carving took place out of sight, and the meal usually involved several courses served over a period of two or more hours. If the guests were hungry, so much the worse: Politeness required attending to one's food as little as possible, despite the fact that six or seven forks had been laid out for the purpose.

The late 19th century was the "golden age" of manners in America. There were rules governing how to *tip one's hat* (1881) to someone on the street, how low to bow, and how to greet a person of either inferior or superior social standing. There was even an elaborate code regarding the proper way to leave *calling cards* (1896): Folding the upper right corner meant that the visit was personal; folding the upper left meant that you'd come to offer congratulations; the lower left signified that you'd come to offer your condolences; and the lower right meant that you'd be leaving the city for some time. (By the end of the 20th century the printed *business card*, ever ready for distribution as a means of *networking*, had all but replaced the engraved calling card.)

The 20th century brought more casual behavioral standards. Some blamed it on the increase in the number of working women, the rising divorce rate, the First World War, or the invention of the automobile. The declining interest in etiquette was blamed on television in the 1950s, the hippies or the women's liberation movement in the 1960s, and the popularity of fast food in the 1970s. And in the 1980s–90s people's rudeness was attributed to such influences as the "new money" made on Wall Street and the absence from the home of two-career working parents.

ADVICE FROM THE EXPERTS

Modern etiquette can be said to have developed from about the close of World War I. Between 1918 and 1929, sixty-eight new books on the subject were published, and 78 more were released between 1930 and 1945. Among the more widely referred to were Lillian Eichler's *Book of Etiquette* (1921), Emily Post's *Etiquette* (1922), Vogue's *Book of Etiquette* (1948), and Amy Vanderbilt's *Complete Book of Etiquette* (1952).

Emily Post (1872–1960), a Baltimore-born New York socialite, was the first American to make a career out of dispensing advice on manners. Daughter of the eminent architect Bruce Price, she married Edwin Post at 20 and soon found it necessary to supplement her income. After Post's *Etiquette* appeared, the many letters she received asking for advice about specific social situations led to a popular syndicated newspaper column and successful radio show. It was the first modern etiquette book written for the average person rather than for the upper classes. Her oft-quoted rule was the democratic "consideration for others." Thus, since 1922, Americans have been settling their debates about manners by saying, *"Emily Post* says" or "Ask *Emily Post."*

Amy Vanderbilt (1908–74) succeeded Emily Post as America's professional etiquette expert. She published her first guide to etiquette in 1952. Vanderbilt served as the official *etiquette consultant* for a number of agencies and organizations, including the U.S. Department of State.

Letitia Baldrige updated *Amy Vanderbilt's Complete Book of Etiquette* in 1978. Baldrige served as chief of staff for First Lady Jacqueline

Emily Post in 1912.

Kennedy. In 1985, Baldrige wrote the first guide to manners for business executives.

Judith Martin, better known as *Miss Manners*, was a Wellesley College graduate and *Washington Post* journalist who covered social life at the White House and on Washington's Embassy Row for 25 years. Her first full-length book, *Miss Manners' Guide to Excruciatingly Correct Behavior*, hit the best-seller list in 1982.

MODERN ETIQUETTE DILEMMAS

In the 1990s, the etiquette experts had to dispense advice on everything from the pleasures and pitfalls of the *office romance* to how to deal with children (*boomerangers*) who *returned to the nest* after graduating from college.

Weddings remained one of the most problematic areas. In her *New Manners for the 90's*, Letitia Baldrige guided her readers through the minefield of *interfaith marriages* and *ecumenical wedding services, prenuptial agreements*, and weddings where the bride was already pregnant (formerly referred to as *shotgun weddings* [1927] for the weapon once used by the father of the bride to ensure that the groom made his daughter *an honest woman*). She explained how to word the invitation when the bride's parents are divorced, widowed, or remarried; weighed the advantages of a *sitdown dinner* versus a *grazing* reception (where the guests would spend most of their time standing and eating off small plates with food selected from a buffet); and led her readers through the mysteries of the *bridal registry* (where the bride lists her wedding gift requirements with a local department store).

Entertaining was another area rife with hazards for the host or hostess of the 90s. Baldrige offered advice on how to avoid the complexities of formal dining by giving a *garage party* or *potluck supper* (where each guest is asked to contribute something to the meal) and how to serve *take-out food* (such as pizza or Chinese food). When dining out, Baldrige advised her readers to avoid *table hopping*, accepting or making *cellular phone calls*, and arguing over who's going to *pick up the check*. Miss Manners, in her *Guide to Excruciatingly Correct Behavior*, addressed the confusion over which is more correct: the *Continental style* of eating, where the fork is always held in the left hand, tines pointing down, and the knife in the right; or the *American style*, where the fork is held in the left hand for cutting food and then shifted to the right for eating it.

Other modern dilemmas included the use of *Ms.* (an alternative to *Miss* and *Mrs.* that avoids revealing marital status) in addressing invitations and making introductions, *social kissing* (accompanying a friendly embrace; sometimes referred to as *air kissing* because the women who engage in this practice rarely make actual physical contact), and the etiquette of *smoking*.

ETIQUETTE IN THE WORKPLACE

The development of a post-industrial, post-World War II *service-based economy* shifted the focus of etiquette from the dinner table to the workplace. For many Americans, success on the job came to depend on their ability to remain polite and cheerful, to deal with uncomfortable or adverse circumstances, and to make customers *feel at home*.

Letitia Baldrige was the first etiquette book author to deal exclusively with manners in the business world. Her 1985 book, the *Complete Guide*

"Thank you for not smoking."

— a common sign in residences, 1990s

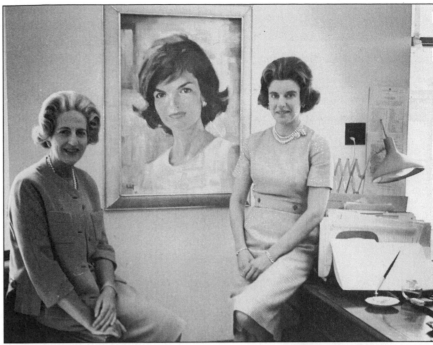

Letitia Baldridge (left) in June 1963 with Nancy Tuckerman, her successor as White House Social Secretary, beneath a portrait of Jacqueline Kennedy.

> "This [voice mail] is the modern equivalent of the butler. Anyone who possesses one should make it behave in a dignified manner."
>
> — *Judith Martin*, **Miss Manners' Guide for the Turn-of-the-Millennium**, *1989*

to *Executive Manners*, talked about proper behavior in the elevator, *door protocol*, and *corporate jet etiquette*. It was followed by *Miss Manners' Guide for the Turn-of-the-Millennium* (1989), Judith Martin's book on the social do's and don'ts of the workplace, covering such sensitive subjects as *sexual harassment* and *children in the office*. Baldrige published her *New Complete Guide to Executive Manners* in 1993.

MANNERS AND THE NEW TECHNOLOGY

The growth of new communications technology since the 1980s has had a significant social impact on Americans. The nearly universal practice of communicating by telephone de-emphasized the status, gender, and age distinctions that once served as cues for polite behavior. Conversely, an increase in telephone rudeness was taken very seriously. Some experts attributed the increased rudeness to the *dis-inhibition* effect afforded by the instant yet impersonal accessibility of devices such as computers and telephone answering machines.

Telephone services that force callers to follow a complicated sequence of *touch-tone* options, that prevent calls from certain people from getting through (*call blocking*), and that enable the receiver to identify the caller before deciding whether or not to pick up the phone (*Caller ID*) raised a number of thorny etiquette questions. Some of the more widespread and controversial ones include:

> "Human interactions are demanding, even simple ones. We still tend to think that human interactions should have some sense of courtesy and formality. On [voice mail] or in e-mail, we don't have to deal with someone's emotional state. . . . I can be less polite and more cursory."
>
> — *Boston College social psychologist Marianne LaFrance in the* **Boston Globe**, *July 21, 1996*

Answering machines, described by Miss Manners as the modern equivalent of the butler, who makes domestic life easier by saying, "Madam is not available. May I tell her who called?"

While some people regarded answering machines as the greatest thing to happen to telephones since *direct dialing*, others found them simply annoying. But they became a fixture in Americans' lives, with most 1990s etiquette experts advising that one record a straightforward

Miss Manners in 1982.

greeting ("Hello, this is_____. I'm sorry I can't come to the phone right now; please leave a message after the beep," or the less personal "Hello, you've reached 555-1212. Please leave a message"). Callers who reach answering machines were advised not to leave "joke" messages and to be as brief as possible, since some machines limited the length of incoming messages. Babbling, fumbling, and rummaging through papers while attempting to leave a message are considered unprofessional.

Once callers got through if they hadn't been *screened out* by the answering machine, some might have to endure listening to the recipient engage in *time-stuffing*, that is to say, doing other things such as read mail, sign documents, load a dishwasher, feed a pet, or put dishes away while taking the call—a process considered just as rude as loudly reprimanding children in side conversations while talking on the phone.

Call waiting, a service that allows a second call to be taken while the line is in use. Miss Manners described the clicking sound of *call waiting* as "incredibly rude," yet acknowledging that it also could be a polite way of easing out of a telephone call that has taken up too much time.

Speakerphone, considered by Letitia Baldrige "an odious contraption" that echoed in your ear and made voices sound strange, giving the caller the unpleasant feeling that others were listening in. When its use is absolutely necessary, she suggested explaining why and asking the caller whether he or she has any objections. She also warned against forgetting to push the *mute button*, which disconnects the *Speakerphone*. It can be very embarrassing if an exchange that was not meant to be shared is transmitted inadvertently.

Voice mail, a service that became particularly popular with businesses in the 1990s, with the downsizing of staff. The phone is usually answered with a recorded greeting and, if the person is not available at the time ("I'm away from my desk . . ."), it instructs the caller to record a message for that person. Failure to respond promptly to *voice mail* came to be considered a serious breach of business etiquette.

Fax machines, evoked etiquette questions when the office fax machine is used indiscriminately to send personal communications (which can be read by anyone who happens to be in the area when the fax arrives), long documents (which use up the receiver's paper supply), and *junk faxes*, which, like their *junk mail* cousins, arrive unsolicited.

Cell phones, popular among business people, some who came to consider receiving a call while playing golf or dining at an expensive restaurant as a status symbol. The constant ringing of phones in once-unlikely places such as concert halls and theaters and the annoyance it represented for others within earshot caused some eating establishments to require their patrons to check all cell phones at the door. And ushers at some theaters routinely began to make *phone sweeps*, asking patrons to leave their cell phones and beepers in the lobby.

Beepers. Etiquette problems arose when people began to get beeped in theaters, restaurants, and places where they posed a distraction for others nearby. For this reason, some 1990s beepers alerted the holder with a vibration rather than a tone.

NETIQUETTE

People using their personal computers to access the *Internet* became part of the latest and most rapidly expanding field for etiquette, sometimes referred to as *netiquette*. The rules here, many of which were still evolving in the late 1990s, usually apply to senders of *electronic mail* and visitors to *chat rooms* where several people discuss an issue of common concern. Typing in all capital letters, for example, is called *shouting* and is considered rude. Another question involves how to address people in *cyberspace*: Should you preface an email message with Dear _____, or is it more appropriate to just plunge right into saying what's on your mind?

Cross-posting or *spamming* is posting the same message in many different locations on the Internet, a practice that makes seasoned Net users angry (it's the Net equivalent of *junk mail*). To convey a particular tone of voice, many users employ *emoticons* (see CYBERSPACE: I HEAR AMERICA CLICKING).

MULTICULTURAL MANNERS

The growing *cultural diversity* of American society began to pose numerous etiquette dilemmas in the 1990s, notwithstanding the historical diversity of the nation from its inception. Examples of issues Americans talked about in terms of *multicultural etiquette* are these few: eating everything on your plate when your hostess is Cambodian indicates that you really want more food; using the All-American "thumbs up" signal in front of an Afghani is the equivalent of making an obscene gesture with your middle finger; and trying to shake hands when you're introduced to a Japanese person can be taken as extremely rude—instead, you should bow and present your business card.

Norine Dresser's *Multicultural Manners* (1996) was one of the latest additions to the etiquette bookshelf. Dresser was a firm believer in familiarizing oneself with the ways of visitors and newcomers, for the simple reason that it made good social and business sense. Her book offered advice on such modern dilemmas as how to greet a Portuguese, how to accept change from a Korean shopkeeper, and what to wear to a Chinese wedding.

Etiquette experts offered classes for preschool children to teach them basic table manners, and seminars for adults who didn't know the difference between a fish knife and a fruit knife. And, as a result of many Americans' concern about the coarsening of behavior and language in the U.S. during the 1990s, organizations such as the *American Foundation for Courtesy Inc.* became active. *Character education* and *basic manners* courses came to be offered in some schools in an effort to move young people to greater *civility* (1561, in the sense "ordinary courtesy or politeness"), the word going back to Latin *civis*, a citizen.

POLITICALLY CORRECT

rying to police the language is an American tradition. Men have traditionally been advised not to use foul language *"in front of the ladies," although nowadays the ladies may prefer to be called* women, *and in many cases they are just as likely as men to pepper their speech with* four-letter words *(see* DIRTY WORDS*). But the arrival of the* civil rights movement *in the 1950s and 60s and the* women's movement *in the 1960s–70s heralded a heightened sensitivity to the biases built into our language, particularly among women (some of whom prefer the spellings* womyn *or* wimmin, *because such words do not contain* -men*) and blacks (many of whom now prefer to be called* African Americans*). Seemingly overnight, men had to change the way they talked about females or risk being branded* male chauvinist pigs *(MCPs). They could no longer freely address women (other than their girlfriends or wives) as* honey, baby, sweetie, *or* sweetheart. *The pronouns "he" and "his," traditionally used to cover both males and females, were replaced with* he/she, s/he, *and* his/hers, *or, to avoid clumsiness, with plural* they/their, *as in* Everyone is entitled to their own opinion. *Giving [a woman] the* once-over *(to look her up and down appraisingly) was no longer considered an innocent case of* elevator eyes, *or simple* girl watching, *but might lead to a serious charge of* sexual harassment *(a term used to describe* sexist *behavior in the workplace, including pressure for sexual favors and sexual jokes and epithets demeaning to women, dramatized by Anita Hill's testimony during the 1991 televised hearings on the nomination of Clarence Thomas to the U.S. Supreme Court) that could land the perpetrator in court—or out of a job. Epithets and nicknames for racial and ethnic groups suddenly became more than crude or insensitive to educated, enlightened Americans: They were* politically incorrect.

There's nothing wrong with trying to rid our language of racist, sexist, and other patently offensive terms—the use of which is a reflection on the user. But by the late 1980s and early 90s, some proponents of polit-

Clarence Thomas testifying before the Senate Judiciary Committee in October 1991, denying allegations of sexual harassment made by former employee Anita Hill.

ical correctness had gone to the extreme of insisting on hypersensitive new usages to replace long-established terms, inviting both consternation and ridicule from the general population. The desire to be *PC* (Politically Correct, 1793, the full form cited in a Supreme Court decision) resulted in national arguments over whether it is too narrowly *ethnocentric* to use *Oriental* (its etymology, from Latin *oriens*, refering to the rising sun in the East and so betraying a Western perspective) instead of *(East) Asian*, or whether people in wheelchairs were *handicapped*, *disabled*, or *physically challenged* (no one dared use the once-common *crippled*). The tangled web woven by the *PC Police* resulted in the elimination of many otherwise accurate and descriptive words, causing a *PC backlash* that gave some radio talk-show personalities the incentive to repeat the very expressions that the PC movement had tried to stamp out.

WAITRON, BRING ME THE CHECK

Feminists were among the first to zero in on job titles, which were rife with *gender-enders* (sex-biased suffixes). In cases where the title used for men was regarded, however incorrectly, as *gender-neutral* (for example, *aviator, actor, author*), use of the feminine form (*aviatrix, actress, authoress*) was spurned. *Policemen* became *police officers, firemen* became *firefighters*, and *salesmen* became *salespeople* or *sales clerks*. One no longer summoned a *waitress* in a restaurant; *server* became a common term, and some preferred *waitron*. The *mail carrier* took the place of the *mailman* or *postman, foremen* became *supervisors*, and *airline stewardesses* were now *flight attendants*. Regulations of the federal *Equal Employment Opportunity Commission*, or *EEOC*, made sure that employers paid attention to using nonsexist job titles and policies. The struggle to avoid offense led to a broader effort to avoid language demeaning to certain occupations. Prostitutes were tagged *sex-care providers*. An employee who lost his or her job was said to be *outplaced, involuntarily at leisure, undergoing a career transition, sidelined, between projects*, or *unwaged*.

> *"Red Riding Hood . . . said, 'Grandma, I have brought you some fat-free, sodium-free snacks to salute you in your role of a wise and nurturing matriarch.' . . . Red Riding Hood said, 'Oh, I forgot you are as optically challenged as a bat. Grandma, what big eyes you have!'"*
>
> — James Finn Garner, **Politically Correct Bedtime Stories**, *1994*

In 1996, Paula Meara is sworn in as the first female police chief in Springfield, Massachusetts, making her the most powerful policewoman in New England.

A gay pride parade in Texas.

Interestingly, it is considered perfectly acceptable for members of racial and ethnic minorities to use terms that would be blatantly offensive if used by the white majority. Some *African Americans* can say *nigger* and get away with it, and homosexuals can call each other *queer*, *faggot*, and *dyke* with impunity. Effeminate men (also known as *queens*) can call each other *girl*, as can *drag queens* (male homosexuals who dress in women's clothes) and *trannies* (transsexuals, or those who have undergone *sex-change operations*). It's okay for an elderly man to refer to someone his own age as a *geezer*, but if a younger person uses the same word he or she is likely to be accused of *ageism*.

THE AGE OF EUPHEMISM

Personal appearance has always been a sensitive issue for Americans, who have nonetheless been quick to come up with colorful descriptive words for those who depart from generally accepted standards. Unflattering nicknames such as *Fatso* and *Skinny* have been around for years, but political correctness dictated that people who are *fat* or even *obese* be referred to as *full-figured, big-boned, stocky,* or *differently sized*. When San Diego State University proposed to hold a fashion show in 1992, it unleashed storms of protest from the *sensitivity establishment*. There were threats to cancel the event on the grounds that it discriminated against everybody, clearly an open-and-shut case of *sizism*.

In terms of physical disabilities, deaf people came to be referred to as *aurally challenged* rather than *hard of hearing* or *hearing-impaired*; blind people were *sightless*; and in terms of personal success (a lack thereof), unsuccessful people came to be called *underachievers* or *individuals with temporarily unmatched objectives*.

A PC GLOSSARY

PC terminology can be amusing as well as amazing. The goal always was to avoid the merest suggestion of any bias, opprobrium, superiority, particular world view or attitude, or assignment of individual responsibility for what once were considered undesirable traits. Consider these exam-

A group of physically challenged people at a Medicaid hearing in Richmond, Virginia, in 1997.

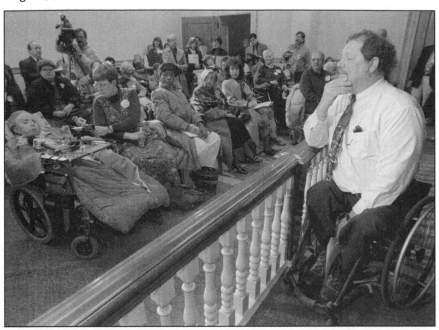

ples of favorite PC expressions of the 1980s and 90s, some used seriously, others tongue-in-cheek:

accommodationist, *traitor.*

acting out, used of a child to denote misbehavior.

Alaskan native, formerly *Eskimo,* now *Inuit.*

birth name, name given to a female child by her biological parents, often kept by a woman after marriage, and once called *maiden name.*

body decolonization, freeing the female (or *fe-person*) to become a lesbian, to escape *heterosexual imperialism.*

Canine-American, a dog living in the U.S. A cat is a *Feline-American.*

challenged, used in combination with an adverb, as in *physically challenged, mentally challenged,* or *visually challenged.*

chemically inconvenienced, drunk or *under the influence.*

deficiency achievement, failure.

developmental education, teaching the *intellectually challenged.*

differently, a word used in combination with sometimes specially coined adjectives to avoid discriminatory labeling, as in *differently abled* (disabled, handicapped), *differently advantaged* (without advantages, poor), *differently aligned* (deviant, anti-social), *differently emotioned* (crazy, hysterical), *differently logical* (illogical by the standards of *linear thinkers*), *differently pleasured* (perverse, kinky), and *differently sized* (too fat, too small, etc.).

discretionary fragrance, a perfume or after-shave.

domestic arts, formerly called *homemaking;* when taught in high school, it is also known as *home economics;* in college, *human ecology.*

economically disadvantaged, poor or *underprivileged,* was superseded by *economically marginalized/exploited,* thus shifting blame to someone else.

femhole, formerly *manhole*, also *personhole* and often (seriously) *utility entrance, personnel access, maintenance hatch*. Any word containing "man" became suspect under the rules of PC; hence *personkind* or *humankind* (though some objected still to the elements *-son-* and *-man-*) in place of "mankind," *freshperson* in place of "freshman," *humyn* in place of "human" in the manner of *womyn*.

gay, homosexual, although *queer* may be preferred by those leading this *alternative lifestyle*.

gender, often used as a replacement for "sex" or "sexual," as in *genderism, gender-bending,* and *person of gender* (woman), but not in set expressions like *sex crime, sexual harassment,* and *sexual misconduct.*

herstory, feminist version of history.

impaired occurs in a number of PC expressions, on the model of *visually impaired* (having to wear eyeglasses); similar words are *inconvenienced* (*orthopedically inconvenienced* should mean something less drastic than missing limbs) and *oppressed* (some used *parasitically oppressed* to mean pregnant).

long-time companion, long-term sexual partner or lover.

negative outcome, a blame-neutral term for failure or loss.

non-decriminalized substance, illegal drug.

non-documented person, illegal alien.

person. the use of this word stresses the individual worth of, say, a *PWA* (Person With AIDS, recently upgraded to *person living with AIDS*) in a way that *AIDS victim* does not. *Victim* is often avoided, except in combinations like *victims' rights groups, child-abuse victims,* and *crash victims. Person of color* is applied to any non-white, especially in contexts encouraging a policy of *inclusion* countering white dominance in positions of authority or prestige.

pharmacologically dependent, drug addict (also called *user*).

seasonal employee, a *migrant worker* or a student holding a summer job.

underrepresented group, any minority group.

   Political correctness has also given rise to a number of new *-isms*. Consider the following:

Afrocentrism, or African American racism, depending on the user's viewpoint; related to the 60s term *Black Pride*. Also meaning the belief that Western and Egyptian cultures are rooted ultimately in Africa.

ageism, discrimination on the basis of age. You seldom hear of *gray hair*; it's *salt and pepper*. Similarly, older people are referred to as *senior citizens*.

biocentrism, the belief that animals are just as important as people (advocated by ecologists, wildlife preservationists, vegetarians, anti-fur radicals, etc.).

colorism, prejudice based on skin pigmentation.

Eurocentrism, bias toward the culture of *DWEMs* (Dead White European Males).

heightism, preferring the tall to the *vertically challenged*.

heterosexism, oppression of non-heterosexuals as a result of *homophobia*, used to describe an aversion to *gays*.

Jesse Jackson, founder of the Rainbow Coalition, with Hazel Dukes (left) and the Reverend Al Sharpton (right), in November 1996 calling for a boycott of Texaco. Charges of racism, discrimination, and a corporate cover-up—bolstered by taped evidence—had been leveled against the oil company by current and former employees.

lookism, too much emphasis placed on physical appearance (also called *face-ism*).

phallocentrism, emphasis on (and overweening pride in) masculinity.

pluralism, another name for *multiculturalism*, but with an emphasis on *entitlements* for minorities. Former New York City Mayor Ed Koch called it *tribal politics*, but his successor David Dinkins called it a *glorious mosaic*—the latter emphasizing the celebration of *ethnicity* and *alternate lifestyles*.

rectocentrism, domination and oppression of *sinistromanualistic* (left-handed) people by the majority, who are right-handed.

sexism, prejudice on the basis of biological gender (usually to the disadvantage of women).

specism, an attitude indicating that one animal species is superior to another.

BEWARE THE BACKLASH

Political correctness led to such extremes in euphemistic terminology that many denounced it as counterproductive. Bumperstickers proclaimed the driver as "Politically Incorrect and Proud of It," and even the academic community, the PC hotbed where *speech codes* became more controversial than dress codes, began to adopt a more tolerant attitude by the mid 1990s.

But the old American boast that *It's a free country* no longer rings as true as it once did. When it comes to *telling it like it is*, Americans who speak their minds freely are bound to offend someone. They may not end up incarcerated, but they could well end up in *sensitivity training*.

POLITICS:
NO TERM LIMITS

*T*he language of America's past has often been the language of America's politics. A study of the American words and phrases in political play begins with the first colonists. From there, the vocabulary moves historically from the causes of the Revolutionary and Civil Wars through the effects of Watergate and the post-Cold War era.

"The conduct of public affairs for private advantage."

— Ambrose Bierce defining politics in The Devil's Dictionary, *1906*

"Politics is the gizzard of society, full of grit and gravel, and the two political parties are its two opposite halves—sometimes split into quarters—which grind on each other. Not only individuals, but states, have thus a confirmed dyspepsia."

— Henry David Thoreau, Life Without Principle, *1863*

"I must not write a word to you about politics, because you are a woman."

— John Adams, letter to his wife, February 13, 1779

American politics has produced a vocabulary of slang and *slang-whanging* (an 1809 term for "angry or empty political talk"), filled with colorful coinages and cynical sayings. That element of cynicism in American government dates to the nation's beginnings; by the time Noah Webster's first dictionary appeared in 1806, for instance, *politically* was already defined not only as "with policy" but also "cunningly." Today's inventive invective—from the attack phrase *you're no Jack Kennedy* to the wise-guy *it's the economy, Stupid* —has sustained that sense of cunning in wicked and wise wordplay.

In fact, the political vocabulary has often blurred the boundaries of humor and insult in its deprecation of government itself. "All politics is applesauce," commented Will Rogers a century ago. A more recent variation, "All politics is local," was propounded by the former House Speaker Tip O'Neill, but the latest language of American government reflects a global concern. Geopolitical movements and international influences have left their stamp on political lingo, welcoming into English a range of foreign terms, from the Russian *glasnost* (openness) to the German *Weltanschauung* ("world view").

The voting booth. Perhaps the only place where a voter is shielded from spin doctors and attack ads.

Tip O'Neill in 1977. He served 36 years in the House of Representatives, the final ten as Speaker. His most remembered observation: All politics is local.

A RACE OF CONVICTS

This early phrase angered the American colonists and was a fairly common insulting sobriquet used by the British. It is traced to Dr. Samuel Johnson's statement, quoted in Boswell's 1791 life of Johnson, that the Revolutionary colonists were "a race of convicts [who] ought to be thankful for anything we allow them short of hanging." It was an awful thing to say, especially insulting because it contained a lot of truth. Between 1607 and 1776, about 40 percent of the English who came to the colonies were convicts, drunks, runaways, debtors, and other such miscreants.

WAR AROUSING ACTS

In 1763 Britain began to pass a series of parliamentary acts that turned the majority of her loyal American subjects into dissidents and revolutionaries. These acts became known to historians as the "War Arousing Acts."

The war cry of *taxation without representation* is attributed to the American lawyer and statesman James Otis (1725–83), who is supposed to have said, "Taxation without representation is tyranny" in 1763 because the colonies were not represented in the House of Commons. There is no written evidence of Otis having said these exact words, but in his 1764 "Rights of the Colonies" he did write, "No parts of His Majesty's dominions can be taxed without their consent."

The Stamp Act, passed in 1765, was a revenue act imposing a stamp tax on publications and legal documents in the American colonies. Newspapers, pamphlets, almanacs, playing cards, and liquor permits, as well as most documents, had to bear a stamp bought from a distributor serving as a tax collector. This tax angered the most vocal forces in the colonies—printers, editors, lawyers, and tavern owners. Nine colonies sent delegates to a Stamp Act Congress in New York City in October 1765. As one would have expected, this congress attacked the Stamp Act as unconstitutional taxation without representation.

"The Sons of Liberty" was originally formed in 1765 in New York City to oppose the Stamp Act. The first radical group to agitate against the British, "the Sons of Liberty" took its name from a phrase used in a pro-American, anti-taxation speech delivered in the House of Parliament on February 6, 1765, by the Irish M. P. Colonel Isaac Barre.

Liberty, part of that group's name, became the watchword of the American Revolution and of America itself. Other "Sons of Liberty "groups were formed elsewhere, notably in Boston with Samuel Adams and Paul Revere (some similar groups took the name "the Sons of America"). Such groups rioted, looted, and hounded the British stamp-tax collectors until most abandoned their task. The Stamp Act was soon repealed, on March 18, 1766, but by then the Sons of Liberty were strong and pressing for independence.

The Sons of Liberty and the wide use of the word *liberty* gave us such American icons as the *Liberty Tree* and the *Liberty Bell*. The original Liberty Tree was an elm tree in Boston on which the first Stamp Act mob there had hanged in effigy the Secretary of Massachusetts Colony, Andrew Oliver. Other cities and towns soon designated dominant trees on their village greens or market squares as "Liberty Trees," and well into the 19th century Americans planted or designated symbolic "Trees of Liberty." The Liberty Bell was originally a symbol of religious liberty, being ordered from London by the Pennsylvania Assembly in 1752 to commemorate the state's 50 years of religious freedom under William Penn's Charter of Liberties. It cracked while being tested after its arrival in America, but was melted and recast here and hung in the steeple of the Pennsylvania State House in 1753. It called the townspeople together on July 8, 1776, to hear the Declaration of Independence read aloud, and it tolled the deaths of Washington and Jefferson, among others.

Teddy Roosevelt made the "White House" its official designation in 1901. It has been the residence of every President except George Washington.

British acts and legislations leading from "taxation without representation" to the Revolutionary War took various names. The Townshend Acts, 1767, were a series of acts named for the British Chancellor of the Exchequer, Charles Townshend, who convinced Parliament that Americans would accept "external" taxes on imports. He was wrong. The Tea Act, 1773, was passed by Parliament to enable the British East India Company to pay the Townshend tea tax. This threatened to give the British company a monopoly on tea, which soon became a symbol of hatred for the British and of American resistance, leading to the 1773 Boston Tea Party. The Intolerable Acts, 1774, sometimes called the Coercive Acts, were Parliament's reply to the Boston Tea Party; they were a series of five acts that closed the port of Boston until the tea was paid for. But Massachusetts refused to pay and called for a "Continental Congress."

The first Continental Congress met in Philadelphia in 1774 to list colonial grievances in a petition to the king—and its members resolved to meet again if King George III didn't redress their grievances. He didn't. They did. On May 10, 1775, the second Continental Congress met and appointed George Washington as Commander in Chief of the Continental Armies, preparing the way for the Revolutionary War and, ultimately, the Declaration of Independence. (See FIGHTING WORDS.)

LAISSEZ-FAIRE

Laissez-faire, inflation, and *bread riots* were all added to the American language during the Panic of 1837 (1837–40). People were talking about the collapse of the wildly inflated prices of land, cotton, and slaves, and the folding of many state banks and the Bank of the United States owing to *inflated money.*

When *inflation* caused the price of flour to rise to $12 a barrel in February and March 1837, poor people broke into New York warehouses to get it, and the state militia was called out to quash the *bread riots.*

President Van Buren expressed his attitude toward the panic by saying, "The less government interferes with private pursuits, the better for the general prosperity." This was called his *laissez-faire* (French "allow to do") attitude, a let-business-alone policy of having no policy, which helped William Henry Harrison defeat Van Buren's reelection bid in 1840.

O.K.

O.K. was a Boston coinage and first appeared in print in the *Boston Morning Post* on March 23, 1839. Meaning "oll korrect," the *k* reflecting a *c* to *k* spelling fad, it had moved to New York City by 1840, with the forming of the new (later to be infamous) Tammany social club, the Democratic O.K. Club. During the rest of 1840, *oll korrect* and *O.K.* became Democratic rallying cries, because the Democratic President campaigning for reelection, Martin Van Buren, was coincidentally called "Old Kinderhook" (he was from Kinderhook, New York, near Albany). Supporters of the Whig candidate, William Henry Harrison, countered that Van Buren had been Andrew Jackson's hand-picked successor and spread the false story that *O.K.* had been Jackson's uneducated way of abbreviating "all correct." Before the end of 1840, *O.K.* was in wide use, found in popular songs. Incidentally, that presidential campaign was a good year for new terms: Van Buren and his *O.K.* lost to Harrison and his slogan "Tippecanoe and Tyler Too."

By the mid 1940s *OK* without periods was the most popular form, vying with the 1929 spelling *okay,* a variant of Woodrow Wilson's 1918 *okeh.* Combined with *A-1* (an 1830s term stemming from its use by Lloyd's Register to designate ships in first-class condition), *A-OK* was introduced into millions of American homes in 1961 during the televised splashdown of astronaut Alan B. Shepard's space capsule when he reported, using a bit of NASA jargon, "Everything's A-OK—dye marker out."

MANIFEST DESTINY

"54-40 or fight!" (1844) was one of the most stirring political slogans in American history, and *Manifest Destiny* (1845) one of the most popular phrases and beliefs. Both grew out of the increasingly expansionist mood of the country after the 1830s and, specifically, out of James K. Polk's presidential election campaign of 1844. That year Polk and the Democrats campaigned on a platform for the "reoccupation of Oregon, the reannexation of Texas" (the nation had agreed to joint occupation of Oregon with Great Britain in 1818 and had given up any of our Louisiana Purchase claims to Texas as part of our agreement to obtain Florida from Spain in 1819). The first part of this platform, the "reoccupation of Oregon, "was translated into the slogan "54-40 or fight! " The second part, "reannexation of Texas," became known as "Manifest Destiny."

"54-40 or fight!" was first used in 1844 by William Allen in a speech before the U.S. Senate. It quickly became the slogan of hundreds of thousands of Democrats (then the "war party"). It meant the U.S. should resolve the Oregon question with Great Britain by fighting, if necessary, for sole occupancy and control of what was then the entire region west of the Rockies from California up to the Alaskan border. After Polk was elected, however, he made a compromise with Great Britain by accepting the Oregon lands only up to the 49th parallel. He compromised because between his election campaign and the negotiations we had annexed Texas, making war with Mexico imminent—and Polk didn't want to fight two wars at once. Thus, despite the slogan, the boundary between the U.S. and Canada wasn't to be the latitudinal measure of 54-40 (54 degrees, 40 minutes), and there was no fight.

Manifest Destiny was the idealistic belief, sometimes the imperialistic creed, that it was God's will (hence our obvious, or manifest, destiny) that the U.S. and its democratic ways should spread from the Atlantic to the Pacific, from Canada to the Rio Grande. The phrase was first hinted at by Andrew Jackson in 1824 when he called the United States "a country manifestly called by the Almighty to a destiny which Greece and Rome . . . might have envied." The actual phrase manifest destiny, however, was first used in the national debate over whether to annex Texas or not. It first appeared in the July-August 1845 issue of the United States Magazine and Democratic Review in an article by its editor, John L. O'Sullivan. Southerners and Democrats especially wanted annexation of the Texas lands as slave states; northern Whigs and abolitionists were against it, not wanting to tip the balance of states in favor of slavery. After annexation took place in December 1845, Manifest Destiny was not forgotten. It was immediately applied to the Mexican War (1846-48) in which we obtained California and New Mexico, and then the concept was enlarged to encompass lands beyond the continental United States, to explain our desire for Cuba in the 1850s, the purchase of Alaska in 1867, and the annexation of Hawaii in 1898.

ABOLITION

"Abolition!" (a 16th-century English noun) was the shout of the colonists in 1765—by which they meant the repeal of the hated British Stamp Act. After the act was repealed in 1766, some colonists liked the word so much they began to apply it widely to the abolition of slavery.

In 1775 the Pennsylvania Society for Promoting the Abolition of Slavery was formed in Philadelphia (the Quakers had started the fight against slavery in 1696); then a similar group was formed in New York. Soon many Northerners were joining the *abolition societies*; by 1840 there were 2,000 such groups with more than 2 million members. Until the 1830s, however, *abolition* didn't necessarily mean abolishing slavery; to many *abolitionists* it merely meant abolishing the slave trade, then perhaps buying the freedom of the existing slaves and sending them back to Africa.

The slave trade did end, on January 1, 1808 (the Constitution had said Congress couldn't ban it before that date), but this ban on importing slaves was poorly enforced and, of course, thousands of slaves were still being born every year in America. From about 1819 until the mid 1850s, the key political theme in America seemed to be whether or not slavery should be allowed to spread. Antislavery and proslavery politicians worked out various compromises, including the Missouri Compromise of 1820 (the admission of Missouri as a *slave state* only by balancing it with the admission of Maine as a *free state*) and the Kansas-Nebraska Act of 1854, which allowed the territories of Kansas and Nebraska to decide for themselves at the time of statehood whether to permit slavery or not. Such local option on slavery was called *popular sovereignty.*

By 1830 the talk among many abolitionists was that stopping the slave trade would never abolish slavery. Thus some of the more radical abolitionists, such as journalist William Lloyd Garrison and his followers, demanded immediate freedom for all slaves, forming the American Anti-Slavery Society in 1833. Now abolition became a militant word, polarizing the country and becoming anathema in the South, which was to call Union troops in the Civil War "abolition soldiers."

Some people had been helping runaway slaves escape northward since at least 1815. Around 1832 this movement grew into the *underground railroad*, a secret cooperating network that smuggled fugitive slaves from house to house, to eventual freedom in the Northern free states or Canada. The underground railroad got its name because railroads were just being introduced in the early 1830s and had caught the public's imagination. By the 1840s the network was often simply called the underground, a word used again in World War II to refer to European patriotic groups fighting the occupying Nazis and then used in the 1960s to refer to radical student groups fighting the American establishment.

The abolitionists gave us further new words and names. Antislavery Democrats included the New York faction called *Barnburners* (because its enemies accused it of being willing to *burn down* the Democratic *barn* to get rid of the proslavery *rats*). *Free soil* (1848) meant states or territories

A political cartoon lampooning the Democratic Party "barnburners," featuring Martin Van Buren as the fleeing "fox" (his nickname), his son at the ladder, and Franklin Pierce in the wagon.

where slavery was not permitted. The modern Republican Party was formed in 1854 after bitter abolitionist opposition to the Kansas-Nebraska Act split both the Democrats and the Whigs, and it soon absorbed the other abolition parties (the *Democratic Party* was founded in 1828). The South violently opposed the new Republican Party, which was against slavery in the new territories, and its "secular candidate" Abraham Lincoln in 1860; they felt *secession* from the Union (1830 in this use) was the only way left to preserve slavery, their economy, and their way of life.

The Fugitive Slave Act of 1850 not only provided a stiff fine and imprisonment for those helping slaves escape but also allowed slave owners to pursue and claim runaway slaves in any state, including free soil states. This so angered the abolitionists that many changed their cry from "Abolition!" to "Emancipation!" Thus after 1850 many who were against slavery called themselves emancipators (the 17th-century English political word emancipation, as in Abraham Lincoln's Emancipation Proclamation, comes from Latin emancipare, meaning "to release from bondage").

RECONSTRUCTION

Even before the Civil War was over, the Union began talking about *reconstruction* (1863) of the South. Thus *Reconstruction* and the *Reconstruction Period* came to mean the 12 years from 1865–77 when the Federal government controlled and Federal troops occupied the South, making the war-ravaged Southern states change their political and social institutions.

"It is rather for us, the living, to here be dedicated to the great task remaining before us—that from these honored dead we take increased devotion to that cause for which they gave the last full measure of devotion—that we here highly resolve that these dead shall not have died in vain; that this nation shall have a new birth of freedom; and that government of the people, by the people, for the people, shall not perish from the earth."—President Lincoln's closing comments, November 19, 1883, at the dedication of the Gettysburg National Cemetery.

"*Each state is a sovereign, and thus may reclaim the grants which it has made to any agent whomsoever.*"

— *Jefferson Davis, Senate Speech, January 21, 1861*

During the 1860s and 70s Reconstruction meant different things to different people. To Presidents Lincoln and Andrew Johnson it meant a quick and compassionate reunion of North and South. To the Northern Republicans who ruled Congress and were to have the final say, Reconstruction meant Federal control of the South until its political, social, and economic institutions were crushed and until, in appreciation, the newly freed slaves could make it a Republican stronghold. To the black South it meant an opportunity to step from slavery into full citizenship, vote, get an education, own land, and earn a living. To the white South, Reconstruction was a humiliating word, a synonym for submission, and many resisted it.

Carpetbagger (1868) was any Northerner who went to the South to gain political power, business advantages, cheap land, etc., during Reconstruction. The carpetbag was a common lightweight piece of luggage of 1840–70, consisting of two squares of carpeting sewn together. Thus, since the 1850s, carpetbagger had meant anyone who traveled fast and light, from carefree vacationers to itinerant businessmen, bankers, and gamblers who moved on before their goods and schemes were found to be fraudulent.

Most Americans had never heard the word *impeachment* until the House of Representatives voted articles of impeachment against President Johnson in 1868. It comes from the 14th-century English verb impeach (meaning "to impede, accuse," via French from Latin impedicare, "to entangle, put in fetters") and is used in the U.S. Constitution. Johnson had tried to follow Lincoln's wishes in his compassionate amnesty and Reconstruction proclamation; he bitterly fought Congress, which tried to get rid of the soft-on-the-South President by impeaching him. The House did impeach, but on May 26, 1868, after a two-month debate, the Senate finally failed to convict him, falling just one vote short of the two-thirds majority necessary to remove Johnson from office.

Radical Republicans (1865) were Northern Republicans who demanded that the Southern states meet stiff requirements before readmission to the Union (radical had been used since 1847 to refer to anyone strongly against slavery). *Scalawag* (1868) was the name Southern Democrats and unreconstructed rebels threw at white Southern Republicans, planters, and businessmen who accepted Reconstruction and cooperated with Northern politicians for their own political and financial gain; the word had meant a rascal or rogue since the 1840s, but its ultimate origin is disputed: It may come from the Gaelic sgalag, servant or rustic, or from Scalloway in the Shetland Islands, known for its dwarf ponies and cattle, thus perhaps coming to mean "a morally stunted person."

The *Solid South* (1876) was originally used to refer both to the solid Republican black vote and to the solid Democratic white vote in the South during Reconstruction. As soon as Reconstruction ended and the whites regained full political power, the Solid South came to mean only the solid Democratic vote. The South generally voted Democratic from 1877 to 1952, when Dwight Eisenhower's landslide finally broke the pattern.

Wave the bloody shirt was what Democrats accused the Republicans of doing throughout Reconstruction and until the 1890s, by which they meant Republicans tried to get votes by waving the bloody shirt of the Civil War, equating the Democrats with the Confederacy and slavery. Federal troops withdrew from the South in 1877, however, and Reconstruction was over.

"Politics makes strange bedfellows."

— *Charles Dudley Warner, editor, 1870, playing on Shakespeare's "Misery acquaints a man with strange bedfellows."*

William Marcy "Boss" Tweed, grand sachem of the Tammany Society—a post once held quite a bit more honorably by Martin Van Buren.

William Howard Taft in 1909 on a "whistle-stop" campaign—so named for the train whistles heard at each stop.

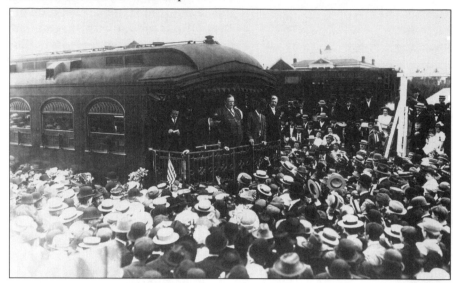

POLITICAL BOSSES

In the early 1870s most Americans were talking about *the Tweed Ring,* a group of corrupt New York City politicians led by William Marcy Tweed (1823–78), better known as Boss Tweed. He had been a leader of Tammany Hall, the New York City Democratic political organization, since 1859 and had absolute power in the party after 1868, controlling patronage and taking for himself positions that brought him power and wealth. But the people liked him, because he gave handouts to the poor and helped immigrants obtain their naturalization papers. In 1869-72 Boss Tweed's Tweed Ring milked New York City of up to $300 million; besides taking kickbacks, the ring used faked leases, false vouchers, and padded bills to steal city money. Tweed was finally jailed for forgery and larceny (1873–75). Though people had spoken of *political bosses* since the 1850s, Boss Tweed gave the term new life, and by the early 1880s *bossism* and *bossdom* were in wide use.

TEAPOT DOME

Teapot Dome was in the news from 1922 to 1929 and became the most talked-about political scandal until the 1990s and Watergate. The name refers to the Teapot Dome Reserve, a 9,321-acre oilfield on public land near Casper, Wyoming, which was set aside in 1915 as an oil reserve for the U.S. Navy. In 1921, President Warren G. Harding, at the insistence of his Secretary of the Interior, Albert B. Fall, signed an executive order transferring the naval petroleum reserves from the Navy to Fall's Department of the Interior. Secretary Fall then entered into secret negotiations to lease Teapot Dome to Harry Sinclair's Mammoth Oil Company and to lease a California naval oilfield to Edward Doheny's Pan American Petroleum Company. For these favors Fall received $223,000 in Liberty Bonds and a herd of cattle for his ranch from Sinclair, and a $100,000 cash "loan" from Doheny.

In 1923 a Senate committee began investigating Teapot Dome, and the country was soon rife with rumors of other corruption in the Harding Administration. While in Alaska in June on a speaking tour, Harding received a long, coded message from Washington, apparently informing him of the widespread corruption about to be exposed. He never recovered from the shock and the shame, took suddenly ill when he reached San Francisco, and died there on August 2, reportedly due to complications from ptomaine poisoning, though the cause of his death was never completely clear.

In February 1924, the Senate's investigative work was done, and in a joint resolution Congress directed President Calvin Coolidge, who had succeeded Harding, to begin civil and criminal prosecution of those involved in fraud and corruption. The oil leases were declared void by the Supreme Court, and Fall was finally convicted of accepting bribery and sentenced to a year in prison in 1929.

A CHICKEN IN EVERY POT

The phrase *A chicken in every pot*, a Democratic attack phrase, headlined a 1928 Republican Presidential campaign advertisement. The ad claimed that "Republican prosperity has put the proverbial `chicken in every pot.'"

Herbert Hoover never used the term himself, but he did use the phrase the full dinner pail in a 1928 campaign statement: "The slogan of progress is changing from the full dinner pail to the full garage."

Democrats managed to exploit both Republican statements in 1932 by creating a pseudo-promise from Hoover: "A chicken in every pot and two cars in every garage."

NEW DEAL

The New Deal was a phrase taken from Franklin Delano Roosevelt's acceptance speech at the Democratic National Convention in Chicago on July 2, 1932: "I pledge you, I pledge myself, to a new deal for the American people." The *Great Depression* was in its third year when Roosevelt won the 1933 presidential election promising "a new deal" for "the fogotten man," and in his inaugural address told the nation, "The only thing we have to fear is fear itself."

New Deal was probably a combination of Woodrow Wilson's New Freedom slogan and Teddy Roosevelt's Square Deal, and was coined either by Judge Samuel Rosenman or Columbia University professor Raymond Moley. The *forgotten man* was a term that the political scientist William Graham Sumner had popularized in his 1883 book *What the Social Classes Owe to Each Other*. F.D.R.'s "The only thing we have to fear is fear itself" was probably based on "Nothing is so much to be feared as fear," from Henry David Thoreau's Journal (1851).

The most significant legislation between the two World Wars, the New Deal introduced new language. *Brain trust* (1933) was first , coined by James Kieran, president of Hunter College, to describe the group of professors who advised Roosevelt and his later intellectual advisers, including social organizer Harry Hopkins (whose programs introduced the terms *underprivileged, social worker,* and *welfare* to millions of Americans).

The *hundred days,* which began on March 5, 1933, marked the period immediately following Roosevelt's inauguration on March 4, 1933. Never had so many reforms and sweeping legislative programs been put into effect in such a short time. On March 12, the new President gave his first evening radio talk, the first of the famous *fireside chats,* a name suggested by Harry Butcher, head of CBS's Washington office; F.D.R. eventually gave 30 of these, beginning with Roosevelt's familiar salutation "My friends. . . ."

Attempting to provide quick recovery from the Depression, the government began to form relief and public works measures, leading to the abbreviations of names into *alphabet agencies.* Sometimes called *alphabetical agencies* when the term was new in 1933, these agencies' initials included *NRA* (National Recovery Administration, 1933), to administer codes of fair business practice; *TVA* (Tennessee Valley Authority, 1933), to build 30 dams in Tennessee and surrounding states; and *WPA* (Works Progress Administration, 1935), to provide jobs in public work and the arts. *Food stamps* were introduced in 1939 as one of the last anti-Depression relief measures.

WATERGATE

Watergate was simply the name of a modern apartment building and office complex overlooking the Potomac in Washington, D. C., until the summer of 1972. Then it became the name of the biggest American political scandal since Teapot Dome, resulting in impeachment proceedings against President Richard M. Nixon and in his 1974 resignation.

It all began the night of June 17, 1972, in a presidential election year, when five burglars were arrested at the offices of the Democratic National Committee located in the Watergate complex. But they weren't really bur-

The Watergate scandal—accompanying the country's prolonged defeat in Vietnam, and following the assassinations of John F. Kennedy, Martin Luther King, and Robert F. Kennedy—helped foster the cynical distrust of government prevalent today.

A president addresses both houses of Congress. Gerald Ford delivering his farewell address in 1977.

glars at all: led by undercover agent James McCord, they had C.I.A. connections and had been paid to break into the Democratic headquarters by Nixon's Committee for the Re-election of the President (or *CREEP*, as it was sometimes called) to plant *bugs* or *taps*. *Bug* (late 1940s) is a concealed recording device; since 1889 cardsharps had used the word to mean a card stuck to the underside of a gambling table, for substitution into one's hand when profitable, and the image remained one of concealment and small size. *Tap* (early 1960s) came from the 1950s police and FBI use of *wire-tap*, an electronic device attached to a telephone or phone wire that taps, or siphons off, its signal so conversation can be secretly heard or recorded; since 1894 gamblers and confidence men had used the verb *wire tap* to mean to attach a line to a telegraph or telephone wire to get, or pretend to get, information on race results before bookies did and thus to be able to, or pretend to be able to, bet on a sure thing.

After Nixon's re-election, the continuing scandal led to Judge John Sirica's Watergate trial. Nixon accepted the resignations of top aides H.R. Haldeman and John Ehrlichman, dismissed White House counsel John Dean, and had Attorney General Elliot Richardson (who had replaced John Mitchell) select Archibald Cox as *Special* Watergate *Prosecutor*. This White House move, however, did not stop the Senate Select Committeee on Presidential Campaign Activities, under the chairmanship of Bible-quoting North Carolina Senator Sam Ervin, from beginning its televised "Watergate hearings" in July 1973. When those hearings revealed that Nixon had made tape recordings of his meetings and telephone calls (as had Presidents Kennedy and Johnson before him), the President, who had denied personal involvement in Watergate, refused to turn the tapes over to the Senate committee or the Special Watergate Prosecutor, even after being subpoenaed, by claiming *executive privilege*.

Prosecutor Cox persistently demanded the tapes, until Nixon had him fired, after Attorney General Richardson and his assistant had resigned rather than do so. The Saturday resignations and firings immediately became known as the *Saturday Night Massacre.* The new Special Prosecutor, Leon Jaworski, asked for all the tapes, and in July 1974 the U.S. Supreme Court ruled against Nixon's claim of executive privilege. By the end of July the House of Representatives passed articles of impeachment against the President. On August 5 he did release the last of the tapes' transcripts, except for a notorious *18-minute gap* that had been mysteriously erased from the tapes. By now even Nixon's staunchest supporters in Congress were convinced that he had been somehow involved in at least the Watergate *coverup* and had tried to obstruct justice. Knowing that he would certainly be impeached and found guilty in the Senate, Nixon resigned on August 7, 1974.

The Watergate scandal had a notable affect on the language. *Coverup*, used since 1942 for an excuse or false story to conceal a real plan or action, became the primary noun for the overall attempt by Nixon, his aides, and his cronies to avoid disclosures of who was responsible for the Watergate break-in. *Dirty trick*, which had meant a malicious or unfair act since 1868, had been used since 1967 for the C.I.A. division that plans espionage and other covert operations: *the dirty tricks department.* *Deep-six*, meaning "sink or destory deliberately," was 1920s Naval slang applied to Watergate evidence carried illegally or surreptitiously. *At that point in time* was used as a highfalutin replacement for *then* in the testimony of several Nixon aides, a borrowing from 1960s academic jargon. And the expression *expletive deleted*, which occurred in transcripts of the famous Oval Office tapes, became inextricably associated with the Watergate scandal.

Leak (1955) was any unofficial or improper disclosure of government or political secrets (also used in the leaking of the *Pentagon Papers* to the press). *Stonewall*, a metaphor for steadfastness taken from Confederate General Thomas J. Jackson's nickname "Stonewall" for standing firm at the first Battle of Bull Run in 1861, was also a cricket term (first cited in Australia in the 1950s) used with contempt to describe delaying or defensive tactics. The words *stonewall* and *stonewalling* were frequently mentioned by Nixon and his associates as the keynote of their *game plan* during the Watergate investigation.

Watergate opened many a related *-gate*. First was *Winegate*, a mid-1970s French scandal about impurities in the best Bordeaux. In 1976, charges of corruption in Congress caused by South Korea became *Koreagate*. Two years later, Congressman Daniel Flood became the focus of controversy in *Floodgate*. Through the late 1980s and early 90s, *-gate* served as the political-scandal suffix of choice, from 1989's *Iraqgate* (about the use of grain credits to supply rocket technology to Iraq), to 1993's *travelgate* (for the dismissal of the White House travel staff in order to replace its head with a relative of Bill Clinton), and to *filegate* (1996–97) denoting unauthorized requests by Clinton White House personnel of FBI files on a large number of American citizens, some previous Bush administration members. It rejoined *water* in the mid-1990s *Whitewatergate*, for hearings on the Clintons' financial dealings in Arkansas before his presidency.

Since Watergate, the language of American politics has been, in turn, international and regional, animalistic and colorful, from *inside the Beltway* terms to the attack phrases of *negative advertising*.

CENTURY'S END

Changes around the world at the end of the 20th century have influenced America's political terminology. The *Cold War* (a 1946 coinage for the nonmilitary conflict between the Soviet Union and the West) led to the 1992 use of *post-Cold War*, for the uncertain East-West relations after the Soviet Union's dissolution. Americans became familiar with adopted Russian words such as *glasnost* (for "openness," as in freedom of speech) and *perestroika* (for "restructuring" of the Soviet economy).

In a *new world order* (George Bush's 1990 use of a 1965 term, stemming ultimately from a Latin slogan first in Virgil, *novus ordo seclorum*,"a new order of the ages" (found on the back of dollar bills), the prospect of peaceful cooperation throughout the world was raised. Many terms with *diplomacy* have marked the foreign policy of the past century. *Dollar diplomacy* (1910) was the term for William Howard Taft's defense of *substituting dollars for bullets* in Central American policy. *Gunboat diplomacy* (1927) referred to Western use of naval force to protect American interests in China during the early 1900s. *Ping-Pong diplomacy* (1970) referred to the opening of relations between the United States and China with games between players from both countries. *Quiet diplomacy* (1976) was Henry Kissinger's term for the importance of

Speaker of the House Newt Gingrich, and to his immediate right, Christian Coalition Executive Director Ralph Reed. On the heels of the successful "Contract with America," the two presented a less popular sequel: the "Contract with the American Family," which called for school prayer and restrictions on abortion.

making private diplomatic moves behind the scenes. First used in 1973, *shuttle diplomacy* meant diplomatic efforts conducted by a mediator traveling back and forth between the major players.

Meanwhile, domestic issues continued to vie with foreign policy for the attention of the American voter. Americans more concerned with domestic problems than foreign disputes sought a *paradigm shift*, historian Thomas Kuhn's 1970 term for reducing the size of bureaucracy and *reinventing government* (1992). The stress on domestic policy has led to several *issue* terms, including *character issue* (1979), the moral fitness (or, more often, unfitness) of a candidate; and *gut issue* (1964), an issue that evokes an emotional or *gut-level* response. *Hot-button issue* (1992, with *hot button* used in politics since 1981), is any issue or term that instantly causes the voter to get agitated or concerned.

Magnet issue (1993) refers to the ability of an issue to cause unification or to draw voters together. *Pocketbook issue* (1970), known in the 19th century as *bread-and-butter*, indicates any economic issue that hits the voter directly in the wallet. *Single-issue politics* (1978) is the use of a single issue (such as abortion or gun control) as the deciding factor in an election, while *wedge issue* (1989), the opposite of a *magnet issue*, is an issue that divides or drives a wedge into a constituency. In 1996, *issues advocacy* was attacked as a loophole in spending laws for elections that allows unlimited amounts of money to urge a position on an issue instead of a specific candidate.

In politics, however, identifying the "issue" is not nearly as important as identifying one's position among myriad possibilities. Members of each party strive to make an opponent's position look like *political extremism* (1964) and their own positions an ideal of *political moderation* (1954), also known as *centrism* (1872), *middle of the road* (1892), or *mainstream* (1963 as a political metaphor). From *left-wing* to *right-wing* (1707 military terms), in the Democrat and Republican and Independent parties, the variations are seemingly endless:

Bleeding heart, a 1930s derogative term for a liberal.

Knee-jerk, an 1876 medical term applied to liberals in 1951 for a supposedly unthinking response to an issue.

Troglodyte, used since 1980 for anybody so reactionary as to seem like a caveman.

Neoconservative, 1955, for any former liberal who has accepted conservative views.

Christian Coalition, a 1990s conservative constituency led by Ralph Reed, champion of the *Christian Right*, espousing traditional *family values* (1966) and attacking abortion and gay rights.

Common sense conservatism, 1996, the philosophy proposed by 1996 Republican candidate Bob Dole to appeal to the mainstream voter, popularized by House Speaker Newt Gingrich in his *Contract With America*, a package of legislation on which he had campaigned in 1994.

STIR UP THE ANIMALS

The nation's first "dark horse." When the 1844 Democratic National Convention was deadlocked, the relatively unknown Governor of Tennessee, James Polk, was given the nomination. He would earn a very narrow victory over Henry Clay in November, as his support of "manifest destiny" helped him overcome his opponent's tactic of repeatedly asking "Who is James Polk?"

From *cattle show* to *zoo plane*, American political vocabulary is rich in animal phrases. This is nothing new; since Aristotle first referred to man as a *political animal*, the imagery has been multiplying.

Stir up the animals (1948), for example, is any action that causes undesirable political controversy or leads to unneeded criticism. In 1993, Dee Dee Myers was the Clinton White House press secretary who called the White House press corps "the beasts." The political parties themselves have proudly adopted beastly symbols: the 1874 cartoons of Thomas Nast in *Harper's Weekly* led to the donkey as the Democrats' symbol and the elephant as the Republican animal.

Those who fear that politics may be going to the dogs can look to the canine metaphors, among them *watchdog committee* (1951), a group appointed to oversee spending and eliminate wastefulness; *that dog won't hunt*, a 1980s Southernism to dismiss an idea as pointless; and *pit-bull politics* (1988), dirty tricks in politics (although George Bush also used the *pit bulls* metaphor to indicate tenacity and fearlessness):

Hail of dead cats, 1943, the raining down of criticism when a controversial public figure leaves political office or appointment.

Cattle show, 1979, a put-down of a public showing of presidential candidates in a primary; this term replaced the equally derisive *beauty contest*.

Copperhead, 1775, the snake; 1809, any hostile person), 1862, a Southern sympathizer in the North.

Dark horse, 1844, an outsider candidate unlikely to win unless the leading contenders become deadlocked. (A *war horse*, on the other hand, has been in political use since the 19th century for any veteran politician, especially one who has survived especially brutal campaigns.)

Lame duck, 1830s, an officeholder known to be leaving office and therefore weakened in power.

Like ugly on an ape, 1948, meaning "completely" or "thoroughly," popularized during the Bush Administration and usually used to describe a full-scale attack of an idea or individual.

Skunk at the garden party, a 1970s phrase for a problem or individual that stands out as undesirable.

Sharks in a feeding frenzy, in use since 1977 to denote overzealous or excessive behavior by journalists fighting over a story. (Since 1968, TV news film crews relegated to a less-important airplane in a presidential campaign have designated that second-order jet the *zoo plane*.)

Colorful coinages have also painted American politics, from *blue smoke and mirrors* (1975, for an illusion used to trick or manipulate) to *redheaded Eskimo* (1986, for a legislative bill affecting a very narrow or nonexistent constituency). Occasionally, animal and color imagery have even combined, from *yellow dog Democrat* (a 1928 Southernism for any party loyalist, one who "would vote for a yellow dog if he ran on the Democratic ticket") to *blue dog Democrats* (a 1980s term from Louisiana where a prominent billboard created by the artist George Rodrigue advertises a blue dog with yellow eyes; in the 1990s, the term came to Washington for maverick Democrats willing to support conservative plans to reduce the Federal deficit—similar to *boll weevils*, the 1950s term used of themselves by Southern conservative Democrats).

INSIDE THE BELTWAY

Often decried as *bureaucratese* (1949) and *gobbledygook* (1943), many Washington words are now derided as being *inside the Beltway* (1977, from the circular highway that surrounds the capital), of more interest to insiders than to the country at large. Much of that lingo takes the form of acronym and cliché.

The short forms, popularized in the 1930s by the alphabet agencies, now include acronyms, abbreviations, and euphemisms. For example, *MEGO* (1969), the acronym for "my eyes glaze over," is used to describe information that is stupefyingly dull despite its importance; *Tanstaafl* (1966), a long acronym for "there ain't no such thing as a free lunch," states the obvious truth that nothing comes without cost. *T-word* (1987) became a euphemism for *taxes* and one of a host of shortenings of unpleasant terms, including the *A-question* for campaign questions about *adultery* and the U-word for *unemployment*. The stand-alone word *isms* (based on the suffix *-ism*) labels philosophies formed from names with this suffix attached, from *McCarthyism* (1950), for the Communist-hunting techniques of Senator Joseph R. McCarthy, to *Buchananism*, a 1996 attempt to belittle the ideas of the ultraconservative candidate Pat Buchanan. *C.Y.A.* was a euphemistic 1970s abbreviation of "cover your ass," particularly popular in deflecting future blame for past actions. Even our leaders turned into acronyms in the 1990s, including the Secret Service's use of *Potus* (for "President of the United States") and *Flotus* (for "First Lady of the United States"); as *Flotus*, Hillary Rodham Clinton's prominence generated references to *co-Presidency* and *the Clintons* to show her elevated position as First Lady.

Cliché, even more prevalent than acronym, has flourished in every level of government. Here are some of the most frequent offenders:

Cautiously optimistic, 1980s, a Reagan comment that has become the standard reply by politicians avoiding a show of undue enthusiasm.

Evil empire, 1983, a Reagan attack on totalitarianism in what was then the Soviet Union.

Fire in the belly, 1882, the trite metaphor for a politician's burning desire or inner spirit of determination to win.

Fishing expedition, 1940, used to label any investigation or in-depth study that lacks focus or goals.

Go ahead, make my day, 1983, a challenge to action that will supposedly result in the pleasure of whoever issues the dare; Ronald Reagan, holding his veto pen, based this imperative challenge on the words of Clint Eastwood in a *Dirty Harry* movie.

Morning in America, 1984, an image of freshness for the country; this cliché, first used in Ronald Reagan's second presidential campaign, may be lifted up as a symbol of political hopefulness or played down as an attack on undue optimism.

Read my lips, 1957, used to insist that listeners pay close attention; at the 1988 Republican National Convention, George Bush promised to tell Congressional leaders wanting to raise taxes, "Read my lips: No new taxes."

Depending on the part of the country a candidate hails from, that person's clichés may well reflect a regional bias. Bill Clinton's Arkansas roots, for example, show up in one of his favorite sayings: "Even a blind hog can find an acorn."

NEGATIVE ADVERTISING

America's politicians have frequently demonstrated the ability to handle invective inventively and to deflect charges of *dirty tricks.* Modern slang-whanging, particularly by Presidents and presidential candidates who must learn to take hits as well as give them, has produced the following:

There you go again, 1980, Ronald Reagan's deft dismissal of Jimmy Carter's attacks during the presidential campaign debates.

Negative advertising, 1980s, a phrase for political commercials used to attack the opponent rather than feature the candidate. The 1990s use of *negative* as a noun refers to any trait or viewpoint that will weigh against a politician's popularity. (To forestall attacks on weak areas, a candidate may use *inoculation,* a 1985 political term for using one's own advertising to admit weaknesses before others can attack.)

Out of the loop, 1985, a usage for "uninformed" or "outside the group"; this phrase, which George Bush employed to deny involvement in Iran-contra deals of arms for hostages, can be used either to attack another person as an outsider or to plead one's own innocence.

Policy wonk, 1984, the standard label for any government worker who enjoys studying the most intricate details of policy and program development; this phrase was applied to both Bill Clinton and Al Gore during their 1992 campaign.

Bubba vote, 1991, a campaign phrase based on *bubba,* a much older term for a Southerner; this label, first used derogatorily, indicates the force of Southern voting, specifically by white conservative males.

Convention bounce, 1980, a sudden temporary rise of a candidate in poll ratings after the national convention of that candidate's party; previously known as a *bump,* this dramatic surge in popularity is usually dismissed as the result of the extensive media coverage of both the candidate and the convention.

Push-polling, 1994, negative advertising by telephone, as political surveying disguises the true intent of pushing voters away from one candidate and toward another.

Spinmeister, 1987, a label for campaign advisers versed in putting their own expert *spin* or analysis onto the public's perception of a speech or event; this term is based on the similar 1984 *spin doctor.*

Sleaze factor. 1983, the charge of widespread minor corruption among a politician's associates or colleagues; Democrats used the term in 1984 to label a pattern of petty corruption in Reagan's Administration.

Teflon-coated, 1983, the attack phrase for a politician who is able to evade or avoid being covered by charges of corruption, levied against Ronald Reagan, alluding to the trademark *Teflon* for nonstick cookware. (See POP CULTURE.)

Buttons from Wendell Willkie's 1940 campaign and Thomas Dewey's 1944 campaign. Both men tried to capitalize on the concerns raised by FDR's seeking of third and fourth terms, but neither managed to garner even 100 electoral votes. Term limits on the Presidency were eventually established in 1951 in the 22nd Amendment to the Constitution.

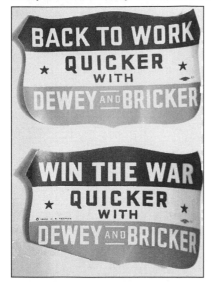

Velcro-coated, 1989, from the trademark *Velcro* for a fabric tape that adheres, this phrase is the opposite of *Teflon-coated* and indicates a politician likely to be hurt by charges of corruption against associates and underlings. Related is *Velcroid* (1992), a political *groupie* who tries to maintain excessive closeness to a political leader.

Bubble (political use since 1992), the figurative protective shield that surrounds a political leader and creates a barrier between that leader and the public; an earlier attack word was *cocoon*, suggesting a nest of security that prevents the leader from seeing the real world.

Déjà voodoo, 1993, an attack (playing on *déjà vu*) on the return of populist economics theories previously disparaged; in 1980, George Bush used *voodoo economics* in his attack on Ronald Reagan's supply-side economic theories months before Bush became Reagan's running mate.

You're no Jack Kennedy, 1988, a leveling charge by one candidate that another has overestimated himself or herself; during the 1988 debate between Vice Presidential candidates, Democrat Lloyd Bentsen attacked Republican Dan Quayle for comparing his own qualifications with those of John F. Kennedy: "Senator, I served with Jack Kennedy, I knew Jack Kennedy. Jack Kennedy was a friend of mine. Senator, you're no Jack Kennedy."

Gridlock, 1980, the urban term for a huge, hopeless traffic jam, applied metaphorically to legislative backup; during his third-party campaign in 1992, Ross Perot pledged to clear up the *legislative gridlock* that had stalled the government for a dozen years.

It's the economy, Stupid!, 1992, reminder of the central issue or theme in a campaign; Bill Clinton's advisers successfully used this mocking motto to keep themselves aware of the major issue during the 1992 campaign.

Smoking gun (a 1970s political variation of the *smoking pistol* in an 1894 Sherlock Holmes story), damaging and undeniable evidence of wrong-doing; the latest variant, perhaps sparked by the cynicism of the times, is the allegation of sexual misconduct in the 1991 phrase *smoking bed.*

Term limits, 1970s, a call for a constitutional amendment to prohibit the habitual return of the same politicians to the same offices.

POP CULTURE

*A*mericans *"talk pop culture," often without realizing that its elements—
especially from commerce, publicity, music, movies, radio, and television—
have permeated our daily vocabulary.*

Marilyn Monroe stands over a
subway grate in the 1955 film *The
Seven Year Itch.*

Pop culture is the sum total of the arts and artifacts and the creativity
behind them that represent generalized mass tastes, widely disseminated
usually on a commercialized basis. *Commercialized* is the key word: figurative uses of registered trademarks occur so often in American writing
that they are part of a pop cultural "shorthand."

THE "BRANDING" OF AMERICAN ENGLISH

All this might be called the "branding" of American English, its chief
impetus and means of dissemination the advertising industry and the
media. And so words are purveyed into the mental *Rolodex*es of Americans:

Cadillac, "Publishers only want to print *Cadillac* names . . . and I sup-
pose I'm a *Volkswagen*" (poet-novelist Ishmael Reed to *Newsweek*,
1975, on his degree of "name recognition").

Kool-Aid, "Sorry is the *Kool-Aid* of human emotions" (Stephen King,
Carrie).

Tabasco, "the *Tabasco*-tempered 11-day walkout" (*Christian Science
Monitor*).

Teflon, "If Ronald Reagan can be said to have a '*Teflon* presidency' in
which negatives don't stick [the expression having been first used by
U.S. Representative Patricia Schroeder in August 1983 in her Colorado
kitchen], then [the judge's] political and judicial career can be
described as 'polyester'—not pretty, but durable" (*Boston Globe*).

And so we worry over *Band-Aid* solutions to problems as we *Xerox* documents; a woman or girl can wear *Barbie* clothes, a First Lady can be
accused of putting together an *Edsel* of a health-care reform plan, a
woman can be called a *Betty Crocker* mom whose family is part of the
Winnebago camping crowd disdained by the *Volvo* set, and a meal in a
fast-food outlet might be called a *Di-Gel* dining experience—in any case,
not a *Princess Cruise* through the language.

WHAT'S IN A NAME?

Yet another trend that plays off the *Walter Mitty, Rube Goldberg* model is
the use of names of the rich, the famous, and the infamous as parts of
speech like adjectives, generic nouns, and verbs. This trend was especially pointed in the later 1980s into the 1990s, and it went well beyond
standard uses like *Chaucerian, Machiavellian, Hitlerite, Stalinization,
Clintonomics, Reaganite, lynch,* and *guillotine:*

Grishamize, to turn an author into a highly lucrative "property" by use
of book-movie tie-ins in an aggressive marketing campaign, a verb

"Make not my father's house a house of merchandise."
　　　　　　　—John 2:16.
Jim and Tammy Faye Baker in 1987.

coined by John Conti, a divisional vice president at Ballantine (1993), referring to best-selling novelist John Grisham: "'We *Grishamized* [author Michael] Crichton'" (to *Publishers Weekly*, December 1993).

Idi Amin, a cruel, despicable leader: "Weirdos change, like anyone else. Jim Jones was everyone's hero until he turned into *Idi Amin*" (Jonathan Kellerman, *Blood Test*, 1986).

Jim-and-Tammyfication, shameless public confessions and self-revelations, named after televangelist Jim Bakker and his wife Tammy Faye when he was exposed in 1987 in a sex scandal and for mishandling church contributions: "A public figure [a politician] has been wounded. And the rest of us have moved one step closer to the *Jim-and-Tammyfication* of America" (*Washington Post*, February 1992).

Willie Horton, a wedge sociopolitical issue used in political attack ads that serve to fragment a voting bloc, going back to the 1989 presidential campaign when Republicans castigated Democratic presidential candidate Michael Dukakis for furloughing violent criminals while governor of Massachusetts. Willie Horton was an African American convicted murderer who had raped a white woman while furloughed from a Massachusetts prison: "[The then-mayor of the District of Columbia, Sharon Pratt Kelly] expressed fear that the Republicans 'might try to make the District the *Willie Horton* of 1992.' She's right in identifying the attack as another form of *Willie Hortonism*" (*Washington Post*, August 12, 1992).

Use of such terms presupposes instant name recognition and instant biographical-character recall on the part of the listener or reader. Parallels are to be seen in language derived from the movies, cartoons, comics, television, and music.

I HEAR AMERICA SINGING

Though the colonists brought with them folk songs and ballads from their native land, they quickly altered the lyrics to fit their new environment and then created their own new songs. The earliest dated American popular song is "Springfield Mountain," which detailed the snakebite death on August 7, 1761 of a man from Springfield Mountain, Massachusetts, now the town of Wilbraham.

So-called dilettante composers wrote *household music* in the mid 1800s and afterward—ballads and other songs that would have been the 19th century equivalent of our own *easy listening* or *elevator music*. The lyrics were in easily understood common language, appealing to the masses. Popular music was born!

But the first real popular music composer of national note was Stephen Foster (1826–64), famed for "O Susannah" (an anthem of the gold-seeking 49ers) and many more.

MINSTRELS
Today a *minstrel* (1864, this sense) show having performers in *blackface* (1869), with *end men* (1865) at each side of the line of performers joshing with the interlocutor, would be considered in bad taste at the least, racist at worst. But in the 19th century the minstrels, a U.S. creation, provided a single source of mass entertainment with their programs of African American songs and melodies, jokes, and impersonations. The first one, called the Virginia Minstrels, performed on February 6, 1843 as part of the Bowery Circus. Yet, all in all, the min-

B.B. King and his guitar, Lucille, entertaining at the Dade County stockade in 1971. King has been playing the blues since 1950, and he received a Grammy Lifetime Achievement Award in 1987.

strels had a significant impact on the development of American popular music—and acting, like the *vaudeville* shows (*vaudeville* cited to 1739 in the sense of a light theatrical piece made up of pantomime, dialogue, and singing, coming from French *vau-de-Vire*, valley of Vire, a southwestern French town where light theatrical songs were written; cited to 1827, a light play or comedy interspersed with songs; cited to 1911, a variety show—a U.S. usage).

RAGTIME

In the 1880s the nation was taken by storm by a popular music movement—ragtime—thanks to the work of itinerant musicians playing pianos in bars, the development of the player piano, and the promulgation of commercial sheet music. *Ragtime* (1897)—characterized by strong Afro-Caribbean dance rhythms and regular, strong drumming—may be a clipped form of *ragged time*, the rhythms executed by the pianist's left hand in playing piano *rags* (also 1897), but the origin is still uncertain. One of the most famous ragtime *piano thumpers* was Scott Joplin.

In 1908 everyone was talking about the new ragtime dance, the *turkey trot*, which resembed just that in the way the dancers moved, with a springing step on the balls of their feet, while jerking their shoulders up and down.

Duke Ellington's music was a blend of blues, jazz, and swing.

LADY SINGS THE BLUES

Blues, with musical roots in African American spirituals, expressed in secular terms the same hopelessness and despair conveyed by the spirituals. The *blues*, originally a shortening of *blue devils*, cited to 1741 and meaning "depression," took on the music sense, influenced by the frequency of *blue notes* in 12-bar sequences. The term in the music context is cited to 1912.

ALL THAT JAZZ

In 1917 the *Literary Digest* informed its readers that an odd new word, *jazz* (also spelled *jas*), had sprung up among popular musicians. The

"The King of Swing," Benny Goodman, in 1940. Goodman was one of the first white bandleaders to play with black musicians.

word is, to this day, of contested and murky origin, though we are reasonably sure that the music it denotes was originally created by a small group of African American and Creole musicians while jamming in New Orleans prior to 1900. We also know that the constituent elements of jazz include slave work songs, African melodies, prisoners' work chants, and various French and Spanish melodies familiar to the Creoles.

As for the origin of the word *jazz*, theories—all unproved for sure—abound: It might be derived form the names of certain African American performers like Jasbo (*Jas*) Brown of Chicago; it might come from *jaser*, a Louisiana Creole word, "to speed up" or "to chatter"; it might be a borrowing from an African language; or it might be a derivation of an American dialect verb meaning to have sex, the last theory prompting Clay Smith to remark that "if the truth were known about the origin of the word 'Jazz' it would never be mentioned in polite society" ("Where is Jazz Leading America?" in *Etude*, 1924). Scholars still aren't sure when the word first appeared, or whether or not the noun or the verb is the older, but the noun is cited to 1913; the verb, to 1917; *jazzy*, to 1919; and *jazzman*, to 1926.

SWING IT!

Swing, which flourished from the 1920s into the 1940s, was the first new music craze to set Americans' tongues wagging with a whole new language, hep talk, used by those wearing zoot suits and flapper dresses (see FASHIONS OF THE TIMES). And along came a host of new dances named the *Suzie-Q*, the *Lindy*, the *jitterbug* (1938), and *trucking*. The advent of the Swing Era really marked the coming-of-age of pop culture.

Swing is a form of jazz played by a large dance band—a *Big Band* (1926) that gives a *Big Band Sound* marked by lively rhythm, simple harmony, and improvisation over a basic melody. Cited to 1899, *swing* was used in the context of "two-step and hot rag *swing*." But Artie Shaw is credited with introducing it on a national scale in the 1930s.

It was left to Charlie "Bird" Parker and John Birks "Dizzy" Gillespie to take the style one step further to the 1940s *beebop* (or *bebop*)—cited to 1944—or just plain *bop* (cited to 1947).

FOLK MUSIC

In the 1950s folk music took off with the Kingston Trio's "Tom Dooley," whose roots lay in the 100-year-old Blue Ridge Mountain ballad spelled and titled "Tom Dula." Kids flocked to *hootenannies* (cited to 1925, origin unknown, in the sense "a gadget"; perhaps first used in the sense "a gathering of people for entertainment" in July 1940 by *Washington New Dealer* editors Bertha and Terry Pettus with reference to a series of political fundraising events involving dinners, dancing, and stage entertainment all in one). At the hootenannies folk singers performed with the audience joining in.

COUNTRY MUSIC

The Grand Ole Opry radio/television show—the longest-running such show in U.S. history—means country music, originally called *hillbilly music*. This moniker was originally selected many years ago by Ralph Peer of Okeh Records, when he asked fiddler Al Hopkins what Hopkins called his band. Hopkins indicated that they were just a bunch of North Carolina and Virginia *hillbillies*, and so his band became known as The Hillbillies. And so the term *hillbilly music* was born. *Billboard* magazine is credited with devising the term *country-and-western* (cited in print to 1960), abbreviated as *C&W*, then becoming simply *country*.

Garth Brooks singing the National Anthem at the 1993 Super Bowl, while actress Marlee Matlin signs for the deaf. Brooks combined country lyrics and twang with a rock 'n' roll backbeat and stage show to become one of the highest grossing performers in popular music.

It was country that formed the basis for *rock-a-billy* (1956), a style melding gospel and African American rhythms plus elements of the blues. In the 1980s and 90s yet another popular style had become very popular—a mix of country and rock called, naturally, *country rock*.

ROCK AROUND THE CLOCK

Though the term *rock-and-roll* is cited to 1954, it was on July 9, 1955—when *Billboard* listed "Rock Around the Clock" by Bill Haley and the Comets as the week's Number One single—that *rock-and-roll* reached the national consciousness in a big-time way.

The King of rock-and-roll was Elvis Presley (1935–77), nicknamed "Elvis the Pelvis" at his first big concert on August 10, 1954 at the Overton Park Shell, Memphis, during which he brought the house down with a bump-and-grind version of "That's All Right, Mama." With this performance emerged the first sensational *pop culture icon* (to use 1990s terminology), *icon* deriving from the Greek verb *eikon*, "to resemble." Other such *celebs* (1912) would be, of course, James Dean, Buddy Holly, Marilyn Monroe, Liberace, Prince, Bette Midler, Madonna, Michael Jackson, Bill Cosby, The Beatles, and many more.

Elvis as a *phenom* (around 1890) seized the nation for real on April 3, 1956, when 40 million viewers watched him on Milton Berle's television show. The kids—especially the girls—went crazy over him, and many parents and music critics called him "lewd" and "obscene." Parents worried about an impending fall of civilization, a subsequent TV show banned below-the-waist footage of Elvis while performing, and more than 50,000 people fought over 100 available seats in the studio to watch him on Ed Sullivan's show.

This type of response was equaled only one more time on a national level—with "the British invasion" of *The Beatles*. As with Elvis, parents

"'Elvis Presley is an icon in many ways,' says filmmaker and anthropologist Bill Ferris, the . . . director [of the University of Mississippi Center for the Study of Southern Culture]. 'He is the greatest popular culture figure of our century.'"

— Smithsonian, *November 1995*

Elvis at the 1956 state fair in his hometown of Tupelo, Mississippi, his hips live and uncensored.

were alarmed with the hysteria and affronted by The Beatles' "long" hair, which was far from the big, wild hair later associated with the hippies and *heavy metal* (1974) musicians.

People picked up lyrics from The Beatles' songs and regularly used them in conversation ("I had *a hard day's night* and so I overslept" is typical). When the group eventually broke up, fans worldwide were stunned, and when John Lennon was gunned down and killed in New York City in 1980, the country and most of the youth culture of the world mourned in the manner that they had done on August 16, 1977 when Elvis Presley was found dead in his bathroom.

But fans of Elvis didn't just "let it be." *Elvis sightings* persisted into the 1990s, with *Elvis impersonators* competing in shows across the land. *Elvis lives!* was pronounced by bumperstickers.

WOODSTOCK NATION: IT ROCKED!

On August 15, 1969 at 7:00 A.M. over 400,000 young people began to fill a 600-acre dairy pasture in White Lake, New York near Bethel in Sullivan County to attend the biggest rock music *happening* (1959, in the sense of "an improvised artistic event") in U.S., maybe world, history. It was called the Woodstock Music and Art Fair, a three-day event named after the Woodstock, New York recording studio and Woodstock Ventures, the organizers. Rock bands and folk singers performed to a crowd that grew to over 400,000, the pall of pot smoke heavy in the air and the ground muddy. *Woodstock* came to be a symbol of social protest against racism, President Nixon, the Vietnam War and all wars, hatred, poverty, and the odious Establishment generally. And *Woodstock Nation* came to mean that group of disaffected youth represented by the attendees, who formed a "nation" outside the established nation of the United States in terms of morality, values, and lifestyle. This sing-in and love-in marked the apex of *rock* (1957)—*rock* being popular music played on electronically amplified instruments, with a heavily accented beat and combining elements of country, folk, and blues. Not so coincidentally, the term *acid rock*— songs with lyrics referring to drug use—also is first cited in the year 1969. And along came numerous *rock* uses like *rock album, rock artist, rock band, rock beat, rock culture, rock festival, rock group, rock guitarist, rock lyric, rock music/musician, rock opera* (like *Hair* [1968] which gave us the *Age of Aquarius* in the song "Aquarius" and "Let the Sunshine In"; *Jesus Christ Superstar* [1971], music by Andrew Lloyd Webber; and *Tommy* [1969] with The Who), *rock singer/singing/song*, and *rock star* (all, late 1960s-late 1970s), moving in the late 1970s-early 1980s to *punk rock*, that vulgar, belligerent sound typified by The Sex Pistols.

Out of Woodstock Nation emerged a cult band, The Grateful Dead (who supposedly got their name by looking words up in a dictionary while stoned). They have fans called *Deadheads*. There are Grateful Dead fanzines and a *Deadbase* listing every word ever used in a Grateful Dead song lyric. When Grateful Dead guitarist Jerry Garcia (for whom Ben and Jerry had named an ice cream flavor "Cherry Garcia") died in 1995, Deadheads nationwide realized that the perennial *road trip* of the singer who had once called himself *Captain Trips* while wearing an Uncle Sam hat in concert had at last ended.

Then along came *disco* (late 1970s in the pop music sense, the word a clipping of French *discotheeque*, nightclub), recorded music with strong, repetitive bass rhythms, played by a disc jockey in a nightclub, using an interplay of lights, with New York City's Studio 54 and John

"The New York State Thruway's closed, man."—Performer Arlo Guthrie onstage at Woodstock. Four months later, another massive rock concert proved far less serene than the "three days of peace and love" in Bethel, New York. The Rolling Stones hired the Hell's Angels motorcycle gang to provide "security" for a free show at the Altamont Speedway in Northern California; when four died, including a spectator killed by The Angels, many felt that the "summer of love" had officially ended.

What a long strange trip it's been. Jerry Garcia in June 1995, at one of his last concert appearances. The Grateful Dead's music managed to blend early rock 'n' roll, bluegrass, freeform jazz, country and western, and tribal rhythms.

Travolta's movie *Saturday Night Fever* (1977) synonymous with this relatively short-lived but important craze.

On August 1, 1981, *MTV*, or *music television*, emerged, propelling the styles and values of especially the hip-hop generation and *rap* music to the fore (see YO! AMERICA RAPS). American English has been on a roller coaster ride peopled by *disc jockeys* (1941) and *deejays* (1949) playing nonstop *Top 100*s and *Top 10*s plus *oldies but goodies* (*Oldie*, 1940; *good old oldies*, 1970; *golden oldies*, 1973). The language and the styles of popular music have been on a seemingly never-ending *American Bandstand* (1947, the Dick Clark television show). From the *hokey pokey* (traced via a 1945 *Dance* magazine citation to World War II England), jitterbug, Charleston, rumba, tango, and others, Americans *boogied* (verb, 1930, a clipping of *boogie-woogie*, 1928, a percussive style of piano blues) till they dropped, doing the *limbo* (around 1950, probably ultimately from an African language); the *twist* (popularized in 1960 by Chubby "Let's Twist Again Like We Did Last Summer" Checker—a 10-year phenomenon), the *shimmy* (a wilder, more suggestive version of the twist involving torso and pelvic shaking), the *frug* (1964, origin unknown), the *hully gully* (1964, origin unknown), the *boogaloo* (1960s, with origins in a Black English word, "to dance"), the *monkey* (1964, called by one writer "a hang-loose mating ritual"), the *watusi* (1964, from the name of a people of Rwanda and Burundi, who are more often called the *Tutsi*), the *pony* (1963), the *jerk* (1966, a burlesque kind of twist), not to mention the *Loco-Motion* (from the song of that name, which generated the dance) and the *Mashed Potato* —also the name of a song—both from the early 1960s.

By 1989 the sexually suggestive *lambada* had appeared, the word from Portuguese *lamb(ar)*, to whip + -*ada,* an ending respelled to -*ade*, used in loanwords from Romance languages to mean in English "an action or process," as in *cannonade.* The dance goes back to 1930s Brazil. The fad (thence the word) quickly faded, yielding pride of place in the late 1990s to the *Macarena* (first cited in 1996)—a *line dance* involving arm and hip movements. Whether it, like the *electric slide* (1989), will exhibit staying power is an open question. This is a *conga* line (1935, American Spanish, *Danza Conga*, Congo dance, from *Kongo*, the African people and their language)—yes, a *Mexican hat dance*—of a changing pop music culture. It ranges from Seattle *grunge* to *karaoke* (*karaoke* from Japanese, "empty orchestra," the word meaning the singing, by amateurs, of pop songs, accompanied by prerecorded music). And it continues with *techno* (electronic dance music with a driving beat and psychedelic distortion of sound), popular at 1980s *raves*—all-night dance parties—moving into the 1990s mainstream.

LET'S GO TO THE MOVIES

First, there was *motion picture* and *moving picture* (both, 1896); then the slangy *movie* (1912)—objected to for many years by the powers that be in the industry; *moviemaker* in 1915; *moviedom* in 1916; and *moviegoer* in 1923, with the first motion picture shown to the public on April 23, 1896 in New York City as an "added attraction" to a vaudeville show. This opened the curtain on an industry that would, like its successor and competitor television, indelibly change the texture of American English.

For several years after their initial development, in which Thomas Edison was a key player, motion pictures were, indeed, only a novelty. They were attractions in vaudeville houses and music halls, or entire programs in *store shows* (small stores serving as motion picture theaters by the addition of folding chairs) or *5¢ shows* (because one could see the entire performance of short pictures for 5¢), a term antedating by a century the *dollar houses* of the 1990s where viewers, for modest ticket prices, could see movies run several months after their initial release.

The Great Train Robbery (1905), an 11-minute, 800-foot film containing 14 shots or scenes, was the first movie western. It featured "Bronco Billy" Anderson (real name Max Aronson), the first actor given credit for a role in an American film.

HOLLYWOOD

By 1915 Burbank, Culver City, Glendale, Santa Monica, or any part of Los Angeles or Southern California where movies were made was known as *Hollywood*, and by 1918 *Hollywood* was another word for the American film industry. Between 1905 and 1915 moviemakers and the public firmly established the basic words *cinema* (1909), *film* (1905), and *picture* (1900). Aside from giving us *film* combinations like *film rights*, to a book, play, etc., 1913; *film producer*, 1914; *film star*, 1914; *film actress*, 1919; *film maker*, 1919; and *film goer*, 1919, it gave us *movie house*, 1914, and *movie actor*, 1913. *Movie star*, for both a man and a woman, is cited to 1919; with *movie actress*, in 1924, and *movie queen* following in 1927. *Movie fan* goes back to 1913; *movie-going public*, to 1938; *movie land*, the film industry, especially Hollywood, to 1914; *movie business*, to 1916, which by 1928 became the *movie industry;* and *movie magazine*, to 1929.

Picture show, 1881, originally referred to items made for and seen in peephole devices; it was used in the modern sense from 1896 on. *Picture* dates to around 1900 as short for *motion picture*, and *pic*, a movie, is cited to 1939. The slang term *flick* (from the flickering movement of early screen images) is cited to 1926. But *release*, a motion picture released for exhibition, goes back to 1912.

Longer films were called *feature films* (1911), soon simply *features* (1913), for which the public was willing to pay 10¢ or even 25¢! In 1913 *first run* meant a brand-new picture, one being shown (or *run* through the projector) for the first time in town.

D.W. Griffith's *The Birth of a Nation* established the *feature film*. Based on Thomas Dixon's novel *The Clansman*, it was about the Civil War and the Reconstruction, showing the action through the eyes of two families, one northern, one southern. It opened in New York City in March 1915. Crowds flocked to see it because of its epic scope and spectacular battle scenes, and because it was racially controversial.

Some movies now featured the *stunt actor*, which, since 1904, had meant any actor known for daredevil action feats on screen, but around 1915 had also come to mean special actors who performed such feats for others, such men being called *stuntmen* by the late 1920s. An assistant director soon was called a *yes man* (1924 as movie use, the term from a 1913 T.A. "Tad" Dorgan cartoon in which the "yes men" were assistant newspaper editors praising the work of the editor). The chief assistant to the *gaffer* (the lighting electrician on a set) was recorded by 1937 as a *best boy*.

In 1928 Douglas Fairbanks, the first president of the recently formed (1927) Academy of Motion Picture Arts and Sciences, presented its first

Braveheart director, Mel Gibson (right) in a Scottish Highlands tartan vest, taking the Oscar for Best Picture in 1996.

annual *Academy Awards*, gold-plated statuettes called *Oscars* (origin of the name obscure) designed by MGM's art director, Cedric Gibbon. Eventually the Academy Awards ceremonies came to be called simply *the Oscars.*

COLOR AND COLORIZING

Technicolor was invented by the Technicolor Motion Picture Corp., founded in 1915 by Boston scientist Herbert T. Kalmus to carry on research and to perfect color movies. Dr. Kalmus said he based the corporation's *Technicolor* name on *Tech-* out of respect for his alma mater, Massachusetts Institute of *Tech*nology; *Technicolor* was then first used to refer to the firm's color process in 1917. The first *Technicolor movie* was *The Toll of the Sea* (1922). The next milestone in film color is reflected by the 1979 verb *colorize* and *colorization*—to add color to a previously black-and-white film by means of a computer.

TALKIES

The Jazz Singer, the *talkie* (1913) of all talkies, opened in New York City on October 6, 1927. *The Jazz Singer* featured the vaudeville star Al Jolson, who sang "four songs, including his blackface rendition of "Mammy," in his unmistakable voice, and in one sequence actually spoke a few lines! It revolutionized the movie industry.

The first *all-talking feature* was the 1928 *The Lights of New York*, produced and directed by Bryan Foy. MGM's first picture with sound was its very successful 1928 *White Shadows in the South Seas*, originally filmed as a silent picture but then embellished with a musical score, sound effects, and one word of dialogue, "Hello," added later—as well as Leo the Lion's first roar. (*Sound path* [1921] soon came to be called a *sound track* [1929].)

Adding sound to movies would be like putting lipstick on the Venus de Milo."

— *Mary Pickford, 1925*

To paraphrase Bob Dylan, the times they have a-changed. Al Jolson in Los Angeles in 1948.

The commercial success of *The Jazz Singer* turned movies into talkies and all earlier movies into *silent movies* (1929; the term *the silent screen* first appeared in 1930). In 1929 theater owners were rushing to install sound equipment. And later Imperial Airways showed the first *in-flight movie*, a version of Arthur Conan Doyle's *The Lost World*.

THE SOUND AND THE FURY OF THE 1930S

The 1930s began with many sound movies and ended with the first major Technicolor movies, the 1939 *Wizard of Oz* and David Selznick's *Gone with the Wind* (affectionately known as *GWTW* to Hollywood reporters), based on Margaret Mitchell's best-selling 1936 novel. Americans stepped into the dark movie theaters to forget the harsh glare of the Depression and saw the:

gangster movie, 1934 (the word *gangster* itself dates only from 1896). Warner Brothers led the way with the 1930 *Little Caesar* and the 1932 *Scarface*, both starring Edward G. Robinson. These films made *tough-guy movies* (a mid 1930s term) popular and made stars out of actors who could play the *heavy* (1928 in movie use).

horror movie, 1937, a movie made to send chills down our spines. It became a popular genre with the 1931 *Dracula* and *Frankenstein*, the latter starring Boris Karloff, with RKO's 1933 *King Kong* the first to be called a *monster movie*. (The grandaddy of the subgenre known as *psychothriller* has to be *Psycho* [1960] starring Anthony Perkins as the homicidal Norman Bates, whose gruesome knifing of a woman in a shower caused thousands of women to vow they'd never again shower while home alone; the film also propelled *The Bates Motel* into the language, denoting a weird, out-of-the way motel with an eerily menacing ambiance.) Such movies had been called *thrillers* by the 1920s.

musical, a new movie term that came in with sound movies, from the stage use. Warner Brothers led the way with *42nd Street* (1933), *Gold*

Charlie Chaplin (left) in 1935 on the set of one of his first "talkies," *Modern Times.* He was one of few Hollywood stars who made a successful transition from silent movies.

> "I don't care if he can act; can he talk?"
>
> — *popular Hollywood joke, as said by producers, 1928*

Clark Gable as Rhett Butler and Vivien Leigh as Scarlett O'Hara in *Gone With the Wind*. More than 50 years later, it is still considered by many critics to be the greatest film ever made.

John Wayne as Rooster Cogburn in *True Grit*.

Diggers of 1933, and *Gold Diggers of 1935*, introducing such songs as "Lullaby of Broadway."

western, 1928, earlier called a *cowboy movie* (around 1920), a *gun opera* (1921), and a *horse opera* (1927). The noun *western* was not created by the movies, however; boys had already been reading *penny westerns* and *half-dime, dime,* and *five-cent westerns* since the 1860s. The first movie showing the Wild West had been the 1898 vignette *The Cripple Creek Barroom.*

The western took on new life in the 1930s when, with talkies, cowboy stars began to sing. Tex Ritter became the first movie *singing cowboy.* In 1969 the term *spaghetti western*—one made, usually on a low budget, in Italy—was first recorded.

It would be left to the 1950s–70s to popularize three more major movie genres:

beach party movies. These appeared in 1963, persisted into 1965, and featured gorgeous gals and muscular, handsome guys cavorting innocently on the sand and in the surf to the accompaniment of light pop music (called, aptly enough, *surf music*) in an *endless summer* or one long *spring break.*

biker movies. Probably the real beginning of the kind of raw violence objected to in the 1990s by many parents, the *biker movie* as such emerged in 1954 with *The Wild One*, starring Marlon Brando, detailing a 1947 biker raid on Hollister, a small California town. The violence in these movies, which continued to escalate in ensuing years, reached a sensational high in *The Wild Angels* (1965). The film reflected the violent rebellion that was consuming parts of society in 1965 by showing drug-and-sex orgies, heavy boozing, biker wars, and gang rape. But it was the classic *Easy Rider* (1969) starring Peter Fonda ("Captain America") and Dennis Hopper ("Billy the Kid") that pictured two mellowed-out counterculture guys on their cycles in search of the real America, only to find decay, hatred, and social desolation.

disaster movies, 1974, high adventure films showing how characters react to spectacular disasters, the very first being *The Last Days of Pompeii* (1935). Also jocularly called "shake 'n bakes," they bore titles like *Airport* (1970, the first modern one), *The Towering Inferno* (1974), and *Earthquake* (1974). Another was *The Poseidon Adventure* (1972), in which an ocean liner capsizes. In the late 1990s weather-disaster movies and natural-disaster films like *Twister* were wildly popular.

HOME MOVIES AND DRIVE-INS

Two other terms were to have great impact on the general public: *home movie* and *drive-in*. By the mid 1930s, simple cameras and projectors had been developed that allowed movies to be taken and shown by the amateur in his or her own home.

The term *drive-in* (for a movie theater) first appeared in the patent for a ramp system for a *drive-in*, granted to Richard M. Hollingshead, Jr., of Riverton, New Jersey, on May 16, 1933. Having experimented with showing outdoor movies at night on a screen in front of his garage, Hollingshead then opened the first movie *drive-in* in a 400-car parking lot on Wilson Boulevard in Camden, New Jersey on June 6, 1933, offering a double feature every evening. (The drive-ins also came to be called *passion pits* because of the proclivity of young lovers to neck, pet, and

Twister onscreen in 1996—the first movie shown at this drive-in since, appropriately enough, tornado damage shut the theater down for ten weeks.

maybe even "go all the way" in their darkened cars during the movies.)

With the advent of affordable television sets, *multiplex cinemas* in shopping malls, and the introduction of *home videos*, the drive-in— a uniquely American invention—all but died out.

COMPETING WITH THE TUBE

In rapid succession between 1952 and 1955—in response to competition from TV—we had "three dimensional" or *3-D* movies, *Cinerama* (which helped to proliferate faddish use of *-orama*, meaning "huge") *Cinema-Scope, Panavision,* and so on. Violent comedies with serious messages, usually that war is hell and society is crazy, were created, appealing especially to younger audiences proud of being anti-establishment after the Vietnam War. These included the 1970 *M*A*S*H* and *Catch-22* and the 1975 *One Flew Over the Cuckoo's Nest.* The major success, however, was the innovative *space odyssey,* a term that first appeared in the title of Stanley Kubrick's 1968 *2001: A Space Odyssey,* and then was applied to George Lucas's 1977 *Star Wars* and its sequels *The Empire Strikes Back* and *Return of the Jedi,* in which *special effects* (1937) entered a new dimension. Millions of American children and adults talked about *Luke Skywalker, Princess Leia,* the hairy creature *Chewbacca,* and the robots *R2D2* and *C3PO,* who, with cliffhanger action and the blessing *May the Force be with you* (which became a national saying), fought the evil *Empire.*

Moviemakers now depended on *bankable* (early 1970s) stars, directors, and producers to provide *blockbusters* (1950s, from 1942, a bomb large enough to destroy a city block).

Movies had become such an integral part of American life that they began to alter the way we speak.

THE "SUBTITLING" OF AMERICAN ENGLISH

Americans began to use movie titles figuratively, along with the names of famous movie settings:

Dodge City, any lawless place or very dangerous situation. "Indochina was *Dodge City,* and the Americans were some collective version of Wyatt Earp" (Pete Hammill, screenwriter of *Doc* [1917], who linked his gunfight-at-the-O.K.-Corral scene to the sociopolitical strife that attended the Vietnam War); "'This may not be *Dodge City*,' said a spokesman for the U.S. Marines occupying war-torn Mogadishu, Somalia, in 1993, 'but Wyatt Earp's in town'" (John Mack Faragher, "The Tale of Wyatt Earp: Seven Films," in *Past Imperfect: History According to the Movies* [1995]).

Dr. Strangelove, a hawkish nuclear scientist, as in "A *Dr. Strangelove* who believed in the doctrine of mutual assured nuclear destruction"; derived adjective *Strangelovian*, all from the 1964 Stanley Kubrick film *Dr. Strangelove—Or—How I Learned to Stop Worrying and Love the Bomb*. This black comedy was about an out-of-control nuclear arms race. It starred Peter Sellers as a former Nazi, now a Pentagon weapons guru—the character, Dr. Strangelove, said to be a blend of three real people: Dr. Henry Kissinger, National Security Adviser to the President (later, Secretary of State); Dr. Edward Teller, the atomic bomb scientist on the Manhattan Project during World War II; and Dr. Wernher von Braun, a German rocket scientist who later worked for NASA.

Star Wars, used to denote the Reagan Administration's Strategic Defense Initiative (*SDI*), a plan for an armed satellite network preprogrammed to destroy incoming enemy missiles from "the *Evil Empire*" (the former Soviet Union), a controversial use of Lucasfilm's trademarked title of its film *Star Wars*; "his commitment to *Star Wars* . . . defense," a *Newsweek* citation dated December 31, 1984, is typical of the extended usage. In a lawsuit involving this unwanted crossover, a federal judge noted that "since Jonathan Swift's time, creators of fictional worlds have seen their vocabulary for fantasy appropriated to describe reality."

10, a beautiful woman, as in "She's a *10*," from *10*, the 1979 movie starring Bo Derek—a beautiful jogger with whom a California songwriter in midlife crisis becomes obsessed.

Home Alone, used chiefly of a child, and meaning "having been accidentally or purposely left behind without supervision while the rest of the family goes out of town," used by association with *Home Alone*, the title of a 1992 comedy about an upscale suburban family who inadvertently leave one small son at home by himself as they go on a vacation, and the ensuing misadventures he experiences or causes. The media immediately co-opted the title, using it like this: "'*Home Alone*' Parents Indicted by State on 64 Criminal Counts" (headline, *Washington Post*, February 10, 1993).

Fatal Attraction, used to denote a homicidal female maniac out for blood as the woman scorned, from the 1987 movie *Fatal Attraction*: "There was no such attack, the defense will counter vehemently. The woman wanted to have sex with a Kennedy, then proved to be a '*Fatal Attraction*' psychotic who screamed rape" (*Washington Post*, December 1, 1991).

gump, to muddle through with complaisance, trusting that all will turn out well in the end, from *Forrest Gump*, the 1994 movie starring Tom Hanks, Sally Field, and Gary Sinise, about the life and times of a rather "slow" Alabama boy who manages, through no fault of his own, to become a football star, a war hero, and a multimillionaire: "Are we going to '*gump*' our way through Bosnia, . . . until Serbs and Croats and Muslims live . . . in peace?" (Michael Douglas, *Akron* [Ohio] *Beacon Journal*, August 4, 1994).

Tom Hanks as Forrest Gump, a role for which he earned his second consecutive best actor Oscar in 1994.

Clint Eastwood as Dirty Harry in *Sudden Impact,* the fourth in the hugely popular series. He would later direct and star in *Unforgiven,* a western that treated killing much less lightly, and which has been interpreted as an apology of sorts by Eastwood for contributing to the glamorization of violence.

Catch-22 came to mean a problem for which the only solution is blocked by a circumstance forming part of the problem itself, or by a crazy rule imposed from the outside. This term, which made its way into dictionaries, comes from the title of Joseph Heller's 1961 novel and the movie made of it: "In the *Catch-22* of a closed repertoire, only music that is already familiar is thought to deserve familiarity" (Joseph McLennan). In addition, the term, which can be used as an adjective ("We were caught in a *Catch-22* situation"), has taken on other meanings: an absurd or senseless situation; a self-defeating course of action; and a very disadvantageously tricky predicament.

STAR BILLING: FILM CHARACTERS IN ENGLISH

The *Dirty Harry syndrome* denotes the tendency among some police officers to use excessive force in apprehending criminals; the term derives from the series of Clint Eastwood films centering on Detective Harry Callahan, a.k.a. *Dirty Harry.* On the lighter side, if someone calls the local constabulary "a bunch of *Keystone Kops,*" the reference is to bumbling law officers, taken from Mack Sennett's slapstick comedies produced at his Keystone Studio in Glendale, California. The name *Keystone Comedy* entered the language in 1913, soon coming to mean any frenetic slapstick comedy. The *Keystone Kops,* as the last word was often spelled for humorous effect, first appeared in 1912. This group committed slapstick mayhem to the horror of their goatee-waggling, bug-eyed leader. An *Inspector Clouseau* is an inexpert detective, so called after the 1964–82 *Pink Panther* movies starring Peter Sellers. During the mid 1980s *Rambo motorist/driver* was widely used with reference to an aggressive driver; the name came from the film character John *Rambo* played in the movies by Sylvester Stallone.

Ronald Reagan used the line "Go ahead—make my day" when threatening to veto legislation passed by a Democratic Congress—making up for a Hollywood "B-movie" acting career in which he never had such memorable material to read.

"Who knows what evil lurks in the hearts of men? The Shadow knows."

— *voiceover introduction,* **The Shadow,** *the story of "Lamont Cranston," a man who had learned in the Far East the hypnotic power of clouding other people's minds so that they could not see him as he fought evil.*

"Twenty-five years [after the advent of comic books] that first generation of comic-kids had grown up. . . . They instantly understood 'Aargh!' and 'Zap!' and 'Takatataka.'"

— *Harvey Kurtzman,* **From Aargh! to Zap! Visual History of the Comics,** *1991*

"Before 1929, newspaper strips and Sunday comic sections, important cultural transmitters since the turn of the century, were known as 'funnies,' a term implying humorous intent."

— *William W. Savage, Jr.,* **Comic Books and America, 1945–54,** *published 1990*

ONE-LINERS

Just as lines from Shakespeare's plays made their way into the general language, so too did lines from the movies get in, these typical:

"You ain't heard nothin' yet, folks," Al Jolson, ad-libbing, the first spoken words in *The Jazz Singer*, 1927.

"Here's another fine mess you've gotten us into," Oliver Hardy in the *Laurel & Hardy* comedy movies, 1926–50.

"Frankly, my dear, I don't give a damn," probably the most famous of them all, spoken by Clark Gable as Rhett Butler to Vivien Leigh as Scarlett O'Hara at the end of *Gone with the Wind*, 1939, a use of a previously taboo swear word on screen.

"Here's looking at you, kid," Humphrey Bogart in *Casablanca*, 1943, a film that also give us *"Play it Sam,"* uttered by Ingrid Bergman; *Play It Again, Sam* was the title of a 1969 movie by Woody Allen.

"A man has to know his limitations," Clint Eastwood as Detective Harry Callahan in *Dirty Harry*, 1971.

"I'm mad as hell and I'm not going to take it anymore," *Network*, 1976, a world-famous line by screenwriter Paddy Chayevsky (1923–81), oft repeated by people when under heavy stress.

"Go ahead—make my day!", Clint Eastwood, Detective Harry Callahan, *Sudden Impact*, 1983. (See POLITICS: NO TERM LIMITS.)

TURN ON THE RADIO AND READ THE COMICS

The "Golden Age of Radio" ran from 1920 through 1950. Though early radio focused on music and news, it also devoted considerable air time to afternoon *soap operas* (1939, from their sponsorship by laundry soap manufacturers) like *The Romance of Helen Trent* and adventure-mystery radio dramas like *Sky King* targeted chiefly to adolescents, not to mention comedies like *Amos 'n Andy* and *The Jack Benny Show* and quiz programs such as *Twenty Questions*.

Adventure-mystery shows whose very titles still enjoy pop cultural perpetuity are *The Shadow, Buck Rogers, Superman, Jungle Jim, Terry and the Pirates*, and *Fu Manchu*. *Dick Tracy, Jungle Jim* and *Terry and the Pirates*—action series featuring heroic struggles against all odds pitting good versus evil—began in print in the 1930s, with *Tarzan* and *Buck Rogers* coming out in January 1929. Of these, one of truly lasting impact was *Superman*, created by teenagers Jerry Siegel (the writer) and Joe Schuster (the artist) in the 1930s. Superman first appeared in 1938 in a *comic book* (early 1930s). From 1939 to 1967 Superman appeared as a strip in newspapers and from 1940 to 1951 on the radio with Bud Collyer doing the voiceover, which contained memorable expressions such as "Faster than a speeding bullet!" "It's a bird! It's a plane! It's SUPER-MAN!", and "Superman . . . fights a never-ending battle for truth, justice, and the American way!" "The Man of Steel" became a pop culture icon, whether on the page, on the air, on the screen, or on breakfast food boxes.

Bob Kane's *Batman*, which first appeared in 1939 in a comic book and in the 1940s, was on the radio and in movie serials and became a "campy" show in the 1960s. It generated terms such as *The Dynamic Duo*, referring to Batman and his sidekick Robin (a.k.a. "The Caped Crusader and the Boy Wonder").

"The Mickey Mouse Club Mouseketeers." Annette Funicello, lower left, would eventually trade her mouse ears for a bathing suit in beach movies of the 60s.

Bob Keeshan (left) as Captain Kangaroo in 1971.

In terms of *comic strips* (1920), in their aggregate called *the funnies* (1852), it was Al Capp, the creator of *Li'l Abner*, who gave us some long-lasting terms. His 1934 strip, set in the fictional Kentucky hamlet Dogpatch, gave us the expression *Dogpatch U.S.A.* for any hick town. Here, we also gained *skunkworks* (from his *Skonk Works*) and *Sadie Hawkins Day*, when females are free to aggressively pursue the males of their choice.

Walt Disney's *Mickey Mouse* (originally "Mortimer" in the 1920s) tops them all, however. Since 1928 when the first sound cartoon by Disney appeared—also the first time the name *Mickey Mouse* was used—the character's instant, mass popularity generated *Mickey Mouse*, the bomb-release lever on a World War II combat aircraft; *Mickey Mouse boots*, large, heavy, insulated, bulbous boots worn especially by Air Force and other military personnel in Arctic regions; *Mickey Mouse ears*, rotating police-cruiser lights; *Mickey Mouse habit*, a minor drug addiction; *Mickey Mouse movie*, either a required combat training film or a required (and graphically gruesome) film on sexually transmitted disease for U.S. service personnel; and *Mickey Mouse program*, a trivial computer program (hackers' jargon). *Mickey Mouse* by itself also came to mean "trivial; unimportant."

Another noticeable contribution to the language from the comics and/or cartoons is the "heroic," or "strong," use of the word *Captain* before other nouns in forming a character's name, as in *Captain Marvel* (1940s), *Captain America* (1941), *Captain Video* (1949–55), *Captain Midnight* (1954–56), and *Captain Kangaroo* (1955–), played by Bob Keeshan. His deep pockets full of unexpected treats, he entertained kids on a television variety show that aimed to educate via characters like Word Bird and Mr. Moose.

TELEVISION: THE LAND OF THE COUCH POTATO

Called variously "the apotheosis of modern communicative devices," "a cool medium," and "the gray wasteland," *television* (1907, from French *télévision*) and its programs dominated American life by the 1980s, having been commercially introduced to the U.S. in the early 1940s (at that time only 23 stations were in U.S. operation). After World War II the industry boomed. People rearranged their living rooms to accommodate the new device, readjusted their *rabbit ears* (top-of-the-set antennae) to avoid *snow* (transient dark or light spots on the screen), often battled with their kids over school-night viewing, and sometimes banned TV altogether. Television spawned the *Television Generation*—those born from 1949 on, who have lived under the pervasive influence of *the tube, the box,* or *the boob tube,* some becoming *couch potatoes* (1982) in the process.

Americans often identify themselves generationally with the TV shows they enjoyed in their adolescence. For example, if somebody says, "I'm a member of the *Father Knows Best* generation, " that means he or she grew up in the 1950s, glued to the heartwarming family *situation comedy* (1946; *sitcom*, 1964) of that title starring Robert Young. One who identifies with *The Beverly Hillbillies* pegs oneself as an avid early 1960s viewer, a fan of the 1962–71 sitcom about the newly rich Ozarks family,

Rod Serling in 1961. In a burst of creativity, he wrote 81 *Twilight Zone* scripts during 1960 and 1961.

the Clampetts, who lived—somewhat uneasily at times—in a Beverly Hills "manse." A *Brady Bunch* kind of person is a late-1960s/early-1970s viewer, one who enjoyed the fun around the house of two families combined into a nuclear unit after a widow and a widower got married. If you're a member of the *Dallas generation* you followed every scandal and crisis in the Ewing family from 1978 to 1991 on this, the first real *prime-time* (1958) *soap opera*. Those who bridged the 1980s into the 90s as youthful viewers often associate themselves with *thirtysomething* (1987–91)—the first yuppie drama, and one that encouraged wide use of the combining form *-something*, as in *twentysomething*—or with *The X-files* (1993, high intrigue and drama involving mysterious cases).

LIFE IMITATING TELEVISION

Washington Post columnist E.J. Dionne Jr. calls it "life imitating TV" when names of TV shows and/or their characters are used to denote a person's physical attributes, character, values, or lifestyle. When then-Vice President Dan Quayle objected in 1991 to the family values of *Murphy Brown*, the fictional 42-year-old broadcast journalist who chose, on the show of that title, to bear a child conceived during a brief fling with her ex-husband, Quayle made "life imitate TV"—and the nation heard and read the words *Murphy Brown* hundreds of thousands of times during that presidential election. Here are more:

Fred Flintstone, Neanderthal in physical appearance: "A 53-year-old declared cocaine addict with a *Fred Flintstone* face, somehow beefy and meek at the same time, [he] was arrested with two bags of crack and a loaded .38 revolver" (*Washington Post Magazine*, November 11, 1991); from *The Flintstones*, (1960–66), a parody of suburban life set in the Stone Age, created by Bill Hanna and Joe Barbera.

MacGyver bomb, an explosive device made of a soda bottle filled with a mix of volatile household cleaning compounds, used chiefly by teens to blow up mailboxes: "'I've run across *MacGyver bombs* for a couple [of] years now and made some arrests'" (Taylorville, Illinois arson/bomb squad investigator Richard Sutton to the Springfield, Illinois *State Journal-Register*, May 4, 1995); derived from *MacGyver*, title of the 1985 foreign-intrigue series about a man who uses creatively jerry-rigged devices to fight global criminals.

Starsky and Hutch, heroic cops or civilians who, in pairs, confront dangerously violent situations and save lives: "They were transformed into a civilian *Starsky and Hutch*. They had no choice. . . . Like other passengers [they were] trapped with Tuesday's rush-hour gunman" (*Newsday*, December 9, 1993); derived from the 1975–79 police drama of that title, the lead characters, Detective Dave *Starsky* and Detective Ken *"Hutch"* Hutchinson (played by Paul Michael Glaser and David Soul), tackling some of the roughest cases in Los Angeles.

twilight zone, an ambiguous area between two distinct conditions, such as good and evil, as in "that *twilight zone* between right and wrong," influenced by Rod Serling's *The Twilight Zone*, a 1959–64 sci-fi cult favorite, but also ultimately from the aeronautical meaning of the expression, "the disorientation and lack of certainty experienced by pilots when the horizon disappears from their view, e.g., when landing an aircraft."

Such usages occur so often in speech and print that perhaps someday people will need almanacs of past and present television shows to understand the denotations of a person called an *Archie Bunker* or a *Boss Hogg*

A raised eyebrow and a "Highly illogical" was the closest Leonard Nimoy could come to showing emotion as Mr. Spock on Star Trek.

(an urban or rural bigot, respectively), a family characterized as *Ozzie-and-Harriet* (Middle Americans with a 1950s outlook), a task deemed *Mission: Impossible* (an insuperable challenge), a meeting that turns into a *Gong Show* (a hysterical fiasco), or a hospital that reminds one of *St. Elsewhere* (a dumping ground for indigent patients).

WHO SHOT J. R.?

That was the nation's $64,000 question at the end of the 1979–80 episode of *Dallas*. During the 13 years that it aired, people talked about the members of the Ewing family at their South Fork Ranch as if they knew them personally—the archvillain J. R. (called "that human oil slick" by *Time*), the respected matriarch "Miss Ellie," Bobby Ewing (the good brother), Bobby's complex wife Pam, J. R.'s beautiful and long-suffering wife Sue Ellen, and others.

When J. R. was shot by an unknown attacker and rushed to the hospital in critical condition (at the end of a season, of course), betting parlors took millions of dollars in summer wagers. The whole country talked about the scheduled denouement in the fall season. Even the actors didn't know who shot J. R. for real, because several different endings had been filmed, the final choice guarded in the highest secrecy. Finally, on November 21, 1980, with 80 percent of the U.S. viewing audience tuned in, the country learned that one of J. R.'s former mistresses (Kristin, Sue Ellen's sister) had done it. (J. R. recovered.)

BEAM ME UP, SCOTTY

Star Trek (1966–69) and its movie follow-ups became, by century's end, a pop cultural obsession, with the show's fans known as *Trekkies*. Set in the 23rd century, the starship *Enterprise* explores previously unvisited planets and worlds in a context often posing difficult, unresolved problems attending the human condition. The names of the key characters and those playing them—*Captain* James T. *Kirk* (William Shatner), *Mr. Spock* the half-breed *Vulcan* (Leonard Nimoy, he with the prosthetically pointed ears), Dr. Leonard *"Bones" McCoy* (DeForest Kelley), and Lt. Commander Montgomery *"Scotty"* Scott (chief engineer, James Doohan)—became household names much like the members of the Ewing family, as the valiant crew fought the *Romulans* and the suturedforehead *Klingons*, the latter of whom speak a gutteral language requiring English subtitles (a dictionary of the *Klingon* language was actually published in the late 1990s!). Other words that viewers came to be familiar with were weapons called *phasers*, propulsion systems called *Warp engines*, and the famous *Vulcan salute* (hand raised, palm facing forward, index and middle fingers separated to form a V).

In 1976 the U.S. space shuttle, then called the *Constitution*, was renamed the *Enterprise* after intense lobbying efforts by Trekkies, who initiated a mass-mail appeal to President Gerald R. Ford, making the point that the cultural *telegenicity* (*telegenic*, 1939) of *televised* (1927) hit dramas has permanently affected our society and the words it uses.

TV ONE-LINERS

Even more than is the case with movie lines, TV lines have insinuated themselves into the general language. *Rowan and Martin's Laugh-In* (1968–73) was an unstructured, irreverent comedy *happening* that featured, among other things, a Joke Wall with doors that flew open one after the other to reveal the heads of performers delivering one-liners like "Incest is a relative term." Aside from "Welcome to beautiful downtown Burbank," "Sock it to me!", "Ring my chimes," "Verrrry interesting!"

John Belushi in 1976 in various *Saturday Night Live* "sketches." The word "skit" was banned from writers' meetings, as it signified the type of establishment, *Carol Burnett Show* humor they sought to avoid at all costs.

Roseanne as Roseanne in 1989. Her show offered an unblinking look at middle class family life.

"Television has given a broad range of words and expressions popularity on a scale they never would have achieved on their own. . . . In most cases, the expressions existed prior to their appearance on the air, . . . but television offered the viewing public a fresh and exciting way of using them."

— *University of South Florida professor Robert O'Hara, to* Sky *magazine, April 1993*

(spoken in a thick German accent by Arte Johnson wearing a Nazi helmet), and "Here come de judge!", by far the most high-profile expression was "You bet your sweet bippy!". It was used by people so much that a UN diplomat—a nonnative speaker of English—was impelled to inquire of a U.S. counterpart, "What is it you mean by 'bippy'?" The word *bippy*—a euphemism for *ass*—and the entire expression were introduced to the nation by this TV show in January 1967, to be exact. Classed as a "nonce word of uncertain origin" by some etymologists, *bippy* is entered in several dictionaries. All of which is appropriate for a word deriving from the very same show that repopularized the preexisting common expression "Look that up in your Funk and Wagnall's."

Saturday Night Live, begun in 1975, starring (originally) Chevy Chase, John Belushi, Dan Aykroyd, and others, with guests like George Carlin, was the first network *underground comedy show*. Emphasizing rebellion, outrage, drug use, and sex, it was in-your-face *late-night viewing*. It became so popular, especially among young adults, that they would either give parties to watch the show or leave other people's parties early to get home to watch it. One of its most long-lasting linguistic contributions is the end-of-sentence negation *"Not!"*, as in "George Bush and his Administration are doing a fine job. *Not!*". This usage continued in currency to the end of the 1990s. Another expression that didn't originate on the show, but gained currency by way of it, particularly in its sarcastic, arrogant, drawn-out oral delivery, is Steve Martin's famous "Excuuuuuse me!", with stress on the *-u-* and on *me*. By century's end this locution had achieved the negative connotation and impact long attached to the opener "With all due respect," in which *disrespect* is really meant.

"*Wild and crazy guys*" is still another slang fixture in English that goes back to this show, the reference being to "We're just a couple of wild and crazy guys," a line said by Martin and Aykroyd, who played the swinging (and geeky) Czech brothers Jorge and Yortuk Festrunk, who loved the West as opposed to their drab Iron Curtain motherland, but loved big American tits more.

Ken Shapiro, producer of *The Groove Tube* (1972), was quoted by Doug Hill and Jeff Weingrad in their book *Saturday Night: A Backstage History of Saturday Night Live* (1986) to the effect that *Saturday Night Live* was a "a gorgeous subculture, with their own language, their own jokes." Clearly, part of their own language has become part of ours in the same manner that the languages of brands, popular music, the movies, and television, plus the names of well-known people have infiltrated American English—subtly and boldly—in what might be called a pop cultural work-in-progress, with many ephemeral terms and others that live on long beyond their originators.

TV Catch Phrases

These expressions, chosen from an array of hundreds, are examples of the perpetuity of television-generated language:

"It's How-w-wwdy Doody Time!", *Howdy Doody*, 1947–50, featuring a freckle-faced marionette so named; responsible also for propelling *peanut gallery* into wide national use. But the show's most high-profile linguistic contribution is most certainly the interjection *cowabunga*, used by one of yet a new generation of TV characters, Bart Simpson of the 1990s show *The Simpsons* (he, famous for being an "Underachiever and proud of it"). This term, of "fanciful" origin, and used since the 1950s by surfers to indicate astonishment or great enthusiasm, was probably coined by *Howdy Doody* writer Eddie Kean to be said by Chief Thunderthud—then spelled *kowabonga* and having a decidedly negative meaning.

"Smile, you're on Candid Camera!", *Candid Camera*, 1948–90, produced and hosted by Allen Funt.

"Until we meet again, may the good Lord take a liking to you," Roy Rogers, *The Roy Rogers Show*, 1951–57.

"How sweet it is!", Jackie Gleason on *The Jackie Gleason Show*, 1952–70, pronounced with stress on *sweet* and *is*.

"Just the facts, ma'm," Sgt. Joe Friday, *Dragnet*, 1952–70.

"And that's the way it is. . . .", Walter Cronkite, signoff, *CBS Evening News*, 1962–81.

"Heeeere's Johnny!", Ed McMahon, *The Tonight Show*, 1962–92, introducing host Johnny Carson.

"I know NOTHink!", Nazi stalag guard Sgt. Hans Schultz, *Hogan's Heroes*, 1965–71.

"Aloha, suckers!", Det. Steve McGarrett, Hawaii State Police, *Hawaii Five-O*, 1968–80.

"The devil made me do it!" and "What you see is what you get," *The Flip Wilson Show*, 1970–74, with the second sentence coming to be abbreviated to *WYSIWYG* (pronounced "whizzy-wig"), later used in computer science to denote a desktop publishing system that displays on the screen the text as it will appear in print, and entered in dictionaries published in the early 1990s.

"No good deed ever goes unpunished," Capt. B.J. Hunnicut, *M*A*S*H*, 1972–83, the TV series becoming a cult favorite.

"waxy yellow buildup," e.g., on floors, a chief concern of Mary Hartman, the star character of the late-night satire of soap operas, *Mary Hartman, Mary Hartman*, 1974, an expression picked up and used jocularly by many Americans.

"No problem!", adolescent Theo Huxtable, *The Cosby Show*, 1984– .

"KID: *I'm bored.* ROSEANNE: *Go play in traffic*," Roseanne Conner, the vulgar blue-collar mom played by Roseanne Barr Arnold, *Roseanne*, 1988– .

"Been there, done that," popularized by Bart Simpson on the 1990s hip, antiheroic cartoon show *The Simpsons*.

YO! AMERICA RAPS

*I*n the late 1980s and early 1990s, rap music *burst from the confines of East Coast inner cities, its core market, to make a dramatic leap into mainstream American youth culture. White, middle-class youth embraced black popular culture and black street vernacular on a scale comparable only to the swing and jitterbug craze of the late 1930s, which made Negro jive from the streets of Harlem, Chicago, and New Orleans a part of the American language.*

Rap's roots may be traced to the Bronx and Harlem in the 1970s, where Afrocentric community leaders consciously created a mix of popular cultural expressions as a creative alternative to the devastating culture of *gang violence*. As originally conceived, this new culture was to consist of three components—breakdancing, graffiti art, and rap music—and would be collectively known as *hip-hop*.

Breakdancing was a fad in the early 1980s. With its intensely practiced, acrobatic moves placing it out of the realm of the lay dancer, it was normally performed either on sidewalks (often on top of a collapsed cardboard box, which provided a slippery surface) for tips or in competitions which were likened to *hoofing*, or tap contests, of earlier in the century. After several movies focused on the breakdance phenomenon, including Harry Belafonte's *Beat Street* (1984), the low budget *Wild Style* (1982), *Breakin'* and *Breakin' 2* (1984), and the box-office success *Flashdance* (1983), in which legendary breakdancer Crazy Legs doubled for star Jennifer Beals in a three-minute breakdancing cameo, breakdancing became commercially exploited. Advertisements for Kool-Aid (with multiracial pre-school breaking *crews* dressed in brightly colored *street gear*), Right Guard, Burger King, and Fruity Pebbles (with Barney Rubble of *The Flintstones* spinning on his back) signaled the end of breakdancing as a cultural expression. By 1987, *rap* was on the rise, and breakdancing all but forgotten.

Breakdancing in Manhattan in 1984—back when sneakers were less complicated.

A graffiti artist decorating a New York City subway car in 1977. "Tracy 168" painted personalized names and greetings for $25.

But several words coined by breakdancers survived. The word *break* is a venerable jazz word, used when a singer steps back from the microphone and lets the music and dancing continue; hence its use in the term for solo-oriented breakdancing. In breakdancing, a *breaker* was a dancer, a *crew* was a group or team of dancers, and *breaking* was dancing. The breakdancing term for sneakers—*dogs*—came into widespread popular usage, as did *gear* (clothes) and *box* or *boom box* (a portable tape player with powerful speakers). The various moves (*pediments*) were combined into one of three styles of breakdancing—simple *breaking*, the *electric boogie*, and *uprock*.

The second facet of *hip-hop culture, graffiti art*, never enjoyed even the passing public acclaim that breakdancing did. Other than the homage paid graffiti artists by Norman Mailer, they did not, in the public's eye, escape the stigma of vandalism, although their artistic style had a definite effect on commercial graphic art of the 1990s. Graffiti artists had their own language, in which they were known as *bombers, writers*, or *tag bangers* (artists who left only their signature). An artist kept his rough sketches in a *piece* (clipped from *masterpiece*) *book*, from which he or she produced a *bomb* or *throw-up* (a painting on a subway car or a wall). Using a word also found in the vocabulary of breakdancers, graffiti artists used *bite* to mean to copy another artist's style. *Crew*, meaning "a group of friends," originated as a word referring to a group of graffiti artists who worked together.

By 1985, *rap music* was the foremost element of the hip-hop triad. *Rap* has demonstrated admirable ability to adapt and survive as an English slang term. From its standard English meaning of "a severe blow," *rap* evolved to mean a softer blow. In the mid 18th century, it took on a slang sense of entering a formal complaint or testifying against someone. By the late 1800s in the United States, *rap* also came to mean a prison sentence or blame for a crime.

In the 1960s, *rap* took on a strong new slang life, meaning "to discuss or debate informally," harkening back to a very early meaning of "to express orally." While William Safire has reported early 20th century

Tupac Shakur, one of rap's most successful and notorious singers, was shot to death on September 7, 1996.

uses of *rap* in this sense by Damon Runyon (1929) and Winston Churchill (1933), *rap* did not assume this new meaning in a robust fashion until the late 1960s. Eldridge Cleaver's use of *rap* in a 1965 letter from prison ("He thinks he is another Lenny Bruce . . . and I dig *rapping* with him") was an early recorded usage in the 1960s. College students, hippies, and blacks rapidly began using it. By the late 1960s, *rap* began to appear in mainstream comic strips. Before it could completely vanish from the public's eye, *rap* came back to life with its new, hip-hop meaning.

Rap was first applied to an evolving form of African American music characterized by percussion-driven rhythms, beat-driven rhymes, and an inner-city subject matter and world view in the late 1970s; it appears in two song titles in 1979. As the 20th century neared its close, *rap* continued to be popular.

Rap music had its own technical vocabulary. From the early days of rap comes the expressions *to beatbox* ("to make mouth noises while somebody else raps"), *to scratch* ("to move a record back and forth on a turntable for a percussion effect"), and *the kick* (the beat). Expressions used as synonyms for *rap* included *break, bust out, chat, cut, drop, freak, give it up* (also used to mean "applaud [for]"), *jam, kick, rhyme, rip,* and *throw out.*

Hip-hop was coined in the mid 1970s, even before *rap* took on its new life. In the early stages of what would become known as *rap*, both D.J. Hollywood of Harlem and Loveburg Starski of the Bronx exhorted crowds at late-night New York night clubs "Hip-hop, you don't stop." Afrika Bambaataa, one of the founders of the *hip-hop movement*, took the expression and applied it as a name for the emerging new culture as a whole. *Hip-hop* proved to be a vigorous heir in the line of *hip/hep* derivatives that have proliferated in 20th century American slang.

After building cultural momentum for a decade within the African American community, hip-hop culture burst into the mainstream of popular culture with startling force. Affluent white youth embraced hip-hop and popular black culture, seeing black teenagers, rappers, and athletes as the hip voice of urban culture. Black youth street fashion (conspicuously expensive brand-name sneakers, baggy pants with the waist worn low, hooded sweatshirts, and baseball caps), black youth vernacular, and rap music became emblems of American youth in revolt, or at least American youth in defiance. Journalists coined a number of terms for young white fans of hip-hop culture, including *wigger* (*w*hite + n*igger*), *yo-boy, poser,* and *wannabe*; while none of these terms (except the last, in a generalized sense) gained widespread acceptance in spoken English, they nonetheless bespoke a profound social and cultural phenomenon. Simply put, American youth came to identify strongly with what was presented, and to a large degree marketed, to them as black culture.

Along with the body of black vernacular being imported into mainstream youth culture came the tradition of ritualized, ceremonial insult, long an outlet for suppressed rage in black culture. Before the surge of hip-hop culture, black oral tradition divided ritual insult into two categories, *the Dozens* and *signifying.*

The Dozens, a game of verbal jousting constructed on insults directed in large part toward the mother of one's opponent, was widespread in black culture by the early 20th century. Langston Hughes lyrically glorified the Dozens in the poem "Ask Your Mama," while in *Die Nigger Die!*, civil rights activist H. Rap Brown explained the game as follows: ". . . what you try to do is totally destroy somebody else with words. It's that whole competition thing again, fight each other. . . . The real aim of the Dozens was to get a dude so mad that he'd cry or get mad enough to fight."

Many slang expressions are devilishly hard to trace. Some histories are simply unknown. Others are disputed. Such is the case with *the Dozens* and its variants, including *playing the Dozens, putting someone in the Dozens*, and *shooting the Dozens*. Several of the more prominent explanations for the origin of *the Dozens* are as follows:

- Insulting rhymes that progressed from 1 to 12, describing the lewd acts that the opponent's mother enjoyed.

- Bad luck associated with throwing a 12 while shooting craps.

- English dialect of the 18th century, in which *dozen* meant to stun or daze.

- The slavery-era practice of selling the *dirty dozen*—the 12 least healthy slaves after the passage from Africa—as a group at a bargain rate.

- The assumption that the female house slave was one of the dozens of women who were sexually available to the master.

- Slang name for the raunchy area around Twelfth Street in Kansas City in the 1930s.

Whatever its true etymology, *the Dozens* was firmly integrated in black culture by the end of World War I as a socially sanctioned vehicle for insult.

Signifying is, in the words of H. Rap Brown, "more humane," focusing as it did on the weaknesses and vulnerabilities of one's opponent, not his mother. *Signification* reached its artistic peak in a folkloric

Rapper Snoop Doggy Dogg (right) in 1994. Snoop doesn't let the murder charges he faces keep him from celebrating the American Music Award that has gone to his friend and collaborator, Dr. Dre.

tradition of poems about the *Signifying Monkey*. In this tale, a clever and verbally abusive monkey provokes a lion into picking fights with other big, tough animals. Gloating and feeling proud of himself, the monkey falls from his perch on the limb of a tree safely above the jungle floor and finds himself at the mercy of the lion. In some endings, the monkey once again outwits the lion and escapes, while in other versions the lion kills the monkey.

With the advent of hip-hop culture, the subtle boundaries between *the Dozens* and *signifying* blurred, and the insult-as-art or disparaging put-down came to be known most widely as *dissing*, a term derived from clipping *disrespect* as a verb and one which very quickly worked its way into the American vernacular.

Hip-hop was replete with synonyms for *dissing*, a testament to the important cultural and social role played by the insult. Analogues include *answer, bag, base on, blow away, bust, cap, chop, clown crack, cut, dog, drop the lugs on, fade, heat, get on his case, get above, hike, jam, jone* (or *joan*), *lean on, loud, mount, plant, rank, rib, riff on, scene on, scream* (*cold, hard* or *foul*), *serve, shoot on, signify, slip, snap, sound, step, stomp, talk shit, talk trash, toast, trip on,* and *wolf* or *woof* (including the variations *selling woof tickets* or simply *selling tickets*).

Central among the idiom of praise in the rap-slang idiom were three words—*fly, fresh,* and *phat. Fly* has a distinguished slang lineage. As early as 1724 it was used as slang to mean "sly, cunning, knowing, or smart," and continued in this sense in Charles Dickens's *Bleak House* (1853). *Fly* crept into the language of jazz musicians in the early 1900s, but was relatively dormant until the late 1940s and early 1950s when it enjoyed a run of popularity meaning "handsome, attractive, and smooth." A series of "Superfly" black exploitation movies of the 1970s gave *fly* another moment of fame, but it fell into disuse until revived by rappers who used it both in the 18th century sense ("knowing") and the sense developed in the 1950s and 1960s ("attractive, smooth"). It is used espe-

Members of the rap group Salt 'N' Pepa, from left, Sandi "Pepa" Denton, Deidra "Spinderella" Roper, and Cheryl "Salt" James. In 1995, the group was honored by Governor William Weld of Massachusetts for displaying positive images of young women through their music.

cially by boys describing girls whom they find attractive and sexually appetizing.

Fresh, used since the mid 1980s as a term of approval, was one of the few rap words that can claim its true genesis in the hip-hop culture. Although *fresh* was used in 19th century slang to mean "barely drunk," it was not used as a general term of praise until the late 1970s. Unlike the intense debates over the origin of many slang expressions, there is general agreement that *fresh* owes its newest slang sense to the lyrics of Fantastic Grand Wizard Theodore and the 5 MC's, who rapped, "We're *fresh* out of the pack, you gotta stay back / We got one Puerto Rican and the rest are black." "*Fresh* out of the pack," easily understood as a boast of artistic originality, was soon shortened to simply *fresh*, used as decisive, all-purpose praise.

On first impression, *phat* seemed to have been a catchy invention of the hip-hop culture, meaning "sexy or cool." Some have gone so far as to suggest that *phat* was intentionally forged as an acronym for *Pretty Hips And Thighs*. Putting aside the *ph* spelling, *fat* was used as early as the 17th century as a slang expression for "rich," a usage that persists to today. In the late 1950s and early 1960s, *fat* became a slang word of praise. It was embraced by practitioners of hip-hop with enthusiasm from the start, appearing in writing as *fat* until the early 1990s when *phat* crept in. While playful spellings persist in hip-hop culture, *phat*'s popularity crested in the mid 1990s.

Other words of rap praise included *all that, bad, bitchin', boomin', bumpin', chill, dap, def, dope, sweet,* and *tight.* Hip-hop slang is equally versatile in its vocabulary describing those of low station: *bank, cramped, played, toe up, wack,* and *weak* all deliver powerful messages of condemnation.

Variations on "what's up" were popular, including *S'up? Wassup?* and *Wassup money?* The simple *Yo* (also claimed by the Italian-American community of South Philadelphia), *Ayo, Eh G,* and *Hayo* were all often heard. Hip-hop nouns of address for male friends or acquaintances included *ace, B, cuz, dog, dude, G, homeboy, homes,* and *power*; female versions include *B-girl, girlfriend, homegirl, sista,* and *tender.* Expressive gestures used in greeting included the classic *high five, daps* (a slap of the hands), *pound* (tapping of closed fists), and *props* (tapped closed fists, top and bottom).

The final opportunity in a conversation or encounter for a speaker to establish station, rap farewells were innovative and abundant. Synonyms for "to leave" included *bail, book, bounce, break, clock out, flex, jet, motor, step off* and *tear up.* Instead of a simple "good-bye," a hip-hop aficionado would say *Check ya, Gone, Later, Peace, Peace Out,* or *Sideways.*

When we hear young people using rap words, many are these:

ass-out, extremely.

bank, money.

baller, sombody who is succeeding.

base, to smoke crack cocaine.

beamer, a user of crack cocaine.

blow up, to achieve fame or success.

bones, dominoes.

bump, to play music extremely loudly.

bust a cap, to shoot with a gun.

bust on the scene, to grow famous.

chill, to relax.

clock, to scrutinize or inspect.

cold, completely.

count, the score in a basketball game.

crile, a vial in which crack cocaine is sold.

dead presidents, money.

digits, telephone number.

down, down with, in tune with the latest styles and fashions and music.

face, pride.

fall off, to experience a loss of popularity.

front, to pretend.

gang banger, a gang member.

hacker, a rough and aggressive defensive player in basketball.

hang, to relax, do nothing.

heavy, serious.

Hit me!, call me on my telephone pager.

ho, hoe, any woman, but especially an attractive one (from whore).

hood rat, somebody from one's home neighborhood.

jack up, to assault physically.

kick it, to relax.

kicks, sneakers.

living large, succeeding at an enterprise or project.

mack, a smooth operator.

my bad!, that was my fault—sorry!

pill, a basketball.

pop shit, to boast and swagger.

posse, a group of friends.

profile, to show off.

roller, someone who is succeeding.

scrilla, money.

stupid, extremely.

style, to put on a show.

tapped, broke, without money.

throw down, to enjoy a party.

24/7, to remain vigilant 24 hours a day, 7 days a week.

vogue, to wear stylish clothes.

Word! Word up! I heartily agree with what you said!

GETTING RELIGION

*I*t was politics, chiefly, that prompted adventurous attempts at the English
settlement of Virginia in the 16th century, but later it was religion (13th
century, ultimately from Latin) that brought the first successful English
settlers to Massachusetts Bay. They called themselves **pilgrimes** (1630). The
Pilgrim Fathers, as they are styled in American history (the phrase coming from
an ode by Samuel Davis cited to 1799), were Calvinist dissenters from the
established Church of England, over which Henry VIII made himself the head in
1533 after he could not get the pope to give him the divorce he wanted.

OF PILGRIMS AND PURITANS

The *Pilgrims* were reform-minded *Puritans* (1560s; a derogatory term
assigned to them by their enemies) and were *Separatists* (1608) because
they chose to break from the established Church of England. They were
also known as *Congregationalists* (from *Congregational*, 1639, so called
because individual churches were autonomous congregations) and were
similar in spirit to other English church reform movements of the time.
Unable to establish themselves comfortably in England (where their
movement was illegal) or in Holland (they settled in Leiden from 1609-
20), the Pilgrims secured sufficient financial backing to allow them to
plant a *theocracy* (1622, from Greek *theokratia*, from *the*, God, from *theos*
+ -*kratia*, -cracy, from *kratos*, strength, power) in the New World. About
a third of the 102 passengers on the *Mayflower* were inspired by this religious fervor; the others were seeking adventure or financial advancement, or were servants. They were actually headed for the mouth of the
Hudson River, then being a part of Virginia, but landed (tradition says,
perhaps inaccurately) in December 1620 at *Plymouth Rock* in Massachusetts, having set out the previous September from Plymouth, England.
They had stopped briefly at the tip of Cape Cod (near modern-day
Provincetown), and after exploring the area and agreeing (in the
Mayflower Compact) to stick together, established their permanent settlement at Plymouth on Cape Cod Bay. They built a *common house* as 1620
ended and encountered Samoset of the local Wampanoag tribe on March
11, 1621. They also met Squanto, who taught them how to plant corn,
and Massasoit, the Wampanoag *sachem* (1622) or chief, with whom they
contracted a peace treaty that was to last 54 years. The successful harvest
of 1621 was cause for real celebration, and Governor Bradford declared a
feast for the Pilgrims and their Wampanoag friends, the model for subsequent Thanksgiving celebrations (see THAT HOLIDAY SPIRIT). In 1630
another settlement of non-separatist Puritans established the *Massachusetts Bay Colony* nearby in Boston, but the Plymouth Colony was not
absorbed into it until 1691.

This colony and its New England offshoots were run with *puritanical*
(1607) strictness. Early on, blue laws (see THE WORD OF THE LAW,
subsection High Profile State Laws) in the Puritans' settlement at New
Haven forbade adultery, drunkenness, and failure to attend church or
meeting (the term preferred by Protestant nonconformists since the late
1500s) on the Sabbath (which for them began at sundown on Saturday).
A Connecticut law of the period made it a crime to "run on the Sabbath
day" or "walk in [the] garden, or elsewhere, except reverently to and
from meeting." (Punishments included being fastened to a pillory, put
into stocks, being dunked in water, or, as Nathaniel Hawthorne relates in

Sunday-go-to-meeting-clothes.

The Scarlet Letter, being forced to wear the red letter *A* for *adultery* on one's dress—as did his character Hester Prynne). They dressed simply in severe *meeting clothes* (1775), later *Sunday-go-to-meeting-clothes* (1831) or *Sunday best* (1849). The Bible was their guide, and for many families was the only book in the house.

The Puritans and many Americans who followed their model were *fundamentalists*. But this word did not appear in American print until 1909. The fundamentalist tradition continued through American history (and still remains strong), despite such disparaging characterizations as *Bible beaters, Bible bangers, Bible pounders* (1880s), and *Bible thumpers* (1937). Around 1925 H.L. Mencken coined the term *Bible Belt* (the model for *Snow Belt, Sun Belt, Rust Belt*, etc.) for the region of the country where fundamentalism is "strongest, across its midsection from the Appalachians west into the Plains. It has a strong northern peak extending into Indiana, and it stretches into New Mexico and especially into Arizona. By the late 1990s most Americans did go to church regularly (some 40 percent attending weekly), and they sent the kids to *Sunday school* (1783); many declared they were *born-again*, and religion flourished in *evangelical* (18th century), *charismatic* (1882), *New Age* (1956), and other churches. (*Born-again* derives from John 3:3: "Except a man be born again, he cannot see the kingdom of God.")

PLAIN PEOPLE

In a country where many people advocate full entry of *women into the priesthood* and the use of *inclusive language* (words that are not gender-tagged) in liturgies, hymnals, and revised versions of the Bible, the *Pennsylvania Dutch* (around 1824, the *Dutch* deriving from *Deutsch* "German," reflecting their German ancestry), for one, still cling to their old ways. William Penn, a Quaker, established Pennsylvania in 1682 as a place of religious freedom not encouraged in, for example, many parts of New England. It attracted groups from Germany such as the *Mennonites* (1565, from cleric *Menno* Simons), *Old Order Amish* (1844, from Swiss Mennonite cleric Jacob *Amman*), *Dunkers* (1744, from Pennsylvania

"Kleberg County [Texas] commissioners . . . designated 'Heaven-o' as the county's official greeting. The reason: 'Hello' contains the word 'Hell.'"

— Associated Press, January 17, 1997, the commissioners not knowing that hello (1889), an altered form of hollo, goes back to an Old German greeting in hailing a boat; hullo is the British spelling.

A Pennsylvania Dutch woodcut, depicting the family record.

German) or *Brethren, Renewed Church of the Brethren* (*Moravians*, 15th century), and the *Schwenkfelders* (1882–83).

In addition to religion, there is also superstition: consider the *hex signs* on Pennsylvania Dutch barns (*hex* the noun, 1856, from an 1830 verb *hex*, itself from Pennsylvania German, from German *Hexe*, witch, ultimately from an Old High German word akin to the Middle English word for *hag*). Not until 1850 or so did English become the first language of some of these self-isolated *Pennsylvania German* (1860s) communities, and in their English they still use German constructions such as "Heat the water that it boils," "Leave him have the book," and "The cheese is all" (without *gone* at the end).

AMERICAN RELIGIONS

Besides importing religions, Americans created some of their own. The list is long and extraordinary and each has its own history. One of the best-known is the *Church of Jesus Christ of Latter-day Saints* (*Mormons*).

Others are *New Thought, New Light Presbyterianism*, various *store-front churches*, the *Unitarian Universalist Church, Christian Science, Russellites* and *Jehovah's Witnesses*, gay and lesbian *Metropolitan Churches* and synagogues, and *Black Muslims*. There are innumerable variations on standard Christian denominations, such as the various *Lutheran synods* (*Lutheran*, the noun, dating to 1521; the adjective, to 1530, both, after Martin *Luther* [1483–1546], the German theologian and leader of the Reformation; *synod*, 14th century, ultimately from Greek *sunodos*, meeting or assembly). Others are *Voodoo* (1850, from Louisiana French *voudou*, from [African] Ewe and Fon *vodun*; the religion coming to the U.S. from Haiti), *Rosicrucianism* (*Rosicrucian*, 1624, from New Latin *Frater Rosae Crucis*, Brother of the Cross of the Rose, a translation of German *Rosenkreutz*, the surname of the legendary founder of the society's), and beliefs of various *gurus* (1613, from Hindi, from Sanskrit).

A Scientology bookstore.

Reverend Sun Myung Moon (left) in 1976.

Still more were a *Millennial Church* (with a Messiah), the *International Church of the Four-Square Gospel* (led by "Sister Aimée Semple Macpherson"), the *Church of Elvis Presley*, and various groups whose rituals involve *snake handlers*. Not to mention the "mainstream" Baptists, both Southern and not, both *total immersion* and not, Episcopalians and Anglo-Catholics, Eastern Orthodox and *Uniat* (the latter, cited to 1833 in English, Ukranian, "one in favor of the union of the Roman Catholic and Eastern Orthodox churches"), Roman Catholics and Old Catholics, African Methodist Episcopalians (commonly abbreviated A.M.E.), Transcendentalists, Ethical Culturalists, *Hare Krishnas* (1969, from *Hare Khrishna*, a phrase in a chant, from Hindi), *Moonies* (1974, from Korean evangelist Sun Myung *Moon*, born 1920), and on and on. The *Church of Scientology* (founded in 1954 by science-fiction writer L. Ron Hubbard) had by century's end thousands of churches, missions in over a hundred countries, noted celebrity adherents, and sales of millions of copies of Hubbard's book *Dianetics*.

GIMME THAT OLD-TIME RELIGION

Fundamentalist Christian evangelist Billy Graham in 1966.

In addition we have had *revivalism* (cited to 1815) and *revivalists* (cited to 1820), from Jonathan Edwards ("Sinners in the Hands of an Angry god" still can shake you up mightily) and the *Great Awakening* (1736) to Billy Sunday (most famous of the 700 revivalists *on the sawdust trail* collecting free-will offerings in makeshift tabernacles into the 1920s), Oral Roberts (who began in 1935, followed by his son), and Billy Graham (who started his *crusades* in 1942—"Decide for Christ!") onward to modern *televangelists* (1973), some of whom have wound up rich, some in jail. The *old-fashioned gospel* of Dwight Moody (popular from 1875-99), and preaching that causes listeners to *get religion* and *shout hallelujah*, are still strong.

The Mormons

The *Mormons*, more accurately called the Latter-day Saints, were the "spiritual pioneers" of the American West: They established 350 settlements in Utah, Nevada, Arizona, Wyoming, and Idaho along with a self-sufficient agrarian economy backstopped by their own industries.

The *Mormon Church*, more accurately called the *Church of Jesus Christ of Latter-day Saints*, was founded in Fayette, New York, on April 6, 1830, by Joseph Smith, Jr., who dictated to *scribes* a 600-page tract, *The Book of Mormon.* (The word *Mormon* is the name of the ancient prophet who appeared to Smith, relating to him a sacred history of the Americas—the content of *The Book*.)

After being driven out of New York—and after Smith's murder by a hostile Illinois mob in 1844—the Mormons under Brigham Young (now *sustained* as their new *prophet*) moved onward, settling in the Salt Lake Valley in July 1847.

Some who chose not to follow Young founded the *Reorganized Church of Jesus Christ of Latter Day Saints* in Amboy, Illinois, in 1860, their *president* being Joseph Smith, III. Their headquarters is in Missouri.

Though they once practiced *plural marriage*, they agreed in 1890 to refrain from it after getting into difficulties with the federal government.

The Mormons have their own vocabulary like other denominations. A local congregation is a *ward*. An unpaid *bishop* heads the *ward*. Five to ten *wards* make up a *stake*, headed by a *stake president*. The central church is governed by a *president* or *prophet*, with two *counselors*. The *Council of Twelve Apostles* is the governing body. Members of the *Council of Seventies* serve as administrators.

Millions of Americans, regardless of faith, listen to music sung by the famous Mormon *Tabernacle* Choir, and many others read the *Deseret News*, the famous Salt Lake City newspaper—also operated by the Mormons.

Brigham Young became the second president of the Church of Jesus Christ of Later Day Saints when the religion's founder, Joseph Smith, was lynched. To escape further persecution, Young led the Mormons to Utah, where they founded Salt Lake City in 1847.

CHURCH-RELATED LANGUAGE

The familiar African American use of *brother* and *sister* recalls a more widespread and church-related form of address of the past. Quakers addressed one another as *friend*—they were the (*Religious*) *Society of Friends* from early on—and Mormons refer to themselves as *saints*. (Thus the city of *St. George* in Utah is named for a Mormon farmer, not the canonized dragon-slayer.) Every Jehovah's Witness is a *minister*, but their churches (called *Kingdom Halls*) also have leaders, while the *Quaker meeting* has merely a *clerk*. Christian Science meetings use two *readers* (to read from the Bible and from founder Mary Baker Eddy's *Science and Health with Key to the Scriptures*, 1875) and they have *practitioners* but no clerics per se.

The term *Quaker* reminds us that *god-fearing* (1835) people have also been much ridiculed in America—the name was originally, like that of *Methodists* and *Shakers*, intended to be insulting. Quakers were once officially called *The United Society of Believers in Christ's Second Appearance*, and believed that "agitation of the body" fostered prophecy. Angli-

Christian Scientists

In frail health and afflicted with a spinal malady since her birth in 1821 in Bow, New Hampshire, Mary Baker, later known by her married name of Mary Baker Eddy, tried various forms of physical and mental healing until she was temporarily cured in 1861 by Phineas Parkhurst Quimby of Portland, Maine. Quimby, an ex-clockmaker and hypnotist, was the father of the *New Thought* of "religio-metaphysical" healing; he believed that all illness was "a matter of the mind," due to "wrong thought," and practiced mental-suggestion healing. He was also the teacher of several famous *faith doctors* (an 1828 term), *faith curists* (1883), or *faith healers* (1885) and founder of various *faith cures* (1880s) and religious sects—as well as the creator of much of their vocabulary. Quimby thought he had rediscovered Jesus's healing methods: the future founder of Christian Science agreed, studied his notes thoroughly, and wrote and lectured about his methods for religious audiences.

After Quimby's death in 1866, Mary Baker's frail health returned. While recovering from a bad fall that same year, she read Biblical accounts of Jesus's healing, regained her full health, and discovered and named *Christian Science* (she considered the word *science* to be but another name for God's wisdom). Denying Quimby's influence, she claimed to have founded the religion on principles and divine laws formulated directly from the acts and sayings of Jesus. She began to write, supported herself by teaching students to be faith healers, and in 1875, using her then married name of Mary Baker Patterson, published *Science and Health*. In 1877 she married her third husband, Asa Gilbert Eddy, one of her followers.

She founded and named her *Mother Church*, or *First Church of Christ, Scientist*, in 1879 first in Lynn, then in Roxbury, Massachusetts. (Its Boston edifice was completed in 1895.) This church contained a *Christian Science Reading Room*, the prototype of similar rooms found in most of the Christian Science churches and in many other locations today. In the 1880s and 90s, as Mrs. Eddy's religion grew, many people first began talking about *Christian Scientists*, its *readers*, and its *practitioners*. Another name that Mrs. Eddy added to the language is *The Christian Science Monitor*, the still-active newspaper she founded in 1908, two years before her death.

Christian Science founder Mary Baker Eddy.

"In the year 1866, I discovered the Christ Science or divine laws of Life, Truth, and Love, and named my discovery Christian Science."

— *Mary Baker Eddy*, **Science and Health with Key to the Scriptures**, *1875*

cans laughed at John Wesley's (1703–91) bringing of "method" into Episcopalianism. (He was famous for "Cleanliness is next to godliness," uttered in his *Sermon XCIII, On Dress*.) The Shakers were a branch of the *plain people*. The Shakers gave us an American Messiah (Ann Lee, God the Mother), plain and practical clothes and furniture, the Poland China hog, packets of seeds, the clothespin, the apple parer, and other innovations.

Like every other specialized group, each denomination has its own inside vocabulary. Until recent times, Quakers used formal, biblical *thee* not *you*. They still "affirm" rather than "swear" (an alternative found in many formulas for public oaths).

Holy Rollers

There is no such thing as an organized *Holy Roller* religion or religious group, but the term is a highly derogatory epithet applied by some people to a fervent local sect or to an emotional revival meeting. *Holy Roller* seems to have come into use in 1842 and may first have been used to refer to members of the Sweezyite sect in New York State, who did express their religious zeal by shouting, shaking, and rolling on the floor.

Pulpit oratory has strongly influenced civil rights (the Revs. Martin Luther King, Jr., Ralph Abernathy, and Jesse Jackson to name a few such speakers). Similarly, it has profoundly affected American literature (notably William Faulkner). Radio from the 1930s onward featured the controversial right-wing Father Charles Edward Coughlin (1891–1979); early television, the much-admired showman Bishop Fulton John Sheen (1895–1979). In the 1950s Americans read and talked about *The Power of Positive Thinking* (1952)—one of the first modern *self-help books*—by American cleric Norman Vincent Peale. Protestantism along with Freemasonry informed American thought from the very beginning. Literary critics, in fact, have argued that "a dark thread of Calvinism" runs all through American literature. Others would identify the principal influence as Puritanism, which H.L. Mencken waggishly defined as "the haunting fear that someone, somewhere, may be happy." Certainly the *work ethic* and the *family values* politicians of the 1990s liked to proclaim their roots in Christian religion. Pat Robertson's *700 Club*, the *Christian Coalition*, and the *Christian Right* generally undertook to return Christian morality to American life and politics. Louis Farrakhan of *The Nation of Islam* and promoter of the October 1995 *Million Man March* (to encourage African American independence and ethical values) agreed that "we need a new beginning" and "moral tone is not intolerance." Some Christian Fundamentalists wanted—into the 1990s—to ban the teaching of Evolution and teach only *Creationism* (1880), also called *creation science* (1979), in the schools. Some Christians wanted to return organized prayer to public schools (banned by a Supreme Court decision in 1962; see THE WORD OF THE LAW AND THE LAW OF THE LAND, subsection All Rise: Here Come the Judges).

NEW TRENDS

In later decades of the 20th century so many American priests left the Catholic Church (with vocations falling off so that fewer and fewer new priests were being trained) that people began to talk about the possibility of a *Eucharistic famine*. This did not happen. In a world of uncertainty and rapid change, Americans sought help—spiritual help—in a number of ways, evidenced by a changing language.

Trends in any aspect of society can be tracked by looking at the words used in connection with it. A decided shift toward *spirituality, recovery,* and *self-help* occurred in the general language of religion as the

Jehovah's Witnesses

Charles Taze "Pastor" Russell (1852–1916) organized the *International Bible Student's Association* in 1872. This was the group from which *Jehovah's Witnesses* grew, but he never heard this name—his followers were known as *Russellites*. A wealthy unordained Congregationalist from Pittsburgh, Russell became "pastor" of his independent church there in 1877, preaching that the Second Coming of Christ had been an *invisible return* that had occurred in 1874, since which the world had been in the *Millennial Age*, which would end in 1914 with chaos, a resurrection of the dead, and the establishment of Christ's Kingdom on Earth. In 1879 Russell started a Bible journal that was later called the *Watchtower* (his wife disagreed on who should be editor, leading to their legal separation), then in 1884 founded the *Watchtower Bible and Tract Society*, a flourishing religious publishing house. He circulated 16 million copies of his own religious books and tracts and wrote a weekly sermon that appeared in 2,000 newspapers. Thus, if not widely talked about, he was certainly widely read.

On Russell's death Joseph Franklin "Judge" Rutherford (1869–1941) became the sect's leader. A Russellite convert and its former legal adviser, he de-emphasized the setting of any exact date of Christ's Second Coming and, in 1931, adopted the name *Jehovah's Witnesses* for the sect, along with the slogan "Millions now living will never die." The name *Jehovah's Witnesses* was taken not only to reaffirm the name *Jehovah* as the true God but also to identify those who witness in that name as His specially accredited followers. Thus the *Witnesses* in the U.S. (headquarters are in Brooklyn, New York) are all called *ministers* and keep Jehovah's command to preach the good news of the rapidly approaching God's Kingdom—at their *Kingdom Halls,* by door-to-door evangelism, and by handing out the *Watchtower* and other religious tracts on street corners.

"Do all the good you can,

By all the means you can,

In all the ways you can,

In all the places you can,

At all the times you can,

To all the people you can,

As long as ever you can."

— John Wesley's Rule; note that the derogatory do-gooder *is dated only to 1926, or 135 years after Wesley's death.*

1990s drew to a close. Americans were using (and reading) these kinds of words by 1997—all of them come from popular books classed as *religious* at the time:

communing spiritually with nature

closer spiritual bonding—parent and child (*bonding* a cliché of the late 1980s)

sensitive man

deepening one's path to Buddha-hood

the joyful journey to deeper spirituality

Women of Faith conferences

exercise our inner joy

the inner child

St. Patrick's Cathedral in Manhattan.

the child within us

spiritual retreats

reaching out

interventions to break co-dependency and save a Christian marriage

online religious services—log on to God!

a spirituality on nature (*a* + *spirituality* referring to a book)

Promise Keepers (the Evangelical Christian men's movement)

lack of moral direction (*moral* and *morality* being much used in social, religious, and political contexts in the 1990s)

feminist Christianity

reconnecting with Earth to renew faith

changing a love of power to the power of love

emptying oneself to help others

praying the Scripture in small groups

Biblical critiques of racism

WORDS WITH RELIGIOUS ROOTS

A number of long-standing terms founded in or related to religion and its concerns have been used by Americans on a daily basis, some of these:

acolyte, around 1000, originally an altar boy (from Greek *akolouthes,* follower), now any kind of assistant, especially a slavish follower.

altar boy, 1772, an acolyte; now also a "goody-goody" young man or naive innocent.

amen corner, 1860, a corner in a church that is reserved for those who lead congregational responses; it also has come to mean any group of fervent leaders. The word *amen,* used not only at the ends of prayers and hymns but also as an interjection expressing strong agreement, came into Old English from Latin and Greek, ultimately from Hebrew *'amen,* verily, certainly.

camp meeting, 1803, a series of revival services held outdoors under a tent.

choirboy, 1837, a young male choir member; now also an innocent police rookie, or just a naive, innocent person.

church key, around 1953, a device for opening a bottle of beer, so called it is said for its similarity in appearance to old-fashioned keys used to open church doors.

church mouse, poor as a very poor indeed (there being little to eat in a church).

eleventh commandment, any important instruction not covered by the rest; in American political contexts, especially since the Watergate scandal, it is popularly considered to be "Don't get caught."

eleventh hour, 1826, the latest possible time, from the parable in Matthew 20:1-6, relating to vineyard laborers who were hired at the *eleventh hour,* and then were paid the same as those hired earlier in the day.

fire and brimstone, from the Bible ("Upon the wicked he shall rain snares, fire and brimstone," Psalm 11:6), the torment and tortures of sinners in hell; the adjective meaning highly spirited, as of a sermon.

Gideon Bible, a Bible purchased by the *Gideons* and placed in hotel rooms for travelers since the early 1900s. *Gideon International,* founded as "a Christian organization of American commercial travelers" in 1898-99, was named after *Gideon,* a judge of ancient Israel who is written about in Judges 6:11.

God's acre, 1617, a churchyard.

God squad, any evangelical, proselytizing group.

gosh, 1757, one of many euphemisms for *God* (also *by gar/gosh/gum* for *by God*); *golly* goes back to 1775.

Hail Mary, 15th century, a translation of Medieval Latin *Ave Maria,* the opening words of Catholic prayer to the Virgin Mary consisting of a plea for intercession; *hail-Mary* now used in some sports to denote a very desperate, very long pass, usually at the end of a half or a period or at the end of a game (see THE SPORTING LIFE).

holier-than-thou, 1859, pious and self-satisfied.

Holy Joe, 1874, a military chaplain.

Is the Pope Catholic? jocular equivalent to *are you kidding?*

Judas priest, near-blasphemous exclamation used like *Jesus Christ!* since at least the early 1900s.

Lawd, folksy spelling of *Lord,* used in many dialects; also *Lawdy, Lawsy,* as in *Lawdy mercy!*; also *Law* (for *Lord*), as in "Oh, Law! The cat is inside the Thanksgiving turkey!"

ministry, 14th century, a newer sense being a religiously-sponsored social welfare project, such as a *firewood ministry* in winter for needy clients.

Old Nick, 1668, also *Old Harry, Old Scratch,* three of many names for the Devil. In the 1980s–90s there was much concern periodically across the nation about alleged *satanic rites* and sacrifices; the numeral 666 was alleged evidence of this. Some major corporations even came under attack by groups believing that some corporate logos were satanic in origin.

padre, 1584, a priest or a chaplain, from the Spanish, Italian, or Portuguese for father. priest.

pass the plate, take up any kind of collection, as is done in churches.

plural marriage, euphemistic Mormon term for polygamy.

Quaker guns, 1809, dummy guns, such as cannons made of wood, to deceive a distant enemy.

"Then the Lord rained upon Sodom and upon Gomorrah brimstone and fire."

— Genesis 19:24

Second Coming, 1644, the return of Christ on The Day of Judgment; often used in secular, jocular contexts with regard to a major comeback after a disappearance from public life of a celebrity.

until kingdom come, 1785, the next world, from "Thy kingdom come" (Matthew 6:10), used as an intensive phrase, as in "We can argue about this until kingdom come, if you want."

THE OCCULT

Perhaps most colorful are the believers in the religions (or superstitions) arising from fascination with the occult. They were given a start in America by Andrew Jackson Davis' book *Nature's Divine Revelations* (1847) and the three Fox Sisters (Kate, Margaret, and Leah) who introduced Spiritualism in upstate New York. Into American speech came *medium* (1852, *trance-medium* by 1878), *séance* (already cited in English to 1803), *table-rapping*, etc. From England we imported *clairvoyance* (1840), *clairaudience, telepathy* (1882), and *thought transference,* and by ourselves we came up with *mind-reader* (1887), *past-life regression,* and *channeling,* the last being communication by voice by a disembodied entity through a living human being, much talked about especially in the 1980s. In 1890 William and Isaac Field patented as a toy *Ouija* (combining the French and German words for "yes," as it was supposed to answer questions). It was in 1919—after deaths in the Great War led to a great many attempts to contact *the other side* by all sorts of methods— that Mrs. John Curran declared she could contact the *spirit world* with her *Ouija,* and ever since then the board game has been popular.

THE AMERICAN WAY OF SEX

*T*he courting rituals *on which a man relied in colonial America to win the favor of the woman he loved must seem prehistoric to today's lovers. The* courting stick, *a six-foot-long wooden tube that couples used to whisper* sweet nothings *to each other under the watchful eyes of their parents, is hardly necessary in an age where two people who are interested in* getting it on *can communicate by cellular phone as they drive to work or have* cybersex *on the computer nets to share their* sexual fantasies.

Pushing the sexual envelope in 1908.

Sigmund Freud, the father of psychoanalysis, used methods such as free association of thoughts and dream analysis to unearth hidden sexual motives.

Sexology (1902, the study of human sexual behavior) turned sex into a legitimate field for scientific inquiry, but until well into the 20th century, most Americans remained prudish when it came to discussing their *sex lives*. Alfred Kinsey's 1948 *Kinsey Report,* the first scientific study of Americans' sexual behavior, was attacked from all sides, and the work of William Masters and Virginia Johnson in the 1960s provoked a similar response. The arrival of the *sexual revolution* in the 1960s and 1970s (though it began in the post-World War II 1940s) brought sex out in the open, but it was the prevalence of *AIDS* in the early 1980s that put sexual habits and preferences on the front page of every newspaper in America. In the 1990s, with television talk shows focusing daily on once-taboo subjects like *sexual abuse*, it's not surprising that even pre-teenagers now have a sexual vocabulary that includes terms like *date rape* (a date that ends in a forced sexual encounter), *sexual harassment* on the job (including everything from flirting to obtaining *sexual favors*), and *safe sex.*

There is a matter-of-factness in the way Americans talk about sex these days. But according to *Sex in America: A Definitive Survey* (1994), the majority of Americans are neither *promiscuous* (a 17th century word from Latin, meaning "mixed" or "indiscriminate") nor unfaithful to their spouses. They are, however, a lot less shy.

DREAM GIRLS

Although the fantasy woman of the Revolutionary War soldier is unknown to us, many Civil War soldiers carried drawings of pretty girls clipped from fashion magazines of the day and by the 1880s such actresses as Lillian Russell—"airy, fairy Lillian, the American Beauty"—set the style for pretty girls. In the 1890s Charles Dana Gibson's *Gibson girl* was the mode. The early *flappers* bobbed their hair in imitation of the French prostitutes so highly advertised in World War I. By the 1920s the movies controlled American taste in beauty, giving us such virginal but vulnerable types as Lillian Gish, Mary Pickford, and Norma Talmadge and such man-destroying femme fatales as Theda Bara. The World War II *oomph girls, sweater girls,* and *pinup girls* were also products of the movies. Here are some major types of pretty or alluring girls we have talked about:

the Gibson girl, the typical, idealized 1890s girl as portrayed by (and in a large measure created by) illustrator Charles Dana Gibson in his many drawings for such popular magazines as the old *Life, Century, Harper's, Scribners,* and *Collier's Weekly.* The Gibson girl's soft, wide

Lillian Russell in 1893.

The Gibson girl.

pompadour, parasol, and clothing influenced some styles until the 1930s. She had the 1890s *hourglass* figure.

the Ziegfeld girl, 1907. Florenz Ziegfeld's *Follies of 1907* was a new type of musical *revue,* featuring "the most beautiful girls ever to walk across an American stage," each personally chosen by Ziegfeld himself. By the time of the last annual *Ziegfeld Follies* in 1931, America had gotten used to calling any tall, statuesque girl a *Ziegfeld girl.*

the vamp and *to vamp* were in the language by 1910, referring to an unscrupulous, seductive woman who exploited men. However, as a type of heavily made-up, mysteriously exotic woman, the word and type were popularized by Theda Bara in the 1914 movie *A Fool There Was*, and later by Pola Negri in the 1919 German-made film *Passion*. *Vamp*, of course, is a shortening of the 17th century word *vampire* (via German from an Old West Slavic word for *witch*).

bathing beauty was popularized before the 1920s by the *Mack Sennett Bathing Beauties*. This was the first term for a girl which admitted that to be "pretty" she had to have a good figure as well as a pretty face. In the 20s *bathing beauty contest* also became a popular term, though *beauty contest* dates from the 1890s.

Miss America, the girl chosen as a paragon of beauty and talent in America at an annual national beauty contest. The first winner was Margaret Gorman of Washington in 1921, who was first called "Miss America" the following year. From the late 1930s any pretty, typically American girl was called "a regular Miss America." Today the term (and the pageant) is regarded with disdain by many.

the It Girl. People began talking about *it* (sex appeal) and *the It Girl* in 1928, both due to the 1928 Hollywood movie based on Elinor Glyn's lush, titillating, mildly daring, best-selling 1927 novel *It*. The star of the movie was Clara Bow, billed as *the It Girl;* an *it girl* then came to mean any girl who was full of sex appeal and vivacious gaiety.

sex kitten, 1940, usually in newspaper gossip columns.

glamour girl, 1941, popularized by Hollywood gossip columnists; *glamour puss*, a humorous or disparaging term for a pretentiously glamorous person of either sex.

oomph girl, early 1940s, popularized by Hollywood press agentry. *Oomph* had been in Hollywood use for sex appeal since 1939. (The word *oomph* is expressive of exertion.)

sweater girl, early 1940s, originally Hollywood press agent use for a sexually attractive girl whose ample and well-defined breasts looked good in a sweater. Two things were happening during World War II that popularized this term: women, including defense plant workers, were wearing tight sweaters over shape-enhancing bras, and Hollywood studios and press agents were trying to come up with new sex-appeal words to describe specific stars. The *Oomph girl, sweater girl,* and *pinup girl* all applied to the same type of buxom, sexy girl, and several Hollywood stars and starlets claimed to be "the original oomph girl" or "the original sweater girl." In the mid-1990s *sweater girl* made a comeback in the language of teenagers, proving that in matters of sex if not language, nothing is predictable.

pin-up girl, pinup girl entered the general language during World War II, first appearing in the Armed Forces newspaper *Yank* on April 30, 1943. It became a popular term thanks to U.S. soldiers, sailors, and

Mack Sennett's Bathing Beauties in 1919.

"Kiss me, you fool." Theda Bara "said" this famous line in the silent movie classic, *A Fool There Was.*

Miss Florida of 1927.

pilots who had put up free publicity photographs of movie actresses and models in footlockers, barracks, crews' quarters, airplane cockpits, military truck cabs, and bars all over the world. Betty Grable was probably the most popular *pinup* and Rita Hayworth's famous pinup photo probably the most artistic (a copy is said to have been attached to the first atomic bomb dropped on Hiroshima in 1945).

sex symbol, mid 1950s. A term first used to explain why certain Hollywood stars were so popular, it was soon used by newspapers to describe the most famous movie glamour girls, especially Marilyn Monroe and Brigitte Bardot.

playmate had been used since the 1920s to refer to a *good time girl* (1928) who "seeks men only as playmates." It became a popular term with *Playboy* magazine's monthly *centerfold* photograph of a sexy, scantily clad girl (nude since the early 1970s) called "the Playmate of the Month." The term was well known soon after *Playboy's* first issue in December 1953. *Playboy's Playmate* catered to male sexual fantasies, showing unbelievably long-legged, large-breasted women. *Playboy Clubs* also featured *Bunnies*, the club's waitresses, whose scanty uniforms even came with white cotton tails. By the mid 1960s *bunny* meant a sexually attractive girl, especially one who attached herself to a sport because she enjoyed the social life and the men found with it, giving us *ski bunny* and *beach bunny.*

fox, a sexy girl, from chiefly African-American speech. When heavyweight boxer Muhammad Ali used it in an interview with *Time* in 1963, others started using it across the nation. It is traceable in print to 1961, though probably older, going back to 1958 black jazz usage.

Cosmo Girl dates back to 1965, when Helen Gurley Brown took over as editor-in-chief of *Cosmopolitan* magazine. This was the image of a sexy, fashionably dressed, take-charge young woman in her 20s or 30s, based on Brown's popular 1962 book, *Sex and the Single Girl.*

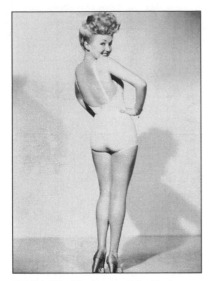

World War II pin-up girls, Betty Grable (above) and Rita Hayworth (below).

Hugh Hefner with six of his bunnies at a Playboy Club in 1962.

X-RATED

Ever since Mary Irwin and John Rice scandalized audiences with the first adult on-screen kiss in 1896, the portrayal of sex in the movies and on television has provoked widespread criticism and controversy. The National Legion of Decency, created by the U. S. Catholic Church in the early 1930s, condemned movies that showed any hint of promiscuity, infidelity, nudity, brutality, or sympathy for evildoers, or that allowed the use of objectionable words (including *damn* in *Gone With the Wind*). Until 1958 the *Legion of Decency,* as it was commonly called (later renamed the *Catholic Film Office*), used a rather complicated *rating system* to grade movies for the acceptability of their content. The popular *Miracle on 34th Street* received a B ("objectionable in part or all") rating because one of the major characters was divorced and unrepentant.

Throughout the 1950s and early 1960s, court rulings supporting constitutional guarantees of freedom of expression combined with changing

A one-penny peepshow at the Louisiana state fair in 1938.

public attitudes concerning morality to make it increasingly difficult to enforce such decency codes. In 1968 the Motion Picture Association of America (MPAA) stopped trying to control movies and turned to categorizing them with a rating system that has been used (with some modifications) ever since:

G (general), all ages permitted.

PG (parental guidance suggested), all ages admitted. By the 1980s this rating meant the movie might contain a few obscenities and perhaps a bit of not-too-explicit sex.

PG-13 (parental guidance strongly recommended; some material may be inappropriate for pre-teenagers).

R (restricted), persons under 17 must be accompanied by a parent or guardian. By the 1980s this rating often meant lots of obscenities or violence, some nudity, or fairly obvious sex.

X, no one under 17 admitted. Since 1968 the term has entered the general language to mean "pornographic," "used for sex," and even "sexy"; thus we speak of *X-rated* books and records, *X-rated* motels, and even *X-rated* (revealing, sexy) attire.

The *NC-17 rating* (*n*o children under 17 admitted) was created in 1990 to allow filmmakers to entice adult audiences without the stigma of an X rating. More risqué than R but not quite as shocking as X, which is usually reserved for *hard-core pornography* (from the Greek *porne*, "harlot," and *-graphos*, "writing," hence "writing about harlots") and ultraviolent films, an NC-17 rated movie usually means less profit than an R-rated one.

In the 1930s, *stag movies* were short, pornographic films shown at *stag parties* for men about to be married (*stag* had been used to mean "for men only" since 1934). In the 1940s, *adult movies* referred to movies in peepshow arcades and in advertisements for pornographic movies that could be purchased through the mail for private viewing or for stag parties. The term was *blue movies* in the 1950s (from the 1864 use of *blue* to

A burlesque theater in Washington, D.C. in 1937.

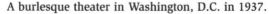

Baltimore's porn district—The Block—in 1976.

Wherever the line was drawn that separated decency and indecency, nearly everyone agreed that *Hustler* editor Larry Flynt went way beyond it. If *Playboy* was naughty and *Penthouse* was dirty, *Hustler* was depraved.

refer to indecent or obscene talk), and in the late 1960s it was *skin flicks*, or commercial pornographic movies shown at a *skin house* (a movie theater openly showing *pornographic movies)*, also a late 1960s term. By 1971, feature-length *porn* (or *porno*) *movies* were being shown both privately and commercially at *porn* (or *porno*) houses. *Deep Throat* (1972), the first widely distributed porno movie featuring explicit sex, made its star, Linda Lovelace, a household name.

The United States Supreme Court has held that government authorities can seize materials that are obscene, sexually graphic, or "patently offensive to an average person" and lacking any "serious literary, artistic, political, or scientific value." But porno continues to flourish, aided by the boom in *adult video stores* and *adult bookstores*. Most people agree that *child pornography* should be controlled, but beyond that, even feminists are often reluctant to join the government's stand against pornography, which raises the strongly objected-to issue of restrictive government censorship. There is growing concern and awareness, however, with the portrayal of violence in general, to which pornography has been linked.

The influence of MTV (Music Television), with its often sexually explicit *rock videos*, was pervasive in the 1980s and 1990s, as were cable television's *Playboy Channel* and *Home Box Office*, routinely exposing viewers to foul language, nudity, and sex scenes. The euphemism *late-night television*, denoting programs with nudity and sex scenes, evolved in the 1990s. Another problem for parents of the 1990s was the *900 number*, a telephone number available to anyone, for a price, to listen to lewd or suggestive talk, termed *phone sex.*

Sexually explicit or violent rock lyrics also aroused controversy in the 1980s and 1990s for their frankness, foul language, or abusiveness. In a 1993 hit song, rap artist L. L. Cool J talks about luring a girl to the back seat of his Jeep so he can "give it" to her "real raw." Not since the birth of rock 'n roll in the 1950s were American adults so appalled by the attitudes expressed by the music their children were listening to. In 1985, Mary ("Tipper") Gore, wife of then-Senator Albert Gore of Tennessee (later vice president) crusaded for *parental warning stickers* on music containing explicit lyrics. A policy of using such stickers was voluntarily begun by record companies in 1990.

BODY TALK

Sex in America almost always involves talk about our own and other people's bodies. Because certain parts of the body weren't talked about in polite conversation, and certain words not recorded, until the 1880s or 90s (or even until the 1930s), many people tend to think that many quite old English words for parts of the body are new and American. But most of these words have been in English for a long time, with a smattering of informal Americanisms added later.

Bosom, breast, and *tit* (meaning *teat*) all date from Old English, before the Norman invasion of 1066. Calling the complete female breasts, especially well-developed ones, *tits, melons, breastworks, boobs, boobies, knobs, knockers* and later *hooters* may be a fairly old practice but such words were not widely used until World War II, when pin-up pictures and the American male's "breast fixation" made them a very popular part of the language. *Headlights* definitely comes from the early 1940s when the shape of the female breasts in the *uplift bras* of the time seemed to match the protruding style of automobile headlights. The *breast implants, push-up bras,* and *Wonderbra* of the 1980s and 1990s are evidence that the American fascination with prominent breasts still drives our spending habits.

Penis (Latin, tail), *cock, prick, member, organ, vagina* (Latin, sheath, scabbard), and *pussy* were all common 17th century words. *Jock* and *jack* have meant the penis since the 16th century (from the familiar names for *John*), hence such terms as *jocker* and *jock* (1915) for sodomite, *jock strap,* and *jack off. Prick* was considered standard until the 18th century, when it began to be considered vulgar. *Dick* became common for penis around the time of the Civil War and men commonly called the testicles *balls* by the 1880s. The jocular *family jewels* also denotes the male genitals. *Clitoris* is a 17th century word (Greek *kleitoris,* small hill).

That leaves the part of the body which seems to have the most synonyms, the *arse* (Old English *aers*), whose variant *ass* is the basic American word. The first colonists brought with them such Old English synonyms for it as *fundament, buttocks, tail, rump, rear, backside,* and *prat. Posterior* was a new British word for it during the early colonial days; then Americans popularized *behind* in the 1780s, *fanny* in the 1860s (from the name *Fanny,* no one knows which Fanny), *beam* and *backporch* in the 1880s, and *can, rear end,* and *rumble seat* in the early 1930s, soon after cars had rumble seats. To show how difficult it is to date words which may be considered vulgar, *buttocks* has been in English since the 13th century, but its short form *butt* is first recorded as having been written in America in 1859!

GOING ALL THE WAY

Bundling was an English custom first reported in America in the 1630s. It was simply a courting couple's getting into bed together—he in his *small clothes* (today we would say *pajamas*), she in her petticoats—and doing a little private talking, kissing, and fondling. In small, chilly colonial houses this was often the only way the couple could have any privacy and keep warm (the girl's family was often clustered around the fireplace in the same room). An extra measure of protection was the *bundling board,* inserted between the couple by more careful parents. Nevertheless, bundling did lead to many of the *six-month children* of colonial days (children born before a couple had been married nine months).

Mating rites spawned a whole new vocabulary in the early part of the 19th century. *Petting* came into the language around 1910, and a *petting party* (1914) was first a party where much petting took place, but by the 1920s it was a private bout of petting for two. *Necking* (1910) seems to have been so called first in the South, then spread to the rest of the country during World War I, being very common from the 1920s into the early 1940s. *Necking* seems to denoted more innocent behavior—"outside the clothing" or "above the waist"—while petting might go much further. The knob fixed to a car's steering wheel, allowing the driver to steer with only one arm, was called a *necker's knob* (early 1940s). A *one-arm driver* was a boy more intent on squeezing his girl than on watching the road .

French kissing (1920s, to insert the tongue into the mouth while kissing) was also called *soul kissing* by the late 1930s. Passionate open-mouthed necking and "love bites" often led to red marks, usually on the neck, called *hickeys* (1920, from the 1913 *hickie, hickey* meaning a "doohickey," a small device or gadget). Other 20th century terms for getting affectionate include *parking* (as on a *lover's lane* or other secluded place; though *lover's lane* dates as early as 1881, in reference to a strolling area frequented by courting couples), *smooching* (1920s, mainly just hugging and kissing), and *submarine watching* (1960s, popularized by rock-and-roll disc jockey Murray the K, originally to sit with one's beloved holding hands and staring dreamily into space, but soon coming to mean serious petting). After the 1950s, most of these activities were regarded as mere *foreplay*; the focus shifted to *having sex*.

Nowadays people who are interested in *having sex* can choose from dozens of colorful phrases to express their intentions: they can *diddle* someone, opt for the more romatic *make love*, or try the Shakespearean *make the beast with two backs* (*Othello*, I,1). They can *get laid* (a term that originally required a female subject but applies to either gender today), *get bent*, or *get it on*. They can go out in search of a little *nookey* (possibly from the Dutch word *neuken*, to fuck), have a *quickie*, or go home for lunch and indulge themselves in a *nooner*. They can *ball, boink, boff, hump, grind, bang*, or *pound* their partner. They can even *jump his/her bones*. They can *have it off* (*with* someone). If all else fails, they can always say they've been *had*.

SEX ON THE NETS

Even though postal laws prohibit selling pornography through the mail, anyone who has a personal computer, a modem, and a credit card can now gain access to sexually explicit material on the vast networks that connect personal and business computers around the globe.

Ever since Jane Fonda, playing the 40th-century science-fiction queen *Barbarella* (1967), denounced "making love" the old-fashioned way as too messy and time-consuming, computer buffs have been exploring the possibilities for having sex without the complications involved in a face-to-face meeting. For most people, *cybersex* is confined to steamy written exchanges, where two people meet in a private *chat room* to share *sexual fantasies*. Net sites can be both intimate and anonymous, making them an ideal place, in some people's minds, for cultivating romantic relationships. An *online encounter* may even lead to an *F2F* (face-to-face) encounter, and it's entirely possible that computer bulletin boards will some day replace *singles bars*, college campuses, and other popular meeting places for the romantically inclined.

The only problem with *cybersex* (also called *teledildonics*, 1990s), is that with present technology the relationship can only proceed as fast as the parties can type, and conversations must be read on the screen. Virtual reality movies in which the audience can participate in the action on the screen can be expected in the future, a decided advance over *computer sex*. In fact, the future of pornography may lie in *cyberporn*, where the sexually adventurous individual can spend an evening home alone with his or her favorite software.

OUT OF THE CLOSET

Homosexual (from the Greek *homo*, same) and related words, or any references to homosexuality, were censored from most family newspapers, radio stations, and movies in America until the mid 1940s. Although love between men was celebrated as *eros* in ancient Greece and flourished in other societies, legal and religious sanctions against homosexual behavior were common in Europe in the Middle Ages, and in Colonial America sexual intercourse between males, or *sodomy* (from *Sodom*, the Biblical city known for its wickedness), was a crime punishable by death. The early colonists also used old English words, such as *bugger* and *buggery* (about 1300, originally meaning "heresy" and "heretic," from the Latin *Bulgaris*, alluding to the Bulgarians' adherence to the heretical Eastern Church) and later *pederast* (1720s, from Greek *paiderastes*, lover of boys). Many would not have known, or admitted knowing, what homosexuality was or that it existed, and those who did associated it primarily with men.

By the 1880s effeminate men, only some of whom were homosexuals, were an acceptable topic of conversation but were often spoken of merely as grown-up *sissies* (1846). The first informal derogatory terms for true homosexual men came into common use during the 1840s, and they were followed by even more offensive words during the next hundred years: *faggot* or *fag* (1905, *fag* a clipped form of *faggot*, itself probably from *fagot*, "bundle, lump, old woman," and going back via three languages—Middle English, Old French, and Old Provençal to a Vulgar

Two women embrace and kiss during the International Dyke March. The 1994 event was billed as the largest such gathering in history, with thousands of lesbians marching in support of gay rights initiatives.

Latin term reconstructed as *facus* and derived from the Greek *phakelos,* also meaning "bundle"). These were followed by *fairy, queer, pansy, fruit* or *fruitcake, limp-wrist* (referring to the stereotypical hand gesture associated with male homosexuals), and *swish*—all of them highly derogatory.

It wasn't until the 19th century that Americans first heard the word *lesbian* (Latin *Lesbius,* referring to Lesbos, birthplace of the 6th century B.C. homosexual poet Sappho) used in reference to homosexual women. Writers in the 1800s described *smashes* and *spoons* (infatuations) between college women, but these relationships never aroused much suspicion until Sigmund Freud (1856–1939) alerted people to the sexual motives underlying everyday behavior. Since then, female homosexuals have been derogatorily labeled *lesbos, bull dykes,* or simply *dykes* (from the 1850s expression *diked out,* meaning dressed up in fancy clothes). The adjective *butch* came from northern British dialect for the youngest male child of a family. Then it came to mean a tough guy, and by the 1940s it was being used to describe a man's very short haircut, which some lesbians adopted. In the 1990s the acronym *LUG* (*lesbian until graduation*), referring to transitory experimentation with homosexuality on college campuses, emerged.

The word *gay* meaning homosexual first appeared in *Underworld and Prison Slang* in 1935, where a *geycat* was defined as a homosexual boy. Prior to that it had been used to describe someone who was addicted to social pleasures and dissipations (1637), and was later applied to prostitutes or women who led an immoral life (1825). By 1955, *gay* was widely acknowledged as an American euphemism for homosexual, and *gays* who flaunted their homosexuality were said to *camp it up* (origin unknown). By the late 1980s into the 1990s *gay* had become the standard word for those whose *sexual preference* was homosexuality, although the formerly derogatory *queer* was adopted by many younger lesbians and gay men to describe themselves.

In the 1950s homosexuals, with Communists, were seen as a security risk—*perverts* whose behavior was the result of an incurable disease. The term *drag queen* (attested in print to 1941, a man who enjoys dressing in women's clothes) came into vogue during this decade—*drag* being an 1850s word for a petticoat worn by a male actor playing a female role because it dragged across the floor when he walked. *Closet queens* (attested in print at least to 1959) were homosexuals who denied their sexuality or who passed as heterosexuals.

The *Stonewall Uprising,* which took place in a Greenwich village *gay bar* in June 1969, marked a turning point for homosexuals. When the New York City police tried to raid the Stonewall Inn, the bar's gay patrons stood their ground and fought back, ushering in a new era of *gay pride,* openness, and activism. Many consider this event the beginning of the *gay liberation movement,* which encouraged homosexuals to come *out of the closet* and stand up for *gay rights.*

It wasn't until 1973 that the American Psychiatric Association decided to remove homosexuality from its list of "mental disorders." Today gay men and lesbians are far more likely to come of out the closet of their own volition rather than being *outed* by others, and acknowledge their *sexual orientation* at an earlier age. And being *queer* (used to describe counterfeit money in the 1870s) is no longer the shameful secret it once was. In *same-sex marriages,* gay couples set up housekeeping and adopt children, and a growing number of employers have provided health insurance and other fringe benefits for *domestic partners.*

In fact, the growing tolerance for non-traditional domestic arrangements, both hetero- and homosexual, has necessitated the coining of new words to describe the partners. While *girlfriend* and *boyfriend* have been

"Jim discovered their language, their expressions. The words 'fairy' and 'pansy' were considered to be in bad taste. It was fashionable to say that a person was 'gay.'"

— *Gore Vidal,*
The City and the Pillar, *1948*

standard terminology in America for decades, they have recently given way to such words as *companion* (usually gay or lesbian), *live-in* girlfriend or boyfriend, and the genderless *significant other*. The acronym *POSSLQ*, for *person of the opposite sex sharing living quarters*, used officially by the U.S. Bureau of the Census, attracted press notice (and some derision) in the 1980s, even making it into some dictionaries.

LOVE IN THE TIME OF AIDS

Nothing inspired more political action and group solidarity among gays than the identification of *HIV* in the early 1980s. (See TO YOUR HEALTH, subsection Aids-related Language) Although the virus and the usually fatal disease it triggers, *AIDS*, were initially linked only to the homosexual population and *intravenous drug users*, the epidemic later spread to the heterosexual population. People engaging in *high-risk activities* such as *casual sex* with multiple partners, sex with strangers, *anal intercourse* with HIV-infected individuals, and the use of unsterilized needles came to be considered highly dangerous in terms of spreading or contracting the deadly virus, which is passed from one person to the next primarily by the exchange of blood, semen, or other *body fluids*. Although AIDS had a devastating impact on the *gay community*, it also served to draw that community together for public action and education.

The advent of AIDS ushered in a new age of frankness in talk about sex, particularly among school-age children, whose *sex ed* (sex education) classes now routinely discuss the importance of *safe sex* (sexual activity in which precautions are taken to avoid acquiring or spreading diseases) and the use of the *condom* (around 1706), a term whose origin is unknown. Teenagers are encouraged to practice *abstinence* (voluntary sexual abstention) until they are old enough to form a *monogamous relationship* (from the Greek meaning "marrying only once"), but reliance on *Just Say No* campaigns is seen by many adults as ineffectual. The Centers for Disease Control and Prevention and the federal government's Health and Human Services Department joined forces in 1993 in a radio and television advertising campaign to prevent the spread of AIDS and other *sexually transmitted diseases* (also known as *STDs*) among young men and women between the ages of 18 and 25. The ads refer to condoms (also called *safes,* and, since at least the 1940s, *rubbers*) as the most effective means of preventing *HIV transmission*.

Condoms today are sold openly in drugstores and grocery stores, and even in specialized *condom shops* or *condom boutiques* offering colorful varieties with special features designed to increase pleasure, such as the *French tickler*. The issue of *condom distribution in school* aroused heated controversy in the 1990s, as some parents thought it encourages early sexual activity among teenagers, of whom half the girls and 75 percent of the boys had had sex by age 18. Dr. Joycelyn Elders, whom President Bill Clinton appointed surgeon general in 1993, will probably go down in history as the *condom queen* for her outspoken support of condoms in an age of rampant teenage pregnancy and sexually transmitted diseases. Dr. Elders will also be remembered for advocating open discussion of *masturbation* (a term of obscure origin first used in the 1850s to describe the practice of "self-abuse," also known colloquially as *choking the chicken, pulling one's pud, spanking the monkey, jerking the gherkin, playing one's trumpet, jacking off, jerking off, beating off, whacking off,* and *playing with oneself*) in the nation's sex education curriculum. *Masturbation,* or *onanism* (about 1741, denoting Judah and Shuah's son *Onan,* who "knew that the seed should not be his . . . and . . . he . . . spilled it on the ground, lest that he should give seed to [his late brother's wife]. . . . And the thing which he did displeased the Lord: wherefore he slew him" [Genesis 38]) was proposed as a means of postponing school children's sexual initiation, thus avoiding the spread of AIDS and other STDs. (In 1994 an American radio station had felt compelled to use the euphemism *self-pleasuring* in place of *masturbation* and *onanism* in discussion of the issue.) For dragging the country's most taboo sex topic into the public forum, Dr. Elders was forced to step down as surgeon general in that same year—1994.

None of this was surprising, however, given the history of America's revulsion against the act, irrespective of the terminology used for it. For instance, Benjamin Rush, a physician and a signer of the Declaration of Independence, had claimed that the act caused vision impairments, memory loss, epilepsy, even tuberculosis. And well into the 19th century, the food barons J.H. Kellogg and Sylvester Graham each had predicted dire fates for *onanists* in their respective best-selling books.

The potential consequences of *unprotected sex* are so much more serious nowadays that it is considered wise for partners to have a frank discussion before they actually *do it*. It is not uncommon for would-be lovers to exchange *sexual histories* or even to get an *HIV test* before sexual involvement. The woman might even provide a condom if the man has failed to bring one, in an effort to avoid at all costs *HIV roulette* (1990), "unsafe sex," a term coined by association with *Russian roulette* and tracing its origins to a 1976 usage of *reproductive Russian roulette* in the British medical journal *The Lancet*.

OUTER SPACE:
THE FINAL FRONTIER

*T*here were no limits to America's commitment to explore the space frontier in 1961. President John F. Kennedy proclaimed "with vigor" America's goal of putting a man on the moon "before this decade is out." The fact that we had a total of less than an hour's experience in space when he made that pledge, all from Alan Shepard's first venture just 20 days earlier, didn't matter.

A SENSE OF MISSION

"Hitch your wagon to a star."

**— Ralph Waldo Emerson,
Society and Solitude,** *1870*

"In a very real sense, it will not be one man going to the moon . . . it will be an entire nation. For all of us must work to put him there."

— John F. Kennedy, State of the Union address, January 30, 1961

"Here men from the planet Earth first set foot upon the moon, July 1969 A.D. *We came in peace for all mankind."*

— plaque left on the lunar surface by astronauts Neil Armstrong and Edwin Aldrin, Jr., July 20, 1969

Technologically speaking, the United States was the most sophisticated nation on earth, and our confidence had been shaken by the Soviet Union's launch of the world's first artificial *satellite* (1880), called *Sputnik,* in 1957. In 1961 Russian Yuri Gagarin had become the first *man in space.* The *space race* was on, bringing with it an entirely new stock of words, including *launch pad* (1958), *orbiter* (1951), *cosmonaut, splashdown,* and *space capsule* (all 1959).

America's efforts in *Space Age* (1946) exploration directed by NASA, the National Aeronautics and Space Administration (created in 1958), changed dramatically over time, especially in the last quarter of the 20th century. Emphasis shifted from competing with the Soviet Union to see who would be the first to set foot on the moon to more utilitarian purposes. These included the reusable *space shuttle* (1969) in the 1970s and missions of scientific discovery from the 70s to the 90s with the launch of numerous *interplanetary space probes, observers,* and observatories,

Astronaut John Glenn, 1962. Glenn went on to become a United States senator from Ohio.

Astronaut Edwin "Buzz" Aldrin "moonwalking" on the lunar surface. Aldrin and Apollo 11 partner Neil Armstrong reached the moon in July, 1969.

like the *Hubble Space Telescope* (launched in 1990; optics repaired in 1993). But can anyone who saw it forget Sunday, July 20, 1969, when the *Apollo 11 moon mission* —*launched* (14th century, "to throw forward," from Middle English, ultimately from Vulgar Latin *lanceare*, "to wield a lance") into space from Cape Canaveral—completed the first *moon landing*? Or, for that matter, can anyone forget when Neil Armstrong said, "That's one small step for man, one giant leap for mankind," as he stepped off the footpad of the "Eagle" capsule onto the moon? (Astronaut Edwin "Buzz" Aldrin's words in describing the *moonscape* [1916] were these: "magnificent desolation.") Spirits were so high following the return of the Apollo 11 crew that many talked seriously about building a permanent base on the moon followed by a manned landing on Mars. Richard Nixon, early in his presidency, declared that it was "the greatest week in the history of the world since the Creation." But with mounting economic and political upheaval in the 70s, we settled on exploring space lessdramatically with *unmanned spacecraft*. "Now, 25 years later, as I look at the Moon, it seems much farther away," Apollo 12 astronaut Alan Bean once mused. "It's kinda drifted away."

DISASTERS AND NEAR-DISASTERS

The American space program also led to tragedy—most notably the explosion of the space shuttle Challenger and the deaths of its seven-person crew on January 28, 1986. The disaster, the worst in the history of the program, occurred 74 seconds after an 11:38 A.M. takeoff from Cape Canaveral. Millions of Americans witnessed it on television. The craft was flying at 1,977 mph 10 miles up and 8 miles *downrange* (1952). The cause was ultimately determined to

"Houston, Tranquility Base here.

The Eagle has landed."

— Neil Armstrong, July 20, 1969,
first message to Earth
from lunar module Eagle upon
landing on the moon

"A major malfunction." The space shuttle *Challenger* after going to "throttle up."

"O brave new world."

— Shakespeare,
The Tempest, *1611*

be the 15-story-tall *booster rocket,* which had a faulty *O-ring.* Perhaps what disturbed Americans most was the death of Christa McAuliffe, a Concord, New Hampshire high-school teacher who had been selected by NASA to be a *citizen-observer* to ride the space shuttle. The terms *criticality* and *O-ring* came to the fore through news reports explaining their association with the tragedy: "NASA and the commission have said the rubber *O-ring* seals in the booster rockets must be redesigned before another shuttle is launched. But these seals represent just one item of about 900 'critical,' or *criticality 1* items, meaning they have no backups in case of failure, and whose failure would cause a catastrophic accident" (*Boston Globe,* March 10, 1986). *Criticality,* first cited to 1756 in the sense "a critical remark or criticism," had been virtually unused in English except during the 1940s–50s in the nuclear industry, in the sense "a critical condition, specifically of fissionable material." It was the worst American space accident since January 1967 when three Apollo astronauts died in a catastrophic fire in a *space capsule* still on the *launch pad.*

Eventually the space shuttle program recovered from its 1986 disaster with the launch of Discovery on September 28, 1988 and continued with about half a dozen launches a year. With the completion of the Endeavour in 1991, the number of shuttles was again up to four, including Atlantis and Columbia (the fleet had been reduced to three after Challenger). Scientists on shuttles routinely studied how fish, newts, and sea urchins behaved in *zero gravity* (cited to 1951), as well as how cells grew and molecules formed.

Apollo 13 achieved *liftoff* (1956) on April 11, 1970. At the time, Armstrong's historic *moon walk* was a recent memory, and 22 previous spaceflight crews had returned to Earth safely, but trouble began on the third night of this flight. Jim Lovell, a veteran of the Gemini spaceflight, was in command; Jack Swigert was the pilot of the *command module* (1962), the vehicle in which the crew traveled; and Fred Haise was pilot of the *lunar module* (1967), the vehicle designed to land on the moon. *Mission Control* in Houston asked for a *cryo stir,* a mixing of liquid oxygen and hydrogen in a fuel cell (1922) to create power and water. Readings indicated almost immediately that there was substantial pressure loss in an oxygen tank and in two of the fuel cells. This was followed by an *undervolt,* or a drop in power, to the electrical system, jeopardizing all of the equipment running from it. A second oxygen tank failed, and the crew was instructed to *power down* and enter the *Lunar Excursion Module* or *LEM* (1967). Mission control analyzed all available options, a process known as *downmoding.* The use of the *LEM* saved the men, and in a storybook ending, the astronauts circled the moon, using its gravitational force for a slingshot effect, and limped home, making a successful *splashdown* six days after launch.

GOING INTO ORBIT

In the 1970s we created the concept of a *flyby,* a *spacecraft* (1930) sent to fly near and observe the moon or a planet. The 60s also saw America build and successfully launch its first *lunar lander* and *rover.* We went on in 1976 with the Viking Mission to put a *lander* and *rover* on Mars. However, after the 1986 Challenger disaster, NASA suspended manned shuttle flights for nearly three years. By the 90s the romanticism as well as the generous federal funding of the Apollo era had ended.

The Magellan orbiter plunged to the surface of Venus on October 12, 1994 after a final experiment to collect data on the planet's gravitational

Early drawings of the space shuttle in 1974. On its first mission in 1981, the shuttle was carried "piggyback" by an Air Force jet.

"The planets in their stations list'ning stood."

— *John Milton,*
Paradise Lost, *1667*

"I felt red, white and blue all over."

— *Edward H. White, Jr., U.S. astronaut, on his walk in space,*
Life, *January 25, 1965*

field. Magellan had been orbiting Venus since August 1990 taking radar images of the planet's surface. What it found was volcanoes, mountains towering above the landscape, and an occasional crater. The planet seems to have undergone a complete upheaval 300 to 500 million years ago in a process called *catastrophism* (1869), the result being the development of a fresh new surface. After 15,034 *orbits* (1696, from Latin *orbita*, path) of Venus, Magellan was maneuvered closer to the planet, while scientists monitored the craft's motion to help planners of future missions refine *aerobraking* techniques.

A Russian *Soyuz* (Russian, "union") rocket, carrying two Russian *cosmonauts* and the first U.S. *astronaut* (1929, *astro-* + *-naut*, as in *aeronaut*, 1784, the *-naut* from Greek *nautes*, sailor) launched in a Russian spacecraft, lifted off on March 14, 1995. The Soyuz craft orbited for two days before *docking* on March 16 with the Russian *space station* (1936) *Mir* (Russian, "peace").

THE HUBBLE AND OTHER TRIUMPHS

Perhaps the most stunning achievement of the U.S. space program in the 1990s was the *Hubble Space Telescope,* named after the astronomer Edwin Hubble, who discovered evidence of the expanding universe in the 1920s. Launched with great expectation in 1990, it soon proved a huge disappointment and embarrassment when it was found that its main telescopic mirror had been incorrectly made. The first optical images sent from the Hubble were fuzzy. A space shuttle mission repaired the flaw in 1993 by installing "eyeglasses" on the Hubble's telescope, and images taken after that were breathtaking. The Hubble repairs were done in the space shuttle Endeavour and by a series of televised *space walks* (NASA's formal term is *extravehicular activity* [1965] or *EVA*), a term first applied in 1965 during the Apollo Mission, that riveted the nation's attention in December 1993. Astronauts repaired or replaced the defective components. When they were finished, each instrument worked exactly as it had been designed to do.

The Hubble, or *HST,* has shown us evidence of other planets orbiting sun-like stars, suggesting the possibility of life beyond Earth. The number of new galaxies photographed by the Hubble indicates billions of other galaxies may exist. Hubble photos show some 1,500 galaxies similar to our Milky Way in a very tiny snapshot of space. Based on their view of that speck, scientists now estimate there may be 50 billion galaxies in the universe, five times the previous estimate. The Hubble has already thrown *Big Bang* (1950) theorists a curve by suggesting that some stars in the universe are older than the universe itself. Estimates for the age of the universe range from eight billion to 20 billion years. Measurements based on Hubble findings have produced some embarrassing disagreements with scientific theory, but such situations often lead to breakthroughs. (The term *Big Bang,* which describes a theory for the origin of the universe emanating from a single explosion event billions of

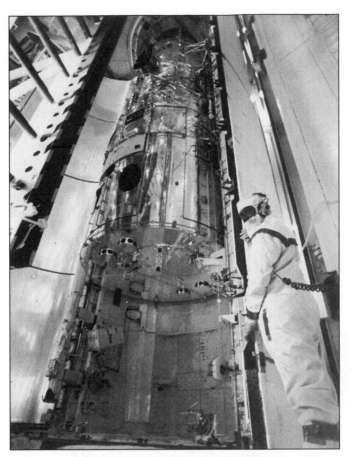

$1.5 billion worth of telescope. The Hubble Space Telescope in 1990 during final preparations for its 15-year mission.

years ago, was actually coined in 1950 by a disbeliever in the idea, astronomer Fred Hoyle.)

At the core of one galaxy Hubble found a *black hole* (1968) as massive as 3 billion suns. Hubble also gave planetary astronomers an unprecedented once-in-a-lifetime view of the massive fragments of *Comet* (before the 12th century, Middle English *comete*, from Old English *cometa*, via Latin from Greek *kometes*, "long-haired," based on *koman*, "to wear one's hair long," from the noun *kome* "hair") Shoemaker-Levy 9 smashing one after another into Jupiter. Hubble altered the way astronomers viewed the formation of *elliptical galaxies*, postulated in 1948. It had been thought that *spiral galaxies*, first viewed in 1913, were the first to evolve in the universe. When spiral galaxies coalesced the resulting amorphous blob would become an *elliptical galaxy*. But Hubble data suggested that *elliptical galaxies* have been around since nearly the beginning of the universe. Hubble also began to focus on *Cepheid variable stars* in distant galaxies, a project intended to provide better estimates of the age and size of the universe.

NASA's *Discovery Program* focused on the study of a nearby *asteroid* (1802, from Greek *asteroeides*, "starlike," from *aster, aster-*,"star") belt. Discovery's overall goal was to design smaller spacecraft with narrowly focused scientific goals, and to build them quickly enough to take advantage of the latest available technology. Future missions were expected to target Mars, the moon, and Mercury. One of the missions, deploying a low-density silica substance known as *aerogel*, was intended to capture dust passing the comet Wild-2. Also new was an *aeroshell*, a broad and blunt shell like a heat shield slowing the probe from 17,000 mph to 900 in a couple of minutes. The probe's final descent was to be cushioned by *air bags* (1969) similar to those used in the automobile industry. Another mission would map the moon's mineral resources. The only big-ticket item left on NASA's budget plate by 1997 was the proposed multi-billion dollar *space station* (a term originating in science fiction in 1936; other terms of the 1920s and 1930s being *space suit*, 1929; *spaceport* for the testing and launching of spacecraft, 1935; and *spaceman*, an astronaut, 1938). An international crew would inhabit this low-orbit outpost, circling the globe every 90 minutes. Fourteen countries began building components of the station, and U.S. shuttles or Russian launch vehicles were scheduled to deliver the parts to space in 36 missions between 1997 and 2002. Future shuttles may be powered by a new rocket technology employing a power plant called an *aerospike engine* (1996), in which the engine's combustion flame is shot along the outside of an inverted cone.

"In the immensity of space there is room for millions of worlds as large or larger than ours, and each of them millions of miles apart from each other."

— Tom Paine,
The Age of Reason, *1794*

"What is it that makes a man willing to sit up on top of an enormous Roman candle . . . and wait for someone to light the fuse?"

— Tom Wolfe,
The Right Stuff, *1979*

Space-age Words from the Space Program

Some space-age *(1946) terms that have made* soft landings *(1960) into general English as a result of their wide usage in the U.S. space program are these:*

affirmative, used by an astronaut or a Mission Control manager, indicating "yes"; also used in *That's an affirmative,* meaning "That's a roger" in pilots' lingo. Its antonym is *negative.*

downlink, cited to around 1969 in print, a communications channel used for reception of a transmittal from a spacecraft; now used as a verb, and also used to denote the transmission itself, not merely from a spacecraft but from a commercial communications satellite. *Uplink,* cited to 1968 in print, a communications channel used for transmittal of data or information *to* a spacecraft; now used like *downlink* as a verb and for the transmission itself. Common in the broadcast industry.

payload (around 1922 in a general vehicular sense) means the people, warhead, or scientific equipment carried by a missile or space flight.

push the envelope, to increase the operating capabilities of a system, especially a high-tech system; used generically now, as in *pushing the envelope of respectability.* Originally pilots' jargon, to exceed the "specs" of the aircraft (e.g. as to G-force loads, speed, or altitude). Variations include *operate outside the envelope,* to challenge the performance limits of an aircraft, system, or program.

throw weight, 1969, the weight of the warhead and guidance system of an intercontinental ballistic missile, also used figuratively, as in *a marketing plan with significant throw weight.*

window, launch window (1962), the time interval within which a spacecraft or rocket must be launched in order to fulfill a given mission; *window,* an area at the limits of Earth's atmosphere through which a returning spacecraft must pass for successful *reentry; window* is widely used nontechnically in expressions such as *window of opportunity, window of vulnerability.*

This brief list shows the futility of early criticism by language purists, especially in the 1960s, of the jargon and technical terms commonly used by NASA personnel, e.g.,

access (verb)	*malfunction*	*phase zero* (the start)
feasibility	*matrix*	*prioritize*
impact (verb)	*nominal* (normal)	*proactive*
input (verb)	*operative*	*scenario*
inoperative	*operationalize*	*time-frame*
interface (verb)	*parameter*	*utilization*
		viable

"A-OK full go."

— Alan B. Shepard, Jr., U.S. astronaut, May 1961, comment upon blastoff by the first American in space, an event that also helped propel the nouns go *and* no-go *into the general parlance.* A-OK *was a widely heard variation on the ever-popular* OK *for a time, and is still encountered in jocular use.*

These and other words, not surprisingly, were fixtures in NASA's lexicon, for they had their roots in the military, early computer science, and the bureaucracy of the U.S. government. NASA is an agency of the federal government, the original astronauts were all military test pilots, and computers from the outset were vital to the program.

Therefore, the world was treated to *real-time* exchanges such as these:

"*T minus 20* seconds and the *countdown* continues to go smoothly. *Guidance release*. . . . We have had *ignition*," "And then go back to *high bit rate* at 6 minutes prior to ignition *per* your *burn cue card* and you can just leave it in *high bit rate* from there on through *AOS*. . . . Have a good *burn*. . . . ," and "CAPCOM: 'And we have word that the *propellant usage* for *T and D* [transposition and docking] was *nominal*.' SWIGERT [astronaut Jack Swigert]: 'What is *nominal*, please?'"

THE SPORTING LIFE

*S*ports play a role in many Americans' lives not unlike that of religion. Fans (an Americanism of the 1880s, first used to describe ardent followers of baseball; a shortened form of fanatic, from Latin fanaticus, "pertaining to religious rites") worship the ground their hero-athletes walk on. They regard certain places where sporting events take place as holy ground—Baltimore's **Camden Yards** (near where Babe Ruth was born), Boston's **Fenway Park**, Chicago's **Wrigley Field**, ("the Friendly Confines" to Cubs fans), New York's **Yankee Stadium** (simply "the Stadium" to Yankees fans everywhere). They set aside special days—**Super Bowl Sunday, Kentucky Derby Day, Patriots' Day** in Massachusetts (for the **Boston Marathon**), **Memorial Day** weekend (for the **Indianapolis 500**)—to witness the spectacles that some of our major sporting competitions have become. They wear **team jerseys**, as well as caps and jackets emblazoned with the colors and logos of their favorite teams. They even make pilgrimages to the "temples" that have been erected in their heroes' honor, such as the **Baseball Hall of Fame** in Cooperstown, New York; the **Football Hall of Fame** in Canton, Ohio; the **Tennis Hall of Fame** in Newport, Rhode Island; and the **Basketball Hall of Fame** in Springfield, Massachusetts.

Among American women and girls, interest in sports, as participants and spectators, is at an all-time high. The widely publicized success of the University of Connecticut's 1994–95 women's basketball team and its star, Rebecca Lobo, inspired thousands of young girls to put away their dolls and start *shooting hoops* in the driveway with their brothers. Softball became an *Olympic sport* for the first time in the 1996 *summer games,* and competition for *Olympic gold* in women's gymnastics and figure skating has sent countless American girls onto *balance beams* and out trying *scratch spins.* A women's boxing champion was crowned for the first time in the 1990s.

Jackie Robinson, the first black major league baseball player in the 20th century, steals home, scoring another run for the Brooklyn Dodgers team. Robinson played for the Dodgers for 10 years (1947–56).

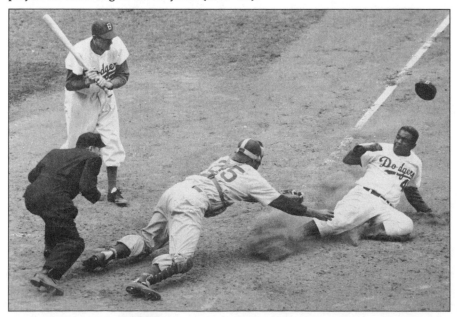

Rebecca Lobo (left) celebrating Team USA's gold medal victory in the 1996 Olympics.

Tara Lipinski skates in the free program at the 1997 World Figure Skating Championships. Lipinski became the youngest ever to win the World Championship. Figure skating has become incredibly popular in the United States, with television ratings that dwarf more traditional spectator sports such as baseball, basketball, and football.

Media attention certainly contributed to the growing interest in American sports, particularly during the quadrennial *Olympic games.* The intense rivalry between ice skaters Nancy Kerrigan and Tonya Harding in 1994, which resulted in a savage attack on Kerrigan as she left the practice rink one day, was only one of many incidents that were exploited by the media. When Olympic diver Greg Louganis hit his head on the diving board in 1988 (and went on to win a gold medal), when *gold-medal favorite* speed skater Dan Jansen failed to win in 1992 shortly after his sister's death but returned for victory in 1994 in *world-record time,* and when American gymnast Kerri Strug executed a gold-medal-clinching vault in 1996 while suffering from a severe leg injury, the television cameras were there to capture not only the *thrill of victory* but *the agony of defeat.* (And during the late 1980s-early 1990s the intransitive verb *medal,* as in "She *medaled* in three events," emerged.) In order to survive, some sports had to remake themselves for TV audiences by simplifying the rules and adding more color and drama. It's no surprise, therefore, that *beach volleyball,* which features young men and women in skimpy outfits romping around on the sand, was added to the Olympics in 1996, while the *modern pentathlon* (which dates from 1912 and entails an awkward combination of horseback riding, swimming, shooting, running, and fencing) was in danger of being dropped from the Olympic schedule.

Three major sports—baseball, football, and basketball—have long dominated the sports scene in America and given us some of our most colorful words and expressions. Almost everyone has used such phrases as *batting a thousand, running interference,* and *slam dunk.* But new sports are constantly emerging, and once obscure ones are gaining in popularity. Football, though it grew hugely in popularity as a *spectator sport* and eclipsed baseball in the 1990s as the *National Pastime,* yielded considerable ground to soccer as the most popular fall sport for boys (in the 1996 presidential race, candidates Bob Dole and Bill Clinton competed for the support of the *soccer moms* who typified middle-class, middle-income female voters). Ice skating by the 1990s was no longer as common as the year-round sport known as *in-line skating,* (*in-line skate,* around 1988), just as ice hockey was overtaken by *roller hockey* and

Gymnast Kerri Strug at the 1996 Olympics, being carried from the gold medal awards ceremony by coach Bela Karolyi.

floor hockey (also known as *deck hockey* or *street hockey*) in many areas. Skiing, traditionally a popular winter sport among the well-heeled, became a sport of the masses in the 1980s and by the 1990s had become something that people in their teens and 20s did before they discovered *snowboarding*. With these new sports constantly expanding our day-to-day language, we may one day talk about *carving* our way to work in the morning and *busting a half-Cab* on a slippery side-street.

THE NATIONAL PASTIME

"Baseball is a public trust. Players turn over, owners turn over and certain commissioners turn over. But baseball goes on."

— Peter Ueberroth, baseball commissioner in the New York Times, *August 9, 1985*

The term *base ball* was first recorded in 1744, when it was a name used in the south of England for the game known as *rounders*. It was played by a batter against a pitcher, a catcher, and two or more additional fielders. The batter hit a soft ball with a flat-sided bat and circled (*rounded*) two bases to score runs. In America, the game became known as *base* (an American soldier wrote of "playing at base" at Valley Forge in 1778), *stick ball* (1832), *goal ball* and *round ball* (1830s), *barn ball* (1840s), *town ball* (1852), and *one old cat, two old cat, three old cat,* or *four old cat* (1850s), the number of *cats* referring to the number of bases. But the ball remained soft because *outs* were made by throwing it at the batter as he ran around the base posts.

In the late 1830s someone had the bright idea of *forcing the runner out* by throwing the ball to the base ahead of him, or by *tagging* him with the ball rather than actually throwing it at him. Since the runner was no longer hit with the ball, a *hard ball* could now be used, which meant that the pitcher could throw it faster and the batter could hit it farther. Modern baseball was born about 1845, when the New York City

Yankee Stadium in 1995, home of some of baseball's most legendary players: Babe Ruth, Lou Gehrig, Joe DiMaggio, Mickey Mantle, and Reggie Jackson.

Knickerbocker Ball Club introduced a code of rules for this new game of hard ball, which was now referred to as the *New York game* or *New York base ball*. The first game under the new rules was played at Elysian Fields in Hoboken, New Jersey in 1846.

By 1871 baseball (which wasn't spelled as one word until the late 1880s) had become America's first mass spectator sport and sports industry. Baseball terms came into the vernacular. People started talking every day about *curve balls* (developed by pitchers in the late 1860s, used figuratively since at least the 1940s to mean an unexpected question or action) and called great successes *home runs* (*home run* dates from 1856, *homer* from 1868; to *hit a home run* means to achieve any objective dramatically). By 1856 baseball was being referred to as *the national game* (which originally meant hard ball as played by the 1845 rules). Later, people took it to mean that this game was the nation's favorite, and it grew into the popular 1920s and 30s term *the National Pastime*. Some other common words and expressions whose meaning can be traced to America's obsession with baseball include:

bat a thousand, like most baseball terms, dates from the late 19th century. The *batting average* is a statistic recorded for each batter, consisting of the ratio of *hits* to *at bats,* expressed to three decimal places. A perfect average is 1.000—hence, *batting a thousand*. The phrase has come into our everyday language to signify excelling at something to perfection.

bush league meant "minor league" in 1909. Now it is used to refer to any small or second-rate sphere of activity.

double header, 1896, originally referred to two games played back-to-back on the same day, usually in an effort to make up for *rain outs*. In 1903 the term was used for two scheduled games for the price of one, a new marketing ploy. Now we use it to mean a double occurrence of almost anything.

first base referred to both the position and the player in the 1840s. To *get to first base* meant "kissing" among teenagers in the 1950s and 60s, with *second base, third base,* and *home run* or *all the way* referring to more intimate stages of sexual contact. *Couldn't get to first base* is also a colloquial expression of failure to accomplish the first step of an undertaking.

foul, foul ball. In the 1860s *foul ball, foul fly, to foul* and *foul ball line* were in use, the last being shortened to *foul line* by 1878. *Foul ball* has meant a contemptible person since the 1920s.

home team dates from the 1880s. Although it was originally used to describe the team on whose field the game was played (as opposed to the *visiting team*), the expression also refers to any group on whose turf a contest is being waged.

major league dates from 1882, and we also use it adjectivally of anything important or prominent. Now every American professional team sport has its major league or leagues, and cities vie to get or keep a *major-league sports franchise,* proof that they are *playing with the big boys.*

Play ball! was first used as the umpire's command or signal to begin a game. By 1901 it also meant "to cooperate." Now we say *it's time to play ball* when we mean it's time to get started or to get serious about something.

rain check in 1890 meant a piece of paper entitling the holder to be admitted to another game free if a game was interrupted by rain before three innings were played. Nowadays, in an era of *domed stadiums,* teams playing in the Sun Belt, and *artificial turf* that can be vacuumed dry after a storm, we associate it with a coupon issued by a store guaranteeing that an item that is on sale but has been sold out may be purchased in the future at the sale price.

rhubarb, for a noisy argument among players or between players and the umpire, or the missed play leading to such an argument, cited in print in this sense to 1943. Used as a slang word today to mean "a heated discussion or argument," it was originally a theatrical term: Actors in mob scenes would say "rhubarb" over and over to simulate the angry, confused sounds of a mob.

shutout first appeared in 1881, referring to a game in which one team fails to score any runs. Now we use it to describe to any situation or contest in which one side has been thoroughly overwhelmed.

World Series. Beginning in 1884 a series of post-season games was usually played each year between the *pennant winners* (1880, of a championship banner in baseball) of the National League and the American Association. By 1888 baseball's *world's championship series* was established, soon to be called the *world's series* (1889) and eventually the *world series.* Though really only a national professional championship series, American marketing hyperbole stuck. It wasn't until midseason 1903 that the new American League was recognized as a full major league (hence the National League's nickname, the *senior circuit*); therefore, the 1903 series was really the first between two major league teams. Now, to call an event *the World Series of* ———— is to define it as a competition involving the very best.

Professional baseball has suffered a loss of prestige in recent years because of frequent and often prolonged *player strikes* and management *lockouts*—not a *strike* in the context of the game, which occurs when a player swings the bat at a pitch but misses (1840s), but a labor dispute in which the players' union refuses to play until they have reached an agreement with management concerning their terms of employment. But baseball terminology is still very much with us. Almost everyone uses

Reggie Jackson hits his first of three home runs in the sixth and final game of the 1977 Fall Classic. Jackson and Babe Ruth are the only players to ever hit three home runs in a World Series game, a feat that helped earn Reggie the name "Mr. October."

expressions such as *strike out* (fail), *go to bat for* (stand up for or support someone), *out in left field* (alone, forlorn, or ignored) *throw (someone) a curve* or *a curveball* (to trick, outwit, or surprise someone else), and *touch base* (to communicate briefly)—even if they don't think of them as baseball-related terms. And you don't have to have *something on the ball* (the desire and ability to succeed, 1912) to know that a *goose egg* (a baseball term of 1866) is a score of zero.

BATTLE FOR THE PIGSKIN

The brutal game once known in England as *kicking the bladder* actually dates back at least to the Roman conquest in A.D. 43. Two hundred years later it was a wild free-for-all in which scores or even hundreds of young men from two places would meet at a midway point and kick, push, shove, and fight for an air-filled pig's, sheep's, or cow's bladder or other object. The name *fut balle* was given the game in the 12th century, when it was first played on a large *field* with boundary lines, with approximately 50 men on each side. It was already causing so many injuries that a number of English monarchs, including Henry VIII and Elizabeth I, tried to ban it. The modern spelling *football* appeared in England by 1650.

Football didn't become respectable until James I of England lifted the ban imposed by Elizabeth I, and the rules against mayhem slowly began to evolve. Physical contact was reduced, and eventually the ball need not be wrestled across the goal to score, but could be kicked between two sticks, or *uprights,* at the end of the field. By 1711 the new term *football match* was a respectable sporting term in England. The English game was, of course, developing into what we Americans now call *soccer* (1889, a clipping and alteration of *association football*), but which the rest of the world still calls, by some variant or translation of English, *football.* In the end, football developed into at least three major games: soccer, Rugby (named after the Rugby School in Warwickshire, England,

An "end run" about to come to a violent conclusion at the hands of the Chicago Bears fearsome middle linebacker, Dick Butkus (51).

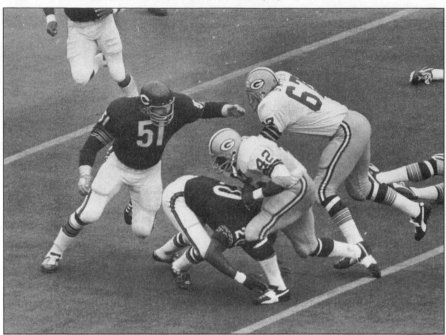

where young William Ellis first picked up the ball and ran with it down the field, a maneuver that had been unthinkable for generations; Rugby developed its own rules by the mid 19th century, and came to use an oval-shaped ball), and our own American football.

In the 1820s some schools were still playing a free-for-all game close to the original, the best-known American one being the traditional *Bloody Monday* game between Harvard freshmen and sophomores, in which as many players from these classes as possible tried to push a ball over a line. This and a similar freshman hazing game at Yale were banned by the schools in the 1830s. America's first intercollegiate college football game or *varsity football game* (*varsity* being an 1845 colloquial shortening of *university*, from English university sporting slang) was a form of soccer using a round ball (called a *leather* since 1868). Princeton played Rutgers in 1869 at New Brunswick, New Jersey, with 25 players per side. The Princeton players used a blood-curdling Civil War rebel yell, which they called their *scarer*, to accompany important plays. But this *football yell* was soon picked up by supporters on the *sidelines*—the *cheering section*, forerunners of today's pompom-wielding *cheerleaders*.

By 1873, when Columbia, Princeton, Rutgers, and Yale agreed to play football by soccer-style rules, it appeared that this would be the model for American football. But in 1872 Harvard had begun playing its own form of the game (called the *Harvard game* or the *Boston game*), in which a player could pick up the ball and run to advance it. Harvard held out for its Rugby-type game and refused to join the new soccer-playing league. The first Rugby game played in the U.S. was between Harvard and Montreal's McGill University in 1874. The game used an egg-shaped ball and provided Americans with their first opportunity to use such British Rugby terms as *drop kick* (1857), *free kick* (1882), *fair catch* (around 1876), and *off sides* (1867). Eventually Yale agreed to play Harvard using the same rules, and soon Princeton, Columbia, and Rutgers joined them. Starting in 1880, Yale's legendary coach Walter Camp introduced the play from *scrimmage* (15th century, from Middle English, a minor battle or skirmish) in place of the Rugby *scrum*, the key role of the *quarterback,* the systems for determining *downs* and for scoring, *tackling* rules, and the standard 11-player team.

Despite the evolution of rules, the game we now know as football and sometimes referred to as *gridiron* retained its reputation for brutality (*gridiron,* 1897, from the grid-like appearance of the field when marked off with *yard lines,* perhaps influenced by the former nickname for our striped American flag, called *the gridiron* from 1812 to about 1900). After a particularly rough game between the University of Pennsylvania and Swarthmore in 1905 in which the bloody, beaten face of defensive linesman Bob Maxwell appeared in a number of newspapers, President Theodore Roosevelt called representatives of Harvard (his alma mater), Princeton, and Yale to the White House to tell them that if such brutal play wasn't ruled out, he would abolish the game by executive order! Some schools, such as Columbia, abandoned the game at this point. Others got together in 1906 and outlawed mass formations and such dangerous plays as *hurdling* (vaulting over players still on their feet), reduced the game from 90 to 60 minutes, increased the yardage need for *first down* (since 1882, each team had to advance the ball five yards in three *downs* or turn it over to the opposing team) from five to 10 yards, added a second *referee,* and legalized the *forward pass* (1903, which had been used as a trick play in informal games).

Sports mushroomed in popularity after World War I, and the advent of television and televised games following World War II made football and its vocabulary a part of American life. With the completion of the Yale Bowl in 1914, *bowl* became a synonym for football stadium; *bowl* later came to mean an annual post-season game played at a major stadium between outstanding teams. Today we have the "Granddaddy of them all," the *Rose Bowl* (1902, though not officially called the *Rose Bowl* until 1923) in Pasadena, California; the *Orange Bowl* in Miami, Florida (1933); the *Sugar Bowl* in New Orleans (1935); the *Sun Bowl* in El Paso (1936); the *Cotton Bowl* in Dallas (1937); the *Gator Bowl* in Jacksonville, Florida (1946); and numerous other post-season bowl games. In fact, watching college bowl games on television has become an American New Year's Day (when several major games are played) tradition.

Coach Vince Lombardi celebrating his Packers' last-second, game-winning touchdown in the 1967 NFL championship game in Green Bay, Wisconsin. The New Year's Eve game against the Dallas Cowboys has been known ever since as the Ice Bowl, for the arctic conditions in which it was played. Lombardi's team would go on to win Super Bowl II against the AFL's Oakland Raiders—though professional football's championship game wasn't actually called the Super Bowl until 1970 when the NFL and AFL merged.

The *Super Bowl,* the most widely watched game of all, is a one-game playoff, originally between the champions of the then-rival National and American Football Leagues, later between the National and American Conference Champions of the merged National Football League. It has been played since 1967 on or around the last Sunday in January. *Super Bowl parties* are common on that day nationwide, as is media hype leading up to the game, and the endless TV commercials in the *pre-game show* and throughout the game (for which sponsors pay hundreds of thousands of dollars for each 30-second spot). The winning coach gets a *call from the White House* in the locker room in addition to a huge trophy, and players look forward to sporting their *Super Bowl rings.*

FOOTBALL LINGO

A *Monday morning quarterback* (1941) is someone who criticizes the actions of others based on hindsight, or who expounds upon what should have been done—an allusion to the weekend football fan who, having seen a game from the stands or on television, proudly offers opinions on how the game would have been played if he had been quarterback. A related term, *grandstand quarterback,* refers to a spectator who continually second-guesses plays throughout the course of a game. Other colorful terms and phrases have come to us by way of football are:

benchwarmer, early 1920s slang for a player who doesn't get into the game, and used colloquially for anyone kept out of the action at work, etc.

end run, originally *end-around run,* was an invention of Amos Alonzo Stagg (1862–1965), legendary coach at the University of Chicago during the late 1890s. By 1902 it was being called an *end run*—an offensive play in which the ball carrier runs around one end of the *line* of players. Today we use this term to describe any attempt to bypass red tape or opposition.

game plan, late 1950s, as the strategy and specific tactics a team plans to use in a game, based on its strengths and the opponents' weaknesses. The term took on political and economic use in 1969, when it became a favorite of President Richard Nixon and several members of his administration who were avid fans of the capital's hometown team, the Washington Redskins. Today any long-range strategy or strategy planned in advance is referred to as a *game plan.*

huddle, a gathering of the players on the field to call the next play out of hearing of the other team, also initiated by Amos Stagg, was a standard part of the game in the early 1920s. By 1929 it had come into general use, meaning to get together for a private, informal conference.

interference, 1894. Blockers are said to *run interference* for the *ball carrier* or *running back,* meaning they ward off or knock down defensive players trying to tackle the runner. Today we use the term to describe any action designed to distract or deflect any sort of imminent trouble.

Ivy League. This term was coined by the *New York Herald Tribune's* Casell Adams in the 1930s to refer to the prestigious eastern colleges where football was developed, known for their ivy-covered buildings. Football's official Ivy League was formed in 1956 (eight universities are represented: Brown, Columbia, Cornell, Dartmouth, Harvard, Pennsylvania, Princeton, and Yale), but today we use the term to describe these eight institutions in any regard, including academic, or anything that is first-rate or the best in its class.

jock, late 1960s, originally a big, dumb college football player. By the mid 70s it meant any athlete, especially one with an excess of brawn and a lack of brains and sensitivity. While related in origin to the horse-racing *jockey* (1825), it mainly carries the connotation of *jock strap* (1915, *jock* having been a slang word for penis since the 16th century), the genital support worn by male athletes.

punt, 1845, origin unknown; to kick a ball in football or soccer; originally in Rugby, to strike it. When a football team punts, it has failed to advance the ball enough for a *first down,* and must kick the ball *downfield* to the other team. The *punter* drops back about 15 yards behind the line of scrimmage to do this. *To drop back 15 and punt* has also come to mean "consider options in a crisis and determine the least troublesome course of action."

scramble, early 1970s in football use. It originally meant to mix and cook (as with eggs, 1864), then in World War II referred to fighter pilots rushing to their planes and taking off as quickly as possible, in no particular order, to intercept approaching enemy aircraft. This connotation of speed and disorganization made *scramble* one of several World War II terms borrowed by football, referring to the quarterback's frantic efforts to evade onrushing tacklers.

scrimmage, first sports use in English Rugby, replaced the *scrummage* or *scrum* (the popular word in England), in which both teams would battle for possession of the ball as it was put into play. In the scrimmage, the ball is snapped back by one side (in a move known as the *hike* or *snap*) to begin play. We also use *scrimmage* in any sport to mean a practice under gamelike conditions, and of any rough-and-tumble fight or confused struggle.

sudden death (*overtime*), early 1970s, referring to an overtime or extra period of no more than 15 minutes, used in professional football if the score is tied at the end of the fourth quarter. It is called *sudden death* because the extra period is over as soon as one team scores. The term had been used in golf since at least the 1950s of a tie-breaker won by the first to win one of the extra playoff holes.

tackle, to knock or force a player to the ground, especially by grabbing his legs or hitting him so that he loses balance and falls, first allowed in 1888. Saying that someone was *tackled from behind* means that he or she was caught off guard.

Corporate America has been especially enamored of football terminology. When a group of business managers or executives get together to come up with a *game plan,* to encourage certain individuals to become *team players,* or to urge someone to *take the ball and run with it,* and not *fumble* it, they are borrowing the language of America's most brutal and beloved game.

Chicago Bulls power forward Dennis Rodman grabbing a rebound. The word "Rodman" may yet enter the language, perhaps to indicate one whose erratic behavior is purposefully outrageous.

BASKETBALL: MADE IN AMERICA

Basketball is the only major sport of purely U. S. origin, though it was invented by a Canadian, (George) James Naismith (1861–1939) in Springfield, Massachusetts, in 1891. Naismith was a *physical education* (1858) instructor at the Springfield Y.M.C.A. Training School, where students had long felt that the marching calisthenics and gymnastics of their winter gymnasium classes (called *gym* by 1897) were boring. The head of the department urged Naismith to invent a game that could be played in a gymnasium, had no bodily contact, used a lightweight ball—for the protection of both the students and the school's facility—and would give each player an equal chance to handle the ball and to make plays. Naismith nailed up a half-bushel peach basket high up at each end of the gym, and the game was called *basket ball*. It was played by five men per team, using a soccer ball until 1894, when the Chicopee Overman Wheel Company, a Massachusetts bicycle manufacturer, began making a slightly larger ball especially for the game, the new ball being called a *basket ball*. A player was sometimes called a *basketballer* or even a *basketeer* into the late 1920s, and his footgear were called *basketball shoes* by 1922.

The original peach baskets of 1891 were joined by wood, leather, and heavy wire baskets and by wood and metal buckets over the next 10 years, with teams using the latter to score *buckets* instead of *baskets.* The first commercial iron *hoop* with a string net basket was made in 1893. Whereas other players, including Naismith's original ones, had to use a ladder to retrieve the ball from the bottom of the basket or bucket, those who used the early hoop-and-string basket could empty it merely by poking the ball out with a pole. Soon, of course, impatient players cut a hole in the bottom of the net basket, and by 1912 the open-bottomed net basket was the only one allowed.

Since the early baskets were attached directly to the gym walls, some players developed the skill of running at top speed toward the wall and then up it a step or two to get a closer shot, such players being said to *climb the wall* (used today to describe a condition of frustrated confinement). *Up the wall* shots were eliminated in 1920, when a new rule dictated that the *backboard* project at least two feet from the wall. In 1939 this rule was improved, dictating that the backboard project four feet from the end line; this allowed for more playing room *under the basket* or *under the boards*, terms which then became common.

Women started to play basketball within a week or two of Naismith's original trial game. *Women's basketball*, originally called *girls' basketball* and *the girls' game*, had six players per team, the three forward players doing all the scoring and the three backcourt players serving merely as guards. It developed from a mistake made by Clara Baer of New Orleans' Newcomb College. She had requested and received a diagram of Naismith's game and mistook its dotted lines, indicating where various players might best execute plays, to be restraining lines. Then in 1895 she published her set of *women's rules*, restricting players to specific areas on the court.

By the mid-1890s, basketball was so popular that the game and its players were monopolizing gyms. Many Y.M.C.A.s began to ban basketball, forcing those teams that wanted to play, usually the better ones, to hire halls to play in. To pay for hiring the hall, the teams charged spectators to watch them play: the birth of *professional basketball*. In fact, it was a group of semi-professional Y.M.C.A. youngsters in 1915 who started all America talking about basketball. Calling themselves the *Original Celtics*, they traveled widely, played "every night and twice on Sunday" during most of the six-month winter playing season, and won 90 percent of their games. They were featured in the first basketball game ever played at New York City's Madison Square Garden, and they dominated the nine-city *American Basketball League* (formed in 1925) to such an extent that the team was banished from the league as "too strong" and disbanded.

The game grew faster and higher-scoring in the 1930s and 40s, and since the rim of the basket was at 10 feet, height became a notable advantage. In the early days the two-handed *set shot,* in which the player sets his feet and takes deliberate aim at the basket, was the main shot. In the 1930s, with players even taller, the *one-handed jump shot* became a necessity, and in the 1940s the *hook shot,* executed with a sweeping motion of one's arm as the opponent is blocked off by the shooter's other arm and body, was widely used (by the 1950s any distant shot was called an *outside shot*). A fast style of play once called *racehorse style,* begun in the 1930s, was perfected by the 1940s University of Illinois *whiz kids* (from the 1908 *whiz,* wizard, expert, plus *whiz* as the sound of a speeding object). The key to this fast style was the *fast break,* perfected in the late 1950s by the professional Boston Celtics, who moved the ball downcourt for a shot in a few seconds with teamwork, *pinpoint passing,* and *hustle.* The players' increased height led to *goal tending* (1937, interfering with an opponent's shot when it was above the basket on its downward arc). Although to *dunk* had meant to shoot the ball through the basket in any way since the 1930s, tall offensive players developed the modern *dunk shot* in the 1950s and the *slam dunk* in the 1970s,

"Playgrounds are the best place to learn the game [basketball], because if you lose, you sit down."

— *Gary Williams, coach, University of Maryland*

Turner Broadcasting chairman, Ted Turner, and Time Warner chairman, Gerald Levin, exchanging a "high-five" (sort of) at the 1995 press conference announcing the merger of the two companies. Later, Turner's confusion over his role would make the Atlanta Braves owner feel like he was "out in left field."

leaping high to stuff or slam the ball down through the basket rapidly or dramatically. The dunk was banned from college play for eight years, beginning in 1968, after UCLA's 7-foot-2-inch Lew Alcindor (who became Kareem Abdul-Jabbar in 1971) dominated the game with it in his first year of college play.

Equipment, rules, styles of play, and team names come and go, but Naismith's game is still giving both players and the American language plenty of exercise. Consider the following terms that have come to us by way of basketball:

high five, 1980s, a contribution of African American urban culture, became widely known in sports, especially basketball, as a quick, dramatic substitute for the traditional handshake or *pat on the butt* in congratulation. The *high five,* developed from an earlier greeting practice of palm-slapping known as *slapping five* (often accompanied by the words "Gimme five" or "Gimme some skin"), is done with one palm or both palms raised high, and the slap can be quite energetic. It is done by players of all levels, in all sports and regions, as well as by fans, and even in non-sports settings.

in your face, 1980s, also from African American culture, is an interjection (sometimes shortened to "Face!") said after succeeding in an aggressive, face-to-face confrontation, as when dunking a basketball despite the close guarding of a defender. (*Face* means *pride.*) The term became generally popular by the late 1980s, and was used as an adjective, as "an *in-your-face* style of political campaigning." (See YO! AMERICA RAPS.)

on the rebound, known since at least the 1920s in its generic sense, may actually have originated in ice hockey, where a defensive team can be caught out of position after a fast shot rebounds off the goalie, and is shot again by another offensive player. The same can happen in basketball, as a missed shot rebounds off the backboard into the hands of an *open man. On the rebound* often is used to describe someone who has recently been rejected in a love affair and whose frayed emotions make him or her vulnerable.

full-court press, an aggressive defensive style of play in basketball that challenges the offensive team all the way down the court, came into general use in the 1970s to mean any constant, exerted effort or pressure brought to bear on a situation. As a basketball defense, the *full-court* (or *all-court*) *press* has been known since at least the 1950s, and developed as a more challenging style of the *man-to-man defense* (the gender-neutral synonym *match-up defense* is now often heard), with every offensive player covered by an assigned defender. Any aggressive team effort, as in business, is called a *full-court press.*

Basketball has created some of the most widely admired—and wealthiest—athletes in America. Michael Jordan, "Magic" Johnson, Larry Byrd, Shaquille O'Neal, Hakeem ("the Dream") Olajawon, and other towering professional players could be seen daily in the 1990s on everything from television commercials to feature-length films, music videos to cereal boxes. They became heroes to America's young people and gold mines to the manufacturers of athletic gear and other consumer goods. Through the long winter months, many Americans spend their leisure hours watching television, and seeing Michael ("Air") Jordan do a *spinning reverse monster slam* is the *armchair athlete's* idea of heaven.

The basketball season extends from October (November for colleges) through much of June, highlighted along the way by the *NBA All-Star Game* (the best players of the professional National Basketball Association) and its *Slam Dunk Competition,* and the *NCAA Tournament* pitting 64 college teams against each other (all members of the National Collegiate Athletic Association) in the month of March (called *March madness* by media and fans alike) for a *single-elimination playoff* culminating with the *Final Four,* the last four teams, one emerging victorious as the *NCAA champion.*

Michael Jordan dunking during the 1996–97 season. Who wouldn't want to "be like Mike?"

FROM PUGILISM TO PARASAILING

"Golf is not a funeral, though both can be very sad affairs."

— *Bernard Darwin, English writer and golfer*

While baseball, football, and basketball unquestionably dominate the sports scene in America, a number of other sports have made significant contributions to American English. From golf, for example, we have *duffer* (from the Scottish word *duffar,* dullard, stupid person; *to duff,* 1897, means to hit the ball badly, to make a bad shot), *dogleg* (1907, any sharp bend or turn), *par for the course* (from Latin *par,* equal, meaning the score an expert golfer is expected to make on a hole or course, playing without errors; used as a slang expression meaning "as expected"), and *hole-in-one* (getting the ball into the hole on the initial shot from the tee; used figuratively to mean an extremely fortunate occurrence). Boxing has given us *knock-down-drag-out* (an 1827 English use for any tough, anything-goes fight), *on the ropes* (1924, American slang for "in a difficult or hopeless situation"), to *throw in the sponge* or *towel* (to give up the struggle, to admit defeat; from the symbolic practice of a boxer's *corner man* actually pitching a sponge or towel into the ring during the course of a fight to indicate that the action should be stopped), *up to scratch* (in the 19th century, a boxer who was knocked down could be helped to his corner, rest for 30 seconds, then had to go unaided to a line drawn or scratched in the center of the ring and resume fighting), and familiar expressions such as *down for the count* (nearly defeated), *take it on the chin* (bear harsh treatment), and *saved by the bell* (rescued from imminent defeat at the last moment).

Floyd Patterson (left) about to take one on the chin from Muhammad Ali (then Cassius Clay) in Las Vegas in 1965.

Few sports caught on as quickly as *snowboarding* did in the 1990s. The sport entails riding down a snow-covered slope on a *snowboard* (1981), somewhat larger than a *skateboard* (1964) but smaller than a *surfboard* (around 1826). Absorbing much of its terminology from skateboarding and surfing, *snowboarding* has also introduced a new language, at this point understood only by the *shredders*—mostly under the age of 25—who avidly pursue the sport. They talk about *carving* (making sharp lines in the snow by turning the board; *Euro-carving* is a more flamboyant style), *big air* (elevation off the snow), *freeriding* (boarding on one's own, not in a competition), *jibbing* (riding on something that is not snow), and *riding fakie* (backward, with feet reversed). An *Indy nose bonk* is grabbing the toeside edge of your board, extending your front leg, and *kissing* (lightly touching) the side of the *hit* (jump) but not colliding with it. A *Cab* or a *half-Cab* (named for Steve Caballero, who devised the move) involves a 360- or a 180-degree spin in the air. When you *sky off*, you leave the surface, gaining a big air. The response from fellow snowboarders when someone executes one of these gravity-defying moves? *Gnarly!* meaning great, excellent, a surfing and skateboarding term.

Snowboarding, a sanctioned Olympic event for the first time at the Winter Games held in Nagano, Japan in 1998, is only one of the *extreme sports* (offering physical challenge and a rush) that became so popular among 1990s youth. *Extreme skiing*, the sport of skiing down steep, rugged, previously unskied terrain and taking high, dangerous jumps, emerged in the early 1980s. *Extreme fighting*,—a no-holds-barred event which continues until the opponent drops—emerged as a controversial sport in the mid 1990s, being banned in some jurisdictions. Other sports included *rock climbing, windsurfing* (1969, a combination of sailing and surfing), *in-line skating* (featured in the opening ceremonies of the 1996 Summer Olympics in Atlanta, Georgia), and *UpSkiing* (early 1990s, a sport that combines skiing with parachuting to propel a skier up a snow-covered mountain or across a frozen lake at 60 miles per hour).

I HEAR AMERICA TALKING . . .
ON THE TALK SHOWS

LET'S TALK IT OVER . . . ON THE RADIO

"Now and again . . . one may find a . . . Hoosier who turns from the lamp to listen to a 'Fireside Chat.'"

— American Mercury,
July 2, 1935

In the *global village* (1960) of mass media, *talk shows* (first recorded in print in 1965) became the backyard fences over which neighbors and strangers began to gossip, argue, lecture, and entertain. The shows may soothe us or shred us, but the culture of talk binds us together and holds us in its thrall. As a nation of *yakkers* (from *yak*, 1949), we just can't seem to say enough. Nor do we tire of listening and watching. There is always a new bone of contention, as we listen to America talking. In *talkathon* (1934) America, the talk show explosion also reflects the disposable culture. Today's hot topic is tomorrow's cold irrelevancy. We get all fired up. We purge ourselves. And we move on to the next thing. The debate ends as the sun goes down on the broadcast day.

Radio talk has been around, of course, since the commercialization of the medium in 1920. That year, commercial radio was born fully-formed on November 2 when Leo Rosenberg became the first human to breathe life into a microphone and throw his voice out into the Pennsylvania night. From Pittsburgh's KDKA, Rosenberg read results of the Harding/Cox presidential contest. By 1923, there were 571 stations on the air.

As Rosenberg stood in that first radio studio—a wooden shack atop the six-story Westinghouse Electric Building—listeners could have imagined him anywhere. That was the wonder of radio. It remains the home of the imagination, as proven so vividly by Orson Welles with his 1938 *War of the Worlds* broadcast, during which he led many in a media-unsavvy nation to believe that Martians had landed.

President Franklin Delano Roosevelt, the first President of the United States to discover the intimate power of the broadcast medium, used the radio for his "Fireside Chats." Roosevelt's discourses from the White House became an anxious nation's addiction. (Over time, *fireside chat* became a generic term for an evening presidential address, on television, to the nation.) (See POLITICS: No Term Limits.)

From 1932 Walter Winchell's gossipy radio chat sessions became the nation's balm during hard times. Winchell was the first personality to adopt an instantly identifiable slogan: "Good evening, *Mr. and Mrs. North and South America* and all ships at sea. Let's go to press. Flash . . ." He was on the air until 1950.

Televisions were supposed to supersede radios in the 1950s, but it didn't happen. Radio talk still flourished. However, it stayed mostly non-consequential and uncontroversial. Arthur Godfrey, the mellifluously folksy radio and (later) TV host, provided some spiciness (for those times); he also was a workhorse, doing three shows a day from New York. He set the standard of a friendly touch that was emulated by other radio talk hosts who reached out in an informal way—broadcasting either from restaurants or their homes. From Chicago, Don McNeill pitched his *Breakfast Club* directly at the stay-at-home 1950s mom.

The *couples shows—Dorothy and Dick, Tex and Jinx, The McCanns*—revolved around domestic fluff and follies. These pleasant folk invited

Talk Show Topics

Americans talked about these and many more hot topics in the 1980s and 90s on radio and television talk shows, the short list illustrating that the topics, more than the vocabulary used in discussing them, speak to the state of the Union:

the location of Jimmy Hoffa's corpse

Hollywood madam Heidi Fleiss

the O.J. Simpson case

assisted suicide

anorexia/bulimia

the Oklahoma City bombing

demonism, satanic rites and cannibalism

the 1996 Olympic Park bombing

Ruby Ridge

reunification of long-separated, separately adopted siblings

militias

the Branch Davidians and the Waco compound assault

gun control

the performer Madonna

birth control and abortion

the downing of TWA flight 800

Rambo motorists

urban gangs

new killer forms of viruses and bacteria

Whitewater

UFOs

welfare reform

adult bed-wetting

animals in toilets

end times, the alleged apocalypse in 2000

Saddam Hussein

Clarence Thomas and Anita Hill

health-care reform

depression

tax reform

sexual harassment in the workplace

drug use

unsafe drinking water

the royal divorces of Di and Fergie

incest

transvestism

gays in the military

gay/lesbian marriage

sexually transmitted diseases, especially AIDS

racism

the Million Man March

violent rap music lyrics

impotence

White House counsel Vince Foster's suicide

multiple orgasms

prostate cancer

atheism

Elvis sightings

the death penalty

affirmative action

the Gulf War

Bosnia

self-esteem

the L.A. riots and the Rodney King case

terrorism, domestic and international

joblessness and homelessness

---

you into their homes for a little chat between commercials. They took no phone calls. They took no prisoners either.

Barry Gray, who dispensed late night wit, wisdom, and wackiness, was a phenomenon, staying on the air via a nationwide network of stations post-midnight for nearly half a century.

Jerry Williams, a Brooklyn, New York-born boy who found his way to Boston via radio stations in New Jersey and Florida, says he invented *two-way talk radio* in the 1950s. By 1957, the technology had advanced enough so that Williams could actually put callers on the air. The phone line for a *phone-in* (1968) thus became a laundry line and the air waves provided a fresh breeze for the public airing of issues, gripes, and complaints. Williams, who in the 1990s, referred to himself as the "dean of talk radio," still presided over a daily show in Boston. He was the grizzled, grumpy veteran of *talkmasters* (also *talkmeisters*)—the legion of local radio rabble rousers in cities and towns all over America who incited the public to pick up their telephones and call in.

The *talkmasters* acted like circus ringmasters moving the show along. They knew how to launch an issue—affirmative action, school prayer, and crime being particularly loaded ones—and put the callers through their paces.

"Go ahead, you're on the air," became the prompt to the next participant cued from the pack holding on a blinking *phonebank* in the talkmaster's studio. A producer in the outer studio would have *pre-screened* the call for content and the extent of the nuttiness factor.

"Thank you for taking my call," became the polite rejoinder as the talk show participant entered the arena before making a point. "Longtime listener, first-time caller" signaled that the caller had finally gathered the courage to join in the dialogue—or the patience to keep calling despite countless busy signals.

Larry King, like Jerry Williams, was Brooklyn-born. He came up via Miami. There, on the radio, he moderated a debate for mayor in 1964 and, in a visionary burst, took reactive phone calls. King defined the art of radio hosting in the early 1980s when his Mutual Broadcasting Corporation radio late-night show took off. Airing from midnight to 5:30 a.m., King's program was the first national two-way talk radio program. King keyed the conversation to the late night hour, setting a varied and non-confrontational tone. King did not pre-screen calls. He allowed his loyal audience of insomniacs and swing-shifters to be freewheeling and fresh, discussing any topic—from Hollywood to hockey, from political figures to lounge singers. In affairs of state, King took no sides, offering all parties equal time.

In 1985, King took a flyer on a fledgling all-news cable network. Ted Turner, the founder of CNN, offered King a slot to bring his talk-show format to television. CNN's *Larry King Live* started as and remained low-tech, *talking heads* TV—King and his guests with callers and conversation. Larry's informal style (usually jacketless and inevitably wearing suspenders) continued, as in radio, to be bipartisan and noncombative, attracting top newsmakers to his program. In 1992, Ross Perot, the Texas billionaire industrialist and presidential candidate, launched his campaign from *Larry King Live*, and garnered 19 percent of the national vote. Top participants in the celebrated O.J. Simpson criminal case used the show as a sounding board in 1994 and 1995, educating the viewing audience on fine points of legal procedure.

Rush Limbaugh had become, by the 1990s, the ultimate sharp-edged partisan of talk radio. A native of Cape Girardeau, Missouri, Limbaugh had worked in public relations and talk radio before he sprang to national prominence in 1990 as host of the *The Rush Limbaugh Show*. Limbaugh unabashedly expressed his fiercely conservative views and won a loyal audience who called themselves *dittoheads*. A best-selling book, *The Way Things Ought To Be*, and a TV show followed. After the 1992 presidential election the Clinton administration, and particularly First Lady Hillary Rodham Clinton, were often the targets of Limbaugh.

In 1995, *shock jock* Howard Stern's on-air vulgarities got him into hot water with the Federal Communications Commission, the broadcasting supervisory agency. Stern—the "dark prince" of the *shock jocks* (the term dating from the late 1980s)—rocked the airwaves with his insults, gamy sexual routines, and bizarre antics. Egged on by his perennially giggling sidekick Robin Quivers—a former military nurse who had been with Stern since 1980—Stern performed such stunts as dropping his pants, sitting on marshmallows, and then describing the resultant discoloration of the marshmallows. Stern was known to regularly ask his guests about their erotic proclivities, and seemed particularly fascinated with lesbianism, prodding female guests to describe any past bisexual experi-

Larry King in 1980.

"A sharp tongue is the only edged tool that grows keener with constant use."

— Washington Irving,
Rip Van Winkle, 1819–20

Howard Stern found his way to New York City after being fired in Washington, D.C. for trying to make light of a fatal plane crash into the 14th Street Bridge.

ences. But Stern discussed anything—his wife's miscarriage, his penis size, and his extreme dislike for various celebrities, including perky TV hostess Kathie Lee Gifford. Occasionally Stern veered beyond the pale— as happened when he played recorded gunshots over a song by murdered Tejano singing star, Selena. Stern later apologized in Spanish.

Don Imus could be styled the thinking man's Howard Stern. While employing similar tactics, Imus—known to his adherents as "I-man"— garnered more mainstream respectability. A political maven, Imus' nationally syndicated morning program originated from a sports radio station in New York City. During the 1992 campaign, candidate Bill Clinton—who successfully worked the *alternative media* of off-network TV programs and radio talk shows—used *Imus in the Morning* as a favored forum. Imus returned the compliment by endorsing Clinton. After Clinton was elected, he continued to go on Imus's show, even as the I-man ridiculed Clinton as a "fat pantload." Other politicians also were regular guests, as well as Washington media heavyweights. Jocular jousting with Don Imus came to be considered a savvy publicity tactic by the inside-the-Beltway crowd.

TALKING . . . TV

In the raucous world of television broadcast talk, Phil Donahue long wore the mantle as king. While milder "chat" show hosts had preceded Donahue—notably Merv Griffin, Mike Douglas, and Dinah Shore—their quasi-entertainment programs derived their content from the factory of Hollywood press agentry. The conversation tended toward the genial and inconsequential.

Donahue did not deliver Hollywood fluff. A product of the heartland, Donahue got his start as an announcer on the University of Notre Dame campus radio station in South Bend, Indiana. After college, he first appeared on television at Dayton, Ohio's WHIO. In 1967, after moving to another Dayton station, WLWD, Donahue created the format that would carry him onward for nearly 30 years. During this initial week on the air, his guests were an atheist activist, single men looking for dates, a gyne-

Phil Donahue on Newt Gingrich impersonator day?

cologist, and a funeral director. He prodded the discussants to delve into controversy and everyday issues.

Donahue was the first to interview a gay man and the first to hold up an anatomically correct male doll. Dayton survived, and Donahue thrived. In 1974, he moved the program to Chicago and *Donahue*—as a syndicated show sold nationwide—was born. Newly divorced and raising five sons, Donahue took up the banner of feminism. For a largely female daytime audience, Donahue—with his rugged Irish good looks, plus a soft heart and a quick wit—raised consciousness. Donahue was all the more provocative because he tangled with guests who flaunted extreme political views or lifestyles. No subject seemed taboo—lesbian mothers, gay male strippers, transvestism. In one memorable show of the mid-1980s about men who wear women's clothes, Donahue put on a dress and wore it throughout the entire hour. While Donahue also distinguished himself by interviewing national candidates and opinion makers, the *fringe-topic* shows became his lasting legacy. And before he went off the air in 1996 (precipitated by his flagship station in New York canceling the program), there were a slew of imitator shows—many of which took the *Donahue* model and went to the outer limits with the format.

Oprah Winfrey featured human frailty. Her guests shared stories about alcoholism, abuse, drug addiction, teenage pregnancy, and the dysfunctional family. Oprah herself confessed that she had been raped and molested by a relative. She was a modern-day *sob sister* who cried on-air (*sob sister* goes back to 1912, first with reference to in-print *sob stories* [1913]). She hugged her guests and members of the studio audience when *they* sobbed on-air. She became so famous, as did her show, that the show came to be known simply as *Oprah*.

Geraldo Rivera was emblematic of the New Wave of *freak talk show hosts* who began popping up in the late 1980s. Rivera, once an investigative reporter for ABC News, got down-and-dirty with his syndicated *Geraldo*. It was the first *tabloid* (1918 in the sense of print journalistic sensationalism) talk show. No topic was too hot for Rivera, whose guests included porn stars and screaming families. Nor was

Jenny Jones on the witness stand during the murder trial that resulted from one of her shows. That the show in question—which featured a gay man revealing a crush to an unwitting straight man who later killed him—was never aired suggests that there is at least one line daytime talk shows won't cross.

Oprah Winfrey in 1995.

Geraldo Rivera, in 1992 on Elvis impersonator day.

Rivera above the participatory stunt: he had on-air liposuction. His nose was broken when a chair was thrown at him during a melee on a 1988 show titled "Teen Hatemongers." The next day he appeared for a taping with black eyes and a facial bandage.

Sally Jessy Raphael mixed Oprah's empathy, Donahue's credibility, and Geraldo's daring. Her trademarks were the red-rimmed owlish eyeglasses she wore as well as a calm, maternal manner amidst the chaos of *screaming heads* (1990s).

Jenny Jones and *Jerry Springer* in the 1990s established themselves as the prime purveyors of *trash talk* and sensationalism. Shows with such titles as "My Sister Stole My Husband" featured the profanity of screaming guests censored with a stream of *bleeps* (1968). Jones made talk show history in 1995 when on a show titled "Secret Admirers" and scheduled for national broadcast, a gay man revealed that he had a crush on another man who was straight. So humiliating was this revelation that the object of this misguided affection allegedly shot and killed the gay man. The incident had a *chilling effect* (see THE WORD OF THE LAW AND THE LAW OF THE LAND) on the content of daytime talk shows. The powerful political trio of William Bennett, former U.S. Secretary of Education, and then-senators Joseph Lieberman (D-Connecticut) and Sam Nunn (D-Georgia) decried daytime talk shows as "cultural rot" and urged an advertiser boycott.

TALKING . . . POLITICS

In the political arena, television has provided unadorned forums for a gaggle of talking heads:

Crossfire, 1982, featured a political-debate format, cablecast on weeknights by CNN. From the "left" and from the "right," hot-button issues were analyzed forthrightly while the cameras focused tightly on the two adversaries hosting the show. The program spawned a new term, *crossfire culture*, the public atmosphere of screaming heads that attends any political fight, and launched the political career of one of its hosts, conservative commentator Patrick Buchanan. *Capitol Gang* was another CNN discussion program that featured journalists matching wits and showing their inside knowledge of Washington goings-on.

C-SPAN. The 24-hour public-affairs cable channel started in 1979 with a staff of four and a television camera trained on debates in the U.S. House of Representatives. Since then, it attracted enough viewers to justify a second channel, *C-SPAN 2*, airing U.S. Senate debates. Besides congressional affairs, C-SPAN also aired press briefings; its founder and president, Brian Lamb, hosted journalists, politicians, and newsmakers in roundtable discussions with viewer *call-ins* from around the country.

Nightline, the ABC late-night news program, on the air since the Iran hostage crisis of 1979, explored a single topic from many angles. Host Ted Koppel handled questions and the flow of the discourse. It was a rare occurrence for an interviewee to sit with Koppel at the anchor desk, becoming a so-called *in-studio guest*. The location of most *Nightline* guests is termed *remote* in broadcasting parlance. Such guests sit on distant sets and talk into a camera while Koppel appears to be debriefing them through a large television screen.

Sunday morning interview shows became a weekly ritual for political junkies and Washington heavyweights. NBC's long-running *Meet the Press*, ABC's *This Week with David Brinkley*, and CBS's *Face the Nation* matched superstar TV journalists with political kingpins.

TALKING . . . TERMS

The language of talk shows is fast and loose on both sides of the television camera:

host, the on-air focus of the show. The host asks the questions of guests, parries with the audience, and carries the microphone. A TV talk show takes on the personality of its host.

green room, a room in a studio where guests can relax before going on the air; it goes back to a 1701 theater-and-concert-hall use; in Elizabethan theaters such rooms were called *tiring* (for *attiring*, or dressing, the performers) *rooms*. Some of these rooms had shrubbery in them, hence, *green*. Though this color is thought to have a relaxing effect on those waiting for *show time*, many such rooms nowadays aren't green at all.

guest, treated with respect or scorn depending on what's said. Celebrity guests are normally thrown *softballs* (easy questions) by the host, while controversial figures get rougher treatment.

hoaxers, guests who claim to be genuine but aren't. Three comics from Canada showed up on Jerry Springer's talk show playing a philandering husband, a babysitter fending off his advances, and the long-suffering wife.

booker, the talk-show employee who sifts through the real people and the hoaxers. A booker must contact the potential guests, entice them, and ensure that they appear on the show. Some bookers will go to any length to get their guests—promising free hotel rooms, limo rides, or airplane tickets.

"Television . . . the new gladiatorial arena."

— *Josephine Hart,* Damage

studio audience, a pop *vox populi,* the modern equivalent of the crowd in the Roman Colosseum.

audience coordinator, the person responsible for putting together each day's studio crowd and for sending out tickets as well as making room for VIPs.

talent coordinator, on lighter talk shows, the staffer who books all the entertainment acts.

publicist, the person in charge of press relations.

intern, the lowest staffer in the hierarchy, responsible for everything from fetching the host's coffee to answering mail and responding to nutty phone calls.

associate producer, also known as *booker* or *a.p.,* the staffer with the challenging assignment of finding and then ensuring that the guests make it to the studio on time.

producer, senior to associate producer and responsible for putting shows together.

senior producer, senior to producer and in overall charge of the daily routine, plus publicity and advertising.

executive producer, the second most important person aside from the host, the chief hand-holder and ego-stroker for the host.

pre-interview, the very important process whereby host, guest, and producers work out all the action and revelations that are supposed to occur so that they will seem spontaneous on the air. The term is also used to refer to the conversation between an interviewee and a producer to discuss possible on-air topics.

pre-production meeting, the gathering of staff to put together final shape of each edition of a show.

talking head, 1968, the simple TV image of a person talking on screen, an image showing, by camera angle, the person's head and part of the upper body. The term came to mean anyone—host or guest—so photographed.

post-mortem, a meeting to assess the show after airing.

media whore, inside term referring to an expert guest—such as a psychologist-author of a self-help book—who makes a career out of dispensing advice on any talk show that books early and often.

TRANSPORTATION:
HITCHIN' A RIDE

*T*he native peoples of North America traveled widely on foot, and the continent was crisscrossed with their paths and trails. From New England down through the South, most of the early colonial roads followed these existing trails. Our language borrowed the **toboggan** *(1829, from Micmac* **topaghan,** *via Canadian French)*, and colonists saw Native Americans using **snowshoes** *(1666)*. The Native Americans' great contribution to transportation was the **canoe** *(1555)*, a Carib word that Columbus brought back to Europe as Spanish **canoa.**

WINDJAMMERS AND STEAMERS

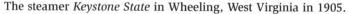

By the 19th century American *schooners* (1716, possibly related to the Swedish dialectal word *skunna,* to skim over the water) and the famed *clipper ships* (1845, from *clip*, "trim, shipshape," which by 1820 had come to mean "to move fast" in America) had evolved into the fastest and largest sailing ships ("Yankee Clippers") of their day. We still use many old sailing terms:

(all) at sea, 1890s.

the bitter end, 1800. In nautical use the term referred to the end portion of a line belayed around *bitts* (timber crosspieces), especially to the end of the anchor rope attached to the massive *bow bitt.*

give a wide berth to, 1794, the sailors' term for not approaching dangerous shoals, shorelines, or other vessels too closely.

keel over, 1896, to fall over unconscious, from the nautical use of *keel over* (1840), to turn a ship over for repairs or maintenance of the hull or bottom.

mainstay, any key support (the extended sense known from 1787, in the writings of Thomas Jefferson), from the huge tarred rope that supported the mainmast.

shipshape, 1860, neat or in proper order.

The steamer *Keystone State* in Wheeling, West Virginia in 1905.

The "unsinkable" *Titanic*, shown here under construction, went down in three hours. It was not found until 1985, off the coast of Newfoundland.

stand by, from the nautical meaning of "be ready," as when preparing for an order to weigh anchor, make sail, etc.

taken aback, caught by a sudden shift of wind onto the forward surface of a sail.

take the wind out of one's sails, 1901, figuratively "to deflate someone's ego."

try a new tack, a *tack* being one leg of the zigzag course a sailing vessel must follow when going upwind.

American shipyards also concentrated on perfecting the *steamboat* (1785), which had proved a commercial success on rivers after Robert Fulton's *Clermont* made its first successful trip up the Hudson River in 1807. By the 1820s *steamers* were reliably crossing the Atlantic. The reliability of steam power allowed commercially viable *lines* (a term used by 1786 for U.S. overland freight services running scheduled routes) of steamers to outdo the risky sail-powered *packet boats* in operating on schedule. And so by the mid 1890s the United States had more shipping tonnage in steam than in sail. By 1899 steamship sailors were derisively calling any merchant sailing vessel a *windjammer* (the latter now popular in the adventure-vacation industry for *barefoot cruises*).

The period between World Wars I and II was the heyday of the great *ocean liners,* after the tradegy of the British luxury liner *Titanic*'s collision with an iceberg on its maiden voyage from Southampton, England, to New York, in April 1912. The ship took over 1,500 people to the bottom of the sea. (The common expression *went down like the Titanic,* "to sink," came from this disaster, in which many Americans—some quite prominent—perished.) Steam-powered, later diesel-powered *turbine engines* made ocean travel commonplace. But as early as 1939, with Boeing's 314 Clipper *flying boat*, commercial air travel cut crossing times from days to hours, and ocean liners could no longer compete for speedy travel. They were redesigned as slow, super-luxurious *cruise ships* (a British concept of the 1720s).

ACROSS THE COUNTRY

The earliest American pioneers had two choices for their westward journey: they could risk the stormy 15,000-mile voyage around Cape Horn (even a fast clipper ship needed more than 100 days), or they could take the shorter but no less perilous *overland route* (1800). Early explorers of North America found a vast network of waterways that drew them deep into the interior. The Great Lakes and the Ohio, Mississippi, and Missouri river systems opened up the entire heartland of America. As more settlers made their way west, they used the rivers to move their goods on rafts and flat-bottomed boats, including the *keelboat* (1780s), the *flatboat* (1822), and the *Kentucky* or *Mississippi broadhorn* (around 1819), a large flatboat with giant steering sweeps projecting from each side.

But serious two-way river and coastal travel only came with the *Mississippi steamboat* (1832) and similar paddleboat steamers. River steamboats were driven by paddle wheels; the main distinction was between *stern-wheelers* and *side-wheelers* (both 1836). The largest of the *riverboats* (1851) were elaborately furnished and carried up to 1,000 passengers. After the Civil War the classic *showboats* (1869) appeared, presenting entertainment to passengers. And a special place in America's memory belongs to the riverboat leadsman's phrase *by the mark, twain,* meaning "two fathoms deep." Samuel Langhorne Clemens (1835–1910), a former river pilot from Hannibal, Missouri, took *Mark Twain* as his pen name in 1862.

The rivers brought Americans to the interior, but beyond them lay a sea that no boat could cross: an ocean of grass called the Great Plains. When *Oregon fever* swept the frontier in 1843, thousands struck out on the *Oregon Trail* toward the fertile Willamette Valley, crossing the plains in *wagon trains* (1849) comprising hundreds of *covered wagons* (1745). The best-known type of these was the *Conestoga wagon* (1750), from *Kanastoge,* the Huron name of the Susquehanna River in Pennsylvania, near where they were first made. By the mid 1840s they were called *prairie schooners* (first used in Iowa for stagecoaches), for the canvas-topped wagons seen above waves of wind-rippling grass did look like distant sailing ships (hence *prairie clipper,* 1870), and some even carried a sail to help their progress through the "sea of grass"). Reflecting this nautical motif, forts and towns on the prairie, especially the *jumping off place* (1830s), Independence, Missouri, were often called *prairie ports* (1848). The culture of the *Conestoga* drivers, who fancied long thin cigars, gave us the slang *stogies* (1853)—short for *Conestoga.*

By the 1850s the overland route was well established. In 1858 John Butterfield's *Overland Mail Company* began to carry mail, packages, and passengers by *stagecoach* from Missouri to California. (Early stage-

A prairie schooner.

coaches—called *Concord Coaches* (1827)—were named for Concord, New Hampshire. Carrying nine passengers, they were pulled by four to six mules or horses.) In 1866 Butterfield sold the company to an old business associate, Henry Wells, who had formed *the American Express Company* in 1850 and organized *Wells, Fargo & Company* in 1852.

THE IRON HORSE

Meanwhile, an ever-growing network of iron rails was stretching westward. The first U.S. passenger railroad, the 1827 *Baltimore and Ohio,* was originally equipped with horse-drawn cars. *Engine* had meant any complex machine since the 17th century and the *steam engine* had been known long before its use to pull railroad cars. Thus we used the older *engine* and *steam engine* more comfortably than that strange new 19th century English word *locomotive* (from Latin *loco,* place + Middle English *motive,* causing to move, from Latin *movere,* to move). Since the cars on railroads were originally pulled by horses, it was also natural to call a locomotive an *iron horse* (1830s) or a *steam horse* (1840s).

The *steam railroads* or *steam cars* (1833) began as long-shot competition to the much-ballyhooed plans for a great canal system (the Erie Canal, from 1825, was one of the only successful canal routes). Arising in an era of boats (especially canal boats), stagecoaches, even *sail cars* (early 1800s), cars propelled by sails (a famous one plying the tracks of the South Carolina Railroad), early railroading borrowed many terms from these older forms of transportation. Thus *All aboard!* (1837), *berth, caboose, crew,* and *gondola* are from ship and boat use, while *accommodation, car, coach, conductor,* and *station* come from stagecoach use. *Train* (via Middle English *trayne* from Latin *trahere,* to drag) was in use in England by 1824 for a string of cars, but it was the late 1840s and early 1850s before the word took hold in America.

The first *transcontinental railroad* was completed in 1869, when the tracks of the *Central Pacific Railroad* from Sacramento met those of the *Union Pacific Railroad* from Omaha at *Promontory Point,* Utah, becoming, in the words of Jessamyn West, the "big iron needle stitching the country together." The railroad introduced or popularized many terms:

baggage car, 1833; *to check* baggage, 1846; *baggage check,* 1848.

cab (on a locomotive), 1859.

caboose (via Dutch from Low German *kabuse,* hovel), first meaning a shack (1839) and then a ship's galley, as on riverboats. In 1861 it was first recorded as the last car on a freight train, containing the crew's kitchen and sleeping quarters. (By the 1990s most railroads had stopped using cabooses.)

car, railway car, 1826; *rail car,* 1834; *train car,* 1856. The first passenger cars on rails were modified coaches, three coach bodies having been run together.

"Casey Jones," popular song about engineer John Luther ("Casey") Jones, who, when his Illinois Central train, called the "Cannonball Express," was about to crash, asked his crew to jump out, applied the brakes himself to save his passengers, and was the only one to die in the crash, which occurred on April 30, 1900.

club car, 1886, a passenger car where drinks and other refreshments are served; *bar car,* 1945; *lounge car,* 1947.

"... I hear the iron horse make the hills echo with his snort like thunder, shaking the earth with his feet, and breathing fire and smoke from his nostrils."

—Henry David Thoreau

"It's a great sight to see a large train get under way. . . . As to the engine, the most pithy and expressive epithet I ever heard applied to it is 'Hell-in-Harness.'"

— George Templeton Strong, 1839

415

conductor, on a stagecoach, 1790; on a horse-drawn railroad, 1826; on a steam railroad, 1832; on a city horsecar, 1860s. *Railroad conductor*, 1842; *train conductor*, 1849.

cowcatcher, 1838, a frame attached to the front of an engine, used to remove obstructions from the tracks.

depot, railroad use first recorded in 1832 (earlier use referred to a storage area), in its French spelling *dépôt*. For years pedants criticized it as an unnecessary American synonym for the perfectly good English word *station*. Longfellow thought it rather quaint, noting in 1842 that a fellow passenger pronounced it to rhyme with "teapot."

derail, 1850, from French *dérailler*, to throw off the tracks, a mix of *dé-*, de + *rail*, itself a borrowing into French from English. It is also used figuratively to mean "frustrate someone's efforts or plans."

diesel, 1894, a type of engine running on liquid fuel rather than coal, named after the German mechanical engineer Rudolf Diesel (1858-1913) and introduced to railroads in 1925.

dining car, 1838. *Diner*, as a railroad dining car, 1890.

engineer, 1832, sometimes called a *pilot* and a *driver* in the early days, a *locomotive engineer* by 1843.

freight car, *burden car*, 1833; *freight train*, *freight*, mid 1840s; freight cars and trains were even then being called *rattlers*.

high ball, a semaphore signal of a large ball raised high to signal engineers to proceed, 1890s. By the 1930s *highball* (it) meant to move at full speed.

hotbox, 1840s, an overheated bearing on a railroad car.

main line, 1841, a principal railroad track or line.

milk train, 1853. Trains carrying milk had the right of way because they held a perishable cargo.

parlor car, 1868, a passenger car with individual chairs.

Pullman, 1867, a car with sleeping accommodations, named after its inventor George M. Pullman (1831–97); also coming to mean a type of suitcase and a long narrow kitchen.

railroad, 18th century mining use in England. *Rail road train* came into wide use in the 1840s; *railroader* appeared in the late 1850s. *To railroad* someone, "to convict someone falsely," appeared in 1877.

railroad crossing, 1834. Until the railroads came most Americans knew a *crossing* (1753) as a place where a river was forded.

railroad time, in good time, with speed, 1864; it also referred to the time standard used by a railroad. Railroad time differed on different lines and as one traveled across the country.

red ball, early 1900s, a fast freight train or cars carrying perishables, marked with a placard bearing a large red circle.

redcap, a baggage porter, 1919. It influenced the development of *sky cap*, 1941, for the equivalent airport worker.

round trip, 1850s.

sidetrack, 1835; *to sidetrack* (a train), 1880. By 1893 to *sidetrack* meant to divert from the main issue, course, or goal.

"It was the way they worked the cord and changed the steam pressure that made the whistle almost . . . talk. . . . There was a regular language of signals—two long blasts for starting up; one long tremolo for approaching a station; and, at grade crossings, the familiar whoooo, whoooo, hoo, whooooooooo! . . . An engineer was a man of importance, admired by young and old, and the whistle was his signature."

— Oliver Jensen, "Farewell to Steam," American Heritage, December 1957

The California Limited in 1905 (left) and one of its parlor cars (right).

snowshed, 1860s, a 40-mile wooden tunnel built to protect the Central Pacific's tracks from avalanches and heavy snows. It covered the turntables, depots, section houses for foremen, sidings, and the workers' homes. As late as the 1950s sections of this huge "railroad barn" still existed.

streamlining, 1909, England. Aerodynamic designs and power from diesel engines led to faster trains with names evoking images of fast flight, such as *Comet, Flying Yankee, Powhatan Arrow, Meteor,* and *Zephyr.*

switch engine, 1867, a small engine used in switching cars and making up trains.

on the track, off the track, 1870s.

whistle stop, 1925, a town too small to be a regularly scheduled stop: if a passenger wanted to get off at one, the conductor would signal the engineer to stop by pulling a signal cord, and the engineer would respond with two toots of the whistle. (See AMERICA'S POLITICAL LANGUAGE.)

Palace Cars for New Arrivals

In the post-Civil War period of opulence known as the Gilded Age, the ultimate sign of social and monetary "arrival" was ownership of a *palace car*, especially one made by the Pullman Palace Car Company. These *private cars*—the forerunner of today's private jets—ranged in price from $50,000 in the 1880s to $300,000 in 1929.

Palace cars were decorated with gold chairs, crystal chandeliers, opulent bedspreads and window treatments, Tiffany table services, brass king-size beds, portraits, and gold plumbing fixtures attached to marble bowls. Servants included French chefs, footmen in powdered wigs, and butlers.

These cars, which in the tradition of railroad engines and the trains themselves bore names like *La Rabida* or *Isabella*, were dubbed *private varnish* by railroad insiders.

A Pullman porter in the 1920s, *sans* red cap.

PUBLIC TRANSIT

The first horse-drawn city buses appeared in the 1820s. They had several nicknames, one of which was *omnibus* (Latin, "for all"), shortened to *bus* by the 1840s. A system of larger horse-drawn cars on rails, called a *street railway*, appeared in 1832, and improvements to the *horsecars* (1833) in the 1850s made them successful for the next 40 years. Larger horsecars not only had a driver but also a *conductor* to collect the *car fare*. By 1886 over 300 American cities had horsecars. Some people also called them *streetcars* (1862).

By the late 1870s people were talking about the new *cable cars* and *electric streetcars*. By 1890 horsecars all across the nation were being replaced by the *electric trolley cars* (from Old French *troller,* to wander, search; actually the *trolley* was the grooved wheel in contact with the current-carrying overhead wire). Eventually *streetcar* virtually replaced *trolley* and stayed in wide use through the 1930s. The common sight of the *motorman* getting out to reposition the trolley wheel back on its wire gave us the popular expression *to be off one's trolley* by 1896.

A turn-of-the-century trolley car in Washington, D.C. This one was on the line that went to the zoo.

New York City built its first *elevated railway* in 1867, the name shortened to *the el* by the late 1880s. America's first *underground electric train* system—the *subway*—was built in Boston in 1897. *Rapid transit* had been applied to elevated railways in the 1880s, but from then on it was to mean subways to most people. From 1905 to the end of the 1930s, *motorbuses* replaced streetcars in most cities, and the first *long-distance buses* appeared in the early 1920s.

The other now-familiar fixture of urban public transportation is the *taxi*. But long before people were shouting for taxis they were shouting for *cabs,* an 1827 English shortening of *cabriolet* (borrowed from French, from *cabriole,* a caper or leap, ultimately from Latin *capreolus,* wild goat), a one-horse carriage with two seats and a folding top. The *hansom cab* (1847, named for its designer, English architect Joseph Hansom) was a two-wheeled one-horse carriage with the driver seated behind and above the passenger compartment. The first *taximeter motor cab* appeared on the streets of New York on October 25, 1907. Soon people were calling them *taximeter cabs*, then *taxis* (all from *taximètre,* tariff meter, coined by a French company that made meters for horse-drawn cabs). *Hack* (1733) was originally short for *hackney* (Old French *haquenée,* from Latin *equus,* horse), an ordinary horse for riding and driving; by 1796 it meant a horse and carriage for hire and later a person who hires himself out for routine work, as a "literary hack." It was first applied to taximeter motor cabs around 1912.

WHEELS

THE BICYCLE

Although the *bicycle*s (the word and the vehicle coming from France; French *bi-*, two + Greek *kuklos*, wheel) first were talked about in England and America in 1868, their popularity was at first limited. The famous *high-wheeler* with pedals attached to a huge front wheel was the first type in wide use, but was hard to ride and uncomfortable (it was also dubbed the *bone-shaker*). By 1880, it was also called simply *bike* and *wheel*. The modern *safety bicycle,* with both wheels the same size and with the pedals powering a *bicycle chain*, came into use about 1885. In 10 years the safety bicycle became simply the *bicycle*, with added improvements such as air-filled rubber tires, *coaster brakes, adjustable handlebars*, and a cushioned *saddle*. The *tandem* bicycle, or *bicycle built for two*, was perfected in the early 1890s.

High-wheelers in 1887.

Mountain biking in West Virginia in 1995.

By the late 1800s about four million Americans were biking. But in the early 1900s the bicycle craze died down as automobiles came along. Bike riding became a limited activity except for children, and remained so through the 1950s. In the 1970s, ecology- and exercise-minded Americans rediscovered the nonpolluting recreational and health benefits of cycling. New and improved designs made the bicycle more popular than ever in America, and the trend continued through the 1990s. The 1990s saw a rise in popularity of such innovations as *mountain biking*, as well as bike-borne messenger and delivery services in urban centers.

THE CAR

Thank Julius Caesar for the word *car*. It was he who used a Gaulish word for wheeled vehicles, and from the Latinized form *carrus* we get the English words *chariot, carriage*, and *car*. American colonists knew *car* only as a poetic word meaning chariot; it wasn't until its use to refer to railroad cars (1826), horsecars, and streetcars in the 19th century that ordinary people used the word much. Since the early 1900s, however, *car* has most often meant one thing to Americans: an automobile.
Automobile (borrowed from French; from Greek *auto-*, self- + Latin via French *mobile*, moving) first appeared in English in the 1880s as an adjective describing various self-propelled vehicles. It soon was applied to the pioneering *horseless carriages* (1895) of the day, powered by batteries or steam engines. The *Stanley Steamer* was the most talked-about automobile of the late 1890s, and was manufactured until 1924. Various gasoline designs were also built before 1900, and the general term for them became *automobile*, already shortened to *auto* by the late 1890s. *Motor-car* was also in use from around 1890; its shortened form *car* was an accepted term by 1910, though well into the 1930s some people still favored *motorcar, motor*, or *machine*.

Henry Ford in his car in 1903. Soon after inventing the assembly line, Ford discovered that with monotonous work comes labor turnover. By doubling his workers' wages to $5/hour, his labor force was stabilized and became potential consumers of his product.

A 1951 Buick Le Sabre ragtop.

Since before 1890 *driver* had become the accepted word for one who could operate a car, although *chauffeur* was also in use (from French *chauffer*, to heat, originally meaning a stoker and then humorously applied to the driver of a steam automobile). From the end of the 1890s new words having to do with cars came fast:

automobile accident, 1882; *car crash*, 1915; *hit-and-run*, 1920s.

fender, 1883; *hood*, 1906; *running board*, 1923; *rumble seat*, 1931.

runabout, 1891; *touring car*, 1903; *station wagon*, 1904 in the motor vehicle sense; *roadster*, 1908, *coupe*, 1918, *sedan*, 1920; *sports car*, 1925; *convertible*, 1918—colloquially also known as a *ragtop*, 1953.

road hog, early 1900s, used of a driver who weaves or blocks two lanes. It had been applied to bicyclists in the 1890s; *road rage*, 1990s, related to *road duels* fought by aggressive motorists.

license plate, 1901. *Vanity plates*, with letter or number combinations selectable by the user, were first used in the mid 1960s.

garage, for an automobile, 1902.

gas, 1905, from *gasoline* (1865).

Model T, 1908, Henry Ford's economical car that made driving accessible to the general populace, also called affectionately the *Tin Lizzie*.

spark plug, 1908, used to mean an energetic leader by the 1930s.

blowout, 1915.

retread (of a tire), 1912.

flivver, 1914, a jocular or disparaging slang term for a car; others include *heap*, 1915; *crate*, 1920; *jalopy*, 1924.

filling station, 1915; *service station*, 1922; *gas station*, 1925.

step on the gas, 1916; *step on it*, 1922; *floor it*, cited to 1950–51.

back seat driver, 1920s.

used car, 1920s; *preowned* or *pre-driven car*, 1980s euphemisms.

"Thanks to the Interstate Highway System, it is . . . possible to travel across the country from coast to coast without seeing anything."

— *Charles Kuralt,*
On the Road, *1985*

Quite a bit less successful than the Model T, the much-hyped Edsel came off Ford's assembly line in 1957. Named after Henry Ford's only son as a tribute, it instead became a synonym for monumental failure.

parking, *parking space*, *parking lot*, 1924; *parking meter*, 1935.

hitchhike, 1925; to *thumb a ride*, late 1930s.

freeway (usually not a toll road), 1930; *thruway*, 1930; *expressway*, 1944; *beltway*, 1952; *parkway*, 1887.

drive-in, 1931 (referring to a filling station).

motor hotel, mid 1940s; *motel*, late 1940s.

hot rod, *drag race*, mid 1940s; *joy ride*, 1909.

interstate, since the 1950s, designated with an "I," as in *I-70* and *I-40*. The even-numbered roads run east-west, the odd north-south.

bumpersticker or *bumper sticker*, 1967.

During the gasoline shortages of the 1970s, many Americans who were stuck in long lines waiting to refill their *gas guzzlers* rethought their automotive priorities. They began to look for smaller, more fuel-efficient, *subcompact cars* or even *econoboxes*, many of them imports. The next two decades saw a revolution in automobile design. At first the accent was on fuel efficiency with better engine design (incorporating *fuel injection*) and lighter weight cars that had many plastic parts and used *front-wheel drive*. By the 1980s new models emerged, including the *minivan* and the *4 × 4s*, besides *custom vans*, *luxury pickups*, and *RVs* (1967, from *Recreational Vehicle*). Much discussed in the mid 90s was the *air bag* (1969), a safety device designed to protect riders by inflating automatically in case of collision. And although there had been *electric cars* before 1900, insufficient battery technology kept them still as a promise for the future into the late 1990s. Indeed, modes of vehicular transport have come a long way from the coaches drawn by horses along America's city streets, having names (some persisting in today's motor vehicles) like *landau, drag, brougham,* and *rockaway* (also called a *station wagon* in 1875, with six seats)—and for winter the *Boston booby*, or *booby hut*, a carriage body mounted on runners.

Wilbur (second from left) and Orville (far right) Wright in Virginia in 1909 with their first "biplane." Its 25-horsepower engine could manage speeds of 42 miles per hour.

THE FLYING MACHINE

Wilbur and Orville Wright received a patent for a *flying machine* in 1906, three years after their first flight near Kitty Hawk, North Carolina. *Aeroplane* was first used in England in 1866 to describe a wing (or geometric) plane, what we would call an *air foil* (1922). In the U.S. the spelling was changed to *airplane* in the late 1890s, and shortened to *plane* by 1910. By 1908 *pilot, hangar, airfield, monoplane,* and *biplane* were known to young and old. World War I brought stories about airplanes and legendary pilots and made *cockpit, prop, airpocket, ceiling, takeoff,* and *tailspin* part of everyone's vocabulary.

Lucky Lindy and the *Spirit of St. Louis.* The years after his heroic trans-Atlantic flight were marred by the kidnapping and murder of his son, and being forced to resign his Air Force commission for anti-war speeches made during World War II.

The zeppelin was invented by a German general named Ferdinand Zeppelin in 1900. Though providing the first commercial air service in 1910, any competitive threat the zeppelin posed to the airplane ended in 1937 with the spectacular crash of the *Hindenburg*.

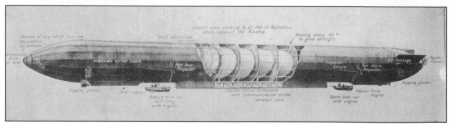

After World War I, pilots *barnstormed* (1928) towns and villages across the country, performing aerobatics and taking paying passengers up for rides. The most famous barnstormer of all was Charles A. Lindbergh, who, in 1927, flew his monoplane *The Spirit of St. Louis* across the nation from its San Diego factory to Long Island's Curtiss Field, setting a transcontinental flight record of 21 hours, 20 minutes. Lindbergh then made the first solo non-stop flight across the Atlantic, from Roosevelt Field on Long Island to Paris, in 33 hours, 30 minutes.

The future of the airplane was now with the *airline* (1914) and the *airliner* (1915). Regular service began between New York City and Atlantic City in 1919, and between Key West and Havana in 1920. In 1930 Ellen Church, a registered nurse, became the first airline *stewardess*, choosing the name "stewardess" herself (it had been used on ships since the 1830s). Later some airlines briefly called their stewardesses *hostesses* or *air hostesses* and some newspapers referred to them as *sky-girls*. Besides reassuring passengers and passing out chewing gum to ease ear pressure after takeoff, stewardesses aided those who had *air sickness*, a term first used by balloonists in the 1780s. They began serving *in-flight meals* from *on-board kitchens* in 1936. By the 1980s more men began to take up the occupation, and the gender-neutral term *flight attendant* (1947) began to replace *stewardess* and *steward* in general use.

National Airport in 1971. With the growing popularity of air travel came long lines at check-in.

In 1936, American Airways put into service the twin-engined, all-metal, 21-passenger Douglas *DC-3*. With its "comfort facilities" (toilets) and "comfortably heated and ventilated" cabin, the DC-3 became the plane that *air travelers* grew to love and trust, introducing them to such terms as *airline ticket, airline reservation,* and *Please fasten your seat-belts.*

Pan American began "daily transatlantic jet service" in 1953 and was the first to fly the Boeing 707 in 1958. Soon we were speaking of the *jet set,* those socialites and celebrities who could afford *to jet* (early 1950s) for fun and frolic on transcontinental routes. In 1970 Pan Am introduced Boeing's new *747,* the first *jumbo jet,* which carried nearly 500 passengers. Soon to follow were *wide-bodied jets; wide-body* (1968) soon became a general term for anything especially large. Tens of millions of *frequent fliers* and others flew every year, and *jet lag* (1969) became a familiar complaint.

TRASH AND GARBAGE

A *mericans have often put -ology onto words with more hope than success in the cause of dressing up, in a starched collar, new and self-consciously marginal fields of scholarly endeavor (think, for instance, of* hamburgerology, *which the McDonald's Corporation has long been refining, with little prospect of academic acceptance, at its Hamburger University in Illinois). But look at the happy fortunes of the word* garbology.

It was coined in the early 1970s to designate a specific academic activity at the University of Arizona at Tucson—the scientific study of modern garbage as a way of understanding modern societies. The analogy was with the way archaeologists study ancient garbage to understand ancient societies. *Garbology* quickly expanded in meaning to include the study of contemporary garbage in all its aspects, from garbage generation through garbage *discard* and on to permanent garbage disposal or temporary reuse. Owing to sometimes lurid reports in the press (the University of Arizona researchers were, after all, picking through the contents of household garbage and conducting excavations of major urban dumping grounds, and were meticulously sorting everything they found by category as if it all held the significance of objects from King Tut's tomb), *garbology* soon achieved national familiarity. It received official recognition—as did the word *garbologist,* meaning a practitioner of *garbology*—in the revised edition (1989) of the *Oxford English Dictionary,* which defined it as "the scientific study of the refuse of a modern society; the investigation of material discarded by a society considered as an aspect of social science."

Garbology as an enterprise was given considerable impetus by the *garbage crisis* of the 1980s, a crisis more in rhetoric than reality, and one characterized by the fear that American society was producing garbage at a rate far outpacing our ability to cope with it. For many, the garbage crisis was symbolized by the *garbage barge,* a vessel named *Mobro 4000,* which in March of 1987, laden with some 3,000 tons of garbage, left a port on Long Island, where there seemed to be no place for the garbage to go, and spent the next 55 days sailing along the eastern seaboard in search of a locale that would be willing to accept it. Although the much-publicized incident came to embody the plight of beleaguered communities running out of garbage-disposal options, the episode was in fact the result of an entrepreneur's miscalculation. Nonetheless, the term *garbage barge* lives on in the public mind. The garbage crisis, meanwhile, abated in the face of economic and environmental corrective measures.

Anything at all can be—and has been!—thrown away (where else do so many of those valuable antiquities in museums come from?), so it is no exaggeration to say that there is potentially a garbage aspect to everything. But most of the common words we use for garbage have a more precise meaning than we realize. *Garbage* itself, for instance, technically should refer only to *wet discards*—items such as food waste or grass clippings. (The origins of the word *garbage,* which probably lie in Anglo-French, remain obscure; its earliest uses involve tasks associated with working in the kitchen. By the 16th century, a *serjeant garbager* in England was a royal officer in charge of the poultry.) *Trash,* another seemingly all-inclusive term, should in fact technically be used only for *dry discards,* such as boxes, paper, bottles, and so on. (The distinction

"'Garbology' is becoming a science, Arnold . . . and just think, we were pioneers in the field."

— one bum talking to another in the Grin 'n Bear It *comic strip*

A *Flying Dutchman* for the 20th century. Here the ghost ship of Richard Wagner's opera, doomed to sail eternally, is a "garbage barge." It is sailing off the coast of Key West in March 1987, seeking port after being refused entry by four states and two countries.

between *wet* and *dry discards* was important in the days when *slops*, or food waste, could be used as an animal feed, and cities sent trucks around expressly to collect it; it came to be useful once again when *composting* [1587, noun, 1829, verb], which requires wet garbage, became popular.) The all-embracing term for wet and dry discards alike is supposed to be *refuse* (14th century), a word whose uncomfortable social niche in the netherworld between daintiness and bureaucratism has earned it no real affection. *Litter* (1730, this sense) is the name for garbage that has been dropped on the ground rather than placed in an appropriate container; an early meaning, going back to the 15th century, was material like straw thrown on the ground for bedding. (The high profile and bright coloring of the kinds of refuse that tend to make up litter—fast-food packaging, disposable diapers, cigarette packages, bottles, and cans—help to explain why lots of people believe that such items constitute a huge proportion of all discards, whereas together they actually constitute only a tiny fraction.) All the refuse from a jurisdiction's homes and businesses is *municipal solid waste*, better known simply by the initials *MSW*. By government definition, *MSW* doesn't include *construction-and-demolition debris* (called *C&D* for short), which is a major but often forgotten tributary of the *solid-waste stream*, and it also doesn't include *hazardous wastes* or *industrial wastes*. *Rubbish* (15th century, from Middle English *robys*) is probably the most encompassing "trash" synonym in ordinary parlance for garbage of all kinds. And we mustn't forget that *garbage*, especially when given the faux-French pronunciation *gar-BAZH*, can refer to anything deemed worthless, physical or metaphysical, sensible or nonsensical, conceptual or concrete.

Needless to say, the "stuff" of garbage has brought into existence terminology that is far more descriptive than the broad and rather dry (even if "wet") terminology already mentioned. At a distance, which is where we like to keep it, garbage appears to be an undifferentiated mass, but upon closer inspection we do see splashes of color: *red-bag waste* is infectious waste from doctors' offices and hospitals, and may consist of anything from discarded bandages to the organic waste (sometimes called *cat food*) left over from surgical procedures; the name comes from the color of the plastic bags put out at health-care facilities for the collection of materials that may constitute *biohazards*. Another category of medical waste, which would include used needles, scalpel blades, and certain other disposable implements, is known by those in the field as *sharps*. As one might imagine, red-bag waste should never be put in a *Blue Box* (the plastic receptacle in which homeowners in many locales place their recyclable materials for collection) and red-bag waste will never receive a *Green Seal* stamp of approval (*Green Seal* is a national organization that certifies a product's environmental beneficence). *Green waste* refers to the byproducts of lawnmowing, plant pruning, and other yardwork—byproducts that account for as much as 25 percent of an average household's garbage, and that could be composted virtually in their entirety. (In Beverly Hills, Garbage Project researchers found that the sod from entire lawns which have been seasonally replaced sometimes gets left out for pickup.) *White goods* refers to used stoves, refrigerators, and other appliances, the term coming from the white-enamel finish with which such appliances were once all painted; white goods tend to be *laterally cycled* from household to household before finding their way into the solid-waste stream, from which they are then typically plucked by scavengers for further reuse, to be cannibalized for parts, or to be crushed for scrap metal. Among recyclers, a shipment of waste paper that consists of a combination of white paper and colored paper is referred to as *tossed salad;* another way in which recyclers refer to materials that have been mixed (i.e., different kinds of paper; different kinds of plastic; plastic with paper; paper with glass) is to say that they are *comingled*. A term that recyclers throw around as if it were well-known to everyone is *OCC*, which simply means *old corrugated cardboard* (a major component in the domestic and international trade in *secondary materials*). *Fluff* is what is left over after a car is crushed—a mixture of pulverized foam, plastic, and glass. Old glass that has been broken up is called *cullet* (the word comes from the glass-making term *collet*, which refers to the collar of glass that remains on a glass-maker's blowing pipe after the glass object itself has been broken off). Cullet may be added during manufacturing as temper to strengthen the bond in new glass.

Whatever the specific form garbage may take, those familiar with its behavior cite what has been called the *Parkinson's Law of Garbage:*

The Fresh Kills landfill in Staten Island, New York is one of the largest man-made objects on the plant, second only to the Great Wall of China.

"Garbage expands so as to fill the receptacles available for its containment." (The law is named for C. Northcote Parkinson, the British civil servant who in 1957 formulated the original Parkinson's Law: "Work expands so as to fill the time available for its completion.") The accumulated garbage is dealt with in a variety of ways. Garbage destined for recycling often gets processed at a *materials-recovery facility*, better known these days by its acronym *MRF*, pronounced "merf." Another large portion of our garbage is burned at incinerators. The incinerator concept was first introduced to the United States in 1885 under the name *cremator*, a designation that understandably achieved little popularity. (The alternative, *destructor*, fared no better.) Incinerators in most cases today are more pleasantly and also more accurately described as *resource-recovery facilities* or *waste-to-energy facilities*—in most cases, they not only burn garbage but also produce steam for electricity. Most garbage, however, is neither burned nor recycled but is disposed of the way most garbage always has been, by simply being deposited somewhere. That "somewhere" was once the common *open dump*, sited mainly for reasons of convenience or, dubiously, of wetlands-reclamation. The modern *sanitary landfill* (1968), a vast repository lined with clay and other materials and located with an eye to doing as little environmental damage as possible, is now the legal standard nationwide. Garbage typically arrives at a *landfill* (1942) in *mother-hen packer trucks*—that is, in ordinary garbage trucks—or in rig-pulled *packer rolloffs* from *transfer stations*. The garbage is dumped, or *tipped*, in return for a *tipping fee*. A single day's worth of garbage is called a *cell*. When enough cells have been deposited to fill one level of a landfill, a new level, or *lift*, is started. Over time every landfill, owing in part to the slow process of biodegradation and also to the consequences of wet weather, produces a noxious gravy called *leachate* (1934); the leachate is removed through pipes and is processed. In addition, a latticework of pipes must be installed to remove and capture the copious amounts of methane gas that landfills produce; the array of protruding pipes is known as a *tree farm*. Despite all precautions, landfills—and also composting facilities—can have a problem with *fugitive odor*, one of many reasons that waste-management facilities rank near the top when it comes to vociferous reactions from potential neighbors.

Although its contribution to solid-waste management is in truth relatively insignificant, the *garbage disposer* (also known as the *garbage-disposal unit*, or simply as a *garbage disposal*) has become both an important labor-saving device and a durable cultural icon. The first commercially available garbage disposer came on the market in 1935, bearing a General Electric trademark, but it wasn't widely sold until the end of the Great Depression and the start of the robust post-World War II civilian economy. Celebrated as "a hunk of better living" by proponents such as Morris M. Cohn, the influential editor of the journal *Wastes Engineering* (and the man who officially bears the title "Father of the Kitchen Garbage Disposer"), the household garbage disposer became a not-unfamiliar feature of upscale new homes in the 1950s, and by the 1970s was standard in most new homes, along with a *garbage compactor*.

Garbage-industry personnel have not escaped the wave of gentrification and pseudo-professionalism that swept over most of occupational America by the mid 20th century. The long-used term *garbage man* has a rough-and-ready utility that has stood it in good stead, but *sanitation engineer*, its overeducated and prospective replacement, has shown more staying power in the face of ridicule than we might have expected. (Sanitation engineers themselves are just as happy with the moniker *cantossers*.) As more and more communities confront the issue of how and

The law of unintended consequences at a recycling center in Philadelphia in 1987. Mandatory recycling had choked the city's main recycling plant, and it was eventually closed because of dangerous and unhealthy conditions.

where to dispose of garbage, a breed of *garbitrageur* has come into being, skilled at *garbitrage*: brokering the export of garbage from one place to another. (*Garbitrage* is derived from the stock-market term *arbitrage*.) Another new breed of garbage entrepreneur is the *briefcase recycler*—a consultant who advises communities on the best way to go about setting up recycling operations. *Briefcase recycler* is meant to be a pejorative term: many such consultants have little practical experience in the byzantine vagaries of the *secondary-materials markets*, and recycling programs have had high failure rates. The world of garbage disposal can be highly politicized, in part because of the growing number of *green consumers* (people who would like to make their purchasing and other economic decisions on the basis of what is in the interest of the planet's environment) and in part because the definition of *environmentally friendly* is not one that well-meaning people can agree on.

Ironically, some of the most efficient and perhaps even most environmentally friendly garbage-disposal efforts are among the most discomfiting to look at. The famous *garbage mountains* so familiar from pictures of Third World cities have given rise to a large local scavenging class—the *pepenadores* in Mexico City, the *zabaline* in Cairo; spurred by desperate poverty, these scavengers recycle volumes of materials that suburban recyclers in America do not dare to dream of. The analogue in the United States is the *Dumpster diver*, typically an impoverished and perhaps also homeless person who forages in *Dumpsters* for redeemable bottles and cans, for food, and for other items of value.

Of course, another type of worker who forages in garbage for items of value brings us full circle: the *garbologist*. Writing about the ancient aboriginal garbage mounds of the American Southwest, the eminent archaeologist Emil Haury observed, "Whichever way one views the mounds—as garbage piles to avoid, or as symbols of a way of life—they nevertheless are features more productive of information than any others."

THE WILD, WILD WEST

*T*he dynamics of the American West are vital in understanding the development of American language. Consider the colorful and expressive Western words contributed to the American vocabulary: **chuck wagon, jerkwater, rip-roaring, hornswoggle, pan out, maverick, six-shooter,** *and the* modern **cappuccino cowboy.** *From the earliest pioneers who left the fringes of the eastern seaboard behind, to the* **49ers** *of California, to the* **cowboys** *who rode the* **Plains,** *to the* **Sagebrush Rebels** *of today, western words have been as varied, free-spirited, dynamic, and intriguing as the West itself.*

ERRAND INTO THE WILDERNESS

"Go West, young man, and grow up with the country."

— Horace Greeley, 1850

"All this to go to a wildernesse, where wee could forecast nothing but care and temptations, onely in hopes of enjoying Christ in his Ordinances."

— Thomas Shepard, Puritan minister of Cambridge, Massachusetts, 1648

Almost as soon as the first English colonists established tenuous footholds on the wooded seacoast of America during the early 1600s, they began calling the seemingly unending forest around them *the wilderness* (13th century, from Old English *wilddeoren*, "of wild beasts").

The first task was to conquer the wilderness. Aside from conventional chopping, they cleared land by *girdling* trees (1650, later called *deadening*, 1785), notching the bark all around so the trees would die. They would use the wood for *lumber* (originally "useless items taking up space"; the "timber" sense developed in America) and fuel, then pull or burn the *stumps* (to be *stumped*, "at a loss," is an Americanism) to create *clearings* (1678). As the land was cleared, *settlements* (1675) built, and the best land taken, some *settlers* (1696) decided to see *wide-open spaces* further inland.

By 1676, *frontier* (ultimately from Old French for "something in front") meant the line of settlements between civilization and the wilderness (in England *frontier* had meant the border or border area between two countries, so this was an entirely new, American meaning). As these settlers or *pioneers* (from Old French *peonier*, footsoldier, later meaning

Main Street in a frontier town. Roswell, New Mexico in the late 19th century.

A wagon train pulling through Swift Station, California.

explorer and settler and cited in this sense to 1817) moved into the interior they moved "back" from the original settlements along the seacoast. Thus, those in the original colonies spoke of the *backlands* (1681), *backwoods* (1709), or *back country* (1746), and the people there were called *backwoodsmen* (1774) and later *backwoods women*. And St. Jean de Crèvecoeur referred to those going there as *frontiermen* (1782).

Since the interior was not only "back" from the coast but, especially in the South, "up" from the coastal plain into the highlands, hills and mountains, *frontiersmen* (the more common spelling) were also said to move *upland* (to high ground, 1637, to the backwoods, 1656) or later *upcountry* (1815). The remote virgin forests or unsettled regions were called *timberland* (1654), *the timber* (this sense, 1792), and the *high timber* (1831) or *tall timber*. Other American terms for the back country were *the bush* (1657) and *the brush* (late 1700s).

As settlers moved west, the term *the West* shifted with them. The migration via the *Oregon Trail* from the 1840s and the Gold Rush to California after 1848 began large-scale American settlement of the area that we think of as the West today. *Wild west*, recorded in 1849, reflected the relative lawlessness of the American West compared with the more "civilized" East. The *wild and wooly West*, perhaps referring literally to uncurried wild horses or the sheepskin chaps of cowboys, appeared during the 1880s.

While the West was being won, the significance of the *frontier* as a concept in American culture and politics became clear. As early as 1893, Frederick Jackson Turner set forth his *frontier theory*, which claimed that the fundamental character of American life had been shaped by the continuous presence of true wilderness on its borders. Americans much later began using *frontier* for areas of intellectual discovery and challenge, from President Kennedy's *New Frontier* to suburbia's *Crabgrass Frontier* (1980s).

"Woodman, spare that tree! Touch not a single bough! In youth it sheltered me, And I'll protect it now."

— George Pope Morris, 1830, "Woodman, Spare That Tree"

NATIVE AMERICANS

When the Pilgrims landed, there were some thousand distinct Native American (Indian) nations. The word *Indian* itself, of course, reflects a notorious linguistic mistake. When Christopher Columbus journeyed to the New World he was convinced he had reached his goal: the Indies of Asia. Hence the native inhabitants he found, of the Carib tribe or nation, he called *Indians*, and the Caribbean Islands he visited were called the *Indies* (later, the *West Indies*, to distinguish them from the Asian or East Indies).

Indian was first used in 1602 to refer to a native of what is now the United States and since then has been a generic term for all peoples indigenous to the Americas. During the late 1960s and early 1970s, *Indian* fell into some disfavor. The term preferred by many became *Native American* (cited to 1925), which had the advantage of distinguishing between inhabitants of the Americas and India.

But many experts and observers agree that people sympathetic to Native American issues do continue to use *Indian* as a term of pride and respect. A great number of Native Americans accept either term, though most would prefer to be called by their tribal names,

Sitting Bull, chief of the Sioux Nation, is a fitting symbol of the uneasy relationship between Native Americans and whites during the late 19th century. He defeated General Custer at the Battle of Little Big Horn in 1876. He toured with Buffalo Bill's Wild West Show during the 1880s. In 1890, he was shot and killed by tribal police when he protested a warrant for his arrest.

"Ye say they all have passed away,

That noble race and brave;

That their light canoes have vanished

From off the crested wave;

That mid the forests where they roamed

There rings no hunter's shout;

But their name is on your waters;

Ye may not wash it out."

— Lydia Huntly Sigourney,
Indian Names

Navaho, Cheyenne, Shoshone, etc. And during the 1990s there was some evidence of a return to the term *Indian.* A leading Native American newspaper, the *Lakota Times,* for instance, returned to using *Indian* instead of *Native American.*

European settlers borrowed thousands of words from the Native Americans, including place-names, words about Native American life and lore, and names for common plants and animals. The first colonists adopted such words largely out of practicality, but there's no doubt they were attracted by the beauty of the sounds as well. "I know not a language spoken in Europe," William Penn wrote, "that hath words of more sweetness or greatness, in accent or emphasis, than theirs."

The words we use in talking about Native Americans include some real Indian words as well as others from our conceptions and misconceptions of the peoples themselves:

bury the ax, 1680; *bury the tomahawk,* 1705; *bury the hatchet,* 1754. A Native American custom, used to symbolize coming to an agreement or making peace.

How! This is actually a western tribal greeting (Sioux, *hao,* Omaha *hau*) first encountered by whites about 1815; however, the Native Americans usually used it not as a greeting but as an expression of impatience.

squaw, 1634, Massachuset *squa, ussqua,* woman, although not necessarily a married one; the colonists then came to use it to mean an Indian wife. White settlers carried the word *squaw* west where Plains Indians viewed it as a white man's word and found it objectionable, as Native Americans do today.

sweat lodge, cited to 1850, a low hut used by western tribes for sweating as a ritual of purification and healing.

Indian summer, 1778, origin much disputed. It could be so called because at this time of warm fall days following a hard frost Indians burned grass to clear and fertilize land and to drive animals in one last fall hunt (early accounts of *Indian summer* stress its "smokiness" or haze). Or it may reflect the fact that Indians were on the move to winter quarters or hunting grounds during these last warm days of fall. Still another theory (1812) holds that the term is derived from the Indian belief that the season "is caused by a wind, which comes immediately from the court of their great and benevolent God Cautantowwit, or the south-western God."

Indians called white people many names, many unflattering. *The Long Knives,* and the *Big Knives,* were first recorded in 1750 as tribal talk for settlers, especially in Virginia, referring to the swords early settlers carried. Indians also called white people *goddams* because the settlers used this expression so often. And Indians welcomed Lewis and Clark with a hearty "son-of-a-pitch," apparently believing this curse, which they had overheard trappers using, was a form of greeting in English.

Tribal words for plants, animals, and landscapes began to appear in our language as soon as the colonists landed. Often the colonists misheard, shortened, or altered the word or phrase (*isquantersquash* from Narraganset [1634] became *squash*), tried to pronounce parts of words like familiar English words (a process called "folk etymology" and most notably represented by *woodchuck*), or took several Indian terms and made a single word out of them. Some are these:

hickory, 1670, a clipping of the obsolete *pokahickory,* itself from Virginia Algonquian *pawcohiccora,* which didn't refer to the tree itself but to a dish made by pounding hickory nuts and water, 1618. *Hickory* was used to mean "firm, unyielding" by 1800.

moose, 1603, of Algonquian origin, related to Massachuset *moos*, moose.

pecan, 1712, Louisiana French *pacane*, of Algonquian origin, related to Ojibwa *pakan*, which actually meant any hard-shelled nut. The colonists reserved the word for the nuts of a specific species.

raccoon, 1608, Virginia Algonquian *raugroughcun*, scraper, scratcher. Early spellings included *arocoun*.

skunk, 1634, of Algonquian origin, related to an Eastern Abenaki word *segank*, the Native American word meaning "a mammal that urinates or sprays."

THE PRAIRIE

Once American settlers began crossing the Appalachians in large numbers after the American Revolution, they encountered the great grassland named the *prairie* by French explorers, trappers, and fur traders. The French frontiersmen also gave us *butte*, a hill (cited to 1805, from French, "the mound behind a target," and still considered a Southwestern word in American English).

After the English colonists picked up *prairie* scores of *prairie* derivatives evolved, including, *prairie chicken* and *prairie dog*; *prairie telegraph* (1800s, the written messages left by pioneers beside wagon trails); *passed over the prairie*, a 19th century euphemism for being raped by Native Americans; *prairie soil* (1817, soil types predominating in areas of tall grass); and *prairie butter* (a batter made from grease, flour and water).

The *Great Desert* (1784) and the *Great American Desert*, first recorded in 1834, were used to describe the extensive grasslands of the western Great Plains, dry and quite treeless by Eastern standards and reflecting an original sense of *desert* as a wild, uninhabited place.

BUFFALO

When Americans began settling west of the Mississippi, the plains teemed with roaming herds of buffalo. *Buffalo* (Italian and Spanish *bufalo* via Latin from Greek *boubalos*), is, of course, a misnomer. *Buffalo* is a word Europeans had used for the African gazelle, a species much smaller and weaker than the *American bison* (1796), but the Spanish explorer Hernando DeSoto was probably applying the nearest equivalent at hand when he first called the animal a *bufalo* in 1544. Because of the importance of the animal and its vast numbers, it became a symbol of the West and many derivative terms developed, such as *buffalo robe* (1723), a buffalo pelt used as blanket, coat, or sleeping bag; *buffalo chips* (1804), dried buffalo dung, a common fuel of the prairie; and *buffalo soldier* (1873), an African American soldier serving in the West after the Civil War. To *buffalo someone* (1870s) meant to confuse, cheat, or intimidate another. It comes not, as we might assume, from the power of a buffalo herd to frighten or threaten someone, but from the perception of the buffalo as a dim-witted, easily terrorized creature. In the 20th century, some ranchers crossbred buffalo with beef cattle to produce *beefalo* (1973), also known as *cattalo*.

FRONTIER LINGO

The frontier proved a rich source of new words and expressions: *rip-roaring* (1834), for noisily exciting; *holdup* (1878), for a robbery at gunpoint; *doing a land office business* (1853), for brisk sales; *rub out* (1849), to kill someone; and *sand* for grit and determination.

Westerners concocted and used colorful lingo. A bowie knife was an *Arkansas toothpick*; coitus interruptus was an *incomplete act of worship*; calf testicles (eaten as delicacies) were *mountain* (or *prairie*) *oysters*; a coffin was a *wooden overcoat*; to *cash in your six-shooter* was to rob a bank; a *California prayerbook* was a deck of cards; a *Kentucky breakfast* was a bottle of whiskey; a *live dictionary* was a schoolmarm. Euphemisms for prostitutes included *calico queen, nymph du prairie, horizontal worker, ceiling expert,* and *frail sister.*

One of the most striking styles of western speech was a fondness for fancified, multisyllabic words, concocted perhaps out of desire to mock the pretensions of the "sophisticated" East, perhaps out of the sheer boredom of frontier life, though some were transported to the West: *discombobulate* (1916, possibly an alteration of *discompose*), to confuse; *squablification* (from *squabble*), quarreling; *hornswoggle* (around 1829, origin unknown), to swindle; and *snollygoster* (1846), a politician who gets into office by nonstop talking, among several meanings (*snollygoster* possibly an alteration of *snallygaster*, mythical creature that was supposed to prey upon children and poultry; itself possibly from a Pennsylvania Dutch *schnelle geeschter*; from Middle High German *snel*, fast, quick + *geist*, spirit). While some of these highfalutin terms, such as *absquatulate* (go away), *skedaddle* (1861, scram, attested in Missouri), and *splendiferous* (splendid) may have Old World connections, they were given form and popularity by American westerners.

Annie Oakley, crack rifle marksman of the 1880s, shot holes in playing cards. Since a free ticket is generally punctured with holes (so it would not be counted with the paid receipts) a free pass is often termed an *Annie Oakley.*

"A fellow who wants office regardless of party, platform, or principles, and who, whenever he wins, gets there by the sheer force of monumental talknophical assumnacy."

— an early definition of *"snollygoster,"* J. L. Dillard, **American Talk,** 1976

An advertisement for "Buffalo Bill" Cody's Wild West Show in 1900. Before he was a showman, Cody was a rider on the Pony Express, a veteran of the Union army, a buffalo hunter (he claimed to have killed 4,000 in a year and a half), and the star of novels by Ned Buntline.

THE GOLD RUSH

The first *gold rush*—in Georgia in 1828—gave us *gold digger* (1830, one who digs for gold; it didn't mean a mercenary woman who preys on men until the early 20th century), *gold region* (1832), and the *gold belt* (1879). Other early gold finds in Illinois, Missouri, Iowa, and the Great Lakes region gave us:

bonanza, 1844, Spanish, literally "calm sea" and figuratively "prosperity," from Medieval Latin *bonacia*, with roots *bon* "good" from Latin *bonus* and the suffix of *malacia* "calm sea," from Greek *malakia*, meaning literally "softness." It came to mean both a lucky discovery of gold and any source of sudden wealth.

to pan for gold, 1833; *to pan out*, to find gold by panning in a river or stream, 1839, which by 1873 gave us the general term *to pan out*, meaning to produce or succeed.

a *prospect*, 1832, in the sense of a location which seems a promising place to search for gold; *to prospect*, 1841; *prospector*, 1846.

The discovery of gold at John Sutter's mill in the Sacramento Valley on January 24, 1848 triggered gold fever in the entire nation and started the *gold rush* (cited 1876). Along with it came the first *forty-niners* (cited 1853; it wasn't generally written *'49er* until the mid 1860s). Between 1849 and 1853 the California gold rush had created or popularized:

mother lode, 1874, a main lode or vein of ore in an area. The term later came to mean "a main source or supply of anything," typically used in the expression *hit the mother lode*.

pard, 1850, short for the American pronunciation of *partner* as "pardner."

piker, a California gold rush term for a cheapskate. The term most likely derives from the popular belief that settlers from Pike County, Missouri were contemptible and stingy.

tenderfoot, 1849, first applied to imported cattle (which were tenderfooted), then to inexperienced people by the '49ers. Easterners were also called *rawheels* because they weren't used to wearing boots.

Sutter's Mill. It is estimated that 100,000 people participated in the gold rush, coming not just from the east, but South America, Asia, and Europe as well. Ten thousand would die from dysentery and other diseases in the first year alone. Lawlessness was nearly as big a threat as infection.

A rodeo rider on a buffalo.

COWBOYS

During the Revolutionary War, *cowboys* (cited to 1623, a tender of cattle or horses) was a term for Loyalists who would lure patriot farmers into ambushes by ringing cowbells. Later it meant a Texan who rustled Mexican cattle. But *cowboy* began to take on its legendary U.S. meaning by the spring of 1867 when the railroad reached Abilene, Kansas, and a 29-year-old livestock trader named Joe McCoy hired ranchers and laborers to drive beef cattle from Texas up the Chisholm Trail to the railhead. Soon McCoy (not, by the way, the source of the phrase "the real McCoy," origin unknown) was shipping half a million head East a year and there were over 5,000 cowboys on the trail. The dry summer and severe winter of 1886–87 and use of *barbwire* (1880) or *barbed wire* (1881)—an American invention—marked the end of the heyday of the cowboy.

THE NEW WEST

From the 1970s through the 90s the West experienced a social, demographic, and political transformation nearly as dramatic as what it had witnessed during the 19th century. Influenced by rising environmental concern, federal agencies began to impose tighter restrictions on the use of federal land by ranchers, miners, and loggers. The U.S. Forest Service and the Bureau of Land Management raised land-use fees and prohibited certain kinds of commercial activity.

Ranchers and sheepherders joined with mining and timber interests to launch a campaign against federal authority in the West. They presented legislative proposals to sell large amounts of federal land to private interests and speed development of natural resources. This populist campaign against government control of federal lands became known as the *Sagebrush Rebellion*, a term that came to national prominence in 1980.

As the Sagebrush Rebellion subsided, the West was rocked by a second and more far-reaching revolution: an inundation of affluent newcomers (a new generation of *dudes* [1877, in the sense of a dandy or fop; in the West, an Easterner or city slicker; origin unknown) from urban areas. Native-born westerners felt invaded and overwhelmed by these affluent newcomers. Two flashpoints were the early 1990s disputes over whether to permit logging in an area inhabited by the spotted owl, an endangered species, and whether to reintroduce cattle-killing wolves into Yellowstone Park.

Old-guard Westerners, sometimes called *Wild Westerners*, developed some choice terms for the newcomers, including *cappuccino cowboys*, *suitcase rancher*, and *white-collar rancher*, the hostility reminiscent of the days when cattlemen and farmers said rude things to and of one another. In Colorado, where new arrivals flocked to areas on the east slope of the Rockies around Denver while natives stayed on the west slope, people began to identify themselves as *East Slopers* or *West Slopers*.

Terms for the strip malls and suburban tracts that sprang up near old mining and cow towns include *rural sprawl* and *oasis civilization*. Native Westerners complained of *tourons* (a blend of *tourist* and *moron*) and argued for *sustainable tourism* that didn't damage the region's natural charms. Small towns—overwhelmed by lavish second homes, expensive restaurants, and luxury boutiques—were said to have been *Aspenized*, that is, turned into another Aspen, Colorado, a tourist mecca of the rich and famous.

PHOTO CREDITS

INDEX

Annie Oakley (ticket), 435

another day, another dollar, 101

answering machine, 53, 305–6

answering service, 53

ante-bellum, 144

Anthony, Susan B., 215, 216, 217

anthracite coal, 197

antiabortion, 291

Antichrist, 189

anti-establishment, 223

anti-freezing protein, 236

anti-oxidant, 252

anti-stalking laws, 293

antitakeover measures, 112

A-OK, 317, 388

A-1, 317

a.p., 411

Appalachian Mountains, 243

Apple Annie, 111

apple pie, 177

April Fool's Day, 271

April vacation, 267

aquacize, 163

aquaculture, 128

A-question, 329

arbitrageur, 112

ARC, 259

archives, 71

area code, 52, 54

Arizona, 238

Arkansas, 238

Arkansas toothpick, 435

Armageddon, 189

armchair athlete, 402

armchair quarterback, 166

Armistice Day, 262

Armstrong, Neil, 383, 384

Arnold, Benedict, 142

aromatherapy, 165

arraignment, 299

arrest, 299

arroyo, 248

arse, 377

article, 72

artificial turf, 394

arugula, 185

ARVIN, 155

Aryan Nation, 189

asanas, 162

asbestos, 77, 128

ashpone, 168

Asian, 309

as if!, 228

Ask the man who owns one, 4

Aspenized, 437

aspirin, 254

ass, 377

ass, piece of, 84, 86

asshole, 81

assisted suicide, 261

associate producer, 411

association football, 395

ass-out, 358

asteroid, 387

Astor, John Jacob, 106

astronaut, 386

at bat, 393

Atlantic Seaboard, 243

Atlantic States, 242

Atlas, Charles, 158

ATM, 101

at-need arrangements, 211

atom bomb, 151

Atomic Age, 151

atomic power plant, 203

at that point in time, 325–26

At the tone the time will be, 51

attorney, 300

auction system, 276

audience coordinator, 411

Auld Lang Syne, 266

Aunt Jemima, 168

auto, 420

Automat, 183

automatic redial, 52

automobile accident, 421

automobiles, 116–17, 420–22

avatar, 77

awakening, 255

A.W.O.L., 144

Axis, 148

AZT, 259

B

Baby Boomer, 225, 227

baby farm, 278

backboard, 400

back care, 212

back country, 432

backcrossing, 231

back door, 79

backlash, 313

backporch, 377

backside, 377

back seat driver, 421

back-to-school time, 267

back-to-the-lander, 187

backwoods, 432

Bacon, Francis, 181

bad (good), 225

badlands, 243

Bad Thing, 77

bad trip, 226

Baer, Clara, 400

bagel, 167

baggage, 85

baggage car, 415

baggies, 140

bag lady, 281, 282

bag man, 281

bagnio, 85

bail, 285

Bailey, F. Lee, 285

bail out, 146

Bain, Alexander, 53

Baker, George, 151

bakery bread, 170

Bakke v. University of California, 290

balance beam, 390

balanced diet, 254

bald lump, 280

Baldrige, Letitia, 303–6

ball-and-socket joint, 252

ball carrier, 398

baller, 358

balls, 377

balmy, 37

Baltimore and Ohio, 415

Bambaataa, Afrika, 355

bamboozle, 113

bamf, 77

banana, 16

banana split, 178

Band-Aid solution, 333

bandwidth, 77

bang, 378

bank, 201, 358

bankable star, 344

banked (fires), 201

Bankhead, Tallulah, 33

banking, 115

banking by phone, 52

bank robber, 57

Bara, Theda, 371, 372, 373

barbarism, 113

barbecue, 174

barbells, 164

Barbera, Joe, 349

Barbie clothes, 333

barbwire/barbed wire, 437

bar car, 415

Bardot, Brigitte, 373

barefoot cruise, 413

barfogenesis, 79

bark up the wrong tree, 10

Barnburners, 319

barnstorming, 424

barracks, 141

barrel stove, 199

barren, 249

Barry, John A., 74

bartering, 110

base, 358

baseball, 392–95

baseboard heating, 202

basket, 399–400

basketball, 399–402

basket case, 146

bass (fish), 172

bastard, 81

bathing beauty, 372

bathing suit, 137

bathtub gin, 29, 36, 40

Batman, 347

batted, 38

batting a thousand, 391, 392

batting average, 392

battle fatigue, 147

Battle of Britain, 148

baud, 77

baud barf, 77

Baudot, Jean Maurice Emile, 77

bawd, 85

bayou, 243, 244

bazooka, 148

beach bunny, 373

beachhead, 148

beach party movie, 343

beach volleyball, 391

Beacon, Aurora Daily, 277

beam, 377

beamer, 358

bombed/bombed out, 38
bomber, 146, 171, 354
bomb shelter, 148
bonanza, 436
bones, 358
bone-shaker, 419
bonnet, 132
Bonney, William H., 57
Bonnie and Clyde, 57, 58
bonny clabber, 169
boobs, 377
boob tube, 348
boogaloo, 339
boogied, 339
book (police), 62
booker, 410, 411
boom (economic), 111
boom and bust, 246
boom box, 354
boomerangers, 304
boomers, 227
boom town, 247
boondocks, 145, 243
booster rocket, 385
boot, boot camp, 145
bootlegger, 29, 41
booty, 57
booze, 23–46
boozehound, 39
boozy, 36
bop, 336
bordello, 85
Borden, Lizzie, 58
Bork, Robert H., 288
born-again, 361
bosom, 377
boss, 8
Boss Tweed, 322
Boston baked beans, 175
Boston game, 396
bot, 79
bottled beer, 26
bottled gas, 202
bottom dropped out, 111
bottom line, 105
boulder (crack cocaine), 64
bounces and shrubs, 32–33
bounty, 141
bourbon, 29
boutique winery, 44

bovine somatotropin, 233
Bow, Clara, 372
bowl (football), 397
bow tie, 136
box, the, 348
boxed, 38
boxing, 402, 403
box stove, 196
boyfriend, 380–81
bozon, 78
bra, 138
bra burner, 219
Braden, Margaret, 278
Brady Bunch, 349
Brady Law, 291–92
brain-damaged, 78
brain death, 261
brain dump, 78
brain fart, 78
brain trust, 323
brainwashing, 152
Branch Davidians, 191, 192
Brandeis, Louis D., 286, 293
Brando, Marlon, 343
brandy, 30
brass, 145
Brathwaite, Fred, 355
bread, 102, 170
bread-and-butter issue, 327
breadline, 111, 276
bread machine, 170
bread riots, 110, 317
break, 354
breakdancing, 353–54
breakfast, 167–69
breakfast food, 168
breaking, 354
breast, 377
breast implant, 377
breeches, 130, 131
Brennan, William J., Jr., 285, 289, 376
Brethren, 362
brewpub, 24
brick stove, 196
bridal registry, 304
brie, 169
briefcase recycler, 430
Brinkley, David, 410
briquette, 201
broad, 87
broadcloth, 130

broad construction, 286
Broadway, 244, 245
brochureware, 78
broke, 107
broker, 108
bronco, 21
Brooks, Garth, 337
brothel, 85
brother, 364
Brown, Helen Gurley, 373
Brown, H. Rap, 355–56
brownie, 178
Browning, Robert, 195
brown nose, 83
Brown v. Board of Education, 287, 288, 290
Bruce, Lenny, 81, 355
Bryan, William Jennings, 102, 296
Bryant, William Cullen, 434
bubba vote, 330
bubble, 331
bubble boy disease, 234
bubbly, 33
Buchanan, Patrick, 410
Buchananism, 329
buck, 102
bucket, 14, 399–400
bucket shop, 109
buckram, 132
buckskin, 132
buckwheat cakes, 169
bud (marijuana), 64
buffalo, 434
buffalo (verb), 434
buffalo chips, 434
buffalo robe, 434
buffalo soldier, 434
Buffalo wings, 172
bugger, 379
bugs (computer), 76, 78
bugs (concealed recording devices), 325
bull (market), 109, 110
bull (police), 62, 279
bull dyke, 380
bulletin board system, 70–71
bullshit, 83, 84
bum, 279
bum a ride, 279
Bumbo, Bombo, 32

bump, 330, 358
bumper sticker, 422
bundling, 377
bundling board, 377
Bundy, Ted, 59
Bunker, Archie, 349
bunned, 38
Bunnies, 373, 374
Burchfield, Robert W., 113
burden of proof, 289
bureau, 11
bureaucratese, 329–30
burgers, 172
burglar, 66
burial court, 211
burial ground, 209
burial society, 206–7
Burma-Shave road signs, 2
burn, the, 246
burnout, 256
Burnside, Gen. Ambrose Everett, 134, 135
bury, 208
bury the hatchet, 433
bus, 419
bush, the, 432
Bush, George, 155, 189, 288, 326, 328, 329, 330, 347
bush league, 393
business card, 303
business suit, 134, 136
business woman, 215
bust (arrest), 61
bust (economic), 111
bust (reduce in rank), 145
bust a cap, 358
busthead, 30
busting a half-Cab, 392
bust on the scene, 358
butch, 380
Butcher, Harry, 324
butt, 377
butte, 434
butter, 169
butter beans, 175
Butternuts, 89
buttocks, 377
button-down shirt, 137
buttoned-down, 137
buyout, 105
Byrd, William, 157
byte-bonding, 74

get inside one's head, 226
get it on, 378
get laid, 378
get off, 87
get one's Irish up, 22
get religion, 363
get-rich-quick scheme, 107
getting in touch with oneself, 226
get to first base, 393–94
Gewürztraminer, 45
geyser, 91
ghetto, 19
ghost town, 246
GHP, 204
Gibbon, Cedric, 341
Gibson, 35
Gibson, Mel, 341
Gibson, William, 69
Gibson girl, 134, 371–72
Gideon Bible, 369
Gideon v. Wainwright, 288
giggle-juice, 33
GIGO, 80
GI Joe, 149
Gillespie, "Dizzy," 336
Gillis, Lester, 57
Gilmore, Gary, 57
"Gimme five," 401
"Gimme some skin," 401
gin, 29
gingerbread, 177
Gingrich, Newt, 283, 327
ginned, 36
gin rickey, 34
Ginsberg, Allen, 222
girdle, 137
girdling trees, 431
girl, 214, 310
girlfriend, 380–81
girls' basketball, 400
girl watching, 308
Gish, Lillian, 371
give a wide berth to, 412
give her the once-over, 308
give me a ring, 51
gizmo, 149
glamor stocks, 110
glamour girl, 372
glasnost, 314, 326

glass ceiling, 220
Gleason, Jackie, 352
Gleick, James, 104
Glenn, John, 383, 385
glitch, 78
global village, 404
global warming, 125
globe stove, 199
Glorious Fourth, 269
glutes, 164
Glyn, Elinor, 372
G-men, 57
Gnarly!, 403
"Go ahead—make my day!," 329, 347
goal tending, 400
goatee, 135
goat whiskey, 37
gobbledygook, 329
gobs and swabbies, 147
God, euphemisms for, 369
goddams, 433
Godey's Lady's Book, 133
god-fearing, 364
Godfrey, Arthur, 89, 404
God's acre, 369
God squad, 369
go-fast, 64
go for the burn, 159
go fuck yourself, 82
go-go funds, 110
go Hollywood, 243
going all the way, 377–78
going into the red, 105
going postal, 59
gold belt, 436
goldbrick, 147
gold certificates, 102
gold digger, 85–86, 436
golden handshake, 105
golden oldies, 339
golden parachute, 105
golden shower, 83
Goldman, Jane, 350
gold-medal favorite, 391
gold region, 436
gold rush, 246–47, 436
gold standard, 102
gold watch, 105
Goldwater, Barry, 154
golf, 402
golly gee, 87
gomers, 255
gondola, 20, 415

gone, 222
gone down the tubes, 101
Gone with the Wind, 342, 343, 347, 374
Gong Show, 350
Good for man or beast, 3
Goodman, Benny, 336
Goodman, Ellen, 51
good time girl, 373
Good to the last drop, 4
Goodwin, Mrs. Wilder, 132
goofer dust, 206
goo-goo eyes, 89
gook, 89
gooseberry fool, 177
goose egg, 395
gopher, 71
Gore, Al, 69, 330
Gore, "Tipper," 376
gork/gorky, 255–56
gosh, 369
gosh darn, 87
go to bat for, 395
gotten, 11
Gotti, John, 60
Gould, Jay, 109, 110
gourmet, 185
government, 117
Go West, 247
goy, 19
Grable, Betty, 373, 374
graffiti art, 354
graft, 60
Graham, Rev. Billy, 363
Graham, Katharine, 87
Graham, Sylvester, 157, 382
grand (in place names), 247
grand (thousand), 102
Grand Army of the Republic, 267–68
grand jury, 284–85, 299
Grand Ole Opry, 336
grandstand quarterback, 398
granny dresses, 138
granny dumping, 283
granny glasses, 138
grape-and-wine boom, 44
grass (marijuana), 64
grate, 194

Grateful Dead, The, 338, 339
grate people, 282
G rating, 375
graveyard, 209
gravlax, 185
gravy, 103
Gray, Barry, 165, 405
gray flannel suit, 137
graying of America, 251–52
grazing, 176, 304
great (in place names), 247
Great American Desert, 434
Great American Smokeout, 255
Great Awakening, 363
Great Depression, 111, 280–81, 324
Great Lakes area, 243
Great Train Robbery, The, 340
Greeley, Horace, 247, 431
green, 121
Green, Nancy, 168
greenbacks, 103
green beer, 272
Greenbelt, 247
green card, 106
green consumers, 430
greenhorn, 247
greenhouse effect, 125–26
greenhouse gases, 126
greening, 128
greenmail, 112
Greenpeace, 121, 122, 124
green politics, 128–29
green revolution, 129
green room, 410
Green Seal, 428
Greenspan, Alan, 111
Greer, Germaine, 218
Gregg, Allan, 227
Gregory, Horace, 11
Greyhound therapy, 282
griddle cakes, 169
gridiron, 397
gridlock, 249, 331
grief counselor, 212
grief therapy, 212
grieving fare, 211
Griffith, D. W., 340

Jefferson, Thomas, 1, 9, 10, 38, 94, 102, 106, 142, 175, 193, 221, 287, 331, 412
Jehovah's Witnesses, 362, 364, 366, 367
jelly beans, 179
Jencks, Christopher, 281
Jensen, Oliver, 414, 416
jerk (dance), 339
jerkin, 130
Jerry, 89
Jersey lightning, 30
Jesus H. Christ, 87
jet lag, 425
jet set, 425
Jews, 19–20
Jezebel, 86
jibbing, 403
Jim-and-Tammyfication, 334
Jim Crow laws, 287–88, 289
jim-jams, 39
jingled, 38
jitterbug, 336
jitters, 39
jock, 377, 398
jockey, 398
jock strap, 377, 398
Joe Sixpack, 187
jogging, 157, 159, 161
Johannsen, Wilhelm, 230
john, 87
johnnycake, 14, 169
Johnny Reb, 88
John Q. Public, 187
Johnson, Andrew, 321
Johnson, Arte, 351
Johnson, Lady Bird, 336
Johnson, Lyndon B., 152, 251, 292
Johnson, Samuel, 2, 119–20, 315
Johnson, Virginia, 371
Johnston, Gen. Joseph E., 268
joint, the, 66
jolly, 36
Jolson, Al, 341, 342, 347
jolt, 31
Jones, Edward D., 110
Jones, Jenny, 409
Jones, John Luther "Casey," 415

Jonestown, 192
Joplin, Scott, 335
Jordan, Barbara, 214
Jordan, Michael, 402
joyful journey to deeper spirituality, 367
joy ride, 422
joy water, 30
Judas priest, 369
judge, 299
judicial activist, 286
jug, the, 66
juice, 30
juiced, juiced up, 38
julep, 32
jumbo jet, 425
jump his/her bones, 378
jumping (on bike), 162
jumping gene, 237
jumping jacks, 160
jumping off place, 414
jump steady, 37
jumpsuits, 139
jungles, 280
jungle stiff, 279
junk bonds, 110
junk DNA, 235
junk faxes, 306
junk mail, 306, 307
junta, 145
juror, 299
jury, 299
jury selection, 299
"Just the facts, ma'm," 352
Just Say No, 6, 65, 381

K

Kaiser, Henry J., 150
Kalmus, Herbert T., 341
kamikaze pilot, 149, 150
Kane, Bob, 347
Kansas, 239
Kaposi's sarcoma, 259
karaoke, 339
Karloff, Boris, 342
Karolyi, Bela, 392
Kasczynski, Theodore, 191
katzenjammers, 39
kayak, 19
keelboat, 414
keel over, 412

keep Britain tidy, 119
keep on truckin', 279
Keeshan, Bob, 348
Kellerman, Jonathan, 334
Kellogg, J. H., 382
Kelly, "Machine Gun," 57
Kennedy, Jacqueline, 138, 206, 305
Kennedy, John F., 66, 153, 158, 190, 331, 383, 432
Kentucky, 239
Kentucky breakfast, 435
Kentucky broadhorn, 414
kerosene heater, 201–2
Kerouac, Jack, 222, 223
Kerrigan, Nancy, 391
ketchup, 172
Kevorkian, Jack, 261
Key, Francis Scott, 142
Key lime pie, 177
keys, 76
Keystone Kops, 346
khaki, 145
KIA, 154
kibitz, 19
kick, 355
kickboxing, 163
kicking the bladder, 395
kick it, 359
kicks, 359
kick the habit, 255
Kieran, James, 324
killer T cells, 259
kill ratio, 154
kilowatts, 204
kincob, 131–32
kindling, 14
King, B. B., 335
King, Billie Jean, 403
King, Larry, 406
King, Rev. Martin Luther, Jr., 17, 366
King, Martin Luther, Jr., Day, 263
King, Rodney, 62–63
Kingston Trio, 336
Kinsey, Alfred, 371
kissing, social, 304
Kissinger, Henry, 326
kitchen terms, 114
kiwi, 185
Klein, Calvin, 130

Klingons, 350
klutz, 19–20
knackwurst, 20
knee-jerk, 327
knickers, 136
knight of the road, 280
knobs, 377
knock, 200
knock-down-drag-out fight, 402
knockers, 377
Koch, Ed, 313
Kodak, 3
kohlrabi, 185
kooks, 190
Kool-Aid, 333
Koppel, Ted, 410
Korean War, 152–53
Koresh, David, 191, 192
kosher, 20, 273
kowabonga, 352
Kraut, 89
Kubrick, Stanley, 344, 345
kudzu, 246
Kuhn, Thomas, 327
Ku Klux Klan, 63, 188–89
Kunstler, William M., 297–98
Kuralt, Charles, 421
Kurtzman, Harvey, 347
Kwanzaa, 274

L

LA, 243
Labor Day, 269
Labor-Management Relations Act, 293
lack of moral direction, 368
lady, 213
LaFrance, Marianne, 305
lager beer, 24, 25, 26
lagniappe, 244
laid-back, 226
laid out, 206
laissez-faire, 317
lallapaloosa, 12
Lamaze method, 250
Lamb, Brian, 410
lambada, 339
lame duck, 328
lameness, 77

lynching, 188, 333
lynch mob, 63

M

Ma Bell, 49
Macarena, 339
macaroni, 185
MacArthur, Gen.
  Douglas, 150
Macaulay, Thomas, 2
McAuliffe, Christa, 385
McAuliffe, Gen.
  Anthony "Old Crock,"
  148
McCarthy, Eugene, 331
McCarthy era, 187, 285
McCarthyism, 329
McDonald's, 184
McDowell, James S.,
  385
Macfadden, Bernarr,
  164
McGrath, Charles, 130
MacGregor, Robert, 35
MacGyver bomb, 349
machete, 145
Machiavellian, 333
macho, 139
McIlhenny, Mary Avery
  and Edmund, 173
mack, 359
McKinley, William, 144
McKnight, George
  Henry, 15
McLennan, Joseph, 346
McLuhan, Marshall, 408
McMahon, Ed, 352
McNeill, Don, 404
McRae, John, 267
McVeigh, Timothy, 65
mad, 113
madam, 85, 87
MADD, 40
Madison, James, 221
Madison Avenue, 2, 244
Mad Magazine, 348
Mae West (life vest),
  150
Mafia, 59–60
Maginot Line, 148
magma, 90
magnates, 107
magnet issue, 327
mahimahi, 185
maiden name, 217, 311

mail, 47–48
  electronic, 55, 69, 307
  junk, 306, 307
  overland, 414–15
mailbombing, 75
Mailer, Norman, 84, 354
mailing lists, 75
mailman, 48
main drag, 278
Maine, 239
mainframe, 68
main line, 416
mainstay, 412
mainstream, 327
Mainstream America,
  187
maître d', 183
maize, 174
major league, 394
make, 82
make love, 378
make the beast with
  two backs, 378
making ends meet, 106
male, 213
male chauvinist, 219,
  308
malice, 289
Malloy, John, 139
malt liquor, 25
Mama-san, 153
mamm, 32
mammies, 17
mammography, 257
man, 213, 220
managed care, 250–52,
  253
mandillions, 130
Manhattan (cocktail),
  34
Manifest Destiny,
  317–18
man in space, 383
manners, 302–7
mantilla, 138
mantle, 194
mantlepiece, 194–95
man-to-man defense,
  402
mantra, 260
manufacturing
  economy, 105
Mao jacket, 139
maple syrup candy, 179
Mapp v. Ohio, 289
marathon, 160–61

Marbury v. Madison,
  288
March madness, 402
Marconi, Guglielmo,
  48–49
Mardi Gras, 244
margarine, 169
margarita, 35
margin, 109
marijuana, 63–64
marked man, 67
market, 108
marketplace of ideas,
  286
mark of the beast, 189
Marryat, Capt.
  Frederick, 11
marshal (funeral), 207
Marshall, John, 284,
  286, 287, 288
Marshall, Thurgood,
  287–88
martial art, 163
Martin, Judith, 303–6
Martin, Steve, 351
martini, 34–35
*Mary Hartman, Mary
  Hartman*, 352
Maryland, 239
marzipan, 179
M*A*S*H, 344, 352
MASH, 153
Mashed Potato (dance),
  339
mashed potatoes, 175
Mason, Donald, 147
Mason, Jackie, 19
Massachusetts, 239
massage, 165
Massasoit, 360
massive retaliation, 152
master, 214
Masters, William, 371
masturbation, 381–82
match-up defense, 402
materials-recovery
  facility, 429
Mather, Cotton, 294
Mather, Increase, 294
matzo, 273
mausoleum, 210
maxi, 139
maximum security
  prison, 67
Maxwell House Coffee,
  4

Mayflower Compact,
  360
May the Force be with
  you, 344
mayo, 167
mazuma, 103
mean gene, 237
Meara, Paula, 309
meatless, 167
medal (verb), 391
Medal of Honor, 144
median strip, 13–14
media whore, 411
medical examiner, 299
Medicare, Medicaid, 251
medium, 370
meeting, 360
meeting clothes, 361
megabucks, 106
Megan's Law, 292
Me Generation, 225
MEGO, 329
melanoma, 257
Mellon, Andrew, 106
melting pot, 15
member, 377
memorial, 208
memorial counselor,
  207
Memorial Day, 267–68
memorial park, 210, 211
memory picture, 212
Mencken, H. L., 361,
  366
Meneninee, 176
Mennonites, 361
menorah, 273
mensch, 20
menu, 182
Mercalli scale, 91
Meridian, 32
merlot, 45
mersh, 2
mesa, 248
messenger RNA, 234
Metalious, Grace, 377
metastasis, 257
meth, 64–65
Mexican hat dance, 339
Mexican War, 143, 318
MI, 258
MIA, 154
Michigan, 239
Mickey Mouse, 348
microbreweries, 24
microburst, 98
microcomputer, 68

micromini, 138
microserf, 228
microwave oven, 180
Midas touch, 107
middle-age spread, 166
Middle America, 242
middle management, 104
middle of the road, 327
midi-skirt, 139
midlife crisis, 256
midwife, 250
mighty mouse, 235
migrant worker, 106, 312
Miklaszewski, Jim, 288
military advisers, 153
military mustache, 135
militia, 141, 189, 190
milk chocolate, 179
Milken, Michael, 109, 110, 225
milk train, 416
Millennial Age, 367
Millet, Kate, 219
millionaire, 101, 106
Million Man March, 366
Milton, John, 386
Mimbo, 32
mind expansion, 223
mind-reader, 370
mind your head, 119
minestrone, 21
minigenes, 232
minimum security prison, 67
minimum wage, 106
miniskirt, 138
minister, 364, 367
ministry, 369
Minnesota, 240
Minnesota mule, 243
minos, 235
Minow, Newton N., 407
minstrel shows, 334–35
mint, 106
mint julep, 32
Minute Men, 142
Miranda rights, 291
Miranda v. Arizona, 290–91
mirliton, 185
Mischief Night, 272
Miss, 214, 304
Miss America, 372
missing children, 65
Mission: Impossible, 350

Mission Control, 385
Mississippi, 240
Mississippi broadhorn, 414
Mississippi steamboat, 414
Missouri, 240
mister, 214
Mr., 214
mistress, 86, 87, 214
Mitford, Jessica, 208
Mitnick, Kevin, 57
mixer, 180
mixology, 31–32
mob, the, 59–60
mobile phone, 54
mobster, 60
moccasin, 131
mod, 138
mode, 79
Model T, 421
modem, 55, 68
Modern Times, 342
Modified Mod, 140
mogul, 107
Mohawks, 139
molasses, 180
molecular xeroxing, 235
mole people, 282
mom and pop ISPs, 71
momentary muscular failure, 164
mommy track, 219
Mondavi, Robert, 44
Monday holidays, 263
Monday morning quarterback, 397–98
money, 102–4, 115
money bags, 107
money market fund, 110
money to burn, 101
monkey (dance), 339
monkey laws, 296
Monkey Trial, 295–96
monkeywrenching, 125
Monmouth cap, 130
Monnet, Jean, 148
monogamous relationship, 381
monokini, 137
Monroe, Marilyn, 333, 373
monster movie, 342
monster slam, 402
Montagu, John, Earl of Sandwich, 170

Montana, 240
Monty Python's Flying Circus, 75
moocher, 278
Moody, Dwight, 363
moola, 103
Moonies, 363
moon landing, 384
moonlighter, 29
moon mission, 384
Moon Pie, 167
moonscape, 384
moonshine, 29, 37
moon walk, 385
moose, 8, 434
moot courts, 297
mop-top hairdo, 138
morality, 368
moratorium, 225
Moravians, 362
morel, 185
More than one million copies sold, 3
Mormons, 362, 364
morning-after, 267
Morning in America, 329
Morris, George Pope, 432
Morris Canal, 246
Morris the Cat, 6
Morse, Samuel F. B., 48
mortician, 207, 208
Morton Salt, 4
mortuary, 207
mosquito, 21
motel, 422
motherfucker, 81, 83, 88
mother-hen packer truck, 429
mother lode, 436
Mother of All Battles, 156
Mother's Day, 271
motion pictures, 339
motorbus, 419
motor-car, 420
motorman, 418
motor-voter law, 293
Motown, 243
Mott, Jordan L., Sr., 198
Mott, Lucretia, 215
mountain bike, 161–62
mountain biking, 419, 420
mountain dew, 29

mountaineer, 243
mountain oysters, 435
mourning jewelry, 206
mouse, 72
mouse trails, 78
Mousketeers, 348
movement, 218, 223, 224
moviedom, 339
moviegoer, 339
moviemaker, 339
movies, 339–47
  competing with TV, 344
  Hollywood, 340–41
  phrases from, 344–47
  ratings of, 374–75
  sex and, 374–76
  talkies, 341–42
movie star, 340
moving pictures, 339
MRF, 429
MRI, 256, 258
Mrs., 214, 304
Ms., 214, 304
MSA, 253
MTV, 228, 339, 376
mudbugs, 244
mudflows, 90
mudheads, 72
MUDs, 72, 77
muffs, 130
mugged, 67
mukluk, 19
mule (drink), 30
mule (drug courier), 64
multiculturalism, 227, 313
multimillionaire, 106
multiplex cinemas, 344
mumbo jumbo, 16
mung beans, 175
munge, 79
municipal solid waste, 427
Murder, Inc., 60
Murphy Brown, 349
Murray the K, 378
muscadine grapes, 42
muscat, 46
mush, 167
mushers, 279
mushroom cloud, 152
music, 334–38
musical, 342–43
music scene, 223
music television, 339

music video, 228
mustache, 135
mustard gas, 147
mute button, 306
mutton-chops whiskers, 135
mutual funds, 110
muumuu, 139
my bad!, 359
Myers, Dee Dee, 328

N

nab, 61
nabob, 107
nachos, 186
Naismith, James, 399, 401
Nankeen, 132
napalm, 154–55
narcotics, 63–65, 252
narco-tunnel, 64
narrow construction, 286
Nast, Thomas, 328
national cemeteries, 211, 212
national debt, 101
national pastime, 391–92
Nation of Islam, The, 366
Native American, 17–19, 432–34
natural childbirth, 250
natural gas, 202
naturopathy, 260
navigating the Net, 72
Navy beans, 175
Nazis, 89
NC-17 rating, 375
near beer, 41
near-meltdown, 123
Nebraska, 240
neck cloth, 135
necker's knob, 378
necking, 378
ned, 102
needle beer, 41
negative advertising, 330–32
negative outcome, 312
Negri, Pola, 372
negroes, 16
neighborhood names, 248

Neighborhood Watch, 63
Nelson, "Baby Face," 57, 58
Neo-Nazis, 189
neon sign, 2
nerd, 72
nervous, 222
Nesbitt, Stephen A., 385
Net (Internet), 69-80; see also cyberspace
netiquette, 74, 307
net police, 76
net potatoes, 74
Network, 347
networking, 303
Neuman, Alfred E., 348
neutral ground, 13–14
Nevada, 240
Nevada divorce, 294
New Age, 165, 361
newbies, 72
New Deal, 323–24
New England, 242
New Frontier, 432
New Hampshire, 240
New Jersey, 240
New Jersey barrier, 14
New Left, 224, 225
new media, 2
New Mexico, 240
New Orleans, 244
newsgroup, 72
new woman, the, 216
New World, 273
New World Order, 189, 326
New Year's, 266–67
New Year's resolutions, 267
New York, 240
New York minute, 243
New York Times Company v. United States, 288
New York Times v. Sullivan, 289
niche, 210
nickname, 79
nicotine addiction, 254
nicotine patch, 254–55
Nifty Fifty, 110
nigger, 310
nightcap, 31
Nightline, 410
night owl, 183

night rates, 51
night riders, 63, 188
NIMBY, 125
Nimoy, Leonard, 350
90-pound weakling, 158
900 number, 52, 376
911, 52
nip, 31
Nixon, Richard M., 225, 324–26, 384, 398
noble (wine), 44
no-bra look, 138
no cake, 168
no-code, 261
no entry, 119
no-fault divorce, 294
"No good deed ever goes unpunished," 352
NOLA, 243
no-man's land, 147
nonalcoholic beer, 40
non-decriminalized substance, 312
non-documented person, 312
non-family abduction, 65
nonsmoking section, 254
noodle, 20
nookey, 378
nooner, 378
"No problem!," 352
Norris, Rev. J. Frank, 296
North Carolina, 240
North Dakota, 241
Northeast Corridor, 242
northeaster, 98
no salt, 167
nose candy, 64
nose paint, 30
nosh, 20, 176
nostrum, 3
"Not!," 351
not-for-profit hospital, 251
not guilty by reason of insanity, 288
Nothin' says lovin' like somethin' from the oven, 6
Nott, Eliphalet, 198
nouvelle cuisine, 181
NOW, 218–19

NRA, 324
NSAIDs, 254
nuclear arms race, 152
nuclear family, 187
nuclear weapons, nukes, 152
nucleotide, 233
nude, 88
nuke (in microwave), 180
number, telephone, 50
nurse-midwife, 250
nurse practitioner, 250
nutritional science, 166
Nutt sisters, 49–50
NYD, 256
nymph du prairie, 435

O

Oakley, Annie, 435
oasis civilization, 437
oath, 300
obese, 310
obesity gene, 237
obscenities, 81–89
OCC, 428
occult, 370
ocean liner, 413
O'Connor, Sandra Day, 287, 288
Odell, Allen, 2
officer, police, 61
office romance, 304
officiate, 206
off one's trolley, 418
off-road biking, 162
off-shore oil well, 203
off sides, 396
off-the-grid, 187
off the track, 417
off the wall, 226
off-topic, 75, 77
O'Hara, John, 378
O'Hara, Robert, 351
Ohio, 241
Oh shit!, 84
oil, 202
oil burner, 202
oil crisis, 125, 203
oil glut, 203
oil heating, 202
oil shortage, 203
oil stove, 201
oinks, 225
O.K./OK/okay, 317

Okies, 100
Oklahoma, 241
Oklahoma City, 66, 191
okra, 167
Old-Fashioned, 31
old-fashioned gospel, 363
oldies but goodies, 339
Old Ironsides, 142, 143
Old Nick, 369
oleomargarine, 169
Olmstead v. United States, 286
Olympic games, 391
Olympic gold, 390
omnibus, 418
onanism, 381–82
oncogene, 234
oncology, 257
one-arm driver, 378
one-handed jump shot, 400
O'Neill, Tip, 314, 315
one old cat, 392
one-step-at-a-time approach, 255
one-world government, 189
on the hip, 222
onions, 176
online community, 74
online encounter, 378
online religious services, 368
online services, 71
online shopping malls, 72
online world, 2
on the make, 87
on the rebound, 401–2
on the road, 279
on the spot, 67
on the track, 417
on the wagon, 40
oomph girls, 371, 372
OPEC, 203
open/close a grave, 208
open dump, 429
open man, 401
open-meeting laws, 293
opera hat, 135
operate outside the envelope, 388
operator, telephone, 49–50, 215
operon, 234

opiates, 252
opossum, 18
Oprah, 408
oral contraceptive, 218
orbit, 386
orbiter, 383
Oregon, 241
Oregon fever, 414
Oregon Trail, 414, 432
Oreo, 17
organ, 377
organelles, 231
organized crime, 59
Oriental, 309
O-ring, 385
ornamental cemetery, 210–11
orographic lifting, 99
orphanages, 278, 283
orphan trains, 278
Orr, Isaac, 199
Oscars, 341
OSHA, 123
osteoporosis, 254
O'Sullivan, John L., 318
other side, the, 370
Otis, James, 315
ouch!, 20
Ouija board, 370
Our most important package is yours, 7
Our repairmen are the loneliest guys in town, 7
outdoor relief, 275
outed, 380
outgassing, 128
out in left field, 395
out of sight, 222
out of the closet, 380
out of the loop, 330
outpatient, 251
outpost, 141
output, 80
outside shot, 400
outsourcing, 104
overfishing, 127
overland route, 413
over the bay, 36
over-the-counter pain reliever, 254
over the hill, 280
over-training, 164
owly-eyed, 38
oxbow, 249
oyster cracker, 170
Oy vay!, 20

ozone hole, 125
ozone layer, 125
Ozzie and Harriet, 349, 350

P

Pacific Northwest, 243
Pacific States, 243
pack a day, 254
package (personnel file), 63
packer rolloffs, 429
packet boat, 246, 413
Paddy wagon, 22, 61
padre, 145, 369
pads, 224
pager, 53
paid and displayed, 119
pail, 14
Paine, Tom, 141, 221, 387
pajamas, 377
palace car, 417
palazzo pants, 139
paleface (corn whiskey), 30
palimony, 294
Palko v. Connecticut, 287
Palmer, A. Mitchell, 66
Palmer, Gen. Bruce, Jr., 153
Palmer, Volney B., 1
panacea, 254
pancakes, 168
pandas (police cars), 63
panel heating, 202
pan for gold, 436
panhandle (geography), 249
panhandler (beggar), 277, 278
panic, financial, 110, 111
pansy, 380
panther sweat, 30
pantsuit, 138
panty hose, 138
Papa-san, 153
paper money, 102
Papin, Denys, 180
parachute, 146
paradigm shift, 327
parcel post, 48
pard, 436

parental warning sticker, 376
par for the course, 402
parish, 244
parka, 243
Parker, Charlie "Bird," 336
Parker, Dorothy, 84, 209
Parkerhouse rolls, 182
Parker, W. H., 3
parking, 378, 422
parking lot, 422
parking meter, 422
parking space, 422
Parkinson, C. Northcote, 429
Parkinson's Law, 428-29
Parkinson's syndrome, 258
parkway, 248, 422
parlor car, 416, 417
parmesan, 21
participatory democracy, 224
partisan, 151
partying, 87
party line, 50–51
passed over the prairie, 434
passing bell, 206
passion pit, 343–44
passive system, 204
Passover, 273
pass the plate, 369
pasta, 21, 185
past-life regression, 370
patch, 254–55
patenting of life, 231
patio, 21
pat on the butt, 401
Patriot Missile, 156
Patriots, 142
patrol car, 63
patrolman, 62
patrol wagon, 61
Patterson, Floyd, 403
Patton, Gen. George S., Jr., 149
Paul, Alice, 216–17
Pauling, Linus, 252
pauper, 276
Pay as you ride, 4
pay babies, 278
payload, 388
pay phone, 51
PC (computer), 68

rock (music), 338
Rock, The, 67
rock-a-billy, 337
rock-and-roll, 337
rock climbing, 403
Rockefeller, John D., 106
rockets, 269
rock opera, 338
rock star, 338
rock videos, 376
Rodell, Fred, 286, 288
rodeo, 21
Rodman, Dennis, 399
Rodrigue, George, 328
Roe v. Wade, 288, 291
roger!, 150
Rogers, Roy, 352
Rogers, Will, 314, 420
Rolfing, 165
rolled stockings, 137
roller, 359
Rollerblades, 162
roller hockey, 391
rolling in dough, 101
Rolling Stones, The, 339
rolling the growler, 26
Rolodexes, 333
ROM, 68
Rombauer, Irma S., 180
rompers, 137
Room with a bath for a dollar and a half, 4
Roosevelt, Franklin D., 42, 111, 147, 148, 149, 205, 264, 315, 324–25, 331, 404
Roosevelt, Theodore, 4, 13, 123, 145, 187, 316, 324
Roquelaures, 132
Roseanne, 352
Rose Bowl, 397
Rosenberg, Leo, 404
Rosenberg trial, 297
Rosenthal, A. M., 81
rosé wine, 45
Rosh Hashannah, 273–74
Rosicrucianism, 362
rosy, 38
rotgut, 30
rough and hard in its youth (wine), 44
Rough Riders, 145

round heels, 87
rounding the bases, 392
round trip, 416
Rowan and Martin's Laugh-In, 350
rowing machines, 157
R rating, 375
RTFM, 75
rubbers, 381
rubbish, 427
rub out, 435
ruckus juice, 29
rugby, 395–96
Ruhlen, Merritt, 16
rum, 27–28
rumble seat, 377, 421
rumhead, 39
rummish, 36
rump, 377
rumpus room, 201
rum row, 41
rumrunner, 41, 42
runabout, 421
runaways, 65
running (on bike), 162
running board, 421
running interference, 391
run something by someone, 226
Runyon, Damon, 355
rural cemetery, 210
Rural Free Delivery (RFD), 48
rural sprawl, 437
Rush, Benjamin, 157, 382
rush to judgment, 300
Russell, Bertrand, 84
Russell, Charles Taze "Pastor," 367
Russell, C. M., 25
Russell, Lillian, 371
Russellites, 362, 367
Russian stove, 199
Rust Belt, 242
rust bucket, 151
rustle up a meal, 280
Rutherford, Joseph Franklin "Judge," 367
Rutt, Chris, 168
Rx, 256
rye 'n' Injun, 170
rye whiskey, 28–29

S

sabotage, 147
Sacco, Niccolo, 295
Sacco and Vanzetti trial, 295
sachem, 360
sack, 150
sad cake, 177
saddle (bike), 419
saddle shoes, 137
Sadie Hawkins Day, 348
sad sack, 151
safes, 381
safe sex, 371, 381–82
safety bicycle, 419
Safire, William, 139, 329, 354–55
Sagebrush Rebellion, 437
sail car, 415
sailing, 413
St. Elsewhere, 350
St. Patrick's Day, 272
St. Patrick's Day parade, 22, 272
St. Valentine's Day, 270–71
salad bar, 176
salamander stove, 199
Salem Witch Trials, 294–95
salesgirl, 215
sales lady, 215
Salisbury steak, 172
Salk, Dr. Jonas, 251
Sally Anne, 105
saloon, 26
salsa, 186
salt bread, 170
Salt 'N' Pepa, 357
salt water taffy, 179
same-sex marriage, 380
Samoset, 360
sampling, 2
Sampson, 32
SAM (surface-to-air missile), 155
San Andreas Fault, 92
sand, 435
sand-nigger, 89
sandstorm, 99
sandwich, 170–71
sandwich board, 2
sandwich man, 2
Sanford's Challenge Heater, 199

san garee, 33
Sanger, Margaret, 217
sangria, 33
sanitary landfill, 429
sanitation engineer, 429
Santa Ana, 98–99
Santa Anna, Gen. Antonio Lopez de, 143
Santa Claus, 266
Saracenic grate, 198
sarcoma, 258
satellite, 383
Saturday Night Fever, 339
Saturday Night Live, 351–52
Saturday Night Massacre, 325
sauce, 30
sauerbraten, 20
Sauterne, 45
savage, 88
Savage, William W., Jr., 347
savanna, 248
saved by the bell, 402
savvy, 21
sawbuck, 102
sawdust trail, 363
Sazerac, 33
scalawag, 321
scalpers, 110
scarer, 396
scarf (verb), 186
scatology, 82
Schaffer, Gloria, 220
Schenck v. United States, 286
Schiffer, Claudia, 140
schlemiel, 20
schlep, 20
schmaltz, 20
schmooseoisie, 408
schmuck, 81
school, 215
school's out, 267
schooners, 412
Schroeder, Patricia, 330, 333
Schwarzkopf, Gen. Norman, 156
Schwenkfelders, 362
SCID, 234
Scientology, Church of, 363

24 hours of sobriety, 255
twilight zone, 349, 350
twist, 339
twister, 97
two for the price of one, 105
T-word, 329
two-time loser, 67
two-way talk radio, 405
tycoon, 107
Tynan, Kenneth, 81
typist, 215

U

U-boat, 147
Udall, Stewart L., 122
Ueberroth, Peter, 392
Ultimate driving machine, 6
ultramarathon, 161
Ultrasuede, 139
Unabomber, 59, 191
unbanked, 101
unconditional surrender, 144, 148, 155
underachiever, 310
underground, the, 151
underground comedy show, 351
underground railroad, 319
underpants, 131
underprivileged, 312, 324
underrepresented group, 312
undertaker, 205, 207
under the basket, 400
under the boards, 400
under the influence, 311
undervolt, 385
underwater sound system, 165
unemployment, 329
unisex, 220
Unitarian Universalist Church, 362
United States, 249
universal reactor, 128
UNIX, 72, 79
unmanned spacecraft, 384

unprintable words, 81–89
unprotected sex, 382
unreasonable search and seizure, 284, 289
until kingdom come, 370
"Until we meet again, may the good Lord take a liking to you," 352
upcountry, 432
upland, 432
uplift bra, 377
uplink, 388
upload, 71
uprights, 395
uprock, 354
upscale market, 3
UpSkiing, 403
up the wall, 400
uptight, 224
up to scratch, 402
up yours, 87
urban cemetery, 210–11
urban cowboy, 188
urban forests, 129
urban sprawl, 247
urban yoga, 163
URL, 79
US, 249
U.S.A., 249
U.S. of A., 249
used car, 421
Usenet, 72
user:
    cyberspace, 73
    drug, 64–65
user-friendly, 80
Utah, 241
U-word, 329

V

vagabond, 280
vagina, 377
vagrant, 280
Valachi, Joe, 60
valentine card, 271
Valentine's Day, 270–71
Valium, 254
vamoose, 21
vamp, 372
vampire, 372
Van Buren, Martin, 317, 319

Vanderbilt, Amy, 303
Van Dyke beard, 135
vanity plates, 421
vanity tombstone, 212
Vanzetti, Bartolomeo, 295
vaporware, 79
varsity football game, 396
vaudeville, 335
vault, 212
V.C., 155
V-chip, 76
vectors, 237
V-E Day, 148
Veeck, Bill, 393
vegan, 176
vegetables, 174–76
vegetarian, 176
Velcro-coated, 331
Velcroid, 331
verdict, 299–300
Verdun, Pierre, 180
vermicelli, 21
Vermont, 241
Vernon, Adm. Edward "Old Grog," 33
vertically challenged, 312
Vespucci, Amerigo, 243, 244
Veterans Day, 262
viable, 291
viatical settlement, 253
vibrant with personality (wine), 44
victim, 312
Vidal, Gore, 380
video on demand, 76
Vienna sausage, 171
Viet Cong, 155
Vietnam War, 152, 153–55, 224, 287, 297
vigilante, 63
vigor, 158
vintner, 42
Virginia, 241
Virginia City, 246
Virginia ham, 173
virtual office, 77
virtual reality, 69, 77, 79, 166
virus, 80
visiting team, 394
vital statistics form, 208
vitamin supplements, 252

viticulture, 42
V-J Day, 148
vodka, 29
Vogel, Virgil J., 238
vogue, 359
voice line, 53
voice mail, 53, 305–7
voice phone, 53
voir dire, 300
volcanoes, 90–91
Volvo set, 333
Voodoo, 362
voodoo economics, 331
voting rights, 286
Vreeland, Diana, 333
Vulcan salute, 350

W

Wabash and Erie, 246
Waco, 66, 192
waffles, 169
wagon trains, 414
waitstaff, 167
Wakefield, Ruth, 178
Walker, Alice, 220
walkie-talkie, 151
walking poles, 161
walkshaping, 161
wall of separation, 287
Wall Street, 108–10, 244
Wambaugh, Joseph, 35
wampum, 104
wandering poor, 276
wannabe, 74, 355
war correspondent, 144
ward, 364
Ward, Artemus, 360
war fever, 142
war hawks, 142
war horse, 328
warm-up, 160
Warner, Charles Dudley, 321
warning, storm, 99
warning out, 276
war on drugs, 63–65
Warp engine, 350
warrant, 289
Warren, Earl, 287
wars, 141–43
    American Revolution, 141–42
    Civil, 143–44, 145, 320
    of 1812, 142–43

wooden overcoat, 435
wood lot, 195
woodshed, 195
Woodstock Nation, 338–39
wood stove, 198
Woodward, Henry, 176
woozy, 38
Word! Word up!, 359
work ethic, 366
workfare, 276
workhouse, 66
working girl, 87
working mother, 228
workout, 160
workplace, 104–6, 117
World Series, 394
World War I, 146–48
World War II, 148–52
World Wide Web (WWW), 70–80
WPA, 324
wraparound, 137
wraparound sunglasses, 140
Wright, James D., 281

Wright brothers, 423
wrist weights, 164
wrongful-death suit, 300
wrong side of the tracks, 246
Wyoming, 242
WYSIWYG, 352

X

Xenomouse, 237
Xerox (verb), 333
Xers, 225, 227–29
X-files, 349, 350
X-rated, 374–75

Y

yack yack bourbon, 37
yahoo, 64
yakkers, 404
yams, 167
Yankee rum, 28
Yankees, 15, 142

yard, 67
yardbird, 67
yard bull, 62, 279
yard of flannel, 33
yegg/yegg man, 280
yellow dog Democrat, 328
yellow journalism, 144
yellow pages, 51
Yeltsin, Boris, 329
yes man, 340
Yiddish, 19–20
Yippies, 224
Yo, 358
yo-boy, 355
yoga, 162–63
yogurt, 179
Yom Kippur, 274
"You ain't heard nothin' yet," 347
Young, Brigham, 364
Young, Robert, 348
You press the button, we do the rest, 3
You're no Jack Kennedy, 331

Yukon stove, 199
yuppies, 225, 226, 227

Z

Zangwill, Israel, 15
zap (in microwave), 180
Zapata mustache, 135
z directories, 80
zep, 171
zeppelin, 146, 424
zero gravity, 385
zero-parent children, 273
zero tolerance, 64
Ziegfeld girl, 372
zilch, 348
zinc, 254
Zinfandel, 45
zip, 89
ZIP code, 48
zonked, 39
zoo plane, 328